Nonfiction Classics
for Students

National Advisory Board

Nonfiction Classics
for Students

Presenting Analysis, Context, and Criticism on Nonfiction Works

Volume 3

Jennifer Smith, Editor

GALE GROUP

THOMSON LEARNING

Detroit • New York • San Diego • San Francisco
Boston • New Haven, Conn. • Waterville, Maine
London • Munich

Nonfiction Classics for Students

Staff

Editor: Jennifer Smith.

Contributing Editors: Anne Marie Hacht, Michael L. LaBlanc, Ira Mark Milne, Daniel Toronto, Carol Ullmann.

Managing Editor, Content: Dwayne D. Hayes.

Managing Editor, Product: David Galens.

Publisher, Literature Product: Mark Scott.

Literature Content Capture: Joyce Nakamura, *Managing Editor*. Sara Constantakis, *Editor*.

Research: Victoria B. Cariappa, *Research Manager*. Sarah Genik, Tamara Nott, Tracie A. Richardson, *Research Associates*. Nicodemus Ford, *Research Assistant*.

Permissions: Maria L. Franklin, *Permissions Manager*. Shalice Shah-Caldwell, *Permissions Associate*. Debra Freitas, *IC Coordinator/Permissions Associate*.

Manufacturing: Mary Beth Trimper, *Manager, Composition and Electronic Prepress*. Evi Seoud, *Assistant Manager, Composition Purchasing and Electronic Prepress*. Stacy Melson, *Buyer*.

Imaging and Multimedia Content Team: Barbara Yarrow, *Manager*. Randy Bassett, *Imaging Supervisor*. Robert Duncan, Dan Newell, Luke Rademacher, *Imaging Specialists*. Leitha Etheridge-Sims, Mary Grimes, David G. Oblender, *Image Catalogers*. Robyn V. Young, *Project Manager*. Dean Dauphinais, *Senior Image Editor*. Kelly A. Quin, *Image Editor*.

Product Design Team: Pamela A. E. Galbreath, *Senior Art Director*. Michael Logusz, *Graphic Artist*.

Table of Contents

Literature: Conversation, Communication, Idea, Emotion

The so-called information age of which we are all a part has given birth to the internet, and so literature—the written word in its many forms—now has vaster, faster avenues in which to circulate. The internet is the latest revolutionary development in communication media. Before the internet, the development of the printing press and the advent of radio and television were equally astonishing events. This great network of circulating words and images amongst persons and populations can be thought of as a vast human conversation.

In conversation, speech arises from the desire to communicate an idea or a feeling or else it follows from an address and is a reply of sorts. How quickly one can formulate a communication or a reply depends upon the nature of the problem or of the address. Does one wish to communicate something simple, such as a command? Or does one wish to meditate on a significant problem or issue in one's personal life? Or in history or science? Is the address a greeting, an email, a painting, a letter, or a novel? Nonfiction works, the subject of *Nonfiction Classics for Students*, are written literary communications of a sustained nature, unlike ephemeral written communications such as emails or memos which are concerned with the immediately occurring events of the day. The length and breadth of the novel form follows from the amount of learning and experience that goes into the making of each novel, and from the amount of information it can convey. Nonfiction works that have become classics are

those which have been particularly moving or influential, or both. These works have changed the way people live, think, and see.

Influential and admired nonfiction works can be thought of as significant events in the traditions in which they are working or to which they are related, traditions such as autobiography, biography, history, science, the essay, and so forth. For example, published diaries such as *Anne Frank: The Diary of a Young Girl* are related to the traditions of autobiography and history. If the diary of this child is so valued by readers it is because, besides being engagingly written, it vividly brings forth an era and a set of world-effecting political disasters and events. Through the words of Anne Frank, the reader enters the world of a bright, hopeful teenager who is, nevertheless, haunted by the fear of her imminent death as the world around her crumbles. To know that this child eventually was captured and died in a concentration camp moves us to be more assiduous and vigilant in our protection of innocents, and we lament this terrible suffering and senseless waste of life.

Yet, if we wish to learn how it was that World War II came about, or who Europe's leaders were and what these leaders' beliefs and ideologies were, then we must turn to the written works which are histories and not autobiographies, works whose subject is not the history of a single person but rather the reconstruction of the social, cultural, and political panorama of the period or age under study. Histories, in turn, are related to the traditions of political and social science. The more polemical or argumentative the history book, the more it is a work of political theory, where facts are important—though not as critical as ideas about how human society works or can be arranged. Through the written word, social and political thinkers and philosophers make their arguments, and societies, cultures, and ways of governing rise and fall.

In the form of nonfiction, scientists make their arguments and present their formulae, and technology and medical, and psychological treatments are changed. It is because of the printed, widely disseminated word that women and other minorities win equal opportunity in the world. Ideas change the world, they are a part of our history. Students of literature enter into this vast human conversation and have the opportunity to contribute to it. *Nonfiction Classics for Students* prepares and equips these students so that his or her entry into this conversation is meaningful.

Nonfiction Classics for Students also presents relevant information and discussion about major figures and ideas. As for what makes a particular autobiography or diary stand out, it is often because the story of the single person seems to speak for many or because it is powerfully and beautifully written. While we do not necessarily demand high artistry from some writers of nonfiction prose, we do expect some degree of fluency from those writers practicing the art of the essay, autobiography, or biography. The various reasons why a particular

work has been or is admired, and its reputation past and current, is also discussed in the pages of *Nonfiction Classics for Students*. In presenting students with discussions of a work's artistry and reputation, as well as of relevant, related traditions, theories, and ideas, *Nonfiction Classics for Students* models a process of reading and systematic study that a student can apply to any work he or she reads.

What this study of and engagement with a work of literature can produce is either a research paper, which is a presentation of what has been learned, or else it can give rise to a reply, a counter-communication. In composing writing in response to a work, a student participates in and contributes to the vast human conversation. The entries in *Nonfiction Classics for Students* suggest relevant topics for classroom discussion. *Nonfiction Classics for Students* is an aid to students who set out to inform themselves responsibly about a particular nonfiction work. This series equips students to contribute meaningfully to the vast human conversation. Are a writer's ideas productive and useful? Does the book teach us important lessons or move us? Do we detect the circulation of heinous ideologies in our present times that remind us of destructive ideologies and beliefs from the past? In reading and learning and communicating, we engage with history; to the extent that we live by what we learn, we make history when we respond to and act on what we have read.

Carol Dell'Amico
Santa Monica College, Santa Monica, California

Introduction

Purpose of the Book

The purpose of *Nonfiction Classics for Students* (*NCfS*) is to provide readers with a guide to understanding, enjoying, and studying nonfiction works by giving them easy access to information about the work. Part of Gale's "For Students" literature line, *NCfS* is specifically designed to meet the curricular needs of high school and undergraduate college students and their teachers, as well as the interests of general readers and researchers considering specific works. While each volume contains entries on "classic" works frequently studied in classrooms, there are also entries containing hard-to-find information on contemporary pieces, including works by multicultural, international, and women authors.

The information covered in each entry includes an introduction to the work and the work's author; a summary, to help readers unravel and understand the events in a work; descriptions of key figures, including explanation of a given figure's role in the work as well as discussion about that figure's relationship to other figures in the work; analysis of important themes in the work; and an explanation of important literary techniques and movements as they are demonstrated in the work.

In addition to this material, which helps the readers analyze the work itself, students are also provided with important information on the literary and historical background informing each work.

This includes a historical context essay, a box comparing the time or place the work was written to modern Western culture, a critical overview essay, and excerpts from critical essays on the work, when available. A unique feature of *NCfS* is a specially commissioned critical essay on each work, targeted toward the student reader.

To further aid the student in studying and enjoying each work, information on media adaptations is provided, as well as reading suggestions for works of fiction and nonfiction on similar themes and topics. Classroom aids include ideas for research papers and lists of critical sources that provide additional material on each work.

Selection Criteria

The titles for each volume of *NCfS* were selected by surveying numerous sources on teaching literature and analyzing course curricula for various school districts. Some of the sources surveyed included: literature anthologies; *Reading Lists for College-Bound Students: The Books Most Recommended by America's Top Colleges;* a College Board survey of works commonly studied in high schools; a National Council of Teachers of English (NCTE) survey of works commonly studied in high schools; Arthur Applebee's 1993 study *Literature in the Secondary School: Studies of Curriculum and Instruction in the United States;* and the *Modern Library*'s list of the one hundred best nonfiction works of the century.

Input was also solicited from our expert advisory board (experienced educators specializing in English), as well as educators from various areas. From these discussions, it was determined that each volume should have a mix of "classic" works (those works commonly taught in literature classes) and contemporary works for which information is often hard to find. Because of the interest in expanding the canon of literature, an emphasis was also placed on including works by international, multicultural, and women authors. Our advisory board members—current high school teachers—helped pare down the list for each volume. If a work was not selected for the present volume, it was often noted as a possibility for a future volume. As always, the editor welcomes suggestions for titles to be included in future volumes.

How Each Entry Is Organized

Each entry, or chapter, in *NCfS* focuses on one work. Each entry heading lists the full name of the work, the author's name, and the date of the work's publication. The following elements are contained in each entry:

- **Introduction:** a brief overview of the work which provides information about its initial publication, its literary standing, any controversies surrounding the work, and major conflicts or themes within the work.

- **Author Biography:** this section includes basic facts about the author's life, and focuses on events and times in the author's life that inspired the work in question.

- **Summary:** a description of the major events in the work. Subheads demarcate the work's various chapters or sections.

- **Key Figures:** an alphabetical listing of major figures in the work. Each name is followed by a brief to an extensive description of the person's role in the works, as well as discussion of the figure's actions, relationships, and possible motivation. Figures are listed alphabetically by last name. If a figure is unnamed—for instance, the narrator in *Pilgrim at Tinker Creek*—the figure is listed as "The Narrator" and alphabetized as "Narrator." If a person's first name is the only one given, the name will appear alphabetically by the name. Variant names are also included for each person. Thus, the full name "Richard Monckton Milnes" would head the listing for a figure in *The Education of Henry Adams,* but

listed in a separate cross-reference would be his more formal name "Lord Houghton."

- **Themes:** a thorough overview of how the major topics, themes, and issues are addressed within the work. Each theme discussed appears in a separate subhead, and is easily accessed through the boldface entries in the Subject/Theme Index.

- **Style:** this section addresses important style elements of the work, such as setting, point of view, and narration; important literary devices used, such as imagery, foreshadowing, symbolism; and, if applicable, genres to which the work might have belonged, such as Gothicism or Romanticism. Literary terms are explained within the entry, but can also be found in the Glossary.

- **Historical Context:** This section outlines the social, political, and cultural climate *in which the author lived and the work was created.* This section may include descriptions of related historical events, pertinent aspects of daily life in the culture, and the artistic and literary sensibilities of the time in which the work was written. If the piece is a historical work, information regarding the time in which the work is set is also included. Each section is broken down with helpful subheads.

- **Critical Overview:** this section provides background on the critical reputation of the work, including bannings or any other public controversies surrounding the work. For older works, this section includes a history of how the work was first received and how perceptions of it may have changed over the years; for more recent works, direct quotes from early reviews may also be included.

- **Criticism:** an essay commissioned by *NCfS* which specifically deals with work and is written specifically for the student audience, as well as excerpts from previously published criticism on the work, when available.

- **Sources:** an alphabetical list of critical material cited in the entry, with full bibliographical information.

- **Further Reading:** an alphabetical list of other critical sources which may prove useful for the student. Includes full bibliographical information and a brief annotation.

In addition, each entry contains the following highlighted sections, set separate from the main text:

- **Media Adaptations:** a list of important film and television adaptations of the work, including source information. The list may also include such variations on the work as audio recordings, musical adaptations, and other stage interpretations.

- **Topics for Further Study:** a list of potential study questions or research topics dealing with the work. This section includes questions related to other disciplines the student may be studying, such as American history, world history, science, math, government, business, geography, economics, psychology, etc.

- **Compare and Contrast:** an ''at-a-glance'' comparison of the cultural and historical differences between the author's time and culture and late twentieth-century Western culture. This box includes pertinent parallels between the major scientific, political, and cultural movements of the time or place the work was written, the time or place the work was set (if a historical work), and modern Western culture. Works written after 1990 may not have this box.

- **What Do I Read Next?:** a list of works that might complement the featured work or serve as a contrast to it. This includes works by the same author and others, works of fiction and nonfiction, and works from various genres, cultures, and eras.

Other Features

NCfS includes ''Literature: Conversation, Communication, Idea, Emotion,'' a foreword by Carol Dell'Amico, an educator and author. This essay examines nonfiction as a lasting way for authors to communicate, as well as the influence these works can have. Dell'Amico also discusses how *Nonfiction Classics for Students* can help teachers show students how to enrich their own reading experiences and how the series is designed to aid students in their study of particular works.

A Cumulative Author/Title Index lists the authors and titles covered in each volume of the *NCfS* series.

A Cumulative Nationality/Ethnicity Index breaks down the authors and titles covered in each volume of the *NCfS* series by nationality and ethnicity.

A Subject/Theme Index, specific to each volume, provides easy reference for users who may be studying a particular subject or theme rather than a single work. Significant subjects from events to

broad themes are included, and the entries pointing to the specific theme discussions in each entry are indicated in **boldface.**

Entries may include illustrations, including photos of the author, stills from stage productions, and stills from film adaptations.

Citing **Nonfiction Classics for Students**

When writing papers, students who quote directly from any volume of *Nonfiction Classics for Students* may use the following general forms. These examples are based on MLA style; teachers may request that students adhere to a different style, so the following examples may be adapted as needed.

When citing text from *NCfS* that is not attributed to a particular author (i.e., the Themes, Style, Historical Context sections, etc.), the following format should be used in the bibliography section:

''The Journalist and the Murderer.'' *Nonfiction Classics for Students.* Ed. Elizabeth Thomason. Vol. 1. Farmington Hills, MI: The Gale Group, 2001, pp. 153–56.

When quoting the specially commissioned essay from *NCfS* (usually the first piece under the "Criticism" subhead), the following format should be used:

Hart, Joyce. Critical essay on ''Silent Spring.'' *Nonfiction Classics for Students.* Ed. Elizabeth Thomason. Vol. 1. Farmington Hills, MI: The Gale Group, 2001, pp. 316–19.

When quoting a journal or newspaper essay that is reprinted in a volume of *NCfS,* the following form may be used:

Limon, John. ''*The Double Helix* as Literature.'' *Raritan* Vol. 5, No. 3 (Winter 1986), pp. 26–47; excerpted and reprinted in *Nonfiction Classics for Students,* Vol. 2, ed. Elizabeth Thomason (Farmington Hills, MI: The Gale Group, 2001), pp. 84–95.

When quoting material reprinted from a book that appears in a volume of *NCfS,* the following form may be used:

Gunnars, Kristjana. ''Life as Fiction: Narrative Appropriation in Isak Dinesen's *Out of Africa*,'' in *Isak Dinesen and Narrativity,* ed. Gurli A. Woods, (Carleton University Press, 1990), pp. 25–34; excerpted and reprinted in *Nonfiction Classics for Students,* Vol. 2, ed. Elizabeth Thomason (Farmington Hills, MI: The Gale Group, 2001), pp. 281–86.

We Welcome Your Suggestions

The editor of *Nonfiction Classics for Students* welcomes your comments and ideas. Readers who wish to suggest works to appear in future volumes, or who have other suggestions, are cordially invited

to contact the editor. You may contact the editor via
E-mail at: **ForStudentsEditors@gale.com.** Or write
to the editor at:

Editor, *Nonfiction Classics for Students*
The Gale Group
27500 Drake Rd.
Farmington Hills, MI 48331–3535

Literary Chronology

1803: Ralph Waldo Emerson is born on May 25 in Boston, Massachusetts.

1817: Henry David Thoreau is born on July 12 in Concord, Massachusetts.

1841: Ralph Waldo Emerson's ''Self-Reliance'' is published.

1854: Henry David Thoreau's *Walden* is published.

1856: Sigmund Freud is born on May 6 in Freiberg, Moravia.

1862: Henry David Thoreau dies of tuberculosis on May 6 at home in Concord.

1865: William Butler Yeats is born on June 13 in Sandymont, Ireland.

1881: Victor Klemperer is born on October 9 in Landsberg-on-the-Warthe in the province of Brandenburg, Germany.

1882: Ralph Waldo Emerson dies of pneumonia on April 27 in Concord. He is buried near the grave of Henry David Thoreau, who had died twenty years earlier.

1899: Sigmund Freud's *The Interpretation of Dreams* is published.

1908: John Kenneth Galbraith is born on October 15 on a farm in Iona Station, Ontario, Canada.

1914: Ralph Ellison is born on March 1 in Oklahoma City, Oklahoma.

1921: John Rawls is born on February 21 in Baltimore, Maryland.

1923: William Butler Yeats is awarded the Nobel Prize for Literature.

1925: Malcolm X is born as Malcolm Little on May 19 in Omaha, Nebraska.

1928: Gabriel García Márquez is born on March 6 in Aracata, Colombia, a small town near the Atlantic coast.

1939: Sigmund Freud dies of cancer in London.

1939: William Butler Yeats dies in Roquebrune, France, and is buried in the land of his ancestors, Sligo, Ireland, in 1948.

1940: Anne Moody is born Essie Mae Moody on September 15 near Centreville, Mississippi.

1940: Annie Ernaux is born on September 1 in Lillebonne, France, in the region of Normandy.

1944: Richard Rodriguez is born on July 31 in San Francisco, California.

1954: Anne Lamott is born in San Francisco, California.

1955: William Butler Yeats's *Autobiographies* is published.

1958: John Kenneth Galbraith's *The Affluent Society* is published.

1959: Susan Faludi is born on April 18 in New York City.

1960: Victor Klemperer dies of a heart attack while attending a conference in Brussels, Belgium.

1964: Ralph Ellison's *Shadow and Act* is published.

1965: Malcolm X dies on February 21. As he steps onto a stage to address a crowd of supporters in Harlem, he is gunned down by three men believed to be associated with the Nation of Islam.

1965: Malcolm X's *The Autobiography of Malcolm X* is published.

1968: Anne Moody's *Coming of Age in Mississippi* is published.

1971: John Rawls's *A Theory of Justice* is published.

1981: Richard Rodriguez's *Hunger of Memory: The Education of Richard Rodriguez* is published.

1982: Gabriel García Márquez is awarded the Nobel Prize for Literature.

1991: Susan Faludi is awarded a Pulitzer Prize for an article written for the *Wall Street Journal* on the Safeway Stores' leveraged buyout and its impact on employees.

1991: Susan Faludi's *Backlash: The Undeclared War against American Women* is published.

1993: Anne Lamott's *Operating Instructions* is published.

1994: Ralph Waldo Ellison dies on April 16 in Harlem with his long-awaited second novel unpublished. The unfinished work is edited after his death by his literary executor and published posthumously with the title *Juneteenth*.

1995: Victor Klemperer's *I Will Bear Witness: A Diary of the Nazi Years, 1933–1941* is published.

1997: Annie Ernaux's *I Remain in Darkness* is published.

1997: Gabriel García Márquez's *News of a Kidnapping* is published.

Acknowledgments

The editors wish to thank the copyright holders of the excerpted criticism included in this volume and the permissions managers of many book and magazine publishing companies for assisting us in securing reproduction rights. We are also grateful to the staffs of the Detroit Public Library, the Library of Congress, the University of Detroit Mercy Library, Wayne State University Purdy/Kresge Library Complex, and the University of Michigan Libraries for making their resources available to us. Following is a list of the copyright holders who have granted us permission to reproduce material in this volume of *Nonfiction Classics for Students (NCfS)*. Every effort has been made to trace copyright, but if omissions have been made, please let us know.

COPYRIGHTED MATERIALS IN *NCfS*, VOLUME 3, WERE REPRODUCED FROM THE FOLLOWING PERIODICALS:

American Literature, v. 68, June, 1996. Copyright © 1986 by Duke University Press. Reproduced by permission.—*Challenge,* v. 36, July-August, 1993 for "The Heresies of John Kenneth Galbraith" by Thomas Karier. Reproduced by permission of the author.—*Colby Quarterly,* v. XXXII, December, 1986. Reproduced by permission.—*Criticism,* v. V, Winter, 1963. Copyright, 1963, Wayne State University Press. Reproduced by permission of Wayne State University Press.—*Eire-Ireland,* v. IX, 1974. Copyright 1974 Irish American Cultural Institute. Reproduced by permission.—*Jour-nal of Economic Issues,* v. XXIII, June, 1989 for "Rereading the Affluent Society" by Robert Heilbroner. Reproduced by permission of the author.—*Melus,* v. 11, Winter, 1984. Copyright MELUS: The Society for the Study of Multi-Ethnic Literature of the United States, 1984. Reproduced by permission.—*The Nation,* New York, v. 267, November 16, 1998. © 1998 *The Nation* magazine/ The Nation Company, Inc. Reproduced by permission.—*Progressive,* v. 57, June, 1993. Copyright © 1993 by *The Progressive,* Inc. Reproduced by permission of The Progressive, 409 East Main Street, Madison, WI 53703.—*Yeats,* v. II, 1984. Copyright © 1984 by Cornell University. All rights reserved. Reproduced by permission.

COPYRIGHTED MATERIALS IN *NCfS*, VOLUME 3, WERE REPRODUCED FROM THE FOLLOWING BOOKS:

Bloom, Harold. From *Sigmond Freud's "The Interpretation of Dreams."* Edited by Harold Bloom. Chelsea House Publishers, 1987. © 1987 by Chelsea House Publishers. All rights reserved. Reproduced by permission.—Busby, Mark. From *Ralph Ellison.* Edited by Warren French. Twayne, 1991. Reproduced by permission.—Frieden, Ken. From *Freud's Dream of Interpretation.* State University of New York Press, 1990. Reproduced by permission.—Martin, Rex. From *Rawls and Rights.* University Press of Kansas, 1985. Reproduced by permission of the author.—O'Meally, Robert G. From *The*

Craft of Ralph Ellison. Harvard University Press, 1980. Reproduced by permission.—Packer, B. L. From *Emerson's Fall: A New Interpretation of the Major Essays.* Continuum, 1982. Copyright © 1982 by B. L. Packer. All rights reserved. Reproduced by permission.—Rowe, John Carlos. From *Through the Custom House: Nineteenth-Century American Fiction and Modern Theory.* Johns Hopkins University Press, 1982. Copyright © 1982 by The Johns Hopkins University Press. Reproduced by permission.—Wolheim, Richard. From "Dreams," in *Sigmond Freud's "The Interpretation of Dreams."* Edited by Harold Bloom. Chelsea House Publishers, 1987. © 1987 by Chelsea House Publishers. All rights reserved. Reproduced by permission.

PHOTOGRAPHS AND ILLUSTRATIONS APPEARING IN *NCfS*, VOLUME 3, WERE RECEIVED FROM THE FOLLOWING SOURCES:

An Alzheimer's patient receives a visitor in a long-term health-care facility, photograph. Prentice Hall, Inc./Simon & Schuster/PH College. Reproduced by permission.—Aschner, Jacob and Samuel, photograph. © Corbis. Reproduced by permission.—Bombed buildings, Dresden, Germany, 1946, photograph. CORBIS/Bettmann. Reproduced by permission.—Civil rights marchers walking along Route 80, photograph. AP/Wide World Photos. Reproduced by permission.—Crowds gathering for Christmas, photograph. © Bettmann/Corbis. Reproduced by permission.—Ellison, Ralph (wearing suit and glasses), photograph. Archive Photos. Reproduced by permission.—Emerson, Ralph Waldo, engraving by S.A. Choff c. 1878. The Library of Congress.—Escobar, Pablo, photograph. AP/Wide World Photos. Reproduce by permission.—Faludi, Susan, San Francisco, California, photograph. AP/Wide World Photos. Reproduced by permission.—Farmer, James, Bogalusa, Louisiana, 1965, photograph. AP/Wide World Photos. Reproduced by permission.—Freud, Sigmund, photograph. The Library of Congress.—Friedan, Betty, 1978, photograph. AP/Wide World Photos. Reproduced with permission.—Galbraith, John Kenneth, photograph. The Library of Congress.—Gregory, Augusta, photograph. The Library of Congress.—Hines, Earl, 1939, Savoy Ballroom, Harlem, photograph by Charles Peterson. Archive Photos, Inc. Reproduced by permission.—Hobbes, Thomas, drawing. Archive Photos, Inc. Reproduced by permission.—Interior of Sigmund Freud's study, photograph. Archive Photos, Inc. Reproduced by permission.—Interior of the study in Ralph Waldo Emerson, photograph. The Library of Congress.—Klemperer, Victor, photograph. The Granger Collection, New York. Reproduced by permission.—Lamott, Annie, photograph. Getty Images. Reproduced by permission.—Malcolm X, photograph. AP/Wide World Photos. Reproduced by permission.—Marquez, Gabriel Garcia, 1982, photograph. AP/Wide World Photos. Reproduced by permission.—Mill, John Stuart, drawing. Archive Photos, Inc. Reproduced by permission.—Muhammad, Elijah, speaking at a press conference, photograph. © Bettmann/Corbis. Reproduced by permission.—"Oedipus and The Sphinx," oil painting by Jean Auguste Dominique Ingres. © National Gallery Collection. By kind permission of the Trustees of the National Gallery, London/Corbis. Reproduced by permission.—Pedestrians walking along Lenox Avenue in Harlem, New York, photograph. © Bettmann/Corbis. Reproduced by permission.—Reduced plan of hand drawn map of Walden Pond, drawing.—Rodriguez, Richard, photograph by Roger Ressmeyer. CORBIS. Reproduced by permission.—Rodriguez, Richard, visiting the Sacred Heart School, photograph by Roger Ressmeyer. Corbis. Reproduced by permission.—Schlafly, Phyllis, photograph. AP/Wide World Photos. Reproduced with permission.—Thoreau, Henry David, drawing. The Library of Congress.—Thoreau, Henry David's birthplace. The Granger Collection Ltd.—Washington, Denzel, in title role in the film "Malcolm X" 1992, photograph. The Kobal Collection. Reproduced by permission.—Wilde, Oscar, photograph. The Library of Congress.—Yeats, William Butler, photograph. The Library of Congress.

Contributors

Liz Brent: Brent has a Ph.D. in American culture, specializing in film studies, from the University of Michigan. She is a freelance writer and teaches courses in the history of American cinema. Entries on *The Affluent Society*, *The Interpretation of Dreams*, and *A Theory of Justice*. Original essays on *The Affluent Society*, *The Interpretation of Dreams*, and *A Theory of Justice*.

Jennifer Bussey: Bussey holds a master's degree in Interdisciplinary Studies and a bachelor's degree in English literature. She is an independent writer specializing in literature. Entry on *I Will Bear Witness: A Diary of the Nazi Years, 1933–1941*. Original essay on *I Will Bear Witness: A Diary of the Nazi Years, 1933–1941*.

Lois Carson: Carson is an instructor of English literature and composition. Original essay on *The Autobiography of Malcolm X*.

Erik France: France is a librarian and teaches history and interdisciplinary studies at University Liggett School and writing and poetry at Macomb Community College near Detroit, Michigan. Original essay on *Operating Instructions: A Journal of My Son's First Year*.

Joyce Hart: Hart has degrees in English literature and creative writing and is a published writer of literary themes. Original essay on *Coming of Age in Mississippi*.

Rena Korb: Korb has a master's degree in English literature and creative writing and has written for a wide variety of educational publishers. Entries on *Coming of Age in Mississippi*, *I Remain in Darkness*, *News of a Kidnapping*, and *Operating Instructions: A Journal of My Son's First Year*. Original essays on *Coming of Age in Mississippi*, *I Remain in Darkness*, *News of a Kidnapping*, and *Operating Instructions: A Journal of My Son's First Year*.

Laura Kryhoski: Kryhoski is currently working as a freelance writer. Original essays on *Coming of Age in Mississippi* and *I Remain in Darkness*.

Jennifer Lynch: Lynch is a teacher and freelance writer in northern New Mexico. Entry on *Shadow and Act*. Original essay on *Shadow and Act*.

Candyce Norvell: Norvell is an independent educational writer who specializes in English and literature. She holds degrees in linguistics and journalism and has done graduate work in theology. Entries on *Self-Reliance* and *Walden*. Original essays on *Self-Reliance* and *Walden*.

Josh Ozersky: Ozersky is a critic, essayist, and cultural historian. Original essays on *The Autobiography of Malcolm X*, *I Remain in Darkness*, *News of a Kidnapping*, and *Oper-*

ating Instructions: A Journal of My Son's First Year.

David Remy: Remy is a freelance writer who has written extensively on Latin American art and literature. Original essay on *News of a Kidnapping.*

Susan Sanderson: Sanderson holds a master of fine arts degree in fiction writing and is an inde- pendent writer. Entries on *The Autobiography of Malcolm X, Autobiographies, Backlash: The Undeclared War against American Women,* and *Hunger of Memory: The Education of Richard Rodriguez.* Original essays on *The Autobiography of Malcolm X, Autobiographies, Backlash: The Undeclared War against American Women,* and *Hunger of Memory: The Education of Richard Rodriguez.*

The Affluent Society

John Kenneth Galbraith

1958

The Affluent Society (1958), John Kenneth Galbraith's most broadly influential book, stands out among works of economic analysis for its accessible writing style, which makes complex economic concepts and arguments understandable to the popular reader. Galbraith's phrase "conventional wisdom," a key concept introduced in *The Affluent Society*, has entered common parlance so pervasively that it is now used to describe a variety of concepts not necessarily related to economic theory.

Galbraith asserts that the conventional wisdom of economic thinking in the United States is based in nineteenth-century European economic theory and is no longer suited to the unprecedented phenomenon of mass affluence achieved by American society in the twentieth century. He criticizes the overemphasis on high rates of production as a measure of economic prosperity, suggesting that other factors may be of greater importance. He further asserts that economic theory must take into account the importance of advertising in artificially creating high rates of consumption to support high rates of production.

Galbraith's central concerns in reassessing the American economy include: the nature of American affluence; the relationship between production, consumption, and advertising; the abiding issue of poverty and economic inequality; and changing factors in such economic concerns as employment,

inflation, and consumer debt. He ultimately advocates a greater emphasis on sales tax over property tax; greater government expenditure on such public services as education and health care; and a national goal of expanding the ''new class'' of citizens able to pursue work they find inherently enjoyable.

Author Biography

John Kenneth Galbraith is one of the most influential economists of the twentieth century. His more than forty books bridge the gap between academic economic theorists and the common reader, with witty, insightful, and accessible bestsellers such as *American Capitalism* (1952), *The Affluent Society* (1958), and *The New Industrial State* (1967). He is credited with having coined key phrases now in common parlance, most notably, ''conventional wisdom.'' His works include memoirs, novels, and art history books as well as the economic treatises for which he has made his name. Galbraith is a liberal who, in addition to writing and teaching, has played an active role in American politics. He has held various government posts and worked as a speech writer for United States Presidents Franklin D. Roosevelt, John F. Kennedy, and Lyndon B. Johnson as well as presidential candidates Adlai Stevenson, Robert Kennedy, and George McGovern.

Galbraith was born on October 15, 1908, on a farm in Iona Station, Ontario, Canada. His parents were Catherine (Kendall) Galbraith and William Archibald Galbraith (a farmer and politician). Galbraith graduated from the Ontario Agricultural College of the University of Toronto in 1931, with a bachelor's degree in animal husbandry. He received a master of arts and a doctorate in economics from the University of California at Berkeley in 1934. From 1934–1939, he was an instructor at Harvard University, in Boston, Massachusetts. During this period, in 1937, he became a naturalized American citizen and married Catherine Atwater, with whom he had four children. From 1939–1942, he worked as an assistant professor of economics at Princeton University, in Princeton, New Jersey. From 1941–1946, during World War II and the post-war years, Galbraith occupied a variety of United States government posts, including the National Defense Advisory Commission, the Office of Price Administration, the United States Strategic Bombing Survey, and the Office of Economic Security Policy. He also served on the editorial board of *Fortune*

magazine from 1943–1948. After the war years, Galbraith resumed his academic career teaching as a lecturer at Harvard University from 1948–1949 and as professor of economics at Harvard from 1949–1975. During the 1960s, he also held various government posts—a key advisor to President John F. Kennedy and a United States Ambassador to India from 1961–1963. From 1967–1968, he served as national chairman of Americans for Democratic Action. From 1970–1971, he was a visiting fellow at Trinity College, Cambridge University, in Cambridge, England. He served as president of the American Economic Association in 1972. In 1975, he became professor emeritus at Harvard University. He and his wife live intermittently throughout the year in Cambridge, Massachusetts; Newfane, Vermont; and Gstaad, Switzerland.

Plot Summary

American Affluence and Conventional Wisdom

Asserting that the United States in the twentieth century is an anomaly in world history due to its unprecedented affluence, Galbraith states that economic theory up to this point is based primarily on societies characterized by poverty and is, therefore, inadequate to addressing the economic condition of the United States in the twentieth century. He introduces the concept of conventional wisdom, which refers to the generally accepted ideas within any given society. Galbraith asserts that conventional wisdom is based primarily on tradition and does not accommodate changes in society and so must be viewed with skepticism. He observes that the early economic theorists—the leading figures being Smith, Ricardo, and Malthus—of the previous centuries based their theories in a world economy characterized by poverty. Galbraith then provides an overview of major currents in economic theory since the Industrial Revolution in the mid-nineteenth century. A predominant current of twentieth-century thought—the ''central tradition'' of economic theory—was the idea that financial crises, such as the depression, are a normal occurrence of economic cycles.

Production

Galbraith traces the major currents of American economic thought in the twentieth century,

John Kenneth Galbraith

particularly the influence of Social Darwinism and Marxism. Galbraith argues that the issue of inequality in the distribution of wealth has become less and less of a concern in American conventional wisdom. Focus has moved instead to the benefits of increased production at all levels of society. He points out that since the 1930s, economic security, both for the business owner and the worker, has steadily increased, as has overall production. With the decrease in concern for economic inequality and the relative elimination of extremes of economic insecurity, Galbraith argues, production has become the foremost concern in economic thought. He elaborates upon the extent to which conventional wisdom in the United States regards production as the essential measure of economic vitality. However, Galbraith notes that, in fact, this concern with production is irrational and inappropriate to the realities of the economy. He stresses that the conventional wisdom is selective in evaluating various types of production so that private sector production is deemed good for the economy while social services provided by the government are considered bad for the economy.

Consumption

Galbraith further observes that, with the steady increase in wages in the United States, luxury items have come to be considered consumer "needs," equivalent to the need for food and shelter in less affluent societies. He points out that it is inaccurate to claim that the production of these luxury items is determined by the "needs" of the consumer; rather, it is the extensive advertising efforts that accompany production, which *creates* the "need" in the consumer. Galbraith insists that contemporary economic theory has failed to take this dynamic, which he calls the "dependence effect," into account. He explains that, after the 1930s, the conventional wisdom of economic thinking became dominated by a stress on the value of high production rates. He observes that, although in recent times the focus on production as a measure of economic vitality has given way to a broader range of concerns, it remains, in the conventional wisdom, the be-all and end-all of national prosperity. He goes on to describe the steady increase in consumer debt from the 1920s to the present, warning that massive consumer debt, while potentially hazardous to the economy, is encouraged in the United States as a corollary to high rates of production and consumption.

Inflation

Galbraith examines economic attitudes about inflation, which, since World War II, has clearly become an inevitable factor in the United States economy. Economists disagree on the cause of inflation, as well as on the possible means of regulating it, conservatives being primarily concerned with the level of product demand in the economy and liberals with the "wage-price spiral," according to which increased wages have a snowball effect on the growth of inflation. Galbraith examines the role of the Federal Reserve System of monetary policy in the United States with which attempts are made to regulate inflation. He goes on to note that the Federal Reserve's primary method of raising interest rates does more to harm small businesses than to protect the consumer against inflation. He concludes that monetary policy is "a blunt, unreliable, discriminatory and somewhat dangerous instrument of price control." He describes the relative merits of monetary measures (as advocated by conservatives) and fiscal policy (as advocated by liberals) in regulating inflation.

Social Balance

Galbraith elaborates upon his argument that the conventional wisdom of American economic thought values high production in the private sector as a measure of a strong economy while denigrating the value of goods and services provided by the government. Thus consumer expenditure on personal goods and services is valued above government expenditure funded by taxes. Galbraith coins the term "social balance" to describe an acceptable relationship between private and public expenditure. He argues that an affluent society is dependent, for the public good, on state expenditures in the areas of the police force, education, public sanitation, public transportation, roads, and the regulation of safety standards for air and water. He argues that public education is an area of government expenditure that is ultimately an investment in private-sector industry. In an age of technology, citizens with a higher education in the areas of science and engineering are necessary to the advance of industry. However, the conventional wisdom, Galbraith observes, does not consider public education to be a valuable investment in economic prosperity. Galbraith further asserts that finding employment for the unemployed is not the best way to cure economic downturns or high inflation. Rather, he argues, an increase in unemployment benefits provided by government would accommodate the unemployed without adding to the problem of inflation. He further contends that a greater emphasis on sales taxes (rather than income taxes) would lead to a greater social balance of private and public sector production. He makes clear that income taxes should

remain but that greater sales taxes would fund government at the state level, thus enabling greater expenditure on such vital public services as education. He asserts that greater government spending in the public sector is the most important factor in reducing poverty.

Education and the New Class

Galbraith puts forth the idea that a "new class" of workers has emerged in the "affluent society" of twentieth-century American life—a class characterized by the opportunity to seek enjoyable employment. He argues that the enjoyment of work is of greater value than either increase in pay or decrease in total hours spent at work. He suggests that the expansion of the class of people who are able to find work they enjoy—rather than the senseless expansion of production rates—should be a national priority. He argues that the most important factor that makes the expansion of this new class of workers possible is increased access to quality education for all citizens. He points out that while the conventional wisdom regards excessive spending on military as a necessity, spending on education is considered a waste. However, he argues that spending on education ultimately increases quality of life while spending on the military—particularly the build-up of nuclear arms—hastens the mass destruction of life.

Key Figures

Henry Charles Carey

Henry Charles Carey (1793–1879) was an American economist and sociologist, who is considered to be the founder of the American school of economics. His major works include: *Essay on the Rate of Wages* (1835), *Principles of Political Economy* (1837–1840), *Principles of Social Science* (1858–1860), and *The Unity of Law* (1872). Galbraith refers to Carey as one of the three "distinctly American figures" in the history of economic theory. Of these three, Galbraith notes, Carey was the exception in that his views were optimistic as to the economic future of society. In contrast to earlier theorists, Galbraith observes, Carey argued that wages had increased over time. Galbraith points out, however, that Carey was not a particularly influential figure in economic theory. He concludes that Carey's work is not a significant factor in the "tradition of American economic thought," and that his books, receiving little serious attention, "moldered and died."

Henry Ford

Henry Ford (1863–1947) was an American entrepreneur who founded the Ford Motor Company. His early success was due to his development of the assembly line as the most efficient means of manufacturing a product. Galbraith mentions Ford as an example of the cultural status enjoyed by early industrialists based solely on their success in the realm of business and regardless of their level of education or intellectual sophistication. Galbraith points out that, in modern America, successful business entrepreneurs no longer hold such celebrity status unless they have distinguished themselves in other realms.

Henry George

Henry George (1839–1897) was an American economist who advocated various measures of tax reform. His major work is *Progress and Poverty* (1879), subtitled "An Inquiry into the Cause of Industrial Depressions and of Increase of Want and Increase of Wealth." Galbraith mentions George as one of the three significant American economic theorists of the last century. He describes George, along with Veblen, as a "prophet of gloom" in his pessimistic outlook on the evolution of economic conditions. Although George did suggest a remedy to these conditions, Galbraith observes, he predicted "continuing poverty combined with increasing inequality and increasing insecurity." Galbraith further notes that the "mood" of those who advocated George's theories "was often one of misanthropic and frustrated radicalism."

Herbert Hoover

Herbert Hoover (1874–1964) was the thirty-first president of the United States, holding office from 1929–1933, during the first few years of the depression. Hoover had earned a widespread reputation for his humanitarian efforts during and after World War I. However, his inability to successfully stem the tide of economic devastation in the early years of the depression caused him to lose public favor, and he lost a second term election to Franklin D. Roosevelt. Galbraith observes that Hoover, in his attempts to address the problem of the depression, subscribed to the conventional wisdom that a balanced budget at the federal level was the most important factor in achieving national economic

Media Adaptations

- Galbraith contributed to the television series, *The Age of Uncertainty,* broadcast by the British Broadcasting Corporation (BBC) in 1977.

---

prosperity. Galbraith points out that this conventional wisdom was soon challenged by economic theorists.

John Maynard Keynes

John Maynard Keynes (1883–1945) was an English economist whose theories became known as Keynesian economics. His major work, *The General Theory of Employment, Interest and Money* (1935–1936) argues that widespread employment of the masses is one of the most important factors in attaining national economic stability and affluence and that, conversely, widespread unemployment spells economic devastation. During the 1930s, his theories had a revolutionary effect on economic thought. Keynes was the most influential economist of the twentieth century. Economists and political leaders from all ideological spectrums were quickly, if reluctantly, convinced of the wisdom of Keynesian economics. Galbraith was greatly influenced by Keynes and mentions his work throughout *The Affluent Society* for its powerful influence in altering the conventional wisdom of economic theory. Galbraith argues that Keynesian economics has become the new conventional wisdom.

Thomas Robert Malthus

Thomas Robert Malthus (1766–1834) was an English economic theorist whose ideas centered on the effect of population growth on economic stability. His major work was *An Essay on the Principle of Population as it Affects the Future Improvement of Society, with Remarks on the Speculations of Mr. Godwin, M. Condorcet, and Other Writers* (1798). Malthus's theories were largely pessimistic, arguing that widespread poverty is an inescapable reality of human economic conditions. Galbraith refers to

Malthus, along with Smith and Ricardo, as one of "the founding trinity" of economic theory in English-speaking nations. Galbraith observes that Malthus was extremely influential in spreading an attitude of pessimism throughout the field of economic theory. He further notes that although Malthus proclaimed massive human poverty to be inevitable, he showed no great concern for the suffering of the masses and proposed no possible solution for their economic condition.

Alfred Marshall

Alfred Marshall (1842–1924) was an English economic theorist who was one of the founders of the school of neoclassical economics. His major work was the *Principles of Economics* (1890). Galbraith mentions Marshall as a significant influence on the prevailing conventional wisdom of economic thought.

Karl Marx

Karl Marx (1818–1883) was a German-Jewish economist, historian, and sociologist, whose extraordinarily influential analysis of political and economic history is known as Marxist theory. His major works include *The Communist Manifesto* (1848), which was written with Friedrich Engels and *Das Kapital* (translated as: *Capital*). Galbraith refers to Marx throughout *The Affluent Society* in terms of his profound influence on modern political movements.

John Stuart Mill

John Stuart Mill (1806–1873) was an English economic theorist and philosopher known as an influential exponent of Utilitarianism. Mill was an early advocate of women's suffrage and was one of the founders of the first women's suffrage society, later known as the National Union of Women's Suffrage Societies, in 1867. In 1869, he published the now classic pamphlet, *The Subjection of Women*. Galbraith mentions Mill as one of the economists whose ideas formed the basis of American economic theory.

J. P. Morgan

See John Pierpont Morgan

John Pierpont Morgan

John Pierpont Morgan (1837–1913) was an extremely powerful American industrial magnate of the early twentieth century. His banking house, J. P. Morgan and Company, organized in 1895, became one of the most powerful in the world. Morgan eventually controlled most of the railroad industry in the United States and was head of one of the most powerful railroad businesses in the world. Morgan organized a variety of mergers and consolidations in major industries, heading such powerful corporations as United States Steel, General Electric, and the International Harvester Company. His industrial empire included banking and insurance companies. Galbraith mentions Morgan among several American business magnates of the early twentieth century. He points out that industrial moguls such as Morgan once held celebrity status and that their business ventures were associated in the public mind with the men who headed them. Galbraith observes that successful business magnates are no longer such visible public personalities in the eyes of the American people.

David Ricardo

David Ricardo (1772–1823) was an English economic theorist credited with systematizing economics as a field of scientific inquiry in the early nineteenth century. He is known for his theory of the "Iron Law of Wages," which asserts that the working wages of the masses of humanity will never rise above subsistence level. Galbraith lists Ricardo, with Smith and Malthus, as one of the "founding trinity of economics." He refers to Ricardo as "the man who first gave economics its modern structure." Galbraith observes that Ricardo, like Malthus, subscribed to the pessimistic theory that massive poverty was an inevitable condition of human economic systems. This conviction became a part of the conventional wisdom of economic theory, formulated in the nineteenth century, which continued to dominate economic thought in the early twentieth century. Galbraith notes that, like Malthus, Ricardo asserted that there was no possible remedy to the condition of subsistence level poverty suffered by the majority of the human population. Galbraith states that, from the mid-nineteenth century, Ricardo's central ideas remained dominant in economic theory but faced competition from the theories of Karl Marx, which offered a remedy to conditions of mass poverty.

John D. Rockefeller

John D. Rockefeller (1839–1937) was an American industrial magnate who founded the Standard Oil Company. His successful business conglomerations led to legislation against monopolies in industry, known as the Sherman Anti-Trust Act of 1890. Later in life, Rockefeller became a philanthropist, and his generous contributions, totaling some $500 million, financed the founding of such institutions as the University of Chicago in 1892, Rockefeller University in 1901, and the Rockefeller Foundation in 1903, among others. Galbraith mentions Rockefeller as an example supporting the theory that, in capitalist society, the rich get richer and richer, thus exacerbating economic inequality between rich and poor. He cites Rockefeller's justification of his extremely aggressive business practices as based on the theory of "survival of the fittest," which suggests that it is the natural order of things for certain people to become financially successful at the expense of many others.

Franklin Delano Roosevelt

Franklin D. Roosevelt (1882–1945) was the thirty-second president of the United States, holding office from 1933–1945. Roosevelt's New Deal policies were designed to bring the United States out of the depression that began with the 1929 stock market crash. Galbraith notes that, at the beginning of the depression, the conventional wisdom of economic theory was that a balanced national budget was the most important factor in achieving economic stability. He points out that Roosevelt was elected in 1932, at the height of the depression, based on this theory. However, by the end of the depression, Roosevelt, reflecting a change in the conventional wisdom, announced that reducing unemployment was the most important remedy to the crisis of the depression.

Adam Smith

Adam Smith (1723–1790) was a Scottish political economist and social philosopher of the Enlightenment. His major work, *An Inquiry into the Nature and Causes of the Wealth of Nations* (1776), put forth the first systematized theory of political economy. During his lifetime, Smith was internationally recognized for his influence on both social science and economic theory. Galbraith refers to Smith, with Ricardo and Malthus, as one of the "founding trinity of economics." He describes Smith as "the first great figure in the central economic tradition." Galbraith notes that Smith was the first influential economist to put forth the idea that the economic condition of the mass of humanity could never rise significantly above subsistence level. Galbraith asserts that this pessimistic eco-

nomic view is "the most despairing dictum in the history of social comment."

Herbert Spencer

Herbert Spencer (1820–1903) was a highly influential thinker of the English Victorian era. Spencer's writing and ideas ranged from the fields of biology to psychology to philosophy to sociology. He was a vocal advocate of individualism. His major work was *The Synthetic Philosophy* (1896). Although Charles Darwin formulated a more accurate theory of evolution, Spencer had put forth an earlier, less developed, theory of evolution; he quickly accepted Darwin's theory as superior to his own. It was Spencer, however, who coined the phrase "survival of the fittest" to describe the process of "natural selection." Spencer applied evolutionary theory to social and economic competition, developing a school of thought that came to be known as Social Darwinism. Galbraith refers to Spencer in terms of the influence of Social Darwinism on American economic thought.

John Strachey

John Strachey (1901–1963) was a British Socialist writer and politician in the Labour Party. Strachey published many influential works on Marxist theory. Galbraith describes him as "the most articulate contemporary English Marxist" of the early twentieth century.

William Graham Sumner

William Graham Sumner (1840–1910) was an American economic theorist, influential as an exponent of Social Darwinism. His major work was *Folkways* (1907). Galbraith refers to Sumner as the "major prophet" of Social Darwinism in the United States.

Frank Taussig

Frank Taussig (1859–1940) was an American economic theorist whose theories of international trade were highly influential in the formulation of American policy during the tenure of President Woodrow Wilson. Galbraith describes Taussig as "the leading figure in the central tradition" of American economic theory.

R. H. Tawney

R. H. Tawney (1880–1962) was an English economic historian. He was a highly influential socialist in the British Labour Party during the 1920s and 1930s. He was also a social reformer and many of his ideas were put into practice during his lifetime. His most influential works were *The Acquisitive Society* (1920) and *Religion and the Rise of Capitalism* (1926). Galbraith refers to Tawney in a discussion of the relative value of high levels of production to the social good.

Thorstein Veblen

Thorstein Veblen (1857–1929) was an American economic theorist whose ideas are based in the theory of Social Darwinism. His most influential work was *The Theory of the Leisure Class* (1899). He coined the now commonly used phrase "conspicuous consumption." Galbraith describes Veblen, along with George, as a "prophet of gloom" in regard to his economic outlook. Galbraith notes that Veblen's economic theory suggests that economic inequality is inherent to human society and that "there is not hope for change" in this fundamental structure.

Themes

Conventional Wisdom

Perhaps the most widespread and lasting impact of *The Affluent Society* is the entrance of Galbraith's phrase "conventional wisdom" into common parlance. The effect of conventional wisdom on attitudes about the economy is a key theme in this book. Galbraith explains that the conventional wisdom about the economy stems from nineteenth-century economic conditions and is, therefore, no longer relevant to the American economy in the twentieth century. However, he observes that many people in positions of power have a "vested interest" in the conventional wisdom in that it serves to maintain the status quo. He also claims that economists have a vested interest in conventional wisdom because it represents the basic assumptions upon which economic theory is based. Throughout the book, Galbraith asserts two main points about conventional wisdom. The first is economists, as well as the general public, must look beyond the outdated assumptions of conventional wisdom to formulate a more realistic assessment of the current American economy. Secondly, Galbraith points out that the conventional wisdom often functions as a

cover for economic policies that in fact run counter to this "wisdom." In essence, Galbraith views conventional wisdom as a mass delusion that must be dissipated to gain a clearer picture of the current status of the economy.

American Affluence

Galbraith's title, *The Affluent Society*, refers to the economic conditions in the United States in the mid-twentieth century. He argues that American society represents a new level of mass economic prosperity never before seen. Because of this unprecedented prosperity, Galbraith argues, economic theory based on the conditions of a population whose great masses of citizens live at a subsistence level is no longer appropriate when applied to the United States in the twentieth century. Galbraith asserts that, given the status of American affluence, economic instability has ceased to be a real issue, either at the private or industry level. In other words, he claims that there is little reason for either the individual citizen or the corporate world to fear economic disaster.

Poverty and Economic Inequality

While Galbraith asserts that the United States enjoys unprecedented affluence, he does not deny the continuing issue of economic inequality. He criticizes current attitudes about the economy, which reinforce a habit of discounting the issue of economic inequality. Rather, Galbraith believes that poverty should continue to be at the forefront of national concerns with the economy. He advocates diverting greater sums of tax revenue into public services to compensate for the disadvantages of poverty. Galbraith is especially concerned with providing the children of poor families with the public services, such as education, health care, and proper nutrition, which would allow them to overcome the poverty suffered by their parents.

Production

A central theme throughout Galbraith's argument is the over-emphasis, according to the conventional wisdom, on the value of high rates of production to a healthy economy. He observes that the near worship of high production rates in the American economic attitude is a major hurdle that must be overcome. He provides a variety of arguments demonstrating the fallacy of the common belief that high production rates are the most significant factor in a prosperous economy. He points to a variety of

Topics for Further Study

- Galbraith frequently refers to the effect of the depression on American ideas about economics. What economic conditions led to the stock market crash of 1929? What effect did it have on the American society and the American economy? What governmental policies were instituted in response to the depression? To what extent were these policies effective?

- Galbraith makes frequent reference to the status of the American economy during World War II. Learn more about the impact of the war on the American economy. What effect did the war effort have on employment rates, inflation, and consumer spending? To what extent did these changes persist in the post-war era?

- Find out more about the current state of the American economy. What are considered to be the strengths and weaknesses of the current econ-

omy? What measures are under consideration for addressing current economic issues?

- Galbraith mentions a number of different economists from throughout European and American history. Pick one of the key figures he mentions and learn more about this person. What are the central ideas of this economist? To what historical and national context was this person responding? To what extent do you find this person's ideas relevant today?

- Galbraith's discussion focuses primarily on the American economy of the twentieth century. Find out more about the economy of another nation. What is the current status of the economy in that nation? What are the central economic problems of that nation today? What measures are being implemented or considered to address these problems?

---

examples of current and past economic conditions which, he argues, demonstrate that production is not the most important factor in the economy. Rather, Galbraith points out that the focus on production causes most people to overlook other values, such as the importance of public services and job satisfaction.

Consumerism and Advertising

In a discussion of the relationship between production and consumption, Galbraith points out what he views as a major fallacy in the conventional wisdom of economic thinking about the United States economy. He notes that, according to conventional wisdom, production rates are determined by a society's *need* for various products, as indicated by rates of consumption. However, he points out that economists continue to overlook the power of advertising in actively *creating* artificially high levels of consumer demand. High rates of production, he argues, do not simply satisfy preexisting needs or desires in the consumer; rather, the industries that produce consumer products simultane-

ously produce advertising campaigns designed to convince consumers of their need for this product. Galbraith argues that the factor of advertising has to be taken into account to accurately assess the real value of high rates of production.

Work and Education

Galbraith argues that yet another fallacy of conventional wisdom is the assumption that a primary benefit of affluence is the opportunity to work fewer hours per week. He asserts that working less is not necessarily the most greatly desired benefit of affluence; rather, he contends, the desire for *enjoyable* work is greater than the desire for *less* work. He claims that there is now a new class of workers who have the luxury of pursuing jobs that satisfy their own interests. He does not deny that income is an important factor in job satisfaction, but notes that interest and pleasure are of at least equal importance. Galbraith observes that the most important factor in membership to this new class of workers is access to higher education. It is primarily with education that citizens are allowed the opportunity to pursue a career that involves work that is enjoyable. He argues that greater expenditure in the area of public education would make it possible for a larger and larger portion of the population to find occupations doing work they like to do. Galbraith asserts that there is no reason an affluent society cannot afford to make this possible.

Style

Stylistic Flourish

Throughout *The Affluent Society*, Galbraith makes use of stylistic flourish to make his points more entertaining and understandable to the general reading public. Robert Lekachman explains, in an introduction to *John Kenneth Galbraith and His Critics* (1972), by Charles H. Hession, "As even casual readers and severe critics of Galbraith usually attest, the man writes a lovely English prose—witty, supple, eloquent." The use of figurative language and Biblical reference, for example, demonstrates Galbraith's frequently praised talent for word play and for coining catchy, original phrases. For example, in the opening chapter, he warns the reader that his book puts forth controversial and original ideas that may challenge generally accepted notions held to be the norm. He criticizes the social atmosphere in which "the bland lead the bland." Galbraith here refers to a Biblical parable from which the commonly used phrase "the blind leading the blind" is often quoted. Thus, through a humorous turn of phrase, Galbraith condemns the "bland" conformity that characterizes defenders of the status quo. While this comment in itself is not central to Galbraith's discussion of economic theory, it demonstrates the stylistic flourish by which he successfully communicated complex ideas to the general public, creating a popular bestseller of what could have been a bone-dry economic treatise.

Epigraphs

Galbraith begins two chapters with epigraphs, or short, pithy quotes, that reflect upon the content of that chapter. In opening chapter 10, for instance, Galbraith quotes from W. Beckerman's article, "The Economist as Modern Missionary" (1956). Beckerman asserts that "the problem of creating sufficient wants . . . to absorb productive capacity may become chronic in the not too distant future." This quote illuminates Galbraith's assertion that

high levels of economic production have come to be considered the "keystone" of economic stability, which is a problem in an affluent society because, in essence, no one really "needs" to buy much more than they already have. Galbraith elaborates upon this epigraph in this chapter by proposing that the industry of advertising has grown astronomically as a means of "creating sufficient wants," which the consumer does not naturally possess. Galbraith thus begins his chapter with an epigraph, a quote from another economist, as a basis upon which to develop his own arguments. In the opening to chapter 17, Galbraith begins with an epigraph quoted from economist R. H. Tawney. Tawney's quote, in essence, asserts that money cannot buy human health and happiness. Throughout the chapter, Galbraith builds upon Tawney's statement in arguing that a sense of "social balance" is needed, whereby the state addresses needs of society not necessarily fulfilled by consumer abundance, such as education and other social services. As Tawney was a well-known social historian, Galbraith lends legitimacy to his own argument through opening his chapter with Tawney's words.

Historical Context

In *The Affluent Society*, Galbraith makes broad sweeping references to such historical occurrences as the Industrial Revolution, the depression, and the launching of Sputnik.

The Industrial Revolution

The Industrial Revolution was not a political revolution but rather a conglomeration of significant historical changes that took place in the economic, social, and political spheres of European culture over the course of the nineteenth century. The changes most commonly associated with the Industrial Revolution were in the transition from primarily agrarian economies, employing farm labor, to primarily industrial economies, employing factory labor. Significant advances in technology also characterize the Industrial Revolution—from transportation technology to energy sources to labor-saving machines. The creation of an urban working middle-class led to new political trends emphasizing reform and increasingly democratic political systems. The Industrial Revolution began in Britain, developing between the years 1760 and 1840. In the early nineteenth century, it began in Belgium, reaching France by mid-nineteenth cen-

Compare & Contrast

- **1950s:** Following the communist victory, a rapid transformation takes place, and the Industrial Revolution belatedly makes its way to China.

  Today: Some consider the age of the Industrial Revolution to have passed into the Information Age—in which advances in computer and information technology have transformed the conditions of labor and production.

- **1950s:** During this post-war period, the United States enjoys an era of booming economic prosperity.

  Today: Although the United States continues to enjoy a period of economic prosperity characterized by the lowest unemployment rates in decades and many average Americans profit from stock market investments during the late nine-

ties, the stock market takes a downturn and workplace layoffs begin in 2001.

- **1950s:** The Soviet launching of the first man-made satellite, Sputnik I, causes the United States to question its own achievements in science and technology. The "space race" begins, and the United States creates the National Aeronautics and Space Administration (NASA) to conduct research and development of space exploration capabilities. The first United States satellite, Explorer, is launched.

  Today: The United States and Russia agree to a joint space station program, part of which involves the United States space shuttle and the Russian Mir space station combining efforts in space exploration.

tury and Germany in the late-nineteenth century. The twentieth century saw the United States and Japan take the lead in the Industrial Revolution as well as strong development in such nations as Russia, China, and India. Galbraith refers frequently to the transformations brought about by the Industrial Revolution, particularly in regard to the historical evolution of economic theory.

The Depression

Galbraith frequently refers to the economic conditions of the depression in the United States, which began with the stock market crash of 1929 and lasted roughly until the beginning of World War II in 1939. The depression era was characterized by extremely high rates of unemployment—as much as 25–30 percent—and a severe decline in rates of industrial production. Through its effects on international trade relations, the depression soon spread from the United States throughout Europe. President Roosevelt, who became president in 1933, initiated a series of policies, collectively known as the New Deal, designed to address the concerns of the depression era. The extent to which the New

Deal was effective is debatable. However, with the advent of World War II in Europe, the demand for wartime materials from American industry effectively ended the depression.

The Cold War and the Launching of Sputnik

Galbraith attributed the success of *The Affluent Society*, upon its first publication in 1958, in part to a key event affecting the period of United States relations with the Soviet Union known as The Cold War: the launching of Sputnik. The Cold War can be dated from the end of World War II, in 1945, until the collapse of the Soviet Union in 1991. During this time, the United States and Russia engaged in a "war" of international relations pitting the communist East against the democratic West. A chief characteristic of the Cold War was the arms race, in which each side expended national resources to stockpile more and more destructive nuclear weapons. A significant event in the Cold War was the successful launching of Sputnik, the first man-made satellite, by the Soviet Union in 1957. Although it had no immediate military application, Sputnik represented, in the American psyche, the potential of the Soviet Union to outdo the United States in technological advances. The subsequent crisis in American public opinion involved a tendency to question the quality of American advances in science and industry, given the economic prosperity of the nation. Galbraith's book was thus published at an opportune historical moment when Americans were hungering for answers to the question of where America may have gone so wrong as to allow a communist nation to outshine the United States in technological achievement.

Critical Overview

"Galbraith may well be the most famous economist of the last half century," observes James Ronald Stanfield, in *John Kenneth Galbraith* (1996). Galbraith's celebrity status with the popular reading public may be indicated by his appearance in a February 16, 1968, *Time* magazine cover story, entitled "The Great Mogul." David Reisman, in *Galbraith and Market Capitalism* (1980), sums up Galbraith's widespread influence in stating that he has "succeeded . . . in stimulating more popular discussion of economic, social and political questions than has any other intellectual of his generation." Senator Edward M. Kennedy, in a foreword to *Perspectives on Galbraith* (1978), by Frederick J. Pratson, exemplifies the level and degree of respect and influence Galbraith has achieved in the realm of public policymakers: "As economist, ambassador, philosopher, professor, writer, skier, and public scold, he has had a continuing and extremely influential impact on an entire generation of American life and national economic policy." Kennedy concludes:

> Galbraith has been a profound, persuasive, and progressive influence on all who care about the future of this country. His role is secure as a giant in the contemporary, intellectual, and political history of America.

Pratson sums up Kennedy's assessment in asserting, "John Kenneth Galbraith is one of the world's most influential individuals." If nothing else, all agree that Galbraith's popular influence, for better or worse, is indicated by the number of phrases he coined which have made their way into common parlance, such as "affluent society," "conventional wisdom," "countervailing power," and

"technostructure." In acknowledgement of his accomplishments, Galbraith in 1997 received the Robert Kennedy Book Award for Lifetime Achievement.

The Affluent Society is the first of a series of books often referred to as the Galbraithian trilogy, the other two being *American Capitalism* (1952) and *The New Industrial State* (1967). First published in 1958, *The Affluent Society* was an immediate popular success, becoming second on the *New York Times* bestseller list and translated into numerous languages. By 1990, it had sold nearly one-and-a-half million copies. Accordingly, reviews in popular periodicals tended toward favorable. Pratson observes that *The Affluent Society* "helped make [Galbraith] an international celebrity, a position which he has held and reinforced ever since."

Among his fellow economists, however, Galbraith's work was given a generally harsh reception. Charles H. Hession, in *John Kenneth Galbraith and his Critics* (1972) comments, "In the years following its publication, *The Affluent Society* stirred up a considerable amount of controversy and debate, in the course of which some basic issues in its analysis and interpretation became evident." At its extreme, criticism of Galbraith by other economists may be exemplified by Sir Keith Joseph and Sir Frank McFadzean in the telling title, *The Economics of John Kenneth Galbraith: A Study in Fantasy* (1977). In a foreword, Joseph exclaims of Galbraith: "His views are idiosyncratic and partisan. He does not support them with any evidence." McFadzean adds, "one searches in vain for evidence to justify his lofty claim that he is actuated by a spirit of scientific inquiry." McFadzean further claims, "His beguiling prose style can easily so anaesthetize the critical faculties of the unwary that they finish by believing that he is making a new and vital contribution to economics."

In his defense, critics commonly point to Galbraith's "unconventional" approach to economics, an approach that challenges the very basis of current economic theories, as a threat to those "conventional" economists whose ideas are in question. Pratson notes that *The Affluent Society* "made great waves because it indicated a harsher and a more complex reality in the so-called happy days of the late 1950s." Stanfield states that *The Affluent Society*

> seized the minds both of those who found its message palatable and those who did not, and became the lightning rod on the discourse about the habitual inclination to identify the good life with the goods life.

On Galbraith's behalf, his defenders point out that he has with difficulty challenged members of his profession to bring their theories more in line with the realities of contemporary political, commercial, and economic life in the twentieth century; as Myron E. Sharpe, in *John Kenneth Galbraith and the Lower Economics* (1973), observes, "Galbraith's job is to push, drag, cajole and finesse economics into the latter half of the twentieth century." Others have noted, however, that Galbraith tends to insult his fellow scholars by neglecting to attribute some of his ideas to the work of those who preceded him; it has been pointed out that he frequently omits footnotes citing the sources of ideas not his own—a legitimate complaint on the part of his critics. Even those who champion Galbraith's ideas concede that his arguments are frequently ambiguous, overstated, or over-general.

The Affluent Society was re-issued in 1998 as a fortieth anniversary edition with a new introduction by the author. It was subsequently named one of the New York Public Library Books of the [twentieth] Century. Stanfield assesses the long-term impact of *The Affluent Society* on American thought, observing, "John Kenneth Galbraith's *The Affluent Society* is one of the most famous books of the last twenty-five years." Stanfield further notes, "The issues of values and public policy raised in *The Affluent Society* remain not only very fresh but also indispensable reading."

Criticism

Liz Brent

Brent has a Ph.D. in American culture, specializing in film studies, from the University of Michigan. She is a freelance writer and teaches courses in the history of American cinema. In the following essay, Brent discusses Galbraith's place in the history of economic theory.

To appreciate the significance of *The Affluent Society* to economic theory, it is useful to place the work of Galbraith within the broader history of economics as a field of inquiry. Galbraith is associated with the American Institutionalist school of economic theory, which arose in the early twentieth century. Below is a brief overview of the history of economic theory, beginning in the late-eighteenth century, and a brief discussion of Galbraith's influence on the conventional wisdom of attitudes about the role of the economist in American society and culture.

The first stage in the history of economic theory has come to be called the English school of classical economics or simply classical economics. The Englishman Adam Smith is generally considered to be the father of classical economics, which is dated from the publication of his seminal text, *An Inquiry into the Nature and Causes of the Wealth of Nations* (also referred to as *Wealth of Nations*) in 1776. Although economics had been a topic of discussion in previous centuries, Smith was broadly influential in developing economics into a distinct field of inquiry. Smith posited that economic conditions, such as price levels, are determined by objective principles that he referred to collectively as the "invisible hand" of the market. Thomas Malthus followed up on the work of Smith with his *Essay on Population,* published in 1798. Malthus's "Malthusian principal" was that the economic conditions of the mass of human populations could not be improved beyond a level of subsistence. David Ricardo was the next prominent figure in the family tree of economic theory. Ricardo's *Principles of Political Economy and Taxation,* published in 1817, elaborated upon many of the ideas first put forth in Smith's *Wealth of Nations.* Ricardo further systematized Smith's early theoretical propositions and developed the idea that an "economic model" could explain market conditions based on a few basic variables. Ricardo's "law of diminishing returns" posited that ever-increasing population expansion cannot ultimately be sustained by a corresponding expansion in the food supply. His "law of comparative costs" described the relationship between price levels in different nations—a set of ideas that became the basis of free trade policies in nineteenth-century Europe.

Because their ideas form the foundation of economic theory, Galbraith refers to Smith, Ricardo, and Malthus as "the founding trinity of economics." He further labels both Ricardo and Malthus "prophets of doom" because of their assertions that widespread poverty is inevitable and without remedy. The classical economists were advocates of *laissez-faire* economics. According to *laissez-faire* (which in direct translation from the French means "allow to do") the economy is best left to run its "natural" course without the intervention of governmental monetary policies. In 1848, John Stuart Mill published his *Principles of Political Economy,* which further systematized Ricardo's theories, even

What Do I Read Next?

- In *An Inquiry into the Nature and Causes of the Wealth of Nations* (1776), economist Adam Smith (whom Galbraith describes as "one of the founding trinity of economics") puts forth the first systematized theory of political economy.

- In his *Essay on Population* (1798), Thomas Robert Malthus (whom Galbraith describes as "one of the founding trinity of economics") offers his theory of the relationship between population growth and economic stability.

- In *Principles of Political Economy and Taxation* (1817), David Ricardo (who is also described by Galbraith as "one of the founding trinity of economics") outlines his highly influential theories of trade and taxation.

- In *American Capitalism: The Concept of Countervailing Power* (1951), Galbraith argues against the over-valuation of competition in industry structure.

- In *The Great Crash* (1955), Galbraith provides an explanation of the economic conditions of the stock market crash of 1929, which led to the Great Depression.

- *The New Industrial State* (1967) is Galbraith's sequel to *The Affluent Society*. It concerns the role of advertising in formulating patterns of consumption and suggests alternatives to the emphasis on competition in the American economy.

- In *The Culture of Contentment* (1992), Galbraith argues for the importance of addressing economic inequality in maintaining a healthy economy.

- In *A Journey through Economic Time: A First-hand View* (1994), Galbraith provides a survey history of the American economy from World War I to the present, focusing on the impact of war on the economy, the economic policies of American presidents, and significant changes in the study of economics.

- *The World Economy since the Wars: An Eyewitness Account* (1994) is Galbraith's introduction to American economic history, written in the style of a memoir.

- In *The Good Society: The Humane Dimension* (1996), Galbraith argues for the importance of public expenditure on programs designed to aid the poor.

---

more clearly articulating support for *laissez-faire* economics. By the late-nineteenth century, however, classical economics had ceased to dominate economic theory.

The period of classical economics is generally said to have ended around 1870. In the late-nineteenth century, modern economics arose out of the theories of "marginalism," which developed into three distinct schools of thought in Austria, Britain, and France. The marginalists were concerned with the value of a product in terms of its use-value to the consumer. William Stanley Jevons was the leading economist of the British school of marginalism. In his major work, *The Theory of Political Economy* (1871), Jevons put forth the "marginal utility theory of value." The Austrian school of economics, another branch of marginalism, was founded by Carl Menger. His major work, *Principles of Economics* (1871), put forth a theoretical model for the relationship between value, price, and utility, known as the "theory of value." Léon Walras developed the French school of marginalism with his seminal work, *Elements of Pure Economics* (1874–1877). He was noteworthy among economists for his formulation of a mathematical analysis combining theories of capital, production, exchange, and money. Between 1870 and the stock market crash of 1929, these three schools of economic theory merged as their ideas were more fully developed and elaborated.

The 1930s was another turning point in the history of economic theory during which several new schools of economics became prominent. The German historical school of economics developed throughout the late nineteenth and early twentieth centuries. The historical economists criticized classical economics for its efforts to formulate abstract theories of market behavior, regardless of specific social, national, and historical conditions. In the 1920s and 1930s, the American school of institutional economics, in which tradition Galbraith is categorized, was highly influenced by German historical economics. The institutionalists saw economic conditions as a function of ever-changing social, cultural, and political contexts, rather than a matter of abstract, objective principles (as did the classical economists). Thorstein Veblen is considered to be the father of institutional economics.

The depression era also gave rise to an increasing concern with "macroeconomics"—the study of the economic conditions of an entire nation as a single system. In "microeconomics," by contrast, economists are concerned with the economic behavior of individual industries and with the population as individual laborers and consumers.

Social Darwinism was a popular theory of economic competition that arose in the 1920s and 1930s, particularly in the United States. The most influential proponents of Social Darwinism were William Graham Sumner and Herbert Spencer. Social Darwinism applied the theories of evolution developed by Charles Darwin to economics. The theory of evolution, which posits that nature functions according to the principal of "survival of the fittest," was applied to societal conditions, with the now-debunked conclusion that those who are wealthy represent a biological imperative according to which they are naturally superior to those who are poor. By corollary, this theory asserts that those who are poor are naturally inferior. Social Darwinism was thus used to justify fierce free-market competition, regardless of its impact on economically disadvantaged segments of society. Social Darwinism is now considered to be without scientific basis and is seen as a justification for racist and classist attitudes regarding socioeconomic inequality.

Perhaps the most widely and significantly influential economist of the twentieth century was the Englishman John Maynard Keynes, whose theories became known as Keynesian economics. His major work, *The General Theory of Employment,*

> " The institutionalists saw economic conditions as a function of ever-changing social, cultural, and political contexts, rather than a matter of abstract, objective principles."

Interest and Money (1935–1936), is described in *Encyclopaedia Britannica* (1994–2000) as "the most influential treatise composed by an economist thus far in the century." Keynes shook the world of economic theory with his assertion that ongoing unemployment should be a central concern in analysis of economic recession (such as the depression). He advocated greater government intervention in creating policies to boost flagging employment rates. Keynes's insight was recognized by economists across the political spectrum, who had no choice but to acknowledge the value of his ideas. Keynes thus completely transformed economic theory. Further, his revolutionary theoretical propositions led governments throughout the world to adopt monetary policies in support of actively addressing high unemployment rates. This commitment to greater government intervention in stabilizing economic conditions led directly to the creation, in the 1940s, of such international institutions of monetary policy as the International Monetary Fund and the World Bank.

During the post-war era of the 1940s and 1950s, the field of economics became increasingly standardized and professionalized. Economists became prominent public figures in the political realm, including economic advisors holding governmental posts. Separate "schools" of economic thought lost significance, as the field of economics burgeoned into a unified discipline with distinct sub-fields. New developments in the field of economics included the increasing use of mathematical models. The new field of "econometrics," developed by Norwegian economist Ragnar Frisch, combined mathematical modeling and statistical analysis to support theoretical propositions. Another new branch of economics that arose in the post-war period was the study of developing, not fully industrialized, nations—a field known as development economics.

During the 1960s, traditional economic theory came under fire, considered a conservative force concerned with justifying the status quo of economic inequality. Economists were challenged to question the social relevance and value of their theoretical propositions and statistical models. The Galbraithian trilogy—*American Capitalism* (1952), *The Affluent Society* (1958), and *The New Industrial State* (1967)—written in the tradition of institutionalism—struck a chord in the politically active, socially concerned counterculture that arose in the United States during the 1960s. Galbraith's emphasis on increased government spending for social services as beneficial to the common good struck at the heart of a generation of youth concerned with social and economic inequality.

Source: Liz Brent, Critical Essay on *The Affluent Society,* in *Nonfiction Classics for Students,* The Gale Group, 2002.

Thomas Karier

In the following essay, Karier discusses how Galbraith's progressive economic ideas, as expressed in The Affluent Society *and other works, are "heretical" to followers of the free market doctrine.*

One of the less-recognized accomplishments of the New Deal was its displacement of scores of entrenched bureaucrats, following twelve years of Republican administrations. Believers in balanced budgets and free markets were out, while believers in jobs programs and government regulation were in. In this atmosphere of change, many liberal reformers were swept into the federal government, including a young Harvard professor named John Kenneth Galbraith. With a degree in agricultural economics from Berkeley, Galbraith was employed by the Agricultural Adjustment Administration in the summer of 1934. Thus began a long and illustrious career—one that included Director of the Office of Price Administration during World War II, Editor at *Forbes,* President of the American Economic Association, and Ambassador to India.

As a Democratic administration once again reorients itself in the wake of twelve years of Republican rule, the life and ideas of John Kenneth Galbraith take on renewed importance. Galbraith is not just another "progressive" economist. His major works, *American Capitalism* (1952), *The Affluent Society* (1958), *The New Industrial State* (1967), and *Economics and the Public Purpose* (1972) contain the foundations of an enlightened economic tradition. Call it progressive, liberal, or socialist—

the viewpoint that emerges from these 1,293 pages offers both a theoretical justification for enlightened government intervention and a blueprint for action.

The importance of a theoretical rationale to justify public policy should not be underestimated. Adam Smith continues to stand as a symbol for almost any policy in which the government is asked to do nothing. He is regularly cited by the opponents of affirmative action, import quotas, minimum wage, union recognition, Social Security, Medicare and Medicaid, government training, farm supports, and welfare. The fact of his death (more than two hundred years ago) has done little to dissipate the enthusiasm of his followers. Some of the most zealous have even been known to wear Adam Smith neckties.

While no one can expect Bill Clinton to distribute Galbraith neckties to his new appointees, a copy of *Economics and the Public Purpose* would be of far greater practical value. The progressive program described in this book is essential to deal with the backlog of social problems inherited from the past twelve years of essentially disengaged administrations. Not only has the concept of progressive public policy atrophied from years of neglect, it has been jolted by the implosion of the planned economies and further diluted by an infiltration of conservative ideas. Galbraith's work provides a model of analysis that could prove useful, if not essential, for resuscitating a progressive agenda.

Market heresy

The influence enjoyed by opponents of enlightened public policy clearly peaked during the 1980s with the ascendance of monetarism, supply-side economics, and Reaganomics. But the popularity of this view has always been strong in policy circles, and has provided Galbraith with a consistent target over the years. And, like Galileo, whose work made him a heretic in the eyes of the church, Galbraith has, on many occasions, found himself in violation of accepted doctrine. He confessed in his autobiography that "One of my greatest pleasures in writing has come from the thought that perhaps my work might annoy someone of comfortably pretentious position." His assault on those wearing the Adam Smith necktie—advocates of laissez-faire and neoclassical economics—must have provided a particularly rich source of enjoyment.

A principal belief of the opponents of public policy concerns the alleged superiority (if not perfection) of the unimpeded market. While many economists (even liberals) are quick to concede this point, Galbraith does not. The problems with competitive markets are fundamental—they are technologically backward. Preoccupied with ensuring their own survival, the typical farmer, the bituminous coal company, and the shoe manufacturer have little interest in devoting huge sums of money to risky endeavors with possible payoffs that are put off many years into the future. Hence, those industries that come closest to meeting the conditions of perfect competition also conduct the least amount of research. Even in agriculture, technological deficiency has been avoided only by the concerted efforts of government and large suppliers.

One of the oldest arguments in defense of markets rests on the belief that markets have an unrivaled capacity for meeting consumer needs and desires. Unlike producers in centrally planned economies, their counterparts in free markets are merely the servants of consumers who remain masters of their own demand. A comforting image, says Galbraith, but not one with much relevance. It is no secret that large firms dedicate substantial funds to advertising and related selling efforts. Firms are in the business of shaping the very demands they are supposed to meet. The obvious conclusion is that actual production is some combination of what individuals desire, and of what firms want to produce.

Among the various strategies devoted to marketing, one must include most research and development devoted to new products. The idea that firms engineer socially useful products is a comforting notion that appeals to industrial engineers and business economists, but the reality is that firms design new products because they are salable. Galbraith asserts that even a comparatively useless product can be salable when its demand responds well to advertising campaigns that promise ''greater sexual opportunity, less obesity, or some significant escape from the crypto-servant role of the housewife.'' Product development and market research are seldom very distant from each other in the corporate organization chart.

While these simple observations take much of the luster off the argument that maintains the perfection of free markets, Galbraith proceeds one step further. If many of the goods currently produced could not be sold without advertising, then how important are these goods? The possibility that some portion of private production is superfluous raises serious doubts about its virtue. We are led to

> **If the 'march of events,' rather than the support of scholars, is the basis for evaluating economic theories, then Galbraith undoubtedly ranks among the leading economists of the century.''**

the unavoidable conclusion that private businesses are just as capable of providing unnecessary goods and services as the commonly maligned government sector.

In addition, market defenders insist on painting a picture of firms as if they had no power over the government, consumers, or even their own prices. Once again, according to Galbraith, the image scores higher for the comfort it affords the powerful than for its relevance. Many large firms not only influence consumers and the state, they also exercise considerable discretion over the prices they set. While liberals can applaud this position, both because of its obvious wisdom and the discomfort it inflicts on the conservatives, they may find themselves in less than full agreement with the remainder of Galbraith's argument.

The problem with power, according to Galbraith, is not that firms produce too little (as suggested by conventional monopoly theory), but that they produce too much. The result is that resources are not underutilized by large firms who make up the planning structure, but are overused. This is a heresy of Galbraithian proportions—one that demands a proper explanation. While the planning sector may lose some sales by charging a higher price, the loss is more than offset by the additional sales arising from massive expenditures on advertising and research and development. Where the conventional monopoly model implies that the U.S. auto industry of the 1960s was underproducing, the reality, in this view, was just the opposite. At the time, more resources were devoted to the manufacture of automobiles than could be justified reasonably. The result was more cars and their complements—roads, parking lots, gas stations, pollution, and highway deaths—than would have existed in a more competitive and less profitable market that did not have the resources to put out a new model every year and advertise it on all the major networks.

Incentives

For those opposed to government intervention, a special place is reserved for the role of market incentives. Supply-side economics of the 1980s was based largely on the belief that taxes sullied these pure incentives and resulted in a stark reduction of productive activity. But this notion has been around for a long time, or at least since 1956. In that year, an address to the National Association of Manufacturers claimed that the prevailing tax structure "destroys the incentive of people to work . . . It makes it increasingly difficult, if not impossible, for people to save."

In response, Galbraith pointed out the obvious (if not inconvenient) fact that the tax structure had changed little for two decades; and yet, the country had enjoyed "years of rapid economic growth." The disincentives associated with the tax system were devastating in theory, but fortunately, nearly invisible in reality. Savings were not particularly low, observed Galbraith, nor would "many businessmen wish to concede that they are putting forth less than their best efforts because of insufficient pecuniary incentive."

Another violation of market incentives, according to government opponents, is the welfare system. Where, they lament, is the motivation to work when one can remain idle and collect welfare? But in Galbraith's view, "The corrupting effect on the human spirit of a small amount of unearned revenue has unquestionably been exaggerated as, indeed, have the character-building values of hunger and privation." His proposal to alleviate poverty included a sizable increase in the average welfare grant; and rather than spending less on the education and development of poor children, as is the common practice, he argued that more should be spent.

While the poor are left to suffer the costs of a poorly functioning labor market, the rest of society has, in Galbraith's estimation, largely distanced itself from the insecurity and risk of the market. The planning system of large corporations and the complementary function of trade unions tend to push risk farther down the corporate ladder. Social Security eliminates much of the risk associated with old age, and federal farm-support programs greatly reduce the anxiety in agriculture. Even Keynesian macroeconomic policy alleviates much of the risk inherent in the overall economy. But unlike most economists who lament the loss of market forces and their highly prized incentives, Galbraith recognizes this development as the product of a progressive economy. After all, human beings are strongly averse to risks involving serious deprivation—especially those related to unemployment, bankruptcy, or depression. It is understandable that a relatively affluent society would develop institutions with the explicit purpose of lessening the impact, or likelihood, of such calamities.

As for the incentives discarded with the risks, the loss is again hardly evident. "The most impressive increases in output in the history of both the United States and other western countries have occurred since men began to concern themselves with reducing the risks of the competitive system." But it will take more than obvious facts to break the spell that the concept of market incentives holds over the average economist. The preservation of market incentives has become a calling for many academics—even those on government payrolls, or with tenure. The irony was not lost on Galbraith, who noted, "Restraints on competition and the free movement of prices, the principal source of uncertainty to business firms, have been principally deplored by university professors on lifetime appointments."

The poverty of public goods

Among the most profound accomplishments of economic conservatives has been their ability to establish a positive image for private production, matched by an equally negative one for public production. While politicians are well-regarded for any increase of the gross domestic product that occurs during their tenure, they are attacked for expansions of government spending. The fact that government spending may be necessary to stimulate economic growth has never been sufficiently appreciated by the populace. The myth that private production is, in some way, superior to public production has persisted long past its usefulness. "Comic books, alcohol, narcotics, and switchblade knives are, as noted, part of the increased flow of goods, and there is nothing to dispute their enjoyment," added Galbraith.

He continued that the prevailing view flies in the face of common sense and makes "education unproductive and the manufacture of the school toilet seats productive . . . Presumably a community can be as well rewarded by buying better schools or better parks as by buying bigger automobiles." The results of such perverse priorities are occasionally so striking that they can't be ignored. In the 1950s, "Some . . . even pointed out that, in the same week the Russians launched the first earth satellite, we launched a magnificent selection of automobile models, including the uniquely elegant new Edsel." But unfortunately, recognition of the problem has been infrequent and fleeting. Private production continues to enjoy an undeserved reputation vastly superior to its public counterpart.

What is the source of this discrepancy that Galbraith would call the social imbalance? One answer is that the private sector does a much better job of promoting itself. It leaves only positive images in the minds of consumers through extensive advertising, sales promotion, and company public relations. There is no comparable advertising by the public sector. Elementary schools, police, social-welfare agencies, public housing, city parks and pools, public transportation systems, and state universities are not at liberty to spend large amounts of their budgets on self-promotion. An exception is the advertising conducted by the government for military recruiting. But, this exception only proves the rule, since military spending has traditionally enjoyed a deeper level of support and funding than other government activities. As such, the public sector is at a distinct disadvantage, leaving it especially vulnerable to the ravages of anti-government pundits.

The role of economics

Economists are fond of examining the role that self-interest plays in economic decisions. Most recently, some economists identified with the public-choice school have won acclaim for examining the self-interest of politicians. But conspicuously absent from the spotlight exposing self-interest are economists themselves. If ever they succumb to a moment of self-examination, they become inclined to view themselves as participants in the honorable pursuit of knowledge, objectively applying the scientific method to questions of great social importance. The suggestion that their work might be slanted in some perverse fashion in order to favor the powerful in society—those in positions to provide jobs, contracts, or grants—is regarded as a profound insult.

Galbraith has ensured himself a reputation as a heretic by applying the same assumption of self-interest to the economist that the economist applies to others. For example, Galbraith has argued that "mainstream economics has, for some centuries, given grace and acceptability to convenient belief—

to what the socially and economically favored most wish or need to have believed." The rewards for embracing the conventional view may be subtle—for instance, in improving access to jobs or obtaining promotions and tenure. In other cases, direct pecuniary rewards may be involved, as occurs when an economist engages in a consulting or research contract with a large corporation. It is seldom clear in such a relationship whether it is the research or the conclusions that have been purchased.

In addition to questioning the motivation of economists, Galbraith has presented repeated challenges to the profession. Neoclassical economics, he observed, fails to describe the big picture only because its proponents are hopelessly engrossed in irrelevant details. It is characterized by "refinement with relevance." Galbraith begins a chapter in *Economics and the Public Purpose* with a quotation by Joan Robinson: "The purpose of studying economics is not to acquire a set of ready-made answers to economic questions but to learn how not to be deceived by economists."

A question of standards

Conventional economists routinely evaluate the merit of economic policies by determining how much the results diverge from those of a competitive market. But once one recognizes the shortcomings of such an approach, how does one distinguish between good economic policies and bad ones? Galbraith again serves as an example.

Any economic argument should not only be believable, it should also hold up over time. "The enemy of the conventional wisdom is not ideas but the march of events." Similarly, "For being right, one may perhaps conclude it is better to have the support of events than of high scholarship." By this criterion (admittedly his own), Galbraith is worthy of a very high score.

In 1952, Galbraith described the inability of centrally planned economies to contend with the wide variety of consumer goods and services necessary to support a modern economy. The problem is largely resolved in the United States by a division of labor. A planning system that encompasses large corporations controls the production of consumer durable goods and natural resources, while a more decentralized market system handles the myriad complexities associated with smaller consumer goods and services. The Soviet economy had no comparable mechanism to handle these latter demands—a shortcoming that Galbraith claimed would only get worse with time. The eventual collapse of the Soviet system in the 1980s was widely believed to be related to this particular deficiency.

Also in 1952, Galbraith observed that very little stood in the way of organizing by government employees. He wrote, ''Schoolteachers, clerical workers, municipal employees, and civil servants have generally avoided organization . . . It seems to me possible that the next group to seek to assert its market power will be the genteel white-collar class. In any case, we cannot assume that efforts by presently unorganized groups to seek market power . . . is finished business.'' In 1962, unions represented only 14 percent of all government employees, but by 1980, the percentage had soared to 36 percent.

While government-sector unions advanced, the overall unionization rate retreated. In 1967, Galbraith wrote: ''The loss of union membership is not a temporary setback pending the organization of white-collar employees and engineers but the earlier stages of a permanent decline.'' Some twenty-five years later, there is still no sign of a let-up in the overall decline of unions.

Time has also been kind to a number of Galbraith's ideas that have been rediscovered by other economists. In 1958, Galbraith discussed the importance of investment in individuals—a precursor of the concept of human capital. ''Since investment in individuals, unlike investment in a blast furnace, provides a product that can be neither seen nor valued, it is inferior. Even the prestige of the word investment itself is not regularly accorded to these outlays.'' Galbraith dedicated an entire chapter in *The Affluent Society* to discussing the underinvestment in public education. He correctly noted the problem: The young have no collateral on which to borrow for an investment in their future. As a result, he concluded, the market, by itself, fails to provide enough investment in education. All of this was in print three years before Theodore Schultz legitimized the notion of investment in human capital with his 1961 article in the *American Economic Review,* entitled ''Investment in Human Capital.'' (Galbraith was not cited.)

This is only one of many instances when Galbraith's work anticipated a contemporary economic theme. America's apparent aversion toward leisure was analyzed in *The Affluent Society* in the 1950s, only to be resurrected in the valuable work of Juliet Schor, *The Overworked American: The Unexpected Decline of Leisure* in the 1990s. Galbraith

pointed out the excessive compensation of corporate executives in the 1970s, but it didn't become a subject of popular debate until the late 1980s. And in *Economics and the Public Purpose*, Galbraith presented a comprehensive account of a dual economy with considerable relevance to later work on dual labor markets and persistent wage differentials in the 1980s. Galbraith's theories have shown remarkable resilience over the years.

There is one more aspect of Galbraith's work that qualifies him as a heretic—his occasional appeal to decency and compassion. Why is this a heresy? An essential lesson in the economics curriculum asserts that the only legitimate defense of a public policy is efficiency. Since efficiency and laissez-faire are often equated by definition, the bias against government intervention is assured. One way to escape this trap is to broaden the criteria for evaluating public policy. This solution is not unknown. The recently formed Society for the Advancement of Socio-Economics is committed to ''alternative approaches'' that are ''morally sound.'' For instance, we could apply compassion, thereby giving more weight in economic policy to those with the least income. It is a value that Galbraith has used effectively in his arguments for government intervention. ''An affluent society, that is also both compassionate and rational, would, no doubt, secure to all who needed it the minimum income essential for decency and comfort.''

The march of events

There was a time during the Great Depression when conventional wisdom condemned government intervention in any form as inimical to economic recovery. As the economy spiraled downward, scholars and pundits alike continued to advocate a balanced federal budget and a tight rein on the money supply. This view was highlighted in a letter written by Herbert Hoover to President-elect Roosevelt in 1932, and later quoted by Galbraith: ''It would steady the country greatly if there could be prompt assurance that there will be no tampering with or inflation of the currency; that the budget will be unquestionably balanced even if further taxation is necessary; that the Government credit will be maintained by refusal to exhaust it in the issue of securities.''

At the time, these policies were based on solid theoretical principles and thus earned the widespread support of the economics profession. Objections were not unheard of and could be entertained in polite company, but it was the turn of events that dealt this view a swift and decisive blow. The economy responded to the immense budget deficits and currency inflation of World War II, not with a relapse, but with an explosion. In fact, the recovery was so profound that growth rates in real GNP that were experienced during the first three years of the War have yet to be replicated.

In hindsight, it is easy to account for this egregious and costly error. Many in the profession were opposed resolutely to government intervention—a commitment that stood above practical evidence and common sense. In Galbraith's view, it reflected ''a marked achievement—a triumph of dogma over thought.'' In this case, it was the ''march of events,'' rather than the consensus of scholars that discredited the prevailing doctrine.

If the ''march of events,'' rather than the support of scholars, is to be the basis for evaluating economic theories, then Galbraith undoubtedly ranks among the leading economists of the century. Opponents of government intervention have benefited immensely from using the work of Adam Smith as a symbol of market efficiency. Progressive advocates of an enlightened government would do well to employ John Kenneth Galbraith in a similar fashion. His work serves as a useful symbol, even if his visage has yet to grace a necktie.

Source: Thomas Karier, ''The Heresies of John Kenneth Galbraith,'' in *Challenge,* Vol. 36, No. 4, July–August 1993, pp. 23–28.

Robert Heilbroner

In the following essay, Heilbroner analyzes The Affluent Society *thirty years after its initial publication and finds that it can serve as a model for ''widening the scope of considerations to which the economic scenarist must pay heed.''*

The Affluent Society was written to awaken American public opinion from its complacent worship of mindless economic growth. It succeeded in its purpose beyond all expectation. Almost immediately upon publication in 1958 the book leaped onto the best-seller list, where it remained for twenty-eight weeks. It was considered of such special importance that the Elmo Roper organization conducted a poll of ''businessmen/trustees'' and economists—the latter selected randomly from the membership list of the American Economic Association, along with an undesignated number of ''unusually prominent'' representatives of the profession—asking for their opinions with respect to its findings. Overall, the business community voted four to one against the

book, either categorically or with some reservations; economists rejected it only by the margin of 41 to 38 percent. A fifth of both groups was unable to make up its mind whether it agreed or not.

Thus *The Affluent Society* made its author, already well known, famous, and may indeed be considered the first step of his subsequent triumphant progress into infamousness. Perhaps most important of all, the book has remained alive both in the intellectual domain and on the public policy agenda to this very day. Whatever corrections we may apply from the privileged position of hindsight, its message remains as relevant as it was on its publication thirty years ago.

In this retrospective consideration and appraisal, I intend to pay Kenneth Galbraith the never entirely welcome compliment of taking his book more seriously than it was perhaps intended to be taken. *The Affluent Society* is a polemic, a tract for its times, but I shall reread it as the first statement of a new theory of capitalist malfunction. Such a change in perspective will inevitably discover things that should be amended or rethought, but Galbraith, who relishes irony, will appreciate that signal achievement is more likely to call down criticism than to win praise. With clear conscience, then, let me get down to business.

The Affluent Society covers many aspects of American society, social and political as well as economic. Not the least of its memorable features are a series of *obiter dicta* of which the best known is doubtless the stinging description of the Conventional Wisdom—the received knowledge, the most important attribute of which is not its truth but its acceptability—as well as a volley of rifleshots that any intellectual gunslinger must envy: ''Wealth,'' the book says on page one, ''is the relentless enemy of understanding.'' I shall leave all these matters aside, however, to concentrate on two propositions that underpin the theory I wish to educe from the work. The first is the assertion that the conventional justification for production—its capacity for fulfillment of inherent human needs—no longer applies to the stage of capitalism in which we live. The second is that the cultivation of private consumption leads to a peculiar kind of economic imbalance. These two propositions interact to form a novel and potentially important theory—or, for reasons I shall come to in due course, meta-theory—of capitalist malfunction. Thus my aim in rereading *The Affluent Society* is to move from the level of polemic to that of theory, losing a great deal of the book's appeal

Crowds gathered for Christmas shopping at New York City's Herald Square. The Christmas shopping season exemplifies the theories of consumerism and advertising that Galbraith discusses in the book

along the way but perhaps gaining another reason for maintaining it on the intellectual agenda.

From this Olympian viewpoint, one consideration strikes us immediately. This is the first time in the history of economic thought that anyone has traced capitalist malfunction to too much, not too little consumption. There is certainly no lack of theories attributing capitalist difficulties to over- or underinvestment, and a powerful train of theory, beginning with Malthus and developing through Marx and Keynes, designates underconsumption as

the cause of economic stagnation or crisis. But never to my knowledge has an *excess* of consumption (not, please note, too high a level of wage payments) been called on to play this role.

Moreover, the nature of the malfunction also changes. The familiar theories of capitalist crisis or stagnation usually lead to the conclusion that the level of expenditures will fall. Nothing of this enters *The Affluent Society*. Instead we find a malfunction of an entirely different kind, namely a tendency for the division of outputs between private and public goods and services to lose their necessary complementarity, with results that do not affect the quantity of shortrun output or the immediate division of functional income payments, but whose consequences for long run growth and quality of life may be very serious.

I shall not spend a great deal of time examining or expanding on the Dependence Effect, as Galbraith entitles his proposition that consumer "wants" are not a given aspect of the human condition, but are conjured up as part of the activity of production itself. In Galbraith's words:

> As a society becomes increasingly affluent, wants are increasingly created by the process by which they are satisfied. This may operate passively. Increases in consumption, the counterpart of increases in production, act by suggestion or emulation to create wants. Or producers may proceed actively to create wants through advertising and salesmanship. Wants thus come to depend on output.

Behind Galbraith's proposition are two vexing questions. The first recalls the long philosophical argument over the division between "needs" and "wants," "necessities" and "luxuries," "entitlements" and "desires," an argument that goes back at least to Bernard Mendeville's designation of all superfluities above subsistence as "luxury" and of the ministration to these luxuries as "vice." Galbraith's position here smacks of a certain moralism (or perhaps Veblenianism), evident in his frequently derisive description of the consumption generated by the Dependence Effect: "The family which takes its mauve and cerise, air-conditioned, power-steered, and power-braked automobile out for a tour." I am myself happier with Adam Smith's spirited attack on Mandeville for blurring the distinction between "self-love" and selfishness. Not all advertising- or emulation-associated consumption merits scorn; and Galbraith makes no attempt to estimate the amount or the proportion that does.

Prior to these admittedly difficult distinctions there is, of course, the question of whether the Dependence Effect exists—that is, whether the "demand" for increased production is itself "produced," whether through the cultural pressures of emulation or by direct contrivance. I see no reason to challenge Galbraith's view on the matter, noting only that it refers to the long-run, not the short-run theory of consumption—that is, to the configuration of preference sets over time, rather than to the convexity or other characteristics of utility functions in a given period. This intertemporal aspect of

> **Whatever corrections we may apply from the privileged position of hindsight, its message remains as relevant as it was on its publication thirty years ago."**

the rising level and changing character of demand means that it is difficult to specify the Dependence Effect in quantitative terms, a matter of some importance to which we will return. Nonetheless, the fact that an economic force eludes our capabilities for measurement does not negate its existence or deny its potential explanatory importance.

Let us then proceed to the second, and more important, of the propositions in question—namely that a socially encouraged expansion of private consumption leads to serious imbalance in the system. This hypothesis must be examined from two points of view: the causes for the imbalance, and the nature and importance of the difficulties it raises.

The Affluent Society suggests that three processes link the Dependence Effect to social malfunction, although only one of them leads to the particular kind of malfunction designated as Social Imbalance. The first of these ties the encouragement of consumption to the exacerbation of inflation. To cite Galbraith:

> If inflation is caused by output pressing generally on capacity, then [the Conventional Wisdom tells us] one need only get more capacity and more output and thus insure that this tension no longer exists. But . . . additional all-around production, even when it can be easily obtained from existing capacity, will pay out, in wages and other costs, the income by which it is bought. We have seen, however, that wants do not have an origin that is independent of production. They are nurtured by the same process by which production is increased. Accordingly, the effect of increased production from existing plant capacity is to increase also the purchasing power to buy that production and the desires which insure that the purchasing power will be used.

The argument strikes me as weak. It assumes that a steady stream of consumer expenditures will continue to generate what Galbraith calls the "unliquidated gains" that allow corporations to raise prices. The argument is cavalier with respect to the countervailing force of market saturation. Saturation is surely the common fate of individual commodities—merely as an illustrative instance, the percentage of homes with television sets rose from 9 percent in 1950 to 87 percent in 1960—which rules out the steadily rightward moving demand curve necessary to produce unliquidated gains for a single company or industry. The analysis therefore comes to hinge on whether a general condition of excess consumption demand could be perpetuated by the Dependence mechanisms. This requires the positing of consumption spending, energized and encouraged by emulation and advertising, as an independent variable in the economic system. As with all theories of consumption-led economic movements, it begs the question of how the desire to increase consumption is translated into sufficient actual purchasing power if investment falters *despite* rising levels of consumption, as can surely be the case with the advent of unfavorable expectations.

A second suggested influence of consumer spending on systemic functioning involves consumer debt. Galbraith ties consumer debt ratios directly to the encouragement of consumption:

> It would be surprising indeed if a society that is prepared to spend thousands of millions to persuade people of their wants were not to take the further step of financing these wants, and were it not then to go on to persuade people of the ease and desirability of incurring debt to make these wants effective. This has happened. . . The Puritan ethic was not abandoned. It was merely overwhelmed by the massive power of modern merchandising.

The dangers of this process are obvious enough. Households increase their indebtedness beyond the limits of prudence, with destabilizing results: ''The effect of the expansion of consumer credit is to add an uncertainty, paralleling that which business borrowing brings to business spending, to the hitherto more reliable consumer spending.''

The evidence is mixed with respect to this second difficulty. Unquestionably the debt/income ratio has risen, as Galbraith expected; and living in an age of payment by plastic, we can appreciate the merits of his claim that a high consumption economy activates its own mechanisms for financing the consumption it encourages. Again merely as illustration, the ratio of household (nonmortgage) debt to disposable income has risen from 8.5 percent in 1929 to 23.6 percent in 1986.

The evidence is less conclusive, however, with respect to the instability added to the system by increased consumer debt. Delinquency ratios from 1979 through 1986—years that included two years of unprecedently high interest rates and a very serious recession—range from a low of 1.94 to a high of 2.32, a considerable percentage increase but hardly a level of failure such as to generate alarm. Indeed, Galbraith himself is guarded as to the destabilizing influence of a high consumer debt society:

> In fact, we really do not know the extent of the danger. A tendency to liquidation of consumer debt, with accompanying contraction in current spending, could be offset by prompt and vigorous government action to cut taxes, increase public outlays, and so compensate with spending from other sources.

I turn now to the last, and to my mind incomparably the most important analytic concept in *The Affluent Society*, namely the hypothesis that the encouragement of consumption leads to social imbalance. Galbraith does not spell out this central tenet of the book in any detail, or in analytic form. The glaring contrast between the opulence of the private sector and the squalor of the public is set forth in striking images (the mauve and cerise automobile drives through a squalid public sector), but the causal analysis needed to raise these images above the level of anecdote is sparse.

The principal argument is that the dependence effect operates with full force on the expansion of private wants and their associated satisfaction by private production, but that no comparable process keeps the public sector abreast of the private. The needed complementarity of private and public goods is illustrated by reference to the externalities of crowding, pollution, and the like: ''As surely as an increase in the output of automobiles puts new demands on the steel industry, so, also, it places new demands on public services. Similarly, every increase in the consumption of private goods will normally mean some facilitating or protective step by the state.'' But whereas ''every corner of the public psyche is canvassed by some of the nation's most talented citizens to see if the desire for some merchantable product can be cultivated, [n]o such process operates on behalf of the nonmerchantable services of the state . . . The inherent tendency will always be for public services to fall behind private production.''

Galbraith is not explicit about the extent or severity of the consequences of social imbalance. There a few remarks about the consequences of the neglect of education and research, the misperception of the relation of national security to production, the neglect of possibilities for improving the nonmaterial standard of living, especially in occupations, and a withering scorn for the quality of the environment that social imbalance brings: "Just before dozing off on an air mattress, beneath a nylon tent, amid the stench of decaying refuse, [the inhabitants of the cerise and mauve vehicle] may reflect vaguely on the curious unevenness of their blessings." Withal, the indictment is general rather than specific; pointed at rather than specified. "In all cases, if these [public] services are not forthcoming," Galbraith writes, "the consequences will be in some degree ill," and again, "Failure to keep public services in minimal relation to private production and use of goods is a cause of social disorder or impairs economic performance." The extent of this disorder or impairment is left unexplored. Nor is there any suggestion of its possible cumulative tendencies over time.

Nevertheless, in my opinion, it is here that the principal theoretical contribution of *The Affluent Society* must be sought. The undersupply of public goods is, of course, a familiar theme from the theory of public goods. What is novel and interesting in the Theory of Social Imbalance are two implications not previously advanced, to my knowledge. The first is that this imbalance constitutes more than a static "misallocation" of resources. It contains the basis for a self-induced qualitative decline in the standard of living. In other words, an important malfunction of advanced capitalism may lie in a deterioration in the quality of life brought about by an endemic tendency of the output of public goods to lag behind that of private goods—a malfunction as specific to capitalism as interruptions in trajectory of growth, although quite different in its source.

A second implication is the possibility that the systematic undernourishment of the public sector becomes more aggravated as a capitalist society achieves higher levels of private affluence. This would be the consequence of rising "required" complementary public spending, accompanied by static or laggard flows of actual expenditure. One would therefore expect that an "affluent" economy would experience a growing awareness of unmet public needs, without, however, any corresponding awareness of the linkage of these needs to private consumption. I should add that such an extension of Galbraith's theory of social imbalance appears to accord very well with the tendencies in modern American capitalism, including that of a near total lack of understanding between the scandal of inadequate infrastructure and the encouragement of private consumption.

Is there, then, the basis for a new, possibly important, theory of economic malfunction in *The Affluent Society*? I shall begin by conceding what might seem to be the game. I do not think it is possible to construct such a theory if we must do so within the rules of the game that have become conventional for our discipline. The reasons for this are several. The empirical basis for the dependence effect, as we have seen, is extremely difficult to isolate and identify. One does not know, therefore, what proportion of consumption flows can be attributed to institutionalized encouragement, the crucial element of the Dependence Effect. In addition, any "gap" between the private and public spheres defies—or at least resists—measurement because one cannot not assume that it is accurately depicted in the ratio of gross national product to gross public expenditures, not all of which, by any means, can be counted as redressing the social imbalance.

At a yet different level of difficulty, the sociopolitical response that generates public compensatory expenditure varies widely from one nation to the next, as witness the contrasts between the reach and depth of the public sector in Sweden or the Netherlands, compared with that in the United States. This would require us to construct theories of differential public responses, a task that is still well beyond the capabilities of public choice economics.

Thus I am not sanguine with regard to the possibility of formulating a theory of Social Imbalance on a par with models of capital crisis or stagnation such as over- and under-investment, wage squeeze, and the like. The necessary elements are too "political" (not to say "social"), the degree of conceptual clarity too loose, the imaginable functional connections too complex. We are left with a scenario, a plausible extension of historical trends, political generalizations, and socioeconomic behavior patterns. This may be the basis for insight or action, but it is not what we are accustomed to call a theory.

Does this then relegate Galbraith's thesis to the discard pile? The question raises issues that are of central importance. At their nub is the capacity of economics to claim for itself a privileged position in the task of social prognosis. From *The Wealth of Nations* forward, economics has held such a position, based on its unique capability of reducing social movements to the analytic level of systems—that is, to schematized representations of motivation and response that can be depicted as having something of the regularity of physical systems of interaction. On the basis of this remarkable hypothesis, economics has built its castles, however Spanish in design or insecure as to footings.

The challenge issued by an effort to embrace a tendency to social imbalance into these theoretical edifices is that of incorporating behavior-response mechanisms that cannot be depicted or even conceived in the clear functional relations of economic laws. Propositions such as the Dependence Effect or the tendency to Social Imbalance are better viewed as meta-theories—causal frameworks that have a prima facie claim to plausibility, but that cannot, both for conceptual and mensurational reasons, be reduced to the clarity of functional equations. There are, in fact, many such meta-theories. Examples that come to mind are the beliefs of the Enlightenment as to the natural "life span" of nations and civilizations, or of the corrupting power of luxury; Lord Acton's famous dictum that "All power tends to corrupt and absolute power tends to corrupt absolutely"; Friedrich Hayek's contention that in bureaucracies "the worst get on top"; Schumpeter's conviction that the bell-shaped curve of talent always prevails; and a dozen other such generalizations respecting social behavior, some enunciated formally, many embedded in the common lore. The behavioral linkages that would enable us to put forward a theory of social imbalance as a tendency of advanced capitalism fall into such an enlarged form of social theorizing.

Is this enlargement possible? Is it desirable? It is certainly not without its risks. Generalizations about historical experience, or political attitudes, or human nature are fragile at best, and more often than not, rationalizations for unannounced, perhaps even unknown, preferences on the part of the judge. I have caught Kenneth Galbraith himself in such a featherweight law of history when he writes: "Conservatives will always prefer inflation to its remedies." Nonetheless, I have two reasons for favoring meta-theories. The first is that, as in the case of Lord Acton's generalization with respect to power, or Joseph Schumpeter's with respect to talent, some meta-theories appear not only to apply with disconcerting force to many cultures and periods, but to emerge from plausible roots in what we know of human socialization. The second reason is that, whether we admit it or not, meta-theories of "history," "human nature" and the like are almost always discernible in the background of our efforts to explain or project the course of things. Better to bring these ideas out into the open, using them where possible to construct scenarios that can there-after be subjected to the usual barrages of criticism, than to pretend that such scenarios do not in fact constitute an important means by which we seek social understanding.

A few last words. I have said that I would pay *The Affluent Society* the perhaps unwelcome compliment of examining it as basis for a general hypothesis with regard to capitalist malfunction. Clearly the book does not purport to be such a theory. The word "capitalism" scarcely appears in it. Its moving forces are described as "we," always a screen against deeper analysis. The tone of raillery gives charm, but serves as a substitute for more demanding considerations.

Nonetheless, I think there is a core of social generalization that gives *The Affluent Society* an importance greater than that of a tract of social indignation. A recognition of complementarities of public goods and private endeavor can be traced back to Adam Smith, who approved of the need for public education as a means of remedying the condition of general ignorance to which he believed a commercial society gave rise. The direction in which Galbraith's book points is that of widening the scope of considerations to which the economic scenarist must pay heed. It is thus an attack against the assumption that one can write penetratingly about society when one's perceptions are constrained by the narrow slits through which economists peer out from their theoretical castles. Better to mount to the turrets, whatever the difficulties of seeking to take in the vast social landscape. The result may not have the rigor of the models of conventional economic theory, but (if I may be forgiven for repeating a line I wrote some years ago), it may also escape the fate of such models, which is mortis.

Source: Robert Heilbroner, "Rereading *The Affluent Society*," in *Journal of Economic Issues,* Vol. XXIII, No. 2, June 1989, pp. 367–76.

Sources

Beckerman, W., "The Economist as Modern Missionary," in *Economic Journal,* March 1956.

"The Great Mogul," in *Time,* February 16, 1968, p. 24.

Hession, Charles H., *John Kenneth Galbraith and His Critics,* New American Library, 1972, pp. x, 95.

McFadzean, Sir Frank, *The Economics of John Kenneth Galbraith: A Study in Fantasy,* Centre for Policy Studies, 1977, pp. vii, 1.

Pratson, Frederick J., *Perspectives on Galbraith: Conversations and Opinions,* CBI Publishing Company, Inc., 1978, pp. ix–xiii, 49–50, 54.

Reisman, David, *Galbraith and Market Capitalism,* New York University Press, 1980, p. 6.

Sharpe, Myron E., *John Kenneth Galbraith and the Lower Economics,* International Arts and Sciences Press, Inc., 1973, p. x.

Stanfield, James Ronald, *John Kenneth Galbraith,* Macmillan, 1996, pp. ix, 41–42, 59.

Further Reading

Galbraith, John Kenneth, *Name-Dropping: From FDR On,* Houghton Mifflin Co., 1999.
Galbraith offers personal anecdotes about his encounters with a variety of United States presidents and other high-level government officials.

———, *A Tenured Professor,* Houghton, 1990.
A Tenured Professor is Galbraith's novel about a professor and his wife who discover a stock market scam that allows them to spend their enormous earnings on liberal causes.

Marx, Karl, and Friedrich Engels, *The Communist Manifesto,* W. W. Norton, 1988.
The Communist Manifesto (originally published in 1848) is the widely read pamphlet outlining Marx's and Engels's basic theories of socialism.

Reisman, David, *Tawney, Galbraith, and Adam Smith,* St. Martin's Press, 1982.
Reisman provides a comparative analysis of the economic theories of Galbraith, Adam Smith, and R. H. Tawney.

Sasson, Helen, ed., *Between Friends: Perspectives on John Kenneth Galbraith,* Houghton Mifflin Co., 1999.
Between Friends is a collection of essays by a variety of people who have encountered Galbraith, both at the professional and the personal level.

Autobiographies

William Butler Yeats

1955

William Butler Yeats's *Autobiographies*, originally published in 1955, is a collection of essays written by a man many consider to have been the greatest poet in the English language. The first essays, "Reveries Over Childhood and Youth" (1915) and "The Trembling of the Veil," (1922), cover Yeats's life through his late twenties. In 1936, another four autobiographical essays were published, "Dramatis Personae," "Estrangement," "The Death of Synge," and "The Bounty of Sweden," extending *Autobiographies* well into the poet's fifties, when he received the Nobel Prize for Literature.

While the information contained in these essays is roughly in chronological order, Yeats's goal seems to be not to catalogue exact details about his life but to deliver a sense of how he became the man he was. The pages of his autobiography are filled with the names of hundreds of friends and enemies and of societies formed and joined, contributing to a picture of a man passionate for Ireland and Irish nationalism. Writing from the vantage point of the early part of the twentieth century, Yeats acknowledges many of his past errors in judgment and admits to some bitterness over attempted projects that did not end well. In the later pages of his autobiography, Yeats covers his years of contributing to the Abbey Theater in Dublin, a place in which he made his long-time dream of an Irish national dramatic movement a reality. In addition, in the essays, Yeats reveals his increasing fascina-

tion throughout his life with the supernatural and mysticism.

Author Biography

William Butler Yeats was born June 13, 1865, in Sandymont, Ireland, to John Butler Yeats, a lawyer who later became a painter, and Susan Mary Pollexfen Yeats. He was the eldest of four children. The Protestant Anglo-Irish society into which Yeats was born was the minority in Ireland but had dominated Irish life and politics for hundreds of years. Unlike most of his fellow Anglo-Irish, who regarded England as their true home, Yeats considered himself primarily Irish, and his passion for Irish independence from England colored his life as an artist from the very beginning. He incorporated Irish heroes and heroines into his poetry and other writings.

As a child, Yeats was not a good student and instead desired to spend time walking around his beloved Irish countryside. Most of Yeats's childhood was spent in London, but he was able to soak up Irish stories and legends during his frequent trips to Ireland to visit relatives. He attended art school in Dublin between 1884 and 1886 and eventually decided that his talent was not in painting.

In 1885, at the age of twenty, Yeats published his first poem in *The Dublin University Review*. Four years later, he published his first book of poems, *The Wanderings of Oisin*. According to a passage in his *Autobiographies*, this collection received high praise from the well-known writer Oscar Wilde. For the next ten years or so, Yeats joined and organized a variety of societies and clubs, such as the Irish Literary Society and the National Literary Society, all of which promoted the independence of Ireland from England through the development of Irish national literature and arts. Yeats's enthusiasm for the politics of Irish independence waned in the final years of the nineteenth century because of what he saw as a tendency toward increasing violence; however, he never abandoned his interest in all things Irish as they related to his writing.

Also during his twenties, Yeats began his lifelong and consuming interest in the supernatural and the occult. He joined Madame Blavatsky's Theosophical Society (an organization that promoted a philosophical system associated with mysticism and that claimed to have insight into the

William Butler Yeats

nature of God and the world) and was also initiated into MacGregor Mathers's mystical society, the Hermetic Order of the Golden Dawn.

While numerous commentators have called Yeats the greatest poet in the English language, he did not limit his efforts to verse. In the early 1890s, he wrote two plays that showed his devotion to the Irish cause of nationalism, *The Countess Kathleen* and *Cathleen ni Houlihan*. Around the turn of the century, he joined forces with his patron, Lady Augusta Gregory, to produce his own and other Irish dramas; the success of their efforts led to the creation of the Irish National Theatre Society and the renovation of Dublin's Abbey Theatre for their company's home. He served as head of the company until about 1915. Beginning in 1915 with the release of *Reveries Over Childhood and Youth*, Yeats published six essays that would eventually be collected into his *Autobiographies* in 1955.

Yeats's one great unrequited love for nearly thirty years was the Irish activist Maude Gonne, widely known for her beauty and her passion for Ireland's independence. At an advanced age in 1917, Yeats married Georgiana Hyde-Lees, a fellow member of the Golden Dawn. The couple had two children. In 1923, Yeats received the Nobel Prize for Literature. He died in Roquebrune, France, in 1939 and was buried in the land of his ancestors, Sligo, Ireland, in 1948.

Plot Summary

Autobiographies comprises six essays describing Yeats's life from childhood through 1923 when he received the Nobel Prize for Literature.

Chapter One: ''Reveries over Childhood and Youth''

The first essay in Yeats's *Autobiographies* covers the author's life through his twenties, beginning with recollections of his maternal grandfather, William Pollexfen, and continuing through the publication of Yeats's first collection of poetry in 1889, *The Wanderings of Oisin and Other Poems*.

Yeats remembers having a very unhappy childhood but is never quite able to specify what caused his unhappiness. He suspects: ''my miseries were not made by others but were a part of my own mind.'' As he grew older, Yeats reports that he became happier.

Yeats writes of the first time he experienced hearing an inner voice as a child, which he decided later was his conscience. When he was an adult, this voice continued to come to him ''at moments of crisis.'' He also remembers experiencing various mystical events, such as witnessing the work of ''faeries'' and seeing a ''supernatural bird.''

When his family moved to London's North End, Yeats found himself involved in many fights with schoolmates who teased him about being Irish. He rarely won these fights and struggled over the fact that he never felt as brave as his grandfather Pollexfen. Eventually the family moved to Bedford Park, a neighborhood of art aficionados.

The first poems Yeats heard were a stable-boy's rhymes. When he was eight or nine years old, his father began reading poetry to him and continued this practice as Yeats grew up. Yeats describes himself as a poor student and not much of an athlete but very interested in collecting bugs and being outdoors. He greatly anticipated the occasions when he was allowed to sail to Ireland and visit his Sligo relatives. Yeats's family moved to Dublin from London when Yeats was fifteen years old.

Yeats's difficulty with his studies continued throughout his teenage years, and he became even more entranced with being outdoors. Yeats even slept in a cave for a period of time, causing great consternation among his teachers.

Yeats attended art school in Dublin from 1884 through 1886 but did not enjoy it. He spent most of his time writing poetry and studying the occult and supernatural. Yeats also frequented a number of clubs and societies involved in political debate and the issue of Irish nationalism—the idea that Ireland should be a country independent from England. He met numerous famous Irish nationalists, including John O'Leary, and began meeting with the Young Ireland Society, organized to promote the idea of Irish nationalism through Irish literature.

Chapter Two: ''Book I: Four Years: 1887–1891''

Yeats writes of the four years during which he met numerous poets and artists who would have lasting effects on his life and would become long-time friends and confidants. Yeats was in his early twenties and obviously excited about the numerous philosophical discussions he shared with his father's friends and others. During this period he met Maude Gonne, the Irish beauty and activist who, while becoming an enduring friend to Yeats, never reciprocated his romantic love.

Yeats was involved with many of the intellectuals and literary achievers of England and Ireland during these four years. For example, when Yeats published his first collection of poetry, *The Wanderings of Oisin and Other Poems*, Oscar Wilde praised the book. He and Wilde spent some time together; Wilde was quite fond of the younger poet's ability to tell Irish folk tales.

Yeats also began his association with Madame Blavatsky and her Theosophical Society and was initiated into MacGregor Mathers's mystical society, the Hermetic Order of the Golden Dawn.

Chapter Three: ''Book II: Ireland after Parnell''

Yeats recounts the years he spent organizing the Irish Literary Society, founded in London in 1891, and the National Literary Society, founded the next year in Dublin. Both societies were formed to promote the independence of Ireland from England through the development of Irish national literature and arts.

One of the primary projects undertaken by the two societies was the New Irish Library. Through this effort, the society arranged to have a number of agreed-upon Irish literary works published and distributed to libraries throughout Ireland. A struggle between Sir Charles Gaven Duffy and Yeats ensued over the editorship of the series. Duffy won the editorship, but eventually in-fighting between Yeats and ''half a dozen young men'' put a stop to the project. Yeats expresses a great deal of bitterness about the effort he put into the project.

The title of this part of the essay refers to Charles Stuart Parnell, Irish politician and founder of the Irish Home Rule Association which supported the idea of Irish autonomy. For many, Parnell's untimely death in 1891 signaled the end of any possibility for a nonviolent settlement of the question of Irish independence. Yeats saw this time as the end of attempting a political solution for Ireland's difficulties and the beginning of an effort to raise the profile of Irish literature and arts to secure a sense of Irish nationalism.

Chapter Four: ''Book III: Hodos Chameliontos''

The title of this section, which, according to Yeats can be translated as ''The Path of Chameleon,'' denotes the multiplicity, confusion, and unpredictability in his life. Yeats recalls with pleasure, though, the times he spent with his uncle George Pollexfen in Sligo, Ireland. During this period, Yeats searched for a unifying philosophy for himself and for Ireland. In support of this effort, he spent many hours experimenting with the symbols he had learned from Mathers's Order of the Golden Dawn. Yeats was convinced through his own experiences that a trained person thinking of a particular symbol could prompt a change in another person's mind.

Chapter Five: ''Book IV: The Tragic Generation''

Here, Yeats writes about the artists and authors he knew in the late 1890s, many of whom met with such difficulties as public condemnation and serious ill health. For example, he remembers the events surrounding Oscar Wilde's downfall. Wilde was found guilty of homosexual acts and sentenced to prison for two years of hard labor. About three years after his release, Wilde died. In addition to Wilde's story, Yeats notes that a number of his artist friends became drunks or went mad during these years.

Chapter Six: ''Book V: The Stirring of the Bones''

In this essay, Yeats recalls with some disappointment the dissolution of what he wanted for Ireland, due to the violence of many Irish activists during the final few years of the nineteenth century and the beginning of the twentieth century. Maude Gonne gained much notoriety during this period for her fiery rhetoric in support of an independent Ireland, but Yeats expresses concern over the violence to come. One high point in this period is his introduction to Lady Gregory. She invited him to stay at her estate in Ireland to recuperate (from poor health), and together they began collecting folk tales from the surrounding countryside and discussing the possibility of a theater devoted to Irish plays.

Chapter Seven: ''Dramatis Personae: 1896–1902''

Yeats relates here, too, his meeting Lady Gregory and how they became close friends. Much of this essay is concerned with the two friends' work on developing an Irish dramatic tradition. Yeats and Lady Gregory founded the Irish National Theatre in Dublin and produced a number of plays, including Yeats's *Countess Cathleen* and Edward Martyn's *The Heather Field*. Florence Farr, an actress for whom Yeats had great respect, appeared in many of their productions.

Chapter Eight: ''Estrangement: Extracts from a Diary Kept in 1909''

This section of *Autobiographies* is a collection of sixty-one diary entries dated from January 14 through March 12, 1909. Most of the brief entries are concerned with Lady Gregory and the Abbey Theatre, Yeats's family, and his consideration of the occult and philosophy.

Chapter Nine: ''The Death of Synge: Extracts from a Diary Kept in 1909''

These fifty entries, dated March 12, 1909 through October 1914, primarily cover John Synge's death in March 1909 and Yeats's remembrances of the playwright whom he called the greatest Irish dramatist. Yeats writes also about Lady Gregory and the Abbey Theatre.

Chapter Ten: ''The Bounty of Sweden''

In this final essay, Yeats writes about receiving the 1923 Nobel Prize for Literature and his trip to Stockholm to receive the award. He also includes the text of his acceptance speech, "The Irish Dramatic Movement."

Key Figures

Mary Battle

Mary Battle was George Pollexfen's housekeeper and had worked for the Pollexfen family for many years. She was "second-sighted," according to Yeats. For example, she would know without being told when her employer was bringing someone unexpected home for dinner and would arrange the table with an extra setting before he arrived. So impressed was Yeats with Battle's psychic abilities and storytelling that much of his book *The Celtic Twilight* "is but her daily speech," he noted.

Madame Blavatsky

Madame Blavatsky was one of the leaders of the Theosophical Society in London, an organization that promoted a philosophical system associated with mysticism and claimed particular insight into the nature of God and the world. Between 1887 and 1890, Yeats was a member of the organization and spent much time at Madame Blavatsky's house discussing theosophy and mysticism. He remembered her as an intelligent and personable woman. Eventually, one of Madame Blavatsky's associates asked Yeats to leave the group after the author expressed doubts about the accuracy of some of the society's beliefs.

Thomas Davis

Thomas Davis, with Charles Gavan Duffy, launched the Dublin newspaper *The Nation,* in which many writers, including Yeats, published verse and prose that underscored the need for Irish independence. From this publication came much of the impetus for what became known as The Young Ireland Movement, a group of writers, again including Yeats, who sought to encourage Irish nationalism and identity through their literary efforts.

Edward Dowden

John Butler Yeats introduced Edward Dowden to his son William. Dowden was a poet and professor who, much to the elder Yeats's disappointment, wrote very little after his first collection of poems and focused primarily on criticism. As a young man, Yeats often talked with Dowden about philosophy and literature.

Sir Charles Gavan Duffy

Charles Gavan Duffy was one of the founders of the newspaper *The Nation,* which published Irish nationalistic poetry and prose. He and Yeats both sought the editorship of the New Irish Library series of books about Irish history and literature, but Duffy got the job. The two also struggled over the direction of efforts to achieve Irish independence in the 1890s, with Yeats on the less radical and less violent side of the argument.

Florence Farr

Florence Farr was an English actress. Yeats wrote a number of plays for her and also cast her in shows at the Abbey Theatre. Like Yeats, she was a member of the Hermetic Order of the Golden Dawn, a mystical society. According to Yeats, she was a beautiful woman with a strong and curious mind who did not fathom all of her gifts. The two had a long and enduring friendship; however, Yeats described their relationship as an "exasperation" because he felt she did not play enough roles that displayed her beauty and skill.

Maude Gonne

In 1889, Yeats met Maude Gonne, an Irish nationalist activist, and began a long but ultimately unrequited romantic pursuit of the woman, who was renowned for her beauty and energy. According to Yeats, "her complexion was luminous, like that of apple-blossom through which the light falls." Her fiery nature was legendary, and in one instance she praised war "as if there were some virtue in excitement itself," wrote Yeats.

Lady Augusta Persse Gregory

Lady Gregory was an Irish playwright who did not begin her writing career until she was middle-aged. She met Yeats in 1896 and became his patron and close friend. Yeats spent much time at her Irish estate, Coole Park, resting from his work and collecting stories and folktales from neighboring farmers and peasants. Lady Gregory and Yeats founded the Irish Literary Theatre, the Irish National Theatre Society, and the Abbey Theatre.

W. E. Henley

W. E. Henley was an English editor and poet. Yeats did not express much love for Henley's poems but acknowledged that his own education began through the regular discussions Henley led at his house in London. The group invited to Henley's meetings also included Oscar Wilde and Rudyard

Kipling, and these and other young men sought out Henley's praise in much of what they did. "Henley was our leader, our confidante," wrote Yeats, remembering that the group listened to Henley partly because he was "quite plainly not on the side of our parents."

Henley started two publications, *Scots* and the *National Observer.* Yeats was a frequent contributor to the *National Observer.* As an Englishman, Henley acknowledged to Yeats that Ireland had the right to independence but also said that England could not allow it. Henley began to deteriorate after the death of his daughter in the mid-1890s, as Yeats noted in his essay *The Tragic Generation.*

Liddell Mathers

See MacGregor Mathers

MacGregor Mathers

MacGregor Mathers, originally named Liddell Mathers, was the English leader of the Hermetic Order of the Golden Dawn. Yeats became a member of the order and, in his words, "began certain studies and experiences that were to convince me that images well up before the mind's eye from a deeper source than conscious or subconscious memory." Members, who included many of Yeats's fellow writers and artists, were required to illustrate that they held some competence in mysticism. Their activities included using powerful symbols to bring about visions.

William Morris

William Morris was an English poet, artist, socialist, and manufacturer and designer of such household items as carpets and furniture. There are references to his designs throughout the text of *Autobiographies.* Yeats attended debates sponsored by the Socialist League at Morris's house and often had supper with Morris after the conclusion of the discussions. Yeats credits Morris for his brief identification with socialism. While Yeats did not express great admiration for Morris's poetry, he did write that he would prefer to live Morris's life "rather than my own or any other man's."

Jack Nettleship

Jack Nettleship was an artist whom Yeats described as "once inventor of imaginative designs and now a painter of melodramatic lions." Yeats met Nettleship through his father and said that his own admiration of Nettleship was based less on the quality of his art and more on a habit formed in Yeats's childhood. Nettleship drank cocoa all day long, according to Yeats, because he had once been an alcoholic and still needed some liquid to sip constantly.

John O'Leary

John O'Leary was a writer and activist for the Irish nationalist cause. He was a member of the Young Ireland Movement before he was twenty. He was arrested, jailed, and then exiled to France before returning to lead the Fenians, a revolutionary society formed in Ireland and the United States in the mid-1850s to secure Irish independence from England by force. He also was the center of an Irish nationalist literary group, the Young Ireland Society, of which Yeats was a member.

Yeats remembered O'Leary as "the handsomest man I had ever seen" and maintained extreme respect and admiration for him. He credited O'Leary's debates and conversations, as well as the books which the activist lent him, with providing the inspiration for "all that I have set my hand to since." O'Leary also helped find "subscribers" for Yeats's first book of poems, *The Wanderings of Oisin and Other Poems.*

Elizabeth Middleton Pollexfen

Elizabeth Pollexfen was Yeats's grandmother and William Pollexfen's wife. In contrast to her husband's stern nature, Mrs. Pollexfen was a generous and kind woman, deeply involved in charity work and skilled in drawing the delicate flowers she grew in her beloved garden.

George Pollexfen

George Pollexfen was one of William Pollexfen's sons and Yeats's maternal uncle and "dear friend." The poet and his uncle shared an interest in the occult, and George Pollexfen spent much time developing his skills as an astrologer and a mystic. Yeats remembered his uncle as appearing much older than his age because of his dour demeanor. Nonetheless, Yeats reported that his uncle was interested in learning about mystical symbols and visions. The two spent much time together collecting stories of supernatural experiences from their country neighbors around Sligo.

Yeats had pleasant memories of his visits to Sligo, where he stayed with George Pollexfen. Mindful of Yeats's interest in being outdoors and in spending time alone, George Pollexfen would patiently arrange meals around his young nephew's erratic comings and goings.

William Pollexfen

William Pollexfen was Yeats's maternal grandfather, a man who inspired both fear and admiration among his contemporaries and in the young Yeats. Yeats wrote that his grandfather never mistreated him, but his demeanor was intimidating. Pollexfen was quiet, even around his wife, and never spoke about the great military deeds he had accomplished as a younger man. He was a large and strong man, had traveled throughout much of the world, and owned a number of ships. With some awe, Yeats noted that his grandfather "had the reputation of never ordering a man to do anything he would not do himself."

T. W. Rolleston

Yeats referred to T. W. Rolleston as "the second Thomas Davis." Rolleston was one of the founding members of the Rhymers' Club in about 1891, a literary group that met regularly to share poetry.

George "A. E." Russell

George Russell, also known as "A. E.," attended art school in Dublin while Yeats was also there. Yeats remembered Russell as the student who would not paint what was in front of him, painting instead what he saw in his visions. Russell eventually became well-known as a poet and a mystic and was one of Yeats's closest friends.

Yeats was always impressed with Russell's versatility, noting that with only a brief background in accounting, Russell accepted a position as a member of a "co-operative banking system." People often called upon Russell to settle arguments. However, Yeats did not have much praise for Russell's efforts at literary criticism.

John Synge

Yeats considered John Synge the "greatest dramatic genius of Ireland." Yeats remembered meeting Synge for the first time in 1896 and not being especially impressed with the younger writer. Eventually, Synge would work closely with Lady Gregory and Yeats at the Irish National Theatre Society and at the Abbey Theatre. His play *The Playboy of the Western World* generated a storm of criticism when it was produced at the Abbey Theatre in 1907 for its depiction of the Irish rural character and its use of Irish Gaelic dialect.

Synge died in 1909 after a long illness. In his essay *The Death of Synge*, Yeats ruminated on the nature of his friendship with Synge.

J. F. Taylor

See John F. Taylor

John F. Taylor

John F. Taylor was a lawyer and an orator who spoke on Irish literature and history to the Young Ireland Society and other groups. While he and Yeats clashed on a number of issues, including Yeats's belief in the supernatural, Yeats admired Taylor for his powerful speaking abilities. Taylor had a reputation for taking on hopeless legal cases and also for his short temper.

Oscar Wilde

Yeats met Oscar Wilde through W. E. Henley's discussion group and was amazed at the Irish poet and playwright's ability to speak fluently, as if he had already written out in his head what he was going to say. Wilde was also an occasional visitor to Yeats's Rhymers' Club in the 1890s.

Wilde praised Yeats's first poetry collection, *The Wanderings of Oisin and Other Poems* and had Yeats to his house for dinner a number of times. During these visits, Wilde enjoyed hearing Yeats tell long Irish folk tales and flattered the younger poet by comparing him with Homer. When Wilde was charged with indecency and faced a prison sentence and hard labor, Yeats and many of his friends came out in support of the famous wit.

John Butler Yeats

John Yeats was Yeats's father. He was a lawyer who had quit the bar to become a painter, but he also enjoyed reading drama and poetry. John Yeats had a huge impact on his son's education and ways of thinking by introducing him to many fellow artists and writers. These people contributed greatly to Yeats's philosophy by including him in various discussions about philosophy, art, and politics. Most of them, according to Yeats, were "influenced by the Pre-Raphaelite movement," a nineteenth-century aesthetic movement that often sentimentalized its artistic subjects and made moral judgments against technological and industrial advancement. Yeats's father never fully agreed with his son's interest in the supernatural. In fact, Yeats commented that it was through his study of the occult and the supernatural that he began to break away from his father's strong intellectual influence.

Susan Mary Pollexfen Yeats

Susan Yeats was Yeats's mother and a woman whom her husband described as being extremely honest in expressing her feelings. Yeats remembered that when they moved back to Ireland after living in London, his mother wanted to live near a body of water. "I have no doubt that we lived at the harbour for my mother's sake," he reminisced, adding that it was not uncommon to see her sitting in the kitchen, listening to a servant—a fisherman's wife—tell stories.

William Butler Yeats

William Butler Yeats, author of *Autobiographies*, was an Irish poet and dramatist who lived from 1865 to 1939. As a young child, he was not a good student and strained against being forced to sit and learn in a classroom. He prefered to learn out-of-doors, even though he claimed in his autobiography that he was not a very muscular youth. Yeats especially enjoyed spending his time listening to others tell stories and fairy tales, which he collected as an adult. He recorded them and incorporated their sense into his poems and stories.

As a young man, Yeats became increasingly interested in the occult and the supernatural, joining Madame Blavatsky's Theosophical Society and MacGregor Mathers's Hermetic Order of the Golden Dawn. Yeats's study of the supernatural, as well as his deep interest in Irish culture and his concern for Irish independence from England informed his poetry and other writings. In the 1920s, Yeats became involved in Irish politics, eventually serving as a senator for Ireland.

Around the turn of the century, Yeats began writing and producing plays that reflected traditional Irish life and folklore. With the help of his patron, Lady Gregory, he founded the Abbey Theatre in Dublin. In 1923, he received the Nobel Prize for Literature. In his autobiography, Yeats reported that after he received the news, he and his wife could not find a bottle of wine in the house and so had to settle for sausages, "as a celebration [was] necessary."

Themes

The Supernatural

Yeats's awareness of the supernatural began at an early age. While living with his grandparents in Sligo, he saw "a supernatural bird in the corner of the room." He relates that he dreamed one night that his grandfather's ship had wrecked. The next morning he awoke to find that his dream had come true. These and other events prompted Yeats to consider the existence of spirits or of an alternative plane of reality and launched his life-long interest in the supernatural.

Autobiographies is filled with stories of unexplained events, spirit contact, séances, and other paranormal activities witnessed by Yeats and others. These experiences, in fact, became an integral part of the folk tales Yeats so eagerly collected in support of a national literature for Ireland. After an episode in the essay, "Reveries Over Childhood and Youth," in which he relates seeing unexplained lights in the countryside near his home, Yeats started telling people that they should accept as true "whatever had been believed in all countries and periods and only reject any part of it after much evidence, instead of starting over afresh and believing what one could prove."

Beginning in the mid-1880s, Yeats joined a number of mystical societies, including Madame Blavatsky's Theosophical Society. After testing some of the society's "esoteric teachings" and challenging them, he was encouraged to leave. He became a member of MacGregor Mathers's Hermetic Order of the Golden Dawn in 1890 and commenced learning about symbols and how they may affect the subconscious mind.

Yeats credits his serious study of the supernatural with helping him take a step away from his family and toward adulthood: "It was only when I began to study psychical research and mystical philosophy that I broke away from my father's influence," he notes.

Nature

Yeats describes himself throughout the text of his autobiography as very connected to the land around him and to nature. Yeats expresses a desire for tactile sensations of nature and describes a period in his young life when he had "a literary passion for the open air." These feelings prompted him to do such things as remove the glass in a

Topics for Further Study

- Research the current religious unrest in Northern Ireland. Write a brief summary of the situation, and then explain how the historical relationship between England and Ireland contributed to this situation.

- Read a brief biography of Yeats. Discuss some differences between the biography and *Autobiographies*. Does one include events or personalities that the other omits? Are any events described differently in the two works?

- Many critics believe that Yeats was the greatest poet in the English language. Read a few of his poems. Do you agree with the critics' opinion? Explain why or why not, using the poems you have selected to support your conclusion.

- In his *Autobiographies*, Yeats writes a lot about his experiences and experiments with the supernatural. Choose one type of supernatural event he experienced—such as visions or extrasensory perception—and investigate what scientists, religious leaders, and philosophers have to say about this subject. How do they differ in their interpretations of such events? Have you ever experienced anything similar to what Yeats referred to in his book? If so, how do you explain what happened to you?

- Yeats was heavily influenced by the English writer William Blake. Research Blake's life and work. Then, in a chart or essay, compare and contrast the two men. What elements in Yeats's life and work do you think were a result of Blake's influence? In what ways were the two men and their work very different?

---

window so that rain could fall on him as he slept. When Yeats was school-aged and the family lived in London, he longed for Ireland and for "a sod of earth from some field I knew, something of Sligo to hold in my hand."

Though he was "delicate and had no muscles," Yeats reveled in the outdoors. When his family moved to Dublin from London, Yeats escaped to the Irish countryside on a regular basis, sleeping some nights in a cave or in the woods surrounding a neighboring castle. His holidays were spent in Sligo with his uncle George Pollexfen, who supported the young poet's outdoor adventures. Uncle George would even arrange meals around Yeats's odd comings and goings. Yeats's "literary passion for the open air" showed itself after his father read aloud from Henry David Thoreau's *Walden;* Yeats decided that he wanted to live as Thoreau had, "seeking wisdom" through a solitary life in the country.

Irish Nationalism and Literature

Yeats was preoccupied with the theme of Irish nationalism throughout his life, even though he was a member of an Anglo-Irish family—a group that generally identified more strongly with England than Ireland in the 1800s. From the time he was a small child, the traditional Irish stories of farmers and villagers and odd relatives fascinated him. One of the high points of his childhood was visiting his relatives in the country, especially his aunt Micky, whose land included "a shut-in mysterious place, where one played and believed something was going to happen." Here the young Yeats could speak to villagers and his aunt about the family's local history and learn about the deeds of his ancestors. He claims that he "cared nothing as a child for Micky's tales," but the entry in his autobiography about his relatives may indicate otherwise. As an adult, Yeats was "delighted with all that joins my life to those who had power in Ireland or with those anywhere who were good servants and poor bargainers."

Even as a child, Yeats felt strongly that his true nationality was Irish, despite his living in London. Yeats remembers when he was a schoolboy in England, and, even though anti-Irish sentiment was rampant, he was "full of pride, for it is romantic to live in a dangerous country." Living in England, in fact, made him long for his country and encouraged his identification as an Irishman. Once he and his sister were so homesick for Ireland that they came close to tears in their desperation for something, even a clump of soil, from Sligo. "It was some old race instinct, like that of a savage," he remembers.

As he grew older, Yeats received inspiration for his poetry and plays from various sources, including John O'Leary, who was president of the Young Ireland Society while Yeats was a member. O'Leary had also once been an activist with the Fenians, a group that struggled with force to free Ireland from England's rule. The conversations and debates at the Society's meetings, as well as the books O'Leary loaned to Yeats, inspired the young poet to take seriously the idea that creating a national Irish literature was critical for Irish independence. Yeats had a dream that "a national literature that made Ireland beautiful in the memory and yet had been freed from provincialism by an exacting criticism" could join together the Catholic and Protestant sides of Irish society. He sought a unified mythology that would create a single national identity and wonders whether "all races had their first unity from a mythology that marries them to rock and hill."

Yeats researched Irish Gaelic language and Irish history to incorporate the legends and traditions into his poetry. Much of his time spent with Lady Gregory at Coole Park was devoted to traveling around the Irish countryside collecting stories from peasants and farmers—including stories filled with fairies—night creatures, and eerie lights appearing by roadsides.

Style

Stream-of-Consciousness Writing Style
In his *Autobiographies*, Yeats writes very long paragraphs, many of which are more than one page in length. This style gives the reader the feeling of someone telling a story with many characters and numerous plots that are all somehow connected. The stream-of-consciousness style allows Yeats to move from topic to topic as they seem to occur spontaneously in his thought, unrestricted by the demands of conventional order.

Commentators on Yeats's autobiographical essays have noted that places and dates are not necessarily accurate; however, these lapses do not generally disrupt the atmosphere of the work. While the individual essays are generally arranged in chronological order, time is not a central organizing device. More important are the individuals and what they did, according to Yeats's memory, and how they affected his life.

Essays
Yeats's *Autobiographies* is comprised of a series of essays published individually. The two essays Yeats wrote on his life through the late 1800s, "Reveries Over Childhood and Youth" and "The Trembling of the Veil," were originally published in 1915 and 1922, respectively. In 1926, these two essays were published as one work. The years from 1896 through Yeats's reception of the Nobel Prize for Literature in 1923 are detailed in four essays: "Dramatis Personae," "Estrangement," "The Death of Synge," and "The Bounty of Sweden." All six essays were collected in 1955 for presentation in one volume as *Autobiographies*.

Historical Context

Irish Nationalism and the Nineteenth-Century Literary Renaissance
The Protestant English were the dominant economic, political, and cultural force in Ireland beginning in the sixteenth century, when they settled large parts of Ireland. Throughout the seventeenth century, these Anglo-Irish, with the support of the British Crown, confiscated land from local Irish Catholics and instituted repressive laws that prohibited Catholics from working in many professions and from owning property. The English language replaced Irish Gaelic as the language of everyday speech and literature, helping to stifle traditional Irish culture.

Britain granted Ireland's Parliament legislative independence in 1780. Even though the entire Irish Parliament was Protestant, it granted to Catholics a number of reforms in religious practice and land ownership—but not the right to vote. Irish Catholics rebelled against English domination in 1798, but their uprising was quelled and the Irish Parliament disbanded. Three years later, the Act of Union made Ireland a part of the United Kingdom.

Compare & Contrast

- **1920s:** In 1923, Yeats wins the Nobel Prize for Literature.

  Today: The Irish poet Seamus Heaney wins a Nobel Prize for Literature in 1995. The 1998 Nobel Peace Prize is awarded to two Irishmen seeking to find a solution to the violence still besetting their homeland. The Nobel Prize Committee describes Roman Catholic co-winner John Hume, leader and one of the founders of the moderate Social Democratic and Labour Party, as "the clearest and most consistent of Northern Ireland's political leaders." The prize's other recipient, David Trimble, Protestant head of the Ulster Unionist Party, "showed great political courage when, at a critical stage of the process, he advocated solutions which led to the peace agreement," according to the Nobel Prize Committee.

- **1920s:** Ireland suffers through the Anglo-Irish War, three years of guerrilla warfare between the Irish Republican Army supporting Ireland's independence from Britain. The Anglo-Irish Treaty creates the Irish Free State consisting of twenty-six counties in the southern Roman Catholic portion of Ireland. The Irish Free State exists within the Commonwealth of Nations with a status equal to that of Canada and only a modified oath of allegiance to the British monarch. Yeats serves as a Free State senator from 1922 through 1928. The remaining six Protestant counties accept limited home rule as Northern Ireland. Many Protestants in Northern Ireland view their separation from the Catholic south and union with Britain as a way to maintain their religion and dominant position. Many Irish Catholics, however, view the partition as simply the most recent evidence of British injustice against the Irish people.

  Today: The Irish Free State is now the sovereign Republic of Ireland, without an oath of allegiance to the British Crown. Northern Ireland remains politically connected to the United Kingdom, and tensions continue between the Catholic minority and the Protestant majority.

- **1920s:** Autobiographies and memoirs such as Yeats's essays are written and published primarily by famous people or those who have held important positions in government, the arts, or science.

  Today: Published autobiographies and memoirs are hugely popular and are written as often by the nonfamous as by the famous. The Internet bookseller Amazon.com lists more than thirty-two thousand titles in this category.

- **1920s:** The monetary award for the 1923 Nobel Prize for Literature, won by Yeats, is the smallest ever issued by the Nobel Committee, 114,000 Swedish kroner.

  Today: The prize for the 2000 Nobel Prize for Literature is nine million Swedish kroner, or about $915,000. This amount is the largest sum of money ever awarded for this prize in literature.

In 1842, Irish poet and activist Thomas Davis and other writers founded a weekly newspaper, *The Nation,* which published the political writing and literature that was later credited with sparking in many Irish a renewed sense of nationalism. Before this, much Irish literature was written merely to entertain or to poke fun at local customs; after the middle of the nineteenth century Irish literature began to focus on political concerns.

Literary activities during the final years of the nineteenth century have prompted historians to refer to this period as the Irish Renaissance. The writers of the time were interested in using traditional Irish folk tales and myths as the inspiration for a rebirth of Irish literature. Irish nationalist activists, including John O'Leary and Yeats, met as the Young Ireland Society, organized to promote Irish nationalism through Irish literature. Yeats helped organize the Irish Literary Society in London in 1891 and the National Literary Society in Dublin in 1892. Both societies were formed to promote the independence of Ireland from England through the development of Irish national literature and arts.

The Gaelic League emerged in 1893 to work toward the reinstatement of Irish as the spoken language of Ireland. That same year, Douglas Hyde published a collection of Irish Gaelic folktales translated into English, and Yeats published *The Celtic Twilight*, a collection of his articles on Irish legends.

The full force of the Irish literary rebirth was felt especially in the theatre. In 1902, Yeats and Lady Gregory founded the Irish Literary Theatre (later called the Irish National Theatre Society), and in 1904, thanks to the contributions of a generous patron, they were able to produce their plays in Dublin's famed Abbey Theatre.

The Abbey Theater

Yeats and his close friend and patron, Lady Gregory, established the Irish Literary Theatre in 1902 in Dublin to encourage Irish playwrights to create dramatic works that addressed life in Ireland. Many Irish writers at that point hesitated to produce works that did not reflect the dominant Protestant English culture, but Lady Gregory and Yeats believed that Irish nationalism could be strengthened through the creation of a national literature. Lady Gregory and Yeats encouraged dramatists to include in their plays Irish peasants, folk tales, history, and mythical heroes and legends.

The theater company appeared in various locations but by 1904 had use of Dublin's Abbey Theatre through the contributions of a wealthy patron, Annie Elizabeth Horniman, and changed its name to the Irish National Theatre Society. The company soon gained a popular following by producing the plays of such dramatic luminaries as Sean O'Casey and John Synge. Synge presented his controversial play *The Playboy of the Western World* at the Abbey Theatre in 1907.

Critics maintain that the quality of the productions at the Abbey declined after Yeats's death in 1939. In 1951, a fire forced the company to move to another theater, but in 1966 the Abbey reopened and by 2001 it contained an acting school as well as a second stage for more experimental productions. The theater also expanded its scope to include classical plays such as those by William Shakespeare and plays by contemporary European playwrights.

Critical Overview

Most criticism on Yeats addresses his poetry, and many critics believe him to be the greatest poet in the English language. However, Yeats's prose has received similar praise. Edmund Wilson, in his book, *Axel's Castle: A Study in the Imaginative Literature of 1870–1930,* wrote that Yeats's prose matured as the writer himself matured. Writing when Yeats was still alive, Wilson praised the poet's prose as disciplined, adding, ''Yeats is today a master of prose as well as a great poet.''

Speaking specifically of one of the essays in *Autobiographies*, ''The Trembling of the Veil'' (originally published as a separate work in 1922), Wilson viewed Yeats's prose style almost with relief, as if it were a gift from a more artful past. ''Yeats has achieved a combination of grandeur with a certain pungency and homeliness,'' he wrote. ''The prose of Yeats, in our contemporary literature, is like the product of some dying loomcraft brought to perfection in the days before machinery,'' he noted. He added, however, that Yeats's prose style indicates that he has ''a mind that is not naïve, as the heart that feels is not insensitive.''

Diane Tolomeo Edwards, in the *Dictionary of Literary Biography,* noted Yeats's deliberateness in ''The Trembling of the Veil,'' even though, according to Edwards, Yeats argues in the essay that genius comes from something that is ''beyond one's own mind.'' Many of Yeats's essays, Edwards maintains, ''seek to demonstrate this belief,'' but Yeats was not always successful because of the essays' deliberate and intentional tone. Edwards suggests, ''Yeats's essays need to be read together. Many ideas get repeated, and their cumulative effect helps one focus more clearly on ideas that may seem elusive.''

In his prose, as well as his poetry, Yeats freely incorporates occult symbols and mysticism combined with Irish nationalism; these elements are certainly present in *Autobiographies*. Critic Theodore Spencer, writing in the book *Literary Opinion in America,* expressed gratitude for Yeats's handling of these challenging subjects in his writings.

Irish poet and playwright Oscar Wilde was a long-time friend and literary advisor to Yeats

"Any one of these might have been the ruin of a lesser talent," argues Spencer, but Yeats surmounts any difficulty in this area. "Perhaps a life of action, and the anger it has sometimes generated . . . has helped to put iron into his style," Spencer reasons.

Also lauding Yeats's handling of mysticism in his writing is B. L. Reid, writing in *Dictionary of Literary Biography*. Reid noted the preponderance of the "visionary" over the visual in Yeats's work, which may express the poet's poor eyesight as well as his ongoing interest in the supernatural. "The gauzy, veiled effects of visual observation down past the turn of the century in Yeats's writings . . . doubtless owed something to poor eyesight," wrote Reid. However, Yeats "always seemed to be able to see what mattered to him . . . [and] his essential seeing was more visionary than visual," Reid adds.

In the end, Yeats's essays, including *Autobiographies*, have been generally praised and respected nearly as much as his plays and poems. In an overarching statement, Edith Stillwell, in her *Aspects of Modern Poetry*, notes her admiration for Yeats's comprehensiveness in *Autobiographies*. "Few artists can have given us so complete a record of the life of their soul—a record which is clothed

in reticence and moves with supreme dignity," she writes.

Criticism

Susan Sanderson

Sanderson holds a master of fine arts degree in fiction writing and is an independent writer. In this essay, she looks at how Yeats's supernatural experiences and stories in Autobiographies *relate to his desire for a unified mythology and national literature for the Irish people.*

Yeats's fondness for myths and legends is well known and much appreciated. Seamus Heaney addressed this issue in *The Atlantic,* acknowledging Yeats's efforts to create a unified cultural identity for Ireland based on stories and myths. From his youth, Yeats was deeply involved in "creating a vision of Ireland as an independent cultural entity, a state of mind as much as a nation-state, one founded on indigenous myths and attitudes and beliefs," noted Heaney.

Yeats's *Autobiographies*, a collection of essays written and published as individual pieces before his death in 1939, deals not only with his interest in traditional Irish rural myths and stories but also with his efforts to understand the spiritual aspects of life. Yeats's interests in Irish culture and in the supernatural in the first half of *Autobiographies* complement each other; in fact, Yeats sought a sense of unity from each of these facets of his intellectual life. These two areas informed and fed each other.

As a young man, Yeats was almost obsessed with creating a unified explanation for many things. "A conviction that the world was now but a bundle of fragments possessed me without ceasing," he admitted as he set out to find singularity in his life. He sought to unify art, the state of Ireland, Irish mythologies, and his own spirituality. He vehemently disagreed with theories of art that proposed "the independence of arts from one another" and thought that all art should be "a Centaur finding in the popular lore its back and its strong legs." In spirituality he sought explanations for supernatural events involving archetypal and primal symbols and images.

Yeats remembered in *Autobiographies* that his interest in Irish folk tales began at a very early age,

What Do I Read Next?

- William Blake, the English artist and writer, had an enormous impact on Yeats. *The Complete Poetry and Prose of William Blake,* edited by David V. Erdman, William Golding, and Harold Bloom and first published in 1965, is widely regarded as the best available source of Blake's works.

- Lady Augusta Gregory, Yeats's patron and close friend, collected stories of Irish heroes and powerful gods in *Irish Myths and Legends.* Originally published in 1904 as *Gods and Fighting Men,* the book has a preface by Yeats.

- Yeats referred to John Synge as the greatest Irish dramatist. All of Synge's play have been collected in one volume, *"The Playboy of the Western World" and Other Plays,* published in 1998 and edited by Ann Saddlemyer. The volume's introduction sets the plays in the context of the times and the Irish Literary Movement, also focusing on Synge's role with the Abbey Theatre.

- Oscar Wilde, who took part in a couple of discussion groups with Yeats and praised the young poet's first collection, published *The Picture of Dorian Gray* in 1890. The novel, about a young man who sells his soul for eternal youth, prompted scandal and attacks on Wilde. Many in the late nineteenth century considered Wilde's book decadent.

- The second revised edition of *The Collected Poems of W. B. Yeats* was edited by Richard J. Finneran in 1996. It includes all of the poems Yeats authorized to be included in such a volume.

---

thanks to relatives. The first "faery-stories" he heard were in the cottages near relatives' houses. He especially enjoyed the numerous colorful stories told by servants. A life filled with tales—many apocryphal and amazing—was the norm for young Yeats, and he could not imagine a life devoid of these. "All the well-known families had their grotesque or tragic or romantic legends, and I often said to myself how terrible it would be to go away and die where nobody would know my story," Yeats writes.

Yeats experienced his first mystical vision while under the care of his grandparents. "I have been told, though I do not remember it myself, that I saw . . . a supernatural bird in the corner of the room," he writes. At about the same time in his childhood, Yeats dreamt of the wreck of his grandfather's ship, describing it before he knew details of the actual event. Yeats remembered the event as a "romantic legend" and noted that his grandfather returned safely from the wreck, riding a blind horse secured for him by the ship's grateful passengers.

In addition to the numerous Irish nationalist organizations Yeats joined as a young adult to pursue his belief that Ireland could be free and independent from England—but only if she could find a single artistic tradition—he also enrolled in two mystical societies that helped to form his nascent spiritual sense. Madame Blavatsky's Theosophical Society appealed to Yeats on the basis of its doctrine that some people have a singular or universal wisdom based on special mystical insight. The other important mystical group he joined was MacGregor Mathers's Hermetic Order of the Golden Dawn, which focused on the use of images and symbols to produce visions.

Yeats's statements about both theosophy and the Order of the Golden Dawn mirrored in various ways his statements about the possibility of political unification in Ireland. While pursuing theosophy, he asserted that all people, "while bound together in a single mind and taste," have always believed that a few hold a singular wisdom and insight. The Golden Dawn sustained his interest through personal experiences, convincing him "that images

> Yeats did not see any distinction between collecting folktales and collecting stories of supernatural experiences to satisfy his spiritual curiosity; these two kinds of tales were often joined in his mind."

well up before the mind's eye from a deeper source than conscious or subconscious memory." The primal and archetypal memories that a people have can bring them together under the banner of a nation, he asserted. "[N]ations, races, and individual men are unified by an image, or a bundle of related images" that somehow speaks to all people and pushes them toward a single purpose, he believed.

This desire for unity was one of Yeats's great convictions and drove him to collect rural Irish legends, to push for a united and free Ireland, and to search for spiritual understanding. Yeats did not see any distinction between collecting folktales and collecting stories of supernatural experiences to satisfy his spiritual curiosity; these two kinds of tales were often joined in his mind. For example, Yeats relates the story of being near the site of an ancient destroyed village and seeing lights or fires moving much too quickly to have been torches carried by humans. On another occasion, the lights returned to the site where he was walking and began a sort of blinking communication with one another. After asking many of the older locals about the lights, he decided to believe "whatever had been believed in all countries and periods, and only reject part of it after much evidence, instead of starting all over afresh and only believing what one could prove." This incident was one of several that prompted Yeats to collect Irish folktales and mythologies and weave them into his literature.

Yeats also joined these two kinds of stories—folktales and stories of supernatural experiences—while working with George Pollexfen, his mother's brother. The two men shared an interest in both the countryside and the supernatural, and they conducted numerous experiments using symbols and images to provoke visions—an activity Yeats learned

as a member of the Golden Dawn. In the midst of this work, Yeats began tracing philosophic ideas back to their origins, certain that there must a "tradition of belief older than any European church and founded upon the experience of the world before modern bias."

In a sense, Yeats was looking for a first image or archetypal symbol that was deep inside everyone, regardless of religion, education, politics, or social status. This search for a single tradition prompted Yeats and his uncle George to study the mystical visions and stories of the rural population. They discovered that the country folks' reported visions were very similar to the visions they themselves had called up with symbols. Mary Battle, Uncle George's housekeeper, was essential in this endeavor, as she regularly experienced visions filled with mythological characters that informed Yeats's writings.

In Yeats's mind, this first image or symbol could unify Ireland's population and galvanize it as it sought independence from England, especially if he incorporated it into his writings. In the truest sense, though, he was not looking for one image but for a series of images that could be transformed into a national mythological literature. "We had in Ireland imaginative stories," he writes, which were well known among the lower and rural classes. Yeats asked himself whether it would be possible to "make those stories current among the educated classes . . . [and] so deepen the political passion of the nation that all, artist and poet, craftsman and day-labourer would accept a common design." For these purposes, Yeats organized the Irish Literary Society, the National Literary Society, the Irish National Theatre Society, and Abbey Theatre, all originally formed to promote the independence of Ireland from England through the development of an Irish national literature.

Yeats's "wildest hopes," though, proved of little immediate benefit to Ireland's independence, for Irish nationalism fractured and fell in a period of extremism and violence. He was crushed. The literature that was produced in the name of Irish nationalism descended into propaganda, and "the past had been turned into a melodrama with Ireland for blameless hero and poet," according to Yeats. But Yeats's interest in unification, in all its aspects, still led him to create what many believe to be the best poetry written to date in the English language.

Source: Susan Sanderson, Critical Essay on *Autobiographies,* in *Nonfiction Classics for Students,* The Gale Group, 2002.

James Olney

In the following essay, Olney compares other "classic" autobiographies with Yeats's, exploring comic and ironic elements within them.

The question that I wish to explore in this paper is a threefold one and might be expressed thus: (1) Why is comedy so largely lacking in what one might describe as classic autobiography? (2) Why, on the other hand, is comedy so prominent (as I believe it to be) in Yeats's *Autobiographies*? (3) What is the nature, and what are the motives, of comedy when it does occur in autobiography? And as a sort of fourth fold completing this threefold question I want to pose a paradox: that though there are not many humorous passages in classic autobiography yet this type, like all varieties of autobiography, might be said to be essentially and in its very nature of the comic mode.

I will begin with a definition of classic autobiography, which is not my own but is as good as any other definition known to me: "A retrospective account in prose that a real person makes of his own existence stressing his own life and especially the history of his personality." It is clear, I think, that the kind of writing performance described or defined here is not likely to produce books notable for humorous or comic effects. When a "real person" undertakes a retrospective account "of his own existence stressing his individual life and especially the history of his personality," he is more likely to be serious or perhaps solemn than he is to be comic and gay. And indeed in that long—*very* long—volume that Philippe Lejeune takes for his archetypal autobiography, the *Confessions* of Rousseau, there is only one joke as far as I can recall, and that one joke has little enough to do with Rousseau's "own existence," "his individual life," or "the history of his personality." The joke, if that is the right way to describe it, comes at the death of a woman with whom Rousseau found brief employment. "I watched her die," Rousseau says. "She had lived like a woman of talents and intelligence; she died like a philosopher . . . She only kept her bed for the last two days, and continued to converse quietly with everyone to the last. Finally when she could no longer talk and was already in her death agony, she broke wind loudly. 'Good,' she said, turning over, 'a woman who can fart is not dead.' Those were the last words she spoke." This scarcely qualifies as a great deathbed speech but at least it does provide, for Rousseau's readers, a couple of lines of levity in more than six hundred pages of very uncomic,

> **Thus we have in the first couple of sections of *Autobiographies* fairly frequent instances of irony exercised by the mature Yeats on the immature Yeats."**

paranoid anxiety—the anxiety of an apologist who has the desperate feeling that his audience is unmoved and unconvinced by his "apology for his own life." If Georges Gusdorf is right when he says that "autobiography appeases the more or less anguished uneasiness of an aging man who wonders if his life has not been lived in vain, frittered away haphazardly, ending now in simple failure," we can see easily enough why it should contain so few laughs—one in the case of Rousseau, none in the cases of Saint Augustine or John Bunyan or George Fox or John Stuart Mill or John Henry Newman (though I do not at all mean to say that these men wrote autobiography for the reasons specified by Gusdorf). Trying to salvage or discover meaning for a life when the life is nearly over may produce a great book but it is not likely to conduce to great risibility. Thus in what I have termed classic autobiography—and it would be easy to multiply examples—one does not find much comedy, and if one goes to such a work with the same expectations as one goes to *Joe Miller's Joke Book* one will be sadly disappointed.

I want now, however, to glance at a certain kind of irony that *is* typical of classic autobiography and indeed that is there almost by definition of the mode. Jean Starobinski concludes his essay "The Style of Autobiography" with these observations about Rousseau's *Confessions* as a sort of dramatization of his philosophy: "According to that philosophy, man originally possessed happiness and joy: in comparison with that first felicity, the present is a time of degradation and corruption. But man was originally a brute deprived of 'light,' his reason still asleep; compared to that initial obscurity, the present is a time of lucid reflection and enlarged consciousness. The past, then, is at once the object of nostalgia and the object of irony; the present is at once a state of (moral) degradation and (intellectual) superiority."

If, as has been claimed, classic autobiography depends for its existence on some sort of conversion in the autobiographer's life, then this great emotional and intellectual divide will almost inevitably be present in, and will indeed rule the autobiography, giving an ironic, if not always nostalgic, distancing to the past. I can clarify what I mean here by reference to Augustine's *Confessions,* which I should describe as a radically ironic but never nostalgic book: radically ironic because the ''I'' narrating understands every event in the narrative differently from the understanding possessed in the past by the ''I'' narrated (the reasons for going from Carthage to Rome for example); but never nostalgic because Augustine did not at all share Rousseau's notion of childhood as a time of innocence, happiness, and joy—quite the contrary. This variety of irony that distances the past narrated self from the present narrating self is surely what Yeats intends in a letter written to his father apropos of *Reveries over Childhood and Youth:* ''While I was immature I was a different person and I can stand apart and judge.'' What Yeats describes is present-tense judgement (''I can stand apart'') of a past-tense condition of being (''While I was immature I was a different person''). Thus we have in the first couple of sections of *Autobiographies* fairly frequent instances of irony exercised by the mature Yeats on the immature Yeats. This, for example, in ''Four Years: 1887–1891'':

> [W]ith women . . . I was timid and abashed. I was sitting on a seat in front of the British Museum feeding pigeons when a couple of girls sat near and began enticing my pigeons away, laughing and whispering to one another, and I looked straight in front of me, very indignant, and presently went into the Museum without turning my head towards them. Since then I have often wondered if they were pretty or merely very young. Sometimes I told myself very adventurous love-stories with myself for hero, and at other times I planned out a life of lonely austerity, and at other times mixed the ideals and planned a life of lonely austerity mitigated by periodical lapses.

This kind of indulgent and semi-comic irony, exercised at the expense of a younger self, is not uncommon in autobiography. (Parenthetically, I might contrast the gentle self-irony of Yeats with the mordant self-irony of the following wonderful and justly famous passage in Augustine: ''But I, wretched young man that I was—even more wretched at the beginning of my youth—had begged you for chastity and had said: 'Make me chaste and continent, but not yet.' I was afraid that you might hear me too soon and cure me too soon from the disease of a lust which I preferred to be satisfied rather than

extinguished.'' This is a very different matter from the Yeatsian self-irony, but it still results from the difference between the understanding possessed by the self then and the understanding possessed by the self now.) To return to Yeats's letter to his father: after the sentence I have been looking at—''While I was immature I was a different person and I can stand apart and judge''—a sentence that provides the logic for a certain gentle self-mockery early in the *Autobiographies,* Yeats goes on to say, ''Later on, I should always, I feel, write of other people,'' and this opens the door not to self-irony but to irony, or more exactly comedy, deployed against others, a comedy that operates according to a vastly different logic from that of self-irony. It is the logic of this other variety of irony and comedy that I want to examine now.

I call upon a couple of passages from other prose writings in Yeats to explain the comedy of the second kind. The first passage I have quoted elsewhere but it is so excellent, both in itself and as rationale for the Yeatsian practice of autobiography, that any apology I might make for repeating it would be more *pro forma* than heartfelt. It occurs in one of Yeats's annual pieces on the Irish theatre gathered together in *Explorations* as ''The Irish Dramatic Movement.'' Speaking of what was then (in 1902) a new troupe, the National Theatrical Company, Yeats says:

> They showed plenty of inexperience, especially in the minor characters, but it was the first performance I had seen since I understood these things in which the actors kept still enough to give poetical writing its full effect upon the stage. I had imagined such acting, though I had not seen it, and had once asked a dramatic company to let me rehearse them in barrels that they might forget gesture and have their minds free to think of speech for a while. The barrels, I thought, might be on castors, so that I could shove them about with a pole when the action required it.

When Yeats titles one of his later volumes of autobiography *Dramatis Personae: 1896–1902,* it does not take much imagination to conceive of the text as a Yeatsian drama, of the family, friends, and acquaintances therein as actors in the drama, each in his or her barrel labeled with the role to be played, and of Yeats as playwright, director, and stage manager, exercising complete control over everybody and everything, complete control over his text and his life, as he shoves the embarreled and imperiled actors about the stage with his pole of comedy and irony.

The second passage, of a somewhat more theoretical nature but still concerned with dramatic literature, comes from a short, intense piece called "The Tragic Theatre." Having remarked that in poetical drama there is supposed to be "an antithesis between character and lyric poetry," Yeats goes on: "Yet when we go back a few centuries and enter the great periods of drama, character grows less and sometimes disappears, and there is much lyric feeling. . . . Suddenly it strikes us that character is continuously present in comedy alone, and that there is much tragedy . . . where its place is taken by passions and motives." Even in Shakespeare's tragicomedy, Yeats says, "it is in the moments of comedy that character is defined, in Hamlet's gaiety, let us say; while amid the great moments, when Timon orders his tomb, when Hamlet cries to Horatio 'Absent thee from felicity awhile,' when Antony names 'Of many thousand kisses the poor last,' all is lyricism, unmixed passion, 'the integrity of fire.'" "When the tragic reverie is at its height," Yeats declares, we never say, "'How well that man is realised! I should know him were I to meet him in the street.'" Finally, Yeats writes, "I think it was while rehearsing a translation of *Les Fourberies de Scapin* in Dublin, and noticing how passionless it all was, that I saw what should have been plain from the first line I had written, that tragedy must always be a drowning and breaking of the dykes that separate man from man, and that it is upon these dykes [that] comedy keeps house." Comedy imagines the world in terms of character, it distinguishes this individual and his folly from that individual and his folly, and it never dissolves the contours of character and social reality in the strains of that pure lyric emotion that Yeats believed specific to high tragedy. "I look upon character and personality as different things or perhaps different forms of the same thing," Yeats wrote to his father. "Juliet has personality, her Nurse has character. I look upon personality as the individual form of our passions. . . Character belongs I think to Comedy." And in *Autobiographies* he confirms this sense of comedy and character when he says, "Tragedy is passion alone, and rejecting character, it gets form from motives, from the wandering of passion; while comedy is the clash of character." It may seem somewhat paradoxical, in light of what I have said about autobiography earlier, that I should now suggest that autobiography, at least of the variety practiced by Yeats, is essentially comic rather than tragic—and indeed that all autobiography, not just that by Yeats, is in one sense always comic, never tragic. We should remark that in a tragedy like *Purgatory,* for example, there is nothing to be called character; there is only lyric passion and the keening song; while in the

Autobiographies, on the other hand, where Yeats intends to catch character with an anecdote, we are offered a string of (as he has it in "Easter 1916") mocking tales and gibes that one imagines were first told, and probably retold many subsequent times, to please a companion around the fire at the club.

Take the character of George Moore first of all. It was apparently Moore's *Hail and Farewell,* with its consistently mocking, and often quite funny, picture of Yeats, that first induced Yeats to start on his autobiographical writings. When I say the picture is quite funny, I don't mean that Yeats found it so; on the contrary—it was largely Moore that Yeats was referring to when he wrote of himself that he had become

> *Notorious, till all my priceless things*
> *Are but a post the passing dogs defile.*

Of the first volume of *Hail and Farewell* Moore wrote to a correspondent: "The reviewers look upon my book as a book of reminiscences, whereas I took so much material and moulded it just as if I were writing a novel, and the people in my book are not personalities but human types. . . [A]s a type of the literary fop one could not find a more perfect model than Yeats." Yeats knew nothing of this letter, of course, but he knew well enough—too well, I should say—what Moore was up to, for it was very much what he was to be up to himself when he published his reminiscences of such type characters as George Bernard Shaw, Oscar Wilde—and Moore. What Yeats did not want and absolutely would not have was someone else taking over his life and his text, creating character for him when Yeats intended to be the comic playwright creating character aplenty for others: he was determined that he would control Moore and not vice versa. The interesting thing is that when Yeats reacted to *Hail and Farewell* in his journal, he did so with polemic and direct attack—"Moore . . . is the born demagogue. . . . He has always a passion for some crowd, is always deliberately inciting them against somebody," and so forth; but when he responds in a piece of autobiography intended for publication, Yeats asserts and maintains control over his life and text not through polemic but through a comic reduction of Moore and an ironic rendering of his foolishness and his pretensions.

> Moore had inherited a large Mayo estate, and no Mayo country gentleman had ever dressed the part so well. . . . Yet nature had denied to him the final touch: he had a coarse palate. Edward Martyn alone suspected it. When Moore abused the waiter or the cook, he had thought, 'I know what he is hiding.' In a

London restaurant on a night when the soup was particularly good, just when Moore had the spoon at his lip, he said: 'Do you mean to say you are going to drink that?' Moore tasted the soup, then called the waiter, and ran through the usual performance. Martyn did not undeceive him, content to chuckle in solitude.

This, which sounds very like a mocking tale to please a companion around the fire at the club, was published after Moore's death but even had it been published during his lifetime there would have been no way for Moore to refute this sly picture of a man who pretends to culture but is undone by a coarse palate. It is as if one could hear Yeats saying to Moore, calling from the text of *Autobiographies* to the text of *Hail and Farewell*, ''You imagine that you are the provider of barrels and that you have one for me titled 'literary fop.' Well, you are wrong: I'm running this show; there is your barrel—that one over there labeled 'pretentious and ill-bred fool, also coarse in palate.' Now get in there and stay in there.''

''Moore's body,'' according to Yeats—and no doubt he thought Moore's body merely the outward form of his soul—''Moore's body was insinuating, upflowing, circulative, curvicular, popeyed.''

> He had gone to Paris straight from his father's racing stables, from a house where there was no culture, as Symons and I understood that word, acquired copious inaccurate French, sat among art students, young writers about to become famous, in some café; a man carved out of a turnip, looking out of astonished eyes. I see him as that circle saw him, for I have in memory Manet's caricature. He spoke badly and much in a foreign tongue, read nothing, and was never to attain the discipline of style. . . . He reached to middle life ignorant even of small practical details. He said to a friend: 'How do you keep your pants from falling about your knees?' 'O,' said the friend, 'I put my braces through the little tapes that are sewn there for the purpose.' A few days later, he thanked the friend with emotion. . . . He had wanted to be good as the mass of men understand goodness. In later life he wrote a long preface to prove that he had a mistress in Mayfair.

And so on, with much more to the same effect.

Yeats's treatment of Shaw and Wilde is somewhat different—they hadn't, after all, tried to make Yeats into a character actor and dispose of him in barrels of their own making as Moore had—but it is still anecdotal, devoted to drawing out character, the stuff of comedy rather than of tragedy. According to that other book of Yeats's, rich in comedy, called *A Vision*, Shaw and Wilde were contrasting types—Shaw of the twenty-first phase, Wilde of the nineteenth, the former entirely styleless, the latter nothing but style—and Yeats so creates them, so deploys them as ''characters,'' as archetypal figures, in his *Autobiographies*. Parenthetically, I might point out here that Moore, too, along with Shaw, was assigned to the twenty-first phase in *A Vision;* and, again like Shaw, he is regularly described by Yeats in the *Autobiographies* as having no style, nor even any awareness that such a thing as style exists. The twenty-first phase is the phase of ''the acquisitive man,'' and Yeats's description of the character of the man of phase twenty-one sounds like nothing so much as an abstraction derived from the figure particularized under Moore's name in the *Autobiographies*. One might even suppose that Yeats has in mind the fact that Moore was to be typed as ''the acquisitive man'' when he says that he ''acquired copious inaccurate French'' sitting in a Paris café. To return to Shaw: *Arms and the Man,* Yeats says,

> seemed to me inorganic, logical straightness and not the crooked road of life. . . . Shaw was right to claim Samuel Butler for his master, for Butler was the first Englishman to make the discovery that it is possible to write with great effect without music, without style, either good or bad, to eliminate from the mind all emotional implication and to prefer plain water to every vintage, so much metropolitan lead and solder to any tendril of the vine. Presently I had a nightmare that I was haunted by a sewing-machine, that clicked and shone, but the incredible thing was that the machine smiled, smiled perpetually.

Thus for Shaw. As for Wilde, Yeats speaks of his ''fantasy'' having ''taken . . . [a] tragic turn,'' and he says that ''men who belong by nature to the nights near to the full are still born, a tragic minority, and how shall they do their work when too ambitious for a private station, except as Wilde of the nineteenth Phase, as my symbolism has it, did his work?'' But though Wilde might have been a tragic figure in his own right, in the life he lived, he is not that in Yeats's text; rather he is an archetypal figure, a man of phase nineteen, a character actor, like Ernest Dowson, assigned a humorous role in the comedy that Yeats calls ''The Tragic Generation.''

> A Rhymer had seen Dowson at some café in Dieppe with a particularly common harlot, and as he passed, Dowson, who was half drunk, caught him by the sleeve and whispered, 'She writes poetry—it is like Browning and Mrs. Browning.' Then there came a wonderful tale repeated by Dowson himself, whether by word of mouth or by letter I do not remember. Wilde had arrived in Dieppe, and Dowson pressed upon him the necessity of acquiring 'a more wholesome taste.' They emptied their pockets on to the café table, and though there was not much, there was enough if both heaps were put into one. Meanwhile

the news had spread, and they set out accompanied by a cheering crowd. Arrived at their destination, Dowson and the crowd remained outside, and presently Wilde returned. He said in a low voice to Dowson, 'The first these ten years, and it will be the last. It was like cold mutton'—always, as Henley had said, 'a scholar and a gentleman,' he now remembered that the Elizabethan dramatists used the words 'cold mutton'—and then aloud so that the crowd might hear him, 'But tell it in England, for it will entirely restore my character.'

However tragic Wilde's life may have been, however tragic Dowson's life may have been, they both assume bit parts as comic characters in *The Life of W. B. Yeats,* he the master dramatist and stage manager, in control both of his own life and of the lives of others who play minor roles, hostile or friendly, in the one grand design.

The other attempt on his life—other than George Moore's, I mean—that Yeats intended to counteract by writing his life himself was Katharine Tynan's rather awkward effort at homicide in a book she called *Twenty-five Years: Reminiscences,* which was published exactly contemporaneously with Moore's *Hail and Farewell* (Moore's three volumes were published in 1911, 1912, and 1914; *Twenty-five Years* appeared in 1913). Tynan, instead of presenting Yeats as a literary fop and a pretender to an aristocratic heritage that was never his, as Moore had done, chose instead to twit Yeats and make fun of him for his interest in the occult. Now, I think that Yeats's relationship to occult matters was much more complex and his attitude a good deal more ambivalent than Tynan recognized—indeed, he was more ambivalent and skeptical about the occult than his critics have in general recognized. This is why those who were seriously engaged in occult practices and who gave their whole heart to the occult are regularly treated with much humor by Yeats in the *Autobiographies.* Mme. Blavatsky, for example, whom Yeats describes in a wonderful phrase as "a sort of female Dr. Johnson," is surrounded and, as it were, held off by a string of anecdotes and comic tales designed to qualify very carefully any commitment Yeats might be supposed to have made with regard to occult practices. Likewise McGregor Mathers and the man Yeats describes as "an old white-haired Oxfordshire clergyman, the most panic-stricken person I have ever known": they are all rendered as comic figures in a way they would not have been had Yeats been a wholehearted enthusiast for the magic they engaged in. The following scene with the aged clergyman may be taken as typical. "Has your alchemical research had any success?" Yeats asks him. "Yes, I once made the elixir of

life," the old gentleman responds. "A French alchemist said it had the right smell and the right colour"—then Yeats interrupts to tell the reader, "the alchemist may have been Eliphas Levi, who visited England in the 'sixties, and would have said anything"—and the clergyman again: "but the first effect of the elixir is that your nails fall out and your hair falls off. I was afraid that I might have made a mistake and that nothing else might happen, so I put it away on a shelf. I meant to drink it when I was an old man, but when I got it down the other day it had all dried up."

For a final example of the uses of comedy and irony in the *Autobiographies,* then, I turn to the contrasting accounts given by Katharine Tynan and Yeats of a séance the two of them attended in Dublin. Here is Katharine Tynan's account of what she calls "a spiritualistic seance in which I participated most unwillingly" (among other reasons, presumably, because she was a Roman Catholic):

> In spite of my protestations my host gently but firmly made me take a part. We sat round a table in the darkness touching each other's hands. I was quite determined to be in opposition to the whole thing, to disbelieve in it, and disapprove of it as a playing with things of life and death. Presently the table stood up slowly: the host was psychic. There were presences. The presences had communications to make and struggled to make them. Willie Yeats was banging his head on the table as though he had a fit, muttering to himself. I had a cold repulsion to the whole business. I took my hands from the table. Presently the spirits were able to speak. There was someone in the room who was hindering them. By this time I had got in a few invocations of my own. There was a tremendous deal of rapping going on. The spirits were obviously annoyed. They were asked for an indication as to who it was that was holding them back. They indicated me, and I was asked to withdraw, which I did cheerfully. The last thing I saw as the door opened to let me pass through was Willie Yeats banging his head on the table.

Passing from this account to Yeats's own in *Reveries over Childhood and Youth* one seems to hear him murmur, "Oh, you want to play hard ball, do you? Right . . ." and he starts thus: "Perhaps a year before we returned to London, a Catholic friend"—Katharine Tynan, of course—"brought me to a spiritualistic séance," and then he sets the scene: half a dozen people seated around a table, the medium asleep sitting upright in his chair, the lights turned out, and so on:

> Presently my shoulders began to twitch and my hands. I could easily have stopped them, but I had never heard of such a thing and I was curious. After a few minutes the movement became violent and I stopped it. I sat motionless for a while and then my whole body

moved like a suddenly unrolled watchspring, and I was thrown backward on the wall. I again stilled the movement and sat at the table. Everybody began to say I was a medium, and that if I would not resist some wonderful thing would happen. I remembered that Balzac had once desired to take opium for the experience' sake, but would not because he dreaded the surrender of his will. We were now holding each other's hands and presently my right hand banged the knuckles of the woman next to me upon the table. She laughed, and the medium, speaking for the first time, and with difficulty, out of his mesmeric sleep, said, 'Tell her there is great danger.' He stood up and began walking round me making movements with his hands as though he were pushing something away. I was now struggling vainly with this force which compelled me to movements I had not willed, and my movements became so violent that the table was broken. I tried to pray, and because I could not remember a prayer, repeated in a loud voice-

'Of Man's first disobedience and the fruit
Of that forbidden tree whose mortal taste
Brought death into the world, and all our woe . . .
Sing, Heavenly Muse.'

But the conclusion to this account, so far as Katharine Tynan is concerned, comes in the next line: "My Catholic friend had left the table and was saying a Paternoster and Ave Maria in the corner."

Briefly, I would suggest that in this very funny and quite typical passage we can see the mature Yeats directing irony at his own immature self à la Starobinski; we can see him, by the distancing effect of the comedy, holding in balance commitment and non-commitment with regard to spiritualistic phenomena; and we can see him taking his life back from Katharine Tynan by making her a minor—even unnamed—comic figure in his own drama rather than agreeing to be an actor in a play—and that play a farce—scripted by someone else.

One final remark on the tragic and the comic: Yeats, as everyone knows, calls one section of his *Autobiographies* "The Tragic Generation," and a tragic generation it no doubt was; but all is "changed, changed utterly" when the autobiographer makes it a part of his own triumphant story, transforming it into an element of his text and thus making of a figure or an event that is locally or in itself tragic a detail in a larger pattern that taken overall must play as comedy. This is the sense, mentioned earlier, in which any autobiographer, taking command of his life through inscribing it in a text, triumphs over insignificance, dead ends, and momentary tragedies by the very act of writing his autobiography. I believe that in certain sports they say that the best defense lies in offense, and one might put the matter this way: that to defend and preserve his life, Yeats

adopts the strategies of comedy and irony, but he subtly transforms those defensive tactics into offensive ones, so that in the end he is triumphant, in text as in life, the actor become also the dramatist and the stage manager, and free thereby to live his life as he will.

Source: James Olney, "The Uses of Comedy and Irony in *Autobiographies* and Autobiography," in *Yeats: An Annual of Critical and Textual Studies,* Vol. II, edited by Richard J. Finneran, 1984, pp. 195–208.

Dillon Johnston

In the following essay, Johnston examines Yeats's attempts to define himself and integrate various aspects of his personality in Autobiographies.

Although an access has been opened to Yeats's autobiography by two astute essays on this work as well as by the many recent studies of this newly discovered genre, at least three critical problems continue to block a full understanding and appreciation of this autobiographical masterpiece. First, it is not clear which edition to prefer, the 1926 *Autobiographies* or *The Autobiography* of 1938. Secondly, and most significant, both works seem built on contrary intentions: the memoirist's desire to define his own place in a fluctuating and discontinuous society and the apologist's efforts to recreate an integral self—an essential, unique, and continuous self-image. Finally, the conclusions to both works seem to abandon the apologist's problem and to offer a somewhat artificial solution to the problem of disunity in society.

A careful critical re-reading can establish that *Autobiographies* is the more unified and controlled work, and that the apparently antithetical intentions—the recreations of both a historical and an integral self—are fulfilled in this edition. And finally, in both editions, the concluding images of unified cultures are less conclusive than they appear, and in their intentional inconclusiveness, they comment as much on Yeats's self as on his society.

Critics agree that "Reveries Over Childhood and Youth" and "Trembling of the Veil," which constitute *Autobiographies*, are superior to the four sections added in the 1938 edition—"Dramatis Personae," "Estrangement," "Death of Synge," and "Bounty of Sweden," although they disagree over how much authority to grant to the more complete 1938 edition. Ian Fletcher, in the most perceptive study yet of the autobiographical writings, decides, somewhat arbitrarily, to consider only the first three parts, although they were never printed separately, and to disregard "Estrangement," "Synge," and "Sweden" because they are "disjunct, aphoristic, the raw material for composed autobiography." On the other hand, Joseph Ronsley in his thorough study, *Yeats's Autobiography,* argues for the acceptance of the entire 1938 edition, "although it seems fragmentary and lacks unity of form," in preference to the 1926 edition which "actually appeared to be more unified . . ." Further on, Ronsley describes "the pattern evolving out of his [Yeats's] struggle for unity in both his own life and that of his country" as it appears in the 1938 edition: "*The Autobiography* begins as if it were the beginning of the world. It closes, in Yeats's vision of unity of culture as the ultimate stage in the world's spiritual evolution, as if the apocalypse had at least drawn nearer." Ronsley fails to recognize that this pattern is completed in the first two parts and that only recurrence is added to the pattern and then only by "Bounty of Sweden." "Dramatis Personae" is both narrow in scope and poorly organized. Its original intention, to eulogize Lady Gregory, is outweighed by the less admirable attempt to redress the errors of Moore's *Hail and Farewell,* errors that remain more colorfully and attractively stated than Yeats's defensive rebuttal. "Estrangement" and "Death of Synge," written in diary form, abandon the apologetic intention and slacken into aphorism and memoir. And although "Bounty of Sweden" extends the search for a unified culture, it comments only ironically and indirectly on Yeats's search for a unified self-image, for "unity of being." Whereas the 1938 edition becomes what H. G. Wells called "cosmobiography," comments on civilization from a limited perspective, the 1926 edition, which Ronsley admits "appeared to be more unified," achieves actual unity through a dramatic interweaving of intentions. Therefore I will concentrate in this study on *Autobiographies,* which is comprised only of "Reveries" and "Trembling of the Veil."

The plot of *Autobiographies,* which is organized initially by place and later by dramatic conflicts, reveals the development of Yeats's identity in four fairly distinct stages: first, the child inherits an identity from his West Ireland ancestors; secondly, he loses direct possession of this inherited identity as a consequence of his father's uprooting of the family, and he achieves a negative identity by reacting to his father and then to the modern forces ultimately responsible for his father's and his

A section of the book is devoted to Yeats's relationship with Irish playwright Lady Augusta Gregory, with whom he collected Irish folktales and founded the Irish National Theatre in Dublin

deracination; and, thirdly, he defines himself in terms of six groups in Dublin and London. The fourth phase, in which Yeats separates himself from each group and develops a unique self-image, is only suggested in the direct narration of the events of Yeats's life. Yeats's integral self actually emerges in a pattern of repeated actions; the pattern is developed through certain static effects, through the autobiographical point of view, and through a concatenation of mythological images.

Before considering Yeats's integral self as it appears in this pattern, we should discuss in more detail the plot of his apparent growth. The initial stage of Yeats's self-development is set in Sligo and the west of Ireland prior to his tenth year. Although his early years were actually almost as vagrant as his later, in *Autobiographies* the hero is deep-rooted, drawing sustenance for his later life from family and folk. His principal concerns, here, are to separate all his people—the Butlers, his most ancient forebears, and the Yeatses, Middletons, and Pollexfens—from the paudeens and hucksters he found so inimical to

> **Although his early years were actually almost as vagrant as his later, in *Autobiographies* the hero is deep-rooted, drawing sustenance for his later life from family and folk."**

modern Ireland, and to establish his grandfather, William Pollexfen, as the standard of heroism for all of *Autobiographies*. After recounting some of his grandfather's fabulous exploits, Yeats says, "Even today when I read *King Lear* his image is always before me and I often wonder if the delight in passionate men in my plays and in my poetry is more than his memory."

In addition to this proud family tradition, Yeats inherits the histories and myths associated with so many locations near his Sligo home. He recalls, "The servants' stories . . . interested me. At such and such a house . . ." To the anecdotes that follow Yeats adds this comment: "All the well-known families had their . . . legends, and I often said to myself how terrible it would be to go away and die where nobody would know my story." This opportunity to develop his own "story," to have an identity compounded of family and place and imagination, is his inheritance. From this he is separated by his father's move to London and their subsequent alternations between Dublin and London.

Yeats clearly associates the first move to London with a loss of identity. He writes, "At length when I was eight or nine an aunt said to me, 'You are going to London. Here you are somebody. There you will be nobody at all.'" The English places are mythless for Yeats—"I was a stranger there. There was something in their way of saying the names of places that made me feel this." This instinctive longing for "sacred places," which prevents him from putting down roots in his new soil, persists throughout adolescence and up to the moment of writing, connecting the child and the youth to the autobiographer:

> A poignant memory came upon me the other day while I was passing the drinking fountain near Holland Park, for there . . . I longed for a sod of earth from some field I knew, something of Sligo to hold in my hand. It was some old race instinct. . . .

This lost inheritance is sought in each subsequent phase of Yeats's development, and the values of Sligo are later transformed into his theories of unity of being and unity of culture.

Separated from all other sources of identity, Yeats still had his father as a model for development. Although he could imitate his father in his style of painting and speaking, he was forced to react against him when Jack Yeats diverged from the traditional values with which Yeats had been imbued in Sligo. The first reaction he records was during childhood: "My father's unbelief had set me thinking about the evidence of religion and I weighed the matter perpetually with great anxiety . . ." But more serious differences developed in adolescence over their divergent theories of art. The son continues to admire Blake and Rossetti and the Pre-Raphaelite practice of painting heroic, literary subjects after the father has abandoned Pre-Raphaelitism. Yeats attributes the father's apostasy to the influence of "Victorian science" against which Yeats had "a monkish hate." Furthermore, the father and son also differed over their preferences in poetry: the father argued for dramatic statement while his son contended that personal utterances are the only noble poetry.

Yeats's emphasis on this filial rebellion typifies that of most post-Romantic autobiographers, who wish to demonstrate that their essential qualities were not completely dependent on their parents' influence. When Ronsley argues that "the relationship between his father and himself which he describes in 'Reveries' . . . is suffused with an atmosphere of rebellion, but in the end they shared more beliefs than they quarreled on," he is actually describing a reconciliation that took place in the life rather than in *Autobiographies*, and he is ignoring Yeats's stages of development. Yeats expands this conflict over theories of art and literature to include other contrasting values. The father was an agnostic, an empiricist, a free-trader, and a follower of Mill, while the son was a spiritualist, a dreamer, an oligarchist, and a student of Blake and Rossetti. Finally, and most significant, the father believed in progress and followed the fashion whereas the son sought an image from a past age that would free him from the flux of time.

The rootless, anti-traditional tendencies of the age, of which his father is merely a victim, become Yeats's ultimate antagonists. He reacts specifically to English empiricism of Irish journalism or, as in this quotation, Parisian art and its advocates: "'A man must be of his own time,' they would say, and if I spoke of Blake or Rossetti they would point out his bad drawing and tell me to admire Carolus Duran and Bastien-Lepage." But more frequently he groups his antagonists as "the Huxley, Tyndall, Carolus Duran, Bastien-Lepage rookery."

Soon Yeats discovers he is not alone in his reaction to his father's generation and their mechanistic and scientific values. Yeats writes:

> I was to discover others of my own age, who thought as I did, for it is not true that youth looks before it with the mechanical gaze of a well-drilled soldier. Its quarrel is not with the past, but with the present, where its elders are so obviously powerful and no cause seems lost if it seem to threaten that power.

At this point in *Autobiographies* the hero began to associate himself with various groups and to take on their values, in my term, to "define" himself. The remainder of the book takes on the aspect of a memoir, giving detailed sketches of many of Yeats's contemporaries while emphasizing the relation of the hero to each individual and each group. We finally know what this hero sought in each group, what lessons he learned, and what effect each group had on his search for unity of being and unity of culture. This period of self-definition begins toward the close of "Reveries" and continues into the chapter entitled "Ireland After Parnell." In this stage Yeats suggests a basis for his own distinction from each group, although he is not fully distinguished until the fourth stage, beginning in "Ireland After Parnell" and culminating in the last scene of *Autobiographies*.

Yeats first associated with a group of Irish patriots loosely formed around the heroic figure of John O'Leary. This old Fenian spoke in phrases worthy of "some heroic Elizabethan play" and in other aspects was reminiscent of Yeats's Lear-like grandfather. O'Leary led his group in opposing Gavan Duffy's attempt to impose a false history on Ireland and in seeking heroic images in Ireland's past by which to educe a cultural renaissance. All six groups with which Yeats aligned himself pursued some historical ideal—except the second, the circle of W. E. Henley. Yeats was drawn to Henley because he championed youth in their conflict with the older generation. Yeats writes, "I think we listened to him, and often obeyed him, partly because he was quite plainly not upon the side of our parents." As he was to Henley's and O'Leary's cliques, Yeats was first attracted to the socialist debates at William Morris's house by the heroic figure of the leader who, Yeats recalls, "reminded

me of my old grandfather in Sligo ..." While desiring to alter the future, this group rooted its politics in Morris's medieval ideal. The Theosophists and Hermetic students, two other groups with which Yeats associated, also sought images from the past and recognized strong leaders. Mme Blavatsky was "a great passionate nature" and Macgregor Mathers "a figure of romance."

Of the six groups in and out of which Yeats wandered, he suggests that the last, the Rhymers, contributed most to his self-definition. They lacked a grandfather-figure and philosophical ideals, yet "all were pre-Raphaelite" and "not one had hearkened to the feeblest caw, or been spattered by the smallest dropping from any Huxley, Tyndall, Carolus Duran, Bastien-Lepage bundle of old twigs ..." He suggests through his collective pronouns that he felt a greater unanimity within this group than in the other five groups: "We read our poems to one another;" "Our clothes were ... unadventurous;" "We were all seemingly equal. ..."

All six groups are introduced in the first half of *Autobiographies*. In line chapters entitled "Ireland After Parnell" and "The Tragic Generation" Yeats returns to these groups to distinguish himself from individual members or to recount a break with the group. In establishing these distinctions, Yeats has begun the narration of his fourth phase, in which he developed his positive identity.

Yeats dissociated himself from several of these groups because of a conflict of ideals: the Marxists in the Socialist League denied the existence of his spiritual world and the Theosophists were too fond of abstraction, a divisive and isolating force. From other individuals and groups Yeats became separated by the passage of time which revealed some failure by the other party. Henley's group was an unstable coalition which divided over Wilde's fall, and the Rhymers collapsed as a generation with the close of the old century.

In considering the tragic lives of the Rhymers and of individuals in other groups, Yeats contrasts their pursuit of an ideal self-image with his own quest for unity of being. Most of these individuals attempted to fulfill a romantic self-concept based on an image from the past which, later to be "the mask," Yeats here describes in these terms:

> Every passionate man (I have nothing to do with mechanist, or philanthropist, or man whose eyes have no preference) is, as it were, linked with another age, historical or imaginary, where alone he finds images

that rouse his energy. Napoleon was never of his own time, as the naturalistic writers and painters bid all men be, but had some Roman emperor's image in his head. . . .

Of the other characters in *Autobiographies* only Wilde, Sharpe, and Verlaine consciously sought this "anti-self," this "emotional antithesis to all that comes out of their internal nature," but all of the characters in their conscious or unconscious pursuit of images are judged by Yeats according to the degree to which they achieved a state of unity of being.

Curtis Bradford maintains that these judgments are systematic and suggests that Yeats had fully developed "his analysis of personality-types in terms of the phases of the moon." Yeats's analyses, however, are obviously closer to the poetic, sometimes vague, language of *Per Amica* . . . than to the abstract and diagrammatic analyses of *A Vision*. "Unity of being," for example, Yeats can only define metaphorically—like "a perfectly proportioned human body" or like "a musical instrument so strung that if we touch a string all the strings murmur faintly"—and he cannot explain in what relation one must be to the mask to achieve this condition. Yeats does not insert mechanically into each character-sketch this theory that every passionate man seeks an anti-self. While at times he explicitly states that he is judging the characters according to their success in this search, as this summary of three character studies illustrates: "I have described what image—always opposite to the natural self or the natural world—Wilde, Henley, Morris, copied or tried to copy . . . ," at other times the theory is only a submerged standard.

The failures of his friends to achieve a unified self Yeats attributes ultimately to the rootless, divisive age. A permanent relation to the mask can be achieved only in a society that relates ancient images to everyday tasks through custom and a shared mythology. This unity of culture the hero sought at first for all of Ireland. He dreamed of restoring the Irish mythology and so disseminating a common literature "that all, artist and poet, craftsman and day-labourer would accept a common design." Later in the narrative the disillusioned hero reduces his expectations: "The dream of my early manhood, that a modern nation can return to Unity of Culture, is false; though it may be we can achieve it for some small circle of men and women, and there leave it till the moon bring round its century." *Autobiographies* concludes with the suggestion that the hero has found, if not unity of being, at least the

basis for this in an elite coterie drawn together by a common culture. Around Lady Gregory had gathered a poet, a dramatist, a politician, and a benefactor of the arts, united by a love of Irish tradition. Prefigured by supernatural dreams and placed at the conclusion of *Autobiographies*, the meeting with Lady Gregory symbolizes Yeats's unity of culture, achieved in a "small circle of men and women."

To this point, I have described the plot as having a beginning and four stages of progressive development and a definite end, while I have ignored the cross-weavings of spatial organization, fused point of view, and mythological allusions, which tend to obscure chronology and reduce the progressive effect of the plot, to emphasize patterns of recurrent actions, and ultimately to convey the idea that Yeats's self-image is static and perpetual.

Although *Autobiographies* does reveal four stages in Yeats's growth, within each stage there is little sense of progressive development. The plot is organized within these four phases geographically or dramatically so that the narration moves from place to place or from one group to another rather than from one month or year to the next, a method Yeats suggests in his opening paragraph—"All thoughts connected with emotion and place are without sequence"—and later attributes to a quirk in his memory: "I only seem to remember things dramatic in themselves or that are somehow associated with unforgettable places."

Much of "Reveries" is organized by place. Some sections recount interesting events that occurred in one location over a long period of time, while others tell of Yeats's own association with a place without regard for chronology. From the autobiographer's perspective the different moments during the early stages of his life are merged in a habitual past tense:

> When my father gave me a holiday and later when I had a holiday from school I took my schooner boat to the round pond sailing it very commonly against the two cutter yachts of an old naval officer. He would sometimes look at the ducks and say . . . The pond had its own legends. . . . Sometimes my sister came with me, and we would look into all the sweet shops and toy shops on our way home. . . .

While the usual narrative transition is temporal—"the following month," "next," "after this"—Yeats's narration moves more often from place to place than from moment to moment. The beginning of section three on page 22 is a typical transition: "Some six miles off towards Ben Bulben and beyond the Channel, as we call the tidal river between Sligo and the Rosses, and on top of a hill. . . . ''

Yeats is not interested, as the autobiographers Wordsworth and Ruskin were, in the visual appearance of a place; he sees only the human associations established by one people living in one place for a long period of time. When Ruskin contemplates a scene, he views formations and colors and recalls his past self, while Yeats recollects past history as well as his past self. Of course, descriptions of his ''holy places,'' places rich with human associations, serve as a preface to his theory of unity of culture, expressed later in *Autobiographies*. And organization by place allows Yeats to discuss with freedom the historical and personal themes associated with each location. For example, Sligo suggests the ideal of a unified culture; Ballisodare, an area even more remote than Sligo, is rich with legends and fairy tales; Bedford Park represents Pre-Raphaelitism; London, generally, is the modern deracinated population; Liverpool is the transition between the modern and old worlds. Yeats can juxtapose places in his narration to contrast ideas, as he does on the first page when he recalls a room in Ireland, where ''some relative once lived,'' and then remembers a room in London, where he felt threatened by unfamiliar children in the streets. Or he can make direct comparisons between London and Dublin, as he does on page 191 where he contrasts the romantic faces of the Dublin peasants with the ''fat blotched'' faces of the London poor.

The conclusion to the quite long section V in ''Reveries'' illustrates how Yeats's organization by place and theme allows him to disregard chronological progression. The section does represent a period in Yeats's life, his ''year or two'' at North End in London, but it concentrates on the environs of North End and their associated memories. The last five pages of this section discuss Hammersmith School and the theme of ''companionship and enmity.'' The hero nurtured his distinction from his schoolmates and attempted to develop himself, in his ''enmity,'' according to certain heroic ideals. In the final paragraph, the first sentences discuss an American runner, whom the hero admired; then follows a sentence on heroism and his schoolboy dreams of himself as a hero; then a recalled statement by his father: ''One day my father said, 'There was a man in Nelson's ship at the battle of Trafalgar, a ship's purser, whose hair turned white; what a sensitive temperament; that man should have achieved something!''' Yeats's next sentence concludes the section: ''I was vexed and bewildered,

and am still bewildered and still vexed, finding it a poor and crazy thing that we who have imagined so many noble persons cannot bring our flesh to heel.'' The anecdote of Nelson's purser exemplifies only in a metaphorical, poetic (and humorous) manner Yeats's conclusion about our bringing our ''flesh to heel.'' The organization of this paragraph illustrates, in a general way, the organization of the entire *Autobiographies*. Organization by place breaks down strict chronological narrative and allows Yeats to move freely from one idea to a related theme, from thematic statements to poetic statements, and from an idea in the mind of the immature hero to the same idea developed by the autobiographer.

Organization by ''things dramatic in themselves,'' the dominant organizational method in the last third of ''Reveries'' and in ''Trembling of the Veil,'' also permits Yeats to minimize chronology and to emphasize themes. The character sketches, which comprise the last portion of *Autobiographies*, are dramatic in that they portray individuals in conflict with themselves and with their milieu. These sketches are significant thematically because they illustrate Yeats's theory of the mask by showing various possible relations between individuals and their self-images. Most of the sketches include Yeats's impressions of the individual gathered over a period of time. Consideration of the character's particular problem often leads Yeats into abstraction and, as in the scenes organized by place, into poetic connections. For example, in his consideration of A. E.'s misdirected energies, Yeats praises A. E.'s religious imagination and regrets his political involvement and, then, concludes with a poetic comment on politics: ''Is it not certain that the Creator yawns in earthquake and thunder and other popular displays, but toils in rounding the delicate spirals of a shell?''

The sections in which Yeats describes a location or a character and some theme, often conclude with this type of rhetorical question, with a metaphorical statement, or with a stanza or line of Yeats's latest poetry. Each of these conclusions renders the mature autobiographer's complex and sometimes profound thought on the young hero's subject of inquiry. As a consequence, the distinctions between the youth and the adult and between the different stages of development are obscured. In the manner of Gosse in *Father and Son,* Yeats sometimes merely imposes the adult's knowledge on the child, as when he says, ''To-day I add to that first conviction . . . this other conviction, long a mere opinion vaguely or intermittently apprehended,'' or when he says, ''I thought there could be no aim for poet or artist except expression of a 'Unity of Being' . . . though I would not at the time have used that phrase.'' More often, however, the autobiographer's intrusion is interrogative or poetic, elevating the youth's inquiry to a complex or metaphysical level but not resolving it. For example, after a consideration of Aubrey Beardsley, Yeats asks, ''Does not all art come when a nature . . . exhausts personal emotion in action or desire so completely that something impersonal . . . suddenly starts into its place . . . ?'' The question suggests Yeats's idea of *Spiritus Mundi* about which he had written in *Per Amica*. It is a more complex question than he would have asked in 1890, but a question for which the mature Yeats has only a tentative hypothetical answer. The poetic conclusions function in a similar way by substituting for simpler questions almost impenetrable symbols which raise greater questions. On page 238, Yeats concludes an inquiry about the possibility of achieving a unified culture with this statement: ''One thing I did not foresee, not having the courage of my own thought: the growing murderousness of the world;'' followed by the opening stanza of ''The Second Coming,'' a conclusion which displays the complex and symbolic level to which the hero's initial inquiries about culture have been raised.

Ultimately, as a result of this ''interrogative method,'' this connection of the child's question to the adult's elaboration of that question, Yeats presents an image of himself as a perpetual enquirer, one who constantly asks questions about his self and his society and who finds not answers but questions of a more complex nature. This self-image does not correspond to Yeats's anti-self, which is ''proud and lonely,'' ''hard and cold,'' much like Shelley's figure of Ahasuerus. As he states, the attempt to assume one's mask is ''an intellectual daily recreation'' which requires an alternation between the Will and the Mask and which can never be finally successful.

Yeats's self-image arises not merely from the point of view and from the organization of plot but also from the recorded action of the hero, who is constantly attempting to remake himself to fit an image which varies over the years. We have read of the youthful hero ''walking with an artificial stride in memory of Hamlet'' or wearing a ''tie gathered into a loose sailor-knot . . . like Byron's tie in the picture''; of the slightly older adolescent frequenting a club ''to become self-possessed, to be able to play with hostile minds as Hamlet played''; and of the

young man inquiring after Morris or Mathers and seeking out Madame Blavatsky to find in these heroic figures a self-defining image.

Yeats's integral self is not his anti-self, not Ahasuerus the cold savant, but Yeats in search of this mask, or Ahasuerus the Wandering Jew. On page 212, when Yeats suggests Ahasuerus as the type of his mask, he presents a long passage from Shelley's poem. The page-length excerpt, however, describes not Ahasuerus but the search for Ahasuerus by Mahmud who must go through an elaborate *passage duré* to encounter his symbol of wisdom and experience. He is told, ''Few dare, and few who dare / Win the desired communion.'' Yeats supports this self-image with other literary images—Hamlet, Athanase, Alastor, Manfred—which represent the perpetual wanderer or the divided self seeking a unity. A suggestion of the Ancient Mariner in the ''Preface'' to ''Reveries'' seems intended to introduce the image of the poet errant: ''Sometimes when I remember . . . the past, I wander here and there till I have somebody to talk to. Presently I notice that my listener is bored. . . . ''

This self-image is supported in *Autobiographies* by a mythical-historical pattern which emerges from Yeats's images and from his overt statements. During the eight years in which Yeats wrote the two books of *Autobiographies*, he was developing the elaborate psychological and historical system presented finally in *A Vision*. When Yeats admits his responsibilities as a historian in *Autobiographies*, he writes, ''As I have set out to describe nature as I see it, I must not only describe events but those patterns into which they fall. . . .'' Yeats's historical vision, which measures historical events by a mythology or paradigm and which minimizes chronology and physical causality, is similar to the historical view of other modern writers, who, in the words of Joseph Frank, 'spatialize' time by ''transmuting the time-world of history into the timeless world of myth.''

The myth that underlies *Autobiographies* is based on a Biblical teleology converted to a cyclic historiography. ''Reveries'' opens, as Ronsley has remarked, with a reference to the Biblical Creation: ''My first memories are fragmentary and isolated and contemporaneous, as though one remembered some first moments of the Seven Days.'' Although Yeats recalls much unhappiness during his Sligo childhood, he represents West of Ireland as a lost Eden, the land of his youth from which he is forever exiled. In this Eden, his grandfather, William

Pollexfen, was God: "He was so looked up to and admired that when he returned from taking the waters at Bath his men would light bonfires along the railway line for miles. . . . I think I confused my grandfather with God . . ." As I have shown, Pollexfen continued to represent, after the hero had left Sligo, the standard of nobility. Then in the penultimate paragraph of "Reveries," Yeats describes the death of this god-figure and the ensuing chaos: "Before he was dead, old servants of that house where there had never been noise or disorder began their small pilferings, and after his death there was a quarrel over the disposition of certain mantelpiece ornaments of no value." The apocalypse should follow to accord with the suggested Biblical teleology, but in "Reveries" the pattern is incomplete. *Autobiographies* concludes with Yeats, the time-conscious autobiographer, speaking of his situation in 1915:

> For some months now I have lived with my own youth and childhood . . . and I am sorrowful and disturbed. . . . All life weighed in the scales of my own life seems to me a preparation for something that never happens.

Frank Kermode has described in *The Sense of An Ending* man's need to create a fictional end to the world to give our own lives a sense of completion. Although Western man traditionally has shaped history according to a Biblical teleology, which moves from Creation to Apocalypse, the modern writer has such a strong "sense of an ending" that he represents himself as suspended in the period preceding the Apocalypse, and living with "eternal transition, perpetual crisis."

Yeats infuses "Trembling of the Veil" with the sense of a still moment of crisis, in which he awaits the answer to his question, "What rough beast slouches toward Bethlehem to be born?" Out of respect for this dark chiliasm, we must re-examine the apparently affirmative conclusion of *Autobiographies*. The book closes with Yeats's predetermined meeting with Lady Gregory. He recalls the sessions with two aristocratic patrons, Lady Gregory and a French Count, which led to the establishment of the Irish Theatre:

> On the sea coast at Duras, a few miles from Coole, an old French Count, Florimond de Bastero, lived for certain months in every year. Lady Gregory and I talked over my project of an Irish Theatre looking out upon the lawn of his house, watching a large flock of ducks that was always gathered for his arrival from Paris, and that would be a very small flock, if indeed it were a flock at all, when he set out for Rome in the autumn.

Following this, Yeats specifies the accomplishments of some members of this group—of Yeats, Hugh Lane, Shawe-Taylor, John Synge—under Lady Gregory's personal influence, and adds: "If that influence were lacking, Ireland would be greatly improverished, so much has been planned out in the library, or among the woods at Coole."

In tone this is like the conclusion of "Bounty of Sweden," where Yeats represents Sweden as a paragon of cultural unity. However, the Swedish conclusion is more impressionistic and romanticized than the Irish scene, and as a poetic ideal it is certainly less realizable than the ideal represented by the Coole Park coterie.

Yet, if this "small circle of men and women" has achieved under Lady Gregory's influence a temporary unity of culture, it is only a momentary stasis in the advance of history toward the impending Apocalypse. Through the description of the seasonal peregrinations of the Count, enforced by the image of migrating fowl, a familiar symbol in Yeats's poetry for historical recurrence, Yeats suggests the repetitive cycles of history. The very distance the narrator maintains from his twenty-year-old scene and the fact that those who comprised the circle had passed into obscurity or ignominy suggest that they could not reverse history's decadent course. "They came like swallows and like swallows went," he says of them elsewhere. He concludes *Autobiographies* by commenting on this unified, elite group: "I have written these words . . . that young men to whom recent events are often more obscure than those long past, may learn what debts they owe and to what creditor." The statement recalls to the reader an earlier pronouncement characterizing, in an appreciative tone, the attitude of youth: "Its quarrel is not with the past, but with the present, where its elders are so obviously powerful . . ." The ironic echo suggests that this small circle, which preceded from no immediate cause and which found its pattern in eighteenth-century culture, would effect no change in the next generation or in the inexorable, gyring course of history. Yeats achieves a similar ironic reversal in "Bounty of Sweden," where the conclusiveness of the court-image is undercut by a curious final paragraph. Ronsley praises this conclusion, saying Yeats wished to "give Ireland a model on which to build the unity of culture that the Stockholm Town Hall symbolized." He fails to recognize that the concluding paragraph—

> While we are packing for our journey a young American poet comes to our room, and introduces himself.

''I was in the South of France,'' he says ''and I could not get a room warm enough to work in, and if I cannot get a warm room here I will go to Lapland.''

—reminds us of such poems as ''The Man Who Dreamed of Faeryland'' and suggests that the quest originates in the poet's romantic, insatiable nature and is therefore interminable.

A year or so after the publication of *Autobiographies* Yeats wrote to Sean O'Casey advising him about the proper treatment of history in literature: ''The whole history of the world must be reduced to wallpaper in front of which the characters must pose and speak.'' In *Autobiographies* the action of the hero and the historical background form a complementary design. Between a lost Eden and a suspended Apocalypse the hero wanders in a patterned course of seeking and finding and seeking again on a higher level. The patterned search begins in Eden, where the hero's unhappiness was caused by his own nature, and continues, Yeats suggests, beyond the temporary stasis at Coole Park toward some larger, more inclusive symbol of unity, such as the Swedish court. But Yeats's self-creating entelechy will demand that this image, too, must be transcended. Consequently, the pattern of self-seeking and self-creating is complete in *Autobiographies*, and its recurrence in ''Bounty of Sweden,'' the last section of *The Autobiography*, suggests its perpetuity.

Source: Dillon Johnston, ''The Perpetual Self of Yeats's *Autobiographies*,'' in *Éire-Ireland*, Vol. IX, No. 4, 1974, pp. 69–85.

Sources

Edwards, Diane Tolomeo, ''William Butler Yeats,'' in *Dictionary of Literary Biography*, Volume 98: *Modern British Essayists*, edited by Robert Baum, Gale Research, 1990, pp. 328–41.

Heaney, Seamus, ''All Ireland's Bard,'' in *Atlantic Monthly*, Vol. 280, No. 5, November 1997, pp. 155–60.

Reid, B. L., ''William Butler Yeats,'' in *Dictionary of Literary Biography*, Volume 19: *British Poets*, edited by Donald E. Stanford, Gale Research, 1983, pp. 399–452.

Spencer, Theodore, ''The Later Poetry of W. B. Yeats,'' in *Literary Opinion in America*, edited by Morton Dauwen Zabel, Harper, 1962, pp. 270–81.

Stillwell, Edith, ''William Butler Yeats,'' in *Aspects of Modern Poetry*, Duckworth, 1934, pp. 73–89.

Wilson, Edmund, ''W. B. Yeats,'' in *Axel's Castle: A Study in the Imaginative Literature of 1870–1930*, Scribner's, 1931, pp. 26–63.

Further Reading

Bogan, Louise, ''William Butler Yeats,'' in *Atlantic Monthly*, Vol. 161, No. 5, May 1938, pp. 637–44.
     This article, published not long before Yeats's death in early 1939, expresses appreciation of the aging poet and dramatist and includes an overview of his life and accomplishments.

Cahill, Thomas, *How the Irish Saved Civilization: The Untold Story of Ireland's Heroic Role from the Fall of Rome to the Rise of Medieval Europe*, Nan A. Talese/Doubleday, 1995.
     This book covers, in a relatively light manner, the early history of Ireland, including the legends and myths of many characters in whom Yeats was interested in his search for a unifying Irish literature.

Foster, R. F., *W. B. Yeats, A Life*, Vol. 1: *The Apprentice Mage 1865–1914*, Oxford University Press, 1997.
     This is the first in a planned series of two biographical volumes on the life of Yeats. In this volume, R. F. Foster covers the writer's life through his middle years, when he was especially involved in Irish drama and in running the famed Abbey Theatre.

Shaw, Robert B., ''Tragic Generations,'' in *Poetry*, Vol. 175, No. 3, p. 210.
     In this article, Robert Shaw compares the state of poetry at the end of the twentieth century with poetry at the end of the nineteenth century, with an especially close examination of those poets Yeats referred to in his essay ''The Trembling of the Veil'' in *Autobiographies*.

The Autobiography of Malcolm X

Malcolm X

1965

The Autobiography of Malcolm X is the life story of Malcolm Little: son of a Baptist minister, wide-eyed teenager in Boston, street hustler and prison inmate in New York, faithful and energetic member of the Nation of Islam, and, finally, Muslim pilgrim determined to create an organization for all blacks regardless of their religion. It is also a tale of, as the author puts it, a "homemade" education pursued in the schools, on the streets, in prison, and at the feet of his mentor Elijah Muhammad. Many considered Malcolm X's separatist philosophies (later softened) disturbing and in direct opposition to those of the period's other well-known black activists, including Martin Luther King, Jr., who argued for integration and nonviolent confrontation.

While the book received high praise when it was first published in 1965, it immediately engendered questions about its authorship. The book is unusual in that it was transcribed and constructed by Alex Haley from thousands of hours of conversations he had with Malcolm X in the early 1960s. In fact, while Malcolm X did read drafts of the book, he never lived to see it in print. In early 1965, a trio suspected to have been associated with the Nation of Islam gunned him down as he was about to give a speech in Harlem. Haley, then a recently retired Coast Guard member working as a journalist, went on to write the critically acclaimed family history, *Roots.*

In 1966, *The Autobiography of Malcolm X* received an Anisfield-Wolf Book Award, and in 1992, it was produced as a film.

Author Biography

Since his father was both a minister and an activist for Marcus Garvey's Back-to-Africa movement and his mother had such light skin she could pass as a white woman, Malcolm X seemed almost predestined to a life of challenging America's racial status quo. Born on May 19, 1925, in Omaha, Nebraska, as Malcolm Little, Malcolm X experienced a childhood marked by violence and poverty. While his mother was pregnant with him, white men threatened to burn down the family's house. When Malcolm was six, white supremacists murdered his father, plunging the family into years of hunger and deprivation.

Though Malcolm was a good student, a school career counselor told him that because he was black, he could aim only as high as a job as a skilled laborer. He soon set out on a path that led to a dead-end period of his life, filled with drugs and crime in Boston and then in New York City. While Malcolm was in jail, his brothers and sisters encouraged him to follow Elijah Muhammad, head of the Nation of Islam, as they were doing. The Nation of Islam is a religious and cultural organization founded in the early 1930s in Detroit by W. D. Fard and advocating Islam and economic self-determination for African Americans. Malcolm became a member of the Nation as soon as he was released from prison in 1952.

Malcolm's enthusiasm for Islam as preached by Elijah Muhammad—who taught that white men were devils and that complete separation of the races was the only solution to racism in America—prompted his rise through the ranks of the Nation of Islam. He dropped his last name and replaced it with X to symbolize the identity and history that whites had stripped from blacks during slavery. In January 1958, Malcolm X married Sister Betty X, a fellow member of the Nation of Islam and a nursing student. They had six daughters.

Malcolm X developed a national reputation as an angry black activist, attracting the attention of various law enforcement agencies and the Federal Bureau of Investigation, which were concerned that his ideology promoted racial violence. Muhammad continued to rely on Malcolm X more and more,

until jealousy and Muhammad's sexual indiscretions caused an irreparable rift between the two in 1963. Muhammad expelled Malcolm X from the Nation, and Malcolm X began hearing that members of the Nation were planning his death.

During a pilgrimage to Mecca soon after his expulsion, Malcolm X experienced a second conversion of sorts: he decided that the Islam he had practiced under Muhammad's tutelage was not the true Islam. In 1964, he established his own organization to minister to blacks of all faiths and another organization called the Organization of Afro-American Unity that planned to unite blacks all over the world against racism.

In 1959, Alex Haley had written an article for *Reader's Digest* on Malcolm X and the Nation of Islam. In early 1963, Haley persuaded Malcolm X to tell him his life story, and the two men met often for conversations that Haley eventually transcribed and structured as *The Autobiography of Malcolm X*. On February 21, 1965, as Malcolm X stepped onto a stage to address a crowd of supporters in Harlem, three men believed to have been associated with the Nation of Islam gunned him down. Later that year, Malcolm X's autobiography was published to widespread acclaim.

Plot Summary

Chapter One: "Nightmare"

The Autobiography of Malcolm X begins with Malcolm Little telling about his years as a trouble-making but clever child in the 1930s. His father, Earl Little, is a Baptist preacher who advocates the "back-to-Africa" philosophy of black activist Marcus Garvey. Once, their house is burned down, and another time it is damaged—both times by groups of white men. His mother, Louise, is made a widow when Earl is murdered; then the state welfare agency tries to break up the family. Eventually, fighting against the state and struggling to keep her children fed becomes too much for Louise, and she is committed to a mental asylum. The children are sent to various foster homes in the region.

Chapter Two: "Mascot"

Malcolm is expelled from school when he is thirteen years old, and state officials move him to a detention home. Though Malcolm is a very popular student at the white junior high school and is elected the seventh-grade class president, he later feels that he was simply a ''mascot'' for the school.

His half-sister Ella invites him to visit her in Boston for the summer, a visit that changes his life by showing him a world outside his small town. When he returns to school the next fall, a school counselor tells Malcolm that he should not consider becoming a lawyer because he is black. Ella invites him to move to Boston.

Chapter Three: ''Homeboy''

Malcolm lives with Ella in the ''snooty-black'' neighborhood of Boston. But Malcolm is attracted to the ''town ghetto section,'' where he meets Shorty, a pool hall employee. The two strike up an immediate friendship, and Shorty finds Malcolm a job shining shoes at the famous Roseland State Ballroom. Shorty also initiates Malcolm into the various aspects of city living, including straightening his hair through a painful process called ''conking.'' Looking back, Malcolm sees this as his ''first really big step toward self-degradation,'' trying to look like a white man.

Malcolm X

Chapter Four: ''Laura''

Malcolm quits his shoe shining job to devote more time to dances at Roseland. Ella then finds him a job at the ice cream parlor, much to his dismay. While working, he meets Laura, a studious young girl who isn't haughty like the other customers. Malcolm and Laura attend Roseland dances, where he introduces her to the seamy side of life. Malcolm is meanwhile accepting the advances of Sophia, a rich, attractive white woman who gives him money.

Chapter Five: ''Harlemite''

Ella helps Malcolm get a job as a dishwasher on the train between Boston and New York. After only one day in New York, Malcolm decides to live in Harlem, the center of American black life in the 1940s. Malcolm eventually takes a job as a waiter at his favorite bar in Harlem, Small's Paradise. Meanwhile, Malcolm goes out at night, dancing, drinking, and smoking marijuana.

Chapter Six: ''Detroit Red''

Malcolm is barred from Small's after offering a prostitute to an undercover policeman, so his friend Sammy the Pimp helps set him up selling marijuana to his numerous musician contacts.

Chapter Seven: ''Hustler''

Malcolm next turns to robbery with Sammy. But their friendship cools after Sammy draws a gun on Malcolm during a fight. Malcolm begins to use cocaine on a regular basis. Racial tensions increase in Harlem, and Malcolm moves into the numbers racket and other illegal pursuits. He experiences many brushes with danger and death during this period.

Chapter Eight: ''Trapped''

West Indian Archie, with whom Malcolm has placed thousands of dollars worth of bets, is gunning for Malcolm because he believes that Malcolm is trying to cheat him and make him look weak. Others are also targeting Malcolm, who is now a drug addict, using cocaine, opium, and Benzedrine, and smoking marijuana regularly. Sammy finally calls Malcolm's old friend, Shorty, who takes him back to Boston.

Chapter Nine: ''Caught''

In Boston, Malcolm's friends can hardly believe how mean and hard he has become. Malcolm begins to think about what hustle he will choose next. He decides on house burglary and gathers Shorty, Rudy, Sophia, and her sister into a gang to steal from wealthy Boston homes. They are very successful until Malcolm is caught leaving a stolen watch for repair at a shop.

Chapter Ten: "Satan"

Not quite twenty-one years old, Malcolm is sentenced to jail for the burglaries. The other inmates consider him so mean and irreligious that they call him "Satan." Malcolm meets Bimbi in jail, the first man he has ever known who could command respect simply with words. Bimbi impresses on him the importance of learning, which prompts Malcolm to take a few extension courses in jail. Various members of Malcolm's family start converting to an American Muslim sect called the Nation of Islam and mention in their letters to Malcolm their leader, Elijah Muhammad, who teaches that "the white man is a devil." Malcolm is impressed enough to begin the process that culminates in his own conversion.

Chapter Eleven: "Saved"

Still in jail, Malcolm begins his daily correspondence with Elijah Muhammad, learning about history, religion, and philosophy. He also starts proselytizing (recruiting outsiders to one's cause or faith) other inmates about the Nation of Islam, meanwhile expressing disdain for those blacks, especially intellectuals, who favor integration of whites and blacks.

Chapter Twelve: "Savior"

In the summer of 1952, Malcolm is released from prison and moves immediately to Detroit to be near his family and their local Nation of Islam temple. He becomes involved in recruiting more Nation members, meanwhile becoming closer to Muhammad. In 1953, Malcolm is named an assistant minister of Temple Number One. He replaces his last name with X to commemorate the fact that when blacks were brought to the United States they lost their real names and were instead given meaningless slave names.

Chapter Thirteen: "Minister Malcolm X"

Muhammad expresses his faith in Malcolm X by sending Malcolm X to his old haunt, New York City. Despite not having spent any time thinking about women since his conversion, Malcolm X decides that it was now time to take a wife. In 1958,

he chooses Sister Betty X, a nursing student and Nation instructor, as his wife.

Chapter Fourteen: "Black Muslims"

By the late 1950s and early 1960s, a documentary about the Nation, a book, and numerous newspaper articles are exposing more and more people to the organization. Malcolm X appears on television and radio debates, where he speaks against integration and for separation of races. Muhammad, because of his own declining health, gives Malcolm X a larger role in the running of the Nation.

Chapter Fifteen: "Icarus"

In this chapter, Malcolm X explains his separatist philosophy, his disdain for other organizations that claim to help blacks, and how his message was received in the late 1950s and early 1960s.

Chapter Sixteen: "Out"

In 1961, Muhammad's health continues to worsen, and Malcolm X's frustration with the Nation's lack of action on various issues grows. The story breaks about Muhammad's illegitimate children, throwing Malcolm X into a period of torment and doubt. Muhammad silences Malcolm X for a comment about the Kennedy assassination he considered inappropriate, and threats against Malcolm X's life surface. After much anguish, Malcolm X officially breaks from the Nation of Islam to start his own organization for blacks of all faiths.

Chapter Seventeen: "Mecca"

Malcolm X makes a *hajj,* or pilgrimage, to Mecca in Saudi Arabia. He is impressed with the sense of brotherhood he feels while on the *hajj* and also with the "color-blindness" of the Muslim world's religious society. In response, he softens his previously strong stance against whites and issues a letter to his new mosque outlining his beliefs.

Chapter Eighteen: "El-Hajj Malik El-Shabazz"

Malcolm X, during his *hajj* in Saudi Arabia, takes the Arabic name El-Hajj Malik El-Shabazz. He is treated as a visiting Muslim dignitary during another trip he takes to other parts of the Middle East and Africa. Malcolm X comes to a number of different conclusions during this trip, including that

African-American leaders should travel extensively overseas to give them alternative solutions to "the American black man's problems." In addition, he admits that his previous statements about white people were too sweeping.

Chapter Nineteen: "1965"

The final chapter of the book outlines how Malcolm X sees his philosophy changing and how he anticipates the change will affect the organization he is starting, the Organization of Afro-American Unity. He mentions in this chapter the great possibility of his assassination.

Chapter Twenty: "Epilogue"

This part was written by Alex Haley, Malcolm X's collaborator on the autobiography, after the Muslim leader's murder. Haley discusses how the book came to be, the difficulties in getting information about Malcolm X, and the events leading up to and following his death.

Key Figures

Amilah

Amilah (or Gamilah, as mentioned in Alex Haley's epilogue) was Malcolm X and Sister Betty's fourth daughter, born in 1964.

West Indian Archie

West Indian Archie was "one of Harlem's *really* bad Negroes," according to Malcolm. Still, Malcolm placed many numbers bets with Archie during the mid-1940s, when Malcolm himself was working in the numbers business. Archie threatened to kill Malcolm over a misunderstanding about money, but Shorty and Sammy arranged to have Malcolm leave town.

Attallah

Attallah was Malcolm X and Sister Betty's first daughter, born in 1958. She was named after Attilah the Hun, who sacked Rome.

Bimbi

Malcolm met Bimbi in jail. Bimbi, an old burglar, encouraged Malcolm to read and study and

Media Adaptations

- *The Autobiography of Malcolm X* was primary source material for 1992's *Malcolm X,* directed by Spike Lee and starring Denzel Washington as Malcolm X, Angela Bassett as Betty Shabazz, and Al Freeman Jr. as Elijah Muhammad. Spike Lee and Arnold Perl wrote the screenplay, which was produced by Forty Acres and a Mule Filmworks. The movie was nominated for Academy Awards in the categories of best leading actor for Washington and best costume design.

- James Baldwin adapted portions of the autobiography for a screenplay published by Dial in 1973, entitled *One Day When I Was Lost: A Scenario Based on Alex Haley's "Autobiography of Malcolm X."*

was the first man Malcolm had ever met who commanded respect simply with his words.

Sister Clara

Sister Clara was married to Elijah Muhammad and was, according to Malcolm X, a "dark, good wife."

Ella Mae Collins

Ella was one of Malcolm's father's three children from a previous marriage. Malcolm first met her while he was in seventh grade, and he considered her the proudest black woman he had ever seen. She owned property in Boston and was successful enough in business to help bring a number of her relatives from Georgia to live in Boston. The summer Malcolm spent in Boston with her changed his life, especially when he saw the contrast between the small town he lived in and the big city. The next year, he moved to Boston to live with her.

After a while, Malcolm decided that Ella was a snob and dismissed her efforts to help him. She wanted Malcolm to improve himself, but as a teenager and young adult he was only interested in having fun. After Malcolm converted to Islam, he encouraged her to convert as well. After a number of years, she converted and even set up a language school for young Muslim girls. She also loaned Malcolm the money to make his pilgrimage to Mecca.

Earl

Earl was one of Malcolm's father's three children from a previous marriage. He lived in Boston. When he became an adult, he was a successful singer who went by the name Jimmy Carleton.

El-Hajj Malik El-Shabazz

See Malcolm X

Ilyasah

Ilyasah (from Ilyas, Arabic for Elijah, according to Malcolm) was Malcolm X and Sister Betty's third daughter, born in 1962.

Elijah Karriem

See Elijah Muhammad

Laura

Malcolm met Laura while working at an ice cream parlor in Ella's ritzy black neighborhood. Although she came from a "good" family and was studious, Laura distinguished herself to Malcolm by her friendliness. Ella became very fond of Laura and encouraged Malcolm to see her often. He loved taking Laura to dances, but she had to lie to her family about where she was going. According to Malcolm, their relationship started Laura on the downward path involving drugs, alcohol, and prostitution, for which he blamed himself.

Reverend Earl (Early) Little

Earl Little was Malcolm's father, a Baptist preacher who also advocated the "back-to-Africa" teachings of Marcus Garvey. He chose to do this kind of work because, according to Malcolm, he had seen three of his brothers killed by white men. A large man, well over six feet, and not typically intimidated, Little had to move his large family around more than he would have liked because much of his preaching angered many local whites. He was murdered in 1931 by a white racist group in Lansing, Michigan, when Malcolm was about six years old.

Earl treated Malcolm a bit better than he treated his other children; Malcolm always wondered whether this favoritism was because his skin was lighter than the other children's. Earl had eleven children, three from a previous marriage and eight with Louise, Malcolm's mother. Louise and Earl fought often, usually over Louise's dietary restrictions.

Hilda Little

Hilda was Malcolm's quiet older sister. He remembers that she served as his "second mother." After their father died, Hilda helped around the house by taking care of the younger children while Louise went to work.

Louise Little

Louise Little was Malcolm's mother, born in Grenada to a black woman who had been raped by a white man, according to Malcolm. She had very light skin and was often mistaken for a white woman. This fact helped her get jobs as a maid after her husband died, but as soon as her white employers realized that she was black—often when one of her children dropped by where she worked—she would be fired.

Louise had definite ideas about what she and her family should eat. For example, she refused to allow her children to eat rabbit or pork, and very often these restrictions were the source of fights that erupted between her and her husband. She occasionally had visions, and the day Earl was murdered she had a vision of his death.

After Earl died, the state welfare officials tried to take Louise's children away. Eventually she broke down under the stress of trying to rear her eight children alone. The house fell into disrepair, and the state placed all of her children in different homes and placed her in a mental asylum for twenty-six years. In 1963, her son Philbert removed her from the asylum and took her in.

Malcolm Little

See Malcolm X

Philbert Little

Philbert was one of Malcolm's older brothers who distinguished himself by enjoying his father's preaching, while Malcolm found it confusing. When Philbert and Malcolm weren't fighting with each other, they ganged up against other children. Philbert converted to the Nation of Islam before Malcolm did and became a temple minister in Lansing, Michigan.

Reginald Little

Reginald was one of Malcolm's younger brothers and was always in ill health due to a hernia. Malcolm worked to have Reginald look up to him in the same way that Malcolm respected Wilfred. When Reginald was a teenager, he joined the merchant marine, but he left it and moved in with Malcolm in Harlem in the mid-1940s. Malcolm secured his brother a safe ''hustle,'' or illegal way to make money, selling cheap clothes for about twice their worth, and was always impressed with Reginald's poise and street smarts. Reginald converted to the Nation of Islam but was kicked out for immoral activities before Malcolm left prison. He ended up in a mental asylum.

Robert Little

Robert was one of Malcolm's younger brothers. He spent time at Michigan State University, doing postgraduate work in psychology.

Wesley Little

Wesley was one of Malcolm's younger brothers.

Wilfred Little

Wilfred was the first child Earl had with Louise. Malcolm, as a child, felt very close to Wilfred and looked up to him, especially after their father was murdered. After his father's death, Wilfred quit school and took a job to help support the family. He converted to the Nation of Islam and became a temple minister in Detroit.

Yvonne Little

Yvonne was Malcolm's younger sister, born in 1929.

Mother Marie

Mother Marie was Elijah Muhammad's mother. Malcolm X loved to sit and listen to her tell stories about Elijah's childhood and humble beginnings.

Mary

Mary was one of Earl Little's three children from a previous marriage. She lived in Boston.

The Messenger

See Elijah Muhammad

Elijah Muhammad

Elijah Muhammad was the shy and slightly sickly leader of the Nation of Islam organization for some forty years from the mid-1930s. He and Malcolm first met after extensive correspondence while Malcolm was in jail. Malcolm, for the twelve years after he left prison and until his split with the Nation of Islam, revered Muhammad as if he were a god and served him as a minister and close advisor. Malcolm credited Muhammad for much of his knowledge about the world as well as for his rise from street-smart hustler to respected leader. The two shared an almost father-son relationship.

Muhammad came from a very poor background in Georgia, where he was born Elijah Poole. He had only a fourth-grade education and was sickly but worked to follow and spread the teachings of Master W. D. Fard. Fard taught Muhammad about Islam and that it was the best religion for American blacks. Eventually, Muhammad became a minister at one of Fard's temples and received the name Elijah Karriem. Muhammad's rise in the Nation of Islam was a steady one but was filled with setbacks such as the nearly six years he spent in jail for draft-dodging.

Malcolm X and Muhammad started to part ways in the early 1960s, after reports of Muhammad's illegitimate children surfaced and after Malcolm X became frustrated with the Nation's unwillingness to take stronger action on a number of issues. The final break occurred when Malcolm X made public statements about the Kennedy assassination, forcing Muhammad to ''silence'' him for ninety days.

Mr. Ostrowski

Mr. Ostrowski was Malcolm's English teacher at Mason Junior High School. Like many of the other teachers, he made racist jokes during class. When Malcolm was in eighth grade, Mr. Ostrowski asked him what he wanted to do with his life. When Malcolm answered, ''be a lawyer,'' Mr. Ostrowski told him that blacks could not be lawyers. This incident crystallized Malcolm's discontentment about living in a small town after having spent the summer in Boston with Ella.

Elijah Poole

See Elijah Muhammad

Qubilah

Qubilah was Malcolm X and Sister Betty's second daughter, born in 1960.

Rudy

Rudy was one of Shorty's friends in Boston and was half Italian and half black. He worked for an employment agency that hired him out to wealthy white families as a waiter when they needed catering help for parties. His knowledge of wealthy households made him indispensable when Malcolm decided to gather together a burglary gang. Rudy, along with everyone else in the gang, eventually went to jail for the robberies.

Sammy the Pimp

Sammy the Pimp was one of Malcolm's best friends while he lived in Harlem during the 1940s. He was from Kentucky and had the reputation of having the best-looking whores in Harlem. Sammy "helped" Malcolm in a variety of ways, including getting him started in selling marijuana. Malcolm and Sammy partnered on a few robberies, but their relationship cooled when Malcolm hit Sammy's girlfriend and Sammy threatened him with a gun. However, Sammy later helped save Malcolm's life after Malcolm had angered dangerous people in Harlem. Sammy called Shorty, who came to Harlem and took Malcolm back to Boston.

Shorty

Malcolm met Shorty at a Boston pool hall soon after he moved there to live with Ella. He was from Lansing, Michigan, where Malcolm spent a few years of his childhood. Shorty found a job for Malcolm (whom he took to calling "Red") as a shoeshine boy at the famous Roseland State Ballroom. As well, he introduced Malcolm to all that the city had to offer, including drinking, gambling, expensive clothes, and women. Shorty helped save Malcolm's life by answering Sammy's call to take Malcolm back to Boston when he was threatened in Harlem.

Sophia

Sophia, a well-to-do and attractive white woman, fell for Malcolm after she saw him and Laura dance together in Boston. They became a couple, breaking Laura's heart. Sophia gave Malcolm money that helped him move out of Ella's house and in with Shorty. Malcolm X noted in his book that having a white, attractive girlfriend was an important status symbol for a black man during that period in Boston. After Malcolm moved to Harlem, Sophia visited him, even after she married a wealthy Boston man. She was eventually arrested with Shorty and Malcolm for armed robbery.

Sister Betty X

Sister Betty X served as an instructor to the women members of the Nation of Islam in housekeeping and hygiene. She was a nursing student when Malcolm X first noticed her and began to consider the possibility of their marriage. He did not waste much time courting her, dismissing the concept of romance, but asked her to marry him in a 1958 telephone conversation after the two had spent a minimal amount of time together. Malcolm X considered her a good Muslim wife who stood by him through good and bad times.

Malcolm X

Malcolm X had dramatic beginnings as the child of a Baptist preacher and his wife who were often threatened by gangs of angry whites. His father spread the ideas of black activist Marcus Garvey, and his mother was a light-skinned black woman from Grenada. He had seven brothers and sisters. Malcolm was a clever child who learned very early the value of making a fuss about anything that didn't please him. After his father was murdered and his mother was committed to a mental hospital, the family was split up and Malcolm went to live with the Gohannas family, who had previously fed him when his mother couldn't provide any food.

Throughout his early life, Malcolm X proved himself to be a ingenious man, combining street smarts with basic psychology to get what he wanted. He collected a number of nicknames based on the reddish tint of his skin and hair, for example,

"Red" and "Detroit Red." Eventually he became a drug addict and a criminal and was sent to jail for breaking into homes. In prison he discovered books and was converted to Elijah Muhammad's Nation of Islam. This experience forever changed him and made him appreciative of education and hard work.

Malcolm, who took the last name X to symbolize the identity that was taken from blacks by whites during the American period of slavery, became a powerful speaker and leader who represented the Nation of Islam. But his style of organizing and leading varied greatly from Muhammad's. He also became bitterly disappointed at Muhammad's moral failings. Malcolm was ejected from the Nation but was excited to begin a new organization, the Organization of Afro-American Unity, reflecting his then less-harsh view of whites and an interest in internationalizing the black struggle.

Themes

Oppression and Slavery

One of Malcolm X's greatest desires was to open other African Americans' eyes to the history of black oppression and slavery in the United States and the world. The book's opening chapter immediately presents Malcolm's mother pregnant with him, struggling to save her family and home as white men threaten to harm them. By the end of the same chapter, the family's house has been burned down, and Malcolm's father has been murdered by a gang of white supremacists. Malcolm X's life has been defined by the oppression of his family and friends. His own abilities are ignored by a school counselor who dismisses young Malcolm's desire to become a lawyer or some other professional.

As an adult member of the Nation of Islam, Malcolm X uses the violent history of slavery and oppression in the United States to shock those he tried to reach with his preaching. "I wouldn't waste any time to start opening their eyes about the devil white man," he remembers. "The dramatization of slavery never failed intensely to arouse Negroes hearing its horrors spelled out for the first time." Even after he is expelled from the Nation of Islam, Malcolm X continues to tell the story of how poorly blacks have been treated in the United States, reminding his listeners that the poor treatment did not

end when slavery was abolished. He tells fellow dinner guests in Ghana that racial violence in the United States is not unexpected, since "black men had been living packed like animals and treated like lepers."

Religious Conversion

Much of *The Autobiography of Malcolm X* is devoted to the author's conversion to Islam. Malcolm's conversion experience is classic in that he had fallen to the depths of depravity just before he embraced Islam through Elijah Muhammad and his Nation of Islam. His conversion takes place in prison, a place in which Malcolm has enough time and solitude to study and think. Malcolm leaves prison with all the fervor and energy of a new convert, impatient to spread his new awareness among his fellow blacks. To signify even further his separation from his old life, he takes a new name, Malcolm X.

Malcolm X later experiences a second conversion, to that which he calls in his book "the true Islam." After his expulsion from the Nation of Islam, Malcolm X travels to Mecca on a religious pilgrimage, or *hajj*. On this *hajj* he has his second conversion after seeing the various skin colors of the Muslims around him during prayers. His political ideals change, and he decides that, while black people must work together on a global basis to change their condition, his earlier blanket condemnation of the white man was wrong. He writes a letter, in fact, to his followers back in the United States explaining that he has been "blessed by Allah with a new insight into the true religion of Islam and a better understanding of America's entire racial dilemma."

Leadership

One of the reasons for Malcolm X's split from the Nation of Islam is his disagreement with Elijah Muhammad about the style of leadership undertaken by the organization. Throughout the book, Malcolm X notes that he is a man of action. "All of my life, as you know, I had been an activist, I had been impatient," he says when remembering how he almost couldn't sit still in his eagerness to bring more converts to the Nation of Islam.

Muhammad's style is less assertive. After Malcolm X assumes a more involved role within the Nation, he expresses concerns about these differ-

Topics for Further Study

- *The Autobiography of Malcolm X* is a book that was "told to" Alex Haley and published after Malcolm X's death in 1965. After finishing the book, conduct independent research on Malcolm X and his life, not using his autobiography. Do you find any important incidents that are missing from the book or things that others remember in a different way? Create a chart that shows your findings.

- Investigate what was taking place in the United States and around the world from the late 1920s until the mid-1960s. Create a time line that shows some important events for each decade and place them alongside important events from the autobiography.

- Malcolm X, Elijah Muhammad, and Martin Lut-

her King, Jr., were important African-American leaders during the 1950s and 1960s. Who are the important black leaders today? List three, and tell why you chose them.

- Learn about the history of Islam and different forms of the religion practiced at different times and in different areas of the world. Make a chart showing the major forms of Islam, their important differences, and where they are practiced.

- What do you think the rest of Malcolm X's life would have been like if he had not been murdered? Use what you know about him, and about the plans he had when he died, to write a one-page summary of what he might have done if he had lived to be an old man. Also, tell what the impact of his activities might have been.

ences. Malcolm X recalls, "If I harbored any disappointment whatsoever, it was that privately I was convinced that our Nation of Islam could be an even greater force . . . if we engaged in more *action*." Malcolm X is a more forceful leader than his mentor, able of capturing the minds and hearts of diverse crowds of people. Many believe that this prompted the jealousy that developed between the two great men's supporters, ending in Malcolm X's ejection from the Nation and, ultimately, his death.

Self-Discovery through Education

The years in prison give Malcolm X the chance to contemplate who he is as well as what he can make of himself. He is aided by a surprisingly good library in jail, of which Malcolm X takes full advantage. As well, he takes correspondence courses in a variety of subjects—even Latin! It's in prison that he also learns about the Nation of Islam and decides to change his life through Elijah Muhammad's organization.

But for Malcolm X, the learning and self-discovery does not stop once he converts to Islam

and leaves prison. Almost literally, he sits at the feet of his mentor, Muhammad, and learns the critical pieces of history that will help form his theories about race relations and politics. Malcolm X fervently believes all that Muhammad tells him, which, of course, makes it just that much harder when he discovers the suspect nature of Muhammad's interpretation of history, as well as his moral failings. This sets Malcolm X up for another phase of self-discovery, in which he seems to get even closer to his true self—out on his own, ejected from the Nation of Islam.

Style

Foreshadowing

Malcolm X uses foreshadowing to highlight how far his life has taken him as well as to prepare his readers for disappointment and trauma. For example, early in the book he speaks of his successes as well as of his less admirable points. When he moves to Boston, he relates, he hears about Harvard Law School. "No one that day could have told me I would give an address before the Harvard Law School Forum some twenty years later," he continues. A few sentences down the page, he hints, "I didn't know how familiar with Roseland I was going to become," referring to the many nights he spent dancing and partying at the famed ballroom.

Malcolm X's references to his death increase as the autobiography moves toward its finale. Much of this, of course, has to do with his awareness that some in the Nation of Islam want him dead after his split from the organization; but Malcolm X's allusions to his own death are still remarkable in their context. For example, he says that he considers each day to be "another borrowed day" and that he is living each day "as if [he were] already dead."

Point of View

This autobiography was "told to" another party, Alex Haley, who edited and organized the information Malcolm X related to him in numerous conversations. Nonetheless, the book is written in the first person, with Malcolm X as the "I" in the story. It is written in a conversational style, almost as if the author is sitting across from the reader. Malcolm X's life is presented in a chronological fashion, opening with his birth and ending in 1965 just before he is murdered.

The reader of any autobiography should realize that the information in the book is selected from all of the events in the subject's life. Events and conversations are remembered through the lens of time; in this book, Malcolm remembers events decades after they took place. In addition, there were two people who made judgments about what would appear in the autobiography: Malcolm X *and* Alex Haley. In fact, in his epilogue, Haley notes that he had to struggle to keep Malcolm X speaking about his own life and not about Elijah Muhammad and also that some of the stories Malcolm X told him may have been somewhat stretched.

Historical Context

Struggle for Civil Rights in the 1950s and 1960s

Until a number of court cases struck down segregation of the races in the United States, blacks were barred or restricted—sometimes by law—from a variety of public venues, such as restaurants, neighborhoods, golf courses, schools, and movie theaters. The 1954 U.S. Supreme Court decision *Brown vs. the Board of Education of Topeka* made separate schools for blacks illegal. Over the next couple years, the Supreme Court handed down a series of decisions invalidating segregation of golf courses, swimming pools, and beaches.

Some historians see Rosa Parks's spontaneous 1955 refusal to give up her seat in the front of a Montgomery, Alabama, bus to a white man as the first step in the American civil rights movement. Parks, an African-American woman, was arrested and fined for violating the city's segregationist laws about where she was allowed to sit. Four days later, Dr. Martin Luther King, Jr., a young Baptist minister in Montgomery, urged a local bus boycott, and various black organizations supported his effort. By 1956, the boycott supporters won a small but critical victory when a federal district court issued an injunction prohibiting the racial segregation of buses in Montgomery.

The boycott and subsequent events catapulted King into the national limelight as a civil rights leader. During the Montgomery protest, King was jailed and his house was bombed. King's philosophy of non-violence attracted a large following in the late 1950s and 1960s. His tactics included peaceful demonstrations and marches, sit-ins at segregated facilities, a willingness to go to jail, and public disobedience to law. While Malcolm X and the Nation of Islam never directly advocated violence to accomplish their goals, neither did they reject the possibility that violence might be necessary—in direct contradiction to King's philosophy. In his autobiography, Malcolm X is somewhat disdainful of leaders such as King and accuses them of being co-opted by whites.

From the late 1950s through the 1960s, African Americans and supportive whites engaged in sit-ins and freedom marches, often at risk to their lives. Many of the demonstrations were met with violence, such as the 1963 confrontation between police and marchers in Birmingham, Alabama. The local police commissioner responded to the largely peaceful demonstration by releasing dogs and using cattle prods against the civil rights protesters. Malcolm X recalled this incident when he spoke with Arabic and African Muslims during his overseas trips in 1963 and 1964.

Compare & Contrast

- **1960s:** In 1962, the Twenty-Fourth Amendment to the U. S. Constitution is proposed and, by 1964, is passed as law. One of its primary features is a ban on poll taxes in federal elections, giving the poor and many African Americans increased ability to vote. In 1965, the Voting Rights Act is passed, temporarily suspending literacy tests intended to restrict voting by African Americans and other minorities. Thanks to these two pieces of legislation, by the end of the decade there are 1,469 African-American elected officials in the United States, according to the Joint Center for Political and Economic Studies.

  Today: Currently, the Joint Center for Political and Economic Studies reports that there are nearly nine thousand African-American elected officials in the United States.

- **1960s:** Malcolm X claims that there are approximately four hundred thousand members of the Nation of Islam in the United States.

  Today: Nearly forty years after Malcolm X's assassination, there are an estimated one hundred thousand Nation of Islam members.

- **1960s:** In 1963, the ''I Have a Dream'' speech by Martin Luther King Jr. galvanizes nearly 250,000 participants in the March on Washington to support pending civil rights legislation.

  Today: Nation of Islam leader Louis Farrakhan headlines the 1995 Million Man March on the Mall in Washington, D.C., that asks participating men to recommit to their families, their communities, and their personal responsibility.

One of the largest civil rights demonstrations of that era was the 1963 March on Washington for Jobs and Freedom, led by King. Nearly a quarter-million Americans of varying backgrounds gathered in front of the Washington Monument to hear King deliver his now-famous ''I Have a Dream'' speech. Malcolm X belittles King and this demonstration in the book, calling the march the ''Farce on Washington'' and claiming that it was little more than an ''integrated picnic.''

Night Life in Harlem

The Cotton Club, a famous Harlem nightclub mentioned by Malcolm X in his autobiography, was open only to wealthy white patrons who wanted to sample some of the bawdy nightlife they had heard about. But African-American club owners opened their own establishments, some of which became popular after-hours spots for many of the black musicians with whom Malcolm spent time in Harlem.

Jazz and swing, two types of music Malcolm X mentioned enjoying while he was street hustler in both Boston and Harlem, gained a wide following from the mid 1930s onward and eventually became the most popular kind of music in the nightclubs frequented by Malcolm and his friends. Most dance establishments and nightclubs in the 1930s and 1940s were racially segregated. If blacks were allowed in white establishments it was usually on one specific night a week—such as the night Malcolm X remembered being reserved for domestic help at the famous Savoy in New York. As well, he remembered dancing to such jazz luminaries as Dinah Washington and Lionel Hampton at places such as the Savoy.

Origins and History of the Nation of Islam

The Islamic religion was founded by the Prophet Muhammad in the seventh century in Mecca, Saudi Arabia. The primary text for Islam is the Koran (or Qur'an), believed by Muslims (or Moslems) to be the final revelation by Allah, or God, to Muhammad. Muslims are to fulfill the five basic requirements, or ''pillars,'' of Islam: belief that there is one God, Allah, and that Muhammad is the Messenger of God; performance of five daily ritual prayers;

giving alms, also known as a religious tax; observance of the dawn-to-sunset fast during the lunar month of Ramadan; and making the *hajj,* the pilgrimage to Mecca.

The Nation of Islam dates back to 1930, when a door-to-door salesman peddling cloth and other items appeared in a Detroit ghetto, telling anyone who would listen that the true religion for African Americans was not Christianity but Islam. He went by various names, but he appears in *The Autobiography of Malcolm X* under the name Master W. D. Fard. He used both the Bible and the Koran in his preaching. The central teachings of the Nation as originally promulgated by Fard include the story of a black scientist named Yakub who, thousands of years ago, created a weaker race of white men who were permitted to have temporary dominance over the Earth. But soon, according to Nation doctrine, there would be an apocalyptic clash between the force of evil (whites) and good (blacks), with blacks winning. It is this theology that Malcolm X rebelled angrily against at the end of his autobiography, embracing, instead, what he called the "true Islam" of Africa, the Middle East, and Asia.

Elijah Muhammad, also known as Elijah Poole, was one of Fard's most trusted lieutenants, taking the reins of the Nation of Islam after Fard's mysterious disappearance in 1934. Muhammad maintained leadership of the Nation for the next four decades, establishing that Fard had been Allah and had appointed Muhammad as his official messenger.

The Nation approached the problems of racism in America in two ways: they urged economic independence for blacks (including a separate nation) and pushed members to recover their identities, which the Nation felt had been stolen from blacks when they were enslaved and brought to America. The Nation encouraged an almost Puritanical ethic for its members, including hard work, frugality, cleanliness, debt avoidance, and the prohibition of alcohol, drugs, smoking, and pork. The Nation of Islam became famous for its restaurants that sold bean pies and whiting—part of Muhammad's efforts to improve the health of the African-American community.

Critical Overview

Many reviewers of *The Autobiography of Malcolm X* agree about the power and desire evident in the book. Truman Nelson, writing in the *Nation* soon after the release of the book, lauds it for its "dead-level honesty, its passion, its exalted purpose." And, according to Warner Berthoff in *New Literary History,* the way Malcolm X blends "his own life story with the full collective history of his milieu . . . gives Malcolm's testimony its strength and large authority."

Malcolm X's conversion to Islam and how that is relayed in the book is a commonly addressed subject in both the book's early and recent reviews. I. F. Stone, in an article for the *New York Review of Books* soon after the book's publication, notes, "To understand Malcolm's experience, one must go to the literature of conversion," such as William James's classic examination *Varieties of Religious Experience.* Berthoff agrees, commenting, "Above all, the book is the story of a conversion and its consequences."

However full of praise the reviewers were after the book's release, though, discussions soon appeared over how much of an impact Alex Haley, Malcolm X's collaborator, had on the final project. The book was published not long after Malcolm X's death, and critics such as David Demarest, Jr., in *CLA Journal* have acknowledged Haley's strong role. Demarest notes, "One is tempted to feel that had the book been entirely Malcolm's, . . . the book would have revealed less of Malcolm than it now does." But Nelson urges readers to "put aside" any misgivings they might have "about a book 'as told to' someone." Haley, according to Nelson, did a marvelous job of revealing the true sense of Malcolm X in the work's tone and words.

Many critics have noted the book's similarities to other famous autobiographies. Carol Ohmann, in the journal *American Quarterly,* compares Malcolm X's autobiography with Benjamin Franklin's *Autobiography,* noting that the two books "resemble each other in the conceptions of the self they convey, . . . and in the ways, looking backwards as autobiographers do, they pattern or structure the raw materials of their own lives." Barrett John Mandel, in the journal *Afro-American Studies,* compares Malcolm X's autobiography to those written by Saint Augustine, John Bunyan, and Jonathan Edwards.

Some have criticized Malcolm's ideologies and philosophies as set forth in his autobiography. Stone, for example, notes that in some passages Malcolm

Denzel Washington as Malcolm X in the 1992 film Malcolm X

"sounds like a southern white supremacist in reverse, vibrating with anger and sexual obsession over the horrors of race pollution." And James Craig Holte, in the journal *MELUS,* argues that Malcolm X's conversion to Elijah Muhammad's form of Islam is a "simple, single-minded vision," especially when contrasted against his later "more complex self-examination" during his pilgrimage to Mecca.

For all of Malcolm X's fiery rhetoric, many reviewers have seen in his autobiography evidence of a man who simply wanted to be accepted into the mainstream of American life. Robert Penn Warren, famed novelist, comments in the *Yale Review* that the activist was ultimately seeking respectability. "In the midst of the gospel of violence and the repudiation of the white world, even in the Black Muslim phase, there appears now and then the note of yearning," he writes. The sense that Malcolm X's philosophy was changing by the end of the book underlines his desire to be understood; in fact, the trip to Mecca gives him a sort of authority and propriety, according to Warren. However, Stone believes that Elijah Muhammad's interest in "the virtues of bourgeois America," with Malcolm X rejecting those more quiet "virtues," was the basis for his and Malcolm X's split.

Ultimately, though, most reviewers agree that *The Autobiography of Malcolm X* is a classic of American literature. Stone believes that the book has "a permanent place in the literature of the Afro-American struggle," and Warren sees it as "an American story bound to be remembered." In fact, in a moment of impressive prescience, Warren states in his 1966 article that the book will no doubt "reappear someday in a novel, on the stage, or on the screen"—predating Spike Lee's movie interpretation of the book by nearly thirty years.

Criticism

Susan Sanderson

Sanderson holds a master of fine arts degree in fiction writing and is an independent writer. In this essay, she examines how Malcolm X, despite the fiery rhetoric, fulfills the image of the classic American success story.

The general reaction among the white community in the United States to Malcolm X and the Nation of

What Do I Read Next?

- *One Day When I Was Lost: A Scenario Based on Alex Haley's "The Autobiography of Malcolm X"* is a 1973 screenplay by James Baldwin.

- *With Ossie and Ruby: In This Life Together* is the 1998 autobiography of Ossie Davis and Ruby Dee. This married couple recalls their fifty years of life together and their experiences on stage and screen starting in the 1940s. As well, they remember their years of political activism and the famous figures, including Malcolm X and Sidney Poitier, they befriended.

- In his hugely successful book, *Roots: Saga of an American Family,* first published in 1976, Alex Haley retells the stories his grandmother told him about his family's past generations going back to the young African relative brought to America as a slave. The book spawned a television mini-series and earned the 1976 National Book Award and a 1977 Lillian Smith Book Award.

- Claude McKay's *Home to Harlem,* originally published in 1928, is the story of two young black men who have different reactions to the colorful street life of Harlem during the 1920s.

- Alice Walker's 1976 book, *Meridian: A Novel,* tells the story of Meridian, a high school dropout and single mother who learns about herself as she becomes a daring civil rights worker.

Islam in the 1950s and 1960s was one of alarm. He and the Nation were painted as fomenting violent revolution just as many whites and some more conservative blacks believed that life was beginning to get better for African Americans.

In *The Autobiography of Malcolm X*, the Muslim leader remembers the heated response to a documentary made in 1959 about the Nation of Islam: "The public reaction was like what happened back in the 1930s when Orson Welles frightened America with a radio program describing, as though it were actually happening, an invasion by 'men from Mars.'" For example, panic erupted around the documentary's revelation that the Nation was teaching its members judo and karate—viewers and the press interpreted these actions as evidence of the Nation's malevolent intentions, even though Malcolm X asked the obvious question, "Why does judo or karate suddenly get so ominous because black men study it? Across America, the Boy Scouts, the YMCA . . . they *all* teach judo!"

In a sense, the public perception of the Nation of Islam *was* that its members were aliens. Their separatist philosophy argued that the solution to America's racial woes was an independent black nation, and their strict moral codes, ultra-conservative demeanor and dress, and dietary restrictions offered to many Americans a frightening snapshot of radical discipline.

The story of Malcolm X is about a man who fulfills the classic American tale of struggle and success based on hard work, self-education, and overcoming mistakes. In fact, his autobiography is much more than a revolutionary guidebook—it is also an outline for how to beat your enemy at his own game and come out way ahead of where anyone thought you would through the mainstream American techniques of education and hard work.

Malcolm's childhood is one hard knock after another. His father is murdered and his mother literally goes insane trying to keep the family together. By the time he is about twelve years old, Malcolm is an orphan ward of the state, living with a foster family. He doesn't despair, though, despite his misfortune, and thrills at being able to beat the older men at hunting, for example. "It was the beginning of a very important lesson in life—that anytime you find someone more successful than you are . . .—you know they're doing something that you aren't," he instructs his readers in one of

> The story of Malcolm X is about a man who fulfills the classic American tale of struggle and success based on hard work, self-education, and overcoming mistakes."

the numerous lessons he presents in his autobiography. Striving at education and learning sustain him until a racist school counselor dismisses his desire to become a lawyer, even though he is at the top of his class. "It was then that I began to change—inside," remembers Malcolm X.

Though he leaves school to hang out on the streets of Boston and Harlem, Malcolm's drive to succeed never falters. During all of the years of hustling, he is always learning and thinking, trying to figure out how to do whatever he is engaged in faster and smarter than the next guy. For example, when the pressure from the Harlem police gets to be too much, Malcolm simply puts wheels on his marijuana sales operation and travels up and down the East Coast, following his musician friends to their gigs and selling to them. It is as if a fire burns in his belly, pushing him to be the best, even if his "best" is robbery or numbers. The more experienced hustlers are his teachers and Malcolm proves himself a willing student. The chapters dedicated to his time in Boston and Harlem are sprinkled with references to Malcolm "learning" about street life and getting his "first schooling" in how to succeed in the ghetto.

Throughout the book, Malcolm makes clear that, despite how much he despises the way whites have treated blacks, he has deep respect for the high points of American culture, especially its educational institutions. While visiting Boston for the first time, he walks past Harvard University; he uses this moment to bring the reader up to date with his accomplishments by dropping the comment, "Nobody that day could have told me I would give an address before the Harvard Law School Forum some twenty years later." Despite the tough-guy talk, his pride at how far he had come is evident in this and many other similar scenes. In one of the

book's later chapters, Malcolm X almost sounds as if he is bragging when he says that according to a *New York Times* poll, he was the second most sought after speaker on college campuses in 1963. A few paragraphs later, he wants to make sure that his readers know that by that same year he had spoken at "well over fifty" colleges, including those "in the Ivy League."

Malcolm X cites education, in fact, as one of the reasons for his ultimate break with Elijah Muhammad and the Nation of Islam. Muhammad, according to Malcolm X, feels intimidated when he speaks to influential and prestigious audiences, worried as he is about the inadequacy of his fourth-grade education; this public work he leaves to Malcolm X. Malcolm loves being around those involved in education and learning, noting, "Except for all-black audiences, I liked the college audiences best. . . . They never failed in helping me to further my own education." Jealous feelings develop over Malcolm X's comfort with the Nation's intelligentsia and add to the reasons Muhammad already has for Malcolm X's banishment.

Malcolm X was a passionate and life-long learner, and he knew that these activities would make it easier for him to succeed at whatever he did in the American culture. In prison he is rescued from the possibility of a life of ignorance by Bimbi, an old burglar who chastises Malcolm for failing to use his brain. In no time, Malcolm is reading everything he can get his hands on, even taking a correspondence course in Latin. His reading material in prison includes Gregor Mendel's *Findings in Genetics, Uncle Tom's Cabin,* and works by Thoreau, Spinoza, Kant, and Nietzsche. The reading habit stuck with him his whole life. "You will never catch me with a free fifteen minutes in which I'm not studying something I feel might be able to help the black man," he notes.

At the end of his life, Malcolm X is acutely aware of his lack of an official education, dissatisfied that he had to rely on his "homemade" education instead. "My greatest lack has been, I believe, that I don't have the kind of academic education I wish I had been able to get," he muses in his autobiography's final chapter. "I don't begin to be academically equipped for so many of the interests that I have." Malcolm X, despite being a severe critic of America, understands the role of education and struggle in the great American success story. Everything Malcolm X did was arranged as a self-education of some sort—even his two conversion experiences. The chapters about his introduction to Elijah Muhammad and Islam contain images that are perfect examples of the student-teacher relationship. And when Malcolm X becomes disenchanted with his mentor's theology and philosophy, he travels to Mecca to gather "new insight into the true religion of Islam and a better understanding of America's entire racial dilemma."

All this is not to diminish the radical and challenging nature of Malcolm X's thinking in his autobiography. However, like many self-made Americans, Malcolm X understood the value of educating himself into the mainstream. By the end of the autobiography, Malcolm X has made some kind of peace with his more revolutionary and incendiary pronouncements against whites, deciding that his earlier blanket indictments against those who did not agree with him, and his association with a rather fanatical group, were all part of his personal ongoing learning process. Sounding almost as conciliatory as his former nemesis, Martin Luther King, Jr., Malcolm X explains his new heart: "Since I have learned the *truth* in Mecca, my dearest friends, I have come to include *all* kinds . . . black, brown, red, yellow, and *white*!"

As I. F. Stone notes in the *New York Review of Books,* even while Malcolm X is undergoing his second conversion, he is still the consummate salesman, the American always thinking of a better way to get something done. "He had become a Hajj but remained in some ways a Babbitt, the salesman, archetype of our American society," writes Stone. Malcolm X was a quintessential American, in fact, despite his earlier rejections of that title. During his stay in Africa, he rejects the idea that he is anti-American or un-American while speaking to an "agent" from some U. S. surveillance group. (He suspects that the person is with either the FBI or the CIA.) In fact, with his American label firmly attached, Malcolm X goes on his pilgrimage to Mecca "doing some American-type thinking and reflecting" about how he might be able to "double or triple" the number of converts to Islam if the colorfulness and energy of the *hajj* is "properly advertised and communicated to the outside world."

Malcolm X's self-education into the America mainstream and his striving always to do things faster and better very nearly allow him to secure a piece of the American dream. Just before his death, according to Robert Penn Warren in the *Yale Review,* Malcolm X was about to make a downpayment on a house in a Long Island Jewish neighborhood. Warren wrote:

> He no longer saw the white man as the 'white devil.' . . . and he was ready, grudgingly, not optimistically, and with a note of threat, to grant that there was in America a chance, a last chance, for a 'bloodless revolution.'

Malcolm X yearned for acceptance, and he knew that one of the primary ways one could earn this in America was by fighting against the odds, through hard work and education—whether in the elite classrooms of the Ivy League or the streets of Harlem. These factors in his life have made him an almost mythological figure, surrounded by stories of victorious struggle, many of which appear in his autobiography.

Source: Susan Sanderson, Critical Essay on *The Autobiography of Malcolm X,* in *Nonfiction Classics for Students,* The Gale Group, 2002.

Lois Carson

Carson is an instructor of English literature and composition. In this essay, she analyzes Malcolm X's book as a spiritual autobiography.

The Autobiography of Malcolm X is not only a searing indictment of racism in America but also the moving story of one man's extraordinary metamorphosis from criminal to convert to religious leader. Among the forms of autobiography elucidated by William C. Spengemann, it most closely resembles the formal paradigm established by *The Confessions of Saint Augustine* in the fifth century. Like the *The Confessions, The Autobiography* has a three-part structure. It begins with an already converted narrator examining the sinful events from his past life that have brought him to the present moment. He not only has to accept the past as part of the Creator's divine plan but also to believe, and convince his readers to believe, that his old sinful life was a necessary part of conversion and the achievement of divine wisdom. In the second section, the converted narrator moves into a meditative search for the timeless wisdom that will enable him to serve the will of Allah. In the final section, having learned that faith is wisdom, he submits completely to Allah's divine will.

In the first section of *The Autobiography* (Chapters 1–9) Malcolm's purpose is both instructive and confessional. The narrative voice is that of the thirty-nine-year-old religious and political leader whose conversion enables him to see and understand Allah's divine plan in his earlier life. His tone

> **The narrator's emotion ranges from unflinching anger toward prejudiced whites, . . . to an awestruck wonder at the power of love Malcolm experienced on his pilgrimage to Mecca."**

is both ironic and angry as he relates Nebraska and Michigan memories that shaped his earlier belief that the white man is the devil. In the middle of the decade known as the roaring twenties, his pregnant mother faces down a group of hooded Ku Klux Klansmen. Several years later other Klansmen burn another of Malcolm's homes and all its contents. Negroes with money live "parasitically" off those without. An English teacher tells Malcolm that becoming a lawyer is "no realistic goal for a nigger." Honest black men can only envision a future as waiters or bootblacks. However, the converted, adult Malcolm, recognizing Allah's divine plan for his life in these past experiences, closes the chapters by recalling his childhood with a genuine prayer: "All praise is due to Allah." Were it not for Allah, he believes that he would have become "a brainwashed Black Christian." Instead, he has used his past experience both to chastise the white race for its historical treatment of blacks and to dramatize both unconscious as well as conscious examples of racism.

While the early chapters of the first section of *The Autobiography* are primarily instructive, the remaining chapters are primarily confessional. Here, the voice is that of the thirty-nine-year-old religious penitent, whose conversion enables him to metaphorically descend to the very nadir of his existence, as he confesses his sins and riotous living. He describes his entrance into the seductive worlds of Roxbury and Harlem where violence, crime, drugs, alcohol, prostitutes, and promiscuity abound. It is a world where innocents like Malcolm and Laura are soon corrupted. Throughout this section, however, Malcolm's words are deliberately chosen not to titillate his readers but rather to demonstrate how seductive music, dance, money, drugs, and the high life can be—especially for a rural teenager who finds himself in a world of glamour and money. In

such a world, an older, married, white woman like Sophia is as attractive to a sixteen-year-old black male as a flashy car. She represents the unattainable, the breaching of a taboo. The narrative voice, moving back and forth from that of the teenage Malcolm to that of the converted Malcolm, delineates the level of degeneration of which Malcolm and all humans are capable. Moreover, Malcolm makes his readers aware that everyone, whether an active participant or detached observer, is culpable. He clearly accepts the past as necessary to Allah's divine plan for his conversion and achievement of divine wisdom. Here, as earlier, he closes this first section of *The Autobiography* with a genuine prayer: "All praise is due to Allah."

In the second section (Chapters 10–12), an imprisoned Malcolm begins his own mental and spiritual search for the timeless wisdom that will enable him to serve the will of Allah before he himself has actually come to know Allah. At first anger rules him so forcefully that he escapes into drugs and spends a lot of time in solitary, pacing for hours "like a caged lion." Without quite understanding why, however, he begins his conversion to Islam by responding to his brother's request not to eat any more pork or smoke any more cigarettes. A chance remark by a fellow Negro prisoner Bimbi, the first man Malcolm has ever seen "command total respect with his words," prods him into taking correspondence courses. Gradually, Malcolm's views of himself and the world undergo a radical change. His history studies present telling evidence of white enslavement of native peoples of color on the continents of Africa and North America. In a lengthy correspondence with Elijah Muhammad, the leader of the Nation of Islam, he learns that the followers of Islam obey the Mosaic laws concerning the eating of pork and other meats. They forbid divorce, fornication, and sexual conduct outside marriage. Drugs and alcohol are also forbidden. The more he reads about their rules, conduct, and beliefs, the more he is convinced that the one true God is Allah and the white man is the devil. Like other converts, he immediately changes his name: he replaces Little with the symbolic letter X, severing himself from an identity imposed by the white slave owner. A new man, Malcolm X, dedicates both his spiritual and physical energies to following the strict conduct dictated by Islam as he becomes a full-time minister of the Nation of Islam.

In the final section of *The Autobiography*, spiritually wounded by Elijah Muhammad's moral laxity and a growing split between him and the leader he had viewed as Allah's unassailable earthly minister, Malcolm makes his own pilgrimage to Mecca. There he experiences a life-altering epiphany (a moment of revelation or sudden understanding). He is surrounded by people of all colors, speaking various languages. Despite the crowds, there is harmony, a quiet sharing of food and space, peace, and tranquility. "America needs to understand Islam, because this is the one religion that erases from its society the race problem," he writes home. "I learned that pilgrims from every land—every color, and class, and rank; high officials and the beggar alike—all snored in the same language." The Black Muslim Malcolm X is transformed by his pilgrimage to Mecca into El-Haij Malik El-Shabazz—a true Islam who makes a side trip to Africa before returning to the United States. His voice at the end of the autobiography is resigned and urgent, fiery and peaceful, as he remembers the violent deaths of his father and five of his father's six brothers. He knows that he too will die by violence, but as he has with earlier events in his life, he accepts what will come as the will of Allah. He is not afraid to die. Urgent about continuing Allah's plans for him in his earthly life, he like Shakespeare, holds up "a mirror to reflect, to show, the history of unspeakable crimes" that one race has committed against another.

In the final analysis, the power of this compelling autobiography results not so much from the harsh facts that Malcolm discloses but from the point of view, the voice, and structure that Malcolm and Alex Haley give to the narrative. The narrator's emotion ranges from unflinching anger toward prejudiced whites, to bitterness resulting from the death and destruction of family members, to an awestruck wonder at the power of love Malcolm experienced on his pilgrimage to Mecca. Throughout his life, Malcolm never stops learning, nor does he ultimately close his mind to ideas that challenge long-held beliefs. Instead, even as his own death looms over him in the hectic last days of his life, he takes the time to write his own spiritual autobiography, to leave the rest of the world the certainty that true wisdom resides in faith.

Source: Lois Carson, Critical Essay on *The Autobiography of Malcolm X,* in *Nonfiction Classics for Students,* The Gale Group, 2002.

Josh Ozersky

Ozersky is a cultural historian and author. In this essay, he discusses how Malcolm X's growth as

Elijah (Poole) Muhammad, Malcolm X's teacher and mentor, who took command of the Nation of Islam after its former leader's mysterious disappearance

a person during the writing of his autobiography enriches it as a work of literature.

The Autobiography of Malcolm X is one of the most famous books America has produced. It stands beside the *Autobiography of Benjamin Franklin, The Narrative of the Life of Frederick Douglass,* and other classics. The figure of Malcolm X, the fiery Black Muslim leader, is charismatic and memorable. And since much, if not all, that is known about Malcolm X comes from the *The Autobiography of Malcolm X* , it's only natural to assume that Malcolm X, his autobiography, and people's image of him are all essentially the same. But this would be a mistake. *The Autobiography of Malcolm X* features hidden depths and false bottoms; the book informs its readers about the man as he changes, grows larger and wiser.

Narrated to Alex Haley over a three year period, *The Autobiography of Malcolm X* came at a key stretch in Malcolm's life. The book clearly owes much to Haley's skill as an editor. As Haley makes clear in his lengthy epilogue, working with Malcolm X required great delicacy. Haley could not

> **Perhaps, if Malcolm X had been assassinated in 1963 instead of 1965, the book would have been self-contained, a testament to one truth."**

tell Malcolm how to tell his own story, but neither could he merely transcribe what Malcolm said, especially since, midway through the project, Malcolm's world was turned upside down.

At its inception, the book was meant to be a testament to the goodness and redemptive power of the Nation of Islam and its leader, a man never referred to other than as "The Honorable Elijah Muhammad." So scrupulously devoted to Muhammad was Malcolm X that his writing skirts the border of propaganda. *The Autobiography of Malcolm X* was frankly conceived as a way to proselytize for the Nation of Islam. In fact, the dedication originally planned for the book read:

> This book I dedicate to The Honorable Elijah Muhammad, who found me here in America in the muck and mire of the filthiest civilization and society on the earth, and pulled me out, cleaned me up, and stood me on my feet, and made me the man I am today.

By the time the book was being written, however, Malcolm had broken with the Black Muslims. The Honorable Elijah Muhammad had turned out not to be so honorable as Malcolm had thought: Muhammad had apparently committed adultery with several members of The Nation, and, Malcolm believed, now sought to destroy Malcolm because of his growing popularity.

This betrayal is the central revelation in *The Autobiography of Malcolm X*. When Haley and Malcolm sat down to write this memoir, it was designed as a conversion narrative, an ancient genre with precedents as far back as *The Confessions of St. Augustine*. The narrator would describe his sinful early days, his awakening at rock bottom, and finish on a triumphal note by describing his career as an apostle and reformed sinner. That was the plan; but somewhere along the way the plan was abandoned. Haley asked Malcolm not to revise the early chapters, in which he wrote so glowingly of "The

Honorable Elijah Muhammad," the "this little, sweet, gentle man." To make changes, Haley said, would be to "telegraph" to the reader what lay ahead. So although Malcolm periodically acknowledges that friction develops later with him, one never gets a sense of it while reading the description of Malcolm's redemption in prison. On the contrary, those chapters are written with the evangelical zeal of a man remembering the central event in his life: his conversion to Islam, or at least the Black Muslims' version of it.

Malcolm X's reputation today is that of a charismatic extremist, a bold, take-no-prisoners truth teller out to liberate his race "by any means necessary." This is the man who narrates the early part of the book. In the middle chapters, in which Malcolm preaches about "white devils," expounding on the evils of the white man, Malcolm seems to fit this stereotype. But in the chapters, "Out" and "Mecca," the supremely self-assured narrator begins to change. His once-unshakable faith in The Honorable Elijah Muhammad is destroyed. He goes to the holy city of Mecca and discovers that his vision of Islam has been narrow and parochial. He does not even know the common prayers recited by Muslims around the world; he is physically incapable of assuming the position Muslims do in prayer. "Western ankles won't do what Muslim ankles have done for a lifetime," Malcolm writes. "When my guide was down in a posture, I tried everything I could to get down as he was, but there I was, sticking up."

The narrative in these chapters echoes Malcolm's initial conversion, as described in the book's middle chapters. Then, for example, Malcolm writes of the difficulty of bending his knees to pray:

> Picking a lock to rob someone's house was the only way my knees had ever been bent before. I had to force myself to bend my knees. And waves of shame and embarrassment would force me back up.

The subsequent remark echoes this one.

In his epiphany in Mecca, Malcolm learns of "sincere and true brotherhood," regardless of skin color. Until this point, the narrative is infused with Malcolm's absolute conviction about racism—an intensely compelling quality of his, one that partially accounts for his force as a speaker. Every page of the *The Autobiography of Malcolm X* prior to this point focuses on one central truth: the evil of white racism as "an incurable cancer." The early chapters describe Malcolm's folly and blindness, his wickedness and self-destructive path. The chapters in prison then describe the clouds parting, revealing the truth which is later confirmed by the experience at Mecca. Perhaps, if Malcolm X had been assassinated in 1963 instead of 1965, the book would have been self-contained, a testament to that particular truth. Because of all that happened to him in those two years, however, the book was changed forever, and the last pages, in which Malcolm presciently writes of his own imminent death, have a special poignancy because of his power to change and grow.

This is not to say that Malcolm's views at the end of the *The Autobiography of Malcolm X* are right or wrong, any more so than his views as a minister of the Nation of Islam, or for that matter his views as Detroit Red, the street hustler. In a sense—and in this is surely something Malcolm X would have deplored—the actual content of the author's convictions really isn't that important. It's possible to read, and even revere, *The Autobiography of Malcolm X* without necessarily having any interest or investment in the problem of race. In all probability, the book will continue to matter long after the historical circumstances surrounding Malcolm X and the 1960s have faded into history.

Source: Josh Ozersky, Critical Essay on *The Autobiography of Malcolm X,* in *Nonfiction Classics for Students,* The Gale Group, 2002.

Sources

Berthoff, Warner, "Witness and Testament: Two Contemporary Classics," in *New Literary History,* Vol. 2, No. 2, Winter 1971, pp. 311–27.

Demarest, David P., Jr., "*The Autobiography of Malcolm X: Beyond Didacticism,*" in *CLA Journal,* Vol. 16, No. 2, December 1972, pp. 179–87.

Holte, James Craig, "The Representative Voice: Autobiography and the Ethnic Experience," in *MELUS,* Vol. 9, No. 2, Summer 1982, pp. 25–46.

Mandel, Barrett John, "The Didactic Achievement of Malcolm X's Autobiography," in *Afro-American Studies,* Vol. 2, No. 4, March 1972, pp. 269–74.

Nelson, Truman, "Delinquent's Progress," in *Nation,* Vol. 201, No. 15, November 8, 1965, pp. 336–38.

Ohmann, Carol, "*The Autobiography of Malcolm X:* A Revolutionary Use of the Franklin Tradition," in *American Quarterly,* Vol. 22, No. 2, Summer 1970, pp. 129–49.

Spengemann, William, *The Forms of Autobiography,* Yale University Press, 1980, pp. 1–2.

Stone, I. F., "The Pilgrimage of Malcolm X," in *New York Review of Books,* Vol. 5, No. 7, November 11, 1965, pp. 3–5.

Warren, Robert Penn, "Malcolm X: Mission and Meaning," in *Yale Review,* Vol. LVI, No. 2, December 1966, pp. 161–71.

Further Reading

Archer, Jules, *They Had a Dream: The Civil Rights Struggle from Frederick Douglass to Marcus Garvey to Martin Luther King and Malcolm X,* Puffin, 1993.

This book comprises the biographies of four of the most prominent civil rights leaders in American history. It covers their mistakes and weaknesses as well as their strengths.

Branch, Taylor, *Parting the Waters: America in the King Years, 1954–1963,* Touchstone Books, 1988.

Parting the Waters is first in a series written by Taylor Branch about Martin Luther King Jr. and the civil rights movement in the United States.

Collier-Thomas, Bettye, and V. P. Franklin, *My Soul Is a Witness: A Chronology of the Civil Rights Era, 1954–1965,* Henry Holt and Co., Inc., 1999.

This book is a survey of the people, organizations, and events that comprised the American civil rights movement, with a day-to-day chronology.

Esposito, John L., *Islam: The Straight Path,* Oxford University Press, 1988.

Esposito gives an overview of the Islamic faith in this book, including its origins and history. It gives an historical context in which to understand the diversity of Islam today.

Evanzz, Karl, *The Messenger: The Rise and Fall of Elijah Muhammad,* Pantheon Books, 1999.

The Messenger is a biography of the famed Nation of Islam leader, Elijah Muhammad, exposing his faults and contradictions.

Backlash: The Undeclared War Against American Women

Susan Faludi

1991

Susan Faludi's bestselling book, *Backlash: The Undeclared War Against American Women*, is a methodically researched and documented work challenging conventional wisdom about the American women's movement and women's gains in achieving equality in the latter years of the twentieth century. Faludi begins the book by looking carefully at then-current myths about the status of women, including the press reports that single career women are more likely to be depressed than other women, that professional women are leaving their jobs in droves to stay at home, and that single working women over age thirty have a small chance of ever getting married. Not only are these myths not true, says Faludi, but they are evidence of a society-wide backlash against women and what they have achieved in recent years. She describes this backlash as a "kind of pop-culture version of the Big Lie" and declares that "it stands the truth boldly on its head and proclaims that the very steps that have elevated women's positions have actually led to their downfall."

In her book, Faludi takes the press to task for failing to challenge the myths about women in the 1980s and especially for spreading, through "trend journalism," stories about how unhappy women are, despite their having reaped the benefits of women's liberation in the 1970s. Faludi challenges the prevailing wisdom that the women's movement is to blame for women's unhappiness; she believes

their unhappiness actually stems from the fact that the struggle for equality is not yet finished.

Faludi uses data from a wide variety of sources, such as government and university studies, newspapers, census reports, scholarly journals, and personal interviews to explore women's status in the 1980s. The personal interviews offer a look at the individuals who are behind the ''backlash'' and, according to Faludi, are hindering women's progress.

Author Biography

Susan Faludi was born in New York City on April 18, 1959 to Steven Faludi, a photographer, and Marilyn Lanning Faludi, an editor. When Faludi's *Backlash: The Undeclared War Against American Women* was released in 1991, the book received honors and postive and negative criticism for its controversial content. Susan Faludi, however, was already familiar with controversy. Faludi covered a number of contentious subjects for her high school and college newspapers. Writing for her high school newspaper, she addressed the issue of whether several on-campus Christian organizations had violated the concept of the separation of church and state. While an undergraduate at Harvard University, she wrote an article on sexual harassment that led to the dismissal of a guilty professor after the article was published.

After graduating from Harvard, Faludi worked for the *New York Times,* the *Miami Herald,* and the *Atlanta Constitution* and soon garnered a reputation as a crusading journalist. She received a 1991 Pulitzer Prize for an article she wrote for the *Wall Street Journal* on the Safeway Stores' leveraged buyout and its impact on employees.

In 1986, Faludi contacted the U. S. Census Bureau about the notorious Harvard-Yale marriage study and discovered that the study's methodology and results—including the much-quoted finding that single, educated, career women over thirty had only a 20 percent chance of ever getting married—were suspect. Though she and other writers reported the errors in the study, most of the national press simply focused on the sensational results. Faludi's interest in discerning the facts from the fictions about women's status in the 1980s prompted her to write *Backlash: The Undeclared War Against American Women.*

Susan Faludi

The book went on to win the National Book Critics Circle Award for Nonfiction in 1991. Since then, Faludi has written for various periodicals, including *Mother Jones* and *Ms.* In 1999, she published her second book, *Stiffed: The Betrayal of the American Man,* a similarly extensive tome on issues American men are feeling. Faludi currently lives and writes in California.

Plot Summary

Chapter One

Faludi begins by stating that, though many may agree that the end of the twentieth century is a good time to be a woman, press reports and surveys indicate that women are unhappy with their lives. Often, this is blamed on a variety of factors related to feminism, such as women working outside the home. ''Women are enslaved by their own liberation,'' claim many commentators who argue against feminism. But Faludi disagrees, arguing instead that women are unhappy because the real work of achieving equality has barely begun. She uses statistics that show that women still make less money and hold more low-status jobs than men and that domestic violence and rape are on the rise:

> The truth is that the last decade has seen a powerful counterassault on women's rights, a backlash, an attempt to retract the handful of small and hard-won victories the feminist movement did manage to win for women.

Chapter Two

Faludi presents a number of what she calls myths, stories "that have supported the backlash against women's quest for equality." Even though these myths have appeared in newspapers and have become accepted facts in America, they are untrue. These myths include the notions that women are finding it more difficult to find husbands, that no-fault divorce laws are to blame for the reduction in the standard of living of divorced women, that professional women are increasingly infertile, that career women have more mental illnesses than non-career women, and that children in day care suffer permanent damage.

Chapter Three

The history of women's rights in the United States is much longer than most people believe, Faludi says, and dates to well before the 1970s, a decade that many today see as the advent of feminism. While backlashes against women's rights can be traced to colonial times, Faludi limits her examination to the backlashes after the four most recent periods of advancement: the mid-nineteenth century, the early 1900s, the early 1940s, and the early 1970s. Currently, she says, Americans are in a backlash phase against the advances made in the 1970s. She also notes that each of the backlash periods included a supposed "crisis in masculinity" and its companion, "a call to femininity."

Chapter Four

This chapter covers how the media, through "trend journalism," helped create the backlash against women's rights and feminism in the 1980s by coining the terms "mommy track," "biological clock," and "man shortage." The press sought to answer the question of why women, after years of advances, still felt dissatisfied. Their answer was that feminism's achievements, not society's "resistance to these partial achievements," were causing the stress among women. The media claimed that there was a trend afoot (personified in the

"New Traditionalist" woman) in which women were choosing home life over careers; this did not have any statistical support, according to Faludi. Media reports were presenting a view of single women as defective, while single men were lauded for making "mature" decisions.

Chapter Five

Here, Faludi addresses how the backlash shaped Hollywood's portrayal of women in the 1980s. While a number of films in the 1970s positively portrayed single women making choices that supported their careers, the 1980s produced a crop of films in which single career women were made to pay dearly for their decisions not to have children and husbands. Faludi points to *Fatal Attraction* as the epitome of anti-feminism in the late 1980s. In the movie, Glenn Close plays a bitter, single, career woman who takes out her anger on otherwise happily married Michael Douglas after a brief affair. In many 1980s films, as in *Fatal Attraction,* Faludi states, the plot involves the feminine "Light Woman" killing the aggressively manly "Dark Woman." The press, however, declared that these movies' themes constituted a trend and found actual women like Close's character to write about.

Chapter Six

According to Faludi, while women largely disappeared from prime-time television programming in the late 1980s (as they did in the late 1950s and early 1960s), "TV's counterassault on women's liberation would be . . . more restrained than Hollywood's." During the mid-1970s, many television series tackled political issues, including feminism. But by the early 1980s, the tide was beginning to turn. The few shows with strong women were toned down to appeal to advertisers. Television in the 1980s condemned women who dared step outside the home, and single career women were usually given angry or neurotic personalities. The only "good" female character in the popular series *thirtysomething* was the angelic Hope, according to Faludi, a stay-at-home mom who was the envy of her careerist female friends.

Chapter Seven

In the 1970s, the fashion industry responded to a push from career women to produce more suits and practical clothing. But in the 1980s, a backlash occurred in which designers decided that fashion would be more feminine and fantastical—even to the point of childishness. One of the chief perpetrators of this "little girl" look was Christian Lacroix, according to Faludi. After a lull in the 1970s in sales of undergarments and lingerie, the industry declared that the 1980s was seeing a boom in this area. However, according to Faludi, this was a press-generated trend and did not reflect reality. A major reason women were not buying lingerie was that the styles in the late 1980s "celebrated the repression, not the flowering of female sexuality."

Chapter Eight

In the 1980s, the beauty industry—including those who encouraged unnecessary plastic surgery as well as those who sold cosmetics—set a standard of femininity for American women that Faludi believes was "grossly unnatural." Even though it may be one of the most superficial of the cultural institutions involved in the backlash, Faludi believes that, because the beauty industry changed how women felt about themselves, it was the most destructive.

Chapter Nine

Faludi discusses the "New Right movement" of the 1980s and its agenda—purported to be pro-family but, in her opinion, was simply anti-women and anti-feminist. Faludi focuses on the women who work for New Right organizations, such as the Heritage Foundation and Concerned Women for America. She notes that even though these organizations claim that women cannot be both good mothers and good career women, the New Right's female leaders are living lives that contradict this sentiment.

Chapter Ten

Ronald Reagan's election to the presidency in 1980 came with the help of many New Right women, Faludi asserts. However, she notes that a by-product of Reagan's victory was that "women began disappearing from federal office"—even women who were conservative and anti-feminist. Faludi adds that Democrats did much the same thing during the 1980s and that no one challenged them.

Chapter Eleven

Faludi argues that "the backlash's emissaries" came not only from the New Right movement but

also from among the numerous writers, scholars, and thinkers who appeared in the mainstream media. In this chapter, she profiles nine of these men and women, not in an attempt to "psychoanalyze" them, she says, but to offer an overview of those who helped make the backlash against women's rights more "palatable for public consumption." They include George Gilder, Allan Bloom, Michael and Margarita Levin, Warren Farrell, Robert Bly, Sylvia Ann Hewlett, Betty Friedan, and Carol Gilligan.

Chapter Twelve

In the 1970s, according to Faludi, commercially popular therapeutic and self-help books directed toward women told their readers that they had the right to be treated with respect. In contrast, similar books published in the 1980s urged women to keep quiet and not challenge the social order. These books also blamed feminism for women's unhappiness and asked their readers to criticize only themselves if their lives were not what they envisioned. Meanwhile, the American Psychological Association amended its standard diagnosis reference to include, according to Faludi, anti-woman definitions for two disorders, masochistic personality disorder and pre-menstrual syndrome.

Chapter Thirteen

The Reagan administration in the 1980s downplayed reports that women were losing status in the workplace, according to Faludi. The press failed to investigate this disinformation campaign and actually participated in publicizing misinformation about the backlash against working women. After the gains made in the 1970s, women particularly in the media, retail, and blue-collar industries suffered in their efforts to secure workplace equality in the 1980s.

Chapter Fourteen

In this chapter, Faludi discusses how the 1980s backlash against women affected their reproductive rights. In 1973, the U. S. Supreme Court declared abortion legal in *Roe v. Wade,* but during the 1980s organizations such as Operation Rescue and many conservative politicians wanted to reverse the result of the ruling. Faludi argues that women's ability to regulate their fertility contributed to dramatic changes "not in the abortion rate but in female sexual behavior and attitudes," and this was frightening to many. According to Faludi, in the 1980s, women were losing the right to make decision regarding the treatment of their bodies while pregnant.

Epilogue

Faludi tells a number of women's personal stories to show that "for all the forces the backlash mustered . . . women never really surrendered." She is, though, somewhat disappointed that women as a whole did not take advantage of their numbers as much as they could have in the 1980s to make their case for equality. "The '80s could have become American women's great leap forward," she believes.

Key Figures

Neil Bennett

Neil Bennett was one of the researchers involved in the 1986 Harvard-Yale marriage study, which concluded that college-educated, never-married women past the age of thirty had a slim chance of ever marrying. Bennett was a Yale University sociologist when stories about the as-yet-unpublished study on women's marriage patterns ran in various media outlets. This study generated the idea that there was a "man shortage" in America, something Faludi denies in her book.

Allan Bloom

Allan Bloom was a professor at the University of Chicago and writer of the bestselling book *The Closing of the American Mind*. While the book has been publicized as a treatise on education, Faludi argues that it was actually "an assault on the women's movement." According to Faludi, Bloom believes that "most faculty jobs and publication rights are now reserved for feminist women" and that women who try to mix a career with rearing children are hurting their families.

David Bloom

David Bloom was one of the researchers involved in the 1986 Harvard-Yale marriage study, which claimed that college-educated, never-married women past the age of thirty had a small chance of ever marrying. Bloom was a Harvard economist when stories about the as-yet-unpublished study on women's marriage patterns ran in various media outlets. This study generated the idea that there was a "man shortage" in America, something Faludi denies in her book.

Robert Bly

Originally a poet and Vietnam-era anti-war activist, Robert Bly re-created himself in the 1980s as a leader in what Faludi calls "the men's movement." This movement, according to Faludi, was based upon the idea that men were becoming "soft" and were out of touch with their masculinity. "In short," she writes, "the Great Mother's authority has become too great." Across the country, Bly held weekend retreats in the woods devoted to reconnecting men with their masculinity through drumming and Native American rituals.

Diana Doe

Diana Doe is a pseudonym for a thirty-five-year-old single, working woman who, though she was a public figure, asked Faludi not to use her real name in the book. Doe bet a doubtful male colleague—who had called her "physically inferior" to younger women—that she would be married by the time she was forty despite press reports in 1986 stating that professional single women over thirty had a 5 percent chance of ever marrying. To help her chances of marriage, Doe decided to get a complete physical makeover through plastic surgery and other techniques. She created a market plan in which she agreed to sell the story of her physical "metamorphosis" to various media outlets and gave herself a stage name: "the Ultimate Five Percent Woman." The "project," as Doe referred to it, required her to mention the names of her plastic surgeon, dentist, exercise trainer, and beautician in articles and during personal appearances in exchange for their services. During the project, Doe appeared on a radio show and received criticism from male listeners who considered her vain and unnatural. Faludi bemoans the case of Doe, noting that first a male colleague criticized her for not being young, and then "men were criticizing her for trying to live up to male-created standards—standards she had made her own."

Greg Duncan

Greg Duncan was a University of Michigan social scientist working with Saul Hoffman. They challenged Marlene Weitzman's argument that divorce was impoverishing women. Duncan used his and Hoffman's research and Weitzman's numbers to conclude that, while women did suffer a drop in their standard of living after divorce, that drop was temporary. According to Duncan and his research partner, women's living standards five years after a divorce were actually higher than they had been before the divorce.

Warren Farrell

As a young academic, Warren Farrell supported the women's movement, writing the "celebrated male feminist tome" *The Liberated Man,* and founding some sixty men's chapters of the National Organization for Women. But by the mid-1980s, Farrell decided that men were more oppressed than women and wrote *Why Men Are the Way They Are,* in which he argued that women had been venting too much anger at men and had exerted too much power over them. He taught classes on men's issues at the University of California School of Medicine at San Diego.

Geraldine Ferraro

Geraldine Ferraro was a member of Congress when Democrat Walter Mondale selected her to be his vice presidential running mate in 1984. Faludi notes that Ferraro's nomination provoked attacks from many conservative politicians and notions that the Democrats had "surrendered" to feminists by choosing her.

Betty Freidan

Betty Freidan was once one of America's most famous feminists, a founder of the National Organization for Women and author of the groundbreaking 1963 book, *The Feminine Mystique.* Faludi writes about Freidan's 1981 book, *The Next Stage,* which argues that the leaders of the women's movement in the 1960s and 1970s had ignored the issues of motherhood and family and had been too confrontational.

George Gilder

George Gilder initially supported feminism and women's rights, according to Faludi, but ultimately made a name for himself as a conservative media commentator and writer. In his words, he decided to become "America's number-one antifeminist" by

Media Adaptations

- Susan Faludi is the reader on the audiotape version of her book, *Backlash: The Undeclared War against American Women.* Publishing Mills produced the audiotape in 1992.

writing such books as *Wealth and Poverty, Sexual Suicide, Men and Marriage,* and *Naked Nomads.*

Carol Gilligan

Many books were published in the 1980s on how women are different from men and about "women's inordinate capacity for kindness, service to others, and cooperation," according to Faludi. During this period, Carol Gilligan wrote *In a Different Voice,* a book Faludi refers to as "one of the most influential feminist works of the '80s." While Gilligan wrote the book to illustrate how men diminished women's moral development, the book was misinterpreted by anti-feminist groups to support discriminatory practices against women.

Sylvia Ann Hewlett

Sylvia Ann Hewlett, a member of the Council on Foreign Relations and other think-tanks, indicted the women's movement in her book *A Lesser Life: Myths of Women's Liberation in America.* The book argued that, while feminism may be helpful to upper-class career women, it is actually harmful to what she calls "ordinary women."

Saul Hoffman

Saul Hoffman was a University of Delaware economist who specialized in divorce statistics and worked with Greg Duncan. They challenged Marlene Weitzman's argument that divorce was impoverishing women, using their own research and Weitzman's numbers. They discovered that, while women did suffer a drop in their standard of living after divorce, that drop was temporary. According to Hoffman and Duncan, women's living standards five years after a divorce were actually higher than they had been before the divorce.

Christian Lacroix

Christian Lacroix was a fashion designer. Faludi writes that Lacroix launched a look called "High Femininity," in which women's bodies were cinched into waist-pinching corsets and reshaped by push-up bras. In his own words, Lacroix created these clothes for women who like to "dress up like little girls." Lacroix and other designers participated in the backlash against feminism by promoting "punitively restrictive clothing," according to Faludi.

Beverly LaHaye

Beverly LaHaye was an example of a paradox for Faludi: a high-powered career woman with a family and yet a supporter of the New Right's conviction that such a life is neither possible nor appropriate. LaHaye founded the anti-feminist organization Concerned Women for America in 1978. In Faludi's book, LaHaye claims that her power and authority did not contradict the concept that men should be the heads of households, as women like her were only seeking "spiritual power" and not earthly power. LaHaye wrote a book outlining this philosophy, *The Spirit-Controlled Woman* and also wrote *The Act of Marriage: The Beauty of Sexual Love,* a book Faludi calls "the evangelical equivalent of *The Joy of Sex.*"

Sherry Lansing

Sherry Lansing was a movie executive responsible for releasing films such as *Fatal Attraction* and *The Accused* in the 1980s. Faludi points to *Fatal Attraction,* the story of a single career woman whose affair with a married man sparks her obsession with him, as part of the evidence of a societal and cultural backlash against women's rights in the 1980s. According to Faludi, Lansing's release of *The Accused,* a film about a woman who is gang-raped while a group of men stand by but don't interfere was a feeble attempt to "polish up her feminist credentials." Faludi questions whether audiences needed to be "reminded that rape victims deserve sympathy."

Margarita Levin

Margarita Levin was a philosophy professor at Yeshiva University, with a specialty in the philoso-

phy of mathematics. She was also, according to Faludi, "an intellectual partner" in her husband, Michael Levin's, "antifeminist writings." Faludi reports that, ironically, many of the typically female jobs in the Levin household, such as child care, were done by Michael Levin as well as by his wife.

Michael Levin

Michael Levin was a philosophy professor who wrote *Feminism and Freedom,* a book arguing that sex roles are innate and that women who attempt to have both family and career are denying these sex roles. He was married to Margarita Levin, also a philosophy professor. Faludi reports that many of the typically female jobs in the Levin household, such as child care, were done by Michael Levin as well as by his wife.

Adrian Lyne

Adrian Lyne directed the 1987 blockbuster movie *Fatal Attraction,* in which a single career woman has an affair with a married man and stalks him after he tries to break off the relationship. Faludi points to this movie as part of the evidence of a societal and cultural backlash against women's rights in the 1980s. She highlights Lyne's role in turning the character of the single woman into "the Dark Woman." According to Faludi, Lyne once commented that unmarried women are "sort of overcompensating for not being men."

John T. Malloy

John Malloy, a former English teacher, wrote the 1977 bestselling book *The Woman's Dress for Success Book.* The book encouraged women to dress for the jobs they wanted. Faludi notes that Malloy was "an advocate for women's rising expectations—and urged them to rely on their brains rather than their bodies to improve their station." She argues that much of the "High Femininity" fashion look of the 1980s was a backlash against what Malloy stood for.

Paul Marciano

Paul Marciano, along with his brothers, created the Guess line of jeans and clothing in the early 1980s. Faludi asserts that Guess found a way to "use the backlash to sell clothes" by developing an ad campaign featuring passive-looking women with strong-looking men. Marciano claimed that the design of the ads reflected his love of the American West and the 1950s, places and periods in which women, he said, "know their place, which is supportive, and their function, which is decorative."

Connie Marshner

Connie Marshner was an executive with the conservative organizations Free Congress Research and Education Foundation and the Heritage Foundation. She was the child of liberal parents who encouraged her to go to school and have a career. Faludi draws a profile of her as a woman who has been helped by feminism—she has had a thriving and powerful career as well as a family—and yet still supports the New Right thinking that a woman cannot have a career and be a mother.

Jeanne Moorman

Jeanne Moorman, a demographer in the marriage and family statistics branch of the U. S. Census Bureau, heard about the Harvard-Yale marriage study from the numerous reporters who called her looking for a comment on it. Moorman attempted to reproduce the survey's results. According to her calculations, the likelihood that college-educated, never-wed women past the age of thirty would marry was considerably greater than the Harvard-Yale study had concluded. Her findings showed that these women were simply getting married later in life, not failing to marry. Moorman's attempts to contact the researchers at Yale and Harvard were ignored at first. When they finally did respond, the researchers were uncooperative and difficult, according to Faludi.

Faith Popcorn

Faith Popcorn was an advertising executive and "leading consumer authority" who became well known in the 1980s for predicting social trends. She admitted that her predictions often came from popular magazines, television shows, and bestselling books, rather than from consumer research. Popcorn predicted that "cocooning" was the major national trend for the 1980s, meaning that people were becoming more interested in staying home and eating "Mom foods" such as meatloaf and chicken potpie. Faludi argues that, while Popcorn may have intended for cocooning to be a "gender neutral concept, the press made it a female trend, defining cocooning not as *people* coming home but as *women* abandoning the office."

Ronald Reagan

Ronald Reagan was elected United States president in 1980 on a conservative social and economic platform. Faludi notes that in a 1982 speech he blamed working women for the tight job market. Reagan said in the speech that high unemployment figures were related to "the increase in women who are working today."

Charles Revson

Charles Revson was the head of Revlon, a cosmetics company. In the early 1970s, he came up with the idea of creating a perfume for women that would celebrate women's liberation and independence. The perfume, Charlie, was a huge success. By the late 1980s, however, the marketing campaign for Charlie was modified, according to a Revson spokesperson, to reflect that "we had gone a little too far with the whole women's liberation thing."

Phyllis Schlafly

Phyllis Schlafly was a part of the conservative New Right political movement in the 1980s. She campaigned against the Equal Rights Amendment (ERA) to the U. S. Constitution. Schlafly was a Harvard-educated lawyer, author of numerous books, and two-time congressional candidate who fought against the ERA because, in Schlafly's words, "it would take away the marvelous legal rights of a woman to be a fulltime wife and mother in the house supported by her husband."

Aaron Spelling

Aaron Spelling was the producer behind the late 1980s television series *Angels '88,* a reprise of his earlier series *Charlie's Angels,* in which, according to Faludi, "three jiggle-prone private eyes took orders from invisible boss Charlie and bounced around in bikinis." Spelling assured the press that his new show was much more advanced than *Charlie's Angels* because the women's boss was a female nurse.

Ben Wattenberg

Ben Wattenberg was a syndicated columnist, senior fellow at the American Enterprise Institute, and author of the 1987 book *The Birth Dearth.* In the book, Wattenberg introduced the concept that American women's decisions to have fewer children would hurt the nation's economy and culture. According to Faludi, Wattenberg and others were urging women to have children based on "society's baser instincts—xenophobia, militarism, and bigotry" by arguing that if white, educated, middle-class women didn't have babies, "paupers, fools and foreigners would." Wattenberg blamed the women's movement and feminism for discouraging women from their more traditional societal roles.

Lenore Weitzman

Lenore Weitzman wrote the 1985 book *The Divorce Revolution: The Unexpected Social and Economic Consequences for Women and Children in America.* According to Faludi, Weitzman's thesis, that the recent no-fault divorce laws in America were systematically impoverishing divorced women and their children, increased the "attack on divorce-law reform" in the 1980s. While Weitzman herself never blamed feminists for no-fault divorce legislation, Faludi notes that those who were promoting and supporting her book did so.

Paul Weyrich

Paul Weyrich, head of the Free Congress Research and Education Foundation, is considered by many to be the "Father of the New Right." The New Right was the conservative political movement that supported Ronald Reagan in the early 1980s and put many conservative Republicans in Congress. In Faludi's book, Weyrich called the late 1980s a period when "women are discovering they can't have it all" and that having a career will destroy their family life. He also said that the New Right movement was different from other conservative movements in that it did not want simply to "preserve the status quo" but to "overturn the present power structure of the country." One of the major pieces of legislation he supported at the beginning of the 1980s was the Family Protection Act, which, according to Faludi, was intended to eliminate federal laws supporting equal education.

Themes

Structure and Functioning of Families

Conservative thinkers and writers object to feminism because it ignores what they see as a woman's natural inclination toward making a home for her children and husband. In their eyes, feminists' endorsement of a woman's ability to maintain a home while pursuing a career threatens the family structure by subverting the man as the traditional head of the household. This, in turn, threatens the country's social and economic structure. Those who view feminism in this way believe that the women's movement is not only encouraging women to work while they have children but also to forgo or delay having children. Faludi is particularly concerned that the backlash against women delaying childbirth encourages press reports that there is an "epidemic" of infertility among career women.

Some conservative commentators, who argue that feminists have encouraged women to remain childless, believe that such urgings place the nation at an economic disadvantage in the world. In her analysis of this argument, Faludi asserts that those who make this case for American women having children can be accused of racism and xenophobia. She believes that they are worried not only about America's economic future but also about the possibility of whites becoming a minority among people of color and foreigners.

Faludi delights in revealing the personal lives of many of the conservative thinkers who oppose feminism, observing that those lives very often run counter to the tenets of their public comments. She writes about a number of the women involved in the New Right who, despite their arguments that careers and motherhood do not mix, are pursuing lives filled with both children and work. She also points out the number of men in these prominent couples who take over the household duties, such as child care and cooking, so that their wives can pursue careers.

Popular Culture in the 1980s

Faludi uses popular culture during the 1980s to buttress her argument that the decade was a period of backlash against women and feminism. Her evidence for this backlash includes examples from the movie industry, television, the cosmetics and beauty industry, the fashion world, and societal trends.

For example, Faludi notes that after a decade filled with television series like *All in the Family,* which tackled tough political issues (including women's rights), television in the mid- to late 1980s featured few programs in which women's issues

Topics for Further Study

- Susan Faludi wrote her book primarily in the late 1980s. Do you think the status of women in the United States has changed since then? What about societal attitudes? Is society in a period of backlash or of advancement for women's rights? Provide specific examples from some of the sectors of society covered in Faludi's book—the entertainment industry, the media, government, and so forth—to support your opinion.

- Faludi mentions quite a few movies as evidence that a backlash against women occurred in the 1980s. Watch one of the movies she says is anti-feminist and write a short essay agreeing or disagreeing with her position. Use specific examples from the movie to make your argument. Has she misinterpreted this movie or is she correct in her evaluation?

- Research the four periods of American history during which Faludi says there were advance-

ments in the status of women. Also research the years following these periods, when Faludi argues that there was backlash against women. Create a time line for each of these advancement and backlash eras, including both events pertaining to women's rights and unrelated national and world events. Analyze and explain any patterns you see.

- Interview a woman you know who has a career and is also a mother. Ask her questions about some of the issues explored in *Backlash*. Choose your questions based on the issues you find most interesting. Then write up your interview in the form of a newspaper feature article.

- Choose someone Faludi interviewed for her book and do research to find out what that person is doing now and whether his or her views have changed.

---

were considered. The rare 1980s show featuring a strong woman was usually under threat of cancellation. In the movies, women were regularly beaten, pitted against each other, or punished for being single. Hollywood supported the backlash by showing American women who were "unhappy because they were too free [and] their liberation had denied them marriage and motherhood," says Faludi. The fashion industry reinforced the backlash, as well, by designing clothing that was either childlike or extremely restrictive and binding.

The Struggle for Equal Rights

Faludi's book is concerned with a period in history—the 1980s—during which women's struggle for equal rights suffered setbacks. She notes, however, that these periods of backlash historically occur after periods of advancement in women's rights. According to Faludi, the mid-nineteenth century, the early 1900s, the early 1940s, and the early 1970s were eras during which American women

saw large gains in their economic and social status. "In each case, the struggle yielded to backlash," asserts Faludi.

Faludi points out that the backlash against women is cyclical. For example, when she speaks of movies in the 1980s, she also looks at the tenor of movies in the 1970s. When she examines 1980s fashions, she also considers what women were wearing in the 1950s, a period of backlash after the advances of the 1940s.

Myths and Their Role in Society

Faludi points out that many in society, including some well-meaning writers and thinkers, have accepted the truth of myths about the status of women in the 1980s. She exposes many of these myths and supposed trends, which have appeared so often in the press that most Americans consider them as fact. For example, Faludi discovered that the Harvard-Yale marriage study, proclaiming that unmarried women after the age of thirty have a very slim chance of ever becoming wed was full of methodological errors. She also challenges stories claiming that single career women suffer from depression in epidemic numbers.

Style

Use of Evidence to Make an Argument

Faludi's book is overflowing with data and information that she believes bolsters her case that the 1980s represented a period of backlash against women and their advances. Her supporting data comes from a wide variety of sources, including newspapers, scholarly and academic journals, personal interviews, and government and university studies. This use of authoritative sources is an important way writers convince readers of their argument; however, some critics have suggested that Faludi uses almost too much factual data and that its volume actually hinders her argument.

Personal Profiles

Faludi also includes short profiles of people she believes were critical to the evolution of the backlash against women in the 1980s. Inclusion of these profiles helps move the book along in a number of ways: reading about specific individuals who contributed to the backlash—even though Faludi obviously disagrees with their philosophy—puts a human face on the philosophy and makes the issues seem less amorphous; and the profiles offer some relief from the pages and pages of data. Faludi is able to point her finger directly at the commentators, writers, politicians, and thinkers who she feels helped the backlash gain momentum.

Historical Context

The Equal Rights Amendment

Despite the apparent simplicity of the language in the proposed Equal Rights Amendment (ERA) to the U. S. Constitution, it was one of the most divisive political issues in the 1970s. The fifty-two words of the amendment were as follows:

1. Equality of rights under the law shall not be denied or abridged by the United States or by any State on account of sex. 2. The Congress shall have the power to enforce, by appropriate legislation, the provisions of this article. 3. This amendment shall take effect two years after the date of ratification.

The issue of an equal rights amendment to the U. S. Constitution first emerged in the 1920s and appeared on a regular basis thereafter. Early opponents to the amendment—including labor unions and social reform groups—cited uncertainty about how the proposal would affect legislation meant to assist women and children. In 1972, the U. S. Congress passed the ERA. The next step was for the legislatures of thirty-eight states (three-fourths of the fifty states) to ratify the amendment by 1979. In about a year, twenty-five states had passed the ERA.

The pace of ratification then slowed tremendously. In 1977, only three more states were needed for the amendment to become part of the U. S. Constitution, but by the 1979 deadline this had not happened. Congress extended the deadline to 1982, but no other states ratified the ERA after 1977, and the amendment failed.

Opposition to the ERA came primarily from political conservatives who feared that the amendment would substantially change the roles of men and women. Phyllis Schlafly, a conservative activist, organized the Stop ERA campaign, based primarily on the issue of the amendment's impact on families. She and others argued that the ERA would bring an end to a husband's obligation to support his wife and children, force the creation of unisex bathrooms, and include women in the military draft.

Abortion Rights

Faludi points out that American women's access to legal abortion was generally uncontested until the last half of the nineteenth century. By the end of the nineteenth century, every state in the union had outlawed abortion except in cases in which the woman's life was in jeopardy. In 1967, the National Organization for Women advocated the repeal of abortion laws, and other organizations, such as the group Zero Population Growth, also saw access to abortion as part of their agendas. By 1969, the National Association for the Repeal of Abortion Laws (NARAL) was founded. NARAL made progress organizing at the state level and had received qualified support from such religious groups as the American Lutheran Church and the United Methodist Board of Church and Society. Soon, four states had eased access to legal abortions.

In 1972, the U. S. Supreme Court ruled in favor of abortion rights activists, deciding in its landmark case *Roe v. Wade* that the Constitution prohibits interference by states in medical decisions between a woman and her physician during the first trimester of a pregnancy. In the later stages of a pregnancy, the court ruled, states could regulate abortion.

The reaction to the *Roe v. Wade* decision was immediate and galvanized a number of groups against access to abortion. The Catholic Church in America issued a statement that its members would be excommunicated if they participated in or received an abortion. Many Christian evangelical groups condemned the ruling as well, claiming that the Supreme Court had rejected morality. The anti-abortion movement, now referring to itself as pro-life, also gained strength and numbers among political conservatives during this period and into the 1980s. Abortion clinics became battlegrounds for the fight between pro-life and pro-choice (those supporting access to abortion) groups.

Critical Overview

When *Backlash* was published in the fall of 1991, it was a popular success and stayed at the top of the *New York Times* bestseller list for months. Numerous critics praised Faludi for her use of compelling data and for the book's timely topic. Wendy Kaminer, writing in the *Atlantic,* called the book a "comprehensive survey of a powerful ten-year backlash against feminism." Faludi's critique of the media's role in maintaining this backlash, according to Kaminer, was "powerful," and she rejected some critics' accusations that the book was based on conspiracy theory. Kaminer, however, did warn readers that Faludi's work was much more descriptive than analytic.

Gayle Greene's review of Faludi's book in the *Nation* was similarly receptive, calling the book a "rich compendium of fascinating information and an indictment of a system." Greene also lauded Faludi's considerable interviewing skills and expressed surprise that the author was able to get her subjects to "blurt out marvelously self-incriminating revelations, offering up the real reasons they hate and fear feminists."

This praise continued in the *Whole Earth Review,* in which Ann Norton admired Faludi's book for its clarity and logical arguments. Norton also appreciated Faludi's use of specific examples in popular culture to drive home her points, making her book accessible to everyone interested in the topic. "This is the book for those who have puzzled and despaired . . . over magazine and newspaper articles and TV news shows declaring the 'death of feminism,'" remarked Norton.

Not all of the reviews were positive however; Karen Lehrman, writing in the *New Republic,* argued that despite the large number of examples, Faludi's assigning malevolent and organized motives to the backlash was the book's undoing. She called Faludi's arguments "dubious" and accused Faludi of seeing "a cabal of villains . . . successfully intimidating a large class of victims: women." Lehrman complained that Faludi's book portrayed women as victims until the very end, where the author admitted that woman have not been totally beaten by the backlash. "Writing this in the introduction would have undermined her portrayal of women as helpless, passive victims of society's devious designs," Lehrman asserted.

Some of the criticism of Faludi's book became quite vehement. Maggie Gallagher, writing for the *National Review,* called Faludi's book "an ignorant, nasty, little book . . . small-minded, crafty, conniving, a disgrace even to journalistic standards, and an insult to women." She pointed to what she claimed was Faludi's misrepresentation of the facts in a number of instances, asserting that "evidence is not Miss Faludi's strong point." Gretchen Morgenson, writing in *Forbes,* condemned the book for shoddy reporting, bad writing, paranoia, and for encouraging women to think of themselves as victims. "In the opinion of this career woman," wrote Morgenson, "*Backlash* is a last gasp of Seventies feminism, a final attempt to rally women to a shrill, anti-male cause that has been comatose for years."

Some critics, while not agreeing with all of Faludi's arguments and methods, still realized the importance of the book. Nancy Gibbs, writing for *Time,* declared that the success of Faludi's book was based on "the resonance of the questions Faludi raises." While Gibbs admitted that Faludi did mishandle some statistics in her book, this "should not be an excuse to dismiss her entire argument." Faludi had, according to Gibbs, inspired both men and women to rethink how they relate to each other, on a personal as well as on a public level.

Lawyer, author, and political activist Phyllis Schlafly at a rally protesting the Equal Rights Amendment (ERA)

Criticism

Susan Sanderson

Sanderson holds a master of fine arts degree in fiction writing and is an independent writer. In this essay, she considers the language Faludi uses in her book and how it contributes to her purpose of sounding the alarm about women's rights.

Some critics have argued that in her 1991 book, *Backlash: The Undeclared War Against American Women,* Faludi constructs a world filled with organized schemes perpetrated by those who wish only ill upon all of America's women. For example, Karen Lehrman, writing in the *New Republic,* charges that Faludi's book is based on a "conspiracy theory" and implies that "a cabal of villains has been at work successfully intimidating a large class of victims: women." After summarily dismissing Faludi's book, Gretchen Morgenson writes in *Forbes,* "if you are naturally paranoid, you may like this book."

Faludi, on the other hand, when asked about the book, denies that she believes in an organized conspiracy against women. During an interview with *Time* six months after the book was released, Faludi responded to the interviewer's question about these allegations. "Anyone who says that can't possibly have read the book. I say about fourteen times that I don't mean there's a conspiracy. This is not a book about hating men," she answers.

In the book's first chapter, where she sets the tone for her work, Faludi makes clear that she does not see the backlash against women in terms of a conspiracy. Referring to the various ways in which the backlash has made itself known in society and popular culture, Faludi remarks that these aspects are "all related, but that doesn't mean they are somehow coordinated. The backlash is not a conspiracy, with a council dispatching agents from some central back room." But, as she points out, the fact that the backlash isn't coordinated or organized does not reduce its destructiveness.

Before completely rejecting these critics' complaints, however, there may be a practical reason why so many have seen a conspiracy theory in Faludi's book. In the first chapter, Faludi explains her plan for the book and also briefly considers the language used to describe the backlash. "Women's advances and retreats are generally described in military terms," she notes, acknowledging the value

What Do I Read Next?

- *Stiffed: The Betrayal of the American Man* is Susan Faludi's second book, published in 1999. In this work, she furthers her studies in gender relations, chronicling the thoughts and words of post–World War II men.

- Simone de Beauvoir's groundbreaking 1953 book, *The Second Sex,* uses history, philosophy, economics, and biology to understand women's roles in the second half of the twentieth century. This book was published well before much thought was given to issues surrounding women's place in the world, and was one of the first books to discuss post–World War II feminism.

- *The Reader's Companion to U.S. Women's History* is a collection of four hundred articles celebrating the role of lesser-known women who have had an impact on American history. Wilma Mankiller, Gwendolyn Mink, Marysa Navarro, and Gloria Steinem edited the collection, published in 1999. Entries include an essay on the role of Native American women and a narrative on the female slave experience.

- American writer Grace Paley has described herself as a pacifist, feminist, and anarchist. Her short stories include characters struggling to understand their roles in a society that often limits behavior based on gender. *The Collected Stories,* published in 1995, brings together more than thirty years of her acclaimed stories.

---

of using such terms as "battle." Tempering this sentiment, though, she goes on to note that by "imagining the conflict as two battalions neatly arrayed on either side of the line, we miss the entangled nature . . . of a 'war.'" While she seems to be saying that she will not use warlike language, such language does appear throughout the book.

A majority of the information Faludi relays in the book is presented as cool, hard data, but an important part of her message is delivered using words that are angry and warlike. By using these types of words, she signals that she believes the struggle between feminists and those opposing feminism to be an ongoing, organized conflict between two forces.

The book does draw lines along which two armies might stand: feminists versus anti-feminists. Even though Faludi claims not to express this image, she has done just that by her use of language. Hardly a chapter is presented that does not depend upon military metaphors or use language to bolster Faludi's argument. She refers to the "*campaign* against no-fault divorce" in one chapter; in another, she claims that the sour 1980s economy pushed society to consider women as "the *enemy*"; and in

yet another chapter Faludi describes how, with the help of 1980s advice writers, "the backlash insinuated itself into the most intimate *front lines.*" Sprinkling such terms throughout the book, Faludi has made it clear that she envisions the opposition of parties involved.

Even chapter titles illustrate conflict: only two of the fourteen chapter titles do not include the word "backlash," and those two remaining chapter titles include the equally strong words "blame" and "war." Other chapter titles include the words "refugee," "occupation," and "invasion."

In the backlash against women, Faludi is not ambiguous about her enemy's identity. Not only does she name names throughout the text, but she also paints unflattering, almost propagandistic portraits of the opposition camp. When she describes photographer Wayne Maser setting up an advertising shoot for the "anti-women" film *Fatal Attraction,* for example, Faludi considers how vain Maser is about his clothing. Randall Terry, founder of the anti-abortion campaign Operation Rescue, is described as "a used car salesman" who jerks his thumb at his wife to indicate that she's not to speak to Faludi.

> " A majority of the information Faludi relays in the book is presented as cool, hard data, but an important part of her message is delivered using words that are angry and warlike.''

Faludi delights, as well, in showing politically conservative thinkers and writers in ironically conflicting situations. Though Gary Bauer, an aide to President Ronald Reagan, once called children's day care ''Marxist'' and urged women to stay at home, his own wife worked for nine years, and they placed their children in, as Faludi jokes, ''this leftist institution.'' Faludi gleefully relates that when asked about the apparent hypocrisy, Bauer claimed that ''his use of day care was 'different' and 'better' because he placed his children in 'home-based' day care—that is, an unlicensed center run out of a woman's living room.'' A visit to conservative authors and professors Michael and Margarita Levin unearths even more unflattering information about the home life of anti-feminists. The Levins argue in their writings that sex roles are innate: men naturally don't like to cook, and women naturally enjoy housework, according to the Levins. When Faludi arrives at their house for an interview, Michael is taking care of the children while Margarita gets ready to teach for the evening. Later, Michael ''emerges from the kitchen to say goodbye. He looks a little chagrined—he's wearing an apron,'' Faludi notes.

Faludi's eye for hypocritical anti-feminists is nothing if not equal opportunity. Those who would claim that Faludi condemns only men should note that anti-feminist women do not escape Faludi's sights; she cites numerous examples of women with children working in high-powered jobs at conservative think tanks while still contending that, for society's own good, women should remain at home with their children.

Though Faludi does create a contentious atmosphere in her book and sets two opposing forces against each other, perhaps her intention isn't to indicate that there is an organized conspiracy against women. Maybe she actually means to show that the fight is not as hidden as a ''conspiracy'' would be; that is, there is no conspiracy, but there is, in fact, a battle.

Ultimately, *Backlash* is a book filled with passion and *chutzpah.* Faludi's passion for her topic is clear from the first page. To write with any less strength and vigor would be to submit to those people who argue that being a woman requires one to be polite, forgiving, and invisible.

This, then, begs the question: Why do Faludi's critics find it surprising that she is up front and even fiery about the backlash, especially when she believes that women's rights are under attack? If Faludi feels the need to sound the alarm, writing in courteous terms will not help achieve her goal of an America in which women are ''just as deserving of rights and opportunities, just as capable of participating in the world's events'' as men.

Source: Susan Sanderson, Critical Essay on *Backlash: The Undeclared War against American Women,* in *Nonfiction Classics for Students,* The Gale Group, 2002.

Susan Faludi with Ruth Conniff

In the following interview, Faludi discusses her views on feminism and its place in American society and the negative reaction to Backlash.

'I think, underneath, all women are feminists. It's just a matter of time and encouragement.'

Susan Faludi, author of the best-selling *Backlash: The Undeclared War Against American Women,* recently gave a speech to a standing-room-only audience at the University of Wisconsin-Madison. Afterwards she appeared on *Second Opinion,* a radio program hosted by The Progressive's Editor Erwin Knoll, and then she spoke with me in the studio for an hour or so. I've incorporated some of her remarks from Erwin's show here, and some she made when we talked again on the telephone after she returned to California, where she is a visiting lecturer at Stanford University. Throughout the interviews, she spoke softly but intensely about her book, her mother, her sudden rise to stardom, and feminism in post-Bush America.

Susan Faludi grew up in New York City and graduated from Harvard in 1981. She went to work as a copy girl at The *New York Times,* and then as a reporter for The *Miami Herald,* the *Atlanta Constitution,* the *San Jose Mercury News,* and The *Wall Street Journal.* In 1991, she won the Pulitzer Prize for her expose of the Safeway leveraged buyout. Since *Backlash* was published last year, Faludi has become a media star, dubbed the torchbearer for a new generation of feminists. Yet, she says, she's more comfortable when she's out of the public eye, working as an anonymous reporter, poking holes in the myths that constrain American women.

One powerful section of *Backlash* is devoted to the movie *Fatal Attraction,* which Faludi says both represented and reinforced backlash resentments and fears about women. Faludi paints director Adrian Lyne as a sexist bully who badgered and humiliated actresses, and went to great lengths to transform the originally feminist script for *Fatal Attraction* into a fable in which the uppity single woman is violently suppressed. In Lyne's most recent movie, *Indecent Proposal,* he takes a passing shot at Faludi—the camera zooms in on a copy of *Backlash* in the hands of a blonde and apparently airheaded secretary. In the next scene the secretary is shown vamping in front of the movie's hero. So much for feminist enlightenment.

[Conniff]: *Did you see* Indecent Proposal?

[Faludi:] Yeah, I did.

What did you think of it, and of Backlash's *little cameo in it?*

Well, I actually heard a reporter who had talked to Adrian Lyne explain that Lyne said he wanted to "tweak me," because I had been so hard on him about *Fatal Attraction.* To which—I don't know—I say tweak away. I think he just threw it in. I don't think there was much thought behind it. I suppose one could spin out a grand textual analysis of why he assigned the reading of *Backlash* to some gum-chewing secretary in spandex, but I think that would be giving more intellectual heft to his reasoning than it deserves.

The reviewer for the Village Voice *called* Indecent Proposal *"the Zeitgeist shocker for the 1990s." (In the movie, Robert Redford's character offers a couple $1 million to let him sleep with the wife.) The reviewer says you won't be able to catch this one in "such easy feminist pincers" as you did* Fatal Attraction, *because it's the wife's choice—it's very subtle and complex. What do you think of that?*

I didn't find that so subtle and complex. That's one of the standard hallmarks of a lot of *backlash* cultural artifacts, that they take feminist rhetoric about choice and use it to attack the whole agenda of feminism.

Do you think it was a backlash movie the way Fatal Attraction *was?*

> **If women were running advertising agencies, if women had control in a real way of television stations, of radio stations, we'd be seeing a whole different world.''**

Sure. I mean it's not the same movie. I'd have to read this review, but I guess what I find irritating is the assumption that anything that is subject to feminist analysis is "easy," that there are only certain reductive feminist ideas. The fact that this movie might have a slightly different spin to it or shows a woman who supposedly is choosing to have an affair doesn't mean it's not open to feminist analysis.

Anyway, you have to see this movie in the context of all these new movies that are coming out about the bartering of women. I see it as more a movie about masculine anxiety. A number of movies out in the last year—from *Falling Down* to *Mad Dog and Glory* (which I actually liked for other reasons)—all seem to express extreme anxiety over men's ability to attract women, hold onto them, support them. And this movie seemed to me to be more about that kind of economic male fear. It seems that it was a struggle between two men, and the woman was really irrelevant. She's the object that's being traded. She has no personality. The movie's about who is going to claim this piece of property. Then there's this very calculating insertion of a scene in which she says, "No, I made the choice to do this." Which I think was just Lyne's attempt to get the feminists off his back.

Do you think there's some hostility there—that the movie is really lashing back at Backlash?

I think the way he dealt with it in the movie, by dismissing it—and in his mind, I'm sure, trivializing it—by putting it in the hands of a dippy blonde secretary is an expression of hostility, sure. That's often how we dismiss what we fear. On the other hand, usually feminist theory is equated with some beast with an SS outfit. I mean that's generally how men who are hostile toward feminists like to portray them.

That brings me to my next question, which is about Camille Paglia.

Speaking of dominatrixes.

What do you think of Paglia's claim that the backlash isn't against women, it's against doctrinaire feminism? I think you've used the phrase "the heiresses of Puritanism" to describe the way feminism is often portrayed. Is there any grain of truth in that?

Well, that assumes that most people are so familiar with feminist doctrine that they would find it pervasive and overwhelming. I mean, she's speaking from within the academy, which is a very different brand of feminism than the average woman on the street is exposed to. Having now spent a year in academia, I can to a degree understand the point she's driving at. I mean, sure—not just in feminist studies but in academia in general there's this sort of narrowing specialization and use of coded, elitist language of deconstruction or New Historicism or whatever they're calling it these days, which is to my mind impenetrable and not particularly useful.

But I think to claim that the *backlash* was inspired by doctrinaire feminism in the world at large is to make the false assumption that people are that deeply steeped in feminist theory, and that so-called doctrinaire feminism has that much sway in the general popular culture, which I don't think it does. I don't think the average American woman was turned off by feminism because of the effect of French feminism in the academy.

But Paglia also has a lot of snappy, vicious things to say about Gloria Steinem. Do you think it's possible that a lot of people share her perception that feminism is just not particularly useful to your average woman?

Well, if you look at public opinion polls, the vast majority of women say that the women's movement is very relevant to their lives. They think the only problem is the women's movement hasn't gone far enough and hasn't made enough change. Gloria Steinem is also consistently one of the most popular women in those polls of "who do you admire most?" She's always up there with Princess Di.

What galls Camille Paglia is that she's not on the Top Ten list. We should just stick her there so she'll be happy and stop haranguing us. If you go back and read her complaint against the so-called feminist establishment there's this recurrent theme of Camille as an outsider battering down the door trying to get in. The bone she has to pick with feminists is not an intellectual one. It's not over theory. It's the fact that she hasn't been invited to the party. There's something a bit sad and certainly misbegotten about this notion she has that there is this feminist establishment that's yucking it up till three in the morning. I mean, in fact, I don't know what parties she's talking about. I haven't been invited to them either. And she should just relax and not feel so left out. I don't want to psychoanalyze her, but it seems that a lot of this resentment is the resentment of someone who perceives herself as an outsider, which is doubly sad because there is no inside club except in her imagination. And if she is spurned by feminists it's because she goes around making claims that no self-respecting feminist woman would want to be identified with, such as sneering at sexual harassment, sneering at feminists for calling attention to the high rate of rape.

Did you see the television coverage on this high-school gang, the Spur Posse, accused of raping girls for points?

No, unfortunately that was when I was out of the country. What was your impression of it?

It was sort of amazing. I saw several boys on a talk show, bragging about their conquests. And then the camera would pan across the high-school campus and show girls' legs in mini-skirts walking back and forth.

It's like the coverage of the William Kennedy Smith rape trial. First you think, great, at least they think this is worthy of coverage. But then you realize that they think it's worthy of coverage because they think of it as an excuse to show body parts or, you know, the offending torn panty-hose in the William Kennedy Smith trial. I don't know how many times they showed the defense lawyer dangling her black, push-up bra. And it sounds like this was another case of a chance to do some cheesecake.

Have you ever been sexually harassed?

In ways that are not particularly dramatic, but fairly mundane and common. At The *New York Times,* when I was a copy girl, one of the editors was notorious and had been reprimanded for sexual harassment, although only with a slap on the wrist, so he continued to harass mostly younger women who were copy girls. He took me out to lunch and sort of ran his hand up and down my leg, telling me how "talented" I was, and how much he wanted to assist my career.

And how did you respond?

You know, like most twenty-one-year-old women on their first job, I guess I responded like a deer in the headlights. I just sat there and then sort of gingerly moved my leg away and said thanks so much for the words of support but I need to get back to the office now. I talked to all of the other copy girls I knew and I sort of let the story get out, but I didn't go formally report it. Part of the reason was the reason why all women hesitate before reporting such things when they're in positions of little power and they're at the bottom rung and desirous of moving up a few rungs. But part of the reason was that I knew it wouldn't help any because of this other woman just a year ago. He had gone a great deal further with her, sort of hauled her back to his apartment and jumped on her. But nothing happened. So for me to go knock on the door of human resources and say, well, this guy put his hand on my knee, was not going to go anywhere. You know, it was also a different climate. This is back in the early 1980s, and sexual harassment was not something that one even complained about. I wonder now if it would be different.

What do you think of the debate over sexual harassment—Catharine MacKinnon's theory of the hostile work environment versus the concern that punishing sexual harassment threatens free speech?

On the one hand, as a journalist I'm not in favor of banning pornography or anything that smells of censorship. For one thing, it's just not very productive. It doesn't make things go away. On the other hand, I do like the ways in which, as women enter the law, because of our social experiences, we approach ideas of law and of what should be a basic right, and what shouldn't, differently. I think if all the founding fathers were founding mothers, the right to bear arms would not necessarily be the first right to pop into our minds. Perhaps the right to have some control over our child-bearing capacity would be a more important place to start. In Canada there's some interesting work being done now with recasting the definition of political refugee to include women who are victims of sexual violence.

In Canada they also now ban pornography. How do you recognize the damage that pervasive misogynist images do and respond to it in a way that isn't restrictive of speech?

On the sexual harassment front, I don't know—part of me thinks we've barely gotten to that point. For all the kicking and screaming about how men can barely flirt without a woman slapping them with a sexual harassment complaint, sexual harassment is still vastly underreported. And women don't rush off to the court when a guy says, ''Oh, you're looking cute today.'' I mean, it just doesn't really work that way.

But my gut feeling is that it's one thing to expand the definition of political refugee and another thing to start slapping restrictions on what can be in printed material or on the air. And I just become very queasy whenever anyone starts saying that certain material is unsuitable for publication, because that can easily be turned against us. Which is why one defends the right of neo-Nazis to march down the streets of suburban America.

So what do you do if you're feeling overwhelmed in a hostile work environment? Or about the proliferation of images of violence against women everywhere in advertising and television?

It's this horrible chicken-and-egg problem because the ultimate solution is to have vast numbers of women in positions of influence and power and presumably few of us will be tacking up pinups of the Playmate of the Month. But that's part of the reason we're not in those positions of power, because of that kind of hostile climate that we're working in. If women were running advertising agencies, if women had control in a real way of television stations, of radio stations, we'd be seeing a whole different world. Maybe the place to start is revising FCC regulations to grant radio licenses to women. Starting at that sort of macro level rather than the level of the pinup. Again, I guess it's the sort of raising hell rather than prohibition approach. Just because I say I feel uncomfortable about banning pornography doesn't mean I don't think women should be screaming bloody murder about it. The best way to get rid of pornography is to change people's way of thinking to the point where it doesn't sell anymore.

I want to ask you another question on the micro level. I gave a speech to a group of high-school kids and the girls' big complaint was that they didn't speak in class and they got shouted down. I watched it happen. Even when I was speaking there were guys leaping up in the audience and interrupting to deliver their opinions on abortion. What would you say to those students?

I have a friend who's writing a book based on that American Association of University Women study that shows that girls have a big plunge in self-esteem at adolescence, and this gender gap occurs between boys and girls. She's been spending a lot of time observing high-school kids in San Francisco Bay Area public schools. And even in the most enlightened classes, where the teacher thinks about it and is very consciously calling on girls, it's still horribly unbalanced.

I saw this myself last year. I was doing a volunteer project teaching writing at the public schools in San Francisco. And the boys, in particular the boys who have nothing to offer, are the ones who are the loudest and just drown out the girls. I don't know. I have a couple of practical thoughts on it. Personally, I wish someone had forced me to go through public speaking and debating classes. I mean a lot of it is that girls don't have the tools. Nobody has taught them how to raise their voices, how to use their diaphragms to project. How to be heard. I went through much of my childhood and college years feeling very oppressed by the fact that no one was listening to me. And then finally someone pointed out, well, no one can hear you.

But this goes on endlessly, In Italy, I was on this show that's billed as the *Phil Donahue show* of Italy—the *Maurizio Costanzo show.* It was a panel, me and eight men, and it was as if I wasn't there. The men would talk, and if I would say something, they'd just keep talking right over me. But if one of them spoke up, they would fall silent. Partly there were certain little tricks they used to do that. The male voice is deeper and all that. Also, we are so trained to be polite, and there's something so awful about a woman who speaks in a loud voice, it's so unfeminine. Maybe that's the area to work on, to change notions about femininity. Teachers could do girls a world of good by glamorizing the loud-mouthed girl. It's still going to be a problem though, no matter how many voice lessons you give to girls. It's a real argument for going to a girls' school. They do learn to speak up.

Surely something has to be done for the guys as well. Isn't it disturbing to read all of the self-esteem literature that tells women if you just fix yourself then all these social problems are going to go away?

Right. That's really true. I mean girls could be heard if the boys weren't shouting so damned loud. Part of the problem is how we define masculinity, rewarding boys for talking at the top of their lungs, for interrupting, for pushing girls and for swaggering and being arrogant, and speaking up when you have nothing to say. Part of it is this idea that the public forum belongs to men. It's the realm in which they are comfortable. And they're taught that in a million different ways. Whereas, by the time we women reach adulthood it's so deeply ingrained in us to feel that we're kind of the mouse in the palace in a public situation or at a lectern.

Do you often run across that famous line, ''I'm not a feminist, but. . . ?''

I've certainly run across that. I tend to operate on the assumption that every self-respecting woman is a feminist, and I sort of act as if they are, saying, ''Of course you're a feminist, too.'' Then let them make the case against it if they like. I think underneath it, all women are feminists. It's just a matter of peeling away the layers of denial and self-protection, and all of the reasons why women back off and try to disavow their own best interests.

I find it really curious that people will always ask me, ''When did you become a feminist?'' That doesn't make any sense to me, because it seems to me that one is always a feminist. It's, ''When did you discover that you were at your core, of course, a feminist?'' I assume all other women are that way, and eventually something will happen in their lives that will make the light bulb go on. It's just a matter of time and encouragement. And I like to think that it helps just standing up in an audience, especially of undergraduates—young women who tend to be more vulnerable and fearful of stating their opinion—and just saying, here I am—I'm a feminist and it didn't destroy my life. Quite the contrary, everything good that's ever happened to me came from that starting point of declaring my feminist belief. When I was speaking in Virginia at this real frat-and-sorority campus, young women came up to me and said that they had always said that they weren't feminists, but that now they understood that they were. And I thought well, gee, it was worth coming all the way across the country just for that.

Who made feminism attractive to you?

I probably owe a lot of that to my mother, who is a strong feminist and never presented it in a pejorative way. In high school, I was already doing my little feminist crusades. I think a lot of women of my generation would have had a similar experience of being in that age group in which your mother experienced the last *backlash,* the postwar feminine mystique, ''a true woman is a woman with a polka-dotted apron, armed with Shake-n-Bake in the kitchen.'' Observing the women's movement come to suburban America, where I spent most of my childhood, and observing the radical and beneficial effects that wrought in my mother's generation, had a profound effect on me. My mother does not believe in being quiet. She's actually far more assertive than I am. I've always admired that about her. She has a very strong sense of social justice, and belief that one should loudly point out injustice.

Did she like your book?

Yeah. She likes to introduce herself now to people as the grandmother of *Backlash*. She has always encouraged me to pursue my work and I don't think she's ever said, ''Why aren't you married?''

Or, ''Hurry up, you're past thirty.'' She's always been far more interested in creative pursuits than maternal and marital ones. And by doing that she's cleared away a huge obstacle that I think a lot of other women face. Not only is the culture telling them that they're worthless if they don't have 2.5 kids by the time they're thirty-five, but their mothers are telling them that. And my mother has never pushed that line. She never thought marriage was such a hot idea so she doesn't see why her daughter has to experience it.

Do you think that things have gotten better or worse for American women since you wrote Backlash?

I think things have gotten a lot better. I hope they do another one of these polls that asks the question, ''Are you a feminist?'' The last time they did that poll was in the late 1980s, and it had done a complete turnaround since the early 1980s, when almost 60 per cent of women said yes, they were feminists. By the late 1980s almost 60 per cent said no, they were not. It would be interesting—now that we've had Anita Hill and a series of consciousness-raising events—to do that poll. In the absence of that, all I can go by is anecdotal evidence. I don't know how reliable that is, in that women I talk to are a sort of self-selecting group. They come to my speeches or book readings because they agree with my point of view. Of course, from my perception it seems like the world has turned feminist.

You were just in Europe. When you got home did you feel better or worse about the status of women in American society?

Certainly on the level of Government policy, a lot worse. I mean even in Italy—you know American women like to think that we have all this liberty

and freedom and a more supportive environment than the Vatican-ruled country of Italy—but there the maternity and social welfare policy is so much more advanced. So it's embarrassing, watching people's jaws drop when you say, ''Yes, we're so proud that we finally passed this family leave act where we get three months of unpaid leave.''

In a curious way, because American social policy makes no provisions for women's needs, child care, maternity leave, etc., and there's so much violence against women here, the lines are much more clearly drawn. In France, for reasons that have nothing to do with concern about women's rights, but with pronatalism and restocking the population, they have these wonderful policies. If you're in the civil service you can take up to four years of maternity leave, about a year of that paid.

On the other hand, right now, because many European governments from Germany to France seem to be swinging to the Right, the United States is in this curious position of experiencing a feminist revival, where women have a sense of hope and possibility about influencing a more liberal government. We're slightly out of sync with the political cycle of our sisters across the water.

What do you think of the way last year was celebrated in the American mass media as the year of the woman?

I think it really was a slogan that sought to buy off women with a few crumbs. It's a way of sort of ending or truncating the revolution, by giving us the veneer of celebratory achievement, a trophy instead of decent pay.

Did it work?

I don't think so. As much as those who are opposed to women's advancement would like to imagine that women are no longer eager to press the Government on abortion rights, workplace rights, etc., women have shown no signs of losing interest. If anything, every day there's a new women's-rights organization, a new campaign on everything from RU-486 to the rights of women in Bosnia. But it's a typical strategy in a consumerist culture to offer a kind of celebrity status in exchange for real rights.

One of the things that's so gratifying about reading your book is that you illustrate connections among very elusive phenomena. You connect individual men's misogyny, and larger, economic for-

ces, and expose a whole sexist structure. Can you succinctly say what happens-how sexism is produced?

I don't think that you can find an easy starting point. We're born into the cultural loop, so it's hard to know where we first entered. By the time you've reached the age of three, you've been inundated by images of proper female and male behavior, and it's hard to dig your way out of that, if your desire is to be more enlightened.

If you're talking about mass culture, 85 to 90 per cent of the screenwriters and scriptwriters who are doing TV and feature films are men. And certainly in the executive suites, the people who are able to green-light a show are almost solidly white, middle-aged, rather panicky, midlife-crisis men. And I think there's this very complicated, unconscious tendency for men especially in Hollywood to compensate for the fact that it's not a traditionally macho job. This goes back centuries—this anxiety among male writers that what they're doing is somehow sissified, because they're writing, not fighting, and then the compensation for that is to treat writing or filmmaking as if it were some sort of male ritual, and to be more macho and more testosterone-ridden in their approach than a man who's doing a blue-collar or more physical job.

So you think that men in intellectual professions are more macho?

Sometimes. I know this is a grotesque generalization. I can think of many examples to counter it. But you do see this in Hollywood—the whole language of ''taking a meeting'' and this swaggering and strutting that goes on. Also, it's just the old corruption of power. If you have a desk the size of Madison Square Garden, after a while you think that you deserve it and your ego should be as large. That's part of it, too. I think there's also this problem of the feedback loop, where once an idea is declared the social norm, it's very hard to remove it. So with something like *Fatal Attraction,* it wasn't just a movie. It became this whole social phenomenon. There were constant references to it, and it became this buzzword that you saw in fashion and beauty ads, you saw in greeting cards, you heard over the airwaves, and that repetition that is so fundamental to American pop culture itself breeds conformity of thought.

What about the hostility and extreme violence toward women—for instance, the ''audience participation'' you've described in theaters that showed

Fatal Attraction, where the men were yelling, ''Kick her ass'' and ''Kill the [b——].'' Where does that come from?

Clearly violence toward women is one of the peculiarities of American culture. A lot of the other aspects of sexism—denouncing the career woman, or saying that women should go back to the home—you find the world over. But this extreme, physical violence is, I think, part of our historical origins. There's a wonderful trilogy—the final volume just came out—by Richard Slotkin. The first one's called *Regeneration through Violence.* The one that just came out is called *Gunfighter Nation.* He talks about an idea that other historians have laid out as well, that from the very beginning American national identity was wrapped up with the sense that in order to create who we were as a nation we had to crush the culture that was already here. That sort of winner-take-all mentality is bred in the bone from the beginning.

That somehow has transferred itself onto gender relations, where there is no middle ground. There's a sense that if you give women an inch they'll take a mile. They always have to be kept in check through extreme means. That's one reason why the rape rate in the United States is fourteen times higher than in England and other cultures that are quite similar to ours in all other ways. Violence is part of proving not only national identity but male identity, the two of which are very hard to separate in this culture.

Do you get accused of being a conspiracy theorist?

I find I do get accused of that all the time, and that's part of the American mentality, too—''Who's to blame? Let's get to the bottom of this and find these three people who organized this thing.'' I mean, Americans love conspiracy theories—Trilateral Commissions and people on the grassy knoll and all that. When the reality is—and I'm sort of baffled by it because it seems so obvious—that far more pernicious than some sort of plot or cabal is that all-pervasive social smog of stereotypes and prejudices. I mean, nobody says that racism is a conspiracy. It's odd.

You once said that within the women's movement, there are things you feel you can't say because you don't want to step on toes. What are those things?

I think I was talking about what happens when you go from being the anonymous journalist to

Feminist leader Betty Friedan (second from left) at an ERA march

being a public figure. In a curious way, becoming a so-called celebrity in American culture silences you. They give you the floor, but then you're suddenly worried about whom you are going to offend. Whereas before, when you're the private journalist, if you're worth anything you want to offend as many people as possible. And that's a very uncomfortable role for me, as a journalist, who would rather, as the Yugoslavian proverb goes, tell the truth and run.

So how do you resolve that tension?

Ultimately, I don't know if it is resolvable. But for me, I try as much as possible to say what I think and be aware when I'm censoring myself and fight it. It's difficult. I think a lot of it goes on at the unconscious level. In many cases, one is simply on the same panel as other people and one doesn't want to offend them. That's just courtesy. But it's very destructive not to be able to argue publicly. For example, I got a lot of flak for criticizing the "difference" wing of feminism, the feminist academics who say that women are special, women are more nurturing, women are more cooperative. I don't agree with that. And I did pick up a sense from some feminists that, no, no, no, you shouldn't be criticizing your sisters. But we're better off for not putting up this false united front. I mean, we're

united in other ways, but by censoring our disagreements or papering them over, we ultimately set ourselves back.

I've also seen a quotation from you in which you refer to your revulsion against the capitalist system—a wonderful comment from a former Wall Street Journal *reporter.*

Yes. somebody called me the next day and said, "Well, I hope you're not planning on returning to the *Wall Street Journal*" Although, actually, I think the *Journal,* putting aside the editorial page which is obviously far to the Right of my beliefs, is much harder on businesses, has written much more critical stories than the average front page of a daily newspaper.

But what about that revulsion for the capitalist system? Why do you feel that way?

I think this goes to the heart of why feminism is so deeply resisted in this country. On one level, feminism is this very uncontroversial idea that women should be treated the same as men, with the same rights and opportunities, the same access to the goodies that a capitalist system provides. But on a much deeper level what feminism is about is not simply plunking a few more women into what was largely a male-designed set of structures and institutions, but it's about overturning the whole applecart and coming up with a way of life that accommodates both sexes, so that it's a more humane and compassionate world.

Source: Susan Faludi with Ruth Conniff, ''Susan Faludi,'' in *Progressive,* Vol. 57, No. 6, June 1993, pp. 35–39.

Sources

Gallagher, Maggie, Review of *Backlash: The Undeclared War against American Women,* in *National Review,* Vol. 44, No. 6, March 30, 1992, pp. 41ff.(2).

Gibbs, Nancy, ''The War against Feminism in Popular Culture, in Politics,'' in *Time,* Vol. 139, No. 10, March 9, 1992, p. 50.

Gibbs, Nancy, and Jeanne McDowell, ''How to Revive a Revolution: Interview with Gloria Steinem and Susan Faludi,'' in *Time,* Vol. 139, No. 10, March 9, 1992, pp. 56ff.(2).

Greene, Gayle, Review of *Backlash: The Undeclared War against American Women,* in *Nation,* Vol. 254, No. 5, February 10, 1992, pp. 166ff.(5).

Kaminer, Wendy, Review of *Backlash: The Undeclared War against American Women,* in *Atlantic Monthly,* Vol. 268, No. 6, December 1991, pp. 123ff.(4).

Lehrman, Karen, Review of *Backlash: The Undeclared War against American Women,* in *New Republic,* Vol. 206, No. 11, March 16, 1992, pp. 30ff.(5).

Morgenson, Gretchen, ''A Whiner's Bible,'' in *Forbes,* Vol. 149, No. 6, March 16, 1992, pp. 152ff.(2).

Norton, Ann, Review of *Backlash: The Undeclared War against American Women,''* in *Whole Earth Review,* No. 75, Summer 1992, p. 110.

Further Reading

Bloom, Allan, *The Closing of the American Mind,* Touchstone Books, 1988.

In this book, University of Chicago professor Allan Bloom expounds on the failings of the American education system. He argues that the social and political crisis of twentieth-century America is truly an intellectual crisis. Some feminists have criticized this book for a dismissive attitude toward women and their professional roles.

Bly, Robert, *Iron John: A Book about Men,* Vintage Books, 1992.

Poet and former anti-war activist Robert Bly was one of the leaders of the men's movement in the 1980s, in which men were encouraged to rediscover their masculinity. This book was one of the critical texts of the movement, providing an examination of what it means to be a man through the story and adventures of the mythical Iron John.

Douglas, Susan J., *Where the Girls Are: Growing Up Female with the Mass Media,* Times Books, 1995.

Susan Douglas has written an analysis of the effects of mass media on American women in the second half of the twentieth century. The book combines hard facts with humor.

Friedan, Betty, *Life So Far,* Simon and Schuster, 2000.

Betty Friedan's autobiography covers her life from her beginning as a labor reporter to her work in founding the National Organization for Women and her work and writings since then.

Gilder, George, *Wealth and Poverty,* Institute for Contemporary Studies, 1993.

This is George Gilder's most well-known book. Considered by conservatives to be a masterpiece, it discusses how to increase wealth and reduce poverty—but many feminists and liberal readers look upon it as a broadside against women's economic roles. Gilder argues that most welfare programs only serve to extend poverty and create victims dependent upon government programs.

Coming of Age in Mississippi

Anne Moody

1968

By the late 1960s, the civil rights movement had seen enormous successes along with tragic losses. Significant anti-discrimination legislation had been passed, but in the view of many civil rights activists, society had not changed enough. The civil rights movement itself was transforming, turning away from the nonviolence of Martin Luther King to a more militant stance epitomized by Malcolm X. Into this confusion, in 1968, Moody published her autobiography, *Coming of Age in Mississippi*. This startling depiction of what it was like to grow up a poor, southern African American captured the attention of Americans around the country, from all social classes and all backgrounds. Moody, intimately involved in the civil rights movement in the first half of 1960s, created an unforgettable image of the inequities and violence that characterized southern society.

Instead of focusing on her years in the civil rights movement, Moody chose to start at the beginning—when she was four years old, the child of poor sharecroppers working for a white farmer. In telling the story of her life, Moody shows why the civil rights movement was such a necessity and the depth of the injustices it had to correct; Moody's autobiography depicts the uphill battle that faced all southern African Americans.

More than thirty years later, Moody's autobiography still retains the power it had for its first readers. Part of the book's long-lasting appeal is its

basic humanity. Despite herself, Moody gets drawn into the fight for civil rights, knowing the challenge is incredibly difficult but knowing she has no other path to take.

Author Biography

Born Essie Mae Moody on September 15, 1940, near Centreville, Mississippi, Moody was the daughter of poor African-American sharecroppers. She was the oldest of nine children. Moody's father left the family when she was only a young child, and her mother supported the family through domestic and restaurant work.

Moody grew up in and around Centreville, where she attended segregated schools. Despite her impoverished circumstances, which led her to work from the fourth grade on, Moody was a good student. She won a basketball scholarship to Natchez Junior College and was in attendance from 1959 through 1961. She then won an academic scholarship to Tugaloo College in Jackson, Mississippi, and received a bachelor of science degree in 1964.

While at Tugaloo, Moody became an activist in the civil rights movement, maintaining involvement with the Congress of Racial Equality (CORE), the Student Nonviolent Coordinating Committee (SNCC), and the National Association for the Advancement of Colored People (NAACP). In 1963, she was one of three young people who staged a sit-in at a segregated Woolworth's lunch counter in Jackson. She also took part in the 1963 march on Washington, D.C.

Moody worked in Canton, Mississippi, for more than a year with CORE to register African-American voters. She faced threats of violence and also was put on the Ku Klux Klan's blacklist during this period. From 1964 through 1965, Moody served as the civil rights and project coordinator at Cornell University.

Becoming disenchanted with certain aspects of the civil rights movement, Moody moved to New York City, where she began to write her autobiography, *Coming of Age in Mississippi*, which was published in 1968. The book has received several national awards.

Aside from her autobiography, Moody has only published one other work, *Mr. Death: Four Stories* (1975). Moody has also worked as a counselor for the New York City Poverty Program.

Plot Summary

Childhood

The narrator of *Coming of Age in Mississippi*, Anne Moody (born Essie Mae) spends her first four years in a sharecropper's shack on a plantation owned by a white farmer. Her parents work long hours in the fields. Daddy begins gambling and takes up with another woman, and eventually he deserts the family. Mama and the children move off the plantation, closer to the town of Centreville. Mama supports the family through domestic and restaurant work but often does not earn enough money even for food.

By the time Anne is in the fourth grade, she works regularly after school and on weekends to help support her family. They move into a house that Mama's boyfriend, Raymond, builds for them. Eventually, Raymond and Mama marry, but Raymond is unable to provide for the ever-growing family. Despite working many hours to help support the family, Anne continues to excel in school. She makes top grades, starts playing basketball, and is elected homecoming queen.

High School

As Anne enters high school, a fourteen-year-old African-American boy is killed for whistling at a white woman. Anne realizes that she has overlooked the racial problems and violence that surround her. She now fears "being killed just because I was black." After the murder, Anne overhears Mrs. Burke and her "guild meeting" discuss the NAACP, and she finds out from her teacher that this organization is trying to improve the situation for southern African Americans. She feels hatred toward almost everyone: whites who kill African Americans and African Americans for not doing anything to stop these actions. The tensions between the white and black communities of Centreville escalate, resulting in the beating of one of Anne's classmates and the deliberate setting of a fire that kills almost an entire family.

These events, and the talk surrounding them, upset Anne greatly, so she goes to spend the summer with Uncle Ed, who lives in New Orleans. When she returns to Centreville, she learns of more racial problems that end with a cousin of hers being run out of town. When she asks her family about it, they just get angry and refuse to talk. Anne gets the feeling that Raymond hates her.

To take her mind off her problems, Anne becomes very busy with studies, extracurricular activities, and work. She also begins to tutor Mrs. Burke's son, Wayne, and his white friends in math. Wayne and Anne become friends, which makes Mrs. Burke angry and nervous. Wayne and Mrs. Burke fight over his relationship with Anne, and Anne quits working for Mrs. Burke after she implies that either Anne or her brother stole from her. Over the next few years, Anne finds work with other people and goes to New Orleans in the summers. She works hard to save money for college.

At the start of her last year in high school, Anne realizes that Raymond has started to desire her sexually. The tension escalates, and one day Anne gets into a fight with Raymond and leaves home. She goes to stay with her father and his wife, Emma, for the last six weeks of school. At first, she gets along well there. However, Emma, housebound because of an injury, starts treating Anne poorly. Two days after her high school graduation, Anne leaves town.

College

Anne gets a basketball scholarship to a two-year junior college in Mississippi. Anne feels like college is a prison. During her second year, Anne meets her first boyfriend, a popular basketball player. She also leads a boycott of the school cafeteria, her first act of political activism.

Anne receives a scholarship to the best African-American senior college in the state, Tugaloo College, where she joins the local NAACP chapter. Tugaloo students are involved in demonstrations throughout Jackson. Anne becomes so involved in her NAACP activities that her grades drop. Anne is then recruited to help register African-American voters in the Mississippi Delta. As Anne and her coworkers convince African Americans to listen to their views, for the first time, she thinks that something can be done to change the way that whites treat African Americans.

The Movement

In her senior year, Anne becomes increasingly involved with the civil rights movement, canvassing and giving speeches. Along with two other students, Anne stages a sit-in at the Woolworth's lunch counter. Despite being physically and verbally abused by the gathering white mob, the students, joined by other demonstrators—some white—remain at the lunch counter for several hours, until the manager of

Woolworth's decides to close the store early. When Anne and her friends leave the store, they discover about ninety police officers, none of whom has prevented the mob violence.

Many more demonstrations take place throughout Jackson. Anne gets arrested for her participation and, along with hundreds of other students, is jailed. Following the event, Anne receives letters from her family and learns for the first time that her actions are causing problems for her family back in Centreville.

Jackson becomes the hotbed of racial agitation. Civil rights leader Medgar Evers is shot to death. Anne and the other workers launch a protest march and are arrested. Thousands of African Americans attend Evers's funeral, and a demonstration ensues. Evers's murder contributes to the confusion and infighting between civil rights organizations.

Anne decides to work at the CORE offices in Canton, Mississippi, though she is warned by local civil rights leaders against doing so. Anne and the other workers face an uphill battle in registering voters. African Americans who support their activities or try to register are often threatened with violence or fired from their jobs. Many African Americans fail the voter registration tests as well. The CORE workers are also threatened with violence.

In August 1963, Anne attends the March on Washington, D.C. Then, on September 15, she learns of the Birmingham church bombing, which kills four young girls. This crime causes Anne to question the movement's nonviolent tactics. However, she continues her work in Canton. When high school students hold a rally, the police begin to harass the CORE workers on an almost-nightly basis. Anne finds out that she has been placed on a Ku Klux Klan blacklist, which makes her even more nervous. She begins to fear for her own life, as well as for her family back in Centreville.

Anne decides to take a break from her work and go to New Orleans to work and live with her sister, Adline. Mama, whom Anne has not seen in several years, comes to visit; however, she and Anne have little to say to each other. The assassination of President John F. Kennedy in November 1963 encourages Anne to participate in CORE activities in New Orleans, but she finds it just as hard to register voters in the city as it has been in Canton.

In May, Anne returns to Tugaloo for graduation, where she learns of plans for an upcoming voter registration drive, so-called Freedom Summer, for which northern college students will come south to help. Anne visits Canton, where the CORE workers have organized Freedom Day to take place. During this march, the police brutally attack a boy, drawing the crowd to the brink of violence and almost putting an end to the protest.

After graduation, Anne returns briefly to New Orleans but then goes back to Canton. However, she is depressed by the situation African Americans face. When she gets to the CORE offices, she finds a bus is about to leave for Washington, D.C., transporting African Americans who will testify in congressional hearings about racial discrimination and injustice in the South. Without hesitation, Anne joins the group on the bus. While the others are singing "We Shall Overcome," Anne thinks about all the violence the whites have bestowed upon the African Americans. She wonders if African Americans will ever achieve their goal of racial justice.

Key Figures

Miss Adams

Miss Adams is the basketball coach at Natchez College. She rules her team strictly, and unlike the rest of the students, Anne speaks up for her rights. Because of Anne's actions, Miss Adams is forced to treat the girls more fairly.

Mrs. Burke

Anne meets Mrs. Burke, "one of the meanest white women in town," while working for Mrs. Burke's daughter, Linda Jean Jenkins. Mrs. Burke thinks that Linda Jean treats Anne too well and constantly tries to convince her to change this behavior. Anne goes to work for Mrs. Burke after Jenkins moves away. While Anne forces her into certain concessions, such as allowing her to use the front door, Mrs. Burke remains bigoted in her beliefs. She also helps stir up other white women against Centreville's African-American community.

Wayne Burke

Wayne is Mrs. Burke's son. He is in the same grade as Anne. During the tenth grade, Anne starts to tutor Wayne and his friends in mathematics, and the two teenagers become friends. Their relationship angers Mrs. Burke a great deal.

Ed Cassidy

Ed Cassidy is the sheriff of Centreville. He is known among the African-American community as the "quiet nigger hater." Despite this label, Anne finds herself turning to him when she runs away from Raymond and Mama's home.

Mr. C. O. Chinn

When Anne arrives in Canton, C. O. Chinn and his wife, restaurant owners, are the wealthiest African Americans in town. C. O. is a powerful man in the town. The African Americans respect him, and the whites fear him. His support of the civil rights workers brings more African Americans to the cause. Because of his involvement, however, C. O. loses his business. At the end of the memoir, Chinn is serving on a chain gang. Despite his difficult situation, when he sees Anne, he waves and tries to look happy.

Mrs. Chinn

Along with her husband, Mrs. Chinn owns a successful restaurant in Canton. She becomes involved with the CORE movement, which leads the Chinns to lose their business. She is very supportive of Anne and the work that she and her colleagues are doing, but by the end of *Coming of Age in Mississippi*, she is depressed with the situation in Canton; the African Americans are afraid to demonstrate, her husband is in jail, and the police are harassing her. She tells Anne, "We ain't big enough to do it by ourselves," a sentiment that Anne seems to take to heart.

Mrs. Claiborne

Mrs. Clairborne is one of the kinder white women for whom Anne works. Mrs. Clairborne and her husband treat Anne with respect, inviting her to sit at the dinner table with them and supporting her efforts in school.

Daddy

Anne's father deserts his family when Anne is only four. From that point on, until her senior year in high school, he has little contact with his three children. Anne lives with him and his wife Emma during the final weeks of high school, and he is pleased to have the chance to spend time with her. The two develop a caring relationship.

Dave Dennis

Dave Dennis is a CORE worker. He works with Anne in Jackson and in Canton.

Diddly

See Daddy

Emma

Emma is Daddy's second wife. Anne goes to live with Daddy and Emma after she leaves home in high school. Emma is a strong, smart woman, and at first, Anne respects her. However, housebound with an injury, Emma starts to feel sorry for herself and takes out her frustration on Anne. Anne and Emma continue their relationship after she moves out of the house, and Emma gives Anne money when she is able to do so.

Doris Erskine

Doris Erskine is a CORE member. She works with Anne in Jackson and decides to join her friend in Canton. However, the threat of violence that she continuously feels there makes her nervous and she irritates Anne.

Medgar Evers

Medgar Evers is the NAACP field secretary. Anne gets to know him during her work in Jackson. Edgers is killed by a white assassin in 1963. His murder scares some civil rights leaders.

Mrs. Linda Jean Jenkins

Anne works for Linda Jean Jenkins, Mrs. Burke's daughter. Linda Jean is a kind, liberal woman. She treats and pays Anne well. Anne is allowed to call Linda Jean by her first name.

Jerry

Jerry is a classmate of Anne's who is beaten by a group of white men. This beating, which results from tensions stirred up by the white "guild" members, worries Centreville's African-American committee.

Reverend King

Reverend King comes to Tugaloo as the new minister. At first Anne mistrusts him because he is white. However, Reverend King takes part in many demonstrations and proves himself a person worthy of respect. Reverend King and Anne become close during their civil rights work.

Lenora

Lenora is from Canton, but she is thrown off the plantation where her father works after voicing frustration over racial injustice. She comes to live and work at Freedom House with Anne.

Mama

Mama is Anne's mother. As the autobiography begins, she is the mother of two children and a field worker. She has little time to spend with her children, even less after her husband deserts her. Mama has the responsibility of raising the children alone and takes various jobs as a maid and a restaurant worker. She relies on other members of her family to help out watching the children, when they can, but she gets little financial support from others.

Mama begins a long-term affair with Raymond, which results in six more children and their eventual marriage. Although Raymond helps Mama and the family by building a house for them, his family, among whom they live, treats Mama with disdain. Mama is perpetually unhappy because of this. Raymond also turns out to be unable to make a living, and as the family expands, more financial responsibility falls on Mama. After Anne leaves home in her senior year, Mama begs her to return. When Mama comes to Anne's high school graduation, Anne sees that her mother appears to have aged many years in just six weeks.

After Anne becomes involved in the civil rights movement, she tries to get her mother involved. Instead, Mama writes her letters asking her to stop such activity and telling her that if she continues, she will not be able to come back to Centreville. Mama continues to write such letters over the next few years. When Mama comes to New Orleans for a visit, Anne and her mother have not seen each other in two years. Although Anne feels the love her mother has for her, the two women are unable to get past their barriers, and they find little connection.

Adline Moody

Adline is Anne's younger sister by about three and a half years. Adline is unlike Anne; as a child, she shows little interest in schoolwork and as an adult, she lacks Anne's discontent with the plight of southern African Americans. Adline and Anne become reacquainted in New Orleans, when Anne takes a break from her CORE work. At first, Adline is uninterested in the mistreatment of African Americans or in improving herself. By the time Anne moves out of the apartment, however, it seems that Anne's accomplishment may inspire Adline to achieve goals herself, such as graduating college.

Anne Moody

Anne Moody narrates her autobiography. She is born to a poor, rural southern African-American family. Although she grows up in abject poverty, Anne is always determined to better herself. She studies hard and makes excellent grades in school. She starts working when she is only in the fourth grade, and she gives some money toward the upkeep of her family, but she also starts saving for college.

When Anne is fifteen years old, Emmett Till is murdered. This example of racial violence sparks Anne's awareness of the social injustice that pervades the South. She comes to hate everyone: whites for treating African Americans so badly, and African Americans, for not standing up for their rights. She learns about the NAACP from a teacher, but this teacher also tells her to take her mind off the killings and beating because the African-American community in Centreville won't take action against such mistreatment. Anne tries to subvert her thoughts by joining many extracurricular activities, such as dance, piano, and basketball. However, she remains acutely aware of the racial violence and tensions that go on in the town, more so than most of the people around her. She plans to leave Centreville as soon as she graduates from high school.

Anne's skill at basketball wins her a scholarship to junior college, which she attends for two years. She has her first experience with social activism at Natchez College, when she leads a boycott of the school cafeteria. Her high grades win her a full-tuition scholarship to Tugaloo College in Jackson, Mississippi, where Anne gets involved with the NAACP. She participates in demonstrations, makes trips to the Mississippi Delta, and is one of three students to stage a sit-in at a segregated lunch counter in Jackson. She is arrested and verbally abused repeatedly for her activities.

Dismayed by the infighting among Jackson's civil rights organizations, Anne volunteers to go to Canton, Mississippi, to work in the voter registration campaign. She thinks she and her fellow CORE workers have a good chance of success because there are so many more African Americans in Canton than there are whites. However, throughout her year in Canton, she is often disillusioned by the attitude of the African Americans. They live in poverty and are scared by the violence of the whites. While in Canton, Anne finds out that she has been placed on a Klan blacklist.

After a year in Canton, Anne goes to New Orleans, unsure if she is leaving the movement for good. However, she finds that she cannot tolerate the air of contentment that surrounds her; she knows that African Americans are being treated unfairly, even if no one else does. After her college graduation, Anne boards a bus for Washington, D.C., with other civil rights workers to testify at congressional hearings on racial inequities in the South. Despite making this journey, Anne wonders if she and her fellow African Americans will ever achieve freedom.

Elmira Moody

See Mama

Essie Mae Moody

See Anne Moody

Fred Moody

See Daddy

Grandfather Moody

Grandfather Moody takes care of the children while Mama is at work. He is ashamed of the way his son treats his family and helps out the family with money.

Miss Ola

Miss Ola is an elderly woman who lives in one of the homes where Mama works. She reads to Anne and helps her with her schoolwork. She teaches Anne how to read, write, and spell.

Miss Pearl

Miss Pearl is Raymond's mother. A mulatto, she dislikes Mama, whose skin is much darker than her own. She treats Mama meanly despite her long relationship with Raymond, which is one of the reasons that Anne comes to dislike Raymond so much.

Raymond

Raymond, a former soldier, is Mama's second husband and the father of six of her children. Raymond fails as a farmer and fails to find decent work. When Anne is in high school, he begins to have sexual thoughts about her, which leads Anne to leave the house permanently. After she has left,

Raymond does not allow Mama to give Anne any money.

George Raymond

George Raymond works with Anne in Canton.

Mrs. Rice

Mrs. Rice is a high school teacher who tells Anne about the NAACP. She also teaches Anne about the way that whites have historically treated southern African Americans. Although Mrs. Rice became ''something like a mother'' to Anne, she gets fired at the end of the year, and Anne never sees her again.

Emmett Till

Emmett Till is fourteen years old when he is killed by a white lynch mob for whistling at a white woman. His murder makes Anne become aware of racial injustice and the problems that African Americans face in the South.

Toosweet

See Mama.

Joan Trumpauer

Joan Trumpauer is a white student who serves as a secretary for SNCC. She asks Anne to participate in the voter registration drive that the organization is starting in the Mississippi Delta. Over the next few years, Joan and Anne work together and become friends.

Themes

Racism

Moody's development and life are greatly shaped by the tremendous amount of racial discrimination and prejudice that African Americans face in the South at the time she is growing up. In the 1940 and 1950s, before Anne joins the civil rights movement, African Americans lacked many essential rights, such as the right to obtain an education equal to those offered to white children, and were often unable to exercise those rights they had, such as the

right to vote. The African-American population of Mississippi face racial injustice in different ways. Most African Americans are relegated to low-paying, menial jobs; schools have inadequate facilities; and African-American farmers are not allowed to produce enough on their land to make a decent living. African Americans also face prejudice in the form of violence. *Coming of Age in Mississippi* provides many examples of beatings and murders inflicted upon African Americans. The provocation for these crimes often stems from wanting to intimidate African Americans or to punish them for doing something that goes against the segregationist codes of the South. The white police force does nothing to prevent these crimes and even participates in them at times.

Some whites in the book are openly and unquestionably racist, such as Mrs. Burke. Like so many other whites, Mrs. Burke thinks that African Americans are inferior and undeserving of proper treatment, and she wants her only contact with them to be in an employer-employee relationship. Other whites whom Anne meets support her as well as the African-American cause. Miss Ola, Mrs. Claiborne, Linda Jean Jenkins, and Mrs. Burke's mother are all people who treat Anne with respect. Revered King, his wife, and Joan Trombauer are examples of whites who work hard and risk their own safety to secure civil rights for African Americans.

However, the African-American community also is racially prejudiced. The mulatto population often looks down on the darker African-American population. Miss Pearl, a ''yellow'' woman with straight hair, dislikes Mama because her skin color is dark. Anne almost turns down the scholarship to Tugaloo because she hears that all the other students are mulattos and fears that they will mistreat her.

Poverty

Anne and her family live in severe poverty. Until they move into the house that Raymond built, Anne never feels like she has lived in a real home. In this home, they have furniture and live in more than two rooms. However, Mama is unable to earn enough money to care for the family well. Meals often consist of bread or beans; meat is an almost unheard-of luxury. When Anne is in junior high school, she has no money to buy school clothes and almost does not attend homecoming, though she is queen, because she does not have the money to buy a dress. Anne also comments on the poverty that she

Topics for Further Study

- *Coming of Age in Mississippi* is divided into four sections. Which do you think is the most powerful section? Why?

- Find out more about urban and rural southern society in the 1940s and 1950s, prior to the beginning of the civil rights movement. Compare and contrast these two environments.

- Conduct research to find out more about a specific aspect or leader of the civil rights movement, such as desegregating Central High School in Little Rock or Martin Luther King, Jr. Write a report analyzing your selected topic or person in terms of the overall movement.

- Find out more about the murder of Emmett Till, Louis Allen, or Medgar Evers. Write an article about this incident that might have appeared in a liberal northern newspaper at the time.

- Watch a movie depicting the civil rights era, such as *Mississippi Burning,* which is about Freedom Summer, or *The Ghosts of Mississippi,* which is about bringing the killer of Medgar Evers to justice. Then conduct research on some of the events portrayed in the movie and write a critique of the film with regard to its historical accuracy.

- Find out about the significant events of the civil rights movement that took place after spring of 1964. Write an epilogue to *Coming of Age in Mississippi* that summarizes these events and their effects on southern African Americans.

- Find out how northern politicians in the 1950s and 1960s responded to the civil rights movement and African-American demands for equality. Write a report on their support, or lack of support, of the civil rights movement.

---

sees in other African-American families. With her first paycheck from CORE, Anne buys school clothes and supplies for two girls who are unable to attend school without these necessities. She sees in these girls echoes of her own life.

Family

In *Coming of Age in Mississippi*, Moody presents a number of estranged families, including Moody's own. Her childhood lacks any positive example of a family; her father deserts the family for another women, and her mother eventually marries a man whose family disrespects and dislikes her. As a teenager, Moody also feels sexually threatened by her stepfather, which causes her to leave home when she is still in high school. Moody sees her natural father rarely throughout her life. She also does not develop close ties with any of her eight brothers or sisters.

The only positive example of a family that Moody has is Emma's kin. In the weeks that she

lives with Emma and Daddy, Moody often goes with them to visit Emma's relatives. Walking inside the family café, Moody immediately "felt the closeness of Emma's family."

When Moody joins the civil rights movement, her actions have serious repercussions on her relationship with her family, which is already strained. She finds herself completely cut off from them. She cannot send letters home, for fear they will bring violence upon the family, nor can she visit. Her mother, however, sends her numerous letters asking her to quit the work and pointing out that Moody is putting her family in danger. When Moody leaves Canton and goes to New Orleans, she sees several family members for the first time in years. While she becomes reacquainted with her sister Adline, with whom she shares an apartment, and her brother Junior, her grandmother won't let her in the house. Mama also comes to visit, but she and Moody have little to say to each other. Moody's isolation hits her most strongly when she attends her college graduation and has no members of her family present, especially since she anticipates that her feeling of being alone will only get worse.

Style

Autobiography

Coming of Age in Mississippi is Moody's fictionalized autobiography, which means that Moody uses fictional and novelistic techniques, such as recreating conversations and presenting events in greater detail than she could possibly remember, to tell the story of her life. Her autobiography covers her life from her earliest memories, when she was about four, until 1963, when she headed to Washington, D.C. It is likely that she chose to end her autobiography at that point because later that year she went to Ithaca, New York, to coordinate civil rights efforts. Thus, *Coming of Age in Mississippi* encompasses her entire civil rights career in the South.

Although the essential events of *Coming of Age in Mississippi* are indisputable, Moody uses authorial liberty to shape them. For instance, she chooses to describe certain events in detail, such as the Woolworth sit-in, while at other times she glides over entire years of her life. This method allows Moody to emphasize what she considers to be the most formative events over the twenty-three years about which she is writing.

Dialect and Dialogue

Moody renders the poor, rural, African-American speech that was commonplace to her background in the 1940s through 1960s. Moody captures nuances of speech such as saying, "Mama them" instead of "Mama and them." She uses standard jargon, such as calling African Americans who kowtow to white people "Toms." The figures in the story rarely speak with proper grammar or enunciation. Even the well-educated Moody demonstrates many lapses in grammar though scenes between her and other CORE members show that she can speak perfect English when she wants. At times, however, she and her colleagues play upon the dialects that surround them. When Lenora and Doris bring guns back to Freedom House, they respond with strong accents to Moody's questions. "'I's ooilin' mah gun,'" says Lenora, and "'This heah baby is a takin' a nap,'" says Doris. Their playfulness in light of a serious incident annoys Moody, and they revert to their more customary way of speaking.

Setting

The setting of *Coming of Age in Mississippi* is the Deep South of the 1940s through early 1960s. This is a region marked by deeply ingrained racism. African Americans have many rights in the law books but in daily life are still enchained by prejudice. Southern society discriminates against them; for the most part, the only jobs available to African Americans are menial ones such as domestics or factory workers. Moody notes that even though she has a college education, the only professional career open to her is teaching.

The physical location where the African Americans live and work further points out the racial injustice inherent to this setting. Her life begins in a sharecropper's shack on a white farmer's plantation. For the most part, her succeeding homes are flimsy, decrepit shacks in neighborhoods that usually lack paved streets and sidewalks. The African-American community in and around Canton, Mississippi, suffers in the same manner. Although African Americans in Canton own a great deal of land, laws prevent them from farming it, so they continue to be tied to the land of white farmers, as they have been for decades.

Historical Context

African Americans in the 1940s

World War II offered increasing economic opportunities for many African Americans as the war machine demanded soldiers and factory workers. Almost one million African-American soldiers served in the armed forces; however, they were forced to serve in segregated units. Most were kept out of combat. Although at first many war plants would not hire African Americans or would only hire them as janitors, the 1941 Fair Employment Practices Committee changed this practice. It helped protect African Americans from employment discrimination. An executive order issued two years later required nondiscrimination clauses in all war contracts. Over time, many African-American workers moved into better-paying industrial jobs.

In the aftermath of World War II, many Americans lost their jobs to returning veterans, and African Americans were particularly affected. Their situation was further worsened when Congress abolished the Fair Employment Practices Committee. African Americans throughout the nation faced

Compare & Contrast

- **1950s:** Before 1965, fewer than six percent of African Americans in Mississippi are registered to vote.

  1960s: After the passage of the Voting Rights Act of 1965, thousands of southern African Americans register to vote. By 1968, some fifty-nine percent of eligible African-American voters in Mississippi are registered.

  Today: In the late 1990s, of the total 1,975,000 of Mississippi voters, 670,000 are African American. Overall in the United States, 23.5 million African Americans are registered to vote, but only 63.5 percent report having voted in the 1996 presidential election.

- **1950s:** Prior to 1962, universities and colleges in the South are not open to African Americans. As they are forced to do at the lower educational levels, African Americans attend their own schools.

  1960s: In 1962, a court order forces the University of Mississippi to admit African-American James Meredith. When he arrives on campus, a riot breaks out. Flanked by armed guards, Meredith attends classes for the rest of the year. He graduates in 1963.

  Today: Affirmative action, a policy that seeks to redress past discrimination through active measures to ensure equal opportunity, is undergoing challenges in the U. S. court system. Opponents claim that affirmative action in school admission policy is illegal because race is being used as a factor in judging applicants. In the late 1990s and early 2000, the admissions policies of several graduate schools are found to be unconstitutional. However, polls reveal that the majority of Americans support affirmative action programs in school admissions policies.

- **1940s and 1950s:** As they have long been doing, white state officials use unfair election rules, poll taxes, literacy tests, and threats of violence and loss of jobs to prevent many southern African Americans from voting or even registering to vote.

  1960s: The Voting Rights Act of 1965 gives the federal government the power to inspect voter registration procedures and to protect all citizens' right to vote.

  Today: The presidential election of 2000 brought about charges of voter disenfranchisement and civil rights abuses. In the aftermath of the election, the U. S. Commission on Civil Rights approves an investigative report that finds the 2000 presidential race in Florida has been marred by injustice. The report states that African-American voters were nine times more likely than white voters to have their ballots discarded as invalid.

- **1940s and 1950s:** African-American labor leader A. Philip Randolph protests lower pay of African Americans in industrial jobs and segregation in the armed forces. His efforts and his threats to organize massive marches on Washington, D.C., help reverse these policies. Throughout the 1950s, the National Association for the Advancement of Colored People (NAACP) focuses on abolishing segregation in public schools in the United States. Civil rights leaders also work to desegregate public transportation systems in the South.

  1960s: African-American civil rights leaders continue their hard work to desegregate all aspects of society, to ensure equal access to jobs and educational opportunities, and to register African-American voters. Their efforts bring about the passage of the Civil Rights Act of 1964 as well as the Voting Rights Act of 1965.

  Today: Despite the progress made in desegregating and equalizing American society, many minorities still feel they lack equal opportunities. A survey conducted in 2001 shows that 87 percent of all African Americans polled said that they still lack full civil rights and that more work needs to be done.

segregation in schools and public places as well as discrimination in housing and employment. Lynchings also continued to take place, particularly in the South. In 1946, civil rights groups urged President Harry S. Truman to take action against racism in American society. Truman responded by creating the multiracial Committee on Civil Rights. The committee's report, published the following year, documented widespread discrimination, civil rights abuses, and violence perpetrated against African Americans. Based on these findings, Truman urged Congress to pass an antilynching law and an anti-poll-tax measure. He worked to end discrimination in federal agencies and the military by banning discrimination in hiring, and he desegregated the military. He also took steps to end employment discrimination by companies holding government contracts.

The Civil Rights Movement in the 1950s

In the 1950s African Americans began to more actively demand their civil rights. The National Association for the Advancement of Colored People (NAACP) had long sought to end segregation in education. The 1952 Supreme Court case *Brown v. Board of Education of Topeka* successfully overturned the "separate but equal" doctrine that had long allowed segregation in public schools. Despite this ruling, by the end of the 1956–1957 school year, most southern schools remained segregated. The school board of Little Rock, Arkansas, was the first in the South to announce that it would follow the *Brown* decision. Nine African-American students were chosen to attend Little Rock's Central High. They faced a mob of angry whites and a line of state-sanction, armed National Guardsmen when they tried to go to school. Guarded by one thousand federal troops, sent by President Dwight D. Eisenhower, the African-American students entered the school, desegregating Central High. The first African-American student graduated from Little Rock's Central High in 1958.

Civil rights leaders also determined to end segregation on southern transportation systems. To challenge the practice of forcing African Americans to ride in the back of city buses, they organized Montgomery's African Americans in a citywide boycott. For close to a year, the African-American population refused to ride the public bus system. In 1956, the Supreme Court declared such segregation laws unconstitutional. By the end of the year, Montgomery had a desegregated bus system. President Dwight D. Eisenhower also passed the Civil Rights Act of 1957—the first civil rights law passed since Reconstruction—making it a federal crime to prevent any qualified person from voting.

Through his role in the Montgomery bus boycott, Martin Luther King Jr., a young Baptist minister, emerged as an important leader in the fight for civil rights. He believed in the use of nonviolent resistance in protests. Some of the earliest protests were sit-ins launched at segregated lunch counters throughout the South, beginning in 1958. More than 50,000 students, African-American and white, took part in such protests, and by the end of 1960, most restaurants were integrated.

The Civil Rights Movement in the 1960s

By the 1960s, several civil rights organizations were active. Congress of Racial Equality (CORE), a northern-based, integrated civil rights group, worked to end segregation in bus facilities, which was ruled illegal by the Supreme Court in 1960. The following year, CORE organized black and white Freedom Riders to travel through the South on public buses. When they reached Alabama, they were attacked by white mobs. In Jackson, Mississippi, state officials arrested the riders. Student Nonviolent Coordinating Committee (SNCC) then sent in new riders to take their place. Over the summer, more than three hundred riders traveled the South to protest segregation. Their actions helped persuade the Interstate Commerce Commission to strengthen its desegregation regulations, and segregation in interstate buses ceased to exist by 1963.

Civil rights workers also had success in desegregating public universities. A violent attack on 1,000 youths marching peacefully in Birmingham, Alabama, in 1963 led to increased support for the civil rights movement. President John F. Kennedy determined to take a stand on civil rights. Civil rights leaders called for the March on Washington, D.C., which drew more than 200,000 people to the nation's capital, to encourage passage of civil rights legislation. The resulting Civil Rights Act of 1964 barred discrimination in employment and public accommodations, and it gave the Justice Department the power to enforce school desegregation.

Registering Voters

Other civil rights activists turned their attention to voter registration. They chose to begin their work in Mississippi, where African Americans made up about forty percent of the population in the state, but only five percent of eligible African-American adults were registered to vote. State officials used a variety of means to prevent them from registering, such as poll taxes, literacy tests, intimidation, and violence. SNCC organizers believed that the state was key to their efforts to get rid of racial discrimination.

McComb, Mississippi, a town of 12,000 citizens with only 250 registered African-American voters, was their first target. Robert Moses of SNCC arrived there in July 1961. In less than a month he had registered six voters as well as been jailed, beaten, and chased by an angry mob. Violence increased with the murder of Herbert Lee, who had worked as Moses's driver. Despite evidence to the contrary, Lee's murder was ruled an act of self-defense. In the midst of arrest and mob attacks, the McComb voter registration drive came to an end.

Although activists continued the drive, the intimidation tactics practiced by southern whites kept many African Americans from registering. In 1963, the Council of Federated Organizations (COFO) conducted two mock elections to show that African Americans in Mississippi were interested in voting. Some 27,000 African Americans voted in the first election and some 80,000—four times the number of registered African-American voters in the state—voted in the second election. In 1963, SNCC decided to recruit white volunteers from northern colleges to come to Mississippi to help in the voter registration efforts. These activists launched Freedom Summer in 1964 and rallied African Americans in Mississippi and in Alabama to register to vote. Their actions, and the violence with which whites met these workers, contributed to the passage of the Voting Rights Act of 1965, which put the voter registration process under federal control and greatly increased the number of registered African-American voters in the South.

Critical Overview

Coming of Age in Mississippi was published in 1968 to overwhelmingly enthusiastic acclaim. Around the country, journalists, reviewers, even politicians, remarked upon Moody's stirring story and the historic chain of events to which she bore witness. Senator Edward M. Kennedy became the spokesperson for the *New York Times* with his 1969 review in which he declared that *Coming of Age*

in Mississippi was "a history of our time, seen from the bottom up, through the eyes of someone who decided for herself that things had to be changed." Kennedy was certainly not alone in his thinking. C. N. Degler also remarked in the *Nation* on the timeliness and importance of Moody's work: "Though the author of this autobiography is only twenty-eight years old, her life has already spanned the revolution that has . . . made racial equality the central issue of our time."

Coming of Age in Mississippi was successful because it evoked for so many readers a picture of a world they could not heretofore imagine. Moody's autobiography brought to life the rampant discrimination and violence inflicted upon southern African Americans on a daily basis, as well as the lengths to which whites would go to perpetuate this oppression. Many reviewers commented on the truthful ring of Moody's prose. Wrote Degler, "Moody's candor and refusal to overdramatize create an air of verisimilitude that is the book's signal achievement." Kennedy asserted that in her work, Moody was "personalizing poverty and degradation and making it more real than any study or statistic could have done."

Although an audience for *Coming of Age in Mississippi* may have developed out of interest in the civil rights movement, which had taken particularly violent turns the summer before the book was published, many readers also appreciated it for its portrayal of the rural southern African-American world. Mary Ellmann maintained in *Nation,* "The first section, Childhood, is different from, and better than, all the rest. . . . It hits the page like a natural force, crude and undeniable and, against all principles of beauty, beautiful." Shane Stevens went much further with his praise in *Book World:* "Some [books] have tried to sketch a picture of these years from the American black man's point of view. *Coming of Age in Mississippi* is, quite simply, one of the very best of them."

However, the attention that Moody's autobiography drew to the civil rights movement, at a time when an American would be hard-pressed to ignore it, was perhaps more important. For, as Senator Kennedy noted, even in 1969 discrimination and inequity still prevailed. In closing his review, Kennedy admonished, "Anne Moody's powerful and moving book is a timely reminder that we cannot now relax in the struggle for sound justice in America or in any part of America. We would do so at our peril."

In the years since its initial publication, *Coming of Age in Mississippi* has evolved into a staple on college reading lists and a key text to understanding the civil rights movement in the United States. While Moody herself moved outside of that sphere, her enduring work has placed her presence and influence firmly within the movement.

Criticism

Rena Korb

Korb has a master's degree in English literature and creative writing and has written for a wide variety of educational publishers. In the following essay, she explores the pervading racism that characterized the southern United States prior to the Civil Rights movement of the 1960s.

Coming of Age in Mississippi is a stark testimony to the racial injustice that characterized the southern United States until the civil rights movements of the 1960s brought lasting changes to the region. African Americans had been given full voting and citizenship rights after the Civil War, but with the exception of a brief period immediately following this conflict, many southern African Americans were unable to enjoy these rights for close to one hundred years. The southern world into which Moody was born in 1940 was one ruled by whites. Her autobiography is filled with incidents that serve as a reminder of this disheartening truth. Seen as a whole, they can help explain Moody's lack of optimism as expressed at the end of *Coming of Age in Mississippi* and her departure from the civil rights movement, which had already occurred by the time she wrote her autobiography.

The racial oppression that Moody describes is insidious because it is so pervasive a part of southern society. Mississippi is a state where a member of the legislature can kill an African American "without provocation" and still be found to have acted in self-defense. The majority of adult African Americans, in Centreville and other rural areas, have come to accept this oppression and try to avoid bringing the anger of the whites upon themselves. They often speak of African Americans who have been killed by whites as going on to a better place in heaven. As a young child, Moody hears adults talking about "Negroes found floating in a river or dead somewhere with their bodies riddled with bullets." The only explanation given to her is that an "Evil

James Farmer, co-founder of the Congress of Racial Equality (CORE) walking next to a picketer. Moody was involved with CORE while a student at Tugaloo College

Spirit" killed these people. Moody is left to figure out for herself that this Evil Spirit is actually the white southerner.

Moody comes to comprehend the African American's place in the white world at the age of fourteen. At this time, Emmett Till, a fourteen years old from Chicago, is killed. Although other teenagers have heard about his murder, Moody is taken by surprise. She recalls how she suddenly "realized I didn't really know what was going on all around me." The African-American complicity in ignoring the murder, which arises out of justifiable fear, is inherent in Mama's reaction: she gets angry when Moody asks about Till's murder and refuses to talk about it. Her reason for doing so is clear when she says, "Eddie them better watch how they go around here talking. These white folks git a hold of it they gonna be in trouble." In contrast to Mama, the racist Mrs. Burke is more than willing to talk about the murder. She explains to Moody that Till was "killed because he got out of his place with a white woman." Perhaps she sees some suggestion of anger on Moody's face, for when Mrs. Burke learns that Moody is the same

What Do I Read Next?

- *Mr. Death: Four Stories* (1975) is Moody's only other published work.

- Richard Wright's autobiography *Black Boy* (1945) uses fictional and novelistic techniques to describe Wright's youth in Mississippi and Tennessee. It is widely considered to be one of his finest works.

- Albert French's novel *Billy* (1995) takes place in rural Mississippi in the 1930s. When ten-year-old Billy accidentally kills a white teenager, he is placed on trial in a courtroom that shows the degree of racism and injustice prevalent in the South at that time.

- *Lay Bare the Heart: An Autobiography of the Civil Rights* (1985) is James Farmer's award-winning contribution to literature of the civil rights movement. Farmer, who founded CORE in 1942, conveys the struggle that he and other civil rights leaders went through to achieve their important goals.

- *I've Got the Light of Freedom: The Organizing Tradition and the Mississippi Freedom Struggle* (1996), by Charles M. Payne, emphasizes the grassroots organization and the individuals involved in the civil rights struggle in Mississippi.

- The Pulitzer Prize–winning *To Kill a Mockingbird* (1961), by Harper Lee, tells the story of a small-town southern lawyer who defends an African-American man accused of raping a white woman.

- *A Way Out of No Way: Writings about Growing Up Black in America* (1996), edited by Jacqueline Wilson, collects works by African-American writers, including Langston Hughes, James Baldwin, Toni Morrison, and Jamaica Kincaid. The pieces deal with such issues as family, race, and coming of age.

---

age as Emmett Till was, she comments, "It's a shame he had to die so soon"—what certainly could be construed as a veiled threat from the "meanest white woman in town." On some level, Moody senses this threat—"when Mrs. Burke talked about Emmett Till there was something in her voice that sent chills and fear all over me." Till's murder and Mrs. Burke's reaction to it give Moody a new fear: "the fear of being killed just because I was black."

From then on, Moody becomes increasingly aware of racial and social injustices. She willingly talks about the incidents of racial violence that take place and actively seeks out information. There are few other members of the community who are willing to talk about these subjects. However, Moody learns from a teacher about the NAACP as well as about "Negroes being butchered and slaughtered by whites in the South." Despite acknowledging this truth, the teacher wants to keep their conversation secret and then advises Moody, "It's not good for you to concern yourself too much about these killings and beatings and burnings," because the "Negroes here ain't gonna do nothing about them." When Moody talks with a schoolmate, Jerry, about his beating at the hands of a gang of white men, he says that his parents wouldn't even take him to the hospital because "they were scared to take me to white doctors." A few weeks later, the occupied house of an African-American family is deliberately set on fire. Along with about a hundred people, Moody silently observes the debris and charred bodies. The expressions on the faces of the African Americans would haunt her forever in their "almost unanimous hopelessness."

Even more appalling is the revelation that African-Americans themselves are sometimes involved in these murderous incidents. Samuel Quinn is killed for attempting to organize the Centreville African Americans into the NAACP. The whites found out about his efforts because he went among the African Americans "he thought he could trust" to get people interested, but "someone squealed." This "someone" is later revealed to be the high school principal who, "[I]t was said . . . also helped plot his death." Also, it was African Americans, not whites, who put the fatal bullets in Quinn.

Her understanding of the racial violence that wracks the South causes Moody to hate people, the whites who were "responsible for the countless murders" as well as the African Americans "for not standing up and doing something about the murders." For a few years, however, Moody attempts to replicate the behavior of the African Americans who surround her. She immerses herself in school activities and studies, and while Quinn's murder brings "memories of all the other killings, beatings, and abuses inflicted upon Negroes by whites" and makes her take to her bed for several days, Moody does not follow through on her fleeting idea of "waging a war in protest against the killings all by myself." Instead, she internalizes her feelings of self- and race-hatred and "slowly began to escape within [her]self again." Her only outward reaction is her sustained plan to leave Centreville and Mississippi.

Forced to remain in the state to obtain a college education, Moody is drawn within a few years into the civil rights movement. While she participates in sit-ins and other demonstrations in the city of Jackson, back in Centreville her protest activities bring threats upon her family. When Moody goes to Canton, in Madison County, a place "where Negroes frequently turned up dead," she finds many of the same problems that existed in Centreville. To intimidate the African Americans and keep them from working with CORE and registering to vote, the whites of Canton rely on violent scare tactics. They shoot at high school students with buckshot pellets. They fire at a pregnant woman who is walking with her two sons. A man rapes a high school girl while she works in the cotton fields and then goes "around talking about it." The African Americans react as anticipated: they drop their participation with CORE and look at Moody as if to say, "Why don't you all get out of here before you get us all killed?"

In Canton, Moody comes to have firsthand experience with the intensity of whites' desire to continue to oppress African Americans. Even the so-called law enforcement officers actively participate in the harassment of the CORE workers, and one police officer in particular seems to target Moody. Even federal officers show disdain for the

> Her understanding of the racial violence that wracks the South causes Moody to hate people, the whites who were 'responsible for the countless murders' as well as the African Americans 'for not standing up and doing something about the murders.'"

rights of the African Americans. FBI officers who come South to find out about the shooting of the Canton teenagers do little to investigate and nothing to prevent such violence from happening again; Moody senses their unspoken words: "'What a shame these niggers have to come into a place and open up a joint like this and cause all this trouble for us.'" In another incident, the FBI impassively observes Canton police officers brutally beat a protest marcher. Another killing might have been prevented if the Justice Department had paid attention to Louis Allen, who identifies a white man as a murder and later reports threats on his own life. However, this law enforcement agency tells Allen, "'We can't protect every individual in Mississippi.'" Moody affirms this base injustice when she notes that "the United States could afford to maintain the Peace Corps to protect and assist the underprivileged of other countries while native-born American citizens were murdered and brutalized daily and nothing was done. "

After more than a year in the civil rights movement, Moody comes to question the workers' ability to bring about change in the South. As Moody heads off to Washington, D.C., on the CORE bus, she brings *Coming of Age in Mississippi* to a close. She ends her story in remembering all the bad things that have happened: "the Taplin burning, the Birmingham church bombing, Medgar Evers' murder, the blood gushing out of McKinley's head, and all the other murders." She thinks of her friends, the Chinns, the first African Americans in Canton to welcome the CORE workers. On this last day, Mrs. Chinn tells her, despite all the work they have done in Canton, "things are even worse than they were before." Mr. Chinn, who has "sacrificed and lost all he had trying to get the Negroes moving,'' is now locked up with a chain gang. She wonders if Mrs. Chinn is right when she says, '''This ain't the way. We ain't big enough to do it by ourselves.''' On the bus to Washington D.C., the other African Americans begin singing ''We Shall Overcome,'' but Anne is left with the following words that echo in her head: ''I wonder. I really wonder.''

Source: Rena Korb, Critical Essay on *Coming of Age in Mississippi,* in *Nonfiction Classics for Students,* The Gale Group, 2002.

Joyce Hart

Hart has degrees in English literature and creative writing and is a published writer of literary themes. In this essay, she compares the personal, social, and historical circumstances surrounding Moody's book with Richard Wright's autobiography Black Boy.

In Moody's autobiography *Coming of Age in Mississippi* readers learn that Moody was born in Centreville, Mississippi. This small Southern town, as it turns out, is only about fifty miles south of Richard Wright's birthplace, Roxie, Mississippi. The proximity of these towns and these writers' shared African-American ancestry make their life stories strangely similar. However, their autobiographies are significantly marked by the different time-frames in which the authors grew up, Wright in the 1920s and 1930s and Moody in the 1950s and 1960s.

Juxtaposing Wright's *Black Boy* and Moody's *Coming of Age in Mississippi* suggests changes in black experience in the South during two turbulent periods and gives views of the development in the U. S. civil rights movement. Conditioned by their environments and times, these writers were driven by a similar combination of fear and anger. However, they chose different paths in their attempts to acquire their own freedom and promote freedom among their peers.

Early circumstances in Moody's and Wright's lives, though separated by nearly thirty years, were comparable, but one important difference. Both writers were born into families of sharecroppers, the most common means during the first half of the twentieth century for African-American families in the South to make their living. Both Moody and Wright lost their fathers, who left their mothers behind to raise the children. One important difference is that Moody's mother had good health and eventually married a man who was able to provide a decent home and minimum meals for his family. Wright's mother, by contrast, had several debilitating strokes and never remarried. While Wright was quite young, he was forced to drop out of school and find menial jobs, pick through the rubble in the street for pieces of coal, and take care of himself and his younger brother without adult help. This pattern of working on his own began before Wright reached the age of ten and continued throughout his childhood. Wright's severe poverty also left him constantly hungry, a condition that continued until he was well past his twenty-fifth year. Although both writers suffered, Wright had less hope for future freedom.

A more obvious difference between the two writers is seen in the social pressures of their early years. So-called Jim Crow laws, under which regulations were created to promote strict segregation, prevailed in the South during both Wright's and Moody's experiences there. However, as Wright was growing up, the Ku Klux Klan was extremely active in enforcing racial separation. The Klan committed acts of brutality, torture, and murder to warning all black people. When African Americans stepped across the invisible but well-defined lines of social conduct as defined by the Jim Crow laws, they knew they would probably be severely punished. Although some social protests in the form of boycotts were carried out during Wright's youth in the South, most members of African-American communities learned survival behaviors that expressed a surface submission to the white supremacists. The KKK was so dominant in the 1920s and 1930s that some Southern U. S. congressmen openly supported activities of the KKK by attending and speaking at Klan meetings without their being considered immoral.

In contrast, during Moody's childhood, slow, but nonetheless dramatic, social changes developed. At first, these changes were subtle and were mostly witnessed by the younger generation. Moody's parents as well as the other adults around her continued to accept the mandates of segregation out of justified fear of KKK reprisals. However, despite the fears of her elders, the very young Moody experienced limited friendship with some white children, who lived close to her neighborhood. The children were curious about one another and shared toys for brief periods of play. This contact contrasts sharply with Wright's experience of brick-and-stone battles between groups of his black friends and groups of young white boys, who lived on the other side of the railroad tracks. They hurled their weapons at one another so violently that serious wounds often resulted.

Moody, on the other hand, relates that the son of one of her white employers openly flirted with her in front of his mother while Moody tutored the boy in Algebra. Two elements stand out in this scene: first, the blatant cross-racial flirtation and, second, the white mother's acknowledgement of Moody's intelligence and exceptional ability in math. During Wright's childhood, whites tended to believe that an education past eighth grade was a waste of time for most African-American children, who would grow up to hold only manual labor jobs. The majority of African Americans, whose poverty forced them to take jobs early, did not challenge these assumptions; few received high school diplomas. Black children were not expected to graduate from high school, let alone go on to college. Thirty years later, however, not only did Moody finish high school and proceed to college, she did so amid discussions, albeit heated ones, about the desegregation of schools.

In Wright's time, the legal precedent of *Plessy v. Ferguson* (1896) still dictated a separate but equal status to white and black populations throughout the states, with the sanction of the U. S. Supreme Court. It was through this court decision that the segregationist Jim Crow laws came into existence. Many prominent black leaders and intellectuals, during this time, became caught up in a debate over how to define the role of African Americans and how to fight for their civil rights. Conflicting philosophies disallowed agreement; the civil rights movement in Wright's time became embroiled in controversy and did not make much progress. Some groups, inspired by Marcus Garvey, advocated creating a Black Nation in the United States or moving to Africa. Another philosophy, based in part on Booker T. Washington's beliefs, stated that blacks should accommodate segregation and make the best of it.

However, during the 1950s, the political climate was changing, fueled in part by a new decision that was to counteract the older decree. From 1951 until 1954, the U. S. Supreme Court heard cases and finally made a decision in the case *Brown* v *Board of Education of Topeka, Kansas*. Due to this landmark ruling, segregation of all schools became unlawful. This court decision was the first major move toward the end of legal segregation in the United States.

Moody did not feel the full effects of desegregation in high school, but she cites that, shortly after

> **Wright had the courage to expose his most personal emotions through his writing; while Moody fought off her fears in an effort to break the barriers that inhibited African-American life."**

her graduation, a new, and supposedly improved, "separate but equal" school was opened in her county under the influence of the 1954 court decision. It was not until she entered her junior year in college that Moody experienced a hint of school integration. She was very nervous about attending Tugaloo College in Jackson, Mississippi, because most of its professors were white. Although Tugaloo was traditionally an African-American college, it did promote an integrated faculty. Moody was also warned by her friends that only "high-yellow" African-American students attended Tugaloo. This comment illustrates prejudice within the black community based on skin color. Moody's skin was dark. In addition to feeling that her skin might be too dark, she also was concerned about her educational background, fearing that the white professors would demand more of her than she could fulfill given the education she received in the impoverished African-American school system. However, she soon rid herself of these apprehensions, especially after her first term grades, which renewed her confidence in her intelligence and preparedness.

With only a ninth-grade education, Wright taught himself. He was a voracious reader. Every night upon returning home from work, he devoured books on psychology, philosophy, sociology, and classic literature. In addition to this study, he found intellectual stimulation by joining young, highly educated adults (mostly white) in writers' groups that had been created during Roosevelt's administration which spanned the Great Depression. At this time, Wright left the South and moved to Chicago in desperation. He feared that if he remained in Mississippi, or in Tennessee where he had subsequently moved, he would be killed. His hunger for knowledge and personal freedom would not be tolerated in the oppressive environment of the South.

In Chicago Wright became interested in the Communist Party, which was at that time the most prominent political movement for equal rights. The Party promoted labor unions, social security, and a brotherhood that promised to be race neutral. Although Wright claimed that he did not have political interests, he eventually influenced the course of the civil rights movement. He influenced others through his writing, which took on an angry tone. His books, *Uncle Tom's Children, Native Son,* and finally his autobiography, *Black Boy,* presented deeply personal, painfully realistic depictions of African-American experience. National bestsellers, his books affected African-American authors who followed Wright and the white population in both the North and South who read them. Many white people in the South would deny that what Wright had described was true, but other, more liberal whites, including Eleanor Roosevelt, the wife of the president, were educated and emotionally moved by Wright's work.

Moody's political activism took a different path. While she also became a writer, she first committed herself to trying to create change in the African-American community. Moody was in college during the 1960s, a decade when the National Association for the Advancement of Colored People (NAACP) was about to achieve some of its goals. Inspired by one of the NAACP's most outstanding speakers, Medgar Evans, Moody took part in a sit-in at a whites-only lunch counter in Jackson, Mississippi. She was assaulted by a group of white hecklers who quickly gathered at the scene, while white police offices stood outside watching—a scene of law enforcement passivity that repeated many times. This was the first of many such acts of defiance against the Jim Crow laws in which Moody was involved. Jackson, Mississippi, was soon the subject of national attention as groups such as the Student Nonviolent Coordination Committee (SNCC) and the Congress of Racial Equality (CORE) focused their activities there. Mississippi was one of the poorest and most radically racist states in the South during the 1960s. Moody was right in the middle of this tension.

Moody worked hard, ending up in jail several times, depleting her health at other times, and trying hard to ignore threats against her life, all in the name of freedom. The main thrust of her political activity was to get Southern black people registered to vote. Although she fought hard, her book, *Coming of Age in Mississippi,* ends on a note of frustration. The precise date at the end of her autobiography is not

clear, but Moody writes the words, "I wonder. I really wonder," referring to her doubts about the effects of all her work. Would the demonstrations, the political rallies, the sit-ins, the fights for voters' rights ever make a difference?

It is also unclear what Moody has done with the remaining years of her life, as she refuses interviews, tired of public attention. Rumors have her living in New York, removed from many of the reminders of her Southern childhood. In the end, Wright's and Moody's lives once again take on similar elements. Wright, frustrated and demoralized by prejudice in the United States, made a permanent move to Europe during the last decade of his life. Both writers, once fueled by the anger caused by injustice, turned their frustrations into unselfish acts. Wright had the courage to expose his most personal emotions through his writing; while Moody fought off her fears in an effort to break the barriers that inhibited African-American life. They chose different ways to voice their antagonism, and then both of them, as if depleted by the intensity of their work, disappeared from the scene.

Source: Joyce Hart, Critical Essay on *Coming of Age in Mississippi,* in *Nonfiction Classics for Students,* The Gale Group, 2002.

Laura Kryhoski

Kryhoski is currently working as a freelance writer. In this essay, she considers Moody's work as it relates to events of the Civil Rights movement.

"I couldn't believe it, but it was the Klan blacklist, with my picture on it. I guess I must have sat there for about an hour holding it," says Moody in her autobiography *Coming of Age in Mississippi.* In Moody's response to the list, it is easy to see that she is different, different, in fact, from many young teenagers of her race, gender, time. She is one of the many voices of the Civil Rights movement, one of the unsung heroes courageously following in the steps of Martin Luther King, Jr., to realize freedom and gain self-respect, for herself and for her people as well.

Early in the autobiography, the author describes her experience as a victim of racial injustice in a vivid example. In a particular moment in a local movie theater, Moody begins to understand the far reaching implications of the color divide, what it is to be black in her own community. Arriving at the same time as her white playmates, Moody and her

Civil-rights activists on the Voter Registration protest march along Route 80 from Selma to Montgomery, Alabama in 1965. Even after gaining the right to vote, African Americans in the South encountered discriminatory tactics that prevented them from registering

siblings are naturally compelled to join their friends in the white lobby. Amidst the joy comes confusion, when Moody, along with her sister and brother, are violently snatched away from their friends; she writes, "when we got outside, we stood there crying, and we could hear the white children crying inside the white lobby." Moody explains, "I never really thought of them as white before. Now all of a sudden they were white, and their whiteness made them better than me." Moody's curiosity, her need to question the world around her, is perhaps also defined at this moment. Moody is determined to discover the meaning the skin color imposes on friendships and the secret to the benefits of being white. Playing the game doctor, she looks over her white friend's "privates," and puzzled, responds, "I examined each of them three times, but I didn't see any differences. I still hadn't found that secret." Moody is not content to accept the role society imposes on her. As a child, she is able to question social convention, and this ability defines her actions throughout the autobiography.

Moody continues to push at the boundaries of society, in part as a way to define her individuality,

her blackness. After the wife of a Klan member mentions the NAACP over tea, Moody asks her mother to elaborate and receives harsh words; Momma commands her never to mention "that word" to "no other white person." Moody responds, "With a momma like that you'll never learn anything." Without hesitation she asks another adult about the organization and is offered five hours of history from a teacher who eventually disappears. As Moody learns about the NAACP, and as events in the community unfold, Moody's refusal to remain silent increases her sense of alienation. In response to the racism and violence surrounding her, Moody states, "I couldn't go on pretending I was dumb and innocent, pretending I didn't know what was going on . . . I was sick of pretending, sick of selling my feelings for a dollar a day." Apart from her racial identity, she is truly a woman of unusual beauty, as well as intellect. These gifts certainly distinguish her from her peers. Moreover, her wisdom, her clarity of vision, and purpose, all set her apart from her classmates. It is this different perception and the willingness to act on it that isolate Moody from the people most familiar to her.

> " The courage Moody demonstrates, in her quest for social equality, is phenomenal considering the humiliation and danger she confronts."

Moody's refusal to accept social limitation and her dogged determination to rise above her family circumstances put her in conflict with those close to her. This conflict further alienates Moody. There is a force moving Moody, a spirit compelling her to do the next right thing. Prior to her attendance at her first NAACP convention she receives a condemning letter from her mother. Moody comments on the probable reaction of her hometown of Centreville to her participation: "I knew I could never go to Centreville safely . . . I kept telling myself that I didn't really care too much about going home . . . it was more important to me to go the convention." This sense of spirit, this willingness to forsake her former life to follow her beliefs about activism, pervades the text. In her quest for civil equality, Moody takes a stand without family support. In letters, her mother repeatedly pleads with Moody, as she summarizes here: "Why was I trying to get myself killed? [Momma] kept asking. What was I trying to prove?" Moody reports that her mother pointed out the uselessness of trying to change racial givens in the South: "Over and over again she said that after I was dead things would still be the same as they were now." Moody's participation in CORE does not come without great personal expense—to support the group's efforts, she sacrifices teenage life, the support of her family, and possibly her future.

The courage Moody demonstrates in her quest for social equality is phenomenal considering the humiliation and danger she confronts. Ketchup, mustard, and sugar are smeared all over her hair and clothing at a lunch counter sit-in at Woolworth's. After another arrest on a hot summer day, Moody and fellow marchers are confined in a police wagon with no water or air with the vehicle's heater left on to torture them. In this instance, her release from the truck does not earn her freedom. Moody and her companions are herded into cattle buildings at the State Fairgrounds, surrounded by barbed wire, guarded with policemen bearing rifles. Her immediate associations are those of Nazi Germany: to her the Nazi soldiers "couldn't have been any rougher than these cops." In another moment, with only the tall grass to disguise her, Moody hides with other residents of Sonny's house to avoid being killed by white vigilantes.

In addition to danger, Moody faces repeated rejection by members of her own race. The role of a CORE worker is not only dangerous but also thankless. Time and time again Moody's work goes unfulfilled. In one instance, she responds to the murder of Medgar Evers by taking the opportunity to recruit students at Jackson State College for a march. After a heartfelt speech, Moody's frustration shows: "How could Negroes be so pitiful? How could they just sit by and take all this [sh—] without any emotions at all? I just didn't understand." Any success in her work is tempered by the prospect of interference by hostile whites. In Canton, for example, Moody speaks of the great success CORE realizes in its ability to gain support of the black community. Although large numbers of blacks register to vote, only a few are actually registered; the rest are rejected by white members of the community who oversee the process. To face such passivity and frustration, to meet danger head on and continue to work for the advancement of Civil Rights despite great personal risk, these traits distinguishes Moody from her fellows. Her vision and what she personally describes as her inability to suppress feelings of discontent motivate her.

Dr. Martin Luther King, Jr., Civil Rights leader, wrote *Why We Can't Wait,* a classic exploration of the events and forces behind the Civil Rights movement. In his "Letter from Birmingham Jail," King discusses what propels the movement in the face of great opposition and at such great personal expense. The objective in a nonviolent direct-action program for King, first and foremost, is "to create a situation so crisis-packed that it will eventually open the door to negotiation." The impact of sit-ins, of peaceful demonstrations is found in the activities of the objectors. By subjecting themselves to violence and abuse without retaliation, King recognized the power of creating crisis to "foster such a tension that the community which has constantly refused to negotiate is forced to confront the issue." In light of racial violence that has historically plagued the black community, King's vision is not hard to understand. He adds, "For years now I have heard the word 'Wait!' . . . This 'Wait' has almost always meant

'Never.'" In King's view, this justice too long "delayed" is "justice denied." The motivations of Moody and countless others are beautifully summed-up by King, as he explains why "we" can't wait.

> when you are harried by day and haunted by night by the fact that you are a Negro, living constantly at tiptoe stance, never quite knowing what to expect next, and are plagued with inner fears and outer resentments; when you are forever fighting a degenerating sense of 'nobodiness'—then you will understand why we find it difficult to wait.

Moody's autobiography *Coming of Age in Mississippi* is more than just the story of a young woman's transitions into adulthood. It is the chronicle of a brave young woman who refuses to sacrifice her self-respect, a woman who stands up for her beliefs, despite great personal cost. The final words of her personal account mirror the frustration of such taxing work. As she sits listening to her friends singing, "We shall overcome," she responds: "I wonder. I really wonder." One has to wonder how such vision, such courage, carried Moody in her journey, and if she, like many of us, is still wondering today.

Source: Laura Kryhoski, Critical Essay on *Coming of Age in Mississippi,* in *Nonfiction Classics for Students,* The Gale Group, 2002.

Sources

Degler, C. N., Review, in *Nation,* January 11, 1969, p. 83.

Ellmann, Mary, Review, in *Nation,* January 6, 1969, p. 26.

Kennedy, Edward M., Review, in *New York Times Book Review,* January 6, 1969, p. 5.

King, Martin Luther, Jr., *Why We Can't Wait,* Penguin, 1964, pp. 79–82.

Stevens, Shane, Review, in *Book World,* December 1, 1968, p. 28.

Wright, Richard, *Black Boy,* HarperCollins Publishers, 1998.

Further Reading

Branch, Taylor, *Parting the Waters: America in the King Years, 1954–63,* Touchstone Books, 1989.
  The first book of a two-volume series, this formidable social history profiles Dr. Martin Luther King, Jr., as well as the other key players and events that helped shape the civil rights movement of the 1960s.

Dittmer, John, *Local People: The Struggle for Civil Rights in Mississippi,* University of Illinois Press, 1995.
  This history covers the fight for racial equality in Mississippi from the post–World War II years through 1968.

Hampton, Henry, ed., *Voices of Freedom: An Oral History of the Civil Rights Movement from the 1950s through the 1980s,* Bantam Books, 1991.
  Creating a fascinating narrative, the creator and executive producer of the PBS series *The Eyes on the Prize* draws on nearly one thousand interviews with activists, politicians, officials, and ordinary people who took part in the civil rights movement.

Hine, Darlene Clark, ed., *The Eyes on the Prize: Civil Rights Reader,* Penguin, 1991.
  One of several companion pieces to the PBS *Eyes on the Prize* television series, this book collects over 100 court decisions, speeches, interviews, and other documents on the civil rights movement from 1954 to 1990.

Hunger of Memory: The Education of Richard Rodriguez

Richard Rodriguez

1981

When Richard Rodriguez published his collection of six autobiographical essays, *Hunger of Memory: The Education of Richard Rodriguez* in 1981, roars erupted from both ends of the political spectrum. His conservative readers and critics were happy to hold him up as a minority student who had benefited from affirmative action but who in the end had rejected such programs as unfair to the real underprivileged—those who were impoverished or had never had the educational opportunities Rodriguez had enjoyed. Others saw in Rodriguez someone alienated from his Mexican-American culture and heritage, having betrayed his fellow Hispanics (a broad term meaning Spanish speakers but used in the United States to denote Americans whose forebears are from a Spanish-speaking country) by his denunciation of bilingual education and affirmative action.

The book follows Rodriguez's early life as it revolves around language and education and portrays how those factors contributed to his transition from childhood to adulthood. In the book's prologue, Rodriguez refers to his work as a ''middle-class pastoral'' in which he ''sings the praises of [his] lower-class past'' while reminding himself how education has assisted with the separation from that past. It is his coming-of-age story, he notes, ''the story of the scholarship boy who returns home one summer to discover the bewildering silence, facing his parents. This is my story. An American story.''

Rodriguez covers his first few confusing months in school, when he didn't speak in class because he didn't feel comfortable with what little English he knew. After a few of the nuns from his school ask his parents to speak English around the house, Rodriguez takes his first steps toward becoming a "public man." Such assimilation into American culture is necessary and valuable, he asserts. As the book progresses, Rodriguez relates the story of his growing up, the power and pain of family ties, the role of the Catholic Church in his life, and his staunch rejection of affirmative action for ethnic and racial minorities in education and in the workplace.

Author Biography

Richard Rodriguez was born on July 31, 1944, in San Francisco, California, to Mexican immigrants Leopoldo and Victoria Moran Rodriguez, the third of their four children. When Rodriguez was still a young child, the family moved to Sacramento, California, to a small house in a comfortable white neighborhood. "Optimism and ambition led them to a house (our home) many blocks from the Mexican side of town. . . . It never occurred to my parents that they couldn't live wherever they chose," writes Rodriguez in *Hunger of Memory: The Education of Richard Rodriguez*, his well-received 1981 autobiography. This first book placed him in the national spotlight but brought scorn from many supporters of affirmative action and bilingual education.

Rodriguez's family was not well-to-do, but his father—a man with a third-grade education who ended up working as a dental technician after dreaming of a career as an engineer—and his mother somehow found the money to send their children to Catholic schools. Ultimately, Rodriguez, who could barely speak English when he started elementary school, finished his academic efforts as a Fulbright scholar in Renaissance literature with degrees from Stanford University and Columbia University. Perched on the edge of a brilliant career in academia, but uncomfortable with what he viewed as the unwarranted advantage given him by affirmative action, Rodriguez refused a number of teaching jobs at prestigious universities. He felt that receiving preference and assistance based on his classification as a minority was unfair to others. This dra-

Richard Rodriguez

matic decision, along with a number of anti-affirmative action essays published in the early to mid-1970s, made Rodriguez a somewhat notorious national figure.

After leaving academia, Rodriguez spent the next six years writing the essays that comprise *Hunger of Memory: The Education of Richard Rodriguez*, aided for part of that time by a National Endowment for the Humanities Fellowship. Before being compiled into book form, many of the essays appeared in publications such as *Columbia Forum, American Scholar,* and *College English. Hunger of Memory* was a hugely successful book, garnering reviews in approximately fifty publications after its release. Critics generally praised the book for its clear and concise prose and for Rodriguez's honesty in revealing his conflicted feelings about being a "scholarship boy," as he refers to himself in the book. In 1983, the book won an Anisfield-Wolf Book Award and a Christopher Award.

Since 1981, Rodriguez has continued his writing career, occasionally serving as an essayist for the PBS series *MacNeil-Lehrer NewsHour* and also working as an editor with the Pacific News Service in California. In 1992, he published *Days of Obligation: An Argument with My Mexican Father*, another collection of previously issued autobiographical essays. The book, which did not receive the same acclaim and admiration as his first book, covers such topics as Rodriguez's Mexican and Indian heritage, his homosexuality, and the AIDS epidemic in San Francisco.

Plot Summary

Prologue: "Middle-Class Pastoral"

In the prologue, Rodriguez introduces himself and his book, referring to it as "essays impersonating an autobiography; six chapters of sad, fuguelike repetition." He makes clear that his purpose in putting together the book was to write about how education moved him from boyhood to manhood.

Chapter One: "Aria"

In this essay, Rodriguez focuses on how the use of language has marked the difference between his public life and his private life. When he was a young child, he spoke primarily Spanish. Spanish was the comfortable language of his home life, while English was the language he heard spoken by strangers outside the home.

Soon after Rodriguez starts attending a Catholic elementary school, the family receives a visit from his teachers, concerned about Rodriguez's poor performance and his siblings' academic achievement. The teachers ask his parents to speak only English in the home. This event changes everything, according to Rodriguez, including how he feels at home with his parents. At first he is frustrated with speaking only English, but the day finally comes when he feels comfortable enough with English to answer a question in class. "The belief, the calming assurance that I belonged in public, had at last taken hold," he remembers.

Though Rodriguez feels that he lost something when he and his family became increasingly Americanized, he stresses that there were also things gained. Two of the most critical were "a public identity" and maturity. For this reason, he does not agree with bilingual education proponents who argue that children not taught in their native languages lose their "individuality." He also does not believe that these "bilingualists" understand the necessity and value of assimilation.

Chapter Two: "The Achievement of Desire"

In this essay, Rodriguez reminisces about his education and the impact it has had on his life. He claims that his success in life is based on how education changed him and separated him from the life he had "before becoming a student."

Throughout this essay, Rodriguez refers to Richard Hogart's book *The Uses of Literacy,* in which he discovered one of the few mentions of the "scholarship boy" by educational theorists. Rodriguez sees himself in Hogart's descriptions of the scholarship boy, and this has helped him understand his experiences.

Rodriguez expresses concern that he was the type of student who, while making good grades, simply memorized information and never developed his own opinions. Like the "scholarship boy," Rodriguez worked for academic success and denied his past. And also like the "scholarship boy," Rodriguez experienced nostalgia for his past. But he notes that while education created a gulf between him and his parents, education also made it possible to care about that fact and to write about it.

Paralleling Rodriguez's education were the increasingly contrary feelings he developed toward his parents. While he did not mean to be rude and hurtful toward them, he found himself becoming angry when they did not seem to be as capable as his teachers. More and more as a student, Rodriguez looked toward his teachers, and not his parents, as role models.

Rodriguez remembers his parents' experiences with education and work. His mother received a high school degree even though, he says, her English was poor. She went to night school, worked as a typist, and was very proud of her excellent spelling ability. His father moved to the United States as a young man, seeking a better life as an engineer. That dream never materialized, and his father worked at a series of unsatisfying low-end jobs that, nonetheless, kept the family comfortable.

Chapter Three: "Credo"

In "Credo," Rodriguez discusses his relationship with the Catholic Church. He remembers that Catholicism "shaped my whole day. It framed my experience of eating and sleeping and washing; it named the season and the hour." Before Rodriguez left home to attend Stanford University, he and his family attended Mass every Sunday and on feast days. The first English-speaking guest at their house was their local priest.

Rodriguez remembers how the Church dominated his education. The nuns' teaching through memorization, while discouraging "intellectual challenges to authority," encouraged learning as a rite of passage. He fondly recalls becoming an altar boy and how this role introduced him to the rituals of life and death.

Rodriguez discusses his current views of the Church. He still goes to Mass each Sunday but is not particularly pleased with the changes the Church has made beginning with the reforms of the 1960s.

Chapter Four: "Complexion"

Rodriguez examines how his dark complexion has defined certain parts of his life. Today he notices, when he walks into a hotel, he is often asked if he has been on vacation. But his mother saw dark skin as a symbol of poverty, and he remembers her admonitions to him to stay out of the sun to keep from tanning, lest he be mistaken for a menial worker.

His mother also worried whether it was appropriate for Rodriguez to mow their neighbors' lawns and was adamant that her daughter not wear a uniform while she worked briefly as a housekeeper for a wealthy woman. But Rodriguez's father was mostly concerned that Rodriguez not get stuck in a factory job that would wear him down and make him a tired middle-aged man like himself.

Rodriguez was never concerned that the darkness of his skin made him subject to racism when he was young but remembers feeling that it made him ugly, especially to women. He tried to distance himself from his body, for example, by never participating in sports as a child.

While Rodriguez was attending Stanford University, a friend hesitantly suggested that he consider a summer construction job. Rodriguez accepted it, in part to show his father that he knew about "real work." Surprisingly, Rodriguez enjoyed the work, but he also realized that his short time in the job prohibited him from completely understanding the nature of physical labor.

Chapter Five: "Profession"

In this essay, Rodriguez questions affirmative action and his role as a "minority student," a term

he feels should never have been "foisted" upon him and one he should not have accepted. He believes that black civil rights leaders in the 1960s were correct in their argument that higher education was not accessible to blacks. However, he also believes that they "tragically limited the impact of their movement" when they focused on race as the only factor in lack of educational access. According to Rodriguez, social class, and not race or ethnicity, is the key indicator for oppression.

The very fact that Rodriguez was a well-educated student, he asserts, made him *not* a minority. "I was not—in a *cultural* sense—a minority, an alien from public life," he writes. In the 1970s, Rodriguez began publishing articles stating his discomfort at being a beneficiary of affirmative action. In response, he received many approving letters from "right-wing politicians" and angry reactions from minority activists. He avoided allying himself with either side.

Rodriguez also addresses the establishment of ethnic studies programs in the 1970s and dismisses these programs as being based on "romantic hopes." He expresses disdain for white students who described themselves as oppressed and complained that minorities were taking their seats in postgraduate professional programs.

Because Rodriguez was uncomfortable with his minority status and the benefits he received through affirmative action, he avoided accepting a permanent teaching position at any of the prestigious schools knocking on his door. He felt he did not deserve the amount of attention he was getting and blamed the situation on the unfair application of affirmative action. Eventually, he refused all of the offers, angering his professors and confusing his parents.

Chapter Six: "Mr. Secrets"

In the final essay, Rodriguez addresses his ambivalent feelings about writing this "intellectual autobiography." When Rodriguez had earlier published a short autobiographical piece, his mother was horrified that he had revealed to the public, specifically to *gringos,* that his education had created divisions between him and his parents.

Rodriguez remembers growing up in an atmosphere where even the smallest bit of family information was considered inappropriate for outsiders' ears. But now, unlike his parents, he believes that there is a place for the "deeply personal in public life."

Key Figures

Father

Rodriguez's father was orphaned at age eight and went to work as an apprentice for an uncle. He had a third-grade education, but when he was twenty, he left Mexico for the United States with the idea of becoming an engineer. He thought a priest would help him get the money for his education, but this didn't happen, and he ended up taking a "dark succession of warehouse, factory, and cannery jobs."

Rodriguez's father went to night school with his wife, but after a year or two he quit and waited for her outside on the school steps. When the children were born, he was working at a "clean job," first as a janitor for a department store, then as a dental technician, but Rodriguez remembers that his father was always consumed by fatigue. He laughed whenever his son complained about being tired from reading and studying; he could not understand how one could become tired from reading and often mocked his son's soft hands. Rodriguez's father never verbally encouraged the children to do well in school.

His father was able to provide for his family a house in a comfortable, middle-class neighborhood "many blocks from the Mexican south side of town." But the family still felt estranged from the white community that surrounded them in Sacramento of the 1950s. Rodriguez remembers that his father was shy only when he spoke English; when he spoke Spanish with family and friends, he was animated and outgoing.

Grandmother

Rodriguez's grandmother spoke Spanish to him when he was a small child. However, he found it more difficult to understand Spanish once he started school and spoke English at home and in class. And while he often did not understand her after his English skills improved, Rodriguez is quick to note this did not lessen the love they felt for each other. She called Rodriguez Pocho—a Spanish word for something that is colorless or bland—to tease him

about not being able to speak Spanish very well. He took it as a name for someone who has forgotten his native society while becoming an American.

The last time Rodriguez saw his grandmother, she told him about her life in Mexico with her husband Narciso and how they lived on a farm. She recalled working as a seamstress and that she had to leave Rodriguez's mother and her brother and sisters to travel to Guadalajara for work. She died a few days later, when Rodriguez was nine years old.

Mother

Rodriguez's mother was born in Mexico and immigrated to the United States as a young girl. She and her husband lived a comfortable, middle-class life in Sacramento, California, and succeeded in buying a house in what Rodriguez refers to as a *gringo* neighborhood. Rodriguez describes his parents as full of optimism and hope for their family's future. Rodriguez's mother had better English skills than did his father. She served as the primary communicator with the *gringo* world beyond the family. After Rodriguez's parents became more confident of their language skills, his mother learned the names of everyone living on their block and purchased a phone for the house.

As a girl, Rodriguez's mother had been given a high school degree by teachers "too careless or busy" to notice that she could not speak English, according to her son. She worked as a typist after high school and was proud that she did not have to put on a uniform to go to work and could spell well without a college degree. After Rodriguez began high school, his mother started back to work again in a typing position. She felt strongly that her children should get all the education possible.

Rodriguez's mother was upset by many of the choices her children made. She complained when her children got older that they were not close, "more in the Mexican style," like other families. When Rodriguez left for Stanford University, one hundred miles from Sacramento, his mother could not understand why the colleges in their town weren't "good enough." When Rodriguez published articles in which he mentioned the family, she was uncomfortable about her private life being exposed, and she wrote to him to ask that he stop writing about the family. She called him Mr. Secrets while he wrote this book because he did not share much about his activities.

Rodriguez sees his parents as having great dignity and aristocratic reserve, and he also portrays their devotion to Catholicism. Both parents wanted their children to be aware that they "are Mexicans" and never to try to pass themselves off as being from Spain.

The Priest

When Rodriguez was about four years old, a white priest from Sacred Heart Church came to the Rodriguez house for dinner. This was a special occasion, as Rodriguez remembers it, because the priest was the first English-speaking dinner guest ever invited to the Rodriguez household. The picture left by the priest was of Christ with a "punctured heart"; it still survives, Rodriguez writes, and has hung on the wall of every house his parents have lived in since.

Richard (Ricardo) Rodriguez

Richard Rodriguez is the son of working-class Mexican immigrants to the United States, raised and educated in Sacramento, California, and the third of four children. Spanish was the language spoken inside his home, and when he came home each day from school, he looked forward to hearing a language that was special because it was spoken only among his family and never with *gringos*. Language made the line between public and private life very discernable for Rodriguez. He always felt like a foreigner outside of the house when he was young, able to speak only a few words of English.

Themes

Childhood

A great portion of *Hunger of Memory* covers Rodriguez's childhood and his transformation into an adult. He is the third child of two middle-class Mexican immigrants in Sacramento and has two sisters and one brother.

Rodriguez describes his childhood as "awkward," primarily because of the tension between his private family life and his more public life outside the household. Before Rodriguez was seven, Spanish was the primary language used in his home. He felt clumsy answering questions in English during class and feared any conversation that went beyond a few basic words. But after a trio of nuns from his

school asked his parents to speak only English with their children, his world began to expand. Soon Rodriguez was less shy in school, and he became "increasingly confident" of his public identity.

While Rodriguez credits learning English with helping him become an adult, he also bemoans the fact that his family life, conducted in English, did not have the same, intimate feeling it once had. He and his brother and sisters spoke less with their parents, and the house became quieter. Eventually, Rodriguez began looking more toward his teachers as examples of what he aspired to. While feeling proud of his increasing abilities in school, Rodriguez also began to feel guilty for moving away from his parents. In addition, he occasionally felt ashamed of his parents' halting English, and these feelings filled him with guilt.

Education

Rodriguez also believes that becoming a student helped him become an adult. However, he is very cognizant that this same education placed a gulf between his beginnings and who he is now. He no longer finds it as easy to speak with his parents as freely as he used to, but he also credits his education with making it possible for him to understand and voice this struggle. "If, because of my schooling, I had grown culturally separated from my parents, my education finally had given me ways of speaking and caring about that fact," notes Rodriguez.

Rodriguez writes with pride about his academic achievements, including his four years at Stanford University, a graduate degree from Columbia University, post-graduate work at the University of California at Berkeley, and a Fulbright Fellowship that allowed him to research John Milton at the British Museum in London.

However, Rodriguez devalues his achievements as a student by characterizing his efforts as mere memorization. "I had been submissive, willing to mimic my teachers, willing to re-form myself in order to become 'educated,'" he admits. As a "scholarship boy" Rodriguez admits that much of his success is attributable to his ability to memorize information, not to his broader intellectual strengths. But he defends this teaching methodology pursued by the nuns at the Catholic schools he attended, arguing that students must learn what is already known before they can embark on original thinking and creativity.

Topics for Further Study

- Rodriguez has structured his autobiography less as a timeline of his life and more around six different but important issues in his life. Choose an issue in your life—education, language, family—and write a few pages on this topic as they might appear in your own autobiography.

- Research affirmative action. From your research, come up with a position on the issue and write a one-page essay aimed at persuading readers to adopt your position. Be sure to include reasons for your stance on affirmative action.

- Pick one scene from Rodriguez's book and write a short, one-act play based on it.

- Rodriguez received a Fulbright Fellowship to study in London. Research this scholarship program and create a presentation explaining the program. What subjects can Fulbright scholars study? Where can they study? Are there any famous people who have received Fulbright Fellowships?

- Have you ever lived in or visited a country whose language is different from your own? If so, what was this like? Did you take language classes or try to pick up the language by talking with people? What things did you find difficult because of your language difference? Write a short essay about this experience.

Race and Ethnicity

Even as a child, Rodriguez was keenly aware of his skin color and that he looked different from the other children in his mostly white neighborhood. Of his entire family, Rodriguez claims to have the darkest skin tone. When he was very young, his aunts would try various concoctions on his face to lighten his skin color, and his mother warned him against spending too much time out in the sun, lest his skin become even darker. She expressed concern that he would become like *los pobres,* the poor and powerless, or *los braceros,* men who labored outside all day.

Rodriguez claims to have heard very few racial slurs directed toward him as a child, and when he did hear one, he remembers being so stunned that he could not answer. But now he marvels at the response that his skin color gets when he is at a nice hotel or a fancy cocktail party. People assume that he has been on vacation or ask him if he has thought about doing any "high fashion modeling."

Catholicism

Rodriguez addresses being Catholic in the essay entitled "Credo." Catholicism marked the passage of time in his early life as well as when he was a student at the neighborhood parochial schools. He remembers taking a break during class to march down the street to the church for prayers, the pictures of Jesus in every classroom, and dedicating his homework to Jesus, Mary, and Joseph. His service as an altar boy during weddings, funerals, and other rites of passage taught him about the full spectrum of life. "Experienced in public and private, Catholicism shaped my whole day," he writes, noting that it saturated his every waking moment until he left home to attend Stanford University.

As an adult, Rodriguez is still a practicing Catholic, but with some reservations. The changes to the liturgy resulting from the Second Vatican Conference in the 1960s have made him feel less close to the church. In an interview with Paul Crowley in *America* in 1995, Rodriguez complained about the "theatrical hand-shaking and the fake translations that characterize the vernacular Mass." In the book, he remarks that these changes stem from the fact that the credo, the part of the Mass where the profession of faith is made, is no longer spoken by the priest but by the entire congregation. This has created a false sense of community, he argues, "no longer reminding the listener that he is alone.'' But while he mourns the Catholic Church of his youth, he still clings to it. ''Though it leaves me unsatisfied, I fear giving it up, falling through space.''

Assimilation and Alienation

Rodriguez is a strong supporter of the idea that those who come to the United States should become assimilated into American society. He believes that those who would encourage non-native Americans to avoid becoming part of public society do them a disservice, not realizing that people do not lose their individuality by becoming part of public society. ''While one suffers a diminished sense of *private* individuality by becoming assimilated into public society, such assimilation makes possible the achievement of *public* individuality,'' argues Rodriguez. And it is from this position that Rodriguez argues against bilingual education, the concept that children should be taught using their first language for a period after they enter school.

The Role of Language

Spanish was the language spoken inside the Rodriguez household; English was the language spoken with the *gringos*. Rodriguez writes that, before the age of seven, when English was imposed upon him, coming home was a relief. ''It became the language of joyful return,'' he says of Spanish.

Once English became the household language and his skills in English improved, Rodriguez's life changed dramatically. For the first time, he felt empowered to raise his hand in class and answer questions. He also began to feel connected to the world outside his house, the world of Americans. But, at the same time, Rodriguez noticed that he and his parents and siblings ''remained a loving family, but one greatly changed.'' Much of the old ease was missing, and there were fewer conversations between children and parents.

Rodriguez's Spanish began to falter after he focused on speaking English, much to the concern of his many aunts and uncles. Even though this loss upset Rodriguez as well, he insists that his relatives were mistaken to assume that Spanish was the only thing holding them together as a family. This is the mistake, he says in the book, that proponents of bilingual education make. ''Dangerously, they romanticize public separateness and they trivialize the dilemma of the socially disadvantaged,'' Rodriguez writes. Only after learning to speak English comfortably did Rodriguez consider himself an American, finally able to acquire the rights due to him as an individual member of society.

Style

Structure

Hunger of Memory: The Education of Richard Rodriguez is a compilation of six essays, some of which were published separately before being included in the book. Each one addresses a critical issue in Rodriguez's life. ''Aria'' looks at the impact trading Spanish for English had on his life at home and at school. ''The Achievement of Desire'' covers Rodriguez's love affair with education and studying but also addresses how being a ''scholarship boy'' created a huge divide between him and his parents. ''Credo'' addresses being a Catholic, and ''Complexion'' looks at Rodriguez's awareness of himself as a Mexican American with dark skin. ''Profession'' deals with the decisions he has made about his academic career. The book winds up with ''Mr. Secrets,'' in which Rodriguez speaks to the struggle his parents have had with the autobiographical essays he has published.

Because these essays are self-contained, they do not necessarily fit together neatly and create a smooth time line of Rodriguez's life and experiences. His writing moves between the periods of his life in each of the essays. In keeping with his assertion that the work is an ''intellectual autobiography,'' Rodriguez structures the book less in terms of passing events and more in terms of his emotional growth and maturity as a citizen and a man.

Point of View and Tone

Rodriguez writes these essays in the first person, and his is the dominant voice throughout. This offers readers direct access to his thoughts and feelings, but readers of any autobiographical writings should be aware that everything the author reveals is colored by personal opinions and beliefs. In *Hunger of Memory*, Rodriguez does not (and should not be expected to) give equal space to those who may disagree with his interpretations of events.

Rodriguez's tone is usually one of pride in what he has accomplished, but he also belittles himself and reveals a few less-than-stellar personal qualities. Often, authors use this technique to make a character appear more human and likeable. Rodriguez's pride in his own academic achievement is mitigated by his argument that what made him a good student was not intelligence but his willingness to memorize whatever he was asked to memorize. When he writes about selecting Stanford University for his undergraduate work, he admits that he did so not only because of its excellent academic reputation but also because ''it was a school rich people went to,'' and he wanted to be around them.

Historical Context

Affirmative Action

Affirmative action refers to a series of federal programs set up to address past discrimination against minority groups and women by protecting these groups against bias and by increasing their representation in the workplace and in educational institutions. These programs emerged from a complicated and hotly debated series of federal laws, presidential directives, and judicial decisions, beginning with the passage of the 1964 Civil Rights Act. This act also created the federal Equal Employment Opportunity Commission. In 1968, the U. S. Department of Labor decided that employers should hire and promote women and minorities in proportions roughly equal to their availability in qualified applicant pools. In 1971, the Supreme Court ruled that the 1964 Civil Rights Act banned not only employment practices in which discrimination against women and minorities was a motive, but those practices that, while not adopted with the intent to discriminate, have a discriminatory impact.

Between 1971 and 1989, several Supreme Court rulings established precedents that restricted some aspects of affirmative action. One of the more famous was the 1978 decision *Bakke v. Regents of the University of California,* in which the court rejected the use of numerical quotas designed to increase university minority enrollment but permitted programs in which race was only one factor of several considered.

Rodriguez's book, which received widespread national attention because of his unexpected stand against affirmative action, was written and published during a period of American history when the issue of affirmative action was contested. Generally, Rodriguez sides with those who argue that affirmative action psychologically harms the individuals it claims to help, creating a caste of people who are never truly assimilated into the mainstream of American public life. Others assert that such programs intensify hostilities toward minorities. Rodriguez also condemns affirmative action programs in education for considering only ethnicity and gender and for failing to recognize that a greater handicap to advancement is years of poor pre-college schooling.

Bilingual Education

The issue of bilingual education in the United States began during the colonial period, and teachers struggled to educate students who spoke only German, Dutch, French, or Swedish. More recently, though, the federal push for bilingual education occurred in 1967, when a bill was introduced in the U. S. Senate amending the 1965 Elementary and Secondary Education Act to help local jurisdictions establish bilingual education programs. The primary goal of this program was to assist the children of new immigrants by providing school lessons taught in their native languages at the beginning of their American educational experience. The first Bilingual Education Act was passed in 1968 and renewed in 1974.

By the mid to late 1970s, serious concerns arose about the effectiveness of bilingual education, especially for Spanish-speaking students. The annual cost of the program grew from $7.5 million in its first year to $150 million in 1979.

Opponents of bilingual education assert that English is the new international language and is required to secure a good job in the United States and also that preserving multiculturalism through language threatens the ''melting pot'' function of the public schools and creates national disunity. Rodriguez sides in his book with the opponents of bilingual education, arguing that success in the United States relies on English skills. ''The bilingualists simplistically scorn the value and the necessity of assimilation,'' he writes. Rodriguez attributes his success, in fact, to learning English early in his education, despite the gulf it created between his Mexican culture and himself.

However, advocates for bilingual education argue that unless non-English-speaking children are taught in their own languages at the start of their schooling, their education will suffer. As well, they believe that the education establishment in the United States should take advantage of the many languages spoken by the new immigrants to give students

Compare & Contrast

- **1950s:** Five million new homes are built between 1945 and 1950; as a result, more than 50 percent of Americans own their own homes. Between 1950 and 1960, 75 percent of metropolitan growth occurs in suburban areas.

  1970s: By 1970, about 40 percent of Americans are living in suburbs; both urban and rural areas are experiencing declines in population. During this decade, about 65 percent of Americans own their own homes.

  Today: The so-called post-suburban age is seeing the rise of ''edge cities,'' areas of planned development on the peripheries of major cities but physically, economically, and culturally independent of the cities. In 2000, about 67 percent of Americans own their own homes, but the home ownership rate is only about 46 percent for Hispanics.

- **1950s:** A weekly comedy show starring Lucille Ball, *I Love Lucy,* is one of the most successful television shows in the history of American broadcasting. First broadcast in 1951, the CBS show develops a loyal following of viewers entertained by its comic depiction of the married life of Lucy and Ricky Ricardo, played by her real-life Cuban husband, Desi Arnaz.

  1970s: NBC has a huge hit from 1974 to 1978 with the situation comedy *Chico and the Man* about two men from very different cultural backgrounds living in East Los Angeles. Freddie Prinze stars as Chico, an ambitious young Chicano (an American of Mexican descent) who is a partner in a garage with the older and cranky Ed Brown, a white man played by Jack Albertson.

  Today: According to many Hispanic groups, fewer and fewer network television roles are going to Hispanics. They point out that one of the few Hispanics in a leading television role is Martin Sheen, who plays the U. S. president on the NBC drama *West Wing.* His real name is Ramon Estevez.

- **1950s:** The issue of government aid to parochial schools is fiercely contested. The Catholic Church opposes all legislation that specifically prohibits

public money from going to church-run schools. In 1950, more than three million American students attend parochial elementary and secondary schools, such as the ones Rodriguez and his siblings attend in Sacramento.

  1970s: Controversies about public support of parochial schools continue. In 1973, the Supreme Court declares unconstitutional a New York State tax provision that grants a tuition tax credit benefit to parents of non-public school students.

  Today: The issue of government vouchers for private schools—payments made by the government to parents or to educational institutions for students' education expenses—is a volatile one. Many parents believe that they should have a choice in where their children are schooled and that the government should foster such choice through tax relief and vouchers.

- **1950s:** The most contested issue in education is the desegregation of the country's public schools. In 1954, the United States Supreme Court decides the case of *Brown v. the Board of Education of Topeka, Kansas.* In its decision, the Court declares that the segregation of races in schools is unconstitutional.

  1970s: With desegregation largely accomplished, the nation's attention turns to affirmative action. After a decade of strengthening affirmative action in education, the United States Supreme Court limits some of its aspects in the 1978 decision *Bakke v. Regents of the University of California.* In this decision, the high court rejects the use of numerical quotas designed to increase university minority enrollment but permits programs in which race is only one of the factors considered.

  Today: Supporters of the goal of a colorblind society continue to challenge advocates of race-conscious solutions to discrimination. The United States Supreme Court has upheld key affirmative action measures in the past, but a series of recent rulings cast doubt on the future of affirmative action.

exposure to a world and a nation that is increasingly diverse.

Critical Overview

Rodriguez's *Hunger of Memory: The Education of Richard Rodriguez* was published in 1981 to a great fanfare of publicity. Here was a young Mexican American who resisted being called a minority and condemned affirmative action programs even though he had benefited from them. He accepted the gulf that lay between his parents and himself as the price immigrants must pay to become assimilated into American culture. And he admitted that when he saw other Hispanic students and teachers on campus striving to maintain their ethnicity and culture by demanding such things as Chicano studies departments and minority literature classes, he was confused. Many critics denounced him as a traitor to his heritage, while others saw him as a clear-headed voice against the political excesses of the 1960s and 1970s.

Paul Zweig, reviewing *Hunger of Memory* in *The New York Times Book Review,* acknowledges that Rodriguez's "superb autobiographical essay" will be "a source of controversy." But he chooses, instead, to focus on the book's literary qualities, calling it "an example of a peculiarly modern sort of book, standing in an honorable tradition that includes Wordsworth's *Prelude* and Proust's *Remembrance of Things Past.*" Rodriguez's story of growing up and moving away from his family is a universal one, argues Zweig, which Rodriguez relates with great success.

In fact, Ilan Stavens in *Commonweal* calls *Hunger of Memory* "a Whitmanesque 'song of myself,' a celebration of individuality and valor in which, against all stereotypes, a Mexican-American becomes a winner." Rodriguez's book is a highly personal meditation, and "his voice is alienated, anti-Romantic, often profoundly sad," according to Stavens. Stavens also praises Rodriguez's literary skills, referring to him as "an extraordinary writer."

Other critics, however, are not as charmed by Rodriguez's language and story of "making it" in middle-class America. Carlos R. Hortas, in an article for *Harvard Educational Review,* asserts that Rodriguez is ashamed that he has "cast aside his Hispanic self, and for this he seeks forgiveness." *Hunger of Memory* is, in Hortas' eyes, Rodriguez's apology for his life and an admission of guilt. "To

be an 'American,'" argues Hortas, "one should not have to divorce oneself from one's ethnic culture and heritage." As well, he accuses Rodriguez of not understanding the "aims of bilingual education."

G. Thomas Couser, in the book *Altered Egos: Authority in American Autobiography,* agrees that Rodriguez's arguments against bilingual education are flawed and that he is at his best when his writing is more personal. "His views on bilingualism do not cohere or convince. His narrative is certainly better at describing the pain that attended his progressive alienation from the intimacy of his Hispanic family."

Hortas also makes a similar observation about Rodriguez's writing strengths. When Rodriguez covers his childhood and the Catholic Church, according to Hortas, his writing is "powerful and compelling . . . and almost lyrically narrated." It is when Rodriguez expresses the reasoning for his political beliefs and actions that his writing is less successful, adds Hortas.

Writing in *Diacritics,* Ramón Saldívar agrees with many critics that Rodriguez has abandoned his culture, writing that *Hunger of Memory* was for Rodriguez a way to seek "redemption." Additionally, Rodriguez's rejection of his culture has caused him to feel "existential anguish," according to Saldívar, and prompted him to address the book to "the most receptive audience imaginable: the right-wing establishment and the liberal academic intelligentsia."

Critics differ on the value of *Hunger of Memory* and disagree on whether it is a book that can be enjoyed as a story of growing up or a book that tells a sad tale of one Hispanic's unwillingness to come to terms with his background. But, however controversial the book may be, Richard D. Woods, writing in *Dictionary of Literary Biography,* asserts that it belongs to "the mainstream of American autobiography." Woods comments that the book's universality is achieved through Rodriguez's "sensitive examination of the complexities of language" and that this is "arguably the most notable accomplishment of the book."

Criticism

Susan Sanderson

Sanderson holds a master of fine arts degree in fiction writing and is an independent writer. In this

Rodriguez on a visit to the Sacred Heart School (Sacramento, California) which he attended as a child

essay, she looks at the universality of Rodriguez's experiences growing up.

Many critics have long considered Rodriguez's memoir *Hunger of Memory: The Education of Richard Rodriguez* a confession and apology for his apparent rejection of his Mexican-American roots. For example, Carlos Hortas writes in *Harvard Educational Review* that Rodriguez wrote his autobiography as "an act of contrition, a confession through which he seeks the forgiveness of Chicanos and other members of 'minority' groups."

Some of these commentators, Hortas included, base their "apology" argument on the perception that Rodriguez seems happiest when he is a very young child, at home, speaking Spanish before the nuns have the talk with his parents that sets his life firmly on the English-speaking road. In a sense, these critics see Rodriguez as a sort of contemporary, Californian Adam: before he is introduced to English (the apple of a certain kind of knowledge), Rodriguez lives in a warm, supportive paradise, wanting for nothing. But after he is forced to abandon that which sustains him and is introduced to the world and to worldliness through English, "paradise" isn't good enough for him anymore, and this

makes him unhappy. Certainly, after a superficial examination of the text, this seems to be the case.

In one scene, for example, Rodriguez admits to rarely leaving the house as a small child and writes that, when he did, he felt uncomfortable. Neighborhood children, primarily white, silently stared as he walked by. The passage in which he returns to his house is written with an almost audible sigh of relief: "I'd hear my mother call out, saying in Spanish . . . 'Is that you Richard?' All the while her sounds would assure me: *You are home now; come closer; inside. With us.*"

This home he returned to was, for Rodriguez, a special place. He remembers being "an extremely happy child at home," a home where he felt "embraced" by the sounds of his parents' voices. His family's use of Spanish, the language spoken almost exclusively inside their home, whispered to Rodriguez, "I recognize you as someone special, close, like no one outside. You belong with us." And later, when Rodriguez is older, he hears someone speaking Spanish and remembers "the golden age of my youth." Indeed, Rodriguez writes of his pre-school youth as an almost intoxicating time that no one would want to leave behind.

What Do I Read Next?

- *The Autobiography of a Brown Buffalo* is a mix of autobiography and novel written by Chicano lawyer and activist Oscar Zeta Acosta. In this 1972 coming-of-age book, Acosta tells the story of his life: his birth in El Paso, growing up in Los Angeles in the 1960s, and becoming a lawyer with the reputation for taking on impossible cases and challenging the status quo.

- Jesus Colon's 1961 collection of essays and other short pieces, *A Puerto Rican in New York and Other Sketches,* reflects his concern for the working class. Some of the pieces are autobiographical.

- Ernesto Galarza's fictionalized autobiography, *Barrio Boy,* tells of the author's birth in Mexico and his years-long migration to California during the Mexican Revolution. In the 1971 book, the author is orphaned but manages to graduate from high school and, like Rodriguez, to attend Stanford University.

- Written in 1950, Octavio Paz's *Labyrinth of Solitude* explores the Mexican psyche through an examination of political power in post-conquest Mexico. Paz, who eventually won the Nobel Prize for Literature, argues for democracy in this book, a stance that placed him at odds with Mexican leaders at the time it was written but won him kudos for his social criticism.

- Richard Rodriguez followed *Hunger of Memory: The Education of Richard Rodriguez* with another collection of autobiographical essays entitled *Days of Obligation: An Argument with My Mexican Father* . This 1992 book was not as well-received as his first work, but Rodriguez expands his subject matter to include the AIDS epidemic, his homosexuality, and the history of California and Mexico.

But after Rodriguez becomes educated and leaves his family's house, his returns are not written of with the same warm glow. Rodriguez remembers the first time he came home from Stanford University for Christmas holiday, and paints the scene in anxious tones.

> The first hours home were the hardest. . . . [L]acking the same words to develop our sentences and to shape our interests, what was there to say? . . . One was almost grateful for a family crisis.

And in the final scene of the book, Rodriguez, as a grown man with a national reputation as an essayist, is home again for another Christmas. The careful mood has not changed much from the first college Christmas. As the holiday festivities break up for the day, Rodriguez's father asks him if he is leaving now for home. "It is, I realize, the only thing he has said to me all evening," notes Rodriguez.

So, yes, Rodriguez's book is filled with sad moments after he begins school and learns English.

But is the pain expressed in the book due to Rodriguez's ambiguity about the value and power of his Hispanic heritage, or simply the result of a natural and inevitable growing up and away from his very close-knit family?

Certainly an argument can be made that, contrary to many critics' contentions that the English language sent Rodriguez down the slippery slope of lost identity, English provided him with a way to be more confident about his place in the world outside of his family's house. This is a confidence that every child must find by one means or another.

When Rodriguez attended class before his English improved—before the nuns asked his parents to speak English at home—he was anxious, fearful, and couldn't imagine participating like all of the other children. He felt like the classic outcast, unable to break the code of meaning in this special new place. Each time one of Rodriguez's elementary school teachers asked him a question in class, he would "look up in surprise and see a nun's face frowning. . . . Silent, waiting for the bell to sound, I remained dazed, diffident, afraid."

But once Rodriguez was forced to speak English with his parents and his siblings, things changed for the better for him at school. After a few weeks of anger and resentment at his parents for demanding English of him, Rodriguez suddenly experienced an epiphany after volunteering to answer a question in class. "I spoke out in a loud voice. And I did not think it remarkable when the entire class understood," he remembers. That day, for Rodriguez, marked a turning point, he writes, a moment when he understood the power of language and his own power as an individual away from his family. He remembers: "That day I moved very far from the disadvantaged child I had been only days earlier. The belief, the calming assurance that I belonged in public, had at last taken hold."

Granted, the weeks before this triumphant classroom moment were marked with frustration and anger on Rodriguez's part. At one point, Rodriguez walked in on his parents speaking to each other in Spanish, but when they saw their son, they immediately changed to English. This was a painful moment of alienation within the family—something Rodriguez had only previously experienced outside of his home. He was being denied entrance into that special place where he used to dwell, that garden of warmth and familiarity. "Those *gringo* sounds they uttered startled me. Pushed me away. In that moment of trivial misunderstanding and profound insight, I felt my throat twisted by unsounded grief," Rodriguez recalls.

As Rodriguez grew up, left for college, and became a man, he experienced other similar moments with his parents—although not all were as strongly colored with anger and rejection—moments when the line between his life as a child and his life as an adult was deeply drawn. For example, Rodriguez's realization in elementary school that he wished to emulate his teachers and not his parents is still strongly etched in his psyche. "I came to idolize my grammar school teachers. I began by imitating their accents, using their diction, trusting their every direction," he says. His parents could not give him what his teachers could: extra help with school work or lists of "important" books to read. Though Rodriguez did not want to admit it as a child, he became embarrassed at his parents' lack of education. He maintains that he never thought them stupid, just that "they were not like my teachers."

> " In a sense, these critics see Rodriguez as a sort of contemporary, Californian Adam: before he is introduced to English (the apple of a certain kind of knowledge), Rodriguez lives in a warm, supportive paradise, wanting for nothing."

There is no denying that *Hunger of Memory* is a sad and moving book. In fact, what may be the book's most poignant moment occurs when Rodriguez returns to California after conducting research on Renaissance literature in London on a Fulbright scholarship. He was "relieved" at how easy it was at first to be around his parents in their house, his old house. "It no longer seemed important to me that we had little to say," Rodriguez remembers. But soon he realized that he had been sidestepping the issue of how much he had changed because of his education. Finally he realized that it was precisely that education that had made it possible for him to think clearly about the ways in which he had changed. "If, because of my schooling, I had grown culturally separated from my parents, my education finally had given me ways of speaking and caring about that fact," he notes.

Rodriguez makes clear in the very beginning of the book what he is most concerned about. *Look,* he seems to be saying, *I am much less interested at this point in my life in my cultural heritage than I am in figuring out how I grew up and what it cost in terms of my relationship with my parents.* He writes:

> Aztec ruins hold no special interest for me. I do not search Mexican graveyards for ties to unnamable ancestors. . . . What preoccupies me is immediate: the separation I endure with my parents. . . . This is what matters to me: the story of the scholarship boy who returns home one summer to discover bewildering silence, facing his parents.

Therefore, the critics' insistence that Rodriguez's angst and sorrow come from his rejection of his culture is not so easily accepted. Rodriguez's concern is more universal. It is about family and individuality and maturity, not about a particular culture and heritage.

The universality of the experiences outlined in *Hunger of Memory* is stressed by many critics, including Paul Zweig in *The New York Times Book Review*. Rodriguez's experiences growing up and moving away from his parents may not be so different from the experiences of many other American youths. And this is what has saved the book from becoming simply a two-hundred-page argument against affirmative action and bilingualism.

As far as rejecting his culture, Rodriguez is adamant that this has not happened and cannot happen. In a 1994 interview with *Reason*, Rodriguez claims that most people see their culture as an unchanging, static thing, while he believes that it is "fluid and experiential." He contends that he belongs to many cultures and has had many different cultural experiences.

> The notion that I've lost my culture is ludicrous, because you can't lose a culture. . . . I'm not my father. I didn't grow up in the state of Colima in western Mexico. I grew up in California in the 1950s.

Source: Susan Sanderson, Critical Essay on *Hunger of Memory: The Education of Richard Rodriguez,* in *Nonfiction Classics for Students,* The Gale Group, 2002.

Gustavo Pérez Firmat

In the following essay, Pérez Firmat explores Rodriguez's non-confessional background, its influence on his undertaking an autobiography, and its impact on the details of his story.

Perhaps because the testimonial impulse is especially strong in emergent literatures, the flowering of imaginative writing by U. S. Hispanics over the last fifteen or twenty years has included many notable memoirs and autobiographies. Indeed, it is hardly an overstatement to say that, up to now, the dominant genre of latino literature has been one or another mode of self-writing—either straightforward memoirs like Ernesto Galarza's *Barrio Boy* (1971) or Esmeralda Santiago's *When I Was Puertorican* (1993); fictional autobiographies like Edward Rivera's *Family Installments* (1982) or Sandra Cisneros's *The House on Mango Street* (1989); or hybrid combinations of prose and poetry, fiction and nonfiction, like Cherríe Moraga's *Loving in the War Years* (1983) or Judith Ortiz Cofer's *The Latin Deli* (1993).

But without a doubt the best-known and most controversial of all latino autobiographies is Richard Rodríguez's *Hunger of Memory* (1982). In the decade and a half since its publication, this small volume has become a fixture in course syllabi and ethnic anthologies. The object of many scathing attacks as well as much fulsome praise, Rodríguez's book has been considered both a paralyzing exercise in self-hatred and an eloquent meditation on the risks and rewards of assimilation. And the author himself has been called everything from a chicano Uncle Tom to a hip William Wordsworth. When I teach this book, which I often do, I'm always struck by the vehemence of some reactions. A few years ago, the final paper of one student took the form of an extended letter, in Spanish, to Rodríguez. After upbraiding him for his abandonment of his mother tongue and his opposition to affirmative action, she ended with the following admonition: "Señor Rodríguez, quiero darle un consejo: *get a life!*"

What my student's comment overlooks, of course, is that autobiography *is* a way of getting a life, an instrument for self-invention. As Paul de Man pointed out years ago, in autobiographical discourse the figure determines the referent as much as the referent determines the figure. Whatever we may think of Rodríguez's views on bilingual education or affirmative action, they are not what his book, as autobiography, is primarily about. The real drama of *Hunger of Memory* lies elsewhere, in the intricate and vexed compositional stance that underlies the book's cultural politics. I would argue, moreover, that even if we are interested in Rodríguez's views on topical issues, we still need to address the tacit conflicts and convictions from which they arise. Before we can fully understand his opposition to bilingual education, for example, we need to grasp the inner dynamic of his relationship with the Spanish language. What I should like to do, therefore, is take a step back from Rodríguez's provocative opinions in order to focus on aspects of the text that are less visible but ultimately more determining.

Let me start with the following proposition: *Hunger of Memory* is the public confession of a man who does not believe in public confessions. Two of the enabling assumptions of autobiography are, first, that there is a gap between the inner and the outer self, between private experience and public expression; and, second, that it is not only possible but desirable to bridge that gap. Although Rodríguez buys into the first of these assumptions, he has grave reservations about the second. Early in the book he reminds us that from the time he was a child, he was taught otherwise—that it is wrong to give public expression to private experience. From the Baltimore catechism that he memorized in parochial school he learned that confession was a sacrament involving a secretive, oral transaction between priest and sinner. As the nuns in parochial school said, it's only the Protestants who bare their souls in public. Catholics do otherwise. Add to this his own parents' disapproval of the smallest acts of public disclosure, and the result is young Richard's deeply-held belief that even the most innocuous bit of personal information is a secret. It is not surprising, thus, that when he is asked to write about his family by a fourth-grade teacher, he produces what he calls a "contrivance," a "fictionalized account" that bears little resemblance to his actual life. Nor is it surprising that, once again contravening a teacher's instructions, he refuses to keep a diary.

But disclosures like these—disclosures about the author's reluctance to disclose—do indicate how precarious an enterprise this autobiography really is. As Rodríguez repeatedly mentions, the lack of precedent for acts of revelation in his earlier life makes him a most unlikely candidate for autobiographer. No wonder, then, his life story paradoxically culminates in a chapter entitled "Mr. Secrets," a nickname that he earns by refusing to talk to his mother about the memoir he is writing. Richard is secretive even about his intention to go public.

Now it is certainly true that Rodríguez intends this moniker ironically. He tells us about his habits of privacy in order to impress upon us the vast differences between the taciturn boy that he was—"I kept so much, so often to myself"—and the self-disclosing man that he has become. By publishing his autobiography, Mr. Secrets has become a tattletale—a metamorphosis with important personal and cultural implications, for it not only breaks with his family's code of secrecy, but also transgresses the Mexican ethic of reserve or *formalidad:* "Writing these pages," he says, "I have not been able to forget that I am not being *formal.*" In a book full of memories, one of the most irrepressible ones seems to be the author's lingering awareness that the act of recollection constitutes a betrayal of sorts. He cannot remember his childhood without at the same time remembering that he is violating his family's trust. This guilt-ridden admission of *informalidad* seems to confirm that he is indeed engaged in revealing "what is most personal." The fact that he was raised not to be *informal* only makes his public confession all the more impressive. As he puts it, "There was a time in

> " Rodríguez's book has been considered both a paralyzing exercise in self-hatred and an eloquent meditation on the risks and rewards of assimilation."

my life when it would never have occurred to me to make a confession like this one."

If we now turn to the book's opening sentences, they do sound like a confession: "I have taken Caliban's advice. I have stolen their books." But this admission of having broken the seventh commandment is somewhat equivocal: the fact is that Richard doesn't steal books, he borrows them from the Sacramento public library. That is to say, once we pause to reflect on these sentences, it becomes difficult to understand exactly what sin Rodríguez is confessing to. Not only is the admission of book theft suspect, but the invocation of Caliban in the very first sentence as if he were the author's brutish muse does not square with the book's tone and content. After all, Rodríguez does not feel enslaved but liberated by his assimilation into North American culture. Whereas Caliban curses Prospero, Rodríguez offers benedictions to the American way, and his finely-wrought and highly self-conscious prose is anything but calibanesque—an example not of *mal-decir* but of *bien-decir.* In addition, a few pages into the prologue Rodríguez himself will forsake Caliban by labelling his text "Ariel's song," an identification subtly reinforced in the title of the first chapter, "Aria."

These equivocations tend to complicate the author's confessional gestures, for they turn *Hunger of Memory* into something other than an informal act of self-disclosure. In actuality, this is an extraordinarily reticent autobiography—a book of revelations that often reads like a mystery story. Even at his most personal, even at his most confessional, even at his most repentant, Rodríguez is nothing if not *formal,* and it is no accident that variations of this word appear throughout the book. He asserts, for example, that the purpose of autobiography is "to form new versions of oneself," and that the end of education is "radical self-reformation." Form, formality, formation, reformation—these notions lie at the heart of *Hunger of Memory*.

Monstrous Caliban—the "freckled whelp" of Shakespeare's play—could never be Rodríguez's muse, for there is little here that could be termed misshapen or unformed. As Ramón Saldívar has pointed out, each of the six chapters is a set piece, a carefully-crafted tableau that organizes the different facets of the author's life around a central theme. Thus, the chapter on his mixed race is called "Complexion"; the one on his faith is entitled "Credo"; and the one on his education, "Profession." Rather than simply narrating his life experiences, Rodríguez distills them, defines them, reduces them to abstractions. This generalizing impulse extends even to the people in his life, not one of whom is identified by a proper name; instead, they are referred to according to their relationship with the author—"my brother," "my sister," "my editor," "the person who knows me best." Even his parents do not escape anonymity—not once does Rodríguez provide their given names. In fact, the only proper name in the whole book is the author's—a situation that, if not unique in autobiographical writing, is certainly extraordinary.

Hunger of Memory moves relentlessly from the individual to the general, from the concrete to the abstract—as the metaphorical hunger of the title already makes evident. Rather than giving narrative shape to his life, as is the case in most autobiographies, Rodríguez opts for a coherence based on the subordination of incident to theme, of content to concept. Instead of telling stories, he offers illustrations; and instead of dwelling on details, he jumps to conclusions. His overriding criterion is intelligibility, a thinker's virtue, rather than narrative interest, the storyteller's goal.

Rodríguez's rationale for this approach is that since he is writing an account of his education, of his "self-reformation," the book should reflect the outcome of this process. And in his eyes, the primary benefit of education is the ability to abstract from experience.

> My need to think so much and so abstractly about my parents and our relationship was in itself an indication of my long education. My father and mother did not pass their time thinking about the cultural meanings of their experience. It was I who described their daily lives with airy ideas. And yet, *positively:* The ability to consider experience so abstractly allowed me to shape into desire what would otherwise have remained indefinite, meaningless longing.

As I read this passage, the first thing that occurs to me is to ask what it means "to shape into desire." Desire can be expressed, repressed, sublimated; it can attach to specific objects or float free. But how does one shape, that is, mold or *form* something into desire? Common twentieth-century wisdom has it the other way around: we don't shape our desires; our desires shape us—and mostly in ways that we don't even realize. The notion of shaping desire verges on the solecistic, but not any more so than the title of the chapter where this passage occurs, "The Achievement of Desire." It seems that when Rodríguez conjugates desire, the real-life grounding of the phenomenon gets lost in abstraction. He treats desire much as he treats hunger—as a figure, as a spiritual or intellectual entity only. Although he asserts at one point that he is engaged in "writing graffiti," the coarse, elemental scribblings that one finds in subways and on bathroom walls have little to do with *Hunger of Memory*'s genteel formulations. Perhaps Caliban could write graffiti, but I doubt that he would know how to shape or achieve desire. In fact, by describing his abstractions as "airy ideas," Rodríguez once again allies himself with Ariel—a connection that in turn suggests that the distinction between shaped desires and indefinite longings recovers the opposition between tame Ariel and unruly Caliban.

In a fine recent essay, Paul John Eakin has called attention to the presence of two voices in this book, one narrative and the other expository. For Eakin, these two voices dramatize the split in Rodríguez's authorial persona between the essayist and the storyteller, and he rightly calls attention to the fact that most of the chapters in the book were written originally as opinion pieces for mainstream publications. What I would add to Eakin's insight is that the two voices are not just distinct but, to some extent, dissonant. Although Rodríguez's deftness makes their mingling seem harmonious, the truth of the matter may be that the expository voice acts to silence or mute the narrative voice. Rather than two voices merging in harmony, the book offers us an active and a passive voice—the active voice of the essayist, and the passive voice of the autobiographer. Rodríguez perhaps admits as much when he describes his book as "essays impersonating an autobiography." Although I will have something to say later about the issue of impersonation, for now I want to highlight Rodríguez's opposition of essay and autobiography. Like the other features we have discussed so far, the primacy of discursive over narrative prose in *Hunger of Memory* makes this book a rather unusual exemplar of modern autobiography.

I would also suggest that the two voices that Eakin hears could well be, at bottom, the shaped voice of desire and the indefinite voice of longing—Ariel's song and Caliban's gabble. And what may be happening here is what often happens elsewhere—desires displace longings; that is, conscious feelings and experiences take the place of recalcitrant or repressed material. It is telling that Rodríguez never relates an incident whose meaning he doesn't understand. He assures us that he is revealing "what is most personal"—and yet we all know that what is most personal is often what is most puzzling. But there is little room for doubt or puzzlement in *Hunger of Memory*. Every fragment of narrative, every anecdote or story is firmly embedded within an expository context that determines its significance. Rodríguez gives his readers less a life than a vita—a conspectus of emblematic incidents and achievements carefully arranged by heading. As a result, we come to the end of the book without knowing very much about large areas of his life. Particularly in the later chapters, he devotes as much time to thinking about autobiography as he does to actually writing one. Rather than an emperor without clothes, Rodríguez is a well-dressed strip-tease artist, but one who insists on his nakedness so often that after a while we actually begin to believe him.

Having come this far, I would like now to pursue the issue of impersonation by turning my attention to a seemingly minor item in the book—a screen door that appears several times—but one that may open the way to a fuller understanding of Rodríguez's vexed autobiographical stance.

Since Rodríguez offers his life as a "parable" about the consequences—good and bad—of leaving home, references to the house where he grew up frame his story. If the first chapter opens by evoking the day he first left his home to go to elementary school, the last chapter concludes by showing the grown-up Rodríguez leaving the house again after a Christmas dinner. Between these two scenes, the house is evoked several times, and almost every time the screen door is also mentioned. Discussing the separation between his home and society, Rodríguez states: "Outside the house was public society; inside the house was private. Just opening or closing the screen door behind me was an important experience." This is how he describes beginning elementary school: "Until I was six years old I

remained in a magical realm of sound. I didn't need to remember that realm because it was present to me. But then the screen door shut behind me as I left home for school." The memory of the door accompanies him even into the British Museum, where he finds himself many years later doing research for his dissertation on Renaissance English literature. Hearing some Spanish academics whispering to each other, he has a flashback: "Their sounds seemed ghostly voices recalling my life. Yearning became preoccupation then. Boyhood memories beckoned, flooded my mind. (Laughing intimate voices. Bounding up the front steps of the porch. A sudden embrace inside the door.)"

Whatever this door may have looked like in reality, in his recollections Rodríguez imagines it as a protective barrier—opaque rather than transparent, occlusive rather than permeable. If his childhood home is a world apart, a Spanish-language fortress, that door is the bulwark that keeps intruders at bay. These symbolic associations become all the more evident once we note the contrast with one other door in the book. Referring to his boyhood friendships with non-Mexican kids on his block, Rodríguez writes. "In those years I was exposed to the sliding-glass-door informality of middle-class California family life. Ringing the doorbell of a friend's house, I would hear someone inside yell out, 'Come on in, Richie; door's not locked.'" Unlike the screen door, which isolates, this door connects. If the screen door is a buffer, the sliding glass door is a bridge. If one keeps out, the other welcomes in; if one encloses, the other exposes (note how the passage begins: "In those years I was *exposed* . . ."). Clearly the idea is that in the typical middle-class household—and let's not forget that Rodríguez thinks of his life as a "middle-class pastoral"—the transition from inside to outside, from private to public, from the family circle to the social sphere, is gradual rather than abrupt. Instead of two separate worlds, there is one continuous, uniform space.

For this reason, the unexpected recurrence in this passage of the key notion of informality is entirely apt. If we take Rodríguez at his word, the story of his education can be summarized as the evolution from working-class Mexican formality to middle-class American informality, an evolution that he images as the replacement of a screen door with a sliding glass door. Moreover, since Catholic confession takes place behind a screen—often a screen with a sliding cover—the image of the sliding glass door also implies a departure from the confessional model. Speaking to a non-Hispanic audience a couple of years after the publication of *Hunger of Memory*, Rodríguez depicted his life as a move "out of my own house and over to yours." The architectural imagery in the book certainly bears out this assertion.

The stumbling block here, however, is that this implicit identification of *Hunger of Memory* with glass rather than screen, with openness rather than enclosure, once again runs counter to our experience of the book. It is hard to see how this autobiography could be read as a literary manifestation of "sliding-glass-door informality"—even the language of this phrase, with its string of modifiers linked together by hyphens, clashes with the book's usual diction. Every writer has his or her favorite punctuation marks, and Rodríguez's is clearly the period. Cobbling together short, clipped phrases, he composes by placing bits of text next to each other and cordoning them off with periods. This is the description of his grandmother: "Eccentric woman. Soft. Hard." Much like the chapters of the book, each of these sentence fragments gives the impression of being a discrete, free-standing unit—a cameo or miniature whose connection to the material that precedes or follows remains unstated.

Since Rodríguez has asserted that "autobiography is the genre of the discontinuous life," it is not surprising that he should write discontinuous, paratactic prose. The style is the man—or at least the mannerism. And there is much in this book that speaks of discontinuity—between past and present, between Spanish and English, between parents and children, between the culture of the hearth and the culture of the city. My point, however, is that the book's dominant idiom is far removed from the agglutinative impetus of a phrase like "sliding-glass-door informality," where everything connects, semantically and typographically. This is true also of the second half of the sentence, with its reference to "middle-class California family life," another agglutinative phrase. But constructions like these are actually quite rare in *Hunger of Memory*. Instead of a life on the hyphen, Rodríguez offers us a portrait in pieces, a mosaic of self-contained, fragmentary poses.

In the end, therefore, his autobiography is more screen than glass. Ironically perhaps, the book is composed in the image and likeness of the house and the family and the culture that the author has supposedly outgrown. In this sense, Rodríguez never leaves his parents' house. As Tomás Rivera once

suggested, there are moments when this book reads like an extended postscript to Octavio Paz's *El laberinto de la soledad* (1950). What Paz did for the *pachuco*, the zoot-suited teenager of the *barrio*, Rodríguez does for the *pocho*, the assimilated teenager from the suburbs. In spite of the author's claims to the contrary, I find *Hunger of Memory* a profoundly Mexican performance, at least according to the portrayal of *mexicanidad* in Paz's classic book. It is in the context of *El laberinto de la soledad* that Rodríguez's characterization of his book as "essays impersonating an autobiography" becomes especially meaningful, as does his self-description as a "great mimic." *Hunger of Memory* may well be an elegant impersonation, an example of mimicry or *simulación*, one more *máscara mexicana*, to allude to one of the best-known chapters in *El laberinto de la soledad*. Paz writes, "el mexicano se me aparece como un ser que se encierra y se preserva: máscara el rostro y máscara la sonrisa. . . Entre la realidad y su persona establece una muralla, no por invisible menos infranqueable" ["the Mexican seems to me to be a person who shuts himself away to protect himself: his face is a mask and so is his smile . . . He builds a wall of indifference and remoteness, a wall that is no less impenetrable for being invisible."] These sentences might also describe the author of *Hunger of Memory*, who may be much less of a *pocho* than he thinks. One man's *muralla* is another man's screen door.

Of course, the question now is: if *Hunger of Memory* turns out to be a wall of words, an artfully reticulated screen, what is it that lies behind it? The short answer to the question is that we don't know, but it is probable that one half of the answer has to do with sexuality, and the other half has to do with language. Although I don't intend to enter here into a discussion of *Hunger of Memory*'s treatment of sexuality, it is worth remarking that Rodríguez's near-total silence about any romantic or sexual involvements in his life cannot be without significance. Limiting himself to a couple of brief, ambiguous references to his "sexual anxieties," Rodríguez writes as if issues of sex or gender had played no part in making him the man he has become. Yet one suspects that his reticence on this score may reflect not that there is little to be said, but that perhaps there is too much. Indeed, part of the problem with *Hunger of Memory*, one of the reasons why it is such a disconcerting book, may be that Rodríguez attributes to culture conflicts and insecurities that have rather—or also—to do with gender.

On the role of language in his life, Rodríguez seems rather more forthcoming, to the point of asserting that "language has been the great subject of my life." But here again the abstractness of the formulation tends to divert attention from the material facts. When Rodríguez makes this assertion, the singular subject masks the plural reality of his experience, and particularly the fact that, until he was six years old, he spoke only Spanish. It is perhaps more accurate to say that the great subject of his life is not language in the abstract but the clash or interference between specific languages—Spanish and English. Nonetheless, the mask is the message: what lies behind the screen door is what always did lie behind the screen door—the Spanish language, those "ghostly voices" that he hears even in so improbable a setting as the reading room of the British Museum (the paradox of hearing voices in a "reading" room was probably not lost on Rodríguez). Although the number of actual Spanish words in *Hunger of Memory* is very small, the book as a whole is haunted by Spanish—not by words exactly, not by a language in the usual sense of the term, but by something less studied and more amorphous, something like a far cry.

In fact, Rodríguez treats Spanish less as a language than a euphoric, logoclastic phonation. He remembers: "Family language: my family's sounds. Voices singing and sighing, rising, straining, then surging, teeming with pleasure that burst syllables into fragments of laughter." For Rodríguez, Spanish is both more and less than a language. It is more than a language because it serves as the channel for deep emotional bonding; but it is less than a language because this channel cannot be used for routine verbal communication. This is why Rodríguez takes the rather bizarre position that Spanish cannot be the language of public discourse—the reason is not because it's Spanish, but because in his mind Spanish is not really a language. This is also why, when he recalls childhood conversations, he generally lapses into a musical vocabulary. Speaking of his banter with his siblings, he says, "A word like *sí* would become, in several notes, able to convey added measures of feelings." The fact that in Spanish *si* is the name of a note on the musical scale only underscores the collapse or "bursting" of words into sounds, of language into music. This is how Rodríguez describes his father's arrival from work in the evenings: "I remember many nights when my father would come back from work, and I'd hear him call out to my mother in Spanish, sounding relieved. In Spanish he'd sound light and free notes

he could never manage in English." Typically, Richard's father doesn't speak words, he sounds notes. Indeed, in this resonant home even the lock on the screen door has a "clicking tongue." Later in the book, when Rodríguez describes the Latin liturgy as "blank envelopes of sound," this phrase could also be applied to his conception of Spanish.

Since the opposite of wordless sounds is soundless words, and since the paradigm of a silent language is writing, Rodríguez's view of language cannot be divorced from the primacy he gives the written over the spoken word. The distinction between Spanish and English folds into the contrast between speech and writing: words first, English only. But by setting things up in this manner Rodríguez snares himself in contradiction. Like a man who tries to hear by making himself deaf, he chooses a medium for recollection that ensures that he will not be able to capture some of his most indispensable memories. But maybe the truth is that he cultivates deafness because he knows that he cannot hear. When he confesses that learning English was his "original sin," the acknowledged guilt may mask unacknowledged embarrassment. Behind or beneath the learned references to Shakespeare and Wordsworth, behind or beneath the poise and polish of the self-conscious stylist, someone babbles, *balbucea*—could it be that Richard is really Caliban after all?

If writing is always a way of dressing wounds, the hurt that Rodríguez dresses and redresses is a wound of language. His English prose is a silent screen, a strategy of *simulación* that works to keep the inside in, as it were, to mute the pangs of a certain kind of inarticulateness, of what we might call the *¡ay!* inside the aria. One of the most crucial components of our self-image is the idea we have of ourselves as language users. Thus, one of the most disabling forms of self-doubt arises from our knowledge or belief that we cannot speak our native language well enough. When Rodríguez gets a summer job that requires him to speak in Spanish with some Mexican coworkers, he confesses: "As I started to speak, I was afraid with my old fear that I would be unable to pronounce the Spanish words." I have witnessed this fear many times in students of Hispanic background. I have seen how they squirm and look away when they think you expect them to speak as if Spanish were their native language. I have often squirmed and looked away myself, feeling that no matter how good my Spanish may be, that it is just not good enough, not what it should be. For people like us, every single one of our English sentences takes the place of the Spanish sentence that we weren't able to write. And if we handle English more or less well, it is because we want to write such clean, clear English prose that no one will miss the Spanish that it replaces.

This is another way of saying that one of the largest appetites in *Hunger of Memory* is a craving for Spanish—one of those "indefinite and meaningless longings" that Rodríguez tries to transcend. And the longing is indefinite and meaningless because it is not a desire for definitions or meanings—those one can have in any language—but a nostalgia for sounds, for bursting syllables, for the untranslatable notes that he heard and uttered as a child. While discussing his passion for music, Rodríguez states: "At one moment the song simply 'says' something. At another moment the voice stretches out the words—the heart cannot contain!—and the voice moves toward pure sound." Like a song, *Hunger of Memory* says a lot of things, but it also contains—and fails to contain—the far cry of Spanish vocables, the *¡ay!* inside the aria. Rodríguez responds to the loss of Spanish sounds by taking refuge in English words—which is why the original title of the book was simply "Toward Words." And yet I find his autobiography valuable and moving not only because of his way with words but also because of the muffled music that one hears in the silences between periods—an unsatisfied and perhaps insatiable hunger that his heart cannot quite contain.

Source: Gustavo Pérez Firmat, "Richard Rodriguez and the Art of Abstraction," in *Colby Quarterly,* Vol. XXXII, No. 4, December 1996, pp. 255–66.

Tomás Rivera

In the following essay, Rivera discovers in Hunger of Memory *"a negation of what is fundamentally the central element of the human being—the cultural root, the native tongue."*

(Editor's Note: Shortly before his untimely death, Tomás Rivera sent me the following essay. Except for minor typographical corrections, I have left the work, described by Chancellor Rivera as written from a "loose personal perspective," as he wrote it. I wish to thank Rolando Hinojosa, Tomás Rivera's literary executor, for advice and permission to publish this essay here. M.P.)

Although I was born in Texas, had lived in many states in the Midwest and had not lived in any Spanish-speaking country, until then, my public voice as well as my private voice was Spanish through my first eleven years. It was in the fifth grade, that *eureka!* to my surprise, I started speaking English without translating. I suppose that at that time I had two public voices as well as two private ones.

Hunger of Memory is an exceptionally well written book. It is a profound book, a personal expression which one learns to respect for its sensibility. To respect this type of sensibility is something I learned in the Spanish-taught "escuelita," which I attended before entering public school at age 7. What Richard Rodriguez has written has great value. However, I have difficulties with concepts in the book which I consider anti-humanistic. For several reasons I consider *Hunger of Memory* as a humanistic antithesis. This book has been controversial for the Hispanic in general and in particular to the Mexican-American or Chicano. This has been the case much more so, I think, because it seems to be so well accepted by the North American public as a key to understanding the Mexican-American and debates related to bilingual education and affirmative action. Thus, it is important to define and perceive the book from different vantage points. Hispanics, Chicanos, and Latinos are not a homogenous group. They are as heterogeneous a kindred group as any that exists in our present society. They are at different levels of development, perception, understanding and as complex and therefore as complete as other human beings. Richard Rodriguez' book is a personal expression, an autobiography, and it must be understood as that in its singularity. It should not be used as a single way or method of understanding the bilingual, bicultural phenomenon of the Hispanic group. I do not know Richard Rodriguez. I have seen him on television. I have read *Hunger of Memory* three times. I intend to read it again for it has much to offer. The work becomes more with each reading.

Richard Rodriguez' essays have a style and tone which complement and establish his concepts. *Hunger of Memory* establishes its tone through patterns based on the ideas of silence and the centrality of language—silence versus non-silence, silence and active language, silence and culture, silence and intelligence. The aggregation of silence seems to indicate that if a person does not speak, he/she lacks intelligence. This is a view generally held by many teachers in the classroom: how can one judge silence? If a child's hand does not go up, if a question is not asked, the teacher's perception is usually that there is a lack of intelligence. Richard Rodriguez insists on the presence of his signal-silence and the public voice. If a person does not speak he/she does not have a public voice. How can one have a personal voice only in silence as the only true aggregate? The author indicates that Spanish was and is his personal voice. But it is an inactive passive voice that became neutered, sterile, and finally silent—dead.

I find underlined throughout the text a negation of what is fundamentally the central element of the human being—the cultural root, the native tongue. As one reads each essay, one progressively recognizes that what is most surprising for Richard Rodriguez is that silence and his basic culture are negative elements, regressive ones. This pattern of negation is softened somewhat when he thinks of his parents and his love for his parents, but he ultimately comes to the thesis that this silence and the consequent inactive community is something regressive or negative. This dealing with silence reminds me of my efforts in struggling with this phenomenon of silence when I studied in Mexico and lived with Mexican families; especially in the rural communities, where I tried to write about what I considered the impenetrable face/masks and their silence. But I never thought for a moment that their masks did not conceal an imagination or thought processes, not that they were not developing and inventing constantly their own world view and perceptions. And that, although they were not speaking to me and hardly to each other, they were not actively thinking. Richard Rodriguez delves into silence, and writes from silence as he himself tells us, "I am here alone, writing, and what most moves me is the silence." Truly this is an active task for him. Yet, with regard to his own family, he sees this silence as a non-force. He finally concludes simplistically, unfortunately, that his personal voice is Spanish and that his active voice is English. Surely, this is a humanistic antithesis.

It is necessary at this point to call attention to his development as a writer. He grew up and was taught in the humanities. The humanities have a clear base—at a minimum the explaining or aiding in the elaboration of a philosophy of life. Surely by the time one is twelve years old or so one has a philosophy of life. By then one has formulated and asked all the great philosophical questions and has even provided some answers. Whether one asks and answers in English or Spanish or in any other tongue is not important. The humanities, and certainly the study of literature, recognize this. As an educated scholar in literature, certainly, and much more so as a Renaissance scholar, Richard Rodriguez should know this. But his thoughts do not recognize this

> **As a writer . . . he fails to analyze those pressures that force conformity and simply attributes negative values to the language and culture of his parents, who have, as he states 'no-public-voice.'"**

fundamental philosophical base. Clearly as a youngster of twelve or thirteen years of age he could not have, but certainly as an academic he could have reflected on the realities of his life, on the sensibility, and on the importance of what he did not know then and what he must now know. The humanities are also, to put it simply, a search for life, a search for form, but most significantly a search for wisdom. In this regard Richard Rodriguez starts out well. His search for life and form in the literary form of autobiography has as a premise the basic core of family life. But then Richard Rodriguez struggles with the sense of disassociation from that basic culture. Clearly, he opts to disassociate, and, as a scholar, attempts to rationalize that only through disassociation from a native culture was he to gain and thus has gained the "other," that is, the "public" world. Without wisdom he almost forgets the original passions of human life. Is he well educated in literature? For literature above all gives and inculcates in the student and scholar the fundamental original elements of humanistic endeavor without regard to race or language, much less with regards to a public voice. The most important ideas that the study of the humanities relate are the fundamental elements and values of human beings, regardless of race and nationality. Ultimately, the study of the humanities teaches the idea that life is a relationship with the totality of people within its circumstance.

Then we come to the question of place and being. In Spanish there are two verbs meaning "to be," *Ser* and *Estar*. This is quite important to *Hunger of Memory*. Being born into a family is equal to being, *Ser*. Education and instruction teaches us to be, *Estar*. Both are fundamental verbs. *Ser* is an interior stage, and *Estar* is an exterior one. To leave the *Ser* only for the *Estar* is a grievous error. Richard Rodriguez implies, at times explicitly, that the authentic being is and can only be in the *Estar* (public voice) and only there is he/she complete. And further, he states that authenticity can only come by being an exterior being in English in the English speaking world. In the Hispanic world, the interior world of *Ser* is ultimately more important than the world of *Estar*. *Honra,* honesty, emanates from and is important to the *Ser*. Richard Rodriguez opts for the *Estar* world as the more important and does not give due importance to the world of *Ser*. He has problems, in short, with the world from which he came. Surely this is an antithesis to a humanistic development.

As with memory, the centrality of language is a constant pattern in the book. For the Hispanic reader the struggle quickly becomes English versus Spanish. His parents do not know the grand development of the Spanish language and its importance beyond their immediate family. However, Richard Rodriguez should, as an educated person, recognize this grand development. Surely, he could have given credit to the development of a language that has existed over six hundred years, which has elaborated a world literature, which has mixed with the many languages of the American continents, which is perhaps the most analytical of the romance languages, and which will be of such importance in the twenty-first century. Instead Richard Rodriguez flees, as a young man, from this previous human achievement. This fleeing is understandable as a symbol of the pressures of the Americanization process. Yet, as a formally educated scholar, reflecting upon that flight, he does not dare to signal the importance that the language has. Instead he sees it as an activity that has no redeeming value. He gives no value to the Hispanic language, its culture, its arts. It is difficult to believe that as an educated humanist he doesn't recognize the most important element of Hispanic culture—the context of the development of the distinct religions in the Spanish peninsula—the Judaic, the Christian, and the Moorish. These distinct cultures reached their apogees and clearly influenced Spanish. As a humanist, surely he must know this. The Hispanic world has elaborated and developed much in the history of ideas. Richard Rodriguez seems to indicate that the personal Spanish voice lacks the intelligence and ability to communicate beyond the sensibilities of the personal interactions of personal family life. This is intolerable. Hispanic culture has a historical tradition of great intellectual development. He does not recognize the so-called "original sin" of the American continents. What is this *pecado original* that Hector

Murena wrote about so eloquently? It is simply the act of transplanting the European cultures to the American continents. The conquest by the Europeans of what is today Hispanic America is one of the most fundamental struggles for justice. The Laws of Burgos, established in Spain before the conquest of Mexico, held above all that the Indian was a man of the world. This was a fundamental axiom. The evolved mestizo nations struggled through a racist colonial empire, but there was a mixture of races. This was less evident in the English-speaking world. I mention this because it appears to me that one of the greatest preoccupations of Richard Rodriguez is that he "looks" Indian. He speaks of his father as looking and being white. He speaks of his mother as looking Portuguese. It surprises me that as an educated humanist in 1982 he would still have that type of complex, colonized mind. He feels out of place in Bel Aire in L.A. because he looks Indian. He worries about what or how he will be perceived by the "Anglo." These are honest and sincere perceptions. I respect his feelings. He does, however, remind me of students I had in the 50s and 60s who were struggling with their brownness.

The Hispanic colonial period evolved a racism based mainly on color and, of course, class. The colonial mind was preoccupied with color. When a child born to a couple was darker than the parents, he/she was called a "*salto a tras,*" a jump backwards, but if the child was lighter, he/she was considered a "*salto adelante,*" a jump forward; and if the child was the same color as the parents, a "*tente en el aire,*" suspended. At times Richard Rodriguez clearly illustrates a colonized mind. His reactions as a young child are understandable. As a writer, however, while interpreting these sensibilities well, he fails to analyze those pressures that force conformity and simply attributes negative values to the language and culture of his parents, who have, as he states "no-public-voice."

It is well to recall briefly the formation of the Mexican nation and its history as it went from a political to an intellectual emancipation from 1811 to 1917. It took the Mexican nation over 100 years and 50 civil wars to evolve an independent, clear, and creative character. It is a unique nation. By 1930 the Mexican character was distinct—its art, music, literature, and culture were unique. It had developed a unique identity and character; it had accepted the mestizo. Surely, Richard Rodriguez must recognize, now that he is educated, that his parents came from a culture that was distinctly Mexican, and nonimitative, that his parents represent a culture with a singular identity. He offers, however, no recognition of the cultural uniqueness of his parents. Mexican culture had gone through its colonial and imitative period, its struggle for intellectual emancipation, and had arrived as an authentic, unique nation. His parents, therefore, recognize much better than Richard Rodriquez who the ''gringos'' are. This is a constant motif in the book. His parents know who they are themselves. They are no puzzle unto themselves. Richard Rodriguez says that change is a constant and should be constant and he argues that in order to change or to have the dynamics of change it is necessary to leave behind his Mexicanness, represented by the silence of the personal voice, the non-public voice, and his distinct cultural attributes. By gaining the other public voice, he asserts, he will become more authentic. Truly, this is antithetical to a humanistic education.

Richard Rodriguez' views remind me of two excellent books. The first one was published in 1930 by Samuel Ramos, *El perfil del hombre en la historia de Mexico* (The Profile of Man in the History of Mexico), and the other was published in 1950 by Octavio Paz, *El laberinto de soledad* (The Labyrinth of Solitude). *El perfil* discusses the inferiority complex of the Mexican. *El laberinto* reflects on the silence and the bursting out from that silence of the Mexican psyche. They are books eloquent in their perceptions of silence and the negativistic attitudes about the Mexican psyche. Samuel Ramos writes about *el pelado*; Octavio Paz has a marvelous chapter on *el pachuco* and now with Richard Rodriguez there is a total book on *el pocho* or what he considers to be *el pocho*. *El pelado, el pachuco* and *el pocho* can be considered alienated persons at the margins of culture. They do not represent the totality of the Hispanic culture in general, nor, in particular, the Mexican or Mexican-American culture. These are books about extreme people. What the *pelado,* the *pachuco,* and what Richard Rodriguez symbolize is a type of graffitti. By saying this, I do not seek to demean Richard Rodriguez' endeavor at all, but simply to point out that the most important element of graffitti is that it is an expression. Done in silence. Powerful. Exact. It calls out attention to itself as it saying ''I want to understand myself,'' ''I want you, the passerby, to understand me. I am at the (extreme) margin. I want to be; I hunger to be part of your memory.'' Graffitti beckons us. It calls to tell us that they *are* us—in an extreme way, that they exist between cultures, but outside a culture.

In spite of its humanistic antithesis, *Hunger of Memory* has an authentic dimension. Perhaps the most important element here is that Richard Rodriguez is a reflection of a North American education. Is he a reflection of the English professor or the place of preparation which doesn't really give him perceptions other than those of the English-speaking world? There is, ultimately, I believe, a lack of understanding of world culture; especially lacking is an understanding of the Hispanic world. It is a reflection of a North American education. He calls himself Caliban in ''Mr. Secrets.'' Who is Caliban? He is a slave, a monster, a character in Shakespeare's last play. Caliban represents the puppet, the person who is controlled. Caliban in *The Tempest* was driven by material instincts only. ''Mr. Secrets,'' the last chapter, is especially clear on this concept. Is Caliban a reflection of a North American education? Is it an indication of an education which refuses to acknowledge as important only that which is tied to the northern European cultures? Is it an attitude of non-inquiry in the teaching of humanities? Aren't racist impositions, Adamic and nativistic concepts and attitudes quite prevalent?

The great surprise of many of our students who study abroad is that of finding out that not everything is originated (truly) in the United States, and that in reality our cultural history is quite short and in many instances limited. Richard Rodriguez is saying that he now has a public voice, an authentic one. Before he did not. He now believes that he is more real, and this is absurd. The dimension that Richard Rodriguez gives the North American public in his book fits well within North American intellectual circles because he has ironically justified his context by ''being'' not one of ''them,'' but rather by having become one of ''us.'' The North American public accepts Richard Rodriguez quite well and much in the same manner that it accepted Oscar Lewis' studies of the poor in Puerto Rico and Mexico. In this manner, knowledge of the unknown is accepted, simplified, and categorized. One has to ask if Richard Rodriguez has a community now? Did he have a community in the past? Does he think that now because he has published and has been accepted as a good writer that he now has community? Richard Rodriguez exists between two cultures, but he believes it more important to participate in one world than the other. But it is possible to participate in many worlds profoundly and, without losing, but rather gaining perception and appreciation from all.

I want to place in opposition to Richard Rodriguez's work a body of Chicano literature which has precepts as profound and as well written. This body of expression has not had the same acceptance. Some of it is written in Spanish, some in English, and some in a mixture of both languages. It is not recognized well, basically because the works have not been published nor merchandized by major American publishing companies. In these Chicano works there is little hunger of memory, and much hunger for community. If Richard Rodriguez has hunger of memory, Chicano literature hungers for community. Those who labored, in the 1960s and 1970s and into the 1980s to establish a literature, accepted the task to develop a literature in the United States and that it was to be in languages understandable primarily to the Mexican-American community. The endeavor was a basic challenge to North American literary dominance. In 1965, there were few works written by writers of Mexican extraction in the United States. There were no courses being taught in Chicano literature. Today there are courses taught in Chicano literature in a total of 135 universities at the undergraduate and graduate level. It is recognized as a body of literature either as part of Mexican literature, as part of American literature, or as an offshoot of Hispanic-American literature. It has several intellectual bases, but this literature does not interest Richard Rodriguez even as a curiosity—even though, paradoxically, he is now inextricably part of that contribution.

The Chicano writers I have in mind were hungry for community. The manner of establishing that community was through remembrance and rediscovery of commonalities of the culture plus the need to accept the community in all its heterogeneity—that is, with all its virtues, with all its flaws, With all its energy, with all its apathy. It was important to recognize and to develop the basic elements of our community. Martin Buber's idea that ''Community is the aspiration of all human history'' was clearly before us. The Mexican-American as part of human history had to develop that community, to be part of it, or leave it. Rebecca West says that ''Community is conversation,'' and the Mexican-American community has not been silent since then. What the Chicano writer did was establish a community where there was a definite place, where dialogues could develop, and where the values of the community could be elaborated. There was little concern regarding acceptance by the larger/majority population. There is a more visible Chicano/Mexican-American community today because Chicano writers aided in underlining the realities that made up the community. Clearly Richard Rodriguez regards

that community as living in silence. Actually that is why he is very alone. What one senses in *Hunger of Memory* is that his parents no longer speak. Ironically his parents speak louder than he. The sensibility of his writing effort, I dare say, does not come only from his training in the English language, but from those early day experiences when he was taught, I am sure, the way to invent himself in the world by his parents.

I said earlier that Richard Rodriguez reminds me of students I had in college in the 1960s who were embarrassed to organize themselves, who did not want to bring their parents to college to participate in college activities because their parents wouldn't know how to dress, and students who hardly respected the few Chicano professors who were then around. Truly, these students had the same type of colonized mind dramatized by Richard Rodriguez—honest, authentic, and naïve, particularly at this later date.

What *Hunger of Memory* therefore reveals is one more step in the intellectual emancipation of the Mexican-American. It represents a significant intellectual step because such views are so clearly articulated. His parents know who they are, who they were, and who the gringos were. They didn't stop talking to him because they didn't understand him, but because he no longer saw the significance of their life. Richard Rodriguez lost the memory of all the philosophical questions they had helped him face and answer long before he walked into the English-speaking world. A writer is lonely only if he has lost the sense of his community's aspirations and the integrative values. His parents are the thesis of his statement. Sometimes, he feels frustrated because they have not read Garcia-Marquez, Ruben Dario, but then he never read these writers to them. He hungers for a memory that could be so close, yet he doesn't seem to realize that satisfying this appetite is within reach.

Hunger of Memory is thus a humanistic antithesis for several reasons. First, because its breadth and dimension is so narrow, unaware as it is of the traditions that should inform it. Second, it is ultimately an aggregation of cultural negations. Richard Rodriguez prizes as authentic only that which he learns in the classrooms. Third, he underlines the silence of culture as negative. Finally, Richard Rodriguez believes that it is only through English that he thinks he can elaborate what is correct and not correct for the community as a whole.

In his last chapter, "Mr. Secrets," as the family is leaving, and everyone is standing outside, his mother asks him to take a sweater to his father because it is getting cold. The last words of the book are "I take it [the sweater] and place it on him. In that instant I feel the thinness of his arms. He turns. He asks if I am going home now, too. It is, I realize, the only thing he has said to me all evening."

Here Richard Rodriguez tells us that his father has been silent all evening. What he doesn't tell us is that he (Richard Rodriguez) has also been silent. He does not tell us about *his* own type of silence. If he has a hunger of memory it is mainly because he does not choose to communicate his more intimate memories. Can anything be that painful? Where is the real *honra*, the real *Ser*? The only positive cultural attributes which he signals throughout his book are those relative to the English-speaking world. Richard Rodriguez understands the needs for memory, but does not dare recover it totally. Why? The title is the thesis, but the content is the antithesis of the very title. This is a classic work, 1930 Mexican vintage, clearly seeking approbation of an inferiority complex. As Samuel Ramos stated in *El perfil del hombre,* it is not that the Mexican is inferior: it's that he thinks he is inferior. This was the legacy of Spanish colonization. Richard Rodriguez apparently decolonizes himself by seeking to free himself from a personal voice, but in so trying he will likely enter another colony of despair.

Source: Tomás Rivera, "Richard Rodriguez' *Hunger of Memory* as Humanistic Antithesis," in *Melus,* Volume 11, No. 4, Winter 1984, pp. 5–13.

Sources

Couser, G. Thomas, "Biculturalism in Contemporary Autobiography: Richard Rodriguez and Maxine Hong Kingston," in *Altered Egos: Authority in American Autobiography,* Oxford University Press, 1989, pp. 210–45.

Crowley, Paul, "An Ancient Catholic: An Interview with Richard Rodriguez," in *America,* Vol. 173, No. 8, September 23, 1995, pp. 8ff.(4).

Hortas, Carlos R., "*Hunger of Memory: The Education of Richard Rodriguez:* Book Review," in *Harvard Educational Review,* Vol. 53, No. 3, August 1983, pp. 355–59.

Postrel, Virginia, and Nick Gillespie, "The New, New World: Richard Rodriguez on Culture and Assimilation," in *Reason,* Vol. 26, August 1, 1994, pp. 35ff.(7).

Saldívar, Ramón, "Ideologies of the Self: Chicano Autobiography," in *Diacritics,* Vol. 15, No. 3, Fall 1985, pp. 25–34.

Stavens, Ilan, "*Hunger of Memory: The Education of Richard Rodriguez:* Book Review," in *Commonweal,* Vol. 120, No. 6, March 26, 1993, pp. 20ff.(3).

Woods, Richard D., "Richard Rodriguez," in *Dictionary of Literary Biography,* Vol. 82: *Chicano Writers, First Series,* edited by Francisco A. Lomeli and Carl R. Shirley, Gale Research, 1989, pp. 214–16.

Zweig, Paul, "The Child of Two Cultures," in *New York Times Book Review,* February 28, 1982, pp. 1, 26.

Further Reading

Beckwith, Frances J., and Todd E. Jones, eds., *Affirmative Action: Social Justice or Reverse Discrimination?,* Prometheus Books, 1997.
> Frances Beckwith is an opponent of affirmative action, while Todd Jones supports these programs. They have edited a collection of articles and essays addressing this issue and provided readers with a cool-headed approach to understanding it.

Kingston, Maxine Hong, *The Woman Warrior: Memoirs of a Girlhood among Ghosts,* Vintage Books, 1989.
> Maxine Hong Kingston's memoir of growing up Chinese in Stockton, California, is the story of a young girl living in two worlds. She hears from her mother amazing stories of China, filled with the supernatural, but she lives among the non-Chinese, the American "ghosts," in California.

Stavens, Ilan, *The Hispanic Condition: Reflections on Culture and Identity in America,* HarperPerennial Library, 1996.
> Ilan Stavens brings his own experiences to this examination of the history and attitudes of Hispanics in the Americas. Stavens's experiences include his childhood as a middle-class Jew living in Mexico City and as a white Mexican student moving into a diverse Latino community in New York City.

Suro, Roberto, *Strangers among Us: Latinos' Lives in a Changing America,* Vintage Books, 1999.
> Journalist Roberto Suro considers the issues critical to understanding Latino immigration to the United States. He covers topics such as poverty, bilingual education, and the relationship of Latinos to other ethnic groups.

The Interpretation of Dreams

Sigmund Freud

1899

Sigmund Freud (1856–1939) is universally considered the "father" of psychoanalysis, and many date the birth of psychoanalytic theory from the 1899 publication of *The Interpretation of Dreams* (copyright 1900). Although Freudian theory, since its inception, has been relentlessly attacked from all sides, critics and proponents alike agree that Freud's ideas have exerted a profound influence on twentieth-century thought and culture.

Throughout *The Interpretation of Dreams*, Freud analyzes his own dreams as examples to prove his new theory of the psychology of dreams. Freud makes a distinction between the "manifest," or surface-level, dream content and the "latent," or unconscious, "dream thoughts" expressed through the special "language" of dreams. He posits that all dreams represent the fulfillment of a wish on the part of the dreamer and maintains that even anxiety dreams and nightmares are expressions of unconscious desires. Freud explains that the process of "censorship" in dreams causes a "distortion" of the dream content; thus, what appears to be trivial nonsense in a dream, can, through the process of analysis, be shown to express a coherent set of ideas. The "dream work" is the process by which the mind condenses, distorts, and translates "dream thoughts" into dream content. Freud proposes that the ultimate value of dream analysis may be in revealing the hidden workings of the unconscious mind.

The Interpretation of Dreams presents Freud's early theories in regard to the nature of the unconscious dream psychology, the significance of childhood experiences, the psychic process of "censorship," the "hieroglyphic" language of dreams, and the method he called "psychoanalysis."

Author Biography

Sigismund Solomon Freud was born into a Jewish family in Freiberg, Moravia, on May 6, 1856. His father, Jacob, was a wool merchant, and his mother, Amalie Nathansohn, was Jacob's second wife. When Sigmund was born, his father was forty and his mother only twenty. The family moved to Leipzig in 1859 and to Vienna a year later where Freud remained until a year before his death.

In 1873, Freud enrolled in the University of Vienna to study medicine. Upon completing his degree, he obtained a position as lecturer in neuropathology at the University of Vienna and set up a private medical practice in an office adjoining his home. In 1895, he co-published *Studies in Hysteria* with Joseph Breuer in which they described their new method of the "talking cure." In 1886, he married Martha Bernays with whom he had six children.

A watershed event in Freud's life was the death of his father in 1896 to which he responded by embarking on several years of rigorous self-analysis of his feelings toward his father. In the process, he developed a new method of interpreting dreams as an expression of unconscious feelings. The result of this self-analysis was *The Interpretation of Dreams*, which was first published in 1899 and which marks the birth of psychoanalysis.

A series of publications followed as Freud's reputation grew and in spite of the amount of controversy regarding his theories. In the *Psychopathology of Everyday Life* (1904) and *Jokes and Their Relation to the Unconscious* (1905), Freud developed the theory that everyday slips-of-the-tongue, as well as casual jokes, express unconscious desires that are repressed from direct expression; the term "Freudian slip" came to describe this phenomenon.

Beginning in 1902, Freud's office became the locus of a weekly meeting of Jewish psychologists known as the Psychological Wednesday Circle. In

Sigmund Freud

1908, they renamed themselves the Vienna Psychoanalytic Society, which soon became an international organization.

Freud's introduction to American scholars was heralded in 1909 by his series of lectures given at Clark University, in Worcester, Massachusetts, along with his colleagues Carl Jung and Sandor Ferenczi. These lectures were later published as *Five Lectures on Psychoanalysis* (1910), which remains a classic introduction to Freudian theory.

Freud also published a series of case studies, which have come to be known by such names as "Dora" (1905), "Little Hans" (1909), the "Rat Man" (1909), and the "Wolf Man" (1918). He continued to develop his basic theories throughout the 1920s and 1930s. Significant publications during this time include *Beyond the Pleasure Principle* (1920), *The Ego and the Id* (1923), *Civilization and Its Discontents* (1930), and *Moses and Monotheism* (1939).

In 1938, Freud was forced to move with his family to London to escape the clutches of Nazi forces that had annexed Austria. Freud had developed cancer of the jaw (most likely from his lifelong habit of excessive cigar-smoking) and died of cancer in London in 1939.

Plot Summary

Freud opens *The Interpretation of Dreams* by stating the nature of his theoretical accomplishment in writing the book:

> In the following pages I shall provide proof that there is a psychological technique which allows us to interpret dreams, and that when this procedure is applied, every dream turns out to be a meaningful, psychical formation which can be given an identifiable place in what goes on within our waking life.

The Scientific Literature on Dreams

Freud provides an overview of the scientific and theoretical findings on the interpretation of dreams up to that point in history. He notes that the first written work on dream psychology dates back to the ancient Greek philosopher Aristotle's tract *On Dreams and Dream Interpretation*. However, he claims that no convincing theory of dream interpretation has yet been formulated; he asserts, "In spite of being concerned with the subject over many thousands of years, scientific understanding of the dream has not got very far." He laments that "little or nothing touching the essential nature of the dream or offering a definitive solution to any of its riddles" has been accomplished.

All Dreams Are Wish Fulfillments

Freud observes that, while scientific opinion has come to dismiss the idea that dreams can be interpreted, "popular opinion" has "stubbornly" held on to the notion that dreams do indeed have meaning. He asserts that, contrary to the reigning scientific opinion, he will prove that it is possible to interpret dreams using a scientific method.

He explains that dreams have an "ulterior motive" whereby their meaning is other than it appears on the surface. He proposes a method by which a patient is encouraged to relax the normal impulse to "censor" unwanted thoughts to more easily call to mind the associations that the dream evokes. Freud refers to this state of mind as "uncritical self-observation"; the process was later called "free association."

Freud then proceeds to analyze a dream of his own by isolating its separate elements and describing the amalgam of personal associations that cluster around each element. He concludes that this dream "represents a certain state of affairs as being as I would wish it to be."

Freud's fundamental conclusion about dreams is that "wish-fulfillment is the meaning of *each and every* dream, and hence there can be no dreams besides wishful dreams." Further, dreams are not meaningless but are in fact "constructed by a highly elaborate intellectual activity."

Dream Distortion

Freud further asserts that even anxiety dreams and dreams that seem unpleasant at the surface level are in fact, when analyzed, revealed to be imaginary wish-fulfillments. He makes a distinction between the "manifest" content of the dream and its "latent" content; thus, while the "manifest" content may be distressing, the "latent" content, when analyzed, is always the fulfillment of a wish.

He explains that the process by which the latent content is disguised by the manifest content is via the mechanism of "dream distortion." He compares this process to that of "censorship"—whereby, even in sleep, the mind of the individual works to cover up his or her real desires through the invention of "pretense." He describes these two opposing impulses—the urge to express a desire and the effort to censor the expression of that desire—as "two psychical forces," which together act as the "originators of dream formation in the individual." While one of these forces works to express the wish, the other "imposes a censorship on the dream wish and by this censorship distorts its expression."

He states that the anxiety experienced by a dream with a "painful content" is in part an expression of the dreamer's effort to deny the desires expressed by the dream: "everyone has wishes he would not like to communicate to others, and wishes he prefers not to admit to himself." Taking into account the process of dream distortion, Freud amends his conclusion regarding the meaning of dreams to the statement: "the dream is a (disguised) fulfillment of a (suppressed, repressed) wish."

Freud suggests that the ultimate value of dream interpretation to the psychoanalyst may be that it reveals insight into the workings of the unconscious mind.

The Material and Sources of Dreams

Freud points out that there are three primary sources from which the material of dreams is constructed. First, dreams always draw material from impressions made during the day before the night in which the dream takes place; he refers to this dream material as the "remnants," or "remains," of "impressions'' made during the preceding day. Second, dream content can be drawn from what he calls "somatic sources''—actual physical impressions made upon the sleeper; for instance, a person who goes to bed thirsty may dream that he is drinking a glass of water. Third, Freud asserts, dream content is drawn from childhood experiences that may be long-forgotten in the waking mind of the dreamer.

He notes that it has often been observed that dream content frequently draws from seemingly trivial impressions, made either the previous day, during sleep, or in childhood. One tends to dream, not about the most important event of the day, but of the most insignificant matters. However, Freud insists that while the "manifest" content of dreams is trivial, their "latent" psychic meaning is never trivial. He explains this phenomenon as one of "psychical displacement," whereby important psychological matter is expressed in the dream by a process of "displacement" onto representative dream material that seems to be insignificant. Thus, Freud asserts that it is his "strict and single-minded opinion" that no dream is trivial in its "latent" content, for "the dream never wastes its time on trifles."

The Dream Work

Freud refers to the mind's process of dream formation as the "dream work." The "manifest dream content" includes the images, characters, dialogue, and so forth that appear in the dream. Freud describes the manifest dream content as being like a "rebus," or "picture puzzle"; as such, it is "given as it were in the form of hieroglyphs whose signs are to be translated one by one into the language of dream thoughts."

The first element of the "dream work" is the process of "condensation." Freud here refers to the phenomenon in dreams by which many ideas may be "condensed" into a single image; for example, a single character in a dream may, in the form of a "composite figure," be identified by the dreamer as representing three different people.

The second element of dreams is that of "displacement," whereby one element within a dream may stand as a substitute for an idea that it does not literally represent; for example, the figure of a queen in a dream may represent the mother of the dreamer.

The third element is that of representation—the phenomenon by which ideas are expressed through a dream in non-verbal ways. One task of the dream

analysis is thus to translate dream images into verbalized "dream thoughts."

"Secondary revision" is the process by which the conscious mind of the dreamer intrudes upon the dream thoughts to impose an artificial coherence to the dream. For instance, it sometimes occurs that a dreamer, while still in the midst of a dream, has the thought, "After all, it's only a dream." This process of "secondary revision" continues after waking, when the dreamer attempts to recall the dream as a coherent narrative. The effect of this process is that "the dream loses its appearance of absurdity and incoherence and approaches the pattern of an intelligible experience." When the "secondary revision" does not impose this veneer of intelligibility, "we are helpless in the face of a meaningless heap of fragmentary material."

However, Freud states that this apparent coherence of the dream is the work of the conscious mind, the function of the agency of "censorship," which seeks to obscure the "latent" meaning of the dream, rooted in the unconscious desires of the dreamer. To analyze a dream, the coherence imposed by the process of "secondary revision" must be ignored so that the "latent dream content" may be accessed.

Key Figures

Josef Breuer

Josef Breuer (1842–1925) was an Austrian physician with whom Freud co-wrote *Studies in Hysteria* in 1895. Their findings were based on Breuer's work with a patient, referred to by the pseudonym "Anna O.," who suffered from hysteria. Breuer found that Anna O.'s symptoms were relieved after he put her in a state of mind resembling hypnosis and she described an early childhood experience that had brought on her illness. Anna O. called this process the "talking cure," a term that Freud and Breuer adopted to describe their new method. By the late 1890s, Freud, in his characteristic way, found that his intense ten-year-long friendship with Breuer had cooled, in part due to differences regarding psychoanalytic theory. However, Freud considered Breuer, and not himself, to be the true father of psychoanalytic theory. In *The Interpretation of Dreams*, Freud refers to Breuer by the pseudonym "Dr. M." in describing his appearance in the "Irma" dream. Freud had this dream the night after writing down the case history of a patient

Media Adaptations

- A fictionalized account of the life of Freud was the subject of *Freud*, the 1962 Hollywood movie directed by John Huston and starring Montgomery Clift in the title role.

- *Introductory Lectures on Psychoanalysis*, by Sigmund Freud, was recorded on audiocassette by Audio Scholar, read by Sydney Walker, in 1990.

- *Sigmund Freud* is a biographical video recording of the life of Freud, first broadcast as part of a television series. It was produced by A&E Home Video and distributed by the New Video Group in 1997.

named Irma to present it to Breuer for further consultation. In the dream, Breuer appears with several colleagues who examine Irma. In this same dream, Breuer appears as a "composite figure" with one of Freud's brothers; he makes the association between the two that "I was out of humor with both of them" for rejecting suggestions he had recently made to them. Freud concludes that the dream is in part a wish-fulfillment in which he portrays "Dr. M." (Breuer) as an incompetent physician, thus reassuring *himself* of his own professional competence, which had been put into question (in his waking life) with regard to his only partial success in treating Irma.

Brücke
See Ernst Wilhelm von Brücke

Fleischl
See Professor Ernst Fleischl von Marxow

Wilhelm Fliess
Wilhelm Fliess (1858–1928), a Berlin physician, was a close friend of Freud's and an important

professional influence. An unfortunate incident occurred in 1895 when Freud referred a patient of his, a female hysteric, to Fliess for an operation on her nose. Freud at that time subscribed to Fliess's theory that the nose and the sexual organs were linked. Because of his own theory that hysteria was sexual in nature, he thought that by operating on her nose, Fliess might be able to cure the patient of hysteria. After the operation, however, the patient suffered from near-fatal nosebleeds. When a different physician examined her, he found that Fliess had accidentally left half a meter of gauze in her nasal cavity. This was quite an embarrassment to Freud, who nonetheless felt obliged to defend his friend's professional competence. The figure of Fliess, referred to as "my Berlin friend *Fl.*," appears in several of Freud's dreams, as described in *The Interpretation of Dreams*. One of these dreams is sparked by criticism in a professional journal of Fliess's recent book. Freud, fearing professional criticism of his own work, has a dream in which he stands in for Fliess and the book critic is discredited. Freud's dream is thus a wish-fulfillment that those who may come to criticize him professionally are unfounded in their opinions. Freud uses this as an example to demonstrate that "there is no dream that is not prompted by egoistic movies." In this dream, for example, the dreamer (Freud) "makes my friend's case my own." Another dream is sparked by Freud's concern that Fliess may soon die as the result of a recent operation. The dream recalls associations with a past habit on the part of Freud of arriving late to work. In Fliess's case, Freud fears he may arrive in Berlin (where Fliess lives) "too late"—that Fliess will already be dead. *The Complete Letters of Sigmund Freud to Wilhelm Fliess, 1877–1904*, edited by Jeffrey Masson, was published in 1985.

Amalia Freud
Amalia (maiden name Nathansohn) Freud (1835–1930) was Freud's mother. In *The Interpretation of Dreams*, he describes a dream in which one figure, a woman in a kitchen rubbing dough between her hands to make dumplings, evokes associations with his mother. In another dream, from age seven or eight, he dreamed that his mother had died. In these dreams, his mother is associated with both nourishment and death. Freud's strong childhood attachment to his mother and his corresponding feelings of jealousy toward his father became the basis of his theory of the *Oedipus complex*, one of the fundamental theories of psychoanalysis.

Anna Freud

Anna Freud (1895–1982) was Freud's youngest child. In *The Interpretation of Dreams*, Freud describes a dream from Anna's second year of life. She had gotten sick in the morning and was given nothing more to eat for the rest of the day. Her nurse had attributed the illness to eating too many strawberries. That night, Anna was heard to utter in her sleep: "Anna F[r]eud, strawberry, wild strawberry, scrambled eggs, mash." Freud observed that this was clearly the expression of a wish-fulfillment on the part of the child, who had been denied food of any kind and strawberries in particular: "the menu no doubt included everything that would have seemed to her a desirable meal." Having been told that she had eaten too many strawberries, Freud notes, "she took her revenge in her dream for this annoying report." As an adult, Anna maintained a very close relationship with her father, becoming his constant companion toward the end of his life. She also made a name for herself as a psychoanalyst in her own right, pioneering in the fields of child and adolescent psychology. From 1925 to 1928, she served as chairman of the Vienna Psychoanalytic Society. In 1938, she fled Nazi-occupied Vienna with the Freud family to settle in England. In 1947, she founded the Hampstead Child Therapy Course and Clinic in London, serving as director from 1952 until her death in 1982. *Anna Freud: A Biography,* by Elisabeth Young-Bruehl, was published in 1988.

Jacob Freud

Jacob Freud (1815–1896) was Freud's father. Freud's process of mourning his father's death in 1896 inspired the years of self-analysis that resulted in the writing of *The Interpretation of Dreams.* Throughout the book, Freud mentions several dreams that include either direct or indirect associations with his father. In many of these dreams, Freud expresses concern that he impress his father with his professional accomplishments. Freud recalls that his father had once said to his mother of the young Sigmund, "nothing will come of the boy" (as in, he will never amount to anything). He explains the impact of such a comment on his unconscious mind:

> It must have been a terrible blow to my ambition, for allusions to this scene occur in my dreams again and again and are invariably connected with enumerations of my successes and achievements, as though I wanted to say: 'You see, something did come of me.'

Freud's early childhood attachment to his mother and his consequent jealousy toward his father became the basis of one of his fundamental theories of psychoanalysis: the *Oedipus complex.* Freud drew from the Greek myth of Oedipus, who, as ordained by fate, unwittingly kills his father and marries his mother. Freud theorized that a universal developmental stage for all (male) children is the feeling of strong sexual attachment to the mother and a corresponding desire to kill the father, whom he sees as his arch rival.

Joseph Freud

Joseph Freud was Freud's uncle. Freud had negative associations with his uncle, who was imprisoned in 1866 in connection with counterfeit money. He recalls that his father had always told him his uncle Joseph "had never been a bad man, he had been a numbskull." Freud describes a dream in which his uncle Joseph appears as a "composite figure" with two of his colleagues. He concludes that this association served the function of identifying one of these colleagues as a "criminal" and the other as a "numbskull" (although Freud makes clear that, in his waking life, he has nothing but the highest regard for both men).

Martha Freud

Martha (maiden name Bernays) Freud (1861–1951) was Freud's wife, whom he married in 1886 and with whom he had six children. Freud describes several of his dreams that call to mind associations with Martha. In one dream, his patient, Irma, suffers from abdominal pains, which remind him of a symptom suffered by his wife long ago. He observes that this dream included many indications suggesting his concern for the health of his friends, patients, and family. In one of Freud's most famous examples of his own dreams, a simple scenario in which he has just written a monograph on a certain unspecified plant, Freud is able to connect this reference to the plant *cyclamen,* which is his wife's favorite flower. He notes that reference to this flower gives him a sense of guilt because he rarely brings flowers to his wife although she would like it if he did.

Martin Freud

Martin Freud was Freud's second child and eldest son, born in 1889. Freud mentions a dream of Martin's, when he was eight years old, in which, having read stories from Greek mythology the previous day, he dreamed he was "riding in a chariot with Achilles, and Diomedes was the charioteer." Freud uses this as an example of the way in which children's dreams can be interpreted as simple wish-fulfillments. Martin Freud's *Sigmund Freud: Man and Father* was published in 1958.

Mathilde Freud

Mathilde Freud was Freud's eldest child, born in 1887. He describes two of Mathilde's childhood dreams in a discussion that demonstrates the simple wish-fulfillments expressed in the dreams of children. Mathilde is further mentioned in Freud's discussion of his important dream featuring a patient of his named Irma. By association, the dream calls to mind his daughter Mathilde in two different ways: an illness observed in Irma in the dream resembles an illness suffered by Mathilde several years earlier; the name Mathilde also calls to mind a patient of Freud's by the same name whose treatment he had handled badly.

Oliver Freud

Oliver Freud was Freud's third child, born in 1891, whom he named after the famous English statesman Oliver Cromwell (1599–1658). Freud mentions an indirect reference to Oliver in a dream concerning his own ambitious nature. He had named this son after "a great figure in history who had attracted me powerfully when I was a boy." He explains that his own aspirations to greatness were transferred onto Oliver with the act of naming him after a "great figure in history." Freud comments, "It is not difficult to see how the vaulting ambition which the father has suppressed is transferred in his thoughts onto his children."

Sigmund Freud

Sigmund Freud (1856–1939) is universally considered the "father" of psychoanalysis, a term that he first used in 1896. Upon his father's death, Freud began a process of intensive self-analysis, which resulted in the writing of *The Interpretation of Dreams* (1899). This "magnum opus" (as many have called it) puts forth Freud's early theories of the unconscious, which he was to develop throughout the remaining forty years of his life. *The Interpretation of Dreams* includes extensive, detailed analysis of many of Freud's own dreams, as well as those of his friends, family, and clinical patients. He asserts that, contrary to the current scientific opinion, dreams are meaningful and that though they often seem nonsensical and absurd, dreams actually function according to a logic and language different from that of waking life. It is the task of the analyst to "translate" the language of dreams, which re-

sembles a form of "hieroglyphics," or word-pictures, into everyday speech. Through this process, analysis of dream-content can reveal valuable insight into the workings of the unconscious mind.

John

Freud's nephew is referred to in *The Interpretation of Dreams* simply as John. Although John was Freud's nephew, he was a year older than Freud, and the two had been constant playmates throughout their childhood. Freud mentions John in describing a dream that makes reference to "very early scenes of the childhood quarrels" between the two boys. He describes his "complicated infantile relationship" to John as one which became a template for his later relationships, both personal and professional, to other men:

> Until I was almost four we had been inseparable, had loved each other and fought each other; and this childhood relationship has been decisive . . . for all my later feelings for companions of my own age.

Freud's assessment of the effect of his relationship with John on later relations is that "all my friends are in some sense incarnations of this first figure." He elaborates upon this dynamic:

> An intimate friend and a hated foe have always been necessary to my emotional life; I have always been able to create for myself afresh embodiments of both, and not infrequently my childhood ideal went so far that friend and foe coincided in one person—no longer at the same time, of course, or switching repeatedly from one to the other, which was probably the case in my earliest childhood years.

Biographers frequently refer to this dynamic in Freud's life, particularly in discussion of his famous irrevocable falling-out with his once intimate friend and devoted disciple Carl Jung. A similar dynamic was enacted in Freud's relationship to friend and colleague Josef Breuer.

Ernst Wilhelm von Brücke

Ernst Brücke (1819–1892) was a German professor of physiology at the University of Vienna from 1849 to 1891. While in medical school, Freud worked in Brücke's physiological laboratory and through him was influenced by the work of Hermann von Helmholtz. In *The Interpretation of Dreams*, Freud describes one of his dreams, which takes place in Brücke's laboratory where Freud has been assigned the task of dissecting his own pelvis. Upon analysis, Freud associates the dissection of his pelvis with the process of self-analysis, which resulted in the writing of *The Interpretation of Dreams*. The dream also calls to mind an occasion when he was a student and Brücke reprimanded him for arriving late to the laboratory several times. Freud concludes that the dream is in part a wish-fulfillment that he submit his book for publication before it is too "late"—that is, before he grows old and dies.

Professor Ernst Fleischl von Marxow

Ernst Fleischl (1846–1891) was a close friend of Freud's. His death from cocaine addiction was both personally painful and professionally embarrassing to Freud for several reasons. One of Freud's earliest scientific accomplishments was the discovery that cocaine could be used as an anaesthetic, a finding that he published in 1884 (before anyone realized that cocaine use is both habit forming and unhealthy). Freud had encouraged Fleischl to use cocaine (instead of morphine to which Fleischl was already addicted) as a painkiller to alleviate his health problems. Fleischl subsequently developed an addiction to cocaine, which eventually led to his death. Freud mentions several dreams in which Fleischl appears, either directly or by association. In a dream that includes several references to food and nourishment, Freud associates the name Fleischl with the German word *fleisch,* meaning "flesh" or "meat." In another dream, Fleischl appears in a laboratory where Freud studies among several colleagues. In the dream, these colleagues are acknowledged to be dead.

Themes

The Unconscious

Freud makes an important distinction between the conscious and the unconscious mind. The concept of the "unconscious" was not itself Freud's invention and had already been in use at the time of his writing. However, Freud developed his theory of the unconscious far beyond any previous understanding of it. He makes a distinction between "manifest," or conscious, dream content—the surface-level content of the dream, which can be described by the dreamer upon waking—and the "latent," or unconscious, "dream thoughts," which are only revealed upon analysis. He demonstrates that, through dream analysis, it is possible to access

the workings of the unconscious mind, which is less accessible in the waking thought process.

Childhood Experiences

One of Freud's original insights was his assertion of the importance of early childhood experiences on the unconscious mind, as expressed in dream thoughts. He observed that, while dreams draw manifest material from the "remnants" of the previous day, this material could always be linked back to associations drawn from early childhood. More specifically, Freud asserted that the wishes expressed through dreams are always rooted in infantile desires that have been repressed and yet remain an active part of the unconscious psychical life of the adult. Thus, childhood experiences play a significant role in the unconscious mind of the adult dreamer. For example, in analyzing his own dreams, Freud recalled significant events from his childhood, including interactions with his mother and father, as well as a formative friendship with his nephew (who was a year older than he) during his youth.

Psychoanalysis: The "Talking Cure"

The Interpretation of Dreams (1899) followed Freud's book *Studies in Hysteria* (1895), which was co-written with Josef Breuer. In *Studies in Hysteria*, Freud and Breuer put forth their findings that patients suffering from hysteria experienced some relief from their symptoms through a method one patient (given the pseudonym "Anna O.") termed the "talking cure." In a hypnotic-like state, the patients in these case studies described significant childhood experiences that had first brought on their symptoms. Freud and Breuer observed that, through the process of the patient describing these memories, some of the symptoms of hysteria were dispelled. They concluded that hysterics "suffer mainly from reminiscences." This was the beginning of what developed into Freud's method of psychoanalysis, in which his patients were encouraged to describe dreams and childhood experiences that could be clues to their unconscious desires and fears. In *The Interpretation of Dreams*, Freud extended this method, based on his finding that many patients in the process of "free association" spoke of their dreams.

Censorship and Free Association

Freud makes much of the process of "censorship," which functions to conceal unconscious de-

Topics for Further Study

- Read one of the lectures from Freud's *Five Lectures on Psycho-Analysis* (1910). What is his central theoretical point in this lecture? To what extent do you agree or disagree with his conclusions?

- Carl Jung was Freud's most famous disciple with whom he had a falling-out over differences in psychoanalytic theory. Learn more about Jung and his contributions to psychoanalytic theory, particularly his theories of dream psychology. In what ways does Jung's theory of dream psychology differ from that of Freud? To what extent do you find his ideas convincing?

- Learn more about current approaches to psychology and psychotherapy. What are some of the more significant differences between current approaches and those of Freud? What similarities remain?

- Freud's life was deeply affected by the status of Jews in Vienna during the nineteenth and twentieth centuries. Learn more about Jewish life and culture and the expression of anti-Jewish sentiment in Vienna during Freud's lifetime (1856–1939).

- Analyze a recent dream of your own based on Freud's theory of dream analysis. Do you find this analysis of your own dream convincing or insightful? Can you think of another way to interpret the same dream?

- Freud drew some of his most important theories from examples of Greek mythology. Find a collection of Greek myths, such as *Mythology,* by Edith Hamilton, and read one of the myths. What insight does this myth offer into human psychology and behavior?

---

sires from the conscious mind of the individual. Thus, desires and wishes that are deemed unacceptable or inappropriate are "censored" from the conscious thoughts. Further, although unconscious desires are expressed through dream thoughts, the work of censorship functions to distort the content of dreams so that, even in sleep, the wishes and desires of the individual are disguised. Freud later referred to the psychic agent of "censorship" as the "superego."

Freud's method of dream analysis essentially functions to undo the process of censorship to bring to light the buried desires of the individual. The process of treating patients, including the dream analysis, thus requires that the patient be put in a state of mind that relaxes the process of censorship—catches the censor off guard, so to speak. In earlier work, Freud and Breuer used hypnosis to this effect. However, Freud found that, if the patient lies down on a couch and is put in as unguarded a state as possible, a similar result could be reached without hypnosis. Freud called this state one of "unguarded self-reflection" and the process one of "free association," whereby the patient was encouraged to freely express whatever mental associations came to mind in the course of analysis.

The Language of Dreams

Freud's aim in *The Interpretation of Dreams* is to demonstrate that dreams are by no means nonsensical or meaningless but in fact operate in a rational fashion, according to the "language" of dreams. To make sense of dreams, however, the analysis must involve a process of translating the dream into a comprehensible language of "dream thoughts." Freud compares the language of dreams to that of hieroglyphics, which communicate in a series of images that can be translated into spoken language. He further compares the process of dream analysis to that of deciphering a particular word-image puzzle called a "rebus," which is the presentation of a series of apparently unrelated visual symbols, each of which must be interpreted individually to represent a word or sound and then recombined to form a coherent sentence. Freud asserts that the dream analysis similarly requires a process of isolating individual elements of the dream to tease out the multiple associations that each evokes in the dreamer. He explains that dreams only appear to be absurd, trivial, and nonsensical when they are assumed to operate according to the same logic used in waking life. He asserts that the logic upon which dreams operate is *not,* contrary to surface-level appearance, "more negligent, more unreasonable, more forgetful, more incomplete, say, than waking thought"; rather, the logic of the language of dreams "is qualitatively something completely different from" waking thought processes "and so at first not comparable to it." However, when translated through dream analysis, the thought process of dreams reveals glimpses of the rich unconscious life of every dreamer.

Style

Narrative Voice

Freud made a bold move in choosing to write *The Interpretation of Dreams,* a "scientific" treatise, in the *first person* narrative voice—meaning that he inserts himself into the text as an individual, using the pronoun "I." Freud's theoretical insights, which he puts forth in *The Interpretation of Dreams,* are a direct result of several years of intensive self-analysis; thus, he analyses his own dreams as examples to prove his theory of dream interpretation. He explains that to demonstrate his theory, he found that his own dreams provided "an abundant and convenient fund of material coming from a more-or-less normal person and relating to a variety of occasions in daily life," in part due to the fact that "the conditions for self-observation are more favourable than the conditions for the observation of others." He acknowledges at several points throughout the book the personal risk and embarrassment involved in so publicly delving into the depths of his own psyche, thereby revealing many personal feelings about his friends, family, and colleagues:

> Reporting my own dreams, however, turned out to be inextricably tied to revealing more of the intimacies of my psychical life than I could wish or than usually falls to the task of an author who is not a poet, but a scientist. This was painful and embarrassing, but unavoidable; I have bowed to it then, so that I should not entirely do without presenting the evidence for my psychological conclusions.

So strong was his sense of embarrassment at exposing himself in this manner that Freud withheld the book from publication for a year after he had completed writing it.

Nonfiction Genres: Scientific Treatise and Autobiography

Many critics have acknowledged the tension in *The Interpretation of Dreams* between Freud's efforts to present his groundbreaking theory in an *objective* manner acceptable to the scientific community and his choice to present personal material from a *subjective* perspective, based on experiences from his own life. Ritchie Robertson, in an Introduction to the 1999 translation, observes that the book is in part a "semi-disguised autobiography" of Freud, revealing much about his childhood, family of origin, social milieu, and adult relationships. At the same time, Freud took pains to satisfy the requirements of the scientific community, beginning the book with an overview of the "Scientific Literature on the Problems of Dreams" although he was not particularly interested in this material. Translator Joyce Crick refers to this grafting of scientific and personal narrative in *The Interpretation of Dreams,* calling it a "treatise-cum-autobiography." Crick describes several different "registers" in which the book is written. The "theoretical," or scientific, mode is written in the "discursive, formal language of the argued treatise, presenting evidence, argument, rebuttal, qualification, inference." Another major "register" in which the book is written, according to Crick, is the "narrative" mode, used in the "preambles" and descriptions of Freud's dreams.

Literary References and Allusions

Freud is well known for the rich array of literary references on which much of his writing relies. His central theoretical construct of the *Oedipus Complex,* for example, is based on the Greek myth of Oedipus, and the plays *Oedipus the King* and *Oedipus at Colonus,* by the ancient Greek playwright Sophocles (496–406 B.C.). Throughout his prolific body of psychoanalytic theory, Freud draws many examples from the plays of Shakespeare, particularly *Hamlet.* In *The Interpretation of Dreams,* he makes reference to some twenty different literary figures from throughout history, including French, English, and Greek, as well as German, literature. His reliance on examples from world literature in part explains the lasting impact of Freudian theory on the field of literary theory and criticism in the late twentieth century where his influence is as pervasive and enduring as it is in psychology. One may even regard Freud's dream analysis as parallel to literary analysis, as he makes much use of word play and verbal allusion in dissecting the narrative content of his dreams. Some critics have even come to regard Freud himself as a kind of poet of the mind, interpreting the everyday experiences, dreams, and memories of each individual as a literary creation, rife with literary allusion, symbolism, and allegorical or mythological meaning. Jonathan Lear observes, in a 1995 article in the *New Republic,* that one of Freud's greatest contributions is the realization that "creativity is no longer the exclusive preserve of the divinely inspired, or the few great poets," for, "from a psychoanalytic point of view, everyone is poetic; everyone dreams in metaphor and generates symbolic meaning in the process of living."

Historical Context

Freud's Austria

Freud's home of Vienna is the capital of Austria, which was part of the Austro-Hungarian empire, ruled by the Habsburg Dynasty, from the thirteenth to the twentieth century. The Habsburg Empire included areas that are now parts of Poland, Hungary, Czechoslovakia, and Austria.

The Eighteenth Century: Maria Theresa and Joseph II

From 1740 to 1780, the Habsburg Empire was ruled by Empress Maria Theresa, the first woman to occupy this position. In 1737, her husband, Francis Stephen of Lorraine, inherited the title of Holy Roman Emperor Francis I. Thereafter, the house of Habsburg was known as Habsburg-Lorraine. Maria Theresa's right to rule the empire was challenged in the War of the Austrian Succession, which lasted from 1740 to 1748. Upon victoriously settling this power dispute, Maria Theresa successfully instituted wide-reaching reforms in the military, financial, and administrative concerns of the empire, strengthening and consolidating her power in all of these areas. She also implemented a public school system designed to offer education to the lower echelons of society.

Freud mentions the empress Maria Theresa in a dream, which features an image from the reproduc-

tion of a woodcut that appeared in a book about the history of Austria. In Freud's dream, his father stands in the place of the empress, surrounded by a crowd. He concludes that his dream is a wish-fulfillment on his part, as a father himself, "*to be a pure and great presence to one's children after one's death.*"

When Maria Theresa's husband died, her son Joseph II aided her in ruling the empire until her death in 1780, when he became emperor. Joseph II, continuing his mother's policy of reform, reigned until his death in 1790. One of his more significant accomplishments was the declaration of the 1781 Edict of Toleration, which extended religious tolerance to Jews and Protestants. This was a particularly significant change for the Jews of Austria, allowing them to enter universities and occupy trades from which they had previously been banned. In 1781, Joseph II also extended important legal rights to the peasants.

In one dream, Freud makes a statement that refers to the inscription on the pedestal of an equestrian statue to Emperor Joseph II. He concludes that this dream expressed his wish to "raise a monument to my friend," recently deceased, whose name was also Josef.

The Nineteenth Century: The Revolutions of 1848

In February 1848, a revolution centralized in Paris inspired rebellions that broke out in major cities throughout Europe, many of them in the Habsburg Empire. In March, an uprising in Vienna, calling for liberal reform, led to violent confrontation between protestors and authorities. As a concession, the emperor removed from office Klemens Fürst von Metternich, the minister of foreign affairs, whom many viewed as an oppressor and enemy of the people. Nonetheless, rebellion and violence continued in Vienna throughout the year. Rebellion had simultaneously broken out throughout the empire, with varying degrees of success, in Hungary and Italy and among the Slavic and German populations. In May, the emperor and government fled Vienna, fearing for their safety. They returned to the city in August, however, and in October, the Habsburg army regained control of the city, executing many of the revolutionary leaders. Some effort was made on the part of the government to formulate a constitution, but the emperor ultimately defeated this initiative. One genuine concession on the part of the emperor was the full emancipation of the peasants and serfs.

Compare
&
Contrast

- **1278:** The Habsburg Empire acquires Austria and makes Vienna its capital city.

  1860: Freud's family moves to Vienna.

  1867: The Habsburg Empire centralizes authority over Hungary in Vienna, thus creating the Austro-Hungarian Empire.

  1914: World War I is initiated by the assassination of Archduke Franz Ferdinand, heir of the Austro-Hungarian Empire, by a Serbian nationalist.

  1916–1918: With the death of Francis Joseph, Charles becomes emperor of the Austro-Hungarian Empire.

  1918: Following World War I, Emperor Charles is forced to abdicate, and the Habsburg Empire is formally dissolved into several independent nations, including an Austrian republic. Vienna is made the capital of the newly formed republic.

  1938–1945: Austria is occupied by German forces under Hitler, who declares it part of "Greater" Germany. He declares Vienna a German province and renames it "Greater" Vienna.

  1945–1955: In the wake of World War II, Austria is divided into four regions, each occupied by one of the Allied forces. Vienna is divided into four separate occupation zones.

  1955: In the Austrian State Treaty, Austria is reestablished as a sovereign nation, with Vienna as its capital, and is declared a permanently neutral country.

  1990s: Austria joins the European Union in 1995. Austria and Switzerland have come to be known as the "neutral core" of Europe. As a neutral city, Vienna has become an international conference center and home of many world organizations.

- **1781:** Emperor Joseph II of the Habsburg Empire establishes the Edict of Toleration, which extends religious freedoms to Protestants and Jews.

  1873: A stock market crash in Austria inspires virulent anti-Semitism, as many citizens blame Jews for the economic crisis.

  1895: The highly influential anti-Semitic politician Karl Lueger is elected to the Austrian Parliament.

  1897: Lueger becomes mayor of Vienna.

  1938–1945: During the German occupation of Austria, approximately two-thirds of the Jewish population of Vienna flee to escape Nazi persecution. Freud and his immediate family are among those who flee to England. Most of the Jews who remain in Vienna, including four of Freud's sisters, are killed in the Holocaust.

  1972–1981: Suspected Nazi war criminal Kurt Waldheim represents Austria as secretary-general of the United Nations.

  1986–1992: International controversy is sparked by the election of Waldheim as president of Austria in 1986. In 1987, a previously suppressed United States Justice Department report reveals that Waldheim was (as stated in *Encyclopaedia Britannica*) "a key member of Nazi units responsible for executing prisoners, killing civilians, identifying Jews for deportation, and shipping prisoners to slave labour camps." Nevertheless, Waldheim retains office as president until 1992.

  1994: For the first time in history, the Austrian government publicly accepts responsibility for its participation in the Nazi persecution of the Jews. Vienna is the site of the largest ever United Nations World Conference on Human Rights.

Freud describes a dream he had in which the general atmosphere "makes something of the impression of a fantasy transporting the dreamer to the revolutionary year of 1848." He explains that this element of the dream had been sparked by the national celebration in 1898 of the fifty-year anniversary of the revolution. In one part of the dream, Freud identifies himself with one of the student leaders of the 1848 rebellion.

Count Thun

Count Franz Anton Thun was the governor of Freud's native land of Bohemia from 1889 to 1895 when he resigned. From 1898 to 1899, he was prime minister of Austria. In 1911, he was made a prince and was reinstated as governor of Bohemia until 1915. He died in 1916. Count Thun's checkered political career was the result of opposition by both Czech and German nationalists agitating against the rule of the Habsburg Empire.

Reference to Count Thun is made in Freud's "revolutionary" dream, described above. In his "preamble" explaining the actual events of the day, which contributed to the dream content, Freud explains that he had seen Count Thun in a train station on his way to see the emperor. Freud recalls a joke frequently made in the popular press, referring to Count Thun as Count *Nichtsthun,* which means Count "do-nothing" in German. Freud explains that, while in fact Count Thun was going to a "difficult visit to the Emperor," Freud himself is the real Count "do-nothing," as he is on vacation, taking his leisure. Freud concludes that the "spirit of rebellion" that infuses this dream is in part a wish-fulfillment to rebel against the authority of his father, who is associated with Count Thun.

The Twentieth Century

Beginning in 1848, the Habsburg Empire was ruled by Francis Joseph, who reigned until his death 1916. He was succeeded by Charles, whose reign lasted only two years. The empire was formally dissolved in 1918 in the wake of World War I when Poland, Czechoslovakia, and Austria became independent nations.

In 1938, Hitler invaded Austria and declared it a part of "Greater" Germany. Freud's books had been among the first to be burned in Nazi Germany, and the Freud family was put under house arrest for several months until they were given permission to leave the country. Freud, then eighty-two, was forced to sign a document stating that he had not been ill-treated by the Nazis; with great irony, he added, in his own handwriting, "I can most warmly recommend the Gestapo to anyone" (as quoted in the *Encyclopedia of World Biography*). The family took refuge in London where Freud died a year later.

Critical Overview

The Interpretation of Dreams, Freud's magnum opus, was first published in 1899 but was given a copyright date of 1900 to associate it with the new century. This proved prophetic, as the book's impact on twentieth-century thought and culture has been immeasurable.

In a Preface to the third (revised) English edition, Freud himself said of his seminal work—which, he observes, "surprised the world"—that it represents "the most valuable of all the discoveries it has been my good fortune to make," adding that "insight such as this falls to one's lot but once in a lifetime."

Initial Reception

Freud was gravely disappointed by the initial reception of *The Interpretation of Dreams*, which was, according to Ritchie Robertson in an Introduction to the 1999 translation, "muted but respectful"; it sold only 350 copies in the first six years of publication. However, as Freud's reputation as the founder of psychoanalysis grew throughout the first decade of the century, a second printing was called for (1909), and a third was in demand within a year. Over the next ten years, he revised the book for eight different editions, adding a preface with each new printing.

Criticism and Controversy

Freudian theory, though highly influential and much celebrated during Freud's lifetime, was, from its inception, controversial and subject to extensive criticism. Since his death, psychoanalytic theory has been attacked on many fronts. In 1953, Nathaniel Kleitman discovered the phenomenon of rapid-eye-movement (REM) during the dream state of sleep. This and subsequent neurological and sleep-lab research over the past half-century have led many to conclude that Freud was wrong in most, if not all, of his theories of dream analysis. Feminist theory, as early as the 1950s, attacked Freudian theory for being gender biased and having a disastrous effect on societal attitudes toward women. In

The interior of Freud's study, including the famous couch where he treated patients

addition, the development and increasing use of drugs to treat depression and other psychological disorders has tended to throw psychoanalysis as an effective method of treatment into a dubious light.

Freud's Legacy

Peter Gay, author of the much-celebrated biography *Freud: A Life for Our Times* (1988), has made the oft-repeated assessment that "today we all speak Freud," meaning, "his ideas—or ideas that can be traced, sometimes circuitously, back to him—have permeated the language." In a 1999 article in *Time* magazine, Gay quotes the poet W. H. Auden, who, upon Freud's death in 1939, stated, "If often he was wrong and, at times, absurd, to us he is no more a person now but a whole climate of opinion." Gay goes on to assert that although Freud remains controversial, "on one thing the contending parties agree: for good or ill, Sigmund Freud, more than any other explorer of the psyche, has shaped the mind of the 20th century." He adds, "The very fierceness and persistence of his detractors are a wry tribute to the staying power of Freud's ideas."

A 1989 article in *Psychology Today,* marking the fiftieth anniversary of Freud's death, includes comments from leading psychologists concerning Freud's legacy to the twentieth century. Though he remains highly controversial within the profession, "Most agree that we owe a great deal to Freud." Jerome L. Singer describes Freud's legacy as that of "a lifelong exploration that has stirred the imagination of thousands of thinkers in this century." Will Gaylyn concurs that Freud "has influenced our language, perceptions and institutions more than anyone else in the twentieth century." Robert Jay Lifton similarly considers Freud "a great figure who was responsible for one of the great intellectual breakthroughs in our history."

In a 1995 cover story in the *New Republic,* Jonathan Lear, while acknowledging the many legitimate criticisms of Freudian theory, psychoanalysis, and Freud himself, asserts that Freud's most significant contribution to twentieth-century thought withstands criticism of these specifics. He describes Freud as "a deep explorer of the human condition," in the philosophical, religious, and literary tradition of Plato, Saint Augustine, Shakespeare, Proust, and Nietzsche. Freud shares with these great thinkers the "insistence that there are deep currents of meaning, often crosscurrents, running through the human soul which can at best be glimpsed through a glass darkly." Lear notes, "Psychoanalysis . . . is a technique that allows dark meanings and irrational motivations to rise to the surface of conscious awareness.'' He thus attributes the popularity of ''Freud-bashing'' in the late twentieth century to ''a culture that wishes to ignore the complexity, depth and darkness of human life.'' He concludes that ''none of the attacks on Freud addresses the problems of human existence to which psychoanalysis is a response.''

Criticism

Liz Brent

Brent has a Ph.D. in American culture, specializing in film studies, from the University of Michigan. She is a freelance writer and teaches courses in the history of American cinema. In the following essay, Brent discusses expressions of Freud's Jewish identity.

Although Freud was not religious, his identity as a Jewish man in the Austro-Hungarian Empire of the mid-to-late nineteenth century was central to his psychic life, as revealed through the interpretation of his own dreams. He describes strong impressions, dating back to early childhood, which engendered in him a deep sense of injustice in the face of anti-Semitism and a fierce desire to persevere in his professional ambitions, despite the restrictions Austrian society placed on its Jewish population.

While Freud eventually became famous as the ''father'' of psychoanalysis, he began his career as a doctor, making his living from both a private medical practice and as a lecturer in neuropathology at the University of Vienna. Anti-Semitism (prejudice against Jews) caused the delay of a well-deserved promotion at the university for years after Freud had made a name for himself through a number of noteworthy publications. The equally deserved promotions of several of his colleagues were similarly denied or delayed due to their Jewish identity in the increasingly anti-Semitic climate of Austrian public affairs.

In *The Interpretation of Dreams*, Freud describes several dreams that address his ambitious nature (the ''wish'' to be successful) in the face of the virulent anti-Semitism, which cast a shadow over his hopes and ''dreams'' of personal success, as well as over the future of his children. Although he makes the disclaimer, ''I am not, as far as I know, ambitious,'' his biographers frequently comment that Freud, in fact, was exceptionally ambitious.

In one dream, Freud associates two of his colleagues with his uncle Josef. He states in the ''preamble'' to this dream that he had just learned his own name had been proposed for a promotion to the prestigious title of *professor extraordinarius*. Freud explains that he had made a point of not getting his hopes up because he had witnessed the disappointment of several Jewish colleagues who had been denied such promotions. The day before the dream in question, he had also been visited by a colleague who had just learned that, once again, his own promotion had been denied due to ''considerations of religion.''

The ''manifest'' content of the Uncle Josef dream consists of two parts. Freud describes the first part as the thought: ''*My friend R. is my uncle—I feel great affection for him*''; the second part of the dream consists of the image of a ''composite figure,'' combining suggestions of his uncle, his friend R., and another friend, whom he refers to as N. This dream, though very simple at the level of ''manifest'' content, reveals upon analysis a complex cluster of associations expressing the wish that he be promoted on the basis of his own merit rather than being denied promotion on the basis of his religious identity.

Freud explains that the uncle referred to in the dream is his uncle Josef. He notes that he had always had negative associations with this uncle, who in 1866 was sentenced to ten years in prison in connection with the circulation of counterfeit money. He recalls that his father had told him his uncle Josef ''had never been a bad man, he had been a numbskull.'' Thus, through a string of associations, his dream equates his friends R. and N. with his uncle Josef to the effect that it represents R. as a ''numbskull,'' like his uncle, and N. as a ''criminal,'' like his uncle. (He makes it clear that, in his conscious mind, he respects and admires both of these colleagues and has no desire whatsoever to regard them in a negative light.)

Both R. and N. had recently been denied promotions at the university, no doubt because they were Jewish. Freud concludes that this dream is a wish fulfillment in the sense that it provides an *alternative* explanation for these men not getting the desired promotions—thereby discounting the real reason of their being Jewish. Because Freud himself was hoping for a professorship, he wished to imagine that he would not be denied the promotion simply because he was Jewish. He explains, ''if I

What Do I Read Next?

- *The Letters of Sigmund Freud* (1960), edited by Ernst L. Freud, includes a selection from Sigmund Freud's prolific lifelong correspondence to family, friends, and colleagues.

- In *The Ego and the Id* (1923), Freud elaborates upon his fundamental theory of the basic structure of the human psyche, composed of the id, the ego, and the superego.

- *Dreams* (1974) is a collection of Carl Jung's papers on dream psychology.

- *Sigmund Freud: His Life in Pictures and Words* (1978), edited by Ernst Freud, Lucie Freud, and Ilse Grubrich-Simitis, includes a wide array of photographs from throughout Freud's life, as well as a biographical sketch by K. R. Eissler.

- In *The Interpretation of Dreams: Freud's Theories Revisited* (1987), Laurence M. Porter explores critical responses to Freud's theories of dream analysis from the perspective of developments in the field of dream psychology throughout the late twentieth century.

- *Freud: A Life for Our Times* (1988) is the celebrated biography of Freud by Peter Gay, who has written numerous books on Freud's life and work.

- Freud's *Five Lectures on Psycho-Analysis* (1989), which was first published in 1910, is one of his seminal texts. In it he develops the fundamental elements of his theory of psychoanalysis. The 1989 edition is edited by James Strachey and includes a biographical introduction by Peter Gay.

- In *A Primer of Freudian Psychology* (1999), Calvin S. Hall provides an introductory level overview of the central concepts in Freudian theory.

---

can ascribe their rejection to other grounds which do not apply to me, my hopes will remain undisturbed." By imagining his Jewish colleagues to be incompetent or otherwise unqualified, he could conclude that his own qualifications were all he needed—as he is neither a "numbskull" nor a "criminal" and therefore "can look forward to my appointment as professor" without concern for being held back by anti-Semitism. (Although Freud did eventually receive the desired promotion, it was delayed for several years because of his Jewish identity.)

Freud further analyzes a series of dreams that take place in and around Rome and that center on wish fulfillments in regard to the status of Jews in Austrian society.

He mentions that, in a recent visit to Italy, he was disappointed when, having traveled to within eighty miles of Rome, he was obliged for various reasons to turn back before reaching the "Eternal City" he had always wanted to see. Freud makes the connection between his own experience of having to turn back just outside of Rome and the historical experience of Hannibal (247–183 B.C.), the ancient Carthaginian general who fought in the Second Punic War against Rome. Hannibal, though considered a great conqueror, brought his army within three miles of Rome but never successfully entered the city. Freud explains that, in being prevented from seeing Rome, he himself was "following in Hannibal's footsteps; like him, I had not been granted a sight of Rome."

To demonstrate the importance of childhood experiences on the dream life of adults, Freud discusses several strong associations with Rome that date back to his childhood and that continue to influence his dreams. In his dreams of Rome, Freud identifies himself with Hannibal. He notes that Hannibal had been his "warrior ideal" and "favourite hero" while in grade school. When, in high school, he became increasingly aware of the forces of anti-Semitism and "the consequences of being descended from an alien race," the figure of

> Freud's father, Jacob Freud, had been wearing his finest clothes and a new fur hat when a Christian, passing him on the sidewalk, knocked his hat into the street, shouting, 'Jew, get off the pavement!'"

Hannibal, considered a "Semitic" general, "rose even higher" in his esteem.

As Rome is the seat of the Catholic Church, Freud associates it with anti-Jewish sentiment; thus, Hannibal, a Semitic warrior who came close to conquering Rome, became equated in his mind with the efforts of the Jewish (Semitic) people to overcome the oppressive powers of Christendom, as represented by the city of Rome: "Hannibal and Rome symbolized to me the opposition between the tenacity of Jewry and the organization of the Catholic Church." Hannibal becomes an image of Jewish perseverance against the forces of anti-Semitism. (Yet he adds that the current efforts of Jews to overcome anti-Semitism seem as ill-fated as were Hannibal's efforts to conquer Rome.)

Freud elaborates upon the childhood roots of his strong psychical associations with Rome and with Hannibal, as expressed in his dreams. He recalls that, when he was ten or twelve years old, his father related to him an experience of anti-Semitism from years earlier in their native Bohemia. Freud's father, Jacob Freud, had been wearing his finest clothes and a new fur hat when a Christian, passing him on the sidewalk, knocked his hat into the street, shouting, "Jew, get off the pavement!" Passively submitting to this degrading treatment, Freud's father merely stepped into the street to recover the hat. Freud recalls hearing of this passivity on the part of his father with dismay, noting, "That did not seem to me very heroic of the big, strong man who was leading me by the hand."

The young Freud at that time contrasted his father's passiveness with an incident from Hannibal's life in which *his* father "makes his son swear before the domestic altar to take revenge on the

Romans." Again, Hannibal becomes a symbol for Jewish resistance against the oppression of Christian society, as represented by Rome. Freud notes that after he had been told of the former incident in the life of his own father, the courageous and vengeful Hannibal "had a place in my fantasies."

Freud then traces his strong associations with Hannibal, the would-be conqueror of Rome, even further back in his childhood memories. He states that one of the first books he ever read as a child was a history of France and that afterward he stuck labels on the backs of his toy soldiers, designating each by the names of Napoleon's military marshals. He notes that his "declared favorite" of the French marshals among his toy soldiers was André Masséna (1758–1817), a leading general in both the French Revolution and the Napoleonic wars. By a parallel in military accomplishments, Freud later associated the armies of Napoleon with those of Hannibal. Like Hannibal, Masséna represented a Jewish war hero, as he was popularly believed to have been Jewish (although in fact he was not).

Thus, Freud's many dreams of Rome represent a wish, deeply rooted in his childhood psyche, that Jews become triumphant members of society, rather than the increasingly oppressed population of the Austro-Hungarian Empire, which they became over the course of his life.

Ritchie Robertson has pointed out, in an Introduction to *The Interpretation of Dreams*, that the book is as much a work of autobiography on the part of Freud as it is a scientific treatise on the theory of dream psychology. Freud's identity as an ambitious Jewish professional, with high hopes for the future success of his children, is central to his "dreams" of Jewish perseverance in the face of anti-Semitism.

Source: Liz Brent, Critical Essay on *The Interpretation of Dreams,* in *Nonfiction Classics for Students,* The Gale Group, 2002.

Ken Frieden

In the following essay, Frieden examines the role of analyst as both "seducer" and object of transference in psychoanalysis.

Once Freud questions whether the interpreter can provide a neutral statement of a dream's meaning, he implicitly acknowledges the hazards of interpretive manipulation. Because the dream report invariably distorts and revises, Freud can hardly maintain his bipartite model. Even before interpretation begins, the dream report already modifies the dream.

The analogy between dreams and (censored) texts encourages an application of Freud's methods of dream interpretation to his own writings. His bipartite model of meaning conceives the manifest contents as an outer layer that conceals the latent contents; Freud's psychoanalytic approach implies, at the same time, that the dream work is itself essential. For a literary analysis of Freud, this would mean privileging the modes of figuration and conceiving Freud's texts neither as a set of explicit propositions (for example, "The dream is a wish fulfillment") nor as a complex of hidden thoughts (the personal ambition and sexual dynamics revealed by his self-analysis), but as figures, examples, the turns and detours in Freud's particular rhetoric of war and love.

In many respects, the talking cure resembles a battle and a seduction. Freud encourages the transference neurosis while concealing his own emotions. By presenting the mask of a blank screen, he allows full play to the man or woman who mis-takes him for another; by avoiding any concession to the countertransference, Freud assures that he will emerge from the emotional drama unscathed. Freud is thus a seducer in the tradition of Don Juan, who characteristically dominates the passions of others without allowing his own passions to become enslaved. His seductions entail a lack of mutual feeling, in which misguided men and women perceive a nonexistent mutuality. In order to rechannel the patient's (impatient) passion, Freud exploits the authority of the analyst. If the frequency of the sessions and the intimacy of their dialogue is not sufficient to assure that the analysand will fall in love with the analyst, Freud discourages the formation of other emotional bonds during analysis.

Figures of war predominate at certain stages in Freud's discussion of psychoanalysis and dream interpretation. According to one early assertion, psychological normalcy may be determined by the degree of suppression (*Unterdrückung*) of the unconscious by the preconscious; the unconscious must be subjugated to the dominion (*Herrschaft*) of the conscious and preconscious mind. Freud's language introjects a metaphysical battle between the forces of light and darkness, good and evil, heaven and hell. A skeptical age transforms the opposition between life and death—or the worldly and the otherworldly—into that of waking and sleeping. The divine and daemonic mechanisms are within us. "Flectere si nequeo superos, Acheronta movebo": Freud cites Virgil's *Aeneid* on the title page of *The Interpretation of Dreams*. "If I cannot bend the

> In many respects, the talking cure resembles a battle and a seduction. Freud encourages the transference neurosis while concealing his own emotions."

powers above, I will move those of the underworld." He later attributes this drive to the repressed impulses. But Freud ultimately proposes to mobilize and conquer the unconscious powers by delivering them to the rational control of the higher powers, the I.

Another essentially military metaphor is *Besetzung,* typically translated as "cathexis" but more aptly translated as occupation, deployment, or investment. This is one of the key metaphors that date from Freud's *Project* of 1895, although the range of this term shifts in accordance with other developments in psychoanalytic terminology. The early passages refer to "cathected neurons (*besetzte Neurone*)"; assuming an energetics of the psyche, Freud accounts for alterations in quantity by writing of full and empty neurons. After he has explained general psychological events in terms of neural energy transfers, Freud can account for dreams in relation to the emotional investment or wish fulfillment they represent. This terminology continues to operate in *The Interpretation of Dreams*, when Freud discusses the energy transfers and deployments associated with regression and wish fulfillment.

The patient's *Besetzungen* ("cathexes")—charged with love and hate, eros and thanatos, positive and negative transferences—suggest an economic model, but Freud's heart is not merely a neutral cipher on which the patient places a wager. His deceiving heart cannot be conquered. *Besetzen* means to lay siege, to deploy one's psychical forces around another, perhaps even to cut off supplies and force a surrender. A reversal occurs: at first, the patient's *Besetzungen* resemble a military encirclement of the analyst. But Freud slips out of the trap, demonstrating that the campaign was really a battle within the psyche, between the patient's present desires and past affects. The theory of transference insists that all emotional investments in the analyst are irreal, displaced from prior emotions. The patient's laying siege around the analyst turns into an encirclement of the patient by the past. Freudian *Besetzung* implies a military campaign in which the patient is always conquered, occupied (*besetzt*) by the transference neurosis, in a kind of demonic possession or passion play. To become emotionally attached to a person or thing is, in Freud's implicit rhetoric, to engage in strategic warfare. The psychoanalytic patient's surrender is hastened by the imposed condition of abstinence during cure. Deployment and the overcoming of resistance are central to the Freudian method of treatment; the cure mimics a battle of the sexes.

Besetzung is further related to a matrix of terms that Freud does not explicitly consider. The root verb is *setzen,* to set or posit; emotional life, Freud's choice of words implies, is a kind of self-positing. An *Einsatz* is a wager or bet; we place ourselves on the line when we invest in people and objects. The root noun is *Satz,* a sentence (in grammar) or movement (in music); our psychical energy plays itself out by transferring earlier commitments to new positions. The *Satz* does not merely rule over the *Setzungen* by which we posit our work and our passion. To the extent that love repeats previous patterns of emotion, it is a carryover (*Übertragung*) or repetition (*Wiederholung*) that brings back the past in order that we may relive it. The error behind every transference lies in the fiction of replacement, when we act as if another figure could stand in the place once held by the original. The dream itself is an *Ersatz* for hidden thought processes. But *Ersatz* is always a lie that ultimately betrays its counterfeit nature; and the other resists our transferences. *Besetzung* also names the cast of characters in a dramatic production. Wearing a mask of impassive, free-floating attention and sitting beyond the patient's range of vision like a stage director who observes and intervenes in a rehearsal, Freud oversees the play of passions during which the patient remembers, repeats, and (perhaps) works through former emotional commitments. These linguistic resonances lead toward a conception of love and hate as translations (*Übersetzungen*), positive and negative transferences or carryovers (*Übertragungen*) of words and affects. Beyond conscious control, our *Besetzungen* speak a language of desire inside us, or in our relations with others.

The most revelatory essay in this metaphorical field is "On the Dynamics of the Transference," which employs the terms *Besetzung* and *Libidobesetzung.* Freud argues that transference, when it arises during psychoanalysis, can be en-

listed in the service of treatment. He opens by observing that every human being develops a particular cliché in the experience of love. Freud could have called it simply a repetition, but he chooses to frame this peculiarity in the linguistic terms of "a cliché (or even several), which in the course of life is regularly repeated, newly printed out (*abgedruckt*)." Life follows the literary patterns of a printed and reprinted cliché. Childhood relationships are the prototypes, and adults—like belated authors in literacy tradition—are exposed to the danger of simply reproducing their exemplars.

Freud's novel method of cure allows the patient to transfer his or her love cliché onto the analyst within the confines of the analytic session. This transference is immediately associated with resistance to the treatment, and so necessitates a shift in the metaphoric texture, from the image of energy transfer to that of libidinal occupation or deployment (*Libidobesetzung*). Initially, when the patient transfers emotions or linguistic clichés onto the analyst, Freud becomes the object of unexpectedly intense emotional attachments. He strives to remain a blank screen on which the patient's past is projected and analyzed, but countertransference threatens to destroy the illusion of neutrality. The cure searches for blocked libido, and in so doing engages in a mutual struggle. The deployed forces of both patient and analyst maneuver to attain their ends: "Where the analytic research comes upon the withdrawn libido in one of its hiding places, a battle must break out." This battle is highly sexualized, both in its origins and in the metaphors Freud uses to describe it.

The scenario is essentially one in which a man struggles to overcome a woman's resistance to his sexual advances. The scene of *Besetzung* thus reverses, for the patient's initial investment in the noncommitted analyst has become a full-fledged war. Freud elaborates the metaphors of war at the close of his essay: "This battle (*Kampf*) between doctor and patient, between intellect and the life of the drives (*Triebleben*), between recognition and the desire to act (*Agierenwollen*), plays itself out almost exclusively in connection with the phenomenon of transference." Noting the great difficulties entailed, Freud adds that nevertheless "on this field the victory must be won."

Freud's great initial discovery, which shocked his collaborator and senior colleague Josef Breuer, concerned the sexual etiology of hysteria. Freud explained neuroses as the consequence of sexual disturbances. If health resembles a freely flowing hydraulic system, illness appears to result from dammed energies. In the complex drama now called psychoanalysis, a neurotic returns to the points of resistance and blockage in order to overcome these obstacles to health.

The libido cannot be freed unless it is first engaged. Hence, after Freud discovers the phenomenon of transference, he enlists its aid in the treatment. From one point of view, therapy begins as does a gambling session in which the house calls to the patron: "Place your bets!" And the patient places more than a monetary fee on Freud's desk. The serious wager is emotional: the patient makes a bid for love; desire errs. To lose, in this context, is to facilitate a discovery of the mechanisms of erotic error. Pokerfaced, Freud insists that he is merely a blank screen or mirror, the empty illusion onto which the neurotic projects desire, and he proceeds to show that the patient has mistaken the object of love. In Freud's office, desire comes to learn the unreality of its objects; the repetition of emotions is replaced by analytic working through. Place your bets! Not with any prospect of winning the game, but only to discover that your strategies are insufficient and that the house always wins. Accumulating capital throughout the twentieth century, the house that Freud built has become an increasingly potent institution.

At the start of a psychoanalytic treatment, Freud seems to say: invest in me, bet on me, occupy me, bring your abandoned dreams or hidden wishes, and throw your past loves into the cure. The scene of battle is full of surprises, however, for Freud feigns a weak position in order to provoke an effort at conquest. From a position of illusory weakness, Freud turns the tide of the battle, craftily redirecting the patient's deployments back toward their source. After Freud conquers the patient's heart, he points the subdued psyche to the hidden cause of its ignominious defeat. The patient is necessarily the loser—unless a victory over the past ensues.

The repressed paradigm is defeat at the hands of parental figures. Suddenly Freud urges a revolutionary alliance, a joint overthrow of the mother country (or *Vaterland*). Psychoanalysis makes forgotten loves actual, "for ultimately no one can be slain in absentia or in effigy." This concluding metaphor oddly typifies psychoanalytic treatment, because the distinction between real and imaginary slaughter does not obviously correspond to the difference between repeating and working through.

Analysis does, nevertheless, attempt to "slay" parental figures in their absence. Freud suggests that the transference is necessary in order to reawaken slumbering affects that may then be re-educated. Continuing the prior images, a part of the patient appears to capitulate; the working through of repressed libido is figured as a murder. At best, a memory trace of the parental cliché has been destroyed, freeing the repressed energies for new investment. But if the cure appropriates and destroys the patient's love cliché, how can this mangled narrative be replaced? Like a totalitarian regime, psychoanalysis succeeds when it rewrites the history of its subjects, and when the conqueror convinces the conquered that figurative seduction is beneficial.

Out of the metaphorical battles between Freud and his patients arise questions concerning the relationship between psychoanalysis and power. Despite his efforts to maintain scientific neutrality, Freud's methods evidently involve him in rather irregular maneuvers. The founder of psychoanalysis not only engaged in symbolic battles with his patients; he also fought endlessly against his rebellious disciples, and in so doing he expressed his ambition to remain the absolute father of his figurative children.

Freud most explicitly discusses power and ambition when he interprets a minimal dream of "R." that also raises issues concerning the Jewish condition. His preparatory account refers to Jewish doctors in Vienna who have been denied the title of Professor because of "denominational considerations." Prior to the dream, Freud writes, he was nominated for this title, but the experience of his senior colleagues led him to fear the worst. Freud observes somewhat irrelevantly that he is, as far as he knows, "not ambitious." Yet his interpretation of the dream of R. centers around a mixture of positive and negative feelings, tenderness and hostility, toward this colleague. By distortion into its opposite, the latent hostility is transformed into manifest tenderness.

Freud explains this dream distortion by analogy with the social situation of two people in which "the first possesses a certain power, and the second must show respect because of the power." He observes that this condition is rather the rule than the exception: "The politeness which I exercise every day is in large part such a dissimulation; when I interpret my dreams for the reader, I am obliged to make such distortions." Ambition and hostility seethe beneath the surface of Freud's scientific persona; Freud conceives dream distortions on the model of social pretenses. Freud also compares the dream work to the activity of a political writer, who ''has to tell unpleasant truths to those in power,'' and disguises his opinions to escape censorship. Freud suggests that every individual psyche operates as does a political regime. Long before writing his metapsychological essays on the tripartite psyche, Freud postulates the efficacy of distinct mental powers: ''The first forms the wish that is expressed in the dream, while the second exercises censorship on the dream wish and through this censorship forces a distortion of its expression.'' The self internalizes social hierarchies that assure a disparity between its deepest intentions and manifest expressions.

Freud relates a revealing episode of humiliation at a train station. That Freud was sensitive to such experiences is evident from his memory of an affront to his father—as a Jew. A certain Count Thun haughtily passes him on the platform while traveling to see the kaiser. Freud denies that he envies the count, for he is on vacation and pleasantly conceives himself to be the real Count Nichtsthun (''Do-Nothing''). Yet Freud is preoccupied by the evident social hierarchies. Full of ''revolutionary thoughts'' that oppose social divisions, Freud resolves to protest any signs of favoritism. In fact, a certain government official does claim a half-price, first-class seat, and Freud receives an inferior compartment without a lavatory. Freud's uneasy reactions, and the dreams that result, show the significance of the issues involved in this experience. Social hierarchy has found its way into the recesses of the psyche, and this anecdote might be read as an allegory of tensions within Freud the individual.

Freud the interpreter cannot be entirely separated from Freud the seducer. Janus-faced, he looks back in time with a pretense to uncovering past causes that explain the meaning of dreams; through transferences and free associations, he simultaneously engages the dreamer's imagination in ways that project toward future possibilities. Provoked by Freud, the dreamer invents variations on the dream text. The transference ensures that, to some extent, Freud's interpretation of these inventions will be realized or enacted.

The recognition that Freud sometimes employed self-fulfilling prophecies does not disqualify his results. Medical standards forced him to deemphasize this aspect of the analysis, at least in his public statements; he knew that transference was the strongest ''weapon'' of cure, and had good reason to exploit the power of his interpretive influence. At the same time—to meet the expectations of scientific method—he dissimulated this influence. His ancient precursors provided the prophetic model he felt obliged to reject, since he was closer to them in practice, if not in theory, than he could admit.

Freud uncovers the psychological and rhetorical mechanisms that facilitate thematic awareness. Neither themes nor figures, taken alone, constitute his texts; meaning arises out of the interaction between manifest and latent elements. Freud's discussions themselves show distortions analogous to those of the dream work: his examples, allusions, reversals, qualifications, denials, censorships, revisions, metaphors, and analogies all resemble the processes he discusses. This recognition does not justify a moralistic critique. Freud's diction is unusual only in its eloquence; as with all authors, the rhetoric of his manifest contents appears to distort and recast elusive, ''authentic'' meanings. Authenticity and literal meaning are retrospective illusions fostered by an awareness of tropes and transferences.

Psychoanalysts have pragmatic reasons for borrowing and systematizing certain Freudian concepts while revising and rejecting others, but Freud discouraged his followers from conceiving psychoanalysis as a system. A literary approach takes Freud at his word, or takes seriously the ways in which his words signify, by considering the varied forms of his theories, figures, disavowals, and concealed polemics. According to Freud, the tensions expressed by symptoms, slips of the pen or tongue, and transferences characterize everyday life. To read Freud as Freud read is to observe the distortions or disfigurements that are essential to expression and to discern the movement of texts rather than the congealed meanings they seem to produce. This undertaking runs counter to the forms of psychoanalytic practice that demand routines and standardization: while Freud strives to develop scientific techniques, he also associates dream interpretation with the unpredictable methods of art criticism.

The Interpretation of Dreams is at once a treatise, an episodic novel, and a collection of case studies in which theories, confessions, and fantasies compete. Applied to his own texts, Freud's methods of dream interpretation reveal a system in flux, distorted by condensations, displacements, graphic illustrations, and revisions. Freud searches for concealed wishes, and his own writings acknowledge moments of censorship that veil hidden meanings.

As the manifest content of a dream is no random husk behind which the kernel of meaning may be found, however, so Freud's particular dream examples, and the poetic structures of his work, are significant.

Freud's psychological theories are inseparable from the verbal texture of his essays. Recent studies observe some flagrant distortions that have resulted from translation of Freud into English. Yet the present goal is not prescriptive, because no fully adequate translation of Freud into another language is possible. Freud himself anticipated the difficulties that would beset the translator of *The Interpretation of Dreams*. Rather than work toward a better English version of Freud's texts, we may modestly observe linguistic pathways through which his texts operate. The metaphorical range of Freud's ideas cannot be controlled or reduced to a univocal system; at best, the interpreter attends to meaning on multiple registers.

Critics of Freud have repeatedly questioned the scientific status of psychoanalysis. They argue that Freud fails to impose the highest experimental standards upon his nascent science; some current researchers seek to show that psychoanalytic ideas may be verified or falsified, at the same time that other authors emphasize the necessarily speculative, unprovable character of psychoanalytic theory. If we accept the inevitability of figuration, however, there is less reason to be dissatisfied with Freud's procedures. Freud's *Interpretation of Dreams* is consequently more a book about interpretation than it is about dreams. According to his theories, repression and the concomitant disguise necessitate interpretations that return to the hidden form of the distorted dream contents.

The interpreter of Freud's text can hardly extract fixed theses: as the dream work is essential to the dream, rhetorical devices are essential to the dream book. *The Interpretation of Dreams* tells elaborate stories toward an autobiography of its author, in which the demands of scientist and novelist contend. Beyond conscious control, rhetoric governs the psyche and its textual presentation. The operations of the distorting dream work are analogous to figures of speech. What lies beyond, in the textual unconscious? In a footnote, Freud cites James Sully's image of the dream as a palimpsest that "*discloses beneath its worthless surface-characters traces of an old and precious communication*" (quoted in English and italicized by Freud).

Freud's own writings on dreams are palimpsests over ancient sources.

Source: Ken Frieden, "Interpreter and Seducer," in *Freud's Dream of Interpretation,* State University of New York Press, 1990, pp. 37–46.

Harold Bloom

In the following introductory essay, Bloom examines critical responses to Freud's dream interpretation, including reading Freud's work as literature.

Charles Rycroft explains his use of the word "innocence" in the title of his *The Innocence of Dreams* as a reference to "the idea that dreams back knowingness, display an indifference to received categories, and have a core which cannot but be sincere and is uncontaminated by the self-conscious will." Such an explanation is itself innocent and hardly accounts for the polemical force of the title, since the book is largely written against Freud where Freud is strongest, in the interpretation of dreams. The actual rhetorical force of Rycroft's title is that it contains an implicit interpretation of Freudian theory, in effect making the title of what Freud called the "Dream Book" into *The Guilt of Dreams.* So many years after the publication of *Die Traumdeutung* (1900), it is an admirable act of audacity for an experienced psychoanalyst like Rycroft to dissent so completely from the Freudian theory of dream interpretation. But whether Rycroft has much more than audacity to offer in this book is a question that thoughtful readers must decide by returning to the text of Freud. That impetus to return, like analytic audacity, has its own value, and also must be judged a service that Rycroft has helped perform.

These are still the days, in many critical circles, of "French Freud," meaning Jacques Lacan and his influence. Lacan and his admirers assert continuously that the principal virtue of Lacan is that he *has* gone back to the problematics of a serious reading of Freud's text as text. Whether one credits this assertion, or takes precisely the contrary view with Richard Wollheim, who insists that Lacan gives us psycholinguistics and not Freud's psychoanalysis, the issue is clearly one of accurately *reading* Freud. Rycroft takes no part in this debate, but I fear that his performance as a reader of Freud will encourage the disciples of Lacan. Unlike Wollheim, whose *Sigmund Freud* (1971) is a close and formidable reading, and unlike Philip Rieff in this country, Rycroft gives us an account of Freud that I am compelled to judge as a weak misreading. My

An artist's rendering of the Greek mythological figures Oedipus and the Sphinx. Freud's well-known theory of the "Oedipus Complex" says that children go through a stage in their psychosexual development in which they feel a sexual attraction to the parent of the opposite sex

judgment, if correct, will not remove all value from Rycroft's book, since its constructive aspect stems not so much from his argument against what Freud truly never said as it does from his own experience as an analyst.

Rycroft starts out by setting himself against the analogical method that is always central to Freud's work. So Rycroft argues: "Freud maintained that dreams are neurotic symptoms or, to be more precise, are analogous to neurotic symptoms." This is to begin by missing a crucial point, precisely stated by Rieff in *Freud: The Mind of The Moralist:*

> The inclusiveness of Freud's idea of a symptom should be kept in mind: ultimately all action is symptomatic. There are "normal" symptoms, like the dream, as well as somatic symptoms like a facial tic or a paralyzed leg.

Rycroft believes that for Freud "dreams and neurotic symptoms betoken failures of repression."

Freud's largest actual statement about dreams has a different emphasis: *"a dream is a (disguised) fulfillment of a (suppressed or repressed) wish."* Though Rycroft does not say so, I suspect that his reaction away from Freud on dreams begins with his distaste for the crisis-like aspect of *The Interpretation of Dreams*, which seems to me the book's most literary quality. The crisis for Freud was double, involving both the death of his father and the agonistic relationship with Fliess. Doubtless Freud's greatest work pays a price in darkened knowledge because of its origin in Freud's path-breaking self-analysis. Freud's own dreams became for him "normal" occurrences of what in others he would have judged to be the "psychopathological." It can be argued against Freud that the dream need not have been the inevitable paradigm of hallucination, but though the choice was arbitrary, it was analogically workable. Most powerful interpretive models tend to be arbitrary in their origins, but become inescapable in later interpretive traditions. It was *for Freud* that dream-interpretation proved the royal road to the Unconscious. Coming after Freud, we inherit his insight at the expense of his dominance over us.

Rycroft's fundamental dissent from this dominance comes in his account of the Primary and Secondary Processes, an account which is again not Freud's own. But rather than contrast each of Rycroft's summaries with the actual Freudian text, a wearisome process, I advance to Rycroft's list of the four defects he finds in the Freudian relation of Primary Process to dreaming. These are:

> 1) Since everyone dreams, Freud implicitly argues that everyone is neurotic.
>
> 2) To assume that acquiring the capacity for rational or Secondary Process thinking depends on repression of the Primary Process "implies that human beings enter the world totally unadapted to meet it, an inherently improbable assumption."
>
> 3) By supposedly relating imagination and creative activity to the Primary Process, Freud had to characterize them as "in principle neurotic, regressive and symptom-like."
>
> 4) Freud's formulations belong to his "mechanistic assumption that the mind is a mental apparatus within which energy circulates. . . . Unfortunately, however, we really have no idea what mental energy is or what the concept means."

Of Rycroft's four objections, the first has been met already by Rieff's accurate account of Freud's idea of a symptom. The second is indeed Freud's tragic premise, and ultimately explains why there is a civil war in the human psyche, so that the Unconscious and not nature or the state is what most inescapably threatens each of us. The third, to which I will return later, is wholly inadequate to Freud's quite troubled and finally evasive view of art. The fourth begins by accusing Freud of a reductionism that he proudly espoused and then goes on to a complaint that Freud met quite cheerfully by acknowledging that his theory of drives was the necessary mythology that psychoanalysis *had* to exploit. To sum up Rycroft's objections, their common element is an inability to accept what is most basic in Freud's theories of the mind, which means that Rycroft has become another "humanistic" revisionist of Freud, or most simply, if Rycroft is still a psychoanalyst, then Freud was something else.

If I myself were to criticize Freud's theories of dream-interpretation, I would start with what seems to me his most striking notion about dream-thought, which is that such thought is truly marked by clarity, although its clarity has been repressed. For Freud, the manifest "text" of the dream, its telling by the patient to the analyst, carries the stigma of being the work of the Unconscious, but the "latent" content or true significance of the dream is itself not Primary but Secondary Process labor. Something Secondary and rational has been repressed, and the work of analytical interpretation undoes the repression and yields a clear account of a "normal" thought. Jung scorned the Freudian idea here in both respects. For Jung, the true thought at the origin of the dream *and* its true interpretation must both come up out of the Primal or Gnostic Abyss of a truly creative Unconscious. Though I accept Freud and not Jung on dreams, there is little doubt but that Jung shows more affection for dreams than for their interpretations, whereas what delights Freud is what he can make out of dreams. It is in this rather ironic sense that Rycroft actually teaches "the innocence of dreams."

Wollheim, who seems to me as faithful an expositor as Freud could find, usefully emphasizes that the element of wish *in* dreams is not expressed *by* dreams, and so Freud was able to posit what he called the dream-work as something that disguised wish. This must mean that wish is repressed *before* it gets into the dream. Such a conclusion also serves to devalue dreams and reminds us again that the Freudian Unconscious is a deliberate reduction of the rich, dark Abyss of the ancient (and now Jungian) Unconscious.

What gives Freud the interpretive self-confidence to so reduce dreams, and to insist so merci-

> **"If I myself were to criticize Freud's theories of dream-interpretation, I would start with what seems to me his most striking notion about dream-thought, which is that such thought is truly marked by clarity, although its clarity has been repressed."**

lessly that dream-thought, as opposed to dream-work, is at one with his own rationalizing interpretations? Part of the answer, and another vulnerable aspect of Freudian procedure, is that Freud's dream-text for interpretation is partly written by Freud himself, since it is a version of dream that emerges from the analytic session. This means that it is subject to the dynamics of the transference, and so is a telling that takes place within the context of the analyst's authority.

Rieff gallantly attempts to rescue the dream from the full consequences of Freud's authority by seeing every dreamer as a natural poet and intellectual precisely in the effort to outwit his interpreter, the force of culture as personified in Freud: "The chief quality of the dream *as interpreted* is not so much its meaning as the elaborateness of its meaningful disguises." Upon this, two observations: first, that Freud would have disagreed with Rieff here, though my own sympathies are with Rieff, and second, it is exactly this aspect of Freudian interpretation that partly justifies Lacan. If there is so large a gap between the elaborations of manifest content and the simplicity of latent content, then dreams (in their Freudian context of the transference) provoke the Lacanian strong misreading of the priority of signifier over signified or the contrast between rich figuration and poverty-stricken meaning. It is worth recalling that Rieff anticipated many of the major insights of the Lacanian school and indeed set their pattern when he remarked: "In radical opposition to constitutional psychology, Freud puts language before body."

Rycroft would have profited by pondering Rieff again before he too easily dismissed the cunning intensities of Freudian dream-interpretation. Freud characteristically condemns the dream as an unfaithful translation of the dream-thoughts, and so ''a highly incomplete and fragmentary version of them.'' Rieff invokes Hazlitt, with his dictum that ''poetry represents forms chiefly as they suggest other forms, feelings as they suggest other feelings.'' Commenting upon this as analogue to Freud, Rieff catches the essential agonistic relationship between Freud and the dream:

> Assuming a dream never means what it says, that it is always a substitute for something else which cannot be said and leads to further associations which are in themselves substitutes, Freud may compliment a dream so far as to call it an ''exceptionally clever dream production.'' But this is the compliment paid by a gracious antagonist; Freud treated a dream as an opponent in the work of interpretation, trying by its cleverness to outwit the interpreter.

This means that a dream, however elaborate, is only a substitute for a truer text, indeed an interpretive substitute and so particularly suspect. A dream, in the Freudian view, is thus a belated text, an inadequate commentary upon a missing poem. Its plot is probably irrelevant; what matters is some protruding element, some image that seems hardly to belong to the text. In this sense, Freud is a legitimate father to Lacan and Derrida, with their deconstructions of the drive, except that he would have urged them to the abysses of the dream and not of his own texts.

Rycroft, once he has moved on from Freud to various types of dreams, their relations to sleep, and to cultural patterns, transcends the drubbing I have been administering. This makes me wish he had not taken on Freud, but that is the burden of the writing psychoanalyst, who is tempted to a battle he is doomed to lose. Rycroft is drily persuasive when he writes that neither he nor anyone he has known seems to have had what Ernest Jones would classify as a true nightmare, the criteria of Jones's *On the Nightmare* (1910) being too severe for mere reality to satisfy. Similarly, Rycroft is able to use the later Freud against the author of *The Interpretation of Dreams* on the difficult issue of anxious dreams. Anxiety is a subject by which Rycroft's intellect is kindled, and he makes an original contribution (at least to me) when he shows that it is possible to dream *about* anxiety without necessarily having a dream that itself causes anxiety. I wish he had done more, in this book, to demonstrate that Freud's later modifications of his theories of defense and anxiety render his ideas on dreams less valid or stimulating.

Freud is a weaker antagonist on the subject of sleep and the physiology of dreams, which seems to me Rycroft's best chapter. Freud was not much interested in sleep, and he assumed that the function of the dream was just to keep the dreamer from waking. Here Rycroft has the universal advantage of all latecomers: more facts. Freud did not know that there was normal sleep, with several depths, and also paradoxical sleep, during which the sleeper in some ways hovers near wakefulness. Evidently most dreams, perhaps even all, take place during paradoxical sleep, which seems to be as much a necessity as normal sleep. Rycroft will not go so far as to say we sleep in order to dream, but he goes back to the great neurologist Hughlings Jackson (died 1911) who thought that sleep both got rid of the previous day's useless memories and consolidated the necessary ones, probably during dreamless sleep. If Jackson yet proves to be correct, then one function of dreams is quite unlike anything Freud conceived, since without dreams we would be burdened by more data than we could bear.

In a witty, brief penultimate chapter, Rycroft offers a reprise, saying that the manifest content of his book is his attempt to go back beyond Freud (and Jung) to what he calls the traditional, literary view of dreams, with the difference of holding on to certain Freudian ideas, particularly body symbolism in dream imagery and the genetic inheritance of the family romance. The latent theme of the book then would have to be, as he says, the question of the origin of creative or imaginative energy. This is the subject of Rycroft's final chapter, but unfortunately there is little here that is either new or important. Rycroft falls back upon unanalyzed Coleridgean Imagination and undiscussed Keatsian negative capability, while he largely dismisses Freud upon art and artists. Psychoesthetics is a still inchoate field, but Rycroft seems to know nothing of it, whether British, American, or French.

I conclude, in a coda, by suggesting what I wish Rycroft had discussed, if only he had felt more respect for the Freudian achievement in dream-interpretation. Rieff's assertion that psychoanalysis parodies the traditions of religious hermeneutics is still valid and provocative. But psychoanalysis is also a reductive parody of poetry, which may be another way of saying that poetry has always been a transcendental kind of psychoanalysis, a mode marked by patterns of transference and counter-transference, or of influence and in anxieties. Freud spoke truly (and also somewhat anxiously) in his repeated admissions that the poets had been there before him. Certainly Lacan, at his rare best, gives us what the poets have given more fully and freely. Dreams, like psychoanalysis, parody and reduce poems, if we follow Freud by treating dreams in terms of their latent content or ''meaning.'' But dreams, in their manifest content, in plot and imagery, share in the poetic elements that tend to defy reduction and reductiveness.

Freud wanted and needed his reductions, his quest being scientific and therapeutic. As a therapeutic diviner of dreams he is beyond all competition, ancient and modern, and this more because of than in spite of his interpretive overconfidence. But dreams are not poems, not even bad poems, and Freud was too wary to expend his formidable energies in reducing poems. Rycroft has an honorable nostalgia for treating dreams with a more literary respect than Freud accorded them. It would be more interesting to accept Freud's voluntary limitation and then to see just what kind of an enabling act was constituted by this pragmatic disrespect for dreams. Beyond this acceptance, and this seeing, might come a fresh awareness of the multiple ways in which poetry and psychoanalysis converge and yet differ as modes of interpretation. Freud found his peers in the poets because of their *power of interpretation,* but his aims were not compatible with the largest ambitions of poetry, as I think he came to understand.

Source: Harold Bloom, Introduction, in *Sigmund Freud's ''The Interpretation of Dreams,''* edited by Harold Bloom, Modern Critical Interpretations series, Chelsea House, 1987, pp. 1–7.

Richard Wollheim

In the following essay, Wollheim surveys and analyzes Freud's study of dreams.

I shall begin with Freud's study of dreams, which is in many ways the most distinctive and the most remarkable single element in his vast survey of the mind. It is the topic of his most important work, *The Interpretation of Dreams,* which, besides being what its title indicates, is also a work of confession, in that Freud committed to its pages many of the findings of his self-analysis. And Freud continued to feel a special attachment to dream-interpretation, both for the exactness of its findings and for the precious evidence it provided for the deeper workings of the mind in normality and abnormality alike. The view expressed in the maxim *''The interpretation of dreams is the royal road to a knowledge of the unconscious activities of the mind''* is one from which he never wavered.

Let us start with the most general statement about dreams, which is repeated with slight variations at several places: *''A dream is a (disguised) fulfilment of a (suppressed or repressed) wish.''* One feature of this thesis, which calls for immediate comment, can best be brought out by considering an objection to it, now standard: If the wish that finds fulfillment in a dream is invariably disguised, how can we tell of its existence? Or, How can we tell that there is disguise, unless we know of the existence of the wish and what it is? The point that this objection effectively makes is that the thesis falls into parts— the assignment of a fulfilled wish to each dream, and the predication of disguise or concealment of that wish—and, consequently, it insists that there should be separate evidence for each of the two parts of the theory. I shall respect the objection, or its implicit point, to the extent of expounding the two parts of the thesis successively.

First, then, that dreams are wish-fulfillments. This, we can see, is itself a composite thesis: for it traces dreams to wishes, and it asserts that these wishes belong to the primary process. They belong, that is, to that mode of mental functioning within which, characteristically, no distinction is observed between a desire and its satisfaction—indeed, even to use these terms is perhaps anachronistic, in that as yet the difference has not manifested itself. For the wisher the experience is unitary, and, in consequence, dreams cannot be said merely to express a wish, for, wherever the wish belongs to the content of the dream, so also does the fulfillment of the wish. ''A dream does not simply give expression to a thought, but represents the wish fulfilled as a hallucinatory experience.'' And Freud goes on to say that if the wish ''I should like to go on the lake'' instigates a dream, the dream has for its content ''I am going on the lake.''

Freud at various stages considered the objection that not all dreams are wish-fulfillments, and that surely some derive from other types of mental state; the most obvious counterexamples being anxiety dreams. But, with minor exceptions, Freud held to the universality of his thesis, and he was at pains to point out that in every case brought against it there is either an inadequate analysis of the dream or an inadequate conception of the wish. It was in development of the second point—the first we shall have to take up at greater length—that Freud was

> Freud continued to feel a special attachment to dream-interpretation, both for the exactness of its findings and for the precious evidence it provided for the deeper workings of the mind in normality and abnormality alike.''

led to make a distinction in Lecture 14 of the *Introductory Lectures*. ''No doubt,'' he wrote,

> a wish-fulfilment must bring pleasure; but the question then arises ''To whom?'' To the person who has the wish, of course. But, as we know, a dreamer's relation to his wishes is a quite peculiar one. He repudiates them and censors them—he has no liking for them, in short.

Freud then went on to distinguish between two separate people amalgamated in the dreamer, one of whom has the wish whereas the other rejects it, and it is only the former who is satisfied. Freud's distinction could be made, less dramatically, as one not between two different people, but between two different roles—the man insofar as he has the wish, and the man insofar as he rejects it; or, weaker still, we could contrast the satisfaction of the man and the satisfaction of the wish; and the point would hold. A wish can be satisfied, even though the man who has it isn't. Of course, we might press for an explanation why this was so, and the answer in the case of dreams is obviously connected with the deviance of wish or its discrepancy from the man's other wishes. It is no gross anticipation of Freud's argument to say that we are here approaching—though now from the other side, from consideration of its consequences, not its causes—the issue of the ''incompatible'' idea with which Freud had been struggling since the first drafts for the ''Preliminary Communication.'' For the wish that, when satisfied, leaves the wisher unsatisfied is ''incompatible.''

Secondly, the wishes expressed in dreams are disguised. Here we come to a central notion of Freud's, that of the dream-work. To understand this notion, we must first understand a distinction upon which it rests and which he claimed was always to some degree or other misconceived by his critics:

that between the ''manifest content'' and the ''latent content'' of the dream. The manifest content is that which we experience or remember; it constitutes the subject of the dream report. The latent content is that which gives the dream its sense or meaning: it is sometimes called the ''dream-thoughts,'' where these are contrasted with the dream content. On the distinction two points are to be observed. First, the dream-thoughts are not restricted to the wish that instigates the dream. Rather they include the whole setting or context of the wish. Secondly, the distinction between manifest and latent content is a functional distinction: that is, it refers to the role the thoughts play, so that the possibility is open that the manifest and the latent contents may coincide.

Once this distinction is clear, the dream-work may then be regarded as the process, or piece of mental activity, by which the dream-thoughts are converted or transcribed into the dream content. Note ''dream-thoughts'': for it is crucial to Freud's conception of the dream that the latent content of the dream goes piecemeal, element by element, into the manifest content, inside which only a halfhearted attempt is made to mold it into a unity. For this reason a metaphor which it seems natural to invoke in this context, and which Freud himself employed, that of translation from one language to another, is inexact. For the dream lacks that which is most characteristic of a language: grammar, or structure. A more appropriate comparison that Freud makes is to the rebus, or picture puzzle, in which pictorial elements, words, letters of the alphabet appear side by side and it is only by replacing each element with a syllable or word that sense can be made of the whole.

There are four activities in which the dream-work consists: condensation, displacement, representation (or consideration of representability), and secondary revision. On whether the last properly forms part of the dream-work Freud was later to have his doubts. Each of these activities is, more or less, explained by its name.

Condensation is exemplified in the fact that ''the manifest dream has a smaller content than the latent one,'' or, more exactly, that this abbreviation is achieved without omission. Freud lists various results of condensation—such as the preference given to items that occur several times over in the dream-thoughts, and the formation of composite or intermediate figures. But condensation is seen at its clearest in the handling of words or names, which makes it, from an expository point of view, peculiarly vulnerable in translation. It is condensation that prevents there being any neat one-one correspondence between the elements of the manifest content and those of the latent content. And it is also condensation that permits a more general feature of the dream: that is, overdetermination, according to which, for any given manifest content, there can be more than one latent content, or any one dream can express several quite separate wishes.

By "displacement"—or "transference" as Freud sometimes called it in the early years, before the word took on its technical sense in psychoanalytic theory—Freud meant two distinct but related processes. One is that whereby the dream is differently "centered" from the dream-thoughts, so that it does not reflect the relative importance of those thoughts. The other is that whereby elements in the dream do duty for elements in the dream-thoughts, the substitution being in accordance with a chain of association. Displacement is peculiarly connected with the disguise that the dream wears.

The third process, of representation, is the transposition of thoughts into imagery. Freud, in one of his many apt analogies, compared the difficulty under which the dream labors as a representational device to the limitations that, according to classical aesthetic theory, are inherent in the plastic arts of painting and sculpture in contrast to poetry, and he revealed the ingenuity with which the dream-work tries to incorporate the most recalcitrant or abstract material. Freud said—and it may sound surprising—that this third process is "psychologically the most interesting." Possibly what he had in mind is the way in which the plasticity of dreams links them to the prototype of the primary process: the hallucinatory experience of satisfaction.

The processes of condensation and displacement can be economically illustrated from the so-called "Autodidasker" dream from Freud's own experience. One evening Freud's wife, who had been reading some stories which he had given her, by J. J. David, an Austrian writer and a friend of Freud's brother, told him how moved she had been by one of them about a man of great talents who went to the bad: and she then went on, after a discussion of the talents their children might have, to express the wish that a similar fate would not be theirs. Freud reassured her, and talked of the advantages of a good upbringing. That night he had a dream in which two wishes were expressed: one for

his son's future, and the other that his still unmarried brother, Alexander, might have a happy domestic life—and both wishes are represented as fulfilled. The dream fell into two distinct parts. The first consisted simply in the made-up word "Autodidasker." The second was the reproduction of a phantasy recently entertained to the effect that the next time Freud saw a colleague of his, Professor N., he would say, "The patient about whose condition I consulted you recently is in fact only suffering from a neurosis, just as you suspected."

Let us now see how the dream-thoughts that Freud somehow collected are transposed into the dream content by the means we have been considering. As to the dream-thoughts Freud enumerated the following: an author; a good upbringing; Breslau, as a place where a friend of Freud's who had married had gone to live; then the names of two men, both of whom lived in Breslau and who had come to a bad end through women—Lasker, who died of syphilis, and Lassalle, killed in a duel; a novel of Zola's, *L'Oeuvre,* in which the author introduces himself, with his name ingeniously altered, as a happily married character; and the desire, pertaining to both wishes, that Freud might be proved wrong in his fears. The last thought is expressed fairly directly in the second part of the dream, where it is shown as fulfilled—for Freud is apologizing. The other thoughts are all crammed into the first or prefatory part of the dream. Author, Lasker, and Lassalle figure fairly evidently inside "Autodidasker." A good upbringing is represented through its opposite, i.e., "autodidact." *L'Oeuvre* appears more obliquely, in that the transformation, in the book, of Zola's name into "Sandoz" exhibits a parallel to that of "Alex(ander)" into "Autodidasker"—in both cases an anagram of the original is buried at the end of the substitute name, which contains a prefix for disguise.

If this dream very well illustrates the processes of condensation and displacement in action—indeed, in joint action—the third element in dream-work is present to a degree so peculiarly low as to elicit comment from Freud. To illustrate visual representation, I shall follow Freud and cite specific details from dreams. So, a man dreams that he is an officer sitting at table opposite the Emperor: and this represents his putting himself in opposition to his father. Or a woman dreams that she is walking with two little girls whose ages differ by fifteen months; and this represents the fact that two traumatic events of childhood, of which she is dreaming, were fifteen months apart.

As to secondary revision, this is the attempt by the mind to order, to revise, to supplement the contents of the dream so as to make an acceptable or intelligible whole. Even in *The Interpretation of Dreams* Freud distinguished this factor from the rest of the dream-work by pointing out that it makes no new contribution to the dream in the way of representing dream-thoughts not otherwise included, and he suggested that it should be attributed to the very psychic agency that the dream is otherwise intended to evade. In the encyclopedia article of 1922 entitled "Psycho-analysis," Freud definitely excluded secondary revision from the dream-work.

Freud insisted that the dream-work is confined to these three (or four) processes. Other activities, which appear to take place in dreams—mathematical calculations, or the making of a speech—are simply to be regarded as items or elements that constitute the content of the dream. In reporting them, we report not what we did, but what we dreamt of. For in a dream we do not do things, we only dream of doing them.

At this stage, I should perhaps introduce a topic mentioned only briefly in the original text of *The Interpretation of Dreams* but which figured increasingly in later editions, and which is widely assumed to be central to Freud's theory of the dream. I refer to the symbolism according to which there are certain invariants in dream representations so that certain basic thoughts or preoccupations find a regular form of expression: for instance, the parents are represented by kings and queens; the penis by sticks, tree trunks, umbrellas, nail files, or long, sharp weapons; the womb by boxes, cupboards, ovens, or hollow objects like ships. In one way, such symbolism must be classified with the dream-work, since it provides a transition from the latent to manifest content; yet in another way it must be contrasted to it, precisely because it reduces the element of work on the part of the dreamer. It is a corollary of this last point that, where symbolism is employed, the dreamer is unable to associate to his dream. Furthermore, Freud pointed out that, insofar as dream symbolism is found plausible, it exhibits a capacity of the mind more general than the phenomenon of dreaming. In the *Introductory Lectures* Freud spoke of an "ancient but extinct mode of expression" or "a primal language" which legitimizes the occurrence of symbols in dreams: seemingly an old idea with Freud, which we first catch sight of in a letter to Fliess of 1897, where he talks of a new subject, "psychomythology." But in the massive application of symbolism to dream interpretation it would seem that Freud was heavily influenced by a pupil later to go astray, Wilhelm Stekel.

So much for the nature of the dream-work. Two questions now arise, Why is the dream-work necessary? and, Are any limits imposed upon its scope?—of which the first is really about the latent content of the dream and the second about the manifest content.

In answer to the first question, Freud said that the dream-work is necessary because the wish that finds expression in the dream is invariably a repressed wish. In a footnote added in 1909, Freud said that "the kernel of my theory" lies in the "derivation of dream-distortion from the censorship." Two other characterizations of the dream-wish—that it is infantile, and that it is generally (though not always) sexual—are intimately connected with this thesis, but at the time that Freud was writing *The Interpretation of Dreams*, he was not yet in a position to establish the connections.

In answer to the second question, Freud said that the material for the dream comes from varying sources, and in chapter 5 of *The Interpretation of Dreams* he classified them: recent and indifferent events, infantile experiences, somatic needs, and the repertoire of what Freud called "typical dreams"—dreams of flying and falling, of being naked, of examinations, of the death of loved ones. But Freud laid particular weight on the first of these sources. Indeed, he committed himself to the thesis that every dream contains "a repetition of a recent impression of the previous day." The impression itself may have been significant or it may have been indifferent—where significance and indifference mean, respectively, belonging or not belonging to the latent content of the dream.

Putting together the answers to these last two questions, we may now follow Freud in reconstructing the immediate history of the dream. There is a persisting repressed wish, which forms the motive behind the dream. In the course of the day, this wish comes into contact, or forms an association, with a thought or train of thought. This thought has some energy attached to it, independently of this contact, through not having as yet been "worked over": hence the phrase, the "residues of the day." The upshot is that the thought—or an association to it—is revived in sleep, as the proxy of the wish.

The question that remains to be asked about this alliance is, Why should it assert itself while we are asleep? The answer is not that sleep is peculiarly well-disposed to the alliance, but that it prefers it to any more naked version of the same forces. If the wish did not express itself in the disguise of the dream, it would disturb sleep. And so we come to the overall function of dreams: they are *"the guardians of sleep."*

I now want to ask, What is the evidence for the Freudian theory of dreams? I have already argued that we require separate evidence for the two parts of the theory—for the ascription of dreams to wishes, and for the characterization of the wishes as disguised.

The first piece of evidence comes to us just because the thesis that the wishes involved are disguised admits of a few exceptions. There are dreams that directly express wishes. Such dreams, which Freud referred to in *The Interpretation of Dreams* for their evidential value and to which he devoted a whole lecture in the *Introductory Lectures*, are commonest among children. Freud cited the story of his daughter, then nineteen months old, who, after an attack of vomiting, had spent the day without food and in her sleep called out, "Anna Fweud, stwawbewwies, wild stwawbewwies, omblet, pudden." At this time the little girl used to use her own name to express the idea of taking possession of something. Undisguised dreams also occur to people subjected to extreme privation, and Freud quoted from the explorer Otto Nordenskjöld, who tells how on an Antarctic expedition his men would dream of food and drink in abundance, of tobacco piled up in mountains, of a ship arriving in full sail, or of a letter delivered after a long delay for which the postman apologized.

Turning to the great majority of dreams which do not overtly express wishes, Freud adduced evidence to show that these dreams are disguises. The evidence is that we can, i.e., we have a capacity to, undisguise them. In the majority of cases, we can produce associations to each element in the dream in turn, and these associations, after running for a certain while, will terminate on a point that seems natural. Here Freud is using as evidence something he had already used in therapy as a method of collecting evidence; for in therapy he had used the associations themselves, here he is using the fact that such associations are forthcoming. This capacity, Freud argues, finds additional support in the thesis of psychic determinism (which, as we have seen, was equivalent for Freud to a commitment to science), and also in the word-association experiments devised by Wundt and taken up in Zurich by Bleuler and Jung, which constituted "the first bridge

from experimental psychology to psycho-analysis." Of course, the appeal to association as establishing the existence of a disguised thought instigating the dream is plausible only if we already accept the far more general assumption that a man may know something, or something about himself, without knowing that he knows it: a point which Freud thought was proved beyond doubt by hypnosis and hypnotic suggestion.

That the process of association should sometimes run into difficulty is no argument against its evidential value. For if disguise has been found necessary, should we not expect the process of removing it to be attended with difficulty? Indeed, if no difficulty were encountered, disguise would be inexplicable.

If we now assume that dreams are disguises and that they can be undisguised along paths of association, and we then proceed to undisguise them—or "interpret" them, as the activity is usually called—we find that we are led to a wish whose existence can be independently established. Alternatively, if association is not forthcoming, though there is evidently disguise, and we proceed to interpret the dreams as examples of primal symbolism, we once again find ourselves led to wishes that are independently verifiable. This is the third piece of support that the theory receives. A related argument starts from the character of the wishes that dreams express. Given that they are, as Freud tersely put it, "evil," by which he meant evil in our estimation, it is only to be expected that they should find expression in a disguised form. Neither of these last two arguments, it should be pointed out, offends against the evidential requirement that the two parts of the theory should be confirmed separately, for this is compatible with one part of the theory being used to confirm the other.

Fourthly, the infantile form of dreams—for instance, their plasticity—does much to suggest that they have an infantile content, which means, in Freud's view, that they deal with wishes. Or, to use the terminology of *The Interpretation of Dreams*, the regression in dreams is both formal and material.

Nevertheless, much of the plausibility of Freud's theory of the dream must derive from a somewhat more general conception of the mind and its engagement in the primary processes. As Freud later, somewhat laconically, put it:

> It was discovered one day that the pathological symptoms of certain neurotic patients have a sense. On this discovery the psycho-analytic method of treatment

was founded. It happened in the course of this treatment that patients, instead of bringing forward their symptoms, brought forward dreams. A suspicion thus arose that the dreams too had a sense.

By the time Freud came to write *The Interpretation of Dreams*, not merely had his suspicion hardened to a certainty, but the parallel between dreams and symptoms had allowed his two sets of findings to confirm each other.

Finally, I want to turn to the application of the dream theory, to that remarkable feat of prestidigitation, the interpretation of dreams. The dream I shall select is cited in all three places where Freud talked extensively of dreams—*The Interpretation of Dreams*, the essay "On Dreams," and the second section of the *Introductory Lectures*, in the latter receiving its most elaborate treatment.

A lady, who though still young had been married for many years, had the following dream: *She was at the theater with her husband. One side of the stalls was completely empty. Her husband told her that Elise L. and her fiancé had wanted to go too, but had only been able to get bad seats—three for 1 florin 50 kreuzers—and of course they could not take those. She thought it would not really have done any harm if they had.*

As a preliminary the dreamer disclosed to Freud that the precipitating cause of the dream appears in its manifest content. That day her husband had told her that her friend Elise L., approximately her contemporary, had just become engaged. She then produced the remaining dream-thoughts by association to different elements in the dream. Thus: The week before she had wanted to go to a particular play and had bought tickets early, so early that she had had to pay a booking fee. Then on arrival at the theater, one whole side of the stalls was seen to be empty, and her husband had teased her for her unnecessary haste. The sum of 1 fl. 50 kr. reminded her of another sum, a present of 150 florins (also alluded to during the previous day) which her sister-in-law had been given by her husband, and which she had rushed off to exchange, the silly goose, for a piece of jewelry. In connection with the word "three," introduced in a context where we would expect "two," all the dreamer could think of was that Elise, though ten years her junior in marriage, was only three months younger than she. But to the idea in which the word was embedded—that of getting three tickets for two persons—she could produce no associations.

In reaching an interpretation, Freud was struck by the very large number of references, in the associations to the dream, though, significantly, not in the manifest content of the dream, to things being too early, or done in a hurry, or got overhurriedly, to what might be called temporal mismanagement and the absurdity that attaches to this. If we put these thoughts together with the precipitating cause of the dream—the news of her friend's belated engagement to an excellent man—we get the following synthesis or construction: "Really it was *absurd* of me to be in such a hurry to get married. I can see from Elise's example that I could have got a husband *later*." And perhaps, if we take up the ratio between the two sums of money: "And I could have got one a hundred times better with the money, i.e., my dowry." If we pause at this stage, we can observe massive displacement, in that the central dream thoughts, i.e., the preoccupation with time, do not figure in the dream. And there is an ingenious piece of representation in that the important thought "It was absurd (to marry so early)" is indicated simply by a piece of absurdity, i.e., three tickets for two.

But this last element has gone uninterpreted and, since there were no associations to it, Freud invoked the symbolic equivalences of "three" with a man or a husband and "going to the theater" with getting married. So, getting three tickets for 1 fl. 50 kr. and going to the theater too early also express the idea of a marriage regretted: too early, and to a man of low value.

It is to be observed that the link whereby a visit to the theater can symbolize marriage presupposes that marriage is seen in a happy light. For not merely can young wives go to the theater and see all the plays which respectability had hitherto prohibited, but marriage initiates them into an activity which hitherto it had been their secret desire to gaze on: sexual intercourse. (We can see here how a universal symbolism gains its authority from widespread ways of thinking and feeling.) Now this put Freud on the track of another interpretation, showing another wish-fulfillment in the dream, this time relating to an earlier phase in the dreamer's life. For who is not at the theater? Elise, as yet unmarried. So the dream expresses, as fulfilled, an older wish, that she, the dreamer, should see what happens in marriage, and that she should see it before her friend and near-contemporary. In this case, of course, the two dream wishes are not unconnected. Indeed, Freud suggests that the new angry wish could not have instigated a dream without support from the older, more obviously sexual, wish. Within the dreamer's world, "an old triumph was put in the place of her recent defeat."

Source: Richard Wollheim, "Dreams," in *Sigmund Freud's "The Interpretation of Dreams,"* edited by Harold Bloom, Modern Critical Interpretations series, Chelsea House, 1987, pp. 77–87.

Sources

Crick, Joyce, "Note on the Translation," in *The Interpretation of Dreams,* by Sigmund Freud, Oxford University Press, 1999, p. xlii.

Freud, Sigmund, *The Interpretation of Dreams,* translated and edited by James Strachey, Avon Books, 1965, p. xxxii.

——, *The Interpretation of Dreams,* translated by Joyce Crick, with notes and an introduction by Ritchie Robertson, Oxford University Press, 1999.

Gay, Peter, "Psychoanalyst: Sigmund Freud," in *Time,* Vol. 153, No. 12, March 29, 1999, p. 66.

Lear, Jonathan, "The Shrink Is In: A Counterblast in the War on Freud," in *New Republic,* Vol. 213, No. 26, December 25, 1995, p. 18.

"Re-examining Freud," in *Psychology Today,* Vol. 23, No. 9, September, 1989, p. 48.

"Sigmund Freud," in *Encyclopedia of World Biography,* 2d ed., Vol. 6, Gale Research, 1998, pp. 103–06.

"Year in Review 1994," in *Encyclopaedia Britannica Online,* Encyclopaedia Britannica, Inc., 1994–2000 (February 3, 2001).

Further Reading

Beller, Steven, *Vienna and the Jews, 1867–1938: A Cultural History,* Cambridge University Press, 1989.
      Beller provides historical information on the status and culture of Jews in Vienna during a period roughly coinciding with Freud's lifetime, including discussions of anti-Semitism, the intellectual milieu of Jews in Vienna, and the influence of Jewish culture on Viennese society and history.

Buhle, Mari Jo, *Feminism and Its Discontents: A Century of Struggle with Psychoanalysis,* Harvard University Press, 1998.
      Buhle provides an historical overview of the feminist response to Freudian theory as it developed throughout the twentieth century.

Crews, Frederick C., *Unauthorized Freud: Doubters Confront a Legend,* Viking, 1998.
      Crews grapples with the controversial elements of Freudian theory in an attempt to address the many criticisms it has received.

Ferris, Paul, *Dr. Freud: A Life,* Counterpoint, 1998.
      Ferris' biography of Freud is one of the more recent of several that have been published since Freud's death.

Forrester, John, *Dispatches from the Freud Wars: Psychoanalysis and Its Passions,* Harvard University Press, 1997.
      Forrester provides an historical analysis of the many critical responses to Freudian theory throughout the twentieth century.

Freud, Sigmund, *Dora: Analysis of a Case of Hysteria,* edited by Philip Rieff, Collier Books, 1993 (first published in 1905).
      One of Freud's most famous case histories, *Dora* is the account of his analysis of a young woman suffering from symptoms of hysteria.

Hale, Nathan G., *The Rise and Crisis of Psychoanalysis in the United States: Freud and the Americans,* Oxford University Press, 1995.
      Hale provides an historical account of the influence of Freudian theory on American psychological thought in the twentieth century.

Mitchell, Stephen A., and Margaret J. Black, *Freud and Beyond: A History of Modern Psychoanalytic Thought,* BasicBooks, 1995.
      Mitchell and Black provide an historical account of the development of psychoanalytic theory throughout the twentieth century.

Roazen, Paul, *Freud and His Followers,* Da Capo Press, 1992.
      Roazen provides an historical account of Freud's friends, associates, colleagues, and disciples and their impact on the development of psychoanalytic theory.

Robinson, Paul A., *Freud and His Critics,* University of California Press, 1993.
      Robinson offers an overview of critical responses to Freudian theory in the late twentieth century.

I Remain in Darkness

Annie Ernaux

1997

The volume *I Remain in Darkness* is Annie Ernaux's collection of unedited journal entries that she wrote over the last two and a half years of her mother's life. The entries depict Ernaux's highly personal reaction to her mother's decline to Alzheimer's disease. As Ernaux experiences an almost overwhelming onslaught of conflicting emotions, she reflects on her past and, most particularly, her relationship with her mother, Blanche. Although in previously published works Ernaux has explored ties to her family that were fraught with difficulty, *I Remain in Darkness* provides an intensely intimate, immediate portrayal of the bonds between a grown daughter and her dying mother.

Published in France in 1997 and translated into English three years later, *I Remain in Darkness* was for over a decade Ernaux's private chronicle and almost remained so. Ernaux writes in her preface that she initially believed she would not publish her journals, ''Maybe because I wanted to offer only one image, one side of the truth portraying my mother and my relationship with her.'' She had already written about this relationship in *A Woman's Story*, her autobiographical novel about a mother and daughter. However, as several years passed, Ernaux began to question her own wisdom; ''The consistency and coherence achieved in any written work . . . must be questioned whenever possible.'' Read in conjunction with *A Woman's Story*, *I Remain in Darkness* thus provides a multifaceted portrait of the life of a rural, working-class French woman.

Read in isolation from other Ernaux works, *I Remain in Darkness* still tells a poignant story of a powerful love.

Author Biography

Annie Ernaux was born on September 1, 1940, in Lillebonne, France, in the region of Normandy. She grew up in a small town, the daughter of working-class grocers. Her parents sent her to Rouen University, which allowed her to move to a higher social class than her parents occupied. Ernaux graduated with a degree in modern French literature. From 1966 to 1977, she taught French literature at secondary school, in eastern France and outside of Paris. From 1977 to 2000, she was a professor at the Centre National d'Enseignement par Correspondance.

Ernaux published her first novel in 1974. *Les armoires vides* (translated as *Cleaned Out* in 1990) introduced her technique of writing about intensely personal issues and experiences. In 1977, she published *Ce qu'ils disent ou rien*, which has not been translated into English, and four years later, she published *La femme gelée* (translated as *A Frozen Woman* in 1995). Although these three works earned Ernaux modest critical acclaim, she remained a relatively unknown writer.

In 1984, however, *La place* (translated as *A Man's Place* in 1992), Ernaux's memoir of her father, was awarded the Prix Renaudot, one of France's most important literary awards. This recognition helped Ernaux gain a much wider audience. Her next work, *Une femme* (translated as *A Woman's Story* in 1991), published in 1987, solidified her success. This biographical novel related the complex bond between a mother and daughter. Ernaux based it on her own relationship with her mother and began work on it during the final years of her mother's life. Some of the incidents related in it are identical to those in *I Remain in Darkness*. This collection of journals was published as *Je ne suis pas sortie de ma nuit* in France in 1997 and translated into English in 1999.

With the exception of 1991's *Passion simple* (translated as *Simple Passion* in 1993) and 1993's *Journal du dehors* (translated as *Exteriors* in 1996) Ernaux's books all explore similar territory and essentially tell the same story—the story of her life. She is most concerned with exploring her childhood, her relationship to her parents, and her experi-

ences at university. Ernaux continues to publish books, some of which have not yet been translated into English. She currently writes and lives outside of Paris.

Plot Summary

I Remain in Darkness chronicles the decline of Ernaux's mother, Blanche, from Alzheimer's disease. The first sign that something is wrong comes in the summer of 1983, when Blanche faints. Taken to the hospital, the doctors discover that she has not eaten or drunk anything for several days. Ernaux realizes that Blanche can no longer care for herself, and she invites her mother to come live with her and her sons. By December, when Ernaux writes her first journal entry, Blanche is already suffering the loss of memory that comes with Alzheimer's. By January 1984, Blanche can no longer write. Her last words, in a letter to a friend, read, ''I remain in darkness.''

In February 1984, Blanche, prostrate and refusing to eat, is checked into Pontoise Hospital. The ward where she lives is filled with other older patients who also suffer from limited physical and mental capacities. She remains at Pontoise until mid-May, when she is briefly sent to a private nursing home. The situation there is even worse, so she returns to the long-term geriatric ward at Pontoise.

The next year of her life charts her decline. Ernaux notes that her mother seems to have given up on life. For instance, Blanche loses her personal possessions but does not bother looking for them. However, Blanche holds on to enough of her former self to make it clear to Ernaux that she would rather be at her home than in the hospital. She also makes her daughter feel guilty for leaving her behind. The hospital offers few areas of respite for the patients; for recreation, Blanche watches television, eats, or is taken through the garden. Blanche's condition greatly worsens in 1985. She loses the ability to do just about anything for herself, such as walk or feed herself. More and more she comes to remind Ernaux of a child and even a newborn baby.

Throughout her mother's hospitalization, Ernaux continues her regular life. She takes vacations, attends concerts and plays, goes to the museum, gets a divorce, has an affair, teaches class, writes fiction, and wins literary prizes. These events are touched upon but never become a focus. Instead, Ernaux presents the side of her personality that is intensely focused on understanding what feelings she is experiencing, primarily, her relationship with her mother.

Ernaux also reveals that during her mother's hospitalization, she decided to write an autobiographical novel about her mother. She alternates between finding the writing helpful and being unable to write at all. The image of her mother that she records on paper is incompatible with her mother confined in the hospital.

Blanche dies in April 1986. Ernaux is disconsolate at her loss. She is unable to read and constantly thinks about what her writings about her mother mean. Everywhere she goes and everything she does serve as a reminder of her mother.

Key Figures

Blanche Duchesne

Blanche is Ernaux's mother. She is a former grocer from a rural community. Besides Ernaux, she had another daughter who died in childhood. Her husband is already dead.

Blanche lives alone before the onset of her Alzheimer's disease. At first, Blanche goes to live with Ernaux, but within a few months her faculties deteriorate markedly. When she refuses to get up or eat, Ernaux moves her to the hospital where she spends the final years of her life.

During the early stages of her disease, Blanche attempts to maintain, as much as she can, the patterns of her pre-sickness life. For instance, she insists on having her toiletry bag nearby. However, as she grows sicker, even these tokens of normal life are lost to her. Within a year of entering the hospital, Blanche is unable to perform some of the most basic functions, such as chewing food or using the bathroom by herself.

Blanche is proud of her daughter, but she also resents that her daughter does not spend more time with her. As such, she alternates between inhabiting the parental role and the child's role that her illness forces upon her. However, unable to care for herself, she has little choice but to occupy a newly subordinate role in this relationship.

On many occasions, Blanche tells Ernaux how much happier she would be living with her and makes her daughter feel guilty for this decision. Yet, she also loves her daughter. She enjoys simple signs of affection, such as when Ernaux combs her hair.

Annie Ernaux

Ernaux wrote *I Remain in Darkness* when she was in her forties. Her journal entries chronicle her mother's decline from Alzheimer's disease. She begins writing her journal at the onset of her mother's symptoms, when Blanche lives with her. The difficulty of caring for a person with dementia, however, forces Ernaux to put her mother in a long-term geriatric hospital, where Blanche spends the final two years of her life.

At the time her mother becomes ill, Ernaux is in the process of divorcing her husband. She is also having an affair with a man called A. She lives with her two sons.

Ernaux suffers as she watches her mother succumb to the disease. Her feelings are complex, alternating between love and tenderness for her mother, and hatred and even the desire to be cruel. These intense feelings stem from a complicated relationship that the two women have shared over the years, to which Ernaux frequently alludes in her journal entries.

Ernaux deals with the pain of her mother's slow demise in a variety of ways. She sometimes views her mother as a child and casts herself in the role of mother. As a coping mechanism, one which she has used throughout her life, she sublimates her feelings into art and literature. She also begins writing a work of biographical fiction about her relationship with her mother as a means of working through her complicated feelings.

At the end of *I Remain in Darkness*, after her mother's death, Ernaux is disconsolate. The final journal entry reads, ''This morning, after seeing the words 'cubic meter' on a water bill, I remembered that I used to call her Cubby when I was six or seven years old. Tears come to my eyes.'' This ending shows that Blanche will continue to play a strong role in her daughter's life.

Themes

Art

As a writer, Ernaux funnels the events of her life through the lens of art and literature. Throughout *I Remain in Darkness*, she makes references to

Topics for Further Study

- Read Ernaux's *A Woman's Story*. Write an essay comparing the mother-daughter relationship portrayed in both books.

- Do you think Ernaux's memoir benefited from the unedited journal format that she chose? Explain your answer.

- Find out how to care for people with Alzheimer's disease. Then write an article to share with the adult children of Alzheimer's sufferers, giving suggestions on coping with the disease.

- Conduct research to find out more about the causes of Alzheimer's disease and any new discoveries that may help to cure it or help those who suffer from it.

- Do you think Ernaux should have cared for Blanche at home? Explain your answer.

- Describe your perception of the relationship between Ernaux and her mother as presented in *I Remain in Darkness*.

- Think about some difficulty that you have faced in your life. Do you think writing about this difficulty would have been beneficial or harmful to you, or would it have had little effect? Explain your answer.

---

various works of art and literature. For instance, she likens her mother to Courbet's painting, *The Origin of the World,* which shows a woman lying down with her thighs open, showing her respect for the mother who gave birth to her. At another point Ernaux comments on a Goya painting she saw at the Museum of Fine Arts: "But that's definitely not my mother," Ernaux writes. "Neither is the main character in Lolleh Bellon's play *Tender Relations,* which I went to see the other night." Ernaux likens another woman in the hospital to the broken down clock in Ravel's opera, *The Child and the Enchantment.* Another patient recalls to mind Jean-Paul Sartre's *Nausea,* which Ernaux read in high school. All of these references remind the reader of Ernaux's intellectual background, which figures so prominently in her works and in her relationship with her parents, and provides clues into Ernaux's personality. The latter is particularly important in this slim volume that provides no background for the reader.

Aging

The themes of aging and illness are crucial to *I Remain in Darkness.* Ernaux describes not only her mother's deterioration but the loss of physical capabilities in the other patients who live in the nursing home. The inhabitants must be helped to the bathroom or wear diapers. The nurses insist that Blanche

and the other women be tied to their armchairs. With their lives now exposed because they need others to care for their every physical need, they have lost the sense of privacy. More than once Ernaux notes a woman or her mother with her nightgown askew, revealing her vagina. Ernaux also notes how aging takes away her mother's vitality and sense of purpose. She sees her mother as fading and becoming transparent. She generalizes this transformation to aging in general, noting that the same thing has happened to her cat.

Identification

Throughout her journal entries, Ernaux equates herself with her mother. She expresses herself as having a "dual personality." At one time, she is both herself and her mother. Ernaux sees her mother's body as her own; at other times, she sees her mother inside herself. Her mother's future and old age become her own as well. Only in the rarest of instances does Blanche do something to remind her daughter of the separation between the two women. One day, Blanche shouts out the author's name, which she has not used for over a year. "On hearing her voice, I freeze, emotionally drained," Ernaux writes. "The call has come from the deepest recesses of my life, from early childhood." At most times, however, this identification is so strong that

Ernaux loses her sense of herself. Leaving the nursing home one afternoon, "I glance at myself in the mirror once again, just to make sure."

Memory

Toward the end of her mother's life, Ernaux writes, "I feel that nothing has changed since my early childhood and that life is simply a series of scenes interspersed with songs." Indeed, throughout her mother's illness, Ernaux's thoughts constantly return to her childhood. Her journals are filled with remembrances. She often writes of moments that relate to growing up and womanhood, such as when Blanche first discovered that she wore a bra or her childhood fascination with her mother's underwear that was stained from her period. She also recalls significant moments that the two women shared and that somehow relate to Ernaux's present situation. She recalls her mother at her First Communion, then only one year younger than Ernaux is now. Ernaux wonders "'Where are the eyes of my childhood, the eyes that made me?'" Ernaux's memories are the only place she can find her real mother.

Writing

Ernaux, already a prize-winning author at the time her mother becomes ill, uses writing as emotional therapy. While her mother is hospitalized, she begins to write a book about her mother's life. At times, the disparity between the image of her mother that she sees in her memory and the mother that she sees in real life causes her confusion. As her mother's condition worsens, Ernaux makes more references to her writing, further clarifying the relationship this action has to her emotional well-being; sometimes she is unable to write about her mother at all, but at other times writing helps her work through her grief. In her journal, she records her definitive statement about what writing means to her: "an attempt to salvage part of our lives, to understand, but first to salvage."

Style

Diary

I Remain in Darkness is the diary that Ernaux kept throughout her mother's illness. Ernaux decided to publish these notes more than ten years after her mother's death. Although she did place them in chronological order, she otherwise chose not to edit or alter them in hopes of "echoing the bewilderment and distress that I experienced at the time." Because of this authorial decision, Ernaux's journal fails to tell a complete story. However, the author never intended it to do so; this collection of snippets resonates on an emotional level, not a narrative one. Ernaux sacrifices providing readers with background, which likely would have provided a better understanding of the relationship between herself and her mother.

Memoir

While all of Ernaux's novels have been autobiographical in nature, *I Remain in Darkness* is a true memoir, chronicling the exact thoughts that went through Ernaux's mind, as they went through her mind, during the two and a half years that her mother was declining from Alzheimer's disease. Ernaux had already visited this subject in *A Woman's Story*, which portrays the relationship between a working-class, rural woman and her university-educated daughter. Kathryn Harrison pointed out in the *New York Times Book Review* that "there is little inconsistency between the two works," but believed that this memoir "serves as a more intimate revelation of the slow death that prompted her to bear witness to the life that was ebbing." Indeed, Ernaux makes use of the flexibility of the memoir/journal format to reveal the raw feelings that she experienced as they were happening. The fluidity of the memoir form is evident in *I Remain in Darkness*.

Preface

Though not labeled as such, Ernaux provides a preface to *I Remain in Darkness*. This brief section is significant in that it is the only portion of the volume that Ernaux wrote specifically for publication. Ernaux explains to the reader that the choppiness of the text derives from the fact that she did not edit her journal.

The preface is even more significant because it provides valuable information about the journal entries that Ernaux presents. Without this preface, the reader who has no knowledge of Ernaux and her background would fail to understand the importance of *I Remain in Darkness* to Ernaux personally as well as to her body of work. Ernaux writes that her novel *A Woman's Story* was her initial attempt to make sense of her relationship with her mother, but she came to realize that this effort was not representative enough.

Compare & Contrast

- **1980s:** From the 1970s through the 1980s, the number of French women entering the workforce rises. The service sector in France employs the highest proportion of women.

    Today: In recent years, more women in France are working part-time instead of full-time due to a decline in the number of full-time jobs available and a new trend in working patterns.

- **1980s:** As the 1980s open, rural areas are continuing their trend of declining populations.

    Today: At the beginning of the 1990s, France's urban population is 74.5 percent and its rural population 24.5 percent.

- **1980s:** Although Alzheimer's disease was first documented in 1906, people with Alzheimer's had few places to turn to for assistance until 1979. That year, the Alzheimer's Association was founded. Throughout the following decade, the Association disseminates information about the disease and establishes grants to fund research projects.

    Today: In 2000, the Alzheimer's Association co-hosts World Alzheimer Congress 2000, which brings together 5,000 of the world's leading Alzheimer researchers, healthcare professionals, and caregivers. This is the largest global Alzheimer conference.

- **1980s:** With the formation of the Alzheimer's Association, Alzheimer's disease begins to gain more public recognition. In 1983, the U.S. government approves the creation of a task force to oversee and coordinate scientific research on Alzheimer's disease.

    Today: Genetic researchers announce chromosomal findings related to Alzheimer's disease. In 2001, the USFDA approves a fourth drug specifically to treat symptoms of Alzheimer's disease.

Historical Context

The Catholic Church

By the mid-1980s, despite its long history, the Catholic Church in France had experienced a significant decline. While anywhere between 80 to 90 percent of French people professed to be Catholic, a much smaller minority attended church. Atheism was also on the rise. While church attendance was dropping, many French people were embracing less traditional styles of worship. France saw a rise in the number of informal groups who meet regularly for prayer and discussion, often in private homes.

France and the Arts

When the Socialists came to power in 1981, France's cultural scene brightened. François Mitterand, the new president, committed more of France's budget to the Ministry of Culture. Mitterand and his minister of culture, Jack Lang, both wanted to popularize art and bring it closer to people's daily lives. In addition to the well-known arts, such as theater, Lang supported the so-called minor arts. His ministry subsidized institutions and groups that embraced circus performance, costumes, gastronomy, tapestry weaving, and comic strips, among many other forms of art. He also helped individual artists, including writers, composers, and film directors.

The literary trend in the 1980s veered away from an analysis of contemporary French society. Books tended to take place in the past or abroad, or to dwell on private subjects, such as love or childhood. The French novel lacked insightful social criticism, which characterized so many of France's great literature from the past.

Women

The 1970s and 1980s brought greater social and legal equality to French women. Pro-feminine reforms included the legalization of abortion, sixteen weeks' paid maternity leave, and steps toward the achievement of equal pay. The Professional Equality Law of 1982 made sexual discrimination in the workplace illegal. In the art world, Marguerite Yourcenar became the first woman member of the Académie dan Française in 1980. By the 1980s, increasing numbers of French women were joining the workforce.

Critical Overview

By the time Ernaux published *I Remain in Darkness*, she had already written and published *A Woman's Story*, which was based on her mother's life and death. However, the bulk of Ernaux's writing revisits the themes of growing up and familial relationships. As James Sallis writes in *The Review of Contemporary Fiction,* "Annie Ernaux's work is remarkably of a piece, each book circling back to paraphrase, correct, emendate, and reinvent earlier ones." Novelist Kathryn Harrison, writing for the *New York Times Book Review,* points out, however, that the "sympathy between novel and memoir is not a matter of mere repetition." Harrison finds that the latter work "serves as a more intimate revelation of the slow death that prompted her to bear witness to the life that was ebbing."

Some reviewers shared praise for *I Remain in Darkness*. Sallis was of the opinion that was "a very ambitious book." *Publishers Weekly* called it "quietly searing." Harrison was a champion of the volume. To her, the details that Ernaux includes showing her mother's decline had "such emblematic force and terror that the particular becomes universal." Harrison also explores the important themes that Ernaux raises, specifically the inevitability of death and the inability of literature to provide a meaningful truth to life.

Many reviewers, however, expressed differing opinions of the work, often within the same article. Up for the most criticism was the slight, bare nature of the book. "There are wonderful moments of grace here," writes Eileen Murphy in the *Baltimore City Paper,* but she finds the "complete lack of narrative . . . troubling for the reader" and essentially equates Ernaux's work here with "arranging" and not writing.

By contrast, Wilda Williams, in *Library Journal,* notes that while "there is a choppy, unpolished feel to the book," and puts forth the hypothesis that

Ernaux's style may have been deliberate. The length of the work seems not to have bothered Harrison, who writes, "Ernaux renders the plight of the dying with a seemingly effortless economy."

Richard Bernstein, writer for the *New York Times,* is perhaps a counterpart to Harrison. Although he states that the "book certainly has flashes of genius," his criticism outweighs his applause. Not only did he find it to "lack the quiet impact of her others" because it was so "undeveloped," he also questioned the validity of her major theme:

> the idea that an aging person reverts to a kid of childlike dependency, leaving the former child in a state of guilty mastery worried about her own inevitable death is not a thundering revelation.

Criticism

Rena Korb

Korb has a master's degree in English literature and creative writing and has written for a wide variety of educational publishers. In the following essay, she explores the role reversal that takes place in Ernaux's relationship with her mother.

The relationship between Ernaux and her mother, Blanche, lies at the center of *I Remain in Darkness*, but this relationship, long fraught with difficulty, becomes even more complex as Blanche's illness leads the two women into a confusing, inherently unnatural role reversal. As Blanche becomes increasingly sick, fragile, and unbalanced in the last years of her life, Ernaux takes on more of the nurturing duties and emotional characteristics that belong to the parent. Blanche's deterioration, and her daughter's record of it, is a sad testament to only one of the many regrettable effects caused by illness, particularly one as devastating as Alzheimer's disease.

As evidence of her comprehension of this distressing process, Ernaux, in her journal fragments, makes continuous references to her childhood. This inclination is not surprising, for throughout the two and a half years of her mother's illness, Ernaux is constantly forced to re-evaluate their relationship as she sees it irrevocably change. Other people point out some of the ways in which she resembles her mother physically, as well as her inheritance of Blanche's "brusque, violent temper, as well as a tendency to seize things and throw them down with fury." Ernaux also recognizes the similarities that

An Alzheimer's patient receives a visitor in a long-term health-care facility

exist between the relationship she had with her mother while growing up and her mother's relationship with her at the present time. Blanche usually awaits Ernaux's visits impatiently, causing Ernaux to recall her own experience as a child waiting for her mother to pick her up from school. Both of them felt "the same surge of excitement" when the other finally arrived.

While understanding this role reversal intellectually, Ernaux rebels against it emotionally: "now she is my little girl," she writes. "I CANNOT be her mother." This change in dynamic is inherently unnatural, and to Ernaux, it is "agonizing." She

sees her mother regress physically and mentally. At times, her mother even takes on the petulant aspects of a child such as when she refuses to let Ernaux take away the cake wrapper that she is eating. Blanche is "fiercely clenching her fist" with all the might that a stubborn child possesses. Further, in becoming Blanche's mother, Ernaux loses her own mother and now must acknowledge adulthood. One startling day, upon seeing her mother dressed in "a printed dress with flowers, like the ones I wore when I was a little girl," Ernaux, though in her 40s, "realize[s] that it's only now that I have truly grown up." Blanche becomes not only "the personifica-

What Do I Read Next?

- Ernaux's *A Woman's Story* (1991), which was translated from *Une Femme* in 1987, is a novel about the death of a working-class woman as seen through the eyes of her university-educated daughter. Along with the mother-daughter relationship, Ernaux examines class, age, and gender issues.

- French writer Simone de Beauvoir's *Une Morte Trés Douce* (1964), which is translated as *A Very Easy Death,* recounts the death of her mother in a hospital and addresses the issue of aging.

- James Agee's Pulitzer Prize–winning novel *A Death in the Family* (1957) explores the grief one family feels at the loss of a loved one, as seen through the eyes of a child. Agee wrote this novel as a memorial to his own father.

- The best-selling *Motherless Daughters: The Legacy of Loss* (1994), by Hope Edelman (who lost her mother when she was very young), explores the plight of women whose mothers have died and examines how their lives change as a result.

- *Snapshots: 20th Century Mother-Daughter Fiction* (2000), edited by Joyce Carol Oates and Janet Berliner, collects seventeen short stories focusing on mothers and daughters by well-known and lesser-known women authors.

- Verna A. Jansen's mother was diagnosed with Alzheimer's disease in 1988. In *Alzheimer's, the Good, the Sad & the Humorous: A Daughter's Story* (1999), edited by Glenda Baker, Jansen shares her experiences caring for her mother.

---

tion of *time*''—a physical representation of the passage of the years—but also someone who is ''pushing me toward death.''

Ernaux accepts this role as it is foisted upon her, for the circumstances of her mother's illness offer little other choice. It is infrequent that Blanche demonstrates a parental role: pride in showing Ernaux off to patients or in telling others that her daughter won a prestigious literary prize; or when, as Ernaux bends over to check the safety catch of the wheelchair, ''she leans over and kisses my hair.'' Ernaux compares how their roles toward each other have reversed. At times Ernaux feels great tenderness toward her mother, like the day that ''[F]or the first time I touch her like a child who is sleeping.'' She often writes about caring for her mother, for instance; clipping her fingernails, shaving her face, and feeding her. She combs her mother's hair as if her mother were the child, an action that brings her mother great pleasure.

For Ernaux, however, the primary pleasure drawn from this activity is the transformation of her mother back into a ''human being''; although she does care for her mother and wants to make her comfortable, the change in roles still causes Ernaux tremendous conflict. To an extent, Ernaux refuses to demonstrate her love—or even to acknowledge the purity of the those feelings—as a way of rejecting what is taking place: that her mother ''had become a child again, one who would never grow up.''

More often, however, Ernaux acts within the scope of the power of her new position, which is so absolute that her mother obeys her ''fearfully.'' Ernaux acknowledges that when her mother lived with her when her symptoms first started to manifest themselves ''I was (subconsciously?) cruel toward her, panicked at the idea that she was becoming a woman without a past, a frightened woman clinging to me like a child.'' On one level, Ernaux's attitude toward her mother demonstrates the normal feelings of denial that a debilitating, fatal disease like Alzheimer's can engender. At the same time, however, Ernaux's actions partially stem from the desire to punish her mother; this inconsistency of behavior—indeed senseless behavior—shows just how confusing this illness and its ensuing role reversal is for those who are close to its victims.

Ernaux's own conduct also forces her to deal with her belief that, at times, her mother treated her cruelly during childhood. For instance, while clipping her mother's fingernails, Ernaux "can feel the sadistic streak in me, echoing her behavior toward me a long time ago" when "I was terrified of her." However, these snippets are so brief that there is no way for the reader to evaluate Ernaux's childhood with any accuracy.

Ernaux juxtaposes specific statements revealing her mistreatment at the hands of her mother with fond, loving memories. She reports that Blanche commented of her, "She's not nearly as nice as the other one [Ernaux's sister who died in childhood]," or that Blanche "would slap me for the slightest little thing." However, she also recalls the closeness of sharing the same bed with her mother on Sunday afternoons. One set of memories does little to belittle the other set, for Ernaux's writing in *I Remain in Darkness* is more impressionistic in its presentation of raw feeling and emotion than it is objective.

Indeed, true objectivity would be close to impossible in light of the difficult circumstances surrounding the mother and daughter. Ernaux's comprehension that this new relationship creates a power imbalance only enforces her sense of unreality. Blanche is weak, confused, and needy. She relies upon her daughter both for physical and moral support. Ernaux's descriptions of the hospital—reeking of urine, with [sh—] on the floor and patients roaming around unclothed—clearly demonstrate that the staff does not provide well enough for the bodily upkeep of the patients. The eagerness with which Blanche awaits weekly visits, as well as the short portraits of her fellow patients, show that Blanche receives little emotional support.

Ernaux, by contrast, determines how much time and energy she can invest in her mother. At one point, Ernaux enters the hospital for a dangerous, unnamed operation and does not tell her mother that she will be unable to visit for two months. This operation makes her even more aware of her own mortality, so that when she is able to walk on crutches, she chooses not to visit her mother. "I won't go to this temple of old age," she writes, "hobbling 'like an old lady.'" In control of the relationship, Ernaux has the option of putting her own fears and desires above those of her mother, and in this instance, she takes advantage of her authority.

> **Further, in becoming Blanche's mother, Ernaux loses her own mother and now must acknowledge adulthood."**

Ernaux shapes her relationship with her mother to maintain her own emotional detachment, which is a luxury that her mother does not have. Blanche would prefer living at Ernaux's home to staying in the hospital; "I'm sure I'd be happier with you," she tells her daughter. However, Ernaux refuses these pleas, and others, because Blanche's condition has a detrimental effect on her. "I feel like crying when I see how badly she needs my love because I cannot satisfy her demand," she writes. She then immediately juxtaposes her mother's feelings with her own when thinking of her lover—"I think of how badly I want A to love me now, just when he is drifting away from me"—when there really is no similarity between her relationship with A and Blanche's relationship with her. Whether it be consciously or subconsciously, Ernaux is maintaining distance from her mother, despite, or perhaps because of, the older woman's dependence on her.

Despite the imposition of this role reversal, Ernaux never can really function as Blanche's mother. For all the physical or emotional care she can provide, it is impossible for Ernaux to fulfill a mother's most crucial duty: giving a child a sense of security and safety. Ernaux recalls how she felt when, as a child, Blanche took her to visit an uncle in the hospital. "The sun was shining, men and women were walking around in maroon bathrobes: I was so sad and so happy that my mother was with me, a strong, protective figure warding off illness and death." For both Ernaux and her mother, this sense of security can never be recaptured. Instead, Blanche dies, and her body reminds Ernaux of nothing so much as a "sad little doll," while Ernaux lives on with the "devastating pain" of a life without her mother.

Source: Rena Korb, Critical Essay on *I Remain in Darkness*, in *Nonfiction Classics for Students*, The Gale Group, 2002.

Laura Kryhoski

Kryhoski is currently working as a freelance writer. In this essay, she considers the emotional complexities of Ernaux's work as they relate the author's personal experience with a dying parent.

I Remain In Darkness—the final written words of an aging, ailing woman, and the title of a memoir by Ernaux. Composed merely out of ''jottings'' on ''small, undated scraps of paper,'' Ernaux wrote of her ''bewilderment and distress'' experienced in the company of her mother. Her writings have an emotive power precisely because they capture the mix of emotions an individual may feel caring for an elderly mother with brutal honesty. An elderly dependent parent can inspire love, revulsion or disgust, anger, and as a result, guilt and fear. Ernaux's scribblings betray her conflicted feelings. Her account has a surreal or fantastic quality about it, bringing into sharp focus the distorted emotions of the author.

Ernaux describes her mother with revulsion and brutal honesty. The memoir opens with an unattractive description, ''She just sits there on a chair in the living room. Staring straight ahead, her features frozen, sagging.'' This is not a heartwarming, loving description of a relative. One would be hard-pressed to guess that the author is actually talking about her mother, without reading the introduction to the work. This cold, detached, blank description is a reaction shared by someone coping with a nonfunctional, dependent elderly parent. There is no longer a strong mental connection based on shared history between mother and daughter. A daughter pleads, ''Where are the eyes of my childhood, those fearful eyes she had thirty years ago, the eyes that made me?'' At times barely functional, Ernaux's mother is reduced to a crude character or the product of mere observation.

Her mother's presence often evokes a sense of loathing in the author. In describing one visit with her mother, she says, ''Her greedy instincts are back, she leers at the chocolates, tries to grab them with clumsy fingers.'' The baseness of these descriptions contributes not to the image of mother, but of creature. The author again responds, in a situation not unlike countless others recorded among her entries, ''the piece of pastry I put in her hands slips out. I have to pop it into her mouth. I am dismayed at such degradation and bestiality.'' Yet the author uses other moments or absurd cameos, one in particular of a grotesque, ugly, caricature or exaggerated figure, to describe her parent. For example, ''a transsexual with bluish skin'' sparks a subconscious memory of her mother, specifically, her unshaven face. The carnival-like quality of the experience only enhances the unreal, the incomprehensible figure her mother has become.

The vision of the transsexual is unremarkable to the work. At times, old age is cruel, ugly and for Ernaux, not only a dehumanizing experience but a gender neutralizing, or unfeminine one. One scene etched in her memory involves another female patient, who can be seen, ''diaper sheathing her vagina.'' Again, the awkward, the grotesque, and the absurd come alive. ''Such scenes inspire horror,'' says Ernaux, at the sight of a grown woman whose reproductive region is comically cloaked. It is as if the reader has witnessed a genital mutilation. Certainly, Ernaux is not shy to comment on the injustice she feels. ''Here it's different,'' she says, ''There is no horror. These are women.'' There are also countless references in the text to her own mother's exposed vagina, moments of humiliation as seen through Ernaux's eyes. Mentioning the onset of her mother's menopause, ''the change of life,'' she comments that seemingly ''everything had come to an end.'' It's as though her mother's credibility as a woman and, by extension, a human, is attributed to her sexuality.

Denial plagues everyone dealing with a person affected by dementia or senility. The process of mental decline an elderly person undergoes is often subtle. Human nature generally dictates that one look at the softer edges of a situation, the more pleasant the realities, rather than cope with the ugly truths that the author skillfully explores. During the course of her rough emotional ride, Ernaux too often rallies behind her mother, using personal memories and life experiences to provide a logical rationale or framework for her mother's troubling, often child-like behavior. At one point in the memoir the author comments on a moment in which her mother has felt compelled to hide brioche under her skirt. She responds by relating to the incident, calmly stating, ''as a child, I would steal candy from the store and stuff it inside my panties.''

Additionally, life events outside of the geriatric unit also trigger similar responses. When Ernaux speaks of parting with her mother's clothes, she cannot bear it; however, the author immediately recovers when speaking of the sale of antiques left behind from her marriage. She again relates the circumstances to her mother, claiming, ''Parting with these objects means nothing to me. Like my mother, I am letting go of these things.''

Capturing the mental decline of an aging woman, Ernaux's emotional journal also addresses the often shocking childlike state an elderly person can be reduced to in the aging process. Recalling her mother's words plainly, without visible feeling, she shares, ''This morning she got up and, in a timid voice: 'I wet the bed, I couldn't help it.''' The event is again reduced to mere observation. Ernaux's response is matter-of-fact, she describes her mother's words as simply, ''the same words I would use when I was a child.'' The response, in and of itself, is not cruel or harsh when taken in a broader context. Ernaux is responding to the impact these moments have on her. Her cold words only reverberate or echo the sense of abandonment she feels as a suddenly parentless child. During a visit to the geriatric center, a failed attempt to free a cake wrapper from her mother's clutches sadly inspires Ernaux to write, ''She wouldn't let me pull it away from her, fiercely clenching her fist. An agonizing reversal of roles between mother and child.'' The author again expresses, on many levels, no less in a cold statement as opposed to a tearful moment, the emptiness, the loneliness, the seemingly illogical but real sense of betrayal she feels towards her mother for being in such a feeble mental state.

The most revealing aspects of the memoir involve the strong identification Ernaux has with her mother. Her mother's illness seems to have turned her world upside down. Motherless, fearful, alone—Ernaux is the victim of an ongoing trauma, the loss of a parent, and she often cries out in protest. Crying out in the voice of a defiant child, she exclaims, ''The situation is now reversed, now she is my little girl. I CANNOT be her mother.'' There is no longer a mental connection, no longer a shared history between mother and daughter. Ernaux's selfishness masks a deep sense of rage. Somewhere in the midst of coping with her mother's behavior, the author has discovered her own mortality. ''For me, she is the personification of time. She is also pushing me towards death.''

Dr. Robin Robertson, in *A Beginner's Guide to Jungian Psychology,* offers an interesting perspective on the maternal in a discussion of the mother complex. ''Over the course of the years it takes to develop from infant to adult,'' states Robertson, ''each of us acquires a vast number of memories of his or her particular mother.'' What happens with these memories, according to Robertson, is that they

> " Somewhere in the midst of coping with her mother's behavior, the author has discovered her own mortality."

cluster around the archetype or model of the mother (what is understood to mean ''mother'') to form a complex, or group of associations, to the term *mother.* What essentially has happened is that an individual has formed a mother within, or an understanding of a mother with both universal characteristics and characteristics specific to the individual's own mother. Of note is the necessity for all human babies to contain a mother archetype to imprint onto their own mothers. The importance of this psychological component is that this archetype contains the entire human history of interaction between mother and child. In the words of Dr. Robertson, ''A relationship that has been so important for so long gathers energy, energy which shapes the newborn baby's relationship with its physical mother.''

Perhaps this interruption in energy flow has sent Ernaux on an emotional rollercoaster ride. Her maternal instincts tug at her incessantly yet she is unable to come to grips with the role reversal that has taken place between herself and her mother. At one point, torn with guilt at her own inability to comfort her mother, Ernaux says, ''I feel like crying when I see how badly she needs my love because I cannot satisfy her demand (I loved her so desperately as a child).'' In framing her mother's needs against the backdrop of her own desires as a child, Ernaux is drawing on her own maternal instincts.

For Ernaux there is no reciprocity or mutual exchange in roles between herself and her mother. Instead, her mother's emotional demands tend to enrage her. The painful irony for the author is that she is no longer reacting as a demanding child does but fails to respond as a nurturing parent. This failure inspires Ernaux's dismal assessment of her mother's expectations of her: ''the maternal instinct is tantamount to a deathwish.''

The power of *I Remain in Darkness* is truly attributable to Ernaux's ability to economically convey the complexity of emotion as well as the tenor of a relationship between a daughter and her dying mother. Frustration, fear, anger, and longing echo throughout the body of the work, haunting the author even after her mother's death. In the end, finality of the event does not inspire resolution or relief, but darkness.

Source: Laura Kryhoski, Critical Essay on *I Remain in Darkness,* in *Nonfiction Classics for Students,* The Gale Group, 2002.

Josh Ozersky

Ozersky is a critic and essayist. In this essay, he discusses some of the tensions and paradoxes that inform Ernaux's memoir.

First-time readers of Ernaux's *I Remain in Darkness* are often surprised by it. It's a paradoxical book in many ways. It's ostensibly about Ernaux's mother, but Ernaux is in the forefront of nearly every page. It seems underwritten, but in fact it has an intensely focused literary power. It's essentially about thoughts and feelings, but many of its strongest passages describe vivid physical images. It is written with profound love, which is mixed with an equally profound anger and fear. And although it is about the end of a person's life, ultimately it is a testament to life and regeneration.

Ernaux had written a book about her mother prior to this one; soon after her mother's death in 1986, she began writing *A Woman's Story,* which was published in 1988. *A Woman's Story* is a much fuller, more developed work than *I Remain in Darkness,* which largely consists of notes Ernaux jotted down during the years of her mother's decline. However, since the tone and style of these ''notes'' are recognizably the same as those of Ernaux's earlier books, and since that famous style has made her a nationally known figure in France, it is fair to assume that this book is a companion piece, not just raw materials. Ernaux says as much in her introduction, describing it as a way to ''question'' the ''consistency and coherence'' of her earlier work.

But what is this style? On first examination, there seems to be no style at all, just direct communication of Ernaux's thoughts onto ''small undated scraps of paper.'' A typical entry begins,

> I went to see her before going up to Paris. I feel absolutely nothing when I am with her. As soon as the elevator door snaps shut I want to cry. Her skin is getting more and more crackled, it badly needs cream.

This kind of language seems transparent; in fact, it is pound-for-pound much stronger than a wordier style would be, and testifies to the old maxim that ''less is more.'' It may seem like an odd comparison, given that Ernaux is a cerebral Frenchwoman famous for writing about her feelings, but one of the American writers she most resembles is Ernest Hemingway. Hemingway pioneered the technique of writing most expressively by what he didn't say, of letting his silences speak louder than other writers' words. Ernaux also uses language that is sparse and specific, and that shuns over-elaboration to the point of being tight-lipped.

The reason for this is that both writers take the big issues of human life more seriously than we may be accustomed to. Ernaux, like many French writers, tends to write about the elemental facts of human life: birth, death, love, the body. Often in the past, American readers have been impatient with French writers for this reason; Americans take these things for granted, and always find it vaguely ludicrous to talk about them in an abstract way. That is why Ernaux's style is so effective. She never ventures far beyond the (apparent) surface of things. The detail in the above quotation about her mother's crackled skin is not just easy to visualize—it's something you can feel. And more than that, you can sense Ernaux's tension. Dry skin should be moisturized. Thirst should be quenched. Pain should be succored. There's nothing for her to do but to leave that to the nurses, and to go on to Paris. And there's nothing for her to say about it in retrospect.

Nor does Ernaux dwell on the disjuncture between her warring emotions. In one line she tells us, ''I feel absolutely nothing when I am with her.'' In the next, ''As soon as the elevator door shuts I want to cry.'' Ernaux makes no effort to explain away this apparent contradiction. There is no explanation. It's the way she felt. If you've felt that way yourself, you understand. If you haven't, possibly you won't. As with her mother's crackled skin, the fact is allowed to speak for itself—and it does, eloquently.

The combination of spartan and simple language with vast, imposing emotional realities helps drive Ernaux's art. Another is the presence of opposite emotions juxtaposed. Ernaux is filled with pity and love toward her mother (''She leans over and kisses my hair. How can I survive that kiss, such love, my mother, my mother.''), but at the same time feels resentment and even anger (''I can feel the sadistic streak in me, echoing her behavior from long ago. She still loathes me.'') She is haunted by her mother's dissolution, but also preoccupied with thoughts of her own: ''It's crystal clear: she is me in old age and I can see the deterioration of her body threatening to take hold of me—the wrinkles on her legs, the creases in her neck, shown off by a recent haircut.''

None of these tensions are ever reconciled; instead, they supply much of the book's energy. Each self-contained ''jotting'' functions like a haiku, dense with meaning. But the reader rarely gets wrapped up in them, because Ernaux describes the *physical* reality of her mother's condition so bluntly. ''Food, urine, [sh—]: the combination of smells hits one as soon as one leaves the elevator.''

As a result, the book achieves that kind of timelessness and universality which is the aim of the writer's art. Although written in French, *I Remain in Darkness* translates to English without any awkwardness at all—a tribute both to Ernaux and also to Tanya Leslie, her translator. The clarity of her prose and the accomplishment of her writing, however, don't necessarily mean that *I Remain in Darkness* is an easy read. The material is undeniably depressing; and some readers may find it hard to warm up to the narrator, who makes absolutely no effort to win sympathy from anyone. Unlike, say, Frank McCourt in *Angela's Ashes,* or Maya Angelou in *I Know Why the Caged Bird Sings,* readers are not invited to put themselves in her place, to identify with or even to like her.

But who is this narrator? Given the amount of personal information revealed, readers might think they know her fairly well. (Those who have read Ernaux's other memoirs, such as *A Woman's Story* and *Simple Passion*, may feel that they know her intimately.) On the other hand, in *I Remain in Darkness*, there's much that readers are themselves left in darkness about. Who is this woman? Why does she resent her mother so much? What is her life like when she is not visiting the nursing home? What goes on between visits? The more involved one gets in this deeply emotional work, the larger these questions seem to grow.

Finally, Ernaux refuses us access. This is very different from typical memoirs, particularly one dealing with very painful issues. In those books, the author generally wants readers to understand them. Either they have been obscure, like McCourt, or misunderstood, such as Malcolm X. Moreover, they are saving memories of loved ones for posterity— making the past part of the future, with all the skill they can muster. In so many ways, *I Remain in Darkness* is the opposite of such works. The subject of the book, a woman about whom readers know little and whose consciousness is rapidly disinte-

> **The combination of spartan and simple language with vast, imposing emotional realities helps drive Ernaux's art.''**

grating, seems very vivid; while Ernaux herself, intelligent, articulate, and ruthlessly honest about her feelings, seems ghostly, spectral. That is a tribute to Ernaux's powerful, paradoxical art—and to her own courage in leaving so much of herself out of, and so much of herself in, this remarkable work.

Source: Josh Ozersky, Critical Essay on *I Remain in Darkness,* in *Nonfiction Classics for Students,* The Gale Group, 2002.

Sources

Bernstein, Richard, ''When a Parent Becomes the Child,'' in *New York Times,* November 22, 1999.

Harrison, Kathryn, ''As She Lay Dying,'' in *New York Times Book Review,* November 28, 1999.

Murphy, Eileen, Review, in *Baltimore City Paper,* January 10, 2001.

Review, in *Publishers Weekly,* Vol. 246, No. 41, October 11, 1999, p. 54.

Robertson, Robin, *Beginner's Guide to Jungian Psychology,* Nicholas-Hays, Inc., 1992, pp. 41–43.

Sallis, James, Review, in *Review of Contemporary Fiction,* Vol. 20, No. 1, Spring 2000, p. 193.

Williams, Wilda, Review, in *Library Journal,* Vol. 124, No. 19, November 15, 1999, p. 90.

Further Reading

Atack, Margaret, and Phil Powrie, *Contemporary French Fiction by Women: Feminist Perspectives,* Manchester University Press, 1990.
   This study includes a chapter on Ernaux.

Fallaize, Elizabeth, *French Women's Writing: Recent Fiction,* Macmillan, 1993.

Fallaize's study includes a chapter on Ernaux.

Gillick, Muriel R., *Tangled Minds: Understanding Alzheimer's Disease and Other Dementias,* Plume, 1999.

Dr. Gillick creates a composite patient to show the problems that Alzheimer's sufferers and their families face, as well as providing an historical perspective of the disease.

Holmes, Diana, *French Women's Writing: 1848–1994,* The Athlone Press, 1996.

Holmes traces the development of French women's writing over a period of 150 years.

Stephens, Sonia, ed., *A History of Women's Writing in France,* Cambridge University Press, 2000.

This study introduces French women's writing from the sixth century to the present day. Each chapter focuses on a given period and a range of writers. A reference section includes a guide to more than 150 authors and their works.

Thomas, Lyn, *Annie Ernaux: An Introduction to the Writer and Her Audience,* Berg. Pub. Ltd., 1999.

Thomas presents the first book-length study of Ernaux's work, which is intended for general readers as well as for students of French literature.

I Will Bear Witness: A Diary of the Nazi Years, 1933–1941

Victor Klemperer

1995

Victor Klemperer wrote his diaries during the twelve years of Hitler's rule. The English version of *I Will Bear Witness: A Diary of the Nazi Years, 1933–1941* was published in New York by Random House in 1998 (with a second volume covering the years 1942–1945), but the diaries have an interesting history. After Klemperer's death in 1960, his diaries were taken to the Dresden State Library. Walter Nowojski, a former student of Klemperer's, found them and, recognizing their historical value, typed the handwritten diaries in German. Finally, a small Berlin publisher agreed in 1995 to publish the manuscripts in German as a single volume covering the years 1933 to 1945. Klemperer's diary quickly became a bestseller despite its length (1,500 pages) and price (well over sixty dollars).

The diary is considered important as a detailed account of the spread of Nazism in Germany and the reception of Nazi ideals by the population. It represents the unusual perspective of a Jew throughout all twelve years of Nazi power. The diary's unique contribution to the field of Holocaust literature is its step-by-step presentation of the systematic dehumanization and persecution of the Jews in Nazi Germany.

Some readers focus on the fact that Klemperer knew Germans who were sympathetic to him as a Jew at a time when it was unpopular to be so. Others hold the diary up as evidence that the horrors of the Holocaust were widely known at the time, an issue

that has been sharply debated over the years. Regardless of the reader's or scholar's interpretation of the diary, its important historical value is universally recognized.

Author Biography

Victor Klemperer was born October 9, 1881, in Landsberg-on-the-Warthe in the province of Brandenburg, Germany. Klemperer was the youngest in a family of three other brothers and four sisters. When Klemperer was nine, the family moved to Berlin, where his rabbi father, Wilhelm, was summoned to a liberal Reform Synagogue. As an unorthodox rabbi, Wilhelm was supportive of his four sons converting to the national religion, Lutheranism, in adulthood.

Klemperer married a concert pianist named Eva in 1906. His brothers disapproved of the union because they thought Eva was their brother's social inferior. As for Eva's family, some of her relatives disapproved of her marrying a Jewish man. During World War I, he served as a cannoneer in the German army, earning a Distinguished Service Medal. This service, along with his marriage to an Aryan woman, protected him from deportation to the concentration camps that sealed the fates of millions of Jews during Hitler's rule.

Upon returning from his service in World War I, Klemperer worked for a few years as a freelance journalist. In 1920, he accepted a position at Dresden Technical University as a professor of Romance languages and literature. He occupied this position until 1935, when he was forced to retire. After World War II, he was reinstated.

From the age of seventeen, Klemperer kept a detailed diary of his life. He continued writing during the Nazi years, despite knowing that if the Nazis discovered his diary, he would be killed. The exercise of writing his thoughts and interpretations of changing Germany was a necessary outlet for him, and it was also his personal brand of heroism. He was determined to ''bear witness'' to the horrors he saw, no matter the risk.

At the beginning of 1945, Klemperer was one of only 198 registered Jews still in the entire city of Dresden, all of whom were still free because of their marriages to Aryan spouses. On February 13, all Jews who were deemed fit to work were to report for deportation in three days. This meant that their ''privileged'' status would come to an end. Klemperer knew this was a death sentence, so when the Allies bombed the city that very evening, he and Eva took advantage of the chaos and escaped Dresden. Eva tore the yellow star from his clothing, and they kept running for three months until it was safe. After the war, the couple returned to Dresden, and Klemperer joined the Communist Party.

Klemperer died of a heart attack while attending a conference in Brussels, Belgium, in 1960, nine years after Eva's death. His diaries were taken to the Dresden State Library where one of Klemperer's former students found them and, recognizing their historical value, began transcribing them for publication. The diary was a bestseller in Germany, and critics generally voice their hope that the diary will be as widely read in its English translation.

Plot Summary

Chapter One: ''1933''

In *I Will Bear Witness: A Diary of the Nazi Years, 1933–1941*, Klemperer begins by writing of day-to-day cares and his efforts to make progress on building a small house on the plot of land he and his wife have purchased in Dolzschen, just outside Dresden. Although Klemperer finds the house to be worrisome, his wife is desperate for it, so he wants to see it built for her sake.

Klemperer and Eva suffer from a variety of aches and pains. Because of Eva's declining health, Klemperer often does the domestic chores in addition to working as a lecturer at Dresden Technical University. He is a professor of Romance languages and literature, but the Third Reich's influence threatens his position.

The Klemperers are social people, frequently entertaining guests and visiting friends' homes. Hitler's regime sends waves of fear into every corner of their lives, and they express their uncertainty about the future. Klemperer identifies himself strongly with Germany and is outraged at the rise of the current ''un-German'' regime. Even though he no longer adheres to the Jewish faith, the regime sees anyone who is one-quarter Jewish by descent to be a Jew, and the restrictions are already beginning.

Chapter Two: "1934"

Because Klemperer fought at the front in World War I and because he is married to an Aryan (of Indo-European descent), he is protected from the fate of most other German Jews. He continues to worry about Eva, who is both sick and depressed. The only thing that energizes her is gardening on the land in Dolzschen.

In addition, Klemperer's outlook is grim regarding his career, his health, and their financial situation. The house is expensive, and they have only begun landscaping and building the cellar. A much-needed break comes in July when a friend is able to loan them money for their house.

Gradually, the Klemperers' friends begin to seek ways to leave Germany. This sickens Klemperer because he feels completely devoted to his country, especially as it suffers the shame of the Nazi regime.

Klemperer works slowly on his book about French literature and also begins a new study about the Third Reich's use of language.

Victor Klemperer

Chapter Three: "1935"

Klemperer is officially dismissed by the university, which causes him great worry because "retirement" income is half what he has been making. He begins looking for positions in other countries but has no luck. Having no other choice, he writes to his brother and asks for a loan, which is granted.

When the restrictive Nuremberg Laws are enacted, further stripping Jews of their rights, more of the Klemperers' friends move out of the country.

Klemperer enrolls in driving classes so that he will have better mobility, especially since Eva's health leaves her too weak to walk.

Chapter Four: "1936"

Klemperer passes his driving test and purchases an inexpensive car. Although he enjoys the freedom of a car, he finds that it creates a new set of worries. Eventually, he learns to relax and take pleasure in his and Eva's drives. Unfortunately, as the year progresses, his money problems prevent him from driving very often.

Meanwhile, Klemperer makes slow progress on his writing projects. In October, he encounters an obstacle when he is told at the library that Jews are no longer allowed in the reading room. Instead, he will have to take with him whatever books he needs.

To Klemperer's surprise, there are a few Germans who go out of their way to be kind to him because they are sympathetic to the plight of the Jews.

Chapter Five: "1937"

Klemperer is distraught at the news of the deaths (by illness and suicide) of some of his friends. To add to Klemperer's hopelessness, he becomes even more pessimistic about the political situation in Germany. He fears that Hitler will remain in power for a very long time.

Klemperer makes progress on his French literature book and his language study. While both he and Eva suffer from repeated bouts of illness, he also begins to experience harassment, as when an official checks his garden for weeds and forces him to pay a hefty fine.

Chapter Six: "1938"

Klemperer's hopelessness about the reign of the Third Reich becomes more and more pronounced, and he feels certain he will not live to see a new order. To make matters worse, anti-Semitism mounts, and Jews are barred from certain occupations.

Policemen visit Klemperer, asking if he has any weapons. When he answers that he probably has his saber and bayonet from World War I, they search the house until they find the saber, though not the bayonet. Klemperer is taken into custody, not formally charged with anything, and released a few hours later.

Chapter Seven: ''1939''

The Klemperers experience severe depression and ongoing health problems. Klemperer progresses with his work on the literature book, but it is slow. His plans to write a study of the language of the Third Reich are progressing, and he notes his observations on the topic.

Rations and restrictions on purchases make it difficult for Klemperer to secure all of the goods he and Eva need. Although shopkeepers claim there are shortages, Klemperer suspects otherwise.

Someone tries to assassinate Hitler by setting off a bomb. Because the perpetrator is a Jewish man, Klemperer expects the worse for himself and waits for the police to come get him, but they do not.

Chapter Eight: ''1940''

The Klemperers receive terrible news that they must surrender their house and allow someone to rent or buy it. Because of Klemperer's Jewish status, he and his wife are forced to live in a Jewish ghetto called the Jews' House. They find a tenant, Berger, whom they like, and make the deal they are ordered to make.

The Klemperers find the Jews' House cramped, chaotic, and stark, but they try to make the best of it. While not particularly fond of many of the other people living there, they remain friendly for the sake of solidarity. Klemperer notes that the one good thing that has come from moving to the Jews' House is that Eva has learned to enjoy walking again.

More restrictions are placed upon Jews; they are no longer allowed to enjoy public parks or lending libraries. They are also subject to a curfew of eight o'clock, after which they must remain in their ghetto apartments.

Chapter Nine: ''1941''

Klemperer inadvertently violates a blackout (leaving the window curtains open during a bomb-ing raid) and is sentenced to eight days in prison. During his stay, he finds that time moves very slowly, and he feels that he is trapped in a dismal cage. Above him, he hears another prisoner pacing back and forth for hours at a time. Prisoners are not allowed to converse during outdoor exercise times, and every rule comes with a threat of punishment. When he is released, he feels such relief that he is actually happy for a few days.

The most humiliating blow comes when the Jews are instructed to wear identifying yellow stars. Klemperer dreads the day this policy goes into effect, and afterwards Eva does the shopping and other public chores. Klemperer's sense of shame is profound, and he feels that this experience is worse than his prison stay. His only comfort is that the star identifies him to Germans who are sympathetic: He goes to the market and receives produce he would not otherwise be able to secure.

Klemperer writes that there are shocking and terrifying reports of Jews being transported to Poland. All he knows is that they must go with only the clothes on their backs and without any possessions. In world news, Japan declares war on the United States.

When the Nazis plan an inventory of all Jews' household items, Eva must remove Klemperer's diary from their apartment at once. They take it to a friend's house where it will be much safer.

Key Figures

Berger

Berger is an aryan shopkeeper who is chosen as the Klemperers' tenant when they are forced to leave their house and live in the Jewish ghetto. He is sorry that they are getting such a bad deal, but is glad for himself. Sympathetic to the mistreated couple, he is friendly and brings them honey, which the Nazis had forbidden Jews to have.

Harry Dember

A friend of the Klemperers, Dember is a physicist who is very anxious. He characterizes the Jews as hoping for deliverance from an outside force, such as an invasion or German defeat. Dember is bitter and pessimistic and eventually finds work with the University of Constantinople in Turkey.

Eva Klemperer

Eva is Klemperer's Aryan wife. Although many Aryan spouses give in to public and political pressure to leave their Jewish spouses, Eva remains loyal and dedicated to her husband throughout the trying years of the war. She is a concert pianist whose physical ailments and emotional depression prevent her from playing music very often. The only thing that seems to keep her going is the cottage they are trying to build in Dölzschen. She is an avid gardener who thrives on working on the land while they await the money needed to build the house itself.

Throughout the book, Eva suffers from a variety of ailments, ranging from serious dental problems to swollen ankles. Klemperer also describes her frequent anxiety attacks and bouts of hysteria. At the beginning of the book, she still manages to find the energy and strength to work on the landscaping for the house. Klemperer worries about his wife but sees that this is the only activity that brings her any hope or joy, so he allows her to continue working hard. Eva is a woman obsessed with the house, and when Klemperer fears for their financial future, he keeps spending money on the house only for Eva's sake. When she returns home, however, she has no strength for housework, so she lets her husband perform domestic chores.

Georg Klemperer

Klemperer's older brother, Georg, is a successful doctor who has left Germany and is living elsewhere in Europe. His sons live in the United States, and he tells Klemperer that if the situation in Europe worsens, he will go there, too. In 1935, he does so, but he is disappointed that his age prevents him from acquiring the type of position he had expected. He begins working on his memoirs.

At key times, Georg lends Klemperer much-needed money, but he does not understand the resolute patriotism that keeps him in Germany. Georg tries to convince Klemperer to leave Germany and start a new life where it is safe, but Klemperer dismisses his brother's advice because he feels misunderstood.

Victor Klemperer

Klemperer is the diarist whose writings make up the entire text. His father is a rabbi in a Reform

Media Adaptations

- *I Will Bear Witness* was adapted for the stage by Karen Malpede and George Bartenieff and premiered off-Broadway in the 2000–2001 season. It was presented as part of the "Classic Stages / New Visions" series (see the Web site: http://www.nypost.com/theatre/031201a.htm). The one-man show, directed by Malpede and starring Bartenieff, is scheduled to be performed at theaters around the world. For example, The Vassar College's Jewish Studies Program will present *I Will Bear Witness* at the Bardavon 1869 Opera House (see the Web site: http://www.vassar.edu/relations/011107.klemperer.html); *I Will Bear Witness* is also scheduled to be performed at the Ko Fest (see the Web site: http://www.kofest.com/performances).

synagogue, so Klemperer and his siblings are accustomed to very liberal religious practices. Klemperer, like all three of his brothers, converts to Lutheranism in adulthood, a decision that is supported by their father. Still, in Nazi Germany, anyone who has one Jewish grandparent is regarded as Jewish, so Klemperer is subject to persecution. He is spared the deadly fate of the concentration camps, however, by virtue of his marriage to an Aryan woman, Eva, and his service in the German army during World War I.

As the diary opens, Klemperer is a professor at the Dresden Technical University. He loves lecturing and interacting in the academic community but soon realizes that because students are discouraged from taking his courses (Nazi policies limit his effectiveness; for example, he is not allowed to administer tests), he will be forced to retire. Klemperer and Eva have recently purchased a small plot of land in a town just outside Dresden, and they are planning to build a cottage. The Klemperers enjoy an active social life in the beginning, but as their friends gradually leave the country, they come to rely more on each other for meaningful interaction. Klemperer is an avid reader and writer who enjoys reading aloud to Eva, and the two often engage in intellectual discussion. During the course of the diary, Klemperer discusses two major works he is writing. One is an academic survey of eighteenth-century French literature, and the other is a study of the Third Reich's use of language. The latter would become a highly respected study and is still read by historians and language specialists today.

Klemperer expresses his fear of death although his expressions of this fear have a casual, matter-of-course tone. He only expects to live a few more years, an expectation that affects his plans for new projects. When he is particularly disheartened, he often reminds himself that Eva needs him, a thought that motivates him to keep trying to find money, to keep working around the house, and in general to keep trying to improve their situation. He also suffers from a number of ailments, and he is frequently depressed as a result of the disastrous circumstances in which he finds himself.

Despite his difficult lot in life, Klemperer maintains a detailed journal (at great personal risk) in which he writes his thoughts, feelings, and observations. His careful records of the day-to-day struggles of a man in his precarious position give his diary a great deal of historical weight. In addition, the diary fulfills Klemperer's dream of writing his memoirs for publication, an ambition he felt he never accomplished.

Johannes Köhler

Johannes Köhler is an Aryan man who, along with his wife, maintains a very close friendship with the Klemperers. He teaches history and religion and feels tremendous weight on his conscience because of the behavior of government officials. He considers teaching another course less relevant to current events, such as medicine or business. Klemperer refers to Köhler and his wife as the ''respectable'' Köhlers because they are married; in contrast, they have another friend, named Annemarie Köhler, who lives with a man, and so Klemperer jokingly calls them the ''unrespectable'' Köhlers. Klemperer admires Johannes Köhler and his wife because, although they come from a different background than the Klemperers, they deeply despise Hitler's regime.

Auguste Lazar

Auguste ''Gusti'' Lazar is a longtime friend of the Klemperers. She is an author of books for children and young adults. In the dairy, Klemperer refers to her by her married name, Wieghardt. She is optimistic and believes that the Nazi regime will not last. In Klemperer's first entry of 1935, he writes that she expressed her opinion that the regime will not last the year. She later realizes that the regime will last much longer, so she goes into exile in England in 1939, only to return to Dresden in 1949.

Frau Lehmann

Frau Lehmann is the Klemperers' maid, who is eventually forced to stop working for the Klemperers because they are categorized as a Jewish household. Her affection for the couple, however, leads her to visit them occasionally in the evenings.

Lissy Meyerhof

Lissy Meyerhof is a friend of the Klemperers who manages to keep her position as a social worker because of her service as a nurse during World War I. She is industrious and optimistic. After the Klemperers are sent to the Jews' House, she occasionally sends them packages containing such items as socks, coffee, and tea.

Präatorius

Präatorius is the builder contracted by the Klemperers to build their house. While he waits for them to come up with the money needed to begin work, he stays abreast of their financial affairs. Once building begins, he is fair and negotiates with them when unexpected expenses arise.

Sandel

Sandel is a Polish Jew who cheats Klemperer out of 240 marks and refuses to pay it back. He led Klemperer to believe that he could take the money and make more money with it, but instead he spent it while he was drunk. Sandel believes that Klemperer will not report the incident because Jews should protect each other. Klemperer, on the other hand, feels that not reporting it will make his friends think he lacks integrity for protecting a Jew. Reluctantly, he reports it to the police, and even though Sandel admits his wrongdoing, the police tell Klemperer that they can do nothing to recover his lost money. When Sandel tells the police that he was with Nazi officials when he spent the money, the entire matter is dropped. Klemperer is secretly relieved to have the matter behind him.

Jule Sebba

Jule Sebba is a friend of the Klemperers who makes plans to move his family to Israel. He is a lawyer and teacher in Germany, but he plans to open a candle-making business after he moves. Once he arrives in Israel, however, his original business plan fails and he makes a meager living giving cello lessons and performing at music concerts. Before he leaves, he explains to Klemperer that the reason he must go is that the Nazi regime is making life for the Jews bad now, but the situation will only escalate into ''unimaginable and bloody chaos.'' He adds that after the regime finally falls, there will be nothing left because all other institutions and structures have been destroyed.

Johannes Thieme

Johannes Thieme is a young man who lived with the Klemperers for a number of years beginning in 1920. He was like a foster son to them and called them mother and father. When he visits the Klemperers in 1933, he declares his support of the new regime. This disgusts Klemperer, who sees Thieme as a conformist with bad judgment, and he ends the relationship.

Themes

Disillusionment

From the beginning of the diary, Klemperer expresses profound disillusionment with Germany and with his own life. He is disheartened at the way Hitler has assumed power and at how the German people welcome him and believe what he tells them.

On May 13, 1934, Klemperer expresses his disappointment with his fellow Germans:

> The masses let themselves be talked into believing everything. If for three months all the newspapers are forced to write that there was no World War, then the masses will believe that it really did not happen.

Klemperer finds the Nazi regime to be ''un-German,'' and he is disturbed by the ways he sees people in his own circle of friends and colleagues changing to suit the regime.

Klemperer is tormented by his deep love of his country and his complete powerlessness to save it. On March 20, 1933, he writes,

I think it is quite immaterial whether Germany is a monarchy or a republic—but what I do not expect at all is that it will be rescued from the grip of its new government. I believe anyway that it can never wash off the ignominy of having fallen victim to it. I for my part will never again have faith in Germany.

He adds on April 3rd of the same year, ''Everything considered un-German, brutality, injustice, hypocrisy, mass suggestion to the point of intoxication, all of it flourishes here.'' Similarly, on February 21, 1935, he notes, ''The sense of justice is being lost everywhere in Germany, is being systematically destroyed.'' Klemperer's sense of identity is wrapped up in his patriotism, as evident in this comment from the March 30, 1933, entry: ''In fact I feel shame more than fear, shame for Germany. I have truly always felt a German.''

At the same time, Klemperer feels ongoing helplessness in his personal and professional life. He agonizes over his health, Eva's health, money, his career, and his writing. On May 15, 1933, he confides, ''I have given up thinking about things. I feel it's all coming to an end.'' On June 17 of the same year, he asks, ''Does it make any difference at all *what* I spend the remainder of my time doing? Just do something and forget oneself.''

On his birthday, October 9, 1933, he writes,

> Birthday wishes: To see Eva healthy once again, in our own house, at her harmonium. Not to have to tremble every morning and evening in anticipation of hysterics. To see the end of the tyranny and its bloody downfall. See my Eighteenth Century finished and published. No pains in my side and no thoughts of my death.

He immediately adds, ''I do not believe that even one of these wishes will come true for me.'' Klemperer also feels increasingly alone as people around him either leave the country or adopt the new ways. What was once a vibrant social life for the Klemperers becomes a life of quiet disappointment.

He continues to write as an outlet, but at times, even this practice is insufficient. He remarks on November 25, 1938, ''I completely lack the peace of mind to write.'' Still, he manages to complete a lengthy entry.

Perhaps the greatest despair and loss of control experienced by Klemperer is the day when he must wear the identifying yellow star. On September 15, 1941, he writes, ''I myself feel shattered, cannot

Topics for Further Study

- Suppose you were to leave behind a diary that would preserve an important chapter in your life. What part of your life would it be? Consider the events of your life, both personal and historical, and choose the time you feel is most important. Write between seven and ten diary entries in which you relate these events for posterity. Include a short introduction explaining why you have selected this particular time in your life and what you hope readers will learn from reading it.

- Research the Jim Crow laws, which sustained racial segregation in the American South during the first part of the twentieth century. Compare these laws to the Nazis' increasingly restrictive measures inflicted on Jews in Germany. Draw conclusions about the similarities and differences that you identify. Do you think such situations could happen in today's world? Why or why not? How do you think Klemperer would answer this question?

- Choose an event from Klemperer's diary that you found especially intriguing. Find three pieces of music that capture the feeling and atmosphere of that episode. Try to find three pieces that are as different from one another as possible.

- You are a substitute teacher for a high school English class that is finishing a study of Holocaust literature. Prepare for a class discussion. Create a graphic organizer that compares and contrasts Klemperer's diary with Anne Frank's. You will want to generate thought-provoking discussion during your class, so come up with at least three questions that will prompt your students.

- Research a personality test, such as the Myers Briggs test, which is based on the psychological theories of Carl Jung. See if you can determine Klemperer's personality type, paying close attention to such qualities as his academic nature, his competitive streak, his patriotism, his devotion to his wife, and his relationships with his friends. Once you have determined his personality type, read more about that specific profile. What new insights do you gain from this exercise? Explain how it casts one or more of the events of the diary in a new light.

---

compose myself.'' Five days later, he writes, ''Yesterday, Eva was sewing on the Jew's star, I had a raving fit of despair.''

Political Divisiveness

As Hitler's leadership gains momentum in Germany, Klemperer finds himself increasingly at odds with those around him. He is quick to express his opinions and finds himself so infuriated with others that he ends relationships. This happens partly because of the fundamentally incompatible points of view being expressed and partly because Klemperer loses respect for people who readily accept the new ideology rather than resist conformity by thinking for themselves.

On March 17, 1933, Klemperer writes about a visit from Johannes Thieme, a young man who came to stay with the Klemperers in 1920 and called them mother and father for a while. Klemperer writes:

Thieme—of all people—declared himself for the new regime with such fervent conviction and praise. He devoutly repeated the phrases about unity, upwards, etc. . . . He is a poor swine and afraid for his post. So he runs with the pack. . . . [H]e is absolutely at the mercy of every influence, every advertisement, everything successful. Eva already realized that years ago. She says, ''He lacks any sense of judgment.'' But that he would go so far . . . I am breaking with him.

In reviewing the year 1933, Klemperer writes about how he has lost two friends due to political differences. His entry on December 31 reads,

This is the characteristic fact of the year that has come to an end, that I had to break with two close friends, with Thieme because he is a National Socialist [Nazi], with Gusti Wieghardt because she became a Communist.

In April of the following year, he writes that his friend Grete shocks him because she has allowed everything German about herself to fall away and instead takes a completely Jewish point of view of things. Klemperer is unable to understand how anyone can separate such core pieces of his or her identity, and it disgusts him.

Preoccupation with Death

While reading Klemperer's diary, readers may be struck by his casual references to his own death. Although he says he feels horror at death, his tone indicates otherwise. For example, on July 20, 1933, he writes, "But there are countless people who have the strength for some kind of simple belief (or *unbelief*). *I* only have the quite childish horror of the grave and of nothingness—no more than that."

Klemperer seems preoccupied with the deaths of men his age and makes a point of noting their names, ages, and causes of death. On July 20, 1933, he reports, "Frau Blumenfield's brother, the missionary preacher, was here for a visit with his wife, fell ill suddenly and died very quickly after an unsuccessful gallbladder operation, fifty-four years old." At the time of this entry, Klemperer was 52.

On June 11, 1935, he comments on an obituary: "Heiss died on May 31. The obituary notice shook me, not because I loved him, but because the man was my generation, barely five years older."

The historical context of Klemperer's preoccupation with death is important because during the years covered in this volume of his diary, the mass extermination of Jews was not yet in force. In addition, because of the censored press, it is unlikely that he knew the full extent of the violence being committed against Jews throughout Germany. Thus, his preoccupation with death is not an indication that he has resigned himself to dying at the hands of the Third Reich but an indication that he is simply resigned to dying soon.

His feelings about his own death arise from his declining health and his general sense of hopelessness. Klemperer is depressed throughout 1933–1941, so the threat of death is not met with the same sense of dread and panic that a man with a full and happy life would feel. On September 27, 1934, he casually remarks, "But my first year of retirement will begin in 1935, and soon after that I shall be buried."

Style

Detailed Entries

Klemperer's diary is full of minute details about his private life, the books he is writing, and the events occurring in Nazi Germany. These details are what give the diary its historical significance as well as its human dimension. At times, however, readers may find the level of detail a bit difficult to absorb. While the reactions of people to the Third Reich are fascinating, the recurring lists of his and Eva's ailments, as well as notations of the amount of money spent on cat food and of what plants and shrubs have been purchased for landscaping, can seem a bit mundane.

Klemperer had been an avid diarist since the age of seventeen, and it is clear that by the time he reached his fifties, he was not at all self-conscious in his entries. He wrote for himself, not for posterity, which is why the entries often contain minute detail about topics that are of little interest to the reader. They do, however, provide insight into Klemperer's personality and show him to be an ordinary man.

The details about the rise of Nazism, on the other hand, are both intriguing and historically important. Because Klemperer refuses to accept the Third Reich, he is affronted by its appearance in every aspect of his life. He sees it as the reason he is forced to retire from his position as a university professor, and he also sees it in toothpaste packaging; its pervasiveness horrifies him.

On March 22, 1933, for example, he notes, "A young man with a swastika comes into the school on some official errand or other. A class of fourteen-year-olds immediately begin singing the Horst Wessel Song [a Nazi song]." Other images serve as "signs of the times," such as when Klemperer receives a cat magazine displaying a swastika or when, in 1935, the Nazis try to create German names for the months.

Later, the realities of ever-present Nazi power take on a more sinister quality. Klemperer explains on September 18, 1941, that when one person in the Jewish ghetto visits another, he or she rings three times. He adds, "That has been agreed, so that no one catches fright. A simple ring could be the police."

Blend of Formality and Informality

Klemperer's writing is formal in tone but informal at times in content and sentence structure. His diction and vocabulary frequently remind the reader that he is an academic and that he is accustomed to speaking and writing in a lofty, cerebral manner.

He relates the progress of his book on eighteenth-century French literature, and he includes new observations for his study of language in the Third Reich. Such writing is familiar to him, so it finds its way into his personal writing. When discussing his friends, he often describes their fundamental philosophical differences or his close observations as to why he admires or respects them. In such cases, the content is centered on analytical thinking. In these ways, Klemperer's diary is formal.

In other ways, the diary is quite informal. Because Klemperer did not intend the diary to be published, he was comfortable writing incomplete sentences that nevertheless expressed a complete thought. An example is in the March 27, 1933, entry: ''The Köhlers depressed and cautiously gritting their teeth.'' On July 20, 1933, he simply notes, ''Political situation bleak,'' and on July 14, 1934, he writes, ''The terrible uncertainty.'' Such phrases and incomplete comments fully express Klemperer's state of mind at the time of each entry.

In addition, he writes about domestic details such as his love for his cats, the latest gossip about a friend, or Eva's swollen ankle. Together, the formal and informal elements of Klemperer's diary provide a full portrayal of the man behind the diary.

Historical Context

Hitler's Rise to Power

Anne Frank and her family were in hiding from June 1942 to August 1944. World War II lasted from 1939 to 1945, involving the United States, Japan, Russia, and most of Europe. While the causes of the war are complex, historians agree that without Hitler's regime, there would have been no World War II at that time.

Following World War I, Hitler began to develop his idea of a master Aryan race. This vision included enlarging Germany by overtaking neighboring countries. The National Socialist Party, or Nazis, believed in a totalitarian government that

would, in theory, fairly distribute wealth and provide full employment.

Faced with economic hardship and political uncertainty, Germans were responsive to Hitler's impassioned speechmaking. Hitler maintained that radicals and Jews were to blame for Germany's problems, adding that the Aryan race was naturally superior and, thus, destined to rule the world.

In 1933, Hitler became the chancellor of Germany, and, contrary to the terms of the Treaty of Versailles (which ended World War I), Hitler began to build his military. Because these efforts went unchallenged by other European countries, Hitler's war machine was soon well armed. This rearmament created jobs, restored the economy, and stoked national pride, which increased public acceptance of Hitler.

Armed with a strong military, Hitler invaded Austria and Czechoslovakia in 1938 and set his sights on Poland after France and Britain declared war on Germany. The Allies, however, had not been strengthening their militaries, so they were no match for Hitler's forces. In 1939 and 1940, Hitler invaded Poland, Norway, Holland, Belgium, and France. In 1941, he broke his pact with Stalin and invaded Russia.

Hitler's social design involved banning all other political parties, censoring publications that were not pro-Nazi, and forbidding interaction between Jews and Aryans. Increasingly restrictive measures against Jews followed; they were forbidden to hold public office, teach, practice law or medicine, work in the press, or run businesses. Property was seized, fines were imposed, and emigration was stifled. The Nazis had lists of all Jews in each area and forced them to wear identifying yellow stars.

These measures were the reason that Anne Frank's father moved his family to Holland when Hitler came to power in 1933. Hitler's anti-Semitism was absolute, and the Nazis engaged in the systematic killing of ''undesirable'' and ''inferior'' segments of the population that included not only Jews, but also gypsies, the mentally retarded and disturbed, and homosexuals. The Nazis viewed these groups as subhuman and often made them work under harsh conditions so that the regime could capitalize on their labor before killing them.

When defeat of the Nazis was imminent, they continued to kill as many prisoners as possible

Compare
&
Contrast

- **1930s:** Germans often keep private diaries in which they can express their true opinions and feelings. Fear of discovery is a risk, and many diaries are self-censored by using pseudonyms, euphemisms, and vague references.

  Today: In the United States, freedom of speech is a constitutionally protected right enjoyed by all citizens. Americans freely criticize the government and its institutions.

- **1930s:** Klemperer writes on March 17, 1933, that some German papers are permanently banned while others are sometimes banned for a few days. Government control of the press becomes an important means of influencing public opinion and maintaining support for the regime.

  Today: Freedom of the press is protected by constitutional law in the United States. No matter how extreme the point of view, anyone has the right to print a newspaper expressing it. This freedom extends to harsh criticism of the government and its officials.

- **1930s:** On April 20, 1933, Germany celebrates the Day of the Nation, the Fuehrer's (Adolf Hitler's) birthday.

  Today: In the United States, influential leaders do not declare their birthdays national holidays. Only a few such birthdays are recognized in the United States, and each of these birthdays was declared a holiday after the honored person's death as a tribute to that person's life and contribution. Americans recognize Martin Luther King Day (to honor the birthday of the civil rights leader) and President's Day (to honor the birthdays of George Washington and Abraham Lincoln).

- **1930s:** Klemperer's annual salary as a professor of Romance languages and literature at Germany's Dresden Technical University is the equivalent (according to today's foreign exchange rates) of $4300.

  Today: Primarily because of inflation, but also due to increased cost of living and various other economic and cultural differences, the average annual salary of a U.S. professor of Humanities or Liberal Arts is around $65,000.

---

before the Allies could liberate their camps. At the end of the war, six million Jews had been killed, a number representing two-thirds of the world's Jewish population at the time.

Persecution of German Jews

As soon as Hitler became Germany's chancellor, he began enacting laws that would empower his regime and limit the civil liberties of the people. These limitations were especially strict for Jewish citizens. In February of 1933, Nazi officials declared boycotts on Jewish businesses; the next month violence against Jews and their businesses intensified when the Nazis announced that the German police would no longer defend Jewish citizens or their property. Soon, Jewish judges and lawyers were pulled from cases before being forced to retire.

In April, Hitler enacted laws that would reduce the legal rights of Jews and thus pave the way for harsher persecution. Four hundred laws were enacted to seriously limit the freedom of German Jews. Jews could not sit on juries, professional Jews such as lawyers, doctors, and dentists were no longer allowed to practice, university enrollment was reduced, and attendance at cultural events was forbidden.

In September of 1935, the Nuremberg Laws were enacted, which prohibited marriage between Jews and non-Jews, made extramarital relationships between Jews and non-Jews illegal, limited Jews' ability to hire female domestic help, and prohibited Jews from flying German flags. Hitler summarily blamed all of Germany's problems on the Jews, even as the Jewish population began to dwindle.

Once he had reduced their status, he instituted more drastic solutions to what he called the "Jewish Question."

Once the Nuremberg Laws were in place, the elimination of Jews became a top priority in the regime. On November 9, 1938, an event known as *Kristallnacht* ("the night of broken glass") took place. It involved the destruction of two hundred synagogues and a thousand Jewish businesses. In addition to the irreparable property damage, many Jews were beaten and killed.

Because other countries were unwilling to allow German Jews to immigrate, Hitler began forcing Jews to move to ghettoes. This would be the transition step to his "final solution." Reinhard Heydrich, an SS leader, organized the *Einsatzgruppen,* an elite killing squad created for the sole purpose of massacring Jews. However, Heydrich soon found that his squad could not kill people as fast as he would like, and there was a danger to the sanity of the members of his elite group.

The next step was to starve as many of the people in the ghettoes as possible, while using others to construct concentration camps. Many of these laborers were literally worked to death; the lifespan of laborers forced to work on building Auschwitz was only three or four months.

Once the concentration camps were complete, Nazi officials devised very efficient means of genocide. Soon, Jews from all over Europe were transported by train to the concentration camps, where most would meet their deaths. Once they arrived, their heads would be shaved so German manufacturers could use the hair. Any valuables had to be surrendered to the officials at once.

The numbers are staggering. In two months' time in 1942, three hundred thousand Jews from Warsaw were gassed at Treblinka. On one day in July of 1944, officials at Auschwitz killed 34,000 prisoners. In all, 750,000 were killed at Auschwitz, and one and a half million died in Maidanek. By the end of the war, the Nazis had murdered six million Jews.

Critical Overview

Critics overwhelmingly praise Klemperer's *I Will Bear Witness: A Diary of the Nazi Years, 1933–1941* for its accessible style, its compelling story, and its historical significance. Peter Gay of *New York Times*

Book Review comments, "To read Klemperer's almost day-to-day account is a hypnotic experience; the whole, hard to put down, is a true murder mystery—from the perspective of the victim."

Because Klemperer never intended his diary for publication, critics find that it rings true. Omer Bartov of the *New Republic* observes, "Klemperer's diary has the immediacy and the poignancy of unedited notes written in the thick of experience."

That Klemperer dreamed of writing his memoirs but feared they would never be completed is ironic given the global audience his diary has reached. The character of Klemperer himself is, in fact, part of the book's appeal. Critics commend him for his humanity, integrity, courage, and insight. Gay notes that Klemperer's "observations, including pitiless self-examinations, are unblinking; his reflections are remarkable for their precision and their penetrations."

A *Publishers Weekly* reviewer finds that Klemperer's understanding of the ramifications of the rise of Nazism has "the kind of clarity that usually comes with hindsight." As well, commenting at length on Klemperer's character, Bartov writes:

> What is remarkable about Klemperer's diaries is that he has clearly understood the nature of the Nazi regime and the extent of the public's support for Hitler, but refuses to modify his view that those who brand him un-German are themselves un-German. . . . He thus remains the only true German in a country that denies his right to exist there. . . . For all his refusal to accept the realities of his situation, for all his doubts, his terrible loneliness, his terror and his delusions, Klemperer displays remarkable courage in the face of an inconceivable material and psychological catastrophe.

In a review for the *Nation,* Silvia Tennenbaum commends Klemperer as a diarist, noting that the title of the book:

> says it all. Never has a victim observed his victimization with greater insight. Never has a victim described the apparatus of state-inflicted persecution with greater fidelity. Never has the isolation of living in a world that wishes one's people dead been rendered with greater pathos. Every act of cruelty as well as every gesture of kindness is scrupulously recorded.

Literary and historical scholars value *I Will Bear Witness* as a treasure of Holocaust literature. As a first-hand account of what it was like to be in Nazi Germany, the diary provides crucial details about the nuances of Jewish persecution. Tennenbaum goes so far as to proclaim, "Nothing I have read before made the years of Nazi terror so

World War II devastation is evident in this 1946 image of Klemperer's hometown of Dresden, Germany

real.'' In addition, Gay is quick to note ''even the reader familiar with Holocaust material must be gripped by these pages.'' As well, a reviewer for *Publishers Weekly* calls it ''one of the most important [diaries] to come out of Nazi Germany.'' The reviewer adds that the diary's historical contribution is its record of the ''insidious progress'' of policies that reduced the status of Jews in German society.

Richard Bernstein of *New York Times Book Review* praises the book as a diary that is ''full of pain and anger, but also full of shrewd observations

on the nature of the Nazi regime and the quality of the response of the German people to it.'' Furthermore, in *Commentary,* Daniel Johnson praises the diary as a great work that is among the most readable and revealing first-hand accounts of Nazi Germany. As well, Bartov summarizes Klemperer's contribution to Holocaust literature:

> What we have in this extraordinary book, then, is a view of German society under Nazism by the perfect insider who is rapidly transformed by the regime's ideology and its internalization by the population into the ultimate outsider, a Jew in a racist, violently anti-Semitic land which succeeds in bringing about the

social death of its Jewish citizens before it condemns them to physical annihilation.

Comparisons to Anne Frank's diary are inevitable, but critics are quick to note how fundamentally different the two accounts are. A reviewer for *Time* calls Klemperer's diary "richer and more profoundly disturbing" than Frank's diary. Crediting both diaries as valuable and insightful, Johnson points out what he sees as the core difference between the two diaries: "It is Anne Frank's childish naivete that lends her journal its unforgettable charm, and her fate that renders it unbearably poignant; by contrast, the relatively happy end of Klemperer's war is less obviously tragic."

Bernstein acknowledges that while the two accounts show how Nazi rule was experienced by individuals, Klemperer's diary is, after all, that of "a sophisticated, assimilated, cosmopolitan, middle-aged man striving to maintain self-control and dignity as the only world he knows crumbles around him for no reason." Concurring, Tennenbaum finds that Frank's sentimental diary is read tearfully and hopefully while Klemperer's diary is not at all sentimental in its unblinking look at every "shocking" detail. She concludes that Klemperer's diary "allows no tears but breaks our hearts instead."

The diary contains lessons that can be appreciated by virtually any reader. Bartov is especially drawn to the lesson of human nature's tendency to overlook wrongs committed against others, as long as the danger remains distant. He explains,

> The world that we see through Klemperer's eyes is a world in which most (though not all) Germans gradually turned their backs on the Jews, excluding them from their midst partly out of prejudice or conviction, partly out of fear and opportunism, and partly out of indifference and moral callousness.

Other critics find in Klemperer's diary a warning to the present against the repetition of the past. Johnson concludes his review with the following observation:

> Truly to immerse oneself in this modern classic is to find oneself wondering, and not for the first time, whether the mentality of national self-deception and willful ignorance that it so brilliantly depicts will ever, like the ideology of National Socialism, fade into history.

Finally, a reviewer for *Newsweek* remarks, "The overwhelming theme of Klemperer's diary is that it can happen here: modern society can plunge into brutality. Day by day, he shows precisely how."

Criticism

Jennifer Bussey

Bussey holds a master's degree in Interdisciplinary Studies and a bachelor's degree in English Literature. She is an independent writer specializing in literature. In the following essay, she discusses the importance of Klemperer's imagery to help the modern-day reader understand the slow spread of Nazism in Germany.

Contemporary readers of Klemperer's astonishing *I Will Bear Witness: A Diary of the Nazi Years, 1933–1941* are struck by the unexpected details the diarist notes from his daily life. Klemperer demonstrates how the influence of Nazism was pervasive and penetrated every facet of daily life. Further, he shows how the ever-present images of Hitler and the swastika affected the psyches of the citizens of Germany, having a profound influence on the ways they behaved and treated one another. Modern readers, knowledgeable about the horrors of the concentration camps and the inhumanity of the Holocaust, do not understand how such an unimaginable evil escalated.

Klemperer's diary depicts those tiny steps with which Hitler's regime took power and gradually evolved into what is perhaps the most infamous tyranny in history. Klemperer shows how Hitler's officials were so adept at public relations that they were able to garner widespread support. The diary is thus extremely valuable to modern readers because Klemperer provides startling and memorable images of a Germany moving steadily toward the worse.

Klemperer concentrates on two forms of Nazi imagery: ordinary objects and people's behavior. Both are equally disturbing. While shopping, Klemperer encounters everyday objects somehow transformed by the new regime. On March 22, 1933, Klemperer observes, "In a pharmacy toothpaste with a swastika." Eight days later, he notes, "In a toy shop a children's ball with the swastika." Later, on October 30, 1934, Klemperer writes, "I received a magazine with a swastika on the cover: 'The Care of the German Cat.'"

Later, in October of 1939, Klemperer describes walking through a market where many of the retailers' goods were replaced by pictures of Hitler. Klemperer certainly understood that toothpaste, toys, and cat magazines had nothing to with political events, but he also understood that they did have something to do with political strategy.

What Do I Read Next?

- The classic autobiography *Narrative of the Life of Frederick Douglass* (1845) is a thoughtful telling of Douglass's life first as a slave and then as an abolitionist in America. Despite suffering extreme oppression and humiliation, he was determined to become educated so he could be a leader for his people. His recollections of his past are marked by keen observations and a striking ability to recognize hypocrisy and abuse of power.

- Anne Frank's diary, published as *The Diary of a Young Girl* (1952), is often discussed in the context of Klemperer's diary. Frank was a teenage Jewish girl who went into hiding with her family and four other people in Amsterdam after the Nazis occupied Holland. It has become a classic in young adult nonfiction.

- Thomas Keneally's moving novel *Schindler's List* (1993) is based on the true story of German industrialist Oskar Schindler, who was so horrified by the Nazis' mass murder of Jews that he employed thirteen hundred Jews in a manufacturing facility. At great personal and financial risk, he remained dedicated to saving as many Jews as he could.

- Nora Levin's *Holocaust Years: The Nazi Destruction of European Jewry, 1933–1945* (1968) remains one of the key studies of the Nazi persecution of the Jews from the year of Hitler's rise to power through the end of World War II.

- The philosophical question at the center of Simon Wiesenthal's *The Sunflower: On the Possibilities and Limits of Forgiveness* (1998) is whether evil can be forgiven. The author recalls his experience in a concentration camp and the day a dying Nazi soldier asks him to forgive the evils done to the Jews. Over fifty great thinkers, including the Dalai Lama and Desmond Tutu, address this difficult question.

Similarly, when Klemperer tells about the Nazis' attempts to create German names for the months of the year, he sees it as a ridiculous effort, but a potentially dangerous sign. The imprint of the swastika on so many ordinary things sends a clear message that the regime is everywhere and controls everything, and to be outside the regime is to be alone.

While on the surface, such "marketing" measures appear to be a simple means of getting in touch with the people, they are really intimidation. Such tactics were designed to lead to only one conclusion, which Klemperer labels the thought process of Nazism: "Hitler IS Germany."

The other type of imagery Klemperer provides is imagery of people's reactions to the growing Nazi influence. In September of 1935, Klemperer describes signs being displayed by ordinary citizens who have fallen under the spell of Nazism. One sign reads, "Who buys from the Jew, is a traitor to the nation," while another reads, "No Jews do we want, in our fair suburb Plauen."

The schools were a focal point for Nazi efforts. On March 22, 1933, Klemperer describes this disturbing scene:

> Fraulein Wiechmann visited us. She tells how in her school in Meissin all are bowing down to the swastika, are trembling for their jobs, watching and distrusting one another. A young man with the swastika comes into the school on some official errand or other. A class of fourteen-year-olds immediately begins singing the Horst Wessel Song [a Nazi song].

The son of one of Klemperer's friends communicates another school-related incident. The boy was a "passionate Nazi" until he began thinking for himself and became disillusioned with what he saw. Klemperer tells the boy's story on September 27, 1934:

> The leaders—fellow pupils—take more money from us for excursions than they spend. It is impossible to check, a couple of marks always goes into their

> A toothpaste box and a child's ball are not on the same scale as the gas chambers at Auschwitz, but by providing these early images of Hitler's grip on Germany, Klemperer shows how one escalated to the other."

pockets; I know how it's done, I've been a leader myself. . . . One fellow, who was really poor, a leader for some time, is now riding a motorcycle . . .—'Don't the others notice too.'—'They're so stupid,' and then: 'No one dares say anything or talk to the others. Everyone is afraid of everyone else!'

This example of boyhood abuse of power demonstrates how receptive young minds were to the Nazis. They readily accepted positions of power and had no problem taking advantage of one another. Teachers were not immune to Nazi influence, either. On October 19, 1935, Klemperer explains that many teachers provide "character sketches" of their students. Commenting on a Jewish student, one teacher wrote that he "shows all the characteristics of his race." These sketches were designed to help assess the suitability of very small children for the "national community."

Another type of behavior seemed innocent enough but had harsh consequences. Modern readers can readily identify with the practice of making jokes about current events. Apparently, the same was true in Nazi Germany, as Klemperer explains on January 13, 1934. He writes that jokes about conversations in heaven are very popular, and that the best one at the time involves Hitler asking Moses, "But you can tell me in confidence, Herr Moses. Is it not true that you set the bush on fire yourself?"

Klemperer adds, "It was for such remarks that Dr. Bergsträsser, an assistant in the mechanical engineering department—an Aryan, by the way—was sentenced to ten months in prison by the special court."

Klemperer not only shows the reader how people behaved, he offers some explanation as to

why. He writes with great disgust about the manipulation of the media. First, the Nazis banned publications that were not in their favor. Securing "forbidden" newspapers was a serious crime, as Klemperer notes when a friend of his smuggles newspaper clippings with him back from Bohemia.

Second, the National Socialists saturated the newspapers and radio broadcasts with pro-Nazi propaganda, even going so far as to cast news in a more favorable light. They made light of defeats and exaggerated their victories. The effect was that Germans, like Klemperer, began to feel that the Nazi regime would last a very long time.

This "whitewashing" extended to lesser incidents, too. On May 15, 1933, Klemperer writes about a Communist who came under scrutiny by the Nazis:

> The garden of a Communist in Heidenau is dug up, there is supposed to be a machine gun in it. He denies it, nothing is found; to squeeze a confession out of him, he is beaten to death. The corpse brought to the hospital. Boot marks on the stomach, fist-sized holes in the back, cotton wool stuffed into them. Official post-mortem result: Cause of death dysentery, which frequently causes premature "death spots."

Klemperer discusses another Nazi control tactic: preaching against the individual and for the group. By encouraging people to act as a group, the Nazis positioned themselves as the leaders of the groups. In addition, they reduced a lot of dangerous independent thinking that would create resistance to their ideologies and policies.

They reduced the importance of the individual and exalted the importance of the whole, and in so doing made their followers more compliant. To the true followers, nothing was as important (not even themselves) as the good of the regime.

The next step was to provide ongoing "education" for the public, especially for young people, about the Nazi ideology. On September 4, 1934, Klemperer reports, the Reich Educational Ministry declared, "A total science of people and state based on the National Socialist idea is at the heart of the non-denominational school." In other words, the Nazis planned to perpetuate themselves by recruiting and instructing school-aged children attending public institutions.

Readers may notice that most of the examples of Nazi imagery occur toward the beginning of the diary. This is so because the early diary depicts the early years of Nazism, when the signs of the times were subtler and seemingly harmless. A toothpaste box and a child's ball are not on the same scale as the gas chambers at Auschwitz, but by providing these early images of Hitler's grip, Klemperer shows how one escalated to the other. He does modern readers a great service by demystifying the harrowing omnipotence of Hitler, and somehow reminds them that the German people were, after all, people subject to the same influences as anyone else.

Does this mean that Klemperer's diary is a warning not to let the past be repeated? Not necessarily, but it is a tool for understanding how such a dark chapter in world history methodically evolved. Although his diary was never intended for publication, Klemperer's inclusion of these striking images makes Nazi Germany more tangible for readers who otherwise have no context for knowing what it was like.

Source: Jennifer Bussey, Critical Essay on *I Will Bear Witness: A Diary of the Nazi Years, 1933–1941,* in *Nonfiction Classics for Students,* The Gale Group, 2002.

Silvia Tennenbaum

In the following review, Tennenbaum shares her experience reading Klemperer's diary, stating "nothing I had read before made the years of Nazi terror so real."

The closer we get to the millennium, the clearer it becomes that the Holocaust is the defining event of our century. The unspeakable suffering the German nation under Hitler inflicted on the Jews has become the model we refer to when we speak of man's inhumanity to man. We still suffer its aftershocks. It called into question our trust in "civilization" and created a disquietude between Germans and Jews that may take another hundred years to dispel. It is hardly surprising, then, that the Holocaust brought forth a vast outpouring of literature. The victims often clung to hope with a vow to "tell the world what went on here." But when liberation arrived at long last, an odd thing happened. Although the discovery of the death camps was greeted with shock and incredulity, it soon became clear that the world didn't really care to *keep* hearing about them. The end of the war brought joy and relief to the victors, a bad conscience and the wish to forget to the vanquished. Both wanted to return home and tend their own gardens. Only the survivors had nowhere to go; they became a nuisance, emotionally crippled reminders of a chapter in human history that left all who lived through that time feeling guilty.

Many years passed before we heard survivors' voices calling to us. Anne Frank's *Diary of a Young Girl* appeared; the words of Elie Wiesel; the scholarly researches by Lucy Davidowicz and Hannah Arendt; Paul Celan's poetry; Primo Levi's stories; Ida Fink's and Aharon Appelfeld's novels. And countless memoirs, oral histories of ordinary people. Whenever the flood of material—not all of it literature—seemed to crest, another wave came along and swept yet more scraps upon the shore. The need arose to secure Holocaust memories in a safe place—hence the creation of the Holocaust Museum. Such an official ingathering would guarantee that the important original materials had been unearthed, classified, analyzed and computerized. What remained was to sift through it carefully, write commentaries, interpretations and theses.

But closure is hard to come by.

In autumn 1995, fifty years after the end of the war, the Aufbau Verlag, a publishing house in what had been the German Democratic Republic, brought out a 1,600-page diary, written between 1933 and 1945 by a professor of Romance languages named Victor Klemperer. It is a day-by-day account of life in Dresden, in the heart of Nazi Germany, by a baptized Jew who managed not only to survive but to outlive the Third Reich. Its German title, *Ich will Zeugnis ablegen bis zum letzten* (I Want to Bear Witness to the Very End), says it all. Never has a victim observed his victimization with greater insight. Never has a victim described the apparatus of state-inflicted persecution with greater fidelity. Never has the isolation of living in a world that wishes one's people dead been rendered with greater pathos. Every act of cruelty as well as every gesture of kindness is scrupulously recorded.

Among the watchful victims of the Holocaust, Victor Klemperer stands alone. Whereas Anne Frank's *Diary* was used for sentimental purposes—serving as a shrine that welcomes tearful pilgrims and the hope of redemption—Klemperer's work is so utterly unsentimental, so unsparing in its shocking detail, that it allows no tears but breaks our hearts instead.

The massive two-volume edition had become a bestseller in Germany by the time I arrived to spend the winter of 1995–96 in Frankfurt am Main, where I was born. I bought the diaries and began reading them immediately, propped in my bed, night after

❝❝ **Whereas Anne Frank's** *Diary*
**was used for sentimental purposes
. . . Klemperer's work is so utterly
unsentimental, so unsparing in its
shocking detail, that it allows no
tears but breaks our hearts
instead.❞**

night, in a furnished studio at the university's guest house. Achingly spellbound, reading till 2 or 3 in the morning, it still took me almost three months to finish them. (That I was reading them in the land from which my family was exiled when I was 8 years old seemed a bitter, ironic coda.)

This fastidiously factual record, filled with touchingly honest familial details, trivial jealousies, petty quarrels, reports on illnesses, real and imagined, also contains sharp political insights, academic deliberations and vivid descriptions of the author's ever-worsening ordeal. Nothing I had read before made the years of Nazi terror so real.

I began, as it were, to walk in the author's footsteps. I watched his world shrink, month by month, year by year, until what once had been existed only in his memory. The restrictions imposed on the Jews were so bizarre that one might have thought they had sprung from Kafka's fevered imagination. Jews were forbidden to use the telephone, keep pets, go to the movies, subscribe to newspapers, use the library, buy flowers, smoke. They couldn't own typewriters or furs, go for a boat ride down the Elbe, visit a park or be seen on the streets at certain hours.

It wasn't hard to place myself into that world. I knew the landscape well, I had loved it once. I'd come back to search it for traces of my past and found that only the pictures in the museums still spoke to me of bygone days. When the Jews disappeared the beauty of the landscape was diminished, the shapes of the cities changed, the music stopped. No wonder that—except in the homes of friends—I can find no comfort there. Melancholy fills my heart.

No, not melancholy; the word I want is *Wehmut,* or "pain of the spirit."

Victor Klemperer (1881–1960) was born in the small town of Landsberg-on-the-Warthe, in the eastern part of the state of Brandenburg. He was the youngest of eight children of a rabbi. When he was 9, the family moved to Berlin because Rabbi Wilhelm Klemperer received a call to the pulpit of the Reformed Synagogue. The move was greeted with relief by the entire family, not only because life in the German capital was more exciting than life in the provinces but because the congregation did not ask the family to observe strictly orthodox ritual practices.

Growing up in the shadow of three older, successful brothers gave Victor little chance to gain self-confidence. (He was, however, an obsessive diarist from the age of 17.) He quit his studies early, but returned to them sporadically. He found it hard to settle on any one discipline until he was drawn to eighteenth-century French literature and the Enlightenment. He graduated, married in 1906 and sought employment in Berlin as a journalist. He seems to have worked very hard and gained a modicum of success. (The diaries clearly show his competitive streak.) In 1914 he completed his doctorate and found a teaching job—which he left to join the army one year later. (Since he served at the front, he was allowed moments of reprieve during Hitler's reign. But this alone could not have saved him.)

Those youthful years carry the seeds of many of the resentments Klemperer addresses in his journal. He cannot shake his sense of inferiority vis-à-vis his brothers, who helped him out financially now and then and considered him a dilettante. They also disapproved of his marriage to Eva Schlemmer, a pianist and musicologist they thought socially inferior. That she wasn't Jewish obviously didn't matter; they no longer thought of themselves as Jews either. By the time World War I began, all of Rabbi Klemperer's sons had converted in order to advance their careers.

In 1920 Victor received a chair in Romance languages and literature at the Technical University in Dresden. As the diaries begin, in January 1933, he and his wife have just bought a piece of land in Dölzschen, a suburb in the hills above Dresden, and are planning to build a small house. Domestic matters make up a good portion of the text in the first years under Nazi rule and provide us a wonderful, novelistic sense of who Victor and Eva Klemperer—Mr. and Mrs. K.—are. We find out that they have two cats, that they both suffer from depression, that they love the movies and that Eva is a passionate gardener. We learn that the author worries about money, and that his wife is not a devoted *Hausfrau*. We meet their friends and hear the gossip about them. We are told that he likes to read to her. We know whether it's raining outside or the sun is shining, and are privy to his thoughts concerning one or another work in progress. Above all, we are kept abreast of political developments.

The emerging scene envelops us slowly. Each day adds more homey details, but from the very beginning the political situation provides an ominous, though relatively distant, accompaniment. The National Socialists are in power, Hitler has been made Chancellor, the terror has begun. It mounts swiftly, though it hasn't yet reached the middle-class enclaves of Dresden. (On March 22, 1933, K. reports that Blumenfeld's maid has quit, saying she's found a permanent job: "The professor will soon no doubt not be in a position to keep a maid much anymore.") But there is still time for K. to learn to drive, to buy a used car so he can take Eva for drives in the country, where they can briefly forget the endless bureaucratic chicanery: harassment by the Nazi mayor, the loss of his job (in 1935). As more and more of their friends and acquaintances emigrate, their isolation increases.

In the years ahead, the political drumbeat will grow louder, demand more and more of the diarist's attention, until it is finally all that matters. It is death at the door, hunger in the belly, fear in the heart. The greatness of the diaries lies in the way they portray the inexorable push of history against the life of one man and his wife. The machinery of the entire German state is harnessed to "cleanse" the nation of its Jews. I know of no other text that describes the relentless course of this demented idea—which will play itself out on every inch of land conquered by the Wehrmacht—with equal intelligence and humanity. Most Holocaust-memoirs are—by their very nature—limited in vision. They report what can be seen from behind barbed wire, amid the cries of the dying, or what takes place in the sealed ghetto. Great historians may write brilliantly, great novelists movingly, but the great diarist brings you directly into the mind and the belly of his society.

Klemperer was a scholar as well as an acute observer. A photo taken of him, standing in front of his house with Eva, shows a smallish, balding man in a dark three-piece suit, with large ears and sagging shoulders, who stands almost shyly behind his wife. His demeanor is professorial; it strikes the viewer as, well, typically Jewish. Eva is the more conspicuous of the two, in her white summer dress, thick-rimmed glasses, a turban and pearls, holding a cigarette in one hand. She is not a pretty woman. What is evident in the photo is their attachment—they are a couple bound by love. It is a love, I suspect, common to many childless couples.

It was Eva Klemperer who—literally—saved her husband's life. Jews married to gentiles were spared almost to the end, an odd kind of exemption, considering that the Nazis thought of such marriages as *Rassenschande* (miscegenation), which turned the gentile partner into a pariah or, if she was a woman, a whore, and threatened the German *Volk* with the deadly virus of racial impurity.

It was Eva too—depressed, suffering from migraines—who went where he could not go, did what he could no longer do. She stood in line for the meager rations at the grocery store and, above all, she traveled into the countryside every couple of weeks, carrying the diaries to a friend's house, where they were safely stored in a trunk. Had they been found, the Gestapo would unhesitatingly have murdered anyone connected to them, however slight that contact might have been. Among the themes winding their way through the diaries, the most compelling is what Klemperer calls LTI, or *lingua tertii imperii,* the language of the Third Reich.

LTI, published in book form in 1947, is a brilliant study of the way the Nazis distorted and deformed the German language to serve their needs. The party's propaganda apparatus was quick to understand how to utilize the power of radio and talking pictures to manipulate the masses. Once the opposition had been brutally strangled and every independent news source silenced, the government could broadcast its version of the day's events and its hateful diatribes against the Jews to millions without fear of contradiction. The screaming voices of Hitler, Göbbels et al. were heard not only in the kitchen and living room of every German home but in every public place. It was an intrusion no one could escape.

LTI served as the voice of propaganda, but its twisted vocabulary also defined the government's anti-intellectual, anti-humanist *Weltanschauung.* It perfected the deceitful habit of using euphemisms to hide the true nature of a thing. Propaganda and brute terror, hand in hand, sent an entire nation plunging into barbarism.

Klemperer called his work on the diaries his "balancing pole." It kept him from falling into the

Two Jewish internees at a concentration camp in Hungary in 1944. Even though he felt little allegiance to any religion, under Nazi law Klemperer was a Jew and was forced to display the yellow star these prisoners wear

abyss. At age 60 and ailing, he was sent to work in a factory. In winter's freezing weather he had to go out and shovel snow. And still he wrote, passionately and rigorously. As his situation worsened, his entries grew longer. He wanted to keep the German language, the language of Goethe and Lessing, Schiller and Heine, alive. It—more than a sprinkle of baptismal water—was what bound him to Germany and made him feel that he, and not the brutish brownshirts, was representative of the true Germans.

K. introduced LTI by quoting Franz Rosenzweig's dictum *Sprache ist mehr als Blut* (Language means more than blood). In his own diaries he wrote, ''*Der Geist entscheidet, nicht das Blut*'' (the spirit, not blood, is decisive). These assertions defied the mythology of a nation that had, ever since Bismarck coined the phrase ''blood and iron,'' believed fervently in the mystical qualities of the fluid that courses through our veins. Small wonder that German Jews disputed such dogma. In the century and a half before Auschwitz, it was an article of faith for the vast majority of these German Jews that something called the German-Jewish symbiosis existed. Despite an occasional anti-Semitic incident, wasn't there an unshakable bond

between the two nations, and hadn't it engendered a resplendent Jewish renaissance? And wasn't that bond grounded in language? (Didn't the German Jews disparage Yiddish precisely because they—too!—thought it a bastardization of German?) Paul Celan, who wrote, ''*Der Tod ist ein Meister aus Deutschland*'' (Death is a master from Germany), knew the allurement of the ''pure'' German spoken by his mother in the polyglot city of Czernowitz. He continued to write his agonized, intensely lyrical poems in German, even ''after Auschwitz.''

Victor Klemperer felt himself to be German to the marrow of his bones. He firmly believed he could shed his Jewishness more quickly than his Germanness. He shared the fruits of German *Kultur;* the German *Geist* was alive in him. This is why, during the first few years of his long banishment, he so desperately insisted that he embodied what was truly German.

One of the effects of the *lingua tertii imperii* was to sever the connective tissue of language between the Third Reich and its still-trusting Jews. One of the terrible effects of exile—especially for those who live by the word—is to be rendered mute by loss of the mother tongue.

K.'s deep commitment to the French Enlightenment and Revolution was a reflection of the thesis that both had influenced the great German poets and thinkers in the age of Goethe. They fell into bad repute only in a reactionary Germany that came to reject (in the name of Rousseau and Romanticism, K. would argue) the clarity of the spirit for the murk of emotion, mysticism, blood. By 1871 France had become the enemy; after the defeat of 1918 she was the archenemy. K. never fully understood that it was academic suicide, in that time, to champion Voltaire and the *philosophes* and to find any redeeming value in the concept of *liberté, egalité, fraternité.*

It was the very problem of language that kept Klemperer from trying to leave Germany, as others in his family (including his famous cousin Otto) had done. He cannot imagine immigrating to France (to teach the French about their own literature?). Palestine repels him. He makes abundantly clear how hostile he is to Zionism, voicing outrage at the displacement of the indigenous Arab population and comparing the Zionists' goal of ''returning the Jews to the land'' to the ''blood and soil'' philosophy of the Nazis. (In 1998 some of us might think him prescient.)

The prospect of going to America (despite the movies) seems equally hopeless to K. He fears he is too old to learn English and that his work, the one safe harbor in a world gone insane, will crumble. He was probably right. There were some German Jews who were willing to face death (most likely as suicides the night before they were called to report for deportation) sooner than life in a faraway country. The poet Gertrud Kolmar was such a one. Stefan Zweig fled to South America, only to kill himself there. K. decides to bear witness to the bitter end.

In May 1940 the final degradations commence. The Klemperers are forced to move from their home into a ''Jewish'' house in Dresden. Beginning on September 19, 1941, all Jews are required to wear the yellow star. This is a moment of the deepest humiliation for Klemperer. His own words, as they appear in the German edition, make this—and many other subtle points—very clear. The much-edited English edition does not. Perhaps this is the moment to voice my disappointment at the way Random House has handled this project. First of all, it has been three years since the German publication. This might be forgiven if it were the complete edition we held in our hands. It is not. It is volume one of two. This one ends on December 31, 1941. The second (which Random House plans to publish next August)

covers the period from January 1, 1942, until June 10, 1945, when the author and his wife return to their home in Dölzschen.

K. writes, ''*Am späteren Nachmittag stiegen wir nach Dölzschen hinauf*'' (Later that same afternoon we climbed the hill to Dölzschen). This is the last sentence of the diaries as published in Germany. It is profoundly moving in its brevity because it carries the fullness of the unbearable, unbelievable joy that has come to them at last. The twelve bitter years of exile are over.

The two volumes cannot be split asunder like this: Their literary life lies embedded in their seamless totality. Just think—the first eight years of the Third Reich take up volume one, the last three and a half years volume two. This means that an incredible amount of material is crammed into these last, worst years of the Nazi period. Forget about the cuts; they leave out a great deal but might be acceptable if we had the entire narrative before us. In the second volume, the situation for the Jews grows more perilous by the day; K.'s entries become longer and follow one another more closely. At the same time, news of German reverses on the Eastern front has filtered in, and there are moments of hope. One of the few remaining spots where Jewish men can gather and talk freely is the cemetery—the earth of new graves smells fresh, the thick greenery surrounds them with country peace. K.'s writing becomes richer, flows more smoothly and with greater urgency and deeper emotion. K. has decided the diary will be his legacy of heroism.

The description of the final four months of the war takes up 173 mesmerizing pages of the German edition. On February 23, 1945, Klemperer is called to the office of the head of the Jewish community and given some evacuation notices to pass around. His own is not among them, but he feels certain that the end for him is coming. He is mute with horror, but continues to take note of everything around him, so he can record it when he returns home. That very night British planes rain fire on Dresden and reduce most of the city to ashes. The Klemperers are separated but both survive, and when the morning dawns and they see the devastation around them, they realize that they are free: FREE AT LAST! Eva cuts off K.'s detested star and the two of them join the stream of refugees headed south toward Bavaria and the approaching US Army. All this, of course, is missing in this edition, although its editor and translator, Martin Chalmers, briefly refers to it in his preface.

Klemperer and his wife returned to Dresden after the war, which meant living in the Soviet zone and, later, in the GDR. K., who had been a bourgeois liberal and anti-Communist before the war, joined the Communist Party. Given his experience under the Nazis, his alienation from the society he'd known before Hitler and his preference for ''simple'' working-class people, this was hardly surprising. (German conservatives blame him for this.) He lived a full and productive life in East Germany; Eva died in 1951 and he survived her by nine years, perhaps never able to escape the feeling of February 22–24, 1945, when he noted (in my rendition from the German): ''Whenever I looked back at the heap of cinders that had been the city, I had, and still have, the atavistic emotion: *Yahwe!* It was there, in that place in Dresden, where they burned down the synagogue.''

Source: Silvia Tennenbaum, ''A Season in Hell,'' in *Nation,* Vol. 267, No. 16, November 16, 1998, pp. 12–19.

Sources

Bartov, Omer, ''The Last German,'' in *New Republic,* December 28, 1998, p. 34.

Bernstein, Richard, ''How the Little Things Add Up to Horror,'' in *New York Times Book Review,* November 11, 1998.

Brady, Philip, Review, in *Times Literary Supplement,* January 24, 1997, pp. 27–28.

Gay, Peter, ''Inside the Third Reich,'' in *New York Times Book Review,* November 22, 1998.

Johnson, Daniel, ''What Victor Klemperer Saw,'' in *Commentary,* Vol. 109, No. 6, June 2000, p. 44.

Review, in *Publishers Weekly,* October 5, 1998, p. 65.

Review, in *Time,* November 30, 1998, p. 126.

Shapiro, Laura, Review, in *Newsweek,* Vol. 132, No. 20, November 16, 1998, p. 84.

Tennenbaum, Silvia, Review, in *Nation,* November 16, 1998, p. 12.

Further Reading

Hahn Beer, Edith, *The Nazi Officer's Wife: How One Jewish Woman Survived the Holocaust,* Rob Weisbach Books, 1999.
In this memoir, the author recalls her experience as a Jewish woman acting the part of a Christian wife to a Nazi officer. Although her husband knows about her true heritage, he keeps her secret. When he is sent to Russia, she becomes a strong, independent woman who is able to save herself and her infant daughter under the most dangerous circumstances.

Klemperer, Victor, *I Will Bear Witness: A Diary of the Nazi Years, 1941–1945,* translated by Martin Chalmers, Random House, 2000.
This is the second volume of Klemperer's wartime diary. It relates the events leading up to the end of the war, including Klemperer's summons for deportation, his and Eva's escape from Dresden, and the end of the war.

———, *The Language of the Third Reich: LTI, Lingua Tertii Imperii: A Philologist's Notebook,* translated by Martin Brandy, Athlone Press, 2000.
Klemperer's study of the language of the Third Reich is described in his diary. Today, this study is considered one of the most important of its kind in researching the Third Reich.

Schleunes, Karl A., *The Twisted Road to Auschwitz: Nazi Policy Toward German Jews, 1933–1939,* University of Illinois Press, 1990.
Schleunes provides a detailed account of the development of the Nazi regime with regard to their policies toward the Jews prior to the mass executions that took place in concentration camps. Originally published in 1970, this book opened the way for additional historical studies of the Holocaust.

News of a Kidnapping

Gabriel Garciá Márquez

1997

Gabriel García Márquez was approached by his friends Maruja Pachón de Villamizar and Alberto Villamizar in 1993 to write a book about the ordeal surrounding Maruja's abduction. García Márquez recalls that he was working on the first draft when he realized "it was impossible to separate her kidnapping from nine other abductions that occurred at the same time in Colombia." García Márquez decided to broaden his work to include the stories of all these captives, which lengthened the project to almost three years. The result is *News of a Kidnapping*, which was first published in Spanish in 1996 and in English the following year. In this work, García Márquez takes on the gargantuan task of describing the kidnappings and captivity of ten people. He depicts their families' reactions to these events as well as their efforts to free the hostages, but also attempts to place the entire incident in the context of Colombia's long-standing war on drugs and terrorism in general.

The fame of García Márquez—a Nobel Laureate—guaranteed that the American press would pay immediate and close attention to the work. Moreover, the drug problems of Colombia and the United States were—and remain so today—intertwined. The threat of extradition to the United States drove Pablo Escobar, head of the Medellín cartel, to order the kidnappings. However, it is to García Márquez's credit that he roots *News of a Kidnapping* firmly within Colombian soil, for the violence that the drug industry has wrought upon Colombian

society is astronomical, indeed, hardly comprehensible to Americans. *News of a Kidnapping* depicts a world almost as surreal as any of García Márquez's novels, one that may shock American readers but one all too well-known to Colombians.

Author Biography

García Márquez was born on March 6, 1928, in Aracataca, Colombia, a small town near the Atlantic coast. He was raised by his grandparents, who stimulated his imagination with stories of supernatural beings and Colombian history. García Márquez was sent to school near Bogotá, and he enrolled at the National University of Colombia in 1947 to study law. Also that year, he published his first short story in a Colombian newspaper.

By the following year, García Márquez had transferred to school at Caratagena and was also working as a journalist. His discovery of William Faulkner's work at this time inspired him to become a writer. After he moved to Barranquilla in 1950, he continued working as a journalist while also becoming involved with a group of young writers and intellectuals. García Márquez's reading of Franz Kafka's *The Metamorphosis* made him realize that serious literature could be based on fantastical ideas such as his own. He soon abandoned his law studies and decided to pursue a career as a writer.

In 1954, he moved to Bogotá and became a reporter. In 1955, he won an award for the story "One Day After Saturday" and published *Leaf Storm*, his first novella. His newspaper also sent him to Europe but soon thereafter was shut down by the Colombian government. García Márquez spent the next three years in Paris, France, devoting himself to writing fiction. He also toured Eastern Europe and the Soviet Union.

In 1958, when he returned to Colombia, he published another novella, *No One Writes to the Colonel*, in a magazine, and it was published in book form three years later. In 1962, he published the short story collection *Big Mama's Funeral* and his first full-length novel, *In Evil Hour*. He also went to work for the Bogotá branch of a Cuban news agency, which led to extended stays in Havana and New York. He also lived in Mexico for a handful of years.

In 1965, he began to work full-time on the book that would be published to immediate acclaim in 1967, *One Hundred Years of Solitude*. This novel, replete with Colombian history and the magical realism for which García Márquez is known, led to his international literary celebrity.

García Márquez continued to write, producing several novels and novellas, and was awarded the Nobel Prize for Literature in 1982. He undertook the journalistic project *News of a Kidnapping* at the behest of his friends, Maruja Pachón de Villamizar, a kidnapping victim, and her husband Alberto Villamizar. Just after producing this book, in 1996, a group called Dignity for Colombia kidnapped the brother of former president César Gaviria and demanded that, as condition for the release of the hostage, García Márquez be installed as head of state.

In the late 1990s, politics and journalism took up much of García Márquez's time. He contributed to the peace talks between the Colombian government and guerrilla groups by introducing President Andrés Pastrana to Fidel Castro, who facilitated talk with the guerrillas. He also helped restore relations between the United States and Colombia, which had been severely damaged after a major bribery scandal involving President Ernesto Samper. He has also been involved in negotiations to end the civil wars in El Salvador and Nicaragua. In 1999, he became the majority owner of the weekly news magazine *Cambio;* he still maintains close contact with his staff. Today, García Márquez is seen as much more than a literary figure in his country—he is also a symbol of Colombian pride.

Plot Summary

The Kidnappings

News of a Kidnapping opens in Bogotá, Colombia, in November 1990 with the kidnapping of Maruja Pachón de Villamizar and her sister-in law, Beatriz Villamizar de Guerrero. Their abduction is part of a series of high-profile abductions launched by the Pablo Escobar drug cartel, which began the past August. The drug cartel is attempting to change a new governmental policy that could lead to their extradition to the United States should they surrender to Colombian authorities. These drug traffickers are collectively known as the Extraditables.

Eight men and women, all journalists except one, have already been taken and are being held captive. Diana Turbay, accompanied by a news team, was lured into a trap on August 30 when she was offered the opportunity to meet with a guerrilla leader. Marina Montoya was kidnapped on September 18 outside of her restaurant. Four hours later, Francisco "Pacho" Santos was taken from his car.

Maruja and Beatriz are taken to a house in Bogotá, where they share a small room with Marina. For the most part, they are treated harshly during their captivity; for example, they are forced to speak in whispers. Pacho is held in another house in Bogotá, but he faces more amenable conditions with friendly guards and regular access to books and newspapers. Diana's group, held captive in and around Medellín, are split up; throughout their captivity, they are forced to move numerous times.

The Extraditables

The first eight kidnappings are not publicly acknowledged by the Extraditables until October 30. However, Pablo Escobar acknowledges his responsibility in Maruja and Beatriz's kidnapping within days. The Extraditables declare that they will release the hostages and surrender if non-extradition is guaranteed, security for themselves in prison and their families is ensured, and police abuses in Medellín cease. However, President César Gaviria and his administration already approved a decree in September for the capitulation of the traffickers, and while it said that they could have the right not to be extradited, this would be determined on a case-by-case basis. Escobar rejects the decree because it does not state that he and the other Extraditables would definitely not be extradited.

By the time of Maruja and Beatriz's kidnapping, the government and the victim's families have had numerous contacts with the Extraditables. Former President Turbay and Hernando Santos, Pacho's father, attempt to negotiate with Escobar, but President Gaviria refuses to amend the decree at all. The government maintains that its sole position with regard to the narcoterrorists is that they surrender. By November 7, when Gaviria's administration issues the official decree stating the government's capitulation policy, which did not specifically state that the Extraditables would not be extradited, no progress has been made toward releasing the hostages. After Maruja's kidnapping, her husband, Alberto Villamizar, also becomes involved, but he has no more success in getting Gaviria to negotiate.

Death and Release

On December 14, a capitulation decree that modifies September's decree is issued, but the two

Gabriel García Márquez

greatest obstacles to surrender are still in place: the uncertain conditions for non-extradition and a fixed time limit on pardonable crimes, meaning that crimes had to have been committed before September 5, 1990. Escobar objects to the decree, but three Medellín leaders—the Ochoa brothers—who had determined to surrender back in September to begin the process of turning themselves in.

Following this decree, several hostages—Hero Buss, Azucena Liévano, and Orlando Acevedo—are released, but in January, when two drug leaders are killed, Escobar begins to order the execution of the hostages. On January 23, a guard comes for Marina. Her body is found the next day in an empty lot. After an autopsy, her as-yet-unidentified body is buried in a mass grave. The identity of her body is not established until the following week, after the Extraditables announce her murder.

On January 25, the police raid the house in Medellín where Diana Turbay and Richard Becerra are being held on a tip that Escobar is there. Forced by the guards to flee, Diana is accidentally shot by gunfire. She is taken to a hospital where she dies from her wounds. Some Colombians believe that this action was actually a rescue raid—an action which the captors previously had promised to respond to by killing the hostages. President Gaviria orders an investigation to look into the matter. Its findings, released in April, maintain that the decision to raid was based on the chance of catching Escobar. The investigation was unable to determine if Diana was shot by the police or by the captors.

On January 29, a third version of the capitulation decree is issued, which no longer includes a time limit for pardonable crimes and guarantees non-extradition. Although this final version was already in the works, many Colombians believe it is a response to Diana's death. The Extraditables announce that they will cancel the forthcoming executions as well as release one of the hostages.

Pacho has access to television and newspapers, so he knows about Diana and Marina. Maruja and Beatriz, however, are left to wonder what happened to Marina, although one of their guards reveals news of Diana's death. Toward the end of January, they begin to hear rumors that two hostages would be freed; on February 9, Beatriz is released. Once home, she is careful not to reveal clues that would lead to Maruja's whereabouts and a police raid. She also learns of Marina's death.

Negotiating with Escobar

When Maruja is not released, Villamizar decides that he must go to Medellín and meet Escobar face-to-face. His efforts to locate Escobar begin with a visit to the jail where the Ochoas are incarcerated, and they promise to give Villamizar's message to Escobar. Villamizar and Escobar correspond numerous times. Villamizar explains that, in exchange for releasing the hostages, the guarantees for his surrender were in place, his life would be protected, and he would not be extradited. Escobar, however, refuses to surrender because now he wants a guarantee that Colombia's Constituent Assembly will consider the subject of extradition. In April, negotiations improve when Father Rafael García Herreros offers himself as a mediator. Escobar agrees to meet the priest in Medellín, and the two men work out conditions for the drug leader's surrender, which focus primarily on security in his prison. Escobar orders the release of Pacho and Maruja to take place in a few days, on May 20. That morning, Father García Herreros meets with President Gaviria and gives him the details of his talk with Escobar. Maruja is released at 7 o'clock that evening, 193 days after her abduction. Pacho hears the news of her release on the radio, but minutes later, he, too, is released.

Epilogue

On June 19, 1991, in the presence of Villamizar, Father García Herreros and others, Escobar surrenders to the Colombian authorities. He is held captive in a prison in Medellín, which he quickly turns into a "five-star hacienda." He also continues to oversee his business affairs. When the government learns of this situation, Escobar is transferred to another prison, but he escapes in the process. A massive manhunt takes place, which ends with Escobar's death on December 2, 1993.

Key Figures

Orlando Acevedo

Orlando Acevedo is one of Diana Turbay's cameramen. The kidnappers free him on December 17.

Richard Becerra

Richard Becerra is one of Diana's cameramen. He gains his freedom after the police raid that takes Diana's life.

Hero Buss

Hero Buss is a German journalist who travels with Diana Turbay's crew. The kidnappers free him on December 11.

Pablo Escobar

Pablo Escobar is the head of the Medellín drug cartel. At the time of the abductions, Escobar's fugitive, shadowy identity has led some people to doubt his very existence. Escobar has risen from petty thiefdom to heading a multibillion-dollar, international drug industry. In his hometown of Medellín, Escobar provides jobs and charitable services to slumdwellers. After he is imprisoned, Escobar continues to run his drug business. He is shot and killed by Colombian authorities on December 2, 1993, a few months after his escape from prison.

Father Rafael García Herreros

Father Rafael García Herreros is the eighty-two-year-old priest whose efforts are instrumental in bringing about the release of the final two hostages and Escobar's surrender. Father Herreros's well-known television sermonette program "God's Minute," has been running close to forty years before the nightly news. Father Herreros takes it upon himself to volunteer to mediate between Escobar and the government. Escobar accepts this offer and soon after a meeting takes place between the men, the long ordeal—of the hostages and the government's battle with Escobar—ends.

President César Gaviria

President Gaviria took office a mere three weeks before the first kidnapping. Since his campaign, Gaviria worked to create a judicial policy that would bring about an end to narcoterrorism, and this policy became his first priority in office. Gaviria considered extradition an emergency measure that would pressure the criminals into surrendering. With the kidnapping of Diana Turbay and her news team, his resolve is put to the test. Throughout the months of the hostage ordeal, Gaviria refuses to accede to any demands of the drug traffickers that would tarnish the Colombian judicial system, which he is trying to strengthen. Gaviria is also personally touched by the narcoterrorists during this ordeal; shortly before Escobar's surrender, Gaviria's cousin and old friend is abducted and murdered.

Dr. Pedro Guerrero

Pedro is Beatriz's husband.

Azucena Liévano

Azucena Liévano is a young editor on Diana Turbay's new team. She takes notes during her captivity and later uses them to write a book about the experience. She is held with Diana, but on December 13 the kidnappers free her alone.

General Miguel Maza Márquez

General Maza Márquez, responsible for the investigation into the abduction, is the head of the Administration Department for Security. He has held this position for an unprecedented seven years, under numerous administrations, and he considers the war against the drug dealers to be his personal struggle to the death with Pablo Escobar.

Marina Montoya

Kidnapped three months before Maruja and Beatriz, the sixty-four-year-old Marina Montoya owns a restaurant but her political connections make her a target; her brother was the secretary general to President Barco, whose administration had begun the extradition policy and, at the time of the abductions, he serves as Colombia's ambassador to Canada. It is widely believed that Marina was kidnapped in retaliation for the government's refusal to comply with agreements made with narcoterrorists to bring about the release of her nephew, who previously had been abducted and freed. Many Colombians, including Marina, also believe that she has been abducted so that the captors had a significant hostage whom they could kill without thwarting the negotiations for their surrender. Marina develops a close relationship with her guards before the arrival of Maruja and Beatriz to the room where she is kept, and she has a difficult time adjusting to their presence. In the days before her death, Marina seems to foresee what will happen, and she is executed on January 23, 1991, her body tossed in an empty lot.

Fabio Ochoa

Fabio, the youngest Ochoa brother, is a top member of the Medellín cartel. He surrenders in December.

Jorge Luis Ochoa

Jorge Luis, a top member of the Medellín cartel, surrenders under the new decree in January. Of the three brothers, he is of particular help to Villamizar in his efforts to meet Escobar. He also tries to convince Escobar to surrender.

Juan David Ochoa

Juan David is a top member of the Medellín cartel. He surrenders under the new decree in February.

Gloria Pachón

Maruja's sister Gloria is Colombia's representative to UNESCO and the widow of Luis Galán, the former presidential candidate who made a lasting enemy of Escobar by trying to prevent the drug dealer from obtaining a role in Colombia's government as well as by supporting the extradition treaty. He was assassinated by drug traffickers in 1989.

Maruja Pachón de Villamizar

Maruja Pachón de Villamizar is a journalist and the director of FOCINE, the state-run enterprise for the promotion of the film industry, when she is abducted. Like the captives before her, she is kidnapped for political connections; her husband, Alberto Villamizar, is a well-known politician and her sister, Gloria Pachón, is the widow of Luis Galán. The drug traffickers hope that Maruja's kidnapping will put pressure on the government, through Gloria, to accede to their wishes. Maruja remains strong throughout her captivity, refusing to be intimidated by her captors. After Beatriz is released and she remains alone, however, she becomes disheartened, unsure that her husband is doing all he can to win her release and convinced that she will remain hostage for a long time to come. Maruja is released on May 20, after more than six months in captivity.

Rafael Pardo Rueda

Rafael Pardo Rueda is President Gaviria's advisor on security. Under the previous administration, he was in charge of negotiations with the guerrillas and the rehabilitation programs in war zones, and he achieved the peace accords with the M-19 guerrillas. He acts as the mediator between the Colombian government and Maruja and Beatriz's family.

Guido Parra Montoya

Guido Parra Montoya is Escobar's attorney. He was arrested on suspicion of abetting terrorism the year before. He is involved in negotiating the release of the hostages, but he vanishes in February 1990 after overstepping his authority. He is found dead in Medellín three years later.

Nydia Quintero

Nydia Quintero is Diana's mother. She lobbies President Gaviria to change his decree and thus secure the release of the hostages.

Francisco Santos

See Pacho Santos

Dr. Hernando Santos

Hernando Santos is Pacho's father. Along with his close friend Dr. Turbay, he makes early efforts to negotiate with Pablo Escobar and free the hostages.

Pacho Santos

Francisco Santo, nicknamed Pacho, is the editor in chief of the newspaper *El Tiempo*. Pacho is abducted from his car and taken to a house in Bogotá. Unknown to Pacho, he narrowly escapes death in January, when Marina Montoya is killed instead of him. Toward the end of his captivity, Pacho plans a prison breakout, and his failure to do so leads to thoughts of suicide. Pacho is released a few hours after Maruja, on May 20.

Dr. Julio César Turbay

As president of Colombia, Dr. Turbay allowed the extradition to the United States of Colombian nationals for the first time. Along with his close friend Hernando Santos, he makes early efforts to negotiate with Pablo Escobar and free the hostages.

Diana Turbay Quintero

At forty years old, Diana Turbay is a well-known journalist who directs a popular television news show as well as a magazine, both of which she founded. She is also the daughter of former president Julio César Turbay. Diana always held as a central concern the desire to bring peace to her devastated country.

The kidnappers lure Diana with the promise of a meeting with Manuel Pérez, the priest who commands a major guerrilla group. Diana ignored the advice of others and accepted the invitation, most likely because she hoped to open a dialogue on peace between the guerillas and the government. The journal that Diana keeps during her captivity becomes the primary record of this experience; Diana is shot during a police raid on the house in Medellín where she is being held, and she dies soon thereafter.

Alberto Villamizar

Alberto Villamizar, Maruja's husband, is a well-known politician, who counts among his friends President César Gaviria. In 1985, as a representative in the legislature, Villamizar helped pass the first national law against drug trafficking. He also stopped passage of a bill introduced by politicians friendly to Escobar that would have removed legislative support for the extradition treaty. As a result of this action, an assassination attempt was made on him in 1986.

Villamizar aggressively pursues the release of his wife and sister. He urges President Gaviria to alter the decree so that Escobar need not fear extradition. As a last resort, he decides to meet with Escobar himself. Although he is unsuccessful in this effort, Father Herrerros is able to serve as his emissary, and eventually, the men secure the hostages' release and Escobar's surrender.

Beatriz Villamizar de Guerrero

Beatriz Villamizar de Guerrero is Maruja's sister-in-law and press assistant at FOCINE. She is abducted solely because she is with Maruja at the time. She is released on February 8, 1991.

Juan Vitta

Juan Vitta is a writer on Diana Turbay's news team. He sinks into a deep depression during the kidnapping, which leads to a deterioration of his overall health, already compromised because of a prior heart ailment. Because of this, the kidnappers release him on November 26.

Themes

Violence

The violence inherent to Colombian society, made so apparent by *News of a Kidnapping*, has been a long-standing characteristic of the country. A political assassination in 1948 set off a wave of killings between vying parties; it became known simply as "La Violencia." Just as some peace was returning to Colombia, guerrilla groups began to launch their own offensives.

By the 1980s, the drug traffickers were imbuing the country with their own brand of terrorism and violence. In the hands of the drug traffickers, Medellín became one of the most dangerous cities in the world. In the city's first two months of 1991, a massacre took place every four days and about 1,200 murders were committed; of these, almost 500 police officers, upon whom Escobar placed a bounty, were the victims. However, the police also made their contribution to the escalation and randomness of violence. Believing that most of the young men and boys who lived in the Medellín slums were working in the drug industry—there were few other economic options available—police officers engaged in indiscriminate killing. In his attempts to negotiate with the government, Escobar demanded that these actions be brought to an end. National and international human rights organizations protested these human rights abuses as well.

Violence is so commonplace in Colombian society that, in many instances, a violent act draws little attention or reaction. As just one example

among many, when Marina's son goes to Medellín in an unsuccessful attempt to negotiate with Escobar, he notices a girl lying dead by the side of the road. When he points this out to his driver, the man replies without even looking, "One of the dolls who parties with don Pablo's friends."

Terrorism

Colombia of recent decades is rife with terrorism. The guerrilla groups initiated actions, such as the M-19's assault on the Supreme Court, and the drug cartels quickly embrace such strategies as their most effective means for achieving their goals. By 1991, Medellín has become the center of urban terrorism. Journalists, law enforcement officers, politicians—anyone who attempts to thwart the drug traffickers, or even speak against them—can become a ready victim. Oftentimes, the acts of terrorism committed against these targets affect many ordinary Colombians. García Márquez notes that a car bomb set off in February, which killed three low-ranking officers and eight police agents, also killed another nine passers-by and injured 143 others.

The goal of the narcotraffickers in launching the kidnappings is primarily to gain leverage in negotiating with the government and thus avoid extradition. This strategy places a great deal of pressure on the government; García Márquez explains that "after the first bombs, public opinion demanded prison for the terrorists, after the next few bombings the demand was for extradition, but as the bombs continued to explode, public opinion began to demand amnesty."

As President Gaviria continues to withstand the pressure to bargain with Escobar and his cartel leaders, the acts of terrorism escalate. Marina is executed, and more hostages are threatened. When Gaviria eventually agrees to take extradition off the table, García Márquez writes that the president "did not propose negotiations with terrorism in order to conjure away a human tragedy," but rather, "to make extradition a more useful judicial weapon in the fight against narcotraffic by making non-extradition the grand prize in a package of incentives and guarantees for those who surrendered to the law."

It is noteworthy that in the narcotrafficker's drive to pursue this goal, as well as to protect their families and workers, nothing is scared. In March, Escobar threatens to blow up fifty tons of dynamite

Topics for Further Study

- Many reviewers have said that *News of a Kidnapping* is a piece of nonfiction that reads like a novel. Do you agree? Why or why not?

- Find out about the current situation in Colombia. What is the status of the drug trade and what is its relationship to the United States?

- García Márquez, as well as his reviewers, have pointed out economic benefits that the Colombian drug trade brought to the country. Find out more about these economic effects as well as the drug trade's effects on society in general. Analyze the cost benefit of the drug trade for Colombia.

- In the 1980s, both Colombia and the United States declared a War on Drugs. Find out about the American "war" and compare the two.

- García Márquez has played a significant role in the politics and policy of his country. Learn more about the author's sociopolitical activities, particularly those he is currently undertaking.

- Imagine that you were writing a novelization of *News of a Kidnapping*. How would it differ from García Márquez's work? Which characters and events would you focus on? How would you introduce Colombia's history of drug trafficking? Write an outline of the novel.

- Find out more about the extradition treaties that Colombia and the United States have signed in the past. How did most Colombians react to these treaties and why? How did most Americans react to them and why?

---

in one of the country's most historic cities. Dissuaded from doing so, he still maintains, "If police operations in Medellín continued past April, no stone would be left standing in the very ancient and noble city of Cartagena de Indias."

The United States

Although in other media, García Márquez has made public his objections to the extradition policy, in *News of a Kidnapping* he makes few references to the role the United States plays in Colombia's drug wars. However, the northern neighbor's pervasive presence is seen throughout the book—and throughout Colombian society as it is enveloped in the narcoviolence. García Márquez notes the horror that the prospect of being sent to the United States to stand trial and inevitable incarceration evokes in the Extraditables, who are so "terrified by the long, worldwide reach of the United States" that "they went underground, fugitives in their own country." Fear of extradition leads Escobar to order the kidnappings because he hopes they will provide him with bargaining chips. It also contributes to his

death. About to be transferred to another prison, Escobar thinks that the government is actually going to kill him or even turn him over to the United States, so he escapes, leading to the exhaustive manhunt that claims his life.

Style

Narration

García Márquez undertook the project that became *News of a Kidnapping* at the behest of Maruja Pachon de Villamizar, one of the captives, and her husband, the politician Alberto Villamizar, who was instrumental in winning the release of his wife and the surrender of Pablo Escobar. The book originally focused on Maruja's ordeal, but eventually García Márquez decided to include more of the personal remembrances of the other victims as well. Most likely because of this initial focus, García Márquez chooses to open the book with the kidnapping of Maruja and Beatriz, even though these women are the final captives taken by the Extraditables. After exploring their capture, their families' reaction to the news, and their impressions, the narrative delves back several months to chronicle the eight kidnappings that came before it, eventually catching up again to the present, November 1990.

The narration focuses on the victims, describing the conditions the different hostage groups face and their responses to their captivity. It also focuses on their families, showing their efforts to keep up the spirits of the captives. As the captivity lengthens, negotiations become more complex and involve more people—President Gaviria, members of his administration, high-ranking leaders in the Medellín drug cartel, a priest—and the narration carefully explores the relationships between these people and details the actions they take. The narration also includes background about Colombia's drug wars over the past few decades, which is necessary to understanding the significance of the events that García Márquez recounts. The Colombian government faces considerable difficulty and pressure, particularly from the families of the captives, as it attempts to create a workable drug policy that will lead to the capitulation of the drug kingpins.

García Márquez's skill as a writer allows him to mesh all of these complex elements into one cohesive narrative. As Bonnie Smothers writes in *Booklist,* "[H]e tracks the story like a detective, weaving in the voices of all the players, [and] ferreting out the nuances in their relationships."

Audience

News of a Kidnapping was written in García Márquez's native Spanish and then translated into other languages. García Márquez knew that his work would attract foreign readers, most of whom would have little knowledge of the machinations of the Colombian drug wars and the relations between the government and the narcotraffickers. Because his work is directed at this foreign readership, as well as at readers in his own country, who already had a familiarity with the kidnappings, he gives background about the perils of late twentieth-century Colombia. Despite this background information, many readers may have difficulty putting all of the events that García Márquez reports in perspective. In *Commonweal,* Joseph A. Page chastises the American publisher's "failure . . . to provide background information, a simple chronology, or even an index" as "inexcusable."

Reportage

News of a Kidnapping, a piece of reportage, is based on real events and populated with real people. García Márquez draws on interviews, media broadcasts, newspapers, and diaries kept by several of the hostages to produce this account. While his text is imbued with illuminating details about 1990 Colombia as well as about the mindset of the captives, García Márquez maintains the requisite objective tone of the journalist. He makes no judgements about any of the people that figure in the narrative. Instead, he lets the bare facts speak for themselves, as when he writes about Marina being taken from the room she shares with Maruja and Beatriz (and two guards) to her execution, "The fact was brutal and painful, but it was the fact: there was more room with four people instead of five, fewer tensions, more air to breathe."

As an eminent, well-respected Colombian who has played an important role in the country's recent diplomatic and political life, García Márquez also speaks for the Colombian citizenry in *News of a Kidnapping.* He uses the word "we" in relating how Colombians react to the kidnappings, to Escobar, and to the drug war in general. He calls the drug wars "the biblical holocaust that has been consuming Colombia for more than twenty years"; the details that he provides throughout the book seem to prove his assertion.

As with many works of reportage, readers may question whether García Márquez sticks completely to the facts. In an interview with *World Press Review,* García Márquez stated that the book "does not contain a single line of fiction or a single fact that has not been corroborated as far as humanly possible." However, in creating this work, García Márquez, in part, draws upon individual memories of an extremely harrowing period.

Historical Context

The Rise of Drug Trafficking

Narcotics emerged as a major national problem in the late 1970s when Colombia began exporting a great deal of marijuana to the United States. With the profits from marijuana, drug leaders diversified their operations to include cocaine trafficking. Two major drug cartels—Mafia-like organizations—evolved, one in Medellín and the second in Cali. The Medellín cartel was led by Pablo Escobar, Carlos Lehder, and a few other men. Escobar bribed and threatened government officials to ensure their cooperation. He also attempted to get involved in the government himself and was elected to the Congress as a member of the Liberal party.

The Drug War

Violence grew along with the drug trafficking. In 1984, Medellín traffickers assassinated President Belisario Betancur's minister of justice, Rodrigo Lara Bonilla, who had taken an aggressive policy against drug dealers. Betancur invoked his state of siege powers, and extradited thirteen drug dealers to the United States. The Medellín cartel, calling themselves the Extraditables, immediately began a campaign against extradition, which included targeting the treaty's prominent supporters. Drug kingpin Lehder was extradited to the United States in 1987, where he stood trial and received a life sentence plus 135 years. (He was released in 1996.) The Medellín cartel launched an unsuccessful hit on the minister of justice, assassinated the attorney general, kidnapped a candidate for mayor of Bogotá, and bombed a newspaper office, a commercial airliner, and the national police agency.

This narcoterrorism led to an enormous rise in Colombia's murder rate; in 1989, homicide was the leading cause of death in the country. The destructive effects of this violence were perhaps most readily apparent in the 1990 presidential campaign, as three candidates were assassinated, including the poll-leading Luis Carlos Galán. This action led President Virgilio Barco Vargas to declare a War on Drugs, which involved concerted repression of drug dealers. While several leading drug traffickers were arrested or killed, Escobar responded with his own wave of terrorist attacks. Barco also used the weapon of extradition, promising to enforce the new treaty with the United States that would send drug dealers to America to face prosecution and punishment. Barco believed that extradition was an effective resource against drug-related criminal activities.

The End of the Medellín Cartel

César Gaviria Trujillo, elected in 1990, also held a hard-line anti-drug policy, but he believed that extradition should be only one way to fight the war on drugs. Instead, he favored strengthening the Colombian justice and penal system to deal with traffickers nationally. He implemented a policy of plea bargaining, often combined with a reduction of sentences, to win the surrender of drug traffickers. The rewritten constitution of 1991 declared extradition to be unconstitutional, removing the issue from both Colombian politics and the War on Drugs. These efforts led to the surrender of most members of the Medellín cartel, notably Pablo Escobar in 1992. After escaping thirteen months later, in July 1993, Escobar immediately began to carry out internal purges of his organization and launch another terrorist campaign. A special unit tracked down Escobar in December, and shot and killed him, which also brought the end of the Medellín cartel.

The Colombian Economy

One of the reasons that drugs became such big business in Colombia was the troubled economy. Colombia had long been wracked by economic woes. While the discovery in 1985 of a large petroleum reserve was a major boost to the declining economy, the drug trade also provided enormous benefits. The drug industry made annual trade balances positive whereas they were negative for legal goods. Drug dealers put a great deal of money into the construction and the cocaine refining businesses, invested in other businesses, and were a major source of employment. Drug dealers also provided charitable contributions to poor neighborhoods.

During the early 1990s, Colombia entered a new economic order. Gaviria's government lowered tariffs on imports, provided fewer subsidies for the poor, and lessened the government's role in the economy. However, in 1996, inflation rose, gross domestic product declined, and unemployment hit a new high. By 1998, Colombia was in its worst recession since the Great Depression.

Critical Overview

News of a Kidnapping—like any new work by García Márquez—received a great deal of attention when it was first published in Spanish in 1996, and the following year, in English. A welter of reviewers focused their attention on the myriad aspects of the book: its style, the events it depicted, the state of affairs in Colombia, the drug wars. While this book was a marked departure from the magical realism that characterizes García Márquez's fiction, few reviewers found this to be cause for complaint. The dramatic events that García Márquez has to work with easily provided what John Bemrose called in *Maclean's*, ''thrillerlike momentum.'' Indeed, as Michiko Kakutani pointed out in *The Houston Chronicle*, García Márquez ''uses his novelist's instinct for emotional drama to give the reader a wonderfully immediate sense of his subjects' ordeal: their spiraling hopes and fears, their fantasies of escape, their desperation and despair.'' She was not alone in comparing this book to García Márquez's ''most powerful fiction.'' R. Z. Sheppard's commentary in *Time* that *News of a Kidnapping* ''brings together the world's two best-known Colombians, symbolically locked in a struggle for their nation's soul''—García Márquez and Pablo Escobar— illustrates the inherent narrative power of this non-fiction story.

García Márquez started out his career as a journalist, winning important prizes in that field, and reviewers noted that his skill had not lapsed. Wrote Sheppard, ''One can almost hear García Márquez asking, Who? What? Where? When? and Why? on every minutely detailed page.'' Page also pointed out that the ''terse'' style of the book ''reflects a conscious choice to let the hostages tell their own stories without impressing upon them the stamp of García Márquez's imagination.''

Reviewers, however, also noted that the fantastic elements of the crime, and the drug wars in general, brought the book closer to García Márquez's magical realism. Colombia presents a world hardly imaginable for most American readers, a world where law enforcement officers, Congressional representatives, and journalists are gunned down at the will of criminals. As Robert Stone challenged readers of the *New York Times Book Review*, ''[L]et us imagine that we have a President who carries five bullets in his body as the result of an assassination attempt by drug traffickers. Let us imagine that Lady Bird Johnson and Amy Carter have both spent time in the hands of kidnappers.'' As Kakutani pointed out, books like *News of a Kidnapping* remind the reader that the ''magical realism employed by García Márquez and other Latin American novelists is in part a narrative strategy for grappling with a social reality so hallucinatory, so irrational, that it defies ordinary naturalistic description.''

Pablo Escobar

Criticism

Rena Korb

Korb has a master's degree in English literature and creative writing and has written for a wide variety of educational publishers. In the following essay, she explores the surrealistic aspects of Colombia in 1990.

To many North American readers, the world described so starkly in García Márquez's *News of a Kidnapping* is a world hardly fathomable. Upon its publication, numerous reviewers pointed out that the fantastical story could have been drawn from the pages of one of García Márquez's magical realist novels. However, as García Márquez has stated on several occasions, every event in the book represents the truth as best the former journalist could uncover it—testament to the sad fact that in 1990, what North America found to be surreal and shocking, Colombia perceived as quite ordinary. To García Márquez, and to countless of his fellow countrypeople, the assault on the journalists is merely ''one episode in the biblical holocaust that has been consuming Colombia for more than 20 years.'' His statement should really come as little surprise to

What Do I Read Next?

- García Márquez's novella *Chronicle of a Death Foretold* (1981), originally begun as a piece of journalism, is based on a historical incident in which a group of brothers vow to murder the man who ruined their sister's honor. García Márquez won the Nobel Prize for Literature for this work.

- Max Mermelstein married a Colombian and soon found himself enmeshed in the world's most powerful drug cartels. In *Inside the Cocaine Cartel: The Riveting Eyewitness Account of Life inside the Colombian Cartel* (1993), Mermelstein, a star witness against Pablo Escobar, recounts his involvement with the cocaine traffickers, including his eventual betrayal of them.

- *The Art of Fact: A Historical Anthology of Literary Journalism* (1998), edited by Kevin Kerrane and Ben Yagoda, collects some sixty selections of literary journalism written by authors from different countries and in different time periods.

- *The Heart That Bleeds: Latin America Now* (1995) is a collection of Alma Guillermoprieto's essays that originally appeared in *The New Yorker*. Her essays explore Latin America in the early 1990s, including the effects of the Medellín and Cali cartels on Colombia's economy and political culture.

- García Márquez won international celebrity in 1967 with publication of *One Hundred Years of Solitude*. This novel, steeped in the magical realism tradition, is an epic tale of the Buendía family as well as the turbulence that characterizes Latin America, from the postcolonial 1820s to the 1920s.

- Franz Kafka's *The Metamorphosis* (1915) tells the story of Gregor Samsa, who one day awakens to discover that he has turned into a gigantic insect. García Márquez claims this novel as one of his literary inspirations.

---

readers who have any knowledge of modern Colombia, for the country itself, as Olga Lorenzo puts it in *Quadrant,* is "a place where . . . all civil institutions and even civility itself have largely failed."

The perverse history of contemporary Colombia is made manifest in the book's opening pages. After her abduction, Maruja tries to find out exactly which group has taken her; the ensuing exchange between captive and captors succinctly reveals the perverse nature of Colombian society. To her query, "'Who are you people?'" one of the men replies that they are from the M-19, which she instantly recognizes as a "nonsensical reply" since this former guerrilla group has been rehabilitated. Only five years previous, a commando unit from the M-19 had taken the Supreme Court building hostage, leading to a bloody ten-day battle between the guerrillas and the Colombian army, a battle which claimed the lives of some one hundred people,

including half of the Supreme Court Judges. Yet, as a result of peace accords, by the time of Maruja's kidnapping, the M-19 has been legalized and takes an active part in Colombia's political life, even "campaigning for seats in the Constituent Assembly." The group that once was one of the Colombian government's most fierce enemies now is potentially responsible for rewriting the country's constitution.

Maruja's response to the man's reply is equally telling: "'Seriously. . . . Are you dealers or guerrillas?'" In her casual reference to these groups, both of whom have plunged Colombia into serious violence and waves of terrorism that continue to claim the lives of thousands, Maruja demonstrates the sangfroid that Colombians have been forced to adopt. This is the same variety of composure that is seen in Hernando Santos as his nephew tells him that he has to relate some "very bad news." When Hernando discovers that Pacho has been kidnapped he ''breathed a sigh of relief,'' declaring, '''Thank God.''' These two reactions to news of a kidnapping aptly demonstrate, as Lorenzo points out, how Colombians ''live with a constant, primitive fear on the one hand, yet on the other an almost complacent acceptance of violence.''

Pacho's kidnapping is equally revealing, beginning with his abduction from his car, which looks like an ''ordinary red Jeep'' but actually has been bulletproofed, subtly reinforcing the fact that in Colombia, nothing is what it seems to be. García Márquez's narrative also makes it clear how unreal is Colombia's present situation. As soon as Pacho is deposited in an empty room in the safehouse, he ''realized that his abductors had been in a hurry not only for reasons of security but in order to get back in time for the soccer game between Santafé and Caldas.'' However, the abductors want ''to keep everybody happy''; they give Pacho a bottle of liquor and leave him with a radio so he, too, can follow the game.

Unfortunately, their plan does not succeed, for Pacho, a devoted Santafé fan, gets so angry with the tie score that he cannot even enjoy the liquor. This paragraph is a surreal masterpiece. Each sentence presents an utterly ludicrous proposition, but the one that builds upon it is even more so. The paragraph's culminating lines, however, bring the narrative back down to earth and remind Pacho, along with the reader, of the danger inherent to the situation: ''When it [the game] was over, he saw himself on the nine-thirty news on file footage, wearing a dinner jacket and surrounded by beauty queens. That was when he learned his driver was dead.''

Throughout *News of a Kidnapping*, the media plays a powerful role, contributing to the overall absurdism that sometimes overtakes the menacing situation. For example, it provides fodder for even more bizarre incidents at the different safehouses. The newspaper reports on Pacho's kidnapping are ''so inaccurate and fanciful they made his captors double over with laughter.'' Meanwhile, Maruja's guards' reactions to a family television program celebrating her birthday are even more astonishing; they express their hope that ''Maruja would introduce them to her daughters so they could take them out.''

The media's dissemination of information between the captives and their families also verges on the surreal. After a frantic call from one of Maruja's captors about the medicine she needs to take for her circulation problems, a ''mysterious announcement

> **In this world, the bizarre becomes commonplace, the absurd becomes real, and one of the deadliest men alive can also be a man of honor.''**

appeared at the bottom of the screen during the sports segment of a television newscast: 'Take Basotón.''' In keeping with the lack of reality, ''the spelling was changed''—the medicine is really Vasotón—''to keep an uninformed laboratory from protesting the use of its product for mysterious purposes.'' Overall, however, the media fails to fulfill its supposed role of broadcasting truthful information, and this may stem from the fact that the media blitz about the kidnappings resembles entertainment rather than reportage. This inadequacy is perhaps nowhere so succinctly expressed as in a special correspondent's question to a sports editor upon learning that the last two hostages will be released: '''What do you think of the news?'''

Of all the hostages, Pacho, the journalist, maintains the closest relationship to the media and follows current news sources. However, his ties to the media take on an uncanny aura. His family uses the editorial pages of *El Tiempo* to publish personal notes to communicate with him. Toward the end of his captivity, depressed at his failure to escape, Pacho determines to take his own life. The next day, he reads a newspaper editorial in *El Tiempo,* ordering Pacho ''in the name of God not to even consider suicide.'' Later, Hernando Santos tells his son that the editorial had actually been on his desk for three weeks, but ''without really knowing why he had been unable to decide if he should publish it, and on the previous day—again without knowing why—he resolved at the last minute to use it.'' Ironically, the guard who had the job of bringing Pacho the newspaper each day had a ''visceral hatred of journalists''; in a sense, his anger represents the abductors' failed attempts to isolate their hostage.

Escobar himself is the most potent symbol of the surrealism of Colombian society. One of Escobar's haciendas near Medellín is something of a private playground with a zoo populated by ''giraffes and hippos brought over from Africa.'' At its entrance, Escobar displays, "as if it were a small monument, the small plane used to export the first shipment of cocaine." More tellingly, however, is the way the Colombian citizenry reacts to the kingpins, particularly Escobar. As García Márquez writes, "Years earlier the drug traffickers had been popular because of their mythic aura. . . . If anyone had wanted them arrested, he could have told the policeman on the corner where to find them." In his hometown, Escobar is seen as a modern-day Robin Hood for his charitable works in the barrios. "At the height of his splendor, people put up altars with his pictures and lit candles to him in the slums of Medellín," García Márquez tells readers. "It was believed he could perform miracles." More privileged Colombians, such as the politicians, businesspeople, and journalists, are similarly taken in by the Escobar charisma and power. After meeting the drug kingpin, even Father García Herreros declares, "Escobar is a good man."

Further, the methods that Escobar, a "legend who controlled everything from the shadows," employs to throw the police off his tracks mirror the utter lack of reality and openness in Colombia; "He had employees who spent the day engaging in lunatic conversations on his telephones so that the people monitoring his lines would become entangled in mangrove forests of non sequiturs and not be able to distinguish them from the real messages." While García Márquez is simply reporting the facts, he also is making important narrative choices. By using words such as *lunatic* and *non sequiturs* and emphasizing that "real messages" are actually being conveyed, García Márquez heightens the absurdism inherent to Escobar and his society. Escobar delivers one such "real message" to Villamizar in person: "If any of you feels unsafe, if anybody tries to give you a hard time, you let me know and that'll be the end of it." In this world, the bizarre becomes commonplace, the absurd becomes real, and one of the deadliest men alive can also be a man of honor.

Toward the end of the book, Villamizar visits the Ochoa brothers in prison; their entire families are present and the wives "acted as hostesses with the exemplary hospitality of the Medellinese." Villamizar and the three brothers work together in order to devise a plan to get Escobar to agree to a meeting. This collaboration between the politician who prevented the extradition treaty from being blocked by law and three leaders of the Medellín cartel lends a final note to the surrealist atmosphere of Colombia in 1990.

Source: Rena Korb, Critical Essay on *News of a Kidnapping,* in *Nonfiction Classics for Students,* The Gale Group, 2002.

David Remy

Remy is a freelance writer who has written extensively on Latin American art and literature. In the following essay, he examines García Márquez's use of fictional narrative techniques.

Like *The Story of a Shipwrecked Sailor* (1986), a piece of journalism that was later adapted into book form, *News of a Kidnapping* (1997) chronicles actual events that, at first glance, may read as fiction. The book examines a turbulent period in Colombia's history, one that presaged an even more violent time to come. According to García Márquez, he wrote this book so that the "gruesome drama" of the kidnappings would not "sink into oblivion." One of the reasons why *News of a Kidnapping* succeeds as both reportage and literature is García Márquez's use of fictional devices and techniques to reveal, in poignant and memorable detail, the lives of ten individuals held hostage.

In 1990, barely three weeks after César Gaviria took office as Colombia's president, a series of kidnappings occurred that directly challenged his authority and focused the attention of a nation already divided by civil war. The Extraditables, a group of narcotraffickers led by Pablo Escobar, head of the Medellín cartel, abducted various members of the media to guarantee that they would not, as their name indicates, be extradited to the United States, where an effective and unyielding judicial system awaited them. "We prefer a grave in Colombia to a cell in the United States," was their rallying cry. As García Márquez points out with irony, the only choice the drug traffickers had to save themselves was to place themselves in the custody of the state. Before Escobar and the Extraditables are willing to capitulate, however, they engage in "indiscriminate, merciless terrorism" to force the government's position.

To tell the story of such a campaign and the effect it had upon Colombian politics and society required a narrative framework that would accommodate many points of view. García Márquez describes how he solved this problem in the book's Acknowledgments. Upon realizing that the kidnappings "were not, in fact, ten distinct abductions—as it had seemed at first—but a collective abduction of ten carefully chosen individuals, which had been carried out by the same group and for only one purpose," he revised the book's structure. Had García Márquez written solely about the abduction of Maruja Pachón and the attempts of her husband, Alberto Villamizar, to negotiate her release, the narrative would have become, in the author's words, "confused and interminable." The book's narrative structure would have been insufficient for a story of such wide scope.

By narrating events from the perspectives of several characters, a technique he has used often in his fictional writings, García Márquez offers a panoramic view of the crisis and the people it involved. The author also imbues *News of a Kidnapping* with a sense of humanity that makes it easy for the reader to identify with the plight of the hostages. This narrative approach renders the ambiguity and the complexity of their ordeal with a degree of verisimilitude greater than mere journalism could afford.

García Márquez opens the book *in medias res* (in the middle of things) by describing the abduction of Maruja and her sister-in-law, Beatriz. This creates a sense of immediacy that serves to make the abduction more indelible in the reader's mind. Knowing that Maruja and Beatriz were the last of the journalists to be abducted, the reader begins to wonder about the eight previous kidnappings and how they were orchestrated. García Márquez sows the seeds of speculation in the reader's mind and thus brings into play an essential ingredient in the act of storytelling: the reader's imagination. Had he told the story of Maruja and Beatriz's abduction in the past tense, the event would not have been rendered as vividly and, consequently, the narration of the other eight kidnappings would not have unfolded with as profound a sense of anticipation on the part of the reader.

García Márquez then describes the abduction of Diana Turbay, the director of the television news program *Criptón,* and her film crew. The reader is now aware of how the first and last kidnappings occurred. There is a unifying thread to these abductions, and it is through the use of flashback that García Márquez is best able to reveal Escobar's motive. Furthermore, the use of flashback adds more depth to Maruja's story, which is told in present-time and serves as the central focus of the book. By narrating events out of chronological order, García Márquez establishes a dramatic tension within the book that fosters the reader's understanding of Colombian society and politics. Every abduction since the first, that of Diana Turbay and her crew, builds upon the one preceding it, intensifying the drama and suspense. Not until the reader

> " García Márquez sows the seeds of speculation in the reader's mind and thus brings into play an essential ingredient in the act of storytelling: the reader's imagination."

comprehends the final kidnapping in the context of the previous ones can García Márquez begin to explore in depth the Extraditables' demands for amnesty.

Though *News of a Kidnapping* is written in an unadorned, journalistic style—the sentences tend to be declarative, and there is a marked absence of simile and metaphor otherwise found in García Márquez's novels and short stories—it is not without symbolic power. The author uses symbols sparingly but to great effect in recreating the hostages' experience of captivity. He also uses symbols to reveal traits that are essential for understanding character.

In describing the room in which the three women are held captive, García Márquez selects a few details to create an atmosphere of disorientation. Outside there is the sound of heavy automobile traffic. The women believe they are near a café, for they hear the sound of music very late at night. Occasionally, a loudspeaker announces religious meetings. They hear the sound of small planes landing and taking off, yet the women have no idea where they are. Marina Montoya, the older woman who shares a room with Maruja and Beatriz, espouses theories about what will happen next, arousing fear in her companions. Captivity has heightened the women's senses to the point where they have difficulty distinguishing between truth and fantasy. "At night the silence was total, interrupted only by a demented rooster with no sense of time who crowed whenever he felt like it," García Márquez informs the reader. The women's isolation is complete, for not even the laws of Nature can abide under these conditions.

As their period of captivity lengthens, the women cannot be sure if they are being held in the country or in the city. Once again, García Márquez introduces the rooster as a symbol of disorientation. However, the rooster's crowing at all hours of the day and night also provides a clue about the women's location, "since roosters kept on high floors tend to lose their sense of time."

Another hostage, Francisco "Pacho" Santos, the editor-in-chief of *El Tiempo,* experiences a similar phenomenon.

> A disorienting detail was the demented rooster that at first crowed at any hour, and as the months passed crowed at the same hour in different places: sometimes far away at three in the afternoon, other times next to his window at two in the morning.

The rooster is again described as "demented," thus emphasizing the absence of reason in a world riddled with doubt and fear, only now its crowing possesses a ubiquitous quality previously nonexistent. The rooster can be heard both near and far away. Pacho eventually compounds his despair by attempting to use the rooster's crowing to gauge his position in both time and space. "It would have been even more disorienting if he had known that Maruja and Beatriz also heard it in a distant section of the city," adds García Márquez.

Cock-crow, a symbol for the hour of judgment, is heard often and at various times throughout the day instead of only at dawn. The hostages speculate as to when they will be released—or, what is perhaps foremost in their thoughts: when they will be executed—and the symbolic crowing of a rooster emphasizes the uncertainty and anxiety they experience. The cock crows at random and, in light of Escobar's actions, the release or the deaths of the hostages seems equally as arbitrary. García Márquez sums up this experience by telling the reader that, prior to his release, Pacho spent a sleepless night tormented by the "mad rooster—madder and closer than ever—and not knowing for certain where reality lay."

In addition to using symbol to create an atmosphere of disorientation among the hostages and to reflect their inner states of mind, García Márquez uses symbol to delineate specific character traits. Father García Herreros, a priest and the host of a television program entitled *God's Minute,* serves as an intermediary between Villamizar, who acts unofficially on behalf of the government, and Pablo Escobar so that negotiations for the release of the hostages may continue. His presence helps Escobar overcome his reluctance in dealing with Villamizar, and it also makes it easier for Escobar's men, many

of whom are devoutly religious, to turn themselves in once an agreement has been reached.

Father Herreros is a man of many contrasts. García Márquez describes him as an ascetic who "ate little, though he liked good food and appreciated fine wines, but would not accept invitations to expensive restaurants for fear people would think he was paying." He is an honest, trustworthy man, if slightly misguided by his good intentions. García Márquez draws attention to the fact that Father Herreros wears contact lenses to improve his vision, and that he must have his assistant, Paulina, assist him with putting them in and taking them out, for he has never learned to do so himself.

Many obstacles must be overcome before the remaining hostages are set free, as Escobar's demands change constantly, but throughout the negotiations there is the fear on the part of Villamizar and others that Father Herreros, with his reputation for erratic behavior, will prove a liability and cause the negotiations to end abruptly. This fear proves unfounded, however, for he succeeds in meeting with Escobar and, together, the two men compose a document stating the conditions for the drug lord's surrender. As the priest prepares to leave Escobar's compound, complete with giraffes and hippos wandering about the grounds, one of his contacts falls out. He tries to put it back in but cannot. Escobar, ever the gracious host, offers to have Paulina brought to help him, but the priest refuses. Before he leaves the compound, Father Herreros, his lens not yet restored, says a blessing for Escobar's men.

García Márquez notes the priest's contact lenses in order to underscore his naïveté and lack of foresight in dealing with the narcotraffickers. At a press conference announcing the terms of Escobar's surrender, Father Herreros describes the drug lord as "the great architect of peace." He goes on to say that, despite circumstances, "Escobar is a good man." How could the priest have forgotten Escobar's violent past? Rather than condemn Father Herreros for his error in judgment, García Márquez focuses instead on Escobar: "No Colombian in history ever possessed or exercised a talent like his for shaping public opinion. And none had a greater power to corrupt."

García Márquez's use of fictional narrative techniques in *News of a Kidnapping* affords him greater freedom to tell the story of "one episode in the biblical holocaust that has been consuming Colombia for more than twenty years." By telling the story from the perspectives of several kidnap victims, García Márquez unifies their experience at the same time he offers the reader a broad panorama of the complex personalities and events that make this drama not only an engaging work of journalism but a landmark of literature as well.

Source: David Remy, Critical Essay on *News of a Kidnapping,* in *Nonfiction Classics for Students,* The Gale Group, 2002.

Josh Ozersky

Ozersky is a critic and essayist. In this essay, he discusses García Márquez's literary art, and how it is hidden beneath the surface of his novel.

García Márquez is one of the most famous writers in the world, but not for books like *News of a Kidnapping*. García Márquez, who received the Nobel Prize in 1983 and whose novels are read in nearly every language, is associated with a surreal style called "magical realism." *News of a Kidnapping*, on the other hand, seems to be journalism of the starkest kind. Ten people are kidnapped by soldiers of Pablo Escobar's drug cartel. They are prominent people drawn from the very upper crust of Colombian society. One is the daughter of a former President; another is a famous former soap-opera actress with high political family connections; others are prominent journalists. They are kept under armed guard for six months, and there is every reason to think they will be killed. Eventually, all are released and survive, except for two. García Márquez describes their ordeal, and that of their friends and families, in a book that joins Norman Mailer's *The Executioner's Song* and Truman Capote's *In Cold Blood* on the short shelf of masterpieces that define crime journalism and the novelist's art.

But *News of a Kidnapping* is not merely a journalistic account of some kidnappings; it is a novel (of sorts), and one not as far removed from the author's trademark "magic realism" as it might seem. Because García Márquez was originally a journalist, and has spent much of his adult life in the journalistic world, he knows a lot about how news is written. As a result, *News of a Kidnapping* is written with a very level, factual-sounding tone that suggests the most orderly and observant kind of reporting. Even the title suggests journalism.

In fact, the book is written with an artfulness that conceals as much as it tells. For example, García Márquez tells us in his introduction that the book's genesis came in 1993, when "Maruja Pachon and her husband, Alberto Villamizar, suggested I write a book about her abduction and six-month

> *News of a Kidnapping* is a masterpiece; but a masterpiece closer to fiction than to reportage."

captivity, and his persistent efforts to win her release." García Márquez tells us that he realized immediately that the story could not be told without also telling the story of the other nine people who were kidnapped simultaneously by Escobar's forces, for the purpose of persuading the government not to extradite them to the United States. Pachon and Villamizar, though, would be "the central axis, the unifying thread, of this book."

What do we learn from reading this introduction? Because García Márquez is so skilled a writer, it behooves a reader to pay close attention to what he or she is being told. The book is gripping, and it's easy to get lost in the story. But consider that first sentence of the introduction: "In October 1993, Maruja Pachon and her husband, Alberto Villamizar, suggested I write a book." There are several facts, just below the surface, that readers would do well to bear in mind as they read. (There will be others later; and other facts readers won't be told.)

One fact readers can gather if they look closely lie in the couple's names. While it is fairly common in America for wives to keep their names, it is far less so in a Roman Catholic country like Columbia. And in fact, nearly all of the major characters in *News of a Kidnapping* are elite professionals, members of a wealthy class at the very topmost level of Colombian society. Readers hear of the "ghetto boys" who guard the hostages, and war against the police, but hear very little else about them, such as why they are so willing to die for Escobar, or why the police kill them indiscriminately in the Medellín ghettos.

This is not to say that *News of a Kidnapping* is somehow flawed because it is not a sociological treatise on all levels of Colombian society. On the contrary, as an artist, García Márquez isn't obliged to tell us anything he does not think will further his purposes. But insofar as *News of a Kidnapping* presents itself as more-or-less transparent journalism, readers are obliged to think about what they aren't reading.

Beyond his choice of subjects, García Márquez displays supreme literary craftsmanship in his mastery of time and space. Many of his greatest novels, including his masterpiece *One Hundred Years of Solitude*, follow many characters over long periods of time. *News of a Kidnapping* would seem to be an exception, but actually the cross-cutting, multiple perspectives, and meticulous editing would do great credit to movie directors Stephen Spielberg or Martin Scorsese. Readers hardly notice at times as they move from one hostage cell to another, and thence to the office of President Gaviria, and from there to the shadowy settings in which Pablo Escobar moves.

García Márquez also has the novelist's gift for finding the perfect detail, and weaving it into his story. Marina Montoya, the former actress, even under the severest physical and psychological distress, takes care to keep her nails trimmed and painted. It's a poignant and revealing detail, and it makes this woman more real to us, rather than just a "damsel in distress" or faceless victim. When Marina is summoned to what she knows is her imminent murder, she takes special care to make up her face and do her nails. When her body is found, it is unrecognizable at first, because her killers have shot her through the face; but she is eventually identified by her beautiful nails. This is a heart-rending detail, and it simultaneously gives readers an emotional purchase on Marina's death, as well as giving the story the ring of truth. And it is easy to overlook the groundwork that García Márquez has done earlier in the book, preparing us for this moment with his numerous references to Marina and her manicures. As García Márquez told a journalism seminar in 1996, "one must keep the reader hypnotized by tending to every detail, every word. . . . It is a continuous act where you poison the reader with credibility and with rhythm."

As a result of this kind of literary art, readers feel that by the time they are done reading the book they have gained a deep and varied understanding of the complexion of Colombia. They have been high and low, inside the minds of men and women, young people and old, and felt the tension of so many different desperate interests clashing over the fates of the hostages. The upshot is that readers walk away from *News of a Kidnapping* feeling that what they have read represents not just the truth about Colombia, but beyond that some kind of universal human truth. The author, after all, is a great novelist, and has done his level best not to present the kidnappings as a melodrama. The book is dedicated to "all Colombians, guilty and innocent."

It is here where readers would do well to bear in mind the technique of magic realism. With magic realism, supernatural events are thought of as normal—the appearance of an angel, say, or a man levitating off the ground—and treated in precisely the same detailed, matter-of-fact tone that is used in *News of a Kidnapping*. Magic realism isn't effective because amazing things happen; it's effective because those things are woven seamlessly into the texture of everyday life. When people read of two defenseless women being abducted, or of armed captors having a party for their hostages, and even becoming close to them, in one way it seems unimaginable, surreal; but García Márquez never lets any event become *too* amazing.

One side effect of this style, however, is a certain flattening. Because everything is described in such a concrete, detailed, and prosaic way, we tend to lose sight of everything beyond the frame of what readers are being shown and told. García Márquez means for this to happen; but that doesn't necessarily mean that readers need to be unaware of it. *News of a Kidnapping* is a masterpiece; but a masterpiece closer to fiction than to reportage.

Source: Josh Ozersky, Critical Essay on *News of a Kidnapping,* in *Nonfiction Classics for Students,* The Gale Group, 2002.

Sources

Bemrose, John, Review, in *Maclean's,* Vol. 110, No. 35, September 1, 1997, p. 56.

Cato, Susana, "Mirroring Colombia's Drug Terror," in *World Press Review,* Vol. 43, No. 8, August 1996, p. 44.

Kakutani, Michiko, "Fantastic Voyage," in *Houston Chronicle,* June 26, 1997.

Lorenzo, Olga, Review, in *Quadrant,* Vol. 41, No. 11, November 1997, p. 82.

Page, Joseph A., Review, in *Commonweal,* Vol. 124, No. 16, September 26, 1997, p. 20.

Sheppard, R. Z., Review, in *Time,* Vol. 149, No. 22, June 2, 1997, p. 77.

Smothers, Bonnie, Review, in *Booklist,* Vol. 93, No. 17, May 1, 1997, p. 1458.

Stone, Robert, "The Autumn of the Drug Lord," in *New York Times Book Review,* June 15, 1997.

Further Reading

Anderson, Jon Lee, "The Power of Gabriel García Márquez," in *New Yorker,* September 27, 1999.

> This profile of García Márquez discusses the author's role in helping bring peace to Colombia.

Bergquist, Charles, Ricardo Peñaranda, and Gonzalo Sánchez, eds., *Violence in Colombia 1990–2000: Waging War and Negotiating Peace,* Scholarly Resources, 1992.

> This book presents some of the best recent work by Colombian scholars on the continuing crisis of violence that has been plaguing the nation for the past decade. This collection also includes primary documents and testimony from such crucial eyewitnesses as government members, guerrillas, kidnap victims, and human rights lawyers.

Bowden, Mark, *Killing Pablo: The Hunt for the World's Greatest Outlaw,* Atlantic Monthly Press, 2001.

> Bowden chronicles the rise and fall of the world's first narcobillionaire, tracing the prevalence of violence in Colombian history, the manhunt for Escobar, and the role that the United States played in bringing down the drug kingpin.

Bushnell, David, *The Making of Modern Colombia: A Nation in Spite of Itself,* University of California Press, 1993.

> In the first history of Colombia written in English, Bushnell traces the process of Colombia from its struggle for independence through the 1990s.

Leonard, John, "'News of a Kidnapping,'" in *Nation,* Vol. 264, No. 23, June 16, 1997, p. 23.

> This book review provides a good overview of the issues that García Márquez's book raises.

Solanet, Mariana, *García Márquez for Beginners,* Writers & Readers, 1999.

> Solanet introduces readers to the life and work of this acclaimed author.

Operating Instructions

Anne Lamott

1993

Anne Lamott's *Operating Instructions: A Journal of My Son's First Year* was published in 1993. This work chronicles the first year that Lamott, a single mother, and her newborn son, Sam, spend together. Lamott records her thoughts about her unplanned pregnancy, the birth of her child, and the numerous and often challenging responsibilities of parenthood.

Operating Instructions also focuses on baby Sam's development, detailing his numerous achievements during his first year. Lamott explores her relationship with her child as deeply as she does her relationships with her friends (whom she now relies on more than ever) and her relationship with herself. She writes about the adventure of motherhood without losing a sense of herself as a unique individual, and without losing her unique sense of humor.

Author Biography

Anne Lamott was born in San Francisco, California, in 1954, the daughter of the writer Kenneth Lamott. She grew up in Marin County, north of San Francisco. At seventeen, she attended Goucher College in Maryland on a tennis scholarship, where she wrote for the school paper. However, she dropped out after two years and returned to the Bay Area, where she briefly worked for a magazine called *WomenSports*.

Lamott always knew that she wanted to write, and after moving to Bolinas, in Marin, she began to work on vignettes and stories. The discovery that her father was dying of brain cancer inspired her to organize these short pieces into her first novel, *Hard Laughter*, published in 1980 when Lamott was only twenty-six years old. Her next book, *Rosie*, came out three years later.

Lamott had been experiencing alcohol and drug problems, and in the mid-1980s, she quit using these substances, went into rehabilitation, and did not write for six months. When she returned to her craft, she produced the novel, *All New People*, whose publication she refers to in *Operating Instructions*.

With the birth of her son, Sam, in 1989, Lamott became a single mother. Although she had less time to write, Lamott's friends urged her to jot down notes about her daily life and her agent asked to see them. These notes eventually became *Operating Instructions*, published in 1993, which covered the first year of her life with Sam. The book's publication brought Lamott to national prominence.

Since then, Lamott has published both fiction and nonfiction writing. *Bird by Bird: Some Instructions on Writing and Life* came out in 1994. This popular book provides a step-by-step guide on how to write and manage the writer's life. In 1999, Lamott published *Traveling Mercies: Some Thoughts on Faith*, which is a collection of her thoughts about her religious faith.

In addition to her novels and nonfiction books, Lamott was a restaurant critic for *California* magazine from 1988 through 1991 and wrote a book review column for *Mademoiselle* from 1990 through 1992. Until 1999, she regularly published her diary in the online magazine *Salon*. A former teacher at the University of California, she is also the past recipient of a Guggenheim fellowship.

Anne Lamott

Plot Summary

Pregnancy and Birth

Operating Instructions: A Journal of My Son's First Year begins during Lamott's pregnancy. An unmarried, thirty-five year old writer, Lamott decides to keep the baby and raise it herself when the biological father makes it clear that he will not take part in the child's life. In the months preceding Sam's birth, Lamott faces her feelings of loneliness, as well as her joys and her fears.

1989

Sam is born on September 7, 1989. Lamott's best friend Pammy and her brother Steve are in the delivery room with Lamott. When Lamott holds Sam for the first time, she immediately becomes enraptured with her baby.

During the first month of Sam's life, Lamott is exhausted. Sometimes she feels so stressed that she needs to leave the room to get away from Sam. Throughout the long days and nights, Lamott records Sam's accomplishments: crying, losing his hair, smiling, laughing, sleeping through the night, and being introduced to her church. One highlight is Sam's baptism, which takes place when he is nearly two months old. One of Lamott's novels is published during this period.

1990

By January, Lamott notes that Sam is changing every day. She also notices changes in herself. She feels that it is easier to take care of Sam, and she also finds herself less worried. However, her journal entries show the variability of her moods. For example, just five days after writing an optimistic entry about how much easier it is to take care of Sam, she writes, ''I'm mental and defeated and fat and loathsome and I am crazily, brain-wastedly tired. . . . This is maybe the loneliest I have ever felt.''

Lamott also feels a great deal of financial pressure as her savings dwindle precariously. However, she is confident that God will come through for her, and toward the end of January, Lamott's miracle comes when she is hired to be the monthly book columnist at *Mademoiselle* magazine.

Pammy

In April, immediately after returning from a month-long vacation, Pammy discovers a lump in her breast. She is diagnosed with an aggressive cancer. Early in May, Pammy starts chemotherapy, and although Lamott writes that this first round goes well, Pammy becomes very nauseated and tired. In August, the doctor tells Pammy that her cancer cannot be cured. Lamott is devastated by this news, but her journal entries show that she is gradually coming to an acceptance of Pammy's inevitable death.

Sam's First Birthday

Less than a week before his first birthday, Sam takes his first steps. On August 29, Lamott, Sam, Dudu, Rex, and Steve have a small birthday party; a larger one is planned for the weekend. On this day, Lamott reflects on the past year and Sam's birth, as well as thinking about what the future will bring and what kind of person Sam will grow up to become. In an after-note, Lamott reports Pammy's death two years later, in November 1992.

Key Figures

Biological Father

Sam's biological father, whom Lamott does not name, takes no role in Sam's life. When Lamott first told him she was pregnant, he tried to convince her not to have the baby. When Sam is a few months old, he files court papers falsely swearing that he could not be the baby's father.

Brian

Brian, the husband of Lamott's friend, volunteers to be Sam's Big Brother.

Dudu

Dudu is Sam's surrogate grandmother. She and her husband Rex were Lamott's parents' best friends, and they have been part of Lamott's life since childhood. Along with Lamott's mother, Dudu visits often, and Lamott thinks the two older women compete for Sam's affection.

Anne Lamott

Lamott, a writer, becomes pregnant when she is 35. She is unmarried, the pregnancy is unplanned, and the biological father wants no part of the baby's life. Still, Lamott quickly decides to keep the baby.

Lamott's personality contains seemingly conflicting elements. She is liberal but religiously faithful; she is irreverent but sentimental; and she is prone to mood swings. Lamott has published two novels and a third appears shortly after Sam's birth. The time and energy required to care for a baby by herself, however, renders Lamott unable to write anything except the reviews by which she makes her living and the journal that she publishes as *Operating Instructions*.

The entries in her journal reveal that Lamott undergoes the feelings and experiences that are common among new mothers: she feels fat; she finds her baby unbelievably beautiful and smart; she gets frustrated and wonders why she ever had a child; and she wishes she had a moment to herself. However, the first year of Sam's life also brings atypical circumstances. Specifically, her best friend Pammy is diagnosed with terminal cancer, and Lamott struggles to reconcile her joyful feelings and her sorrowful ones.

Sam Lamott

Sam is Lamott's son. In his first year of life, he reaches typical baby milestones: crawling, walking, laughing, smiling, grabbing objects, and other activities. He brings great joy to Lamott's family and friends.

Steve Lamott

Steve is Lamott's brother. He is present at Sam's birth. Although he remains an active presence in Sam's life, he is adamant about not allowing Lamott to make him a father figure.

John Manning

Manning is Sam's father's best friend, but he supports Lamott in her decision to have the baby. He remains a constant friend to the two of them. He is also the person who convinced her to jot down a few notes and observations each day of Sam's first year.

Megan

Megan, a former student in one of Lamott's writing workshops, is Sam's twenty-year-old babysitter. Lamott often considers Megan to be a lifesaver because her help allows Lamott to have a few much-needed hours to herself.

Mom

Lamott's mother lives nearby and spends a lot of time with Lamott and Sam. Mom babysits every Thursday afternoon so Lamott can have some free time.

Pammy Murray

Pammy and Lamott have been best friends since they were children. Pammy, one of Sam's godmothers, is present at his birth, and during the first year of his life, she visits almost everyday. Pammy and her husband are unable to have children, but Sam inspires them to plan to adopt a child. However, Pammy is diagnosed with cancer when Sam is less than a year old. She dies in November 1992.

Peg

Peg, one of Sam's godmothers, is a close friend of Lamott's from the days when both of them drank and used drugs excessively. Like Lamott, she now is in recovery. She helps Lamott with day-to-day activities, such as laundry and bringing over food.

Bill Rankin

Bill is a priest who is also a friend of Lamott's. She discusses any misgivings she has about her religious faith with him.

Rex

Rex is Sam's surrogate grandfather. He and his wife were Lamott's parents' best friends, and Lamott grew up half a mile away from them.

Rita

Rita is Lamott's therapist. Lamott maintains phone contact with her, as needed.

Themes

Single Motherhood

Lamott faces the trials of raising a child without a partner and Sam, though he is unaware of this, faces life without a father. Soon after the discovery of her pregnancy, she knows that Sam's biological father will be of no help to her. Even before Sam's birth, Lamott faces the difficult future as well as a sense of "aloneness." Although she acknowledges to herself that she will probably feel isolated for awhile, the issue of single motherhood remains of great concern to her.

Lamott often feels jealous of her friends who are raising their children with husbands. These women have someone with whom to share their worries, frustrations, and emotional ups and downs. She wonders about her ability to understand and raise a boy. She also worries about the ramifications for Sam of not having a father, which is "a huge thing not to have." She fears that Sam will grieve over his lack of a father. Since she is unable to change this circumstance, she can only hope that her friends and family will provide significant masculine role models for her son.

As a single parent, Lamott also experiences the stress of being responsible—emotionally, financially, and completely—for another human, particularly an utterly helpless one. Her confidence in herself wavers, for instance, in January, after she gets the *Mademoiselle* book reviewer's job. At first she is jubilant and believes that the worst of her insecurities are over, but by March she writes, "I'm just feeling stressed to the nu-nu's today, very tired and unable to keep the house and our life together. It's clear to me that we need a breadwinner." Throughout the narrative, Lamott reveals the range of emotions that she experiences from day to day.

Despite the lack of a husband or partner, Lamott has an enormously helpful support system, includ-

Topics for Further Study

- Read one of Lamott's novels. Compare the style and focus of the novel to *Operating Instructions*. What similarities do you find? Do these titles share any themes?

- Think about an important event in your life. Write a series of journal entries that you might have written at the time. Alternatively, start keeping a journal now, and write a few observations in it everyday.

- Some critics have wondered how Sam Lamott will feel when he is old enough to read and understand *Operating Instructions*. How do you think he might respond? Explain your answer.

- Conduct research into the growth of the single-parent family in the United States in the past few decades. Create a chart that illustrates your findings.

- Lamott makes her dislike of the first President Bush quite clear. How do you think she responded to the election of Bush's son, George W. Bush, to the presidency in 2000? Write a journal entry that Lamott might have written.

- Think about a challenge that you undertook that was very difficult but worthwhile. Were your family and friends supportive of your efforts? How did their reactions influence you and the decisions you made?

---

ing her friends and family. Pammy comes over almost every afternoon. Her mother lives nearby, as do her so-called second parents, Dudu and Rex. Her brother Steve spends a great deal of time with Sam, and her friend Brian volunteers to be a Big Brother. All of these people love Lamott and Sam tremendously, and while they cannot be a father to Sam or a husband to Lamott, they do play an important role in giving Sam the necessary sense of security and helping Lamott get through this difficult year.

Religious Faith

Lamott's faith in God and Jesus is a crucial component of her life and personality. Her faith stems from the simple decision, which she made a long time ago, to believe. For the past several years, she has found tremendous emotional support and love in her church. Her religious beliefs sustain her through difficult times and give her strength because she knows that God is protecting her. Although she acknowledges that believing in God is "sort of ridiculous," she adheres to the conviction that God has a plan for her.

As an example of Lamott's faith, she believes that God will bring a solution to her financial worries, and she sees the *Mademoiselle* job offer as proof of her faith. She also is aware of the fact that whenever her faith wavers, something happens to make her believe again. She records her misgivings about believing in Jesus in her journal, but the next day a man from her church comes over, offering to help in any way. As further testimony to her faith, *Operating Instructions* closes on her musings about whether Sam will grow up to believe in God.

Friendship

The friendships that Lamott has developed throughout her life prove to be of crucial importance to her during Sam's first year, and she celebrates the "minuet of old friendships." She relies on her friends to help her in many different ways. Her friends watch over Sam so Lamott can take care of simple needs, such as bathing. They bring over food and do the laundry. Their most important function, however, may be as people with whom Lamott can share the wonder of Sam. Pammy, Lamott's best friend, particularly takes on this role. Lamott has a great deal of respect for Pammy, calling her "unquestionably the sanest, most grounded and giving person I've ever known," and she relies on Pammy's dependability and love. In many ways, Pammy fulfills the role of partner or husband, as epitomized by Lamott's statement, ''Whenever Sam does anything new or especially funny, my first thought is, Oh, Pammy will love this.''

Style

Humor

One aspect of *Operating Instructions* that many reviewers commented on, and which will likely strike many readers as well, is its humor. Lamott's reflections are witty, irreverent, and astute. She uses humor as a means of expressing her thoughts about life, which are often earnest and somber, without becoming pedantic or heavy. For example, in the book's first few pages she wonders how anyone can have a child knowing that eventually that child will have to go through the seventh and eighth grades. ''The seventh and eighth grades were for me, and for every single good and interesting person I've ever known, what the writers of the Bible meant when they used the words *hell* and *the pit.*'' In the midst of her humorous ruminations about the difficulties of seventh and eighth grade, Lamott shares a simple truth: ''But more than anything else, they were about hurt and loneliness.''

Lamott also uses humor to convey beliefs that are important to her, such as her political beliefs. She tries to ensure that the newborn Sam will not grow up to become a Republican. On his one-month birthday, while watching the television news, she shares her feelings about President Bush. ''Study that face for a second, listen to that whiny voice,'' she commands Sam, and then she rejoices in Sam's looking ''intently at the TV for a few moments,'' before making the ''loudest, most horrible fart I've ever heard.'' An intense liberal, she proclaims, ''My hatred of American conservatives apparently sustains and defines me as much as my love of Jesus does, since I don't think I'm willing to have it removed.'' As she does in other instances, she uses this humor as an introduction to a more serious question; in this case: ''Who would I be without it?''

Lamott revels in the fact that all of her friends also have ''sick senses of humor'' and acknowledges that for the past twenty-five years she and Pammy ''have been so black-humored and cynical.'' This mordant humor particularly comes into play when Pammy gets sick with cancer. ''All day Pammy has been asking me to do favors for her,'' Lamott writes. ''Then she says that I *have* to do whatever she asks because it's her last wish.'' At the same time, Lamott uses humor to avoid the difficult feelings and worries brought on by Pammy's cancer. She feels her friend's impending death very deeply, as she writes in her journal:

> Pammy came by with strawberry sorbet and the new *People* magazine. . . . She's so incredibly kind to us. It would be much easier to think of losing her if she weren't so . . . kind. Maybe I will talk to her about this tomorrow.

Narrative Structure

The narrative is structured as a chronological journal that reflects Lamott's thoughts and observations about the first year in Sam's life as they are occurring. Lamott's journal chronicles typical events in the life of a baby, following Sam's progress as he lifts his head, rolls over, crawls, and eventually walks. The narrative structure also provides a very loose form that allows Lamott to reflect on her own past as well as think about what the future will bring to her and Sam. She includes many musings that have nothing to do with Sam's life, but rather have to do with the feelings that having a child engenders in Lamott. For example, she thinks about her own childhood, her political leanings, and her religious faith.

Writing

During Sam's first month of life, Lamott reflects upon her ideas about writing. She has already published three novels, and a fourth comes out shortly after Sam's birth. She remembers that her father, also a writer, said that their job was to entertain. She writes, ''I think he believed that the best way to entertain the troops is to tell stories, and the ones that they seem to like the best are ones about themselves.'' This statement applies to Lamott's previous novels, all of which draw from her own life experiences. However, the creative writing that Lamott does during this period is primarily her journal, and she feels little interest in fiction writing. This partially stems from being too busy taking care of Sam, but she also feels that she lacks motivation to write because the ''emptiness and desire and craving and feeling and need to achieve'' are now gone. With Sam, the pressure to write has vanished. This statement reflects that Sam brings her a sense of serenity, which stands in stark opposition to the ''rush'' or the ''hit of something, of anything'' that she sometimes desperately craves.

Historical Context

The Bush Presidency

George Bush succeeded Ronald Reagan for the presidency in 1988. On the domestic front, President Bush launched the War on Drugs, which was an organized effort to end the illegal drug trade, both at home and abroad. While it included drug treatment and education efforts, it primarily focused on using law enforcement to put a stop to drug use. The U.S. government also offered legal and financial assistance to get foreign countries to arrest major drug smugglers. In December 1989, Bush authorized the military invasion of Panama to arrest the country's dictator, Manuel Noriega, for drug smuggling. He was convicted by a U.S. federal court in 1992. Bush also signed a bill to update the Clean Air Act, which required that the amount of emissions released into the atmosphere be reduced, and he approved the Americans with Disabilities Act, which guaranteed people with disabilities equal access to public accommodations, transportation, and employment opportunities.

Social Issues in the Late 1980s

By 1991, the number of children living in single-parent households had grown tremendously over the past twenty years. In 1991, some twenty percent of all white children, sixty percent of all African American children, and thirty percent of all Hispanic children lived with one parent, usually their mothers. Single-parent families were more likely to live in poverty, and many single parents faced serious financial burdens.

AIDS (Acquired Immune Deficiency Syndrome), which had come to prominence in the early 1980s, continued to baffle scientists. By the 1990s, this disease was spreading at an alarming rate. Despite efforts of scientists and researchers, no significant progress was made toward a cure. Some activists accused the U.S. government of responding too slowly and with too little money to the AIDS crisis.

The U.S. Economy

Not all Americans approved of Bush's handling of the economy. The stock market had experienced a significant drop in October 1987, and many people began to fear the start of another depression. This decline hit many savings and loans institutions (S&Ls) very hard, as many had made investments that lost a great deal of their worth. Many S&Ls had also made risky loans to real estate developers, and with the collapse of the real estate markets, these loans were not repaid. S&Ls around the country went bankrupt, forcing the U.S. government to pay out billions of dollars in insured depositors' savings.

The stock market decline, the S&L debacle, the costs of the Persian Gulf War, a recession, and a rising federal deficit all contributed to a faltering U.S. economy. By the early 1990s, the economy was seriously weaker than it had been in previous years. The number of Americans who lived below the poverty line increased by more than 2 million in 1990.

America Abroad

President Bush presided over two important foreign issues: the end of the Cold War and the Persian Gulf War. Soviet leader Mikhail Gorbachev had been pushing for reforms that moved the Soviet Union toward democracy, movements which were encouraged by Bush. Gradually, some Soviet republics declared their independence. In November 1989, pro-democracy Germans tore down the Berlin Wall, which had stood since 1961. The following year, West Germany and East Germany reunified. The Soviet Union dissolved in December 1991, as more Soviets rebelled against hard-line party leaders. With the end of the Soviet Union, the Cold War was over.

In January 1991, an America-led United Nations force launched Operation Desert Storm in response to Iraq's refusal to withdraw its troops from neighboring Kuwait. Iraq's leader, Saddam Hussein, had long claimed that the oil-rich nation belonged to his country. After a six-week air offensive, the UN coalition launched a ground invasion, and within days, Iraq agreed to cease-fire conditions, including its withdrawal from Kuwait. President Bush's popularity rose after this successful Persian Gulf War.

Critical Overview

Reviewers lauded *Operating Instructions* for its humorous, poignant portrayal of new motherhood. *Publishers Weekly* called it a "glowing work" and applauded the "wonderfully candid" quality of Lamott's writing, as well as the "quirky humor [that] steadily draws the reader into her unconventional world." In a similar vein, Jon Carroll wrote in *Whole Earth Review* that the book "will make you laugh and cry." Dawna Lee Jonté, of *Belle Lettres,* commented favorably on Lamott's "hilarious accounts of new motherhood . . . [her] poignant affirmation of her newfound faith and sobriety, and heartbreaking acceptance of her best friend's terminal cancer." However, Jonté cautioned that the "pieces don't always work smoothly together; this book uneasily mixes humor and pathos."

Many reviewers found the people who populated the first year of Sam's life engaging, particularly Pammy, who responds to her terminal cancer with courage and dignity. These qualities drew parents and non-parents alike to *Operating Instructions.* As *Kirkus Reviews* pointed out, "One need not be a new parent to appreciate Lamott's glib and gritty good humor in the face of annihilating weariness."

Erika Taylor, writing in the *Los Angeles Times Book Review,* asserted that the best parts of the book are very funny, imbued with a "conversational style that perfectly conveys her friendly self-deprecating sense of humor." Taylor called it a "smart, funny and comforting read." Taylor, however, pointed out one significant flaw with the book: "Much of the writing is completely preoccupied with *her* traumas and *her* joy over *her* baby which, in spite of a lot of charm and wit, feels like spending hours looking at snapshots of a family you've never met."

Operating Instructions brought Lamott national acclaim. Since its publication, she has published two other works of nonfiction—*Bird by Bird* (1994) and *Traveling Mercies* (1999). Both of these works allow Lamott to further discuss issues important to her that she touched on in *Operating Instructions*: writing and religion, respectively.

Criticism

Rena Korb

Korb has a master's degree in English literature and creative writing and has written for a wide variety of educational publishers. In the following essay, she reflects upon the reality of Lamott's fears and joys.

As the title attests, Lamott's *Operating Instructions: A Journal of My Son's First Year* chronicles the first year in the life of Sam Lamott. The journal is filled with her son's accomplishments, her own responses to motherhood, and the other things that are going on in her life during this busy year. For most of her life, Lamott has chosen alternative paths, particularly in dropping out of college and deciding to support herself as a writer. Although before Sam's birth she sees herself as "much too self-centered, cynical, eccentric, and edgy to raise a baby," *Operating Instructions* proves these doubts to be unjustified. Lamott writes about her awareness of both her responsibility to Sam and to herself, a linked responsibility.

The main focus of *Operating Instructions* is Sam's first year of life. Sam takes the expected developmental steps, from lying in his crib to lifting his head, to rolling over, to crawling, to standing, and then to walking. He experiments with making noises. He touches things to learn about them. He develops emotional attachments. None of his actions are out of the ordinary, yet Lamott believes him to be the smartest, most beautiful, child that ever was born, a typical response. Lamott writes about Sam's new tricks as if they are signs of a baby genius. When, at the age of two months, he learns to "comfort himself without the pacifier by sucking on his hands and fists," Lamott declares, "He's very brilliant, this much is clear." She holds a party for his three-week birthday. She celebrates such important days as National Sam Lamott Neck Control Day by changing her answering machine message to reflect this momentous occasion.

Another response that Lamott shares with other new parents is feeling exhausted and worn out all the time. She jokingly questions why she had a child, even acting as if Sam were an item she purchased at the store, one that she could return if she decided it wasn't what she wanted or expected. "Sam sleeps for four hours at a stretch now, which is one of the main reasons I've decided to keep him," she writes when he is nearly seven weeks old. Other times, however, she records her trials less humorously. On October 14, she calls the Pregnancy to Parenthood 24-hour line. Writing with utter candor, Lamott records how she "told the person on the line that I didn't think I was going to hurt him but that I didn't think that I could get through the night." Such a statement illustrates the depth of the strain that Lamott undergoes in caring for her child. The fact that this hotline exists for worried parents shows that Lamott is not experiencing uncommon feelings.

December 1 in her journal depicts the variability of her feelings. The entry for that day begins bluntly: "It has been a terrible day. I'm afraid I'm

What Do I Read Next?

- Ariel Gore's *The Mother Trip: Hip Mama's Guide to Staying Sane in the Chaos of Motherhood* (2000) is a collection of essays showing the highlights and the low points of motherhood. Gore, an outspoken urban mom, gives inspiration, encouragement, and moral support to real-world mothers.

- *Breeder: Real-life Stories from the New Generation of Mothers* (2001), edited by Ariel Gore and Bee Lavender, is a collection of essays about motherhood from Generation X writers.

- *Mother Zone: Love, Sex, and Laundry in the Modern Family* (1992) is the autobiography of Toronto journalist Marni Jackson. It portrays the drama inherent in mother-child relationships in a society that idealizes motherhood while devaluing its importance.

- Perri Klass's collection *Love and Modern Medicine: Stories* (2001) focuses on domestic life as experienced by young couples and families.

- Anne Lamott's *Bird by Bird: Some Instructions on Writing and Life* (1994) drew rave reviews and was a national bestseller. It serves both as a practical guide to writing and as a glimpse into the mind and life of a professional writer.

- Mary Morris's novel *A Mother's Love* (1993) portrays the artist as a single mother. The painter-protagonist of the story was abandoned by her own mother at birth and now must recreate her own life through her art.

- *Shadow Child: An Apprenticeship in Love and Loss* (2000), by Beth Powning, describes a woman's experience giving birth to a stillborn child and how this tragedy affects her marriage and her future mothering.

- Edith Wharton's novel *The Mother's Recompense* (1925) focuses on Kate Clephane, who abandoned her husband and infant daughter. She is summoned back to New York society by her grown daughter, who is intent on marrying a man that Kate once loved. The moral quandary that faces Kate and the ensuing drama startled readers of that time.

---

going to have to let him go. He's an awful baby. I hate him. He's scum.'' Later that afternoon, however, she ''fell right back in love'' with him, and by midnight, she has concluded that the problem lies within herself, not Sam. She writes, ''I don't think I like babies.'' In this progression, Lamott typifies any overstressed, sleep-deprived mother—in other words, any normal mother. The changes in her feelings are not Sam's fault, but are based on the challenges that any new baby poses without meaning to do so. Lamott understands this, yet she still writes passages that sum up a new parent's conflicting feelings, such as this one from November 22:

> I wish he could take longer naps in the afternoon. He falls asleep and I feel I could die of love when I watch him, and I think to myself that he is what angels look like. Then I doze off, too, and it's like heaven, but sometimes only twenty minutes later he wakes up and begins to make his gritchy rodent noises, scanning the room wildly. I look blearily over at him in the bassinet, and think, with great hostility, oh, God, he's raising his loathsome reptilian head again.

Lamott also records surprise at how quickly Sam is growing up—again, a typical parental reaction. By January, when Sam is nearly four months old, she notes that he is changing every day, and moreover, that she is losing her baby. ''He's becoming so grown-up before my very eyes. It's so painful. I want him to stay this age forever,'' she writes. Clearly, a four-month-old baby is hardly grown-up, but Lamott is speaking in comparative terms, as a four-month-old baby bears little resemblance to a newborn. A newborn seems to just sleep and eat, but a four-month-old baby takes many developmental strides, such as showing cognizance of surroundings, making noises for fun, and moving arms and legs on purpose. Lamott's reflection that she wants him to stay at this period in his life forever is typical, and one which she repeats throughout his first year. As she watches Sam grow and reach new goals and develop new awareness, she feels that she is losing him. In June, when Sam is almost ten months old, she writes, "I feel like he's not even a baby anymore. He's becoming a young adult." This statement reflects back to Lamott's pre-birth thoughts, when she already is worried about "that inevitable day when my son will leave for college." This running commentary illustrates a theme common to all parents—the knowledge that one day the child will become independent.

Another difficulty that Lamott faces—and that Sam increases—are financial problems. As a writer, she does not earn a great deal of money. Her only source of financial stability derives from a few ongoing magazine columnist jobs. At one point, she records that she is down to her last $800 in savings and knows that she may be forced to borrow money from Pammy. Despite these serious troubles, when she focuses on the financial drain that having a baby poses, she maintains a sense of humor: "I'm not suggesting he's a deadbeat," she writes, "but I must say he's not bringing in any money on his own. . . . it's so expensive and time-consuming to have a baby, you might as well keep hothouse orchids. At least you can sell them."

Also notable in these journal entries is how, through her relationship with Sam, Lamott develops a new sense of self and of what is important. One day she uses Sam as an excuse for getting out of a party. After doing this, Lamott feels little guilt but rather a "tremendous sense of power." In this instance, being a mother to Sam has given her the courage and opportunity to be true to her own needs and interests.

Lamott also becomes more aware of her relationships with men, which is an important self-discovery for a woman who feels that the men in her past have actually held her hostage to her desire to make them like and need her. When the baby is two months old, Lamott writes that she is still "so taken up by Sam that I don't have to deal with men." To Lamott, this is a positive benefit of motherhood. The next time Lamott meets a man with whom she might have previously become infatuated, she holds herself back. She now recognizes that any romantic or sexual entanglements will affect Sam. "It would be one thing if I could leap into a disastrous romance and it would be just me who would suffer," she

> **" By Sam's first birthday, Lamott has changed significantly, learning more about herself through her relationship with her baby son."**

writes, "but I can't afford to get lost because Sam doesn't have anyone to fall back on." With this statement, Lamott demonstrates her comprehension that, as Sam's mother, she has a greater burden in the choices she makes. Her next comment—"And *I* don't have anyone else to fall back on, come to think of it"—shows a newfound maturity that has been shaped by having to take responsibility for the life of another human.

Despite its subtitle, *Operating Instructions: A Journal of My Son's First year* is more a portrait of Lamott than it is of her son Sam. In October, when Sam is about six weeks old, Lamott writes in apparent wonderment, "I just can't get over how much babies cry. I really had no idea what I was getting into. To tell you the truth, I though it would be more like getting a cat." By Sam's first birthday, Lamott has changed significantly, learning more about herself and life through her relationship with her son.

Source: Rena Korb, Critical Essay on *Operating Instructions: A Journal of My Son's First Year,* in *Nonfiction Classics for Students,* The Gale Group, 2002.

Erik France

France is a librarian and teaches history and interdisciplinary studies at University Liggett School and writing and poetry at Macomb Community College near Detroit, Michigan. In the following essay, he discusses ways that humor, faith, family, and friendship fuel Lamott's resilient approach to life as a first-time mother and persistent writer.

In *Operating Instructions: A Journal of My Son's First Year*, Lamott employs a mixture of humor and pathos, witty observation, remembrance, and anecdote to carry the reader through her first year as a mother. She tells a compelling story that highlights her complicated life issues and resilient faith. Equally, she makes evident the charity and support of a wide variety of friends and relatives who help console and sustain her through many ups and downs.

The calendar structure of the book adds drama to the often-exhausting life changes inherent in the first year of a mother-child relationship. Each entry is dated and usually includes a brief account of baby Sam Lamott's growth and development. These entries are written in a way that allows the reader to gain considerable insight into Lamott's ever-changing feelings and responses.

Lamott, at age thirty-five, painfully but successfully faces the challenge of sustaining her life as a writer while becoming a single parent. Her decision not to have an abortion, but to follow her pregnancy through, results in Sam's birth and her own increasing sense of responsibility. She is not alone in this transition. By this time in her life, she has developed a sense of faith. She has already given up alcohol and drug addictions, and she now turns more energetically to a network of healing people, a sort of mutual aid society.

Lamott's willingness to ask for and receive help represents one of the main themes of the book. She refers to the people closest to her as her "pit crew" (race car terminology for the people who maintain and repair a driver's car and who look after the well-being of the driver, most crucially during the stress of actual races). She also uses the more general term "tribe," a religious and anthropological metaphor for people who help each other at a deep level, to describe other friends and acquaintances from her church and elsewhere. To appreciate how far Lamott has come by the end of the book, one may usefully consider where she came from. Lamott reflects in many journal entries about her past: this is part of her process of healing and living in a healthier, more hopeful way.

When the journal begins, Lamott finds herself pregnant and abandoned by the father of the child. This unnamed man, more than fifteen years older, is the latest and (she hopes) the last in her long string of relationships with men whom she characterizes as "crummy." But Lamott's complex set of problems and issues go further back than any of her boyfriends. They originated from her complicated and difficult family. Situated in the San Francisco area, Lamott and her brothers John and Steve lived in a somewhat dysfunctional household with their parents, Dorothy and Kenneth Lamott. The children were exposed to a mix of left-leaning politics, intermittent Bohemianism, alcohol, drugs, and unconventional people. Lamott experienced many discussions and parties with her parent's friends and acquaintances, including atheists, artists, and political activists. Lamott retained the social consciousness of her parents, but, feeling empty without a sense of religious meaning, she became a practicing Christian after years of stubborn resistance and self-abuse. Her faith plays a major role in the raising of Sam, and many members of the St. Andrew Presbyterian Church of Marin City, California, help and encourage her along the way.

Despite the complications her parents gave her, Lamott did benefit in two very lasting ways. Her father was a strong role model for her as a writer. He kept at his writing regularly, a disciplined habit that Lamott picked up and, despite various addictive distractions and years of self-sabotage, adhered to. During Sam's first year, her novel *All New People* reached the point of publication and distribution. She also wrote a regular column for *California* magazine, kept the journal that became, in published form, *Operating Instructions: A Journal of My Son's First Year*, and was contracted to write another magazine column.

Lamott's mother also provided a strong role model in one particular way: Dorothy Lamott refused to place herself second to anyone. She had gone to law school and had left the family for awhile and moved to Hawaii to pursue her own dreams. By the time Lamott began her journal in 1989, her father was long dead from a brain tumor and her mother was back in California helping with Sam. In the meantime, Lamott had increasingly turned to the rest of her tribe and pit crew to help her find her own way through life.

For many years, Lamott had turned to addictive behaviors to deny the sense of grief and loss brought about by her offbeat upbringing, her parents' divorce, and her father's death, and to avoid having to deal with internal loneliness and longing. Since the time she was a teenager, she had "tried everything in sometimes suicidally vast quantities—alcohol, drugs, work, food, excitement, good deeds, popularity, men, exercise, and just rampant obsession and compulsion—to avoid" facing herself. Finally, when she is pregnant, she faces herself and somehow manages to go on. Though she must do the heaviest work alone, she is consoled and helped by her many friends, one of whom, John Manning, is also a mutual friend of the man who abandoned her.

Three very important members of Lamott's tribe and pit crew include her therapist Rita, her brother Steve, and her long-time friend Pammy

Murray. Rita helps Lamott come to terms with herself and discover forgiveness, including the ability to forgive herself for past excesses. A recovering alcoholic and addict, Lamott relies on Rita "mostly because I had so many variations on the theme of low self-esteem, with conceitedness marbled in, the classic egomaniac with an inferiority complex." Between sessions with Rita, the demands of raising Sam, and continuing at her writing, Lamott learns how to develop and protect her personal boundaries. She learns especially how to avoid distractions and how to be open to people who can and do truly help her. Lamott's brother Steve helps in practical ways, provides comic relief, and serves as a reminder that not all men are "crummy." Of Pammy, her best friend, Lamott writes, "I could not have gone through this, could not be doing it now, without Pammy." When Pammy is diagnosed with cancer during Sam's first year, Lamott is devastated; still, because of Sam, Lamott persists. Though these three people stand out, there are many others who help Lamott persist.

Finally, in addition to faith and the familial community of her tribe and pit crew, Lamott keeps herself and others going with her biting jokes and sense of humor. When not making fun of herself and her neuroses, she devotes many of her sarcastic quips to belittling a range of "crummy" men, including ex-sexual partners, a potential Republican boyfriend (she is a lifelong Democrat) from whom she decides to spare herself, and even George Herbert Walker Bush, the standing president during Sam's first year of life. Lamott describes Bush as reminding every woman of her first "ex-." Her passionate rage against Republicans is humorous as much for its excess as anything else. The diatribes against Bush also provide historical context for *Operating Instructions: A Journal of My Son's First Year*. The San Francisco earthquake of 1989 does this as well. Lamott is able to see humor even during this disaster, for she recognizes and satirizes her obsessive concern for good reviews and sales of her writing even in the midst of the major earthquake.

Reflecting on her son's first year, Lamott realizes that one cannot and need not be in control of all of life's details. It is enough to have a grasp of the important things in life; beyond that, each day is a new adventure to be taken in daily terms. She paraphrases writer E. L. Doctorow's analogy comparing writing and night driving, adapting it to life. At night, one can only see as far as a beam of headlights permits, but if one is careful, that is enough to permit one to successfully drive all the

> **❝ Of Pammy, her best friend, Lamott writes, 'I could not have gone through this, could not be doing it now, without Pammy.' When Pammy is diagnosed with cancer during Sam's first year, Lamott is devastated; still, because of Sam, Lamott persists.❞**

way to one's destination. Lamott further contemplates and explores the main themes of *Operating Instructions: A Journal of My Son's First Year* in two subsequent nonfiction works: *Bird by Bird: Some Instructions on Writing and Life*, and *Traveling Mercies: Some Thoughts on Faith*.

Source: Erik France, Critical Essay on *Operating Instructions: A Journal of My Son's First Year,* in *Nonfiction Classics for Students,* The Gale Group, 2002.

Josh Ozersky

Ozersky is a critic and essayist. In this essay, he discusses an overlooked aspect of Lamott's book—its deep religious underpinnings.

Religion, on the face of it, would seem to be the last thing Lamott's *Operating Instructions* is about. Primarily, it's about a baby: his face is on the cover, and the book's subtitle is *A Journal of My Son's First Year*. Lamott is pro-choice, dislikes Republicans, lives in San Francisco, and is a single mother with liberal convictions. The book is packed with pop-culture references and profanity. Only rarely does the author explicitly talk about God, and then often in a facetious way. But a good case could be made for *Operating Instructions* being an essentially religious book.

To understand how, it's important to understand Lamott, both as an author and as a character in her memoir. Any author who writes about themselves, even if they are as truthful and transparent as possible, still creates a character for the reader. We do the same thing in daily life, every time we choose to speak in a way that we hope will create a favorable impression. Like T. S. Eliot's Prufrock,

> **Part of what makes her such an appealing narrator is that her faith, though strong, is so flawed and fallible, and wedded to what appear to be such unlikely non-religious beliefs.''**

we ''prepare a face to greet the faces that we meet.'' The character of ''me'' in *Operating Instructions* is far and away the most interesting and complex one the reader meets. The reader learns more about her, cares more about her, and is more involved with her than anyone else in the book.

Lamott's character in the book can be contradictory. She is ironic, skeptical, and tough-minded, but also emotional and moody. She is intensely loving—with Sam, with her friends, with her family—but seems to despise herself much of the time. Her tone is primarily a humorous one, with many snappy one-liners and pop-culture references, but the content of much of her writing is profoundly serious.

It is hard not to feel, as one reads the book, that Lamott is talking directly to the reader as the days pass. One begins to feel as if he or she is a part of her extended family—the network of friends, neighbors, and fellow parishioners who are helping her to muddle her way through Sam's first year.

But is this necessarily so? Surely there must be decisions that Lamott had to make. What does she choose to tell readers? What isn't she telling readers? Is there any part of her life that is being concealed? If so, why? And even if readers are getting the complete story, it's only the complete story as she knows it.

This is especially important when it comes to Lamott's religion. Her grip on her own identity is obviously very strong, even for a writer. And she has a laser-like focus on her son. But as Erika Taylor wrote in the *Los Angeles Times,* ''At the base of Lamott's experience is a deep, hard-earned trust in her self and her God.'' But as with motherhood, religion is an ongoing learning experience. And this can be misleading.

Operating Instructions is definitely not a conversion narrative, like *The Confessions of St. Augustine* or *The Autobiography of Malcolm X.* In those books, the authors have transcendent encounters with God, and are forever changed; the authors write from the point of view of people who have found the truth. Lamott's religion, on the other hand, is clearly more of a work in progress. She is beset by doubts. Some of the most revealing passages in the book, in fact, show her inability to take her own faith seriously. Referring to the crucifix, Lamott writes:

I believe in it, and it's so nuts. How did some fabulously cerebral and black-humored cynic like myself come to fall for all that Christian lunacy . . . It, my faith, is a great mystery. It has all the people close to me shaking their heads. It has me shaking my head.

Even as she makes these protests, however, Lamott stresses her belief in the fundamental tenets of Christianity: redemption, resurrection, and the movements of Providence.

Part of what makes her such an appealing narrator is that her faith, though strong, is so flawed and fallible, and wedded to what appear to be such unlikely non-religious beliefs. Lamott is an avid churchgoer, and considers doing Christ's work to be ''the only operating instructions I will ever need.'' But she won't go out with an attractive man because she finds that he voted Republican.

Likewise, she is alternatively beset by a heady mixture of self-pity and self-loathing (''I'm mental and defeated and fat and loathsome and I am crazily, brain-wastedly tired. I couldn't sleep. This is maybe the loneliest I have ever felt.'') and lifted up on the highest flights of rapturous love and gratitude (''Sam was baptized today at St. Andrew's. It is almost too painful to talk about, so powerful, so outrageous and lovely.'').

In some of her other books, most notably *Traveling Mercies*, Lamott dwells more at length on her faith and how she arrived at it. In *Operating Instructions*, she dwells on it more as background, with occasional flares, both positive and negative. In that sense, Lamott's religion is more persuasively painted than if she spent the better part of her narrative discoursing on Christianity. It's precisely because she is so back-and-forth with her faith, because she is so preoccupied with her son and herself, and because the whole period is such a roller-coaster ride for her, that we get such a deep feeling of what it means to her.

What is that religion? It seems to vary with Lamott's emotional state. At moments of weakness or distress, she has the natural impulse of people in difficult straits—God as cosmic cavalry, coming to the rescue. Several times in the course of *Operating Instructions*, Lamott writes or prays to God to help her with specific financial or emotional problems—and is promptly, and positively, answered. This kind of religion is undemanding and innocuous, and seems at odds with the larger spiritual sense Lamott describes at happier moments: "I know we all only talk about God in the most flat-footed way, but I suddenly had that Old Testament sense of God's presence."

At other times, Lamott frankly doubts her own faith. She looks back on all the years when she was addicted to cocaine and alcohol. She feels helpless as a mother. She feels neurotic and unstable. She feels unworthy of her friends. At these times, her faith in God doesn't so much waver as flicker in and out of the narrative. Some critics have taken Lamott to task for being so frustratingly indecisive and vague about God, about calling herself a Christian writer when she so obviously subscribes to no particular doctrine, and has such an undeveloped theological sense.

But this criticism is misguided, and misses the whole point of *Operating Instructions* as a work of literature. If Lamott's feelings and perception of God change as she changes, it isn't because she is weak-minded; it's because she's human. By being so candid and honest in this memoir, she opens herself to criticism of being unstable, flawed, an unworthy receptacle of divine inspiration. That's no problem; it's all true. But she never claimed to be a saint, or to speak for religious people everywhere. She is a religious person, and in writing about the things most important to her, she inevitably brings her ideas about God to bear on them. For a religious person, nothing of any importance can exist in a spiritual vacuum. And for a person who believes in an infinitely powerful deity, nothing of any importance can exist outside of the concept of God's love and will. It's an alien concept for many readers who don't share Lamott's deep-seated faith in the Christian God; but it's one that is bone-deep in her

writing and informs every page of *Operating Instructions*.

Source: Josh Ozersky, Critical Essay on *Operating Instructions: A Journal of My Son's First Year,* in *Nonfiction Classics for Students,* The Gale Group, 2002.

Sources

Carroll, Jon, Review, in *Whole Earth Review,* No. 78, Spring 1993, p. 24.

Jonté, Dawna Lee, Review, in *Belle Lettres: A Review of Books by Women,* Vol. 9, No. 1, Fall 1993, p. 7.

Review, in *Kirkus Reviews,* March 15, 1993.

Review, in *Publishers Weekly,* Vol. 240, No. 12, March 22, 1993, p. 65.

Taylor, Erika, "Keep the Baby and the Faith," in *Los Angeles Times Book Review,* May 9, 1993, p. 2.

Further Reading

Feinsilver, Pamela, "Anne Lamott: The California Writer Talks about the Birth of Her Son and the Rebirth of Her Career," in *Publishers Weekly,* Vol. 240, No. 22, May 31, 1993, p. 30.
  This article presents a good overview of Lamott's life, work, and her inspirations.

Fisk, Molly, "Anne Lamott: One Bird at a Time," in *Poets & Writers Magazine,* Vol. 24, No. 5, September–October 1996, p. 52.
  This interview with Lamott focuses on the success of *Operating Instructions* and *Bird by Bird,* as well as on ideas to help new writers.

Lachnit, Caroll, "Anne Lamott: Taking It Bird by Bird," in *Writer's Digest,* Vol. 7, No. 6, June 1996, p. 30.
  In this interview, Lamott discusses how and why she writes.

Lamott, Anne, *Traveling Mercies: Some Thoughts on Faith,* Pantheon Books, 1999.
  This nonfiction work presents Lamott's religious ideals and beliefs in greater depth.

Montgomery-Fate, Tom, "Vulnerability Is Not Weakness," in *The Other Side,* Vol. 36, No. 2, March 2000, p. 28.
  Montgomery-Fate discusses how Lamott's three works of nonfiction all focus on the process of becoming something—a mother, a writer, and a Christian.

Self-Reliance

Ralph Waldo Emerson

1841

"Self-Reliance," first published in *Essays* (First Series) in 1841, is widely considered to be the definitive statement of Ralph Waldo Emerson's philosophy of individualism and the finest example of his prose. The essay is a fabric woven of many threads, from a journal entry written as early as 1832 to material first delivered in lectures between 1836 and 1839.

Emerson was known for his repeated use of the phrase "trust thyself." "Self-Reliance" is his explanation—both systematic and passionate—of what he meant by this and of why he was moved to make it his catch-phrase. Every individual possesses a unique genius, Emerson argues, that can only be revealed when that individual has the courage to trust his or her own thoughts, attitudes, and inclinations against all public disapproval.

According to the conventions of his time, Emerson uses the terms "men" and "mankind" to address all humanity, and the multitude of examples he gives of individuals who exhibited self-reliance and became great are all men. These factors somewhat date Emerson's presentation; the underlying ideas, however, remain powerful and relevant.

Author Biography

Ralph Waldo Emerson, essayist, poet, and philosopher, was born May 25, 1803, in Boston, Massachusetts. He was the son of William Emerson, a well-known minister, and Ruth Haskins, daughter of a merchant. In 1811, when Emerson was eight, his father died, leaving his mother to rear six children. His aunt, Mary Moody Emerson, was a writer who took an interest in the education of her four nephews. It is likely that she played a large role in Emerson's development as a writer.

Despite the family's poverty after his father's death, Emerson attended Boston Latin School, a private academy. In 1817, at age fourteen, he enrolled, on scholarship, at Harvard College, where he won several prizes for his writing. After graduation in 1821, Emerson worked as a teacher at a school run by his older brother William. In 1825, he enrolled in Harvard Divinity School, and a year later he began a career as a Unitarian minister. Soon, he became chaplain of the Massachusetts Senate.

Emerson married Ellen Tucker, the great love of his life, in 1829. Her death a year and a half later devastated him and took a heavy toll on his religious faith. He resigned his pastorate in 1832, telling his congregation that he no longer believed in celebrating Holy Communion.

After a tour of Europe, Emerson earned a living as a lecturer. In 1835, he married his second wife, Lydia Jackson. They lived in Concord, Massachusetts, and had four children; one died as a boy. In Concord, Emerson became friends with the author Nathaniel Hawthorne and with Henry David Thoreau, fellow transcendentalist and author of *Walden,* who became his student and close friend.

Emerson began to shape his lecture material into essays and books in the early 1840s. These works expound various aspects of Emerson's transcendentalist philosophy. The core of transcendentalism is the idea that truth resides throughout creation and is grasped intuitively, not rationally. From this core belief, Emerson helped fashion American transcendentalism, which particularly stood against materialism, institutionalized religion, and slavery. Emerson's strong belief in the integrity of the individual is summarized in his oft-repeated phrase, ''trust thyself,'' and given full expression in his famous essay ''Self-Reliance,'' published in his *Essays* (First Series) in 1841.

Among Emerson's other well-known works are the pamphlet *Nature,* published in 1836; a second series of *Essays,* published in 1844; and *The Conduct of Life,* published in 1860. He was also a

Ralph Waldo Emerson

poet; among his lasting poems are ''The Concord Hymn,'' ''Ode to Beauty,'' and ''Give All to Love.''

Emerson continued to write and lecture until the late 1870s. He was widely known and respected throughout America and the Western world. Emerson died in Concord on April 27, 1882, of pneumonia. He was buried near the grave of Thoreau, who had died twenty years earlier.

Plot Summary

Genius

Emerson begins ''Self-Reliance'' by defining genius: ''To believe your own thought, to believe that what is true for you in your private heart is true for all men—that is genius.'' Every educated man, he writes, eventually realizes that ''envy is ignorance'' and that he must be truly himself. God has made each person unique and, by extension, given each person a unique work to do, Emerson holds. To trust one's own thoughts and put them into action is, in a very real sense, to hear and act on the voice of God.

Emerson adds that people must seek solitude to hear their own thoughts, because society, by its nature, coerces men to conform. He goes so far as to call society "a conspiracy against the manhood of every one of its members."

Societal Disapproval and Foolish Consistency

Emerson discusses two factors that discourage people from trusting themselves: societal disapproval and foolish consistency. "For nonconformity the world whips you with its displeasure," he writes. He quickly dismisses public censure as a "trifle."

To the second factor, foolish consistency, Emerson gives more attention. Perhaps the most familiar and oft-quoted declaration in this essay or in all of Emerson's writing appears here: "A foolish consistency is the hobgoblin of little minds, adored by little statesmen and philosophers and divines." He reassures readers that what appears to be inconsistency and is judged harshly by others is simply the varied but unified activity of a unique individual. Emerson supports this view with an apt analogy: "The voyage of the best ship is a zigzag line of a hundred tacks." Be true not to what was done yesterday, Emerson urges, but to what is clearly the right course today, and the right destination will be reached.

Self-Worth

Up to this point, Emerson has made a case that individuals have not only a right but also a responsibility to think for themselves and that neither societal disapproval nor concerns about consistency should discourage these. He now writes that individuals who obey the admonition to "trust thyself" should value themselves highly and consider themselves equal to the great men of history. Returning to a point made earlier, Emerson states that when men trust themselves they are actually trusting the divine, which exists in all men and which he calls "the aboriginal Self," "Spontaneity," and "Instinct."

Relation of the Individual to God

Emerson further explores the nature of the relationship between the individual and "the divine spirit." He holds that this relationship is pure and therefore no intermediaries—priest, doctrine, church, scripture, etc.—are needed or helpful. Emerson decries those who "dare not yet hear God himself, unless he speaks the phraseology of . . . David, or Jeremiah, or Paul."

The Highest Truth

Emerson tells readers that he has now come to "the highest truth of the subject": "When good is near you . . . you shall not discern the footprints of any other . . . the way, the thought, the good, shall be wholly strange and new."

Emerson characterizes an individual's experience of the highest truth as a moment of calm during which the soul stands above all passion, above time and space, above even life and death, and experiences pure existence and reality.

Resist Temptation

Here Emerson encourages readers to give up social pretenses such as "lying hospitality and lying affection." Be true to your feelings and opinions in relation to other people, he writes, even the people closest to you; tell them what you really think of them. They may well be hurt at first, he acknowledges, but they will, sooner or later, "have their moment of reason" and learn to be honest themselves. This social honesty is needed, Emerson argues, because pretense has made people weak and afraid of truth, fate, death, and one another.

Effects of Self-Reliance

Emerson writes that increased self-reliance would revolutionize religion, education, and other facets of society. The remainder of the essay is an exploration of four numbered, specific effects of self-reliance, as follows.

First, Emerson writes that self-reliance would radically alter people's religious attitudes and practices. He calls conventional prayer a form of begging, "a disease of the will," and even "vicious." In a society of self-reliant individuals, Emerson says, "prayer that craves a particular commodity" would be replaced by prayer consisting of "the contemplation of the facts of life from the highest point of view." Another valid form of prayer, according to Emerson, is right action.

Emerson builds on this idea by adding, "As men's prayers are a disease of the will, so are their creeds a disease of the intellect." Again, Emerson urges readers to abandon systems of thought built by others and to fall back on their own unique thoughts and ideas, about the divine as about all else.

Second, Emerson writes that self-reliance would replace the "superstition of traveling." "The soul is no traveler," he says. "The wise man stays at home." Emerson explains that he is not against travel for the sake of pursuing art or study but that too many people travel hoping to find a better culture or society than that in America. The wise course, according to Emerson, is to stay home and devote oneself to making America a place to be admired as much as American tourists admire Italy, England, Greece, and Egypt.

Emerson's third point expands on the second. He charges that Americans' minds are as much "vagabonds" as their bodies and that they look to other countries for inspiration in everything from architecture to opinions, valuing "the Past and the Distant" above the present and the near. Emerson's remedy is that Americans should develop their own culture and arts.

The fourth and final effect of self-reliance that Emerson deals with is the progress of society over-all. He holds that people misunderstand the true nature of progress, mistaking advances in science, technology, and material welfare for progress. Every such advance has a cost as great as its benefit, Emerson claims, and does not really benefit individuals or society in meaningful ways. What passes for progress does not make people either better or happier. True progress occurs on an individual, not a societal basis, he writes, and results from looking to self, rather than material things, for fulfillment. Emerson concludes, "Nothing can bring you peace but yourself. Nothing can bring you peace but the triumph of principles."

Key Figures

John Adams

Emerson refers to "great days and victories behind" that "shed a united light," which in turn "throws . . . America into Adams's eye." Emerson may be referring to John Adams (1735–1826), a revolutionary with a combative style who became the second president of the United States.

John Quincy Adams

John Quincy Adams (1767–1848) was the son of John Adams who became the sixth president of the United States. John Quincy Adams was a friend of Emerson's father and later an outspoken critic of Emerson's transcendentalism.

Samuel Adams

Samuel Adams (1722–1803) was a leader of the American Revolution who later served in Congress.

Gustavus Adolphus

Emerson asks, "Why all this deference to . . . Gustavus?" He may be referring to Gustavus Adolphus (1594–1632), a king of Sweden who reclaimed territory held by Denmark, Russia, and Poland.

Alfred

Emerson asks, "Why all this deference to . . . Alfred?" He is referring to Alfred the Great (849–899), a Saxon king who kept the Danes from overrunning southwest England. Known for promoting literacy, Alfred valued learning.

Ali ibn-abu-Talib

Emerson quotes Ali (circa 600–661), the son-in-law of the Islamic prophet Muhammad and his acknowledged successor. Ali's sayings had been published in English in 1832.

Anaxagoras

A Greek philosopher of nature, Anaxagoras (circa 500–428 B.C.) discovered that solar eclipses were caused by the moon obscuring the sun. He attributed growth and development of organisms to power of mind. Emerson says that he was a great man.

Anthony

Emerson declares, "An institution is the lengthened shadow of one man" and lists the hermit Anthony (circa 250–350) as the founder of Monachism, or Christian monasticism. He inherited wealth but renounced it to live a life of Christian asceticism and celibacy. Anthony drew many monks to his hermitages and was later canonized.

Francis Bacon

Recognized by Emerson as an original genius who could have no master, Francis Bacon (1561–1626) was a philosopher and statesman whose inductive method of reasoning influenced scientific investigation.

Jeremy Bentham

Listed as one of those with a "mind of uncommon activity and power," Jeremy Bentham (1748–1832) was an English economist, philosopher, and theoretical jurist. With John Stuart Mill, he advocated utilitarianism, the belief that right actions lead to happiness.

Vitus Behring

Emerson gives Vitus Behring as an example of one who accomplished much with simple equipment. A navigator from Denmark, Behring (also spelled Bering; 1680–1741) explored the Siberian coast. The Bering Sea and Bering Strait are named after him.

Chatham

See William Pitt

Thomas Clarkson

Thomas Clarkson (1760–1846) was the founder of abolitionism. Clarkson formed the British Society for the Abolition of the Slave Trade in 1787 with Granville Sharp and worked unstintingly for an end to slavery in Britain. Slavery was abolished in the British Empire in 1833.

Nicolaus Copernicus

Listed among the number of great men who have been misunderstood, Nicolaus Copernicus (1473–1543) was a Polish astronomer. His theory that the sun, not the Earth, was the center of the solar system was considered heretical at the time.

David

David, the second king of Israel according to the Old Testament, is said to have authored a number of the psalms in the Old Testament book of the same name. Emerson writes that many intelligent people dare not believe that they can hear the voice of God unless it is mediated through the words of men such as David.

Diogenes

The Greek philosopher who founded the school of thought called cynicism, Diogenes (died circa 320 B.C.) was a nonconformist. He espoused a simple life and was known for roaming the streets of Athens in search of an honest man. Emerson says that he was a great man.

Charles Fourier

Listed as one of those with a "mind of uncommon activity and power," Charles Fourier (1772–1837) was a French social theorist who believed that society could be organized into cooperatives.

George Fox

George Fox (1624–1691) was the founder of Quakerism. Fox was a preacher and missionary who founded the Society of Friends (later called Quakers) in England in 1647.

Sir John Franklin

Emerson mentions British Arctic explorer Sir John Franklin (1786–1847) as having the most advanced equipment of the time, in contrast to the equipment available to earlier explorers Henry Hudson and Vitus Behring. Perhaps giving credibility to Emerson's argument that better equipment does not necessarily lead to greater accomplishments, Franklin died in the Victoria Strait while trying to discover the Northwest Passage.

Galileo Galilei

Listed among the number of great men who have been misunderstood, Italian astronomer, philosopher, and mathematician Galileo (1564–1642) supported the theories of Copernicus and advocated the application of mathematics to understanding nature. For this, he was tried in the Inquisition and forced to retire.

Henry Hudson

Emerson gives Henry Hudson as an example of one who accomplished much with simple equipment. An English navigator, Hudson (died circa 1611) explored the North American coast. The Hudson River is named after him.

James Hutton

Listed as one of those with a "mind of uncommon activity and power," James Hutton (1726–1797) was a Scottish chemist, geologist, and naturalist who originated the principle of uniformitarianism, which explains geological processes over time.

Jeremiah

Jeremiah was a fiery prophet of the Old Testament whose activities are recorded in the book of the same name. Emerson writes that many intelligent people dare not believe that they can hear the voice of God unless it is mediated through the words of men such as Jeremiah.

Antoine Laurent Lavoisier

Listed as one of those with a "mind of uncommon activity and power," Antoine Laurent Lavoisier (1743–1794) was a French scientist who developed the theory of combustion. He is often credited with founding modern chemistry.

John Locke

Listed as one of those with a "mind of uncommon activity and power," John Locke (1632–1704) was an English philosopher of the Enlightenment, a movement that advocated reason as a path to understanding God and the universe. Locke developed a systematic theory of knowledge, and his ideas influenced the U.S. Constitution.

Martin Luther

Listed among the number of great men who have been misunderstood, Martin Luther (1483–1546) was a German monk and scholar who questioned the theology, practices, and authority of the Catholic Church. Luther's teachings resulted in the founding of Protestant Christianity, which had far-reaching effects not only on Western Christianity but also on economic, political, and social thought.

John Milton

Mentioned as having "set at naught books and traditions," John Milton (1608–1674) is regarded as one of the greatest English poets. He is well known for his epic poem *Paradise Lost*. Energetic in his defense of civil and religious rights, Milton promoted ideas that conflicted with the Puritan beliefs of his time.

Sir Isaac Newton

Listed among the number of great men who have been misunderstood, Isaac Newton (1642–1727) explained infinitesimal calculus and the law of gravity. He also laid the groundwork for modern optics with his discovery that white light is made of colored components.

Sir William Edward Parry

Emerson mentions British Arctic explorer Sir William Parry (1790–1855) as having the most advanced equipment of the time, in contrast to the equipment available to earlier explorers Henry Hudson and Vitus Behring. Parry reached farther north than any explorer before him.

Paul

Paul the Apostle was one of Jesus' followers and a leader of the early Christian church. His New Testament writings have had a lasting impact on Christianity throughout the centuries. Emerson writes that many intelligent people dare not believe that they can hear the voice of God unless it is mediated through the words of men such as Paul.

Phocion

One of Emerson's "great men," Phocion (circa 402–318 B.C.) was an Athenian general and statesman, a follower of Plato, and known for his integrity.

William Pitt

William Pitt, the Earl of Chatham (1708–1778), was an English statesman who spoke in Parliament in support of American independence. Emerson refers to the "thunder" in Pitt's voice; he was considered the greatest orator of his age.

Plato

Another man who "set at naught books and traditions," Plato (circa 427–348 B.C.) is recognized as one of the greatest Western philosophers of all time. Advocating reason, he encouraged his followers to define their own lives rather than allow others to define them. For this he was labeled a bad influence by those in power.

Plutarch

An author and biographer, Plutarch (circa 46–120) wrote of heroic feats by Greek and Roman soldiers. Emerson notes that "greater men than Plutarch's heroes" cannot be molded by modern knowledge.

Pythagoras

Possibly the first pure mathematician, the Greek Pythagoras (circa 569–475 B.C.) is among Emerson's "misunderstood." The son of a merchant, Pythagoras founded a school in Samos that is still called the Semicircle of Pythagoras in modern Italy. He also founded a philosophical and religious school in Croton, now Crotone, Italy. Both men and women were accepted as his followers.

Scanderberg

Emerson asks, ''Why all this deference to . . . Scanderberg?'' He is referring to George Castriota (circa 1403–1468), an Albanian patriot with the moniker Scanderbeg, who led his soldiers against the Turks.

Scipio

Scipio Africanus the Elder (237–183 B.C.), the greatest Roman general before Julius Caesar, was victorious in the famous Battle of Zama against Hannibal. Emerson notes that Milton called him ''the height of Rome'' in *Paradise Lost.*

Socrates

Another of Emerson's ''misunderstood'' men, Socrates (469–399 B.C.) was Plato's mentor. Although Socrates did not write his beliefs because he felt they were constantly evolving, his ''The Apology,'' as recorded by Plato, advocates finding true knowledge even in the face of sweeping opposition. Because of his insistence on pointing out the lack in morality in his society, Socrates was put on trial. Given the choice to stop teaching or die, Socrates drank a fatal dose of hemlock.

Thor

Emerson urges the readers to ''wake Thor and Woden, courage and constancy.'' Thor is the Norse god of war, also known as ''the Thunderer.''

Gustavus Vasa

Emerson asks, ''Why all this deference to . . . Gustavus?'' He may be referring to Gustavus Vasa (1496–1560), a king of Sweden who proclaimed Christianity in his country.

John Wesley

Emerson declares, ''An institution is the lengthened shadow of one man'' and lists John Wesley (1703–1791) as the founder of the Methodist denomination of Protestant Christianity. An English clergyman and evangelist, Wesley promoted the doctrine of salvation by faith in Christ alone (apart from deeds).

Woden

Emerson urges readers to ''wake Thor and Woden, courage and constancy.'' Woden, also known as Odin, is the Teutonic god of war and patron of those who have died in battle.

Zoroaster

Emerson quotes the *Avesta,* the holy book of Zoroastrianism, a religion founded by the Persian Zoroaster (circa 628–551 B.C.).

Themes

Individualism

''Self-Reliance'' is widely considered Emerson's definitive statement of his philosophy of individualism. This philosophy esteems individuals above all—societies, nations, religions, and other institutions and systems of thought.

Emerson repeatedly calls on individuals to value their own thoughts, opinions, and experiences above those presented to them by other individuals, society, and religion. This radical individualism springs from Emerson's belief that each individual is not just unique but *divinely* unique; i.e., each individual is a unique expression of God's creativity and will. Further, since Emerson's God is purposeful, He molded each individual to serve a particular purpose, to do a certain work that only he or she is equipped to carry out.

This direct link between divinity and the individual provides assurance that the individual will, when rightly exercised, can never produce evil. Individual will, in Emerson's philosophy, is not selfish but divine.

In this context, an individual who fails to be self-reliant—who does not attend to and act upon his or her own thoughts and ideas—is out of step with God's purpose. Such a person, in Emerson's view, cannot be productive, fulfilled, or happy.

On the other hand, a person who is self-reliant can be assured that he or she is carrying out the divine purpose of life. This is true even of those who flout the rules and conventions of society and religion and suffer disapproval as a result. In fact, Emerson points out, those men who are now consid-

Topics for Further Study

- Emerson mentions many accomplished men in "Self-Reliance." List five to ten people who have lived since Emerson's time who are examples of high achievement. Do some research, and then for each person write a sentence or two about some way in which that person exhibited self-reliance.

- Emerson's central premise is that all individuals have the potential to be great, if only they would trust themselves. Do you agree or disagree? Write a persuasive essay that states and argues for your position. Use examples, as Emerson did.

- Emerson was a strong supporter of President Abraham Lincoln. Given what you know about Emerson and Lincoln, why do you think this was

so? Write your answer in the form of a list of possible reasons, and compare your answers with those of your classmates.

- Emerson was a poet as well as an essayist. Write a poem of at least sixteen lines that expresses the main ideas set forth in "Self-Reliance." Your poem may be in any form and style you choose. Feel free to borrow language and examples from Emerson, to use your own, or to make use of both.

- According to Emerson, people owe one another "mutual reverence." Explain what you think he means by this. Explain whether you agree that mutual reverence is called for and why you agree or disagree.

---

ered the greatest of all fall into this category. He gives as examples Pythagoras, Socrates, Jesus, Martin Luther, Copernicus, Galileo, and Isaac Newton.

Nonconformity

Clearly, Emerson's philosophy of individualism leads directly to nonconformity. Most individuals will find that their private opinions and ideas are in agreement with those of others on some points. For example, most people agree that murder and theft are wrong. On those points, nearly everyone can be a conformist. A commitment to live according to one's own ideas about every matter, however, will certainly make every individual a nonconformist on some issues. In Emerson's words, "Whoso would be a man must be a nonconformist."

Originality versus Imitation

The positive side of nonconformity is originality. Self-reliance is not a matter merely of not believing what others believe and doing what others do but, just as importantly, a matter of believing and doing what one is uniquely suited to believe and do. Emerson expects the self-reliant to substitute originality for imitation in every sphere of life.

Speaking specifically of architecture, Emerson explains that originality will yield a product that is superior (i.e., more suited to the needs of the maker) to one made by imitation:

> If the American artist will study with hope and love the precise thing to be done by him, considering the climate, the soil, the length of the day, the wants of the people . . . he will create a house in which all these will find themselves fitted, and taste and sentiment will be satisfied also.

"Insist on yourself," Emerson concludes. "Never imitate."

Past, Present, and Future

Emerson counsels the self-reliant to keep their focus on the present. "Man postpones or remembers," he complains. "He does not live in the present, but with reverted eye laments the past, or, heedless of the riches that surround him, stands on tiptoe to foresee the future." One who lingers in the past wastes one's life in regret; one who looks to the future misses today's duties and pleasures.

It is Emerson's preference for the present over the past that leads him to call consistency foolish.

That a certain belief or course of action was correct, useful, or best in the past does not guarantee that it remains so in the present. Conversely, to leave behind a belief or a way of doing things does not mean that it was not useful at the time or that one was wrong to have pursued it.

To demonstrate the unity and effectiveness of an apparently inconsistent course through life, Emerson uses a sailing journey as a metaphor: "The voyage of the best ship is a zigzag line of a hundred tacks."

The knowledge that one is following the true path to the right destination, despite apparent inconsistencies, gives the self-reliant individual confidence to ignore the taunts of others who deride him or her for changing course.

Cause and Effect versus Fortune

Cause and effect, which Emerson calls "the chancellors of God," are, he argues, the very opposites of fortune, or chance. By self-reliance, man is able to overcome the unpredictable turning of the wheel of fortune. Understanding the principle of cause and effect, the self-reliant individual applies his will wisely to bring about desired effects. To put it another way, through the wisdom of self-reliance, people become masters of their own fates. Just as God is said to have created order out of chaos, so too can men.

Style

Rational Argument

The essay is, above all, a carefully constructed rational argument with the goal of persuading readers to adopt the ideas Emerson promotes. The author uses logic, reasons, facts, and examples to support his position. One example of his use of facts is his reference to two pairs of British explorers to support his argument that advances in technology do not necessarily lead to greater accomplishments. Emerson writes that Henry Hudson and Vitus Behring, who lived in the centuries preceding Emerson's time, achieved great success with equipment much less sophisticated than that used by Sir William Parry and Sir John Franklin, who were famous in Emerson's day. Emerson's contrast here is especially interesting because history bore him out.

While Hudson and Behring's names appear prominently on today's maps to attest to their discoveries, Parry and Franklin are less well-known. In addition, Franklin died six years after the publication of "Self-Reliance" in a failed attempt to find the much sought-after Northwest Passage.

Emerson organizes his ideas so that they lead readers step by step to the conclusion he wishes them to reach. He begins by defining genius. He then explains why he believes that every human being possesses it and goes on to explain how and why this genius is to be expressed—the expression of that inborn genius is the essence of self-reliance.

Emotional Appeal

Emerson's tight rational argument in "Self-Reliance" is complemented by energetic and passionate language that appeals to readers' emotions. Among the more effective techniques here is the use of images from nature: "My book should smell of pines and resound with the hum of insects" and, "before a leaf-bud has burst, its whole life acts; in the full-blown flower there is no more; in the leafless root there is no less." Railing against men's inappropriate feelings of timidity, Emerson accuses them of being "ashamed before the blade of grass or the blowing rose."

References to Persons and Literature

"Self-Reliance" is studded with a multitude of references to famous men and well-known literature. The men mentioned—from ancients to contemporaries of Emerson, from seagoing explorers to philosophers and poets, from the Islamic leader Ali to the founder of Zoroastrianism—are, for the most part, held up as examples of self-reliance and of the greatness it brings. A few of these references are vague enough to leave some question as to exactly which individual Emerson had in mind. The name Adams is mentioned in a context in which it could refer to John, John Quincy, or Samuel. Similarly, Emerson's Gustavus could be Gustavus Adolphus or Gustavus Vasa, both kings of Sweden.

Literary references serve to illustrate or strengthen Emerson's ideas, though some may be obscure to modern readers. To convey that people are unable to forget ideas to which they have pledged themselves in the past, Emerson writes, "There is no Lethe for this." Lethe, in Greek mythology, is a river of forgetfulness.

There are several biblical references. True to Emerson's belief in subjecting all teaching to individual interpretation, he delights in wrenching these out of context and turning the conventional interpretations upside down. For example, declaring that he will express his true thoughts even if doing so should offend those closest to him, Emerson writes, "I shun father and mother and wife and brother when my genius calls me." This is a reference to Matthew 10:37, in which Jesus says, "He who loves father or mother more than me is not worthy of me. And he who loves son or daughter more than me is not worthy of me." Emerson simply replaces Jesus' "me" with "my genius," a substitution that some readers of his time undoubtedly found heretical.

Similarly, the very next sentence is, "I would write on the lintels of the door-post, *Whim.*" This reference is to Exodus 12, in which God tells the Israelites to smear the blood of a sacrificed lamb on their door posts and that this sign will protect them from the coming plague. Emerson conveys that he relies on himself, on his divinely given genius, to protect him from the plagues of life.

Figurative Language

Emerson makes more use of figurative language and literary devices than many essayists. He is particularly fond of using various forms of comparison—simile, metaphor, and analogy—to add color to a work whose primary purpose is to persuade. One passage contains several examples:

> Men do what is called a good action . . . much as they would pay a fine in expiation of daily nonappearance on parade. Their works are done as an apology or extenuation of their living in the world—as invalids and the insane pay a high board. Their virtues are penances.

The essay also contains some striking examples of personification: "Malice and vanity wear the coat of philanthropy," and, "the centuries are conspirators against the sanity and authority of the soul."

Romanticism

Emerson is considered an American icon of romanticism, a philosophical and literary movement that began in Europe in the early eighteenth century. Emerson's philosophy as expressed in "Self-Reliance" largely overlaps the ideas of romanticism, which include the inherent worth of the individual, the importance of personal freedom from religious and social restrictions, and the divinity of nature. French philosopher and writer Jean-Jacques Rousseau was strongly influential in the development of romanticism in Europe, as was the German writer Johann Wolfgang von Goethe, whose work the New England transcendentalists read.

Historical Context

New England Transcendentalism

Transcendentalism took root in New England in the mid-1830s in reaction against the rationalism (emphasis on intellectual understanding) of the Unitarian Church. The philosophy centered around the premise that divine truth is present in all created things and that truth is known through intuition, not through the rational mind. From this core proceeded the belief that all of nature, including all humans, is one with God, whom the transcendentalists sometimes called the Over-Soul. In an essay with that title, Emerson defined God as "that great nature in which we rest . . . that Unity within which every man's particular being is contained and made one with all other."

The term transcendental was borrowed from German philosopher Immanuel Kant (1724–1804), who wrote in his well-known work *Critique of Practical Reason*, "I call all knowledge transcendental which is concerned, not with objects, but with our mode of knowing objects so far as this is possible a priori" (meaning, independent of sensory experience). American transcendentalism was thus clearly linked to similar philosophies that existed in Europe, and it also shared important ideas with Eastern philosophies and religions, including Hinduism. The New England transcendentalists read the Bhagavadgita (sometimes called the Hindu Bible), the Upanishads (philosophical writings on the Hindu scriptures), and Confucius. In addition, Emerson in "Self-Reliance" quotes both an Islamic caliph (religious person) and the founder of Zoroastrianism.

The New England transcendentalists did not confine themselves to literary pursuits but also experimented with putting their philosophy into practice. Some, such as Bronson Alcott and Elizabeth Peabody, focused on educational reform. Peabody and Margaret Fuller applied the principles of transcendentalism to the crusade for women's rights. The group created two experimental communities, Fruitlands and Brook Farm.

Compare & Contrast

- **Mid-1800s:** Transcendentalism, which borrows some elements of Eastern philosophies and religions, takes hold in Massachusetts and influences many American intellectuals and writers.

  Today: Yoga is increasingly popular throughout the United States. Yoga, the Sanskrit word for ''union,'' is a philosophy that was first systematized by the Indian sage Patanjali. The various schools of yoga taught today have some things in common with transcendentalism, such as the beliefs that each individual soul is directly linked to God and that truth is everywhere present in creation and can be experienced intuitively, rather than rationally. While millions of Americans practice only one element of yoga—its regimen of physical postures and exercises—a growing number are adopting the broader philosophy and its more mystical practices, such as meditation.

- **Mid-1800s:** As the Industrial Revolution brings more efficient production of goods—which, in turn, makes goods more abundant and more affordable—Emerson cautions that progress and happiness are not to be found through materialism but by living simply and seeking peace within.

  Today: An informal ABC News poll finds that nearly one-third of Americans spend more than they earn. This accords with statistics that show that, in 2000 and 2001, the monthly savings rate is often negative, meaning that in some months Americans collectively are spending more than they are earning and not saving any money at all.

- **Mid-1800s:** The economy of the American South is based on slave labor, and Americans are deeply divided over whether slavery is morally acceptable. Anti-slavery literature mailed to the South is routinely burned or otherwise destroyed. In the North, abolitionists are sometimes physically attacked. In 1837, abolitionist editor Elijah P. Lovejoy is murdered for his opposition to slavery. Only after a massively destructive Civil War is slavery finally abolished.

  Today: Virtually no person in America would argue that slavery is acceptable. Since the Civil War, black Americans have fought for and won equal rights under the law in all arenas, from voting to property ownership.

But it is the writing of Emerson and Henry David Thoreau that has been the most enduring product of American transcendentalism. Thoreau's ideas about nonviolent resistance to oppressors, especially, were important both to Mahatma Gandhi's campaign against the British in India in the early 1900s and to the American civil rights movement of the 1960s.

Abolitionism

During the three decades before the Civil War, the movement to abolish slavery in the United States steadily gained momentum. An abolitionist newspaper, the *Liberator,* began publication in 1831, and the American Anti-Slavery Society was founded in Philadelphia in 1833. By 1838, there were nearly fifteen hundred anti-slavery organizations in the United States, with nearly a quarter of a million members. The Liberty Party was formed in 1840 to make abolition a central issue in national politics.

Emerson and his fellow transcendentalists spoke out against slavery, as did John Greenleaf Whittier and other writers. *Narrative of the Life of Frederick Douglass, An American Slave,* the autobiography of escaped slave Frederick Douglass, was published in 1845 and became an immediate bestseller. Harriet Beecher Stowe's famous anti-slavery novel, *Uncle Tom's Cabin,* published serially in 1851–1852, gave a tremendous boost to the abolitionist cause. Both books movingly portray the brutal conditions and dehumanizing effects of slavery as it existed in the American South. In addition, the Fugitive Slave Act of 1850, which legislated harsh penalties for escaped slaves who were recaptured, actually strengthened the anti-slavery movement.

Slavery, of course, became a central issue in the Civil War. Abraham Lincoln, of whom the normally apolitical Emerson was a strong supporter, signed the Emancipation Proclamation freeing all slaves in 1863. The proclamation was symbolic, however; enforcement provisions did not back it. Slavery finally ended with the adoption of the Thirteenth Amendment to the United States Constitution in 1865.

Sensibility

During the nineteenth century, the term ''sensibility'' was used to mean adherence to a set of unwritten but all-encompassing rules that governed acceptable social behavior. A person of sensibility observed others closely to learn how things were done and then acted accordingly, being careful never to step outside the bounds of conventional behavior. The term is preserved in the title of Jane Austen's famous novel, *Sense and Sensibility,* first published in 1811. The story follows the lives of two sisters, one of whom lives a life governed by sensibility and the other of whom flouts sensibility and lives by her passions. In accordance with Austen's belief that sensibility led to personal happiness and social order, her sensible Elinor is shown to be the wiser of the two and is rewarded—after many dramatic trials—with the man of her dreams, while sensual Marianne must reform herself before the author allows her to make a happy marriage.

The idea of sensibility as promoted by Austen and by nineteenth-century society in general is exactly that which Emerson argues against in ''Self-Reliance.''

Critical Overview

There are two distinct bodies of criticism of Emerson's work: commentary on his writing and commentary on his thinking. As a writer, Emerson has been consistently praised through the years from all quarters. Joel Myerson, in *Concise Dictionary of Literary Biography: 1640–1865,* quotes Rene Wellek, a highly respected historian of literary criticism, as deeming Emerson ''the outstanding representative of romantic symbolism in the English-speaking world.'' Myerson himself adds:

> Ralph Waldo Emerson is perhaps the single most influential figure in American literary history. More

than any other author of his day, he was responsible for shaping the literary style and vision of the American romantic period, the era when the United States first developed a distinctively national literature worthy of comparison to that of the mother country.

Myerson goes on to cite Emerson's influence on Thoreau, Herman Melville, Walt Whitman, and Emily Dickinson.

Alfred S. Reid, in *Style in the American Renaissance: A Symposium,* writes that he does not admire Emerson as a philosopher but does hold him in high esteem as a writer. He calls Emerson ''a skillful shaper of sentences, a composer of expository essays that move and give pleasure. . . . one of the few great craftsmen of the genre.'' Reid echoes the sentiments of Emerson's contemporary Nathaniel Hawthorne, who is quoted by John C. Gerber in *Reference Guide to American Literature* as having said that he ''admired Emerson as a poet of deep beauty and austere tenderness but sought nothing from him as a philosopher.''

As consistently as Emerson is praised as a writer, ''Self-Reliance'' is considered the pinnacle of his efforts. According to Gerber, ''In many respects 'Self-Reliance' is the capstone of American romanticism.'' Reid concurs: ''Emerson never again achieved such an artful balance of earnest goodness and pungent oratory. . . . No other essay disentangles the truth from the universal soul as this one, or says it with such eclat.''

As a philosopher, Emerson has received more mixed reviews. He was hotly controversial in his own time, especially for this pronouncements against organized religion. Just before the publication of ''Self-Reliance,'' former president John Quincy Adams wrote dismissively of Emerson's philosophy:

> A young man named Ralph Waldo Emerson . . . after failing in the everyday vocations of a Unitarian preacher and schoolmaster, starts a new doctrine of transcendentalism, declares all the old revelations superannuated and worn out, and announces the approach of new revelations and prophecies.

With the passage of time, criticism of Emerson's philosophy has become less emotional and more pointed. Joyce W. Warren, in *The American Narcissus,* faults Emerson for holding some extreme and unbalanced positions. She writes,

> Despite Emerson's insistence on the grandeur of the self, this philosophy in practice necessarily involves the pettiness that is inherent in any systematic refusal to learn from others. . . . Implicit in Emerson's ideas is the provincialism and narrowness of the self-interested person.''

The interior of the study in Emerson's home in Concord, Massachusetts

The Cambridge History of English and American Literature, published in the early twentieth century, declares that Emerson's philosophy was weakened by his failure to fully understand and grapple with the nature of evil:

> He is above all the poet of religion and philosophy for the young; whereas men, as they grow older, are inclined to turn from him . . . to those sages who have . . . a firm grasp of the darker facts of human nature.

The writer goes on, however, with admirable foresight: ''As time passes, the deficiencies of this brief period . . . of which Emerson was the perfect spokesman may well be more and more condoned

for its rarity and beauty.'' And, though the limits and imperfections of Emerson's philosophy are acknowledged, so is his powerful influence on later philosophers and on American culture as a whole. Myerson points out that Emerson's ideas inspired the quintessentially American philosophy called pragmatism, later developed by William James and John Dewey. Reid sums up Emerson's contribution to American culture:

> . . . through his essays flow the vital currents of American culture. Here we find that fulsome blend of Puritanism, Enlightenment, and Romantic idealism that historically make up the early American charac-

ter; here too the democratic idealism, the individualism, the contempt for tradition, and the practical sagacity.

Criticism

Candyce Norvell

Norvell is an independent educational writer who specializes in English and literature. She holds degrees in linguistics and journalism and has done graduate work in theology. In this essay, she discusses three reasons why Emerson's frequent references to famous men weaken his argument in ''Self-Reliance.''

Frequent references to historical figures and famous contemporaries are a hallmark of Emerson's essays, and the technique is prominent in ''Self-Reliance.'' Emerson mentions scores of well-known men from a wide range of cultures, eras, and disciplines. Most of the men are named as positive examples of the traits Emerson associates with self-reliance. For example, in a single sentence Emerson names Pythagoras, Socrates, Jesus, Luther, Copernicus, Galileo, and Newton as great men who were unaffected by society's disapproval. A few are given as examples of men who, through no fault of their own, are too much revered—men whose recorded thoughts and passed-down ideas are wrongly used by average people. The biblical David, Jeremiah, and Paul fall into this group. A few men, such as Islam's Caliph Ali and Zoroastrianism's founder, are quoted.

No matter how Emerson employs each one, his purpose in doing so is to strengthen his argument for self-reliance. For more than one reason, however, the use of these examples seems less effective than other means might have been. A few references are so vague that even scholars who study Emerson are not sure to whom they refer. Emerson habitually uses last names only. When he writes, ''That is it which throws . . . America into Adams's eye,'' it is impossible to know which Adams he had in mind: Samuel, John, or John Quincy. Not knowing which Adams, the reader also does not know which trait or idea or action Emerson means to spotlight.

This vagueness occurs a few times and is frustrating but not a major stumbling block to understanding Emerson's central argument. But Emerson's name-dropping does cause more serious prob-

lems. First, there is a logical inconsistency in using this technique in support of the particular argument Emerson is making in this essay. Second, many of the references become increasingly obscure as time marches on. And third, the fact that all those mentioned are men—and overwhelmingly European or white American men—detracts from Emerson's authority, again increasingly with the passage of time. Each of these three problems will now be considered in greater detail.

The logical inconsistency that is inherent in Emerson's leaning upon one famous shoulder after another is the most serious problem and has nothing to do with cultural changes over time. It is simply that Emerson's core argument that readers should ignore the great men of the past and instead trust themselves should prevent him from using the great men of the past to justify his own thinking. Emerson writes, in essence, that Moses, Plato, and Milton were exemplars of self-reliance and are now regarded as great men; therefore readers should follow in their footsteps. But there is a double contradiction here. First, given that Emerson is preaching ''trust thyself,'' why should he rely on Moses, Plato, and Milton, instead of on himself, to make his point? And second, given that Emerson wants readers to be nonconforming, original individualists, why should they care to become ''great''; i.e., why should they strive to be highly regarded by society or posterity?

An essayist has many different tools available for the building of an argument. Example is only one such tool; Emerson could have limited himself to other tools, such as reasons or facts, and avoided the awkwardness of using examples to support his argument for living life without examples. If he was determined to use examples, Emerson could have used less problematic ones; he might have used himself or, better yet, his readers as examples of the good results of self-reliance. Emerson could have declared that he himself had followed his principle of self-reliance and had thereby become successful and happy. Or, he could have asked readers to recall occasions when they had trusted themselves and had been proven correct. Either of these would have been a valid example in the context of Emerson's argument, and difficult to contest. But instead of taking either of these courses, Emerson made recourse to great men of the past, saying, in effect, that readers should exhibit self-reliance because these men did so and are now considered great. This line of reasoning is directly at odds with many statements throughout the essay.

What Do I Read Next?

- *Essays: First and Second Series* (1990), edited by Douglas Crase, combines all of the essays that Emerson originally published in two separate volumes in 1841 and 1844.

- *''The Concord Hymn'' and Other Poems* (1996) is a collection of Emerson's most well-known poems.

- *Walden* (1854), by Emerson's friend and student Henry David Thoreau, is the world-famous autobiographical record of Thoreau's time spent living in solitude in the woods near Walden Pond, Concord, Massachusetts. *Walden* has become an enduringly popular literary expression of American transcendentalism, individualism, and naturalism.

- *Little Women* (1868) is a classic novel based on the childhood of its author, Louisa May Alcott, the daughter of Emerson's friend and fellow transcendentalist Bronson Alcott. The book tells the story of the March family, following daughters Meg, Jo, Beth, and Amy from childhood to adulthood. The Marches are transcendentalists who value self-reliance, individualism, compassion, and education above material and social achievement.

- Emerson called *Leaves of Grass* (1855), poetry by Walt Whitman, ''the most extraordinary piece of wit and wisdom that American has yet produced.'' It is now considered one of the most important works of poetry in the English language.

Emerson writes, ''There is a time in every man's education when he arrives at the conviction that . . . imitation is suicide.'' Yet he urges readers to imitate Moses, Plato, and Milton, at least in the matter of self-reliance. ''Don't imitate others,'' Emerson seems to say, ''except when the others are doing what I agree with.''

He writes, ''Why all this deference to Alfred, and Scanderberg, and Gustavus?'' Yet he shows deference to a host of other great men and strongly implies that readers should as well.

''Man is timid and apologetic,'' Emerson writes. ''He does not say, 'I think,' 'I am,' but quotes some saint or sage.'' And then he himself quotes both saints and sages. As one final example, Emerson writes:

> When the good is near you . . . you shall not discern the footprints of any other; you shall not see the face of man; you shall not hear any name; the way, the thought, the good, shall be wholly strange and new. It shall exclude example and experience.

Of course, Emerson's own explanation of ''the way'' is heavily tracked with footprints and populated with faces, and it rings with a roll call of

names. Not content to present his own ideas as being ''wholly strange and new,'' Emerson embeds them in a roster of examples and other men's experiences.

Generations of readers attest that this recurring contradiction does not invalidate Emerson's argument, but it does weaken its force. It calls attention to the extreme nature of Emerson's position. While most readers can agree that some degree of self-reliance is good, close readers can also see that Emerson has set a standard for his readers that he as a writer is not able or willing to meet. While exhorting readers to ignore history and other men and rely only on themselves, Emerson repeatedly relies on history and other men.

The second problem with Emerson's wide-ranging references to men of the past is that some of these men have receded into obscurity with the passage of time. Many modern readers have no acquaintance with names such as Clarkson, Lavoisier, Hutton, Fourier, and many others mentioned by Emerson. More recent thinkers and doers have built upon their accomplishments and surpassed their fame, and only specialists in their fields know them. Emerson would say that this is exactly as it should be—that the old should continually be supplanted by the new. But this process does make his essay gradually less accessible and powerful. Even a footnote giving a one-sentence biography of the man behind the name doesn't give today's readers a full understanding of the man's importance in his own time or in Emerson's. (A hundred years from now, a footnote explaining, "Michael Jordan was the greatest basketball player of the twentieth century" would not be sufficient to convey his stature in twentieth-century America.) It would require outside research to grasp why Emerson chose these particular men over others.

In Emerson's defense, it is quite possible that he never foresaw that his essay would endure as long as it has. Perhaps he expected that he would be supplanted just as Clarkson, Lavoisier, and company have been.

Finally, Emerson's exclusion of women and his near-exclusion of non-European men among his examples of greatness perhaps makes him less authoritative to modern readers than he might otherwise be. Emerson can be appreciated for including quotations from Islamic and Zoroastrian religious teachers. And it must be acknowledged that Frederick Douglass, who would have made an outstanding example of self-reliance, would not publish his best-selling autobiography until four years after the publication of "Self-Reliance." Emily Dickinson, practically Emerson's neighbor and a stellar example of self-reliance, was only a child in 1841; her poems would not become widely known and appreciated until the following century.

Still, among the New England transcendentalists there were accomplished women writers and activists who undoubtedly had to overcome societal disapproval in the course of their work and who would have made as good examples of self-reliance as some of the men featured. Also, as an abolitionist Emerson must have been aware of courageous black men and women of his time who were engaged in breaking the chains of history in just the way that Emerson celebrates. That Emerson did not think to preserve their names in his essay along with those of Moses, Plato, and Milton is unfortunate. It is also a sign that, as mightily as he roared against conformity and conventions, he himself sometimes failed to break through them.

Source: Candyce Norvell, Critical Essay on "Self-Reliance," in *Nonfiction Classics for Students,* The Gale Group, 2002.

> Emerson's core argument that readers should ignore the great men of the past and instead trust themselves should prevent him from using the great men of the past to justify his own thinking."

B. L. Packer

In the following essay excerpt, Packer examines Emerson's prescription for self-reform in "Self-Reliance," including some seeming contradictions between his advocation of self and spirituality.

To learn how to achieve this double abandonment we must turn to the best known of Emerson's essays, "Self-Reliance." If "Circles" was an attempt to discern the general laws governing human behavior, "Self Reliance" is an attempt to formulate a code of conduct for the individual believer, to answer the question: "What shall *I* do to be saved?"

Emerson had always conceived of the principle of self-reliance as an answer to the problem of individual salvation; one of his earliest explorations of the topic, a sermon entitled "Trust Yourself," was preached as a commentary upon Matthew 16:26: "For what is a man profited, if he shall gain the whole world, and lose his own soul?" In it Emerson had used a passage from an early journal that already contains the essence of the later doctrine:

> Every man has his own voice, manner, eloquence, & just as much his own sort of love & grief & imagination & action. Let him scorn to imitate any being, let him scorn to be a secondary man, let him fully trust his own share of God's goodness, that correctly used it will lead him on to perfection which has no type yet in the Universe save only in the Divine Mind.

It was the gospel he had been sent that he might preach, the good news he had been chosen to proclaim. The topic was never far from his thoughts. In 1835, when he was chiding himself for his lack of literary productivity, listing things he felt were peculiarly his own, one of the topics was "the sublimity of Self-reliance." As his thought widened and matured, his conception of the principle grew likewise, until it came to signify everything praiseworthy in the universe. If the "universal grudge"

> **When the soul is really present, Emerson insists, all *sense* of dualism ceases; one does not feel like a little self worshipping or trusting or relying on a bigger Self."**

was Emerson's term for the spirit behind every scheme of reform, self-reliance was the name he used to designate the means by which all schemes of reform were to be accomplished. "It is easy to see that a greater self-reliance must work a revolution in all the offices and relations of men," he argues in the essay, "in their religion; in their education; in their pursuits; their modes of living; their association; in their property; in their speculative views." (That Emerson conceived of self-reliance as a *revolutionary* principle is particularly important to remember now, when his attacks on "miscellaneous popular charities" are in danger of making him sound like the most reactionary politicians. The latter should ponder the implications of Emerson's closing remarks—that "the reliance on Property, including the reliance on governments which protect it, is the want of self-reliance" before rushing to claim Emerson as one of their own.) Every subject that had attracted Emerson's attention in the turbulent years just past—the imitativeness of American literature, the "terror of opinion" that made Americans moral cowards, the reliance upon property that engendered that terror, the futility of preaching that teaches the soul to look for help anywhere other than within itself, the necessity of training the soul to conceive of life as a perpetual process of abandonment—can all be treated under the general rubric of self-reliance. The essay as it stands is a kind of gigantic coda to the work of Emerson's decade of challenge. Some have found its very variousness distracting; Firkins, who concedes the essay's greatness, nevertheless complains that it lacks "tone"; there is in the essay "a singularly mixed effect of anthem, eclogue, sermon, and denunciation." Yet he admits that "no essay of Emerson contains so many phrases that are at the same time barbed and winged."

In fact, the success of those phrases in establishing themselves as proverbial may be the greatest obstacle to the enjoyment of the contemporary reader, who may feel at first as though he is thumbing through a particularly worn copy of *Bartlett's Familiar Quotations.* Yet to the reader willing to look beyond the familiar phrases, attentive to the interplay of Emerson's many voices and to the startling redefinition of familiar terms those voices proclaim, the essay will shortly come to seem as strange and difficult as it really is.

It begins with a restatement of themes made familiar by *The American Scholar:* the self-reliant man who has the courage to make his own spontaneous impressions into universal symbols (as Wordsworth had done) will find himself triumphing over the tyranny of time. "Speak your latent conviction and it shall be the universal sense; for the inmost in due time becomes the outmost,—and our first thought is rendered back to us by the trumpets of the Last Judgment." Hence Emerson's First Commandment: "Trust thyself: every heart vibrates to that iron string." What Emerson means by self-trust is given to us, as usual, not by definition but by analogy: it is something like the pure self-centeredness of infancy, something again like the "nonchalance of boys who are sure of a dinner." It is action without self-consciousness, action without concern for (or even awareness of) consequences— the sort of thing Blake had in mind when he praised Jesus as one who "acted from impulse, not from rules."

Unfortunately, this kind of self-trust is nearly impossible for a grown man to achieve; a grown man is "clapped into jail by his consciousness. As soon as he has once acted or spoken with eclat"— and Emerson is surely thinking here of his own experience after the Divinity School *Address*—"he is a committed person, watched by the sympathy or the hatred of hundreds whose affections must now enter into his account. There is no Lethe for this." The point is not that the man is incapable of telling the truth after once speaking with éclat; merely that he can never recapture that purer kind of innocence that consists in being *unaware* of the consequences. An orator who could somehow manage to free himself from this jail of self-consciousness, and "having observed, observe again from the same unaffected, unbiased, unbribable, unaffrighted innocence," would make himself formidable; his opinions "would sink like darts into the ear of men, and put them in fear."

That Emerson is describing not himself but his possible hero, the figure he will later call the Central

Man, is apparent from his use of the conditional mood; his own journals were there to remind him how far he was from his own ideal. One is inclined to suspect that his private chagrin is partly responsible for the uncharacteristic bitterness of the attack he now launches on the chief obstacle to self-trust. ''Society everywhere is in conspiracy against the manhood of every one of its members. Society is a joint-stock company in which the members agree for the better securing of his bread to each shareholder, to surrender the liberty and culture of the eater.'' Hence Emerson's Second Commandment: ''Whoso would be a man must be a nonconformist.''

What follows this assertion is a violent and disturbing paragraph that seems to have been designed to contain something to offend everyone. Emerson begins by advocating, like Yeats, the casting out of all remorse. Later on in the essay he will define ''prayer'' as ''the soliloquy of a beholding and jubilant soul''; he here advances the same startling conception of penitence: ''Absolve you to yourself, and you shall have the suffrage of the world.'' From these sublime heights of self-reliance he grandly condescends to answer the objections of the ''valued adviser'' who used to importune him with the ''dear old doctrines of the church. On my saying, What have I to do with the sacredness of traditions, if I live wholly from within? my friend suggested—'But these impulses may be from below, not from above.' I replied, 'They do not seem to me to be such; but if I am the Devil's child, I will live then from the Devil.'''

The logic of this answer is like the logic of Blake's famous Proverb of Hell: ''Sooner murder an infant in its cradle than nurse unacted desires.'' Emerson is not advocating diabolism any more than Blake is advocating infanticide; the hyperbole is a way of suggesting the real ugliness of the alternative—in Emerson's case, maintaining a dead church, contributing to a dead Bible-society, worshipping a dead God. The word that needs stressing in Emerson's reply is not ''Devil'' but the verb ''live'': it is better to live from the Devil than die with the church. ''For to him that is joined to all the living there is hope,'' as Ecclesiastes puts it in a verse Emerson might have cited here, ''for a living dog is better than a dead lion.''

Harriet Martineau had been impressed with the remarkable good-humor Americans displayed, their kindness and courtesy toward one another. She did not connect this quality, which she admired, with the want of moral independence she deplored, but

Emerson did. ''In this our talking America we are ruined by our good nature and listening on all sides.'' ''Check this lying hospitality and lying affection.'' Self-reliance is impossible without honesty, and honesty sometimes entails a willingness to be rude. Emerson cannot yet claim that he has this willingness; ''every decent and well-spoken individual affects and sways'' him more than is right. But he indulges in a fantasy of rudeness, imagines himself being able to speak the ''rude truth'' first to a proselytizing Abolitionist, then to members of his own family. ''I shun father and mother and wife and brother, when my genius calls me. I would write on the lintels of the door-post, *Whim.* I hope it is somewhat better than whim at last, but we cannot spend the day in explanation.'' The sentences are discreetly blasphemous: they allude both to Jesus' command to leave father and mother for his sake, and to God's directive to the children of Israel to mark with blood the lintel of the doorway, that the Angel of Death might pass over their houses and spare their firstborn. Emerson's redeemer is his genius (a theme he will develop with more explicitness later in the essay); his saving sign is a confession of irresponsibility and even triviality, designed to make the serious men—the controversialists, the paragraph writers—pass over his house as something beneath contempt. It resembles a similar passage in ''Circles'' in its blend of irony and affected innocence:

> But lest I should mislead any when I have my own head, and obey my whims, let me remind the reader that I am only an experimenter. Do not set the least value on what I do, or the least discredit on what I do not, as if I pretended to settle anything as true or false. I unsettle all things. No facts are to me sacred; none are profane; I simply experiment, an endless seeker, with no Past at my back.

Whim is only a provisional term; we hope that it will be replaced by something better than whim at last (what we hope it will be is the force he will later call Spontaneity or Instinct—though these terms are hardly more likely to recommend him to the orthodox) but we cannot spend the day in explanation, for the same reason that the children of Israel could not tarry to leaven their bread when Pharaoh finally agreed to let them go. As Cavell says, Emerson, in writing *Whim* upon the lintels, is ''taking upon himself the mark of God, and of departure. . . This departure, such setting out is, in our poverty, what hope consists in, all there is to hope for; it is the abandoning of despair, which is otherwise our condition.''

But leaving the dead institutions of society behind is only half the task of departure. Our own past acts, as "Circles" points out, are governed by the same law of ossification visible in history as a whole. And leaving behind our own past insights may be even harder than rejecting the counsels of society, for we naturally possess a greater affection for our own past thoughts. Then, too, there is the fear that inconsistency will expose us to ridicule, that hardest of all crosses to bear. Emerson gave evidence early that he was not to be scared from self-trust by the hobgoblin of foolish consistency; the editor of his sermons tells of an incident in which Emerson interrupted his delivery of a sermon to say quietly to the congregation: "The sentence which I have just read I do not now believe," and then went on to the next page.

Such determination to prefer truth to his past apprehension of truth also governs the choice of the example Emerson now inserts into "Self Reliance" to illustrate what he means by having the courage to risk self-contradiction. He had always objected strongly to any Theism that described God as a Person. "I deny Personality to God because it is too little not too much," he wrote in his journal. "Life, personal life is faint & cold to the energy of God." This denial of personality to God was one of the things his auditors had found most offensive about the Divinity School *Address*. The sermon his former colleague at the Second Church, Henry Ware, Jr., had preached in objection to Transcendentalist ideas in September 1838 was called "The Personality of the Deity"; it regarded attempts to reduce God to an abstract set of laws or moral relations as "essentially vicious." The *Christian Examiner* reviewed Emerson's address and Ware's sermon together, greatly to the detriment of the former.

Emerson's doctrine of Divine Impersonality had angered a whole community; the *Address* had helped end his career as a supply preacher in Unitarian pulpits, and for all he knew at the time, it might have ended his career as a lecturer. Yet now, in "Self-Reliance," he warns himself against making an idol of his own theology: "In your metaphysics you have denied personality to the Deity; yet when the devout motions of the soul come, yield to them heart and life, though they should clothe God with shape and color. Leave your theory, as Joseph his coat in the hand of the harlot, and flee." It is only after describing how these menaces to self-trust or abandonment are to be overcome that Emerson will consider the question posed by the trusted adviser whose earlier warnings he had scorned. "The mag-

netism which all original action exerts is explained when we inquire the reason of self-trust. Who is the Trustee? What is the aboriginal Self on which a universal reliance may be grounded?"

The answer he gives, though, concerns not persons but powers: a "deep force" he calls by the triple name of Spontaneity, Instinct, and Intuition. "Gladly I would solve if I could this problem of a Vocabulary," Emerson groaned after the Divinity School *Address*; he knew very well that his effort to topple "the idolatry of nouns & verbs" in which the Deity had been so long addressed would not be easy. It is easy to object to the terms Emerson chooses, particularly easy for those readers to whom the *instinctual* suggests something bestial, the *spontaneous* something irresponsible, and the *intuitive* something irrational. But the risk of being misunderstood is one Emerson will have to run (anyway, "to be great is to be misunderstood") if he expects to find words in any vocabulary that will suggest a *force* felt by the individual as proceeding from within, yet somehow connected to the larger forces of nature, forces that are prior to reflection, self-consciousness, and the sallies of the will, prior even to that primary fall into division that created him as a separate being. "For the sense of being which in calm hours rises, we know not how, in the soul, is not diverse from things, from space, from light, from time, from man, but one with them, and proceeds obviously from the same source whence their life and being also proceed." To explain what he means by this Emerson offers this quiet prose summary of the Orphic chants of *Nature:* "We first share the life by which things exist, and afterwards see them as appearances in nature, and forget that we have shared their cause." What defines us as individuals is that act of forgetting; hence the paradox that intuition is a better pipeline to truth than conscious reflection. "When we discern justice, when we discern truth, we do nothing of ourselves, but allow a passage to its beams. If we ask whence this comes, if we seek to pry into the soul that causes, all philosophy is at fault. Its presence or absence is all we can affirm."

But here, at the heart of the essay, the reader is likely to be troubled by a contradiction. Emerson began by urging us to insist on ourselves, to express what is absolutely peculiar to us as individuals; he now makes it a defining characteristic of the state of true vision that in it "we do nothing of ourselves" but merely "allow a passage to its beams." This is evidently a paradox; it is one that is as central to Emerson's faith as the Incarnation was to traditional

Christianity. Indeed, it is a resemblance Emerson acknowledges later on in the essay with his unobtrusive little epigram: "a man is the word made flesh." *Any* man is the word made flesh, the incarnation of the universal in the particular. "It seems to be true," Emerson had written in that early journal passage concerning self-trust, "that the more exclusively idiosyncratic a man is, the more general & infinite he is, which though it may not be a very intelligible expression means I hope something intelligible. In listening more intently to our own reason, we are not becoming in the ordinary sense more selfish, but are departing more from what is small, & falling back on truth itself & God."

Here Quentin Anderson (with whom, for once, I find myself in complete agreement) makes an important distinction. It is true that Emerson believes in the existence of a realm of spiritual laws that serves as a base for independent moral vision. "But what the early radical Emerson was excited about was not the existence of the base, but the discovery of the primacy of the individual, who can alone realize the claims of spirit." And he concludes: "There is something inclusive that justifies his activity—this is a statement which quickly leads us away from Emerson: *only the activity uniquely mine can manifest the inclusive*—this is a statement which leads us toward an understanding of him."

Emerson, in other words, is less interested in inquiring into the nature of that Aboriginal Self on whom we can rely than in the nature of the procedures the individual must follow in order to open himself, if only momentarily, to that *power* he regarded as the essence of divinity. When he was only nineteen he wrote in his journal that "the idea of *power* seems to have been every where at the bottom of theology"; in another place he noted that power enters "somewhat more intimately into our idea of God than any other attribute." Power is "a great flood which encircles the universe and is poured out in unnumbered channels to feed the fountains of life and the wants of Creation, but every where runs back again and is swallowed up in its eternal source. That Source is God."

In the highest moments, when we are for a moment the channel through which absolute power is flowing, the petty dialectic of self and society, self and past acts of the self, fades away into insignificance; until Emerson can turn on his own vocabulary with withering contempt. "Why then do we prate of self-reliance? Inasmuch as the soul is present, there will be power not confident but agent. To

talk of reliance is a poor external way of speaking." The term "self-reliance" implies dualism, disunion, a poor frightened individual attempting to rely *on* that Aboriginal Self presumed to be within. If this were really the new religion Emerson had come to preach, it would be no better than the one it replaced. In fact, it would remind us of nothing so much as the ruinous narcissism of Blake's Albion, who loses the Divine Vision when he turns his eyes toward his "Self" or Shadow and makes that his God:

> Then Man ascended mourning into the splendors of
> his palace
> Above him rose a Shadow from his wearied intellect
> Of living gold, pure, perfect, holy: in white linen pure
> he hover'd
> A sweet entrancing self delusion . . .

When the soul is really present, Emerson insists, all *sense* of dualism ceases; one does not feel like a little self worshipping or trusting or relying on a bigger Self, but like a power open to that "great flood which encircles the universe." Self-reliance is not an attitude or a virtue; it is a way of acting, and can only be manifested through action. "Speak rather of that which relies, because it works and is." The distinction is made clearer in the section of the essay concerning the application of self-reliance to prayer: Emerson commends "the prayer of the farmer kneeling in his field to weed it, the prayer of the rower kneeling with the stroke of his oar," but lashes out at the kind of prayer that "looks abroad and asks for some foreign addition to come through some foreign virtue" not only because such prayer for a private end seems to him "meanness and theft" but because it "supposes dualism and not unity in nature and consciousness." True prayer knows no such dualism, even in its contemplative phase. Then it is merely "the soliloquy of a beholding and jubilant soul. It is the spirit of God pronouncing his works good."

In a pair of terse epigrams Emerson condenses the wisdom he has acquired in the turbulent years just passed. "Life only avails, not the having lived," is one; it is an admonition not to look for power in the sepulchers of past literature or past religion or past forms of social organization. "Power ceases in the instant of repose" is the second; it warns us that the divinity within us can only be manifested during those brief moments in which the soul, overcoming the deadliness of the past (including its own past), manages to shoot the gulf, dart to a new aim— manages to do this despite its knowledge that the new aim will someday be as deadly as the old. "This one fact the world hates, that the soul *becomes*; for, that forever degrades the past, turns all riches to poverty, all reputation to a shame, shoves Jesus and Judas equally aside.''

The really formidable difficulty of this enterprise suggests why Emerson felt it necessary to invoke Instinct and Intuition as the only forces that can still put us in contact with our own divinity. The conscious intellect, the intellect alone, could draw only one lesson from Emerson's myth of ossification: that all action is the vanity of vanities. Successful creation is a momentary circumventing of that conscious intellect, which will reassert itself soon enough; the real danger for Americans was not that a surrender to Instinct would plunge them into a maelstrom of uncontrollable passions but that even the wildest impulses can scarcely overcome for a moment the national tendencies to caution, imitativeness, and dissimulation. Hence Emerson's insistence upon the necessity of ''surprise,'' as in the closing paragraph of ''Circles''—''The one thing which we seek with insatiable desire, is to forget ourselves, to be surprised out of our propriety, to lose our sempiternal memory, and to do something without knowing how or why; in short, to draw a new circle''—or in the poem ''Merlin'':

> ''Pass in, pass in,'' the angels say
> ''In to the upper doors,
> Nor count compartments of the floors,
> But mount to paradise
> By the stairway of surprise.''

The man who has perfected the art of abandonment has acquired the only kind of affluence that Fate cannot menace. He has acquired ''living property, which does not wait the beck of rulers, or mobs, or revolutions, or fire, or storm, or bankruptcies, but perpetually renews itself wherever the man breathes.''

Source: B. L. Packer, ''Portable Property,'' in *Emerson's Fall: A New Interpretation of the Major Essays,* The Continuum Publishing Company, 1982, pp. 137–47.

Sources

''Emerson: His Failure to Perceive the Meaning of Evil,'' in *The Cambridge History of English and American Literature,* Vol. XV, edited by W. P. Trent, J. Erskine, S. P. Sherman, and C. Van Doren, Cambridge University Press, 1907–1921.

Gerber, John C., ''Emerson, Ralph Waldo,'' in *Reference Guide to American Literature,* 3d ed., St. James Press, 1994.

Khoren, Arisian, '''The Sun Shines Today Also': The Vision and Impact of Ralph Waldo Emerson,'' speech delivered at New York Society for Ethical Culture, June 17, 2001.

Myerson, Joel, ''Ralph Waldo Emerson,'' in *Concise Dictionary of American Literary Biography: 1640–1865,* Gale Research, Inc., 1988, pp. 74–93.

Reid, Alfred S., ''Emerson's Prose Style: An Edge to Goodness,'' in *Style in the American Renaissance: A Symposium,* edited by Carl F. Strauch, Transcendental Books, 1970, pp. 37–42.

Warren, Joyce W., ''Transcendentalism and the Self: Ralph Waldo Emerson,'' in *The American Narcissus: Individualism and Women in Nineteenth-Century American Fiction,* Rutgers University Press, 1984, pp. 23–53.

Wilson, Leslie Perrin, ''New England Transcendentalism,'' in *Concord Magazine,* November 1998.

Further Reading

Cole, Phyllis, *Mary Moody Emerson and the Origins of Transcendentalism: A Family History,* Oxford University Press, 1998.

Mary Moody Emerson, an aunt of Ralph Waldo Emerson, was a writer herself and one of the early adherents of American transcendentalism. This work examines Emerson's influences on her nephew.

Porte, Joel, and Saundra Morris, eds., *The Cambridge Companion to Ralph Waldo Emerson,* Cambridge University Press, 1999.

Intended to provide a critical introduction to Emerson's work, *The Cambridge Companion to Ralph Waldo Emerson* includes new interpretations of Emerson's work. In addition to commissioned essays, the work includes a comprehensive chronology and bibliography.

Richardson, Robert D., Jr., *Emerson: The Mind on Fire,* University of California Press, 1995.

This biography gives a historical perspective on Emerson and his work. It provides inspiring details on Emerson's thoughts and on the societal and political forces shaping the United States in the 1800s.

Versluis, Arthur, *American Transcendentalism and Asian Religions,* Oxford University Press on Demand, 1997.

Part of the Oxford University Press Religion in America series, this book covers the beginning of Transcendentalist Orientalism in Europe and the complete history of American Transcendentalism to the twentieth century, with a focus on how Asian religions and cultures have influenced transcendentalism in the West.

Shadow and Act

Ralph Ellison

1964

In his introduction to *Shadow and Act* (1964), Ralph Ellison describes the essays to come as ''an attempt to transform some of the themes, the problems, the enigmas, the contradictions of character and culture native to my predicament, into what Andre Malraux has described as 'conscious thought.''''

This collection consists of essays written over two decades, spanning Ellison's growth as a literary and social critic, his rise to recognition as a serious fiction writer, and his establishment as a thinker and teacher. The essays are divided thematically into three sections; as the author summarizes, they are ''concerned with literature and folklore, with Negro musical expression—especially jazz and the blues—and with the complex relationship between the Negro subculture and North America as a whole.''

The bulk of the collection consists of the first section, ''The Seer and the Seen,'' in which Ellison uses interviews and essays to address his personal experience of being what he calls ''Negro American,'' of African descent, but specifically American. He draws on classic American authors, particularly Twain, Hemingway, Faulkner, and Richard Wright, and both lauds and criticizes them in an effort to represent his experience. ''Sound and the Mainstream'' explores the way music is fundamental to his life and chronicles the careers and influence of several artists.

Shadow and the Act draws on different aspects of the way African American and Caucasian Ameri-

can culture intersect. In keeping with his lifelong commitment to representing the individual with integrity, Ellison draws on personal anecdotes as well as his sophisticated analyses of literary and musical culture in an effort to chronicle his experience of being an African American.

universities nationwide although his home base, and the heart of his work, was Harlem. He died in Harlem on April 16, 1994, with his long-awaited second novel unpublished. The unfinished work was edited after his death by his literary executor and published posthumously with the title *Juneteenth*.

Author Biography

Ralph Waldo Ellison was born on March 1, 1914, in Oklahoma City, Oklahoma. His father, who died when the author was three years old, named his son for the philosopher-writer Ralph Waldo Emerson in hopes that his son would one day become a poet. In his introduction to *Shadow and Act*, Ellison characterizes his Oklahoma community as a "chaotic" mix of cultural influences, curiously free of the race stigma inherent to the South and Northeast, and the epitome of the American frontier. The jazz scene in Oklahoma City and Kansas City, in particular, had an impact on the author's view of the world; he studied music throughout his childhood, and when he finished high school, traveled to Tuskegee University in pursuit of formal training in classical music. He was a voracious reader all of his life and, while at Tuskegee, Ellison read T. S. Eliot's *The Wasteland*, which moved him greatly and directed him toward a career in writing.

In 1936, after his third year at Tuskegee, he left the South for a summer job in New York City, where he met the author Richard Wright. Newly arrived in New York himself, Wright invited Ellison to write a book review and a short story for his publication, thus initiating Ellison into the world of writing. Wright fostered Ellison's work for the next several years, during which Ellison published articles for magazines sponsored by the New York Federal Writers Project, such as *New Challenge* and *New Masses*. *Shadow and Act* contains work largely from this period and details the author's personal reckonings with race, politics, literature, and music in his American culture. In 1952, Ellison's novel *Invisible Man*, the product of seven years of work, was given the National Book Award. Somewhat autobiographical, the novel draws upon the author's experiences as a young man at a southern university, and the influence the communist party had over him as he explores his identity. The novel brought Ellison national fame, both for its artistry and its controversial content, and it continues to be taught regularly in schools today. Following the success of *Invisible Man*, Ellison began teaching at various

Plot Summary

The title *Shadow and Act* is drawn from a movie review Ellison wrote in 1948 for *Magazine of the Year* entitled "The Shadow and the Act." The title makes reference to the disparity between screen images of African Americans, in effect mere shadows of real people designed to suit the ideas of the mainstream, and the reality of African-American life. The collection as a whole is aimed at representing the same disparity on a broader level; drawing on American folklore, ritual, literature, and music, Ellison illustrates the complicated relationship between American culture as a whole and what he calls the Negro-American subculture. In the course of essays, reviews, and interviews written over twenty-two years, Ellison demonstrates his evolution as a writer and a thinker, makes observations about American culture as a whole, and in particular, represents autobiographically his experience of being black in America.

Section One: "The Seer and the Seen"

The first section of *Shadow and Act* is comprised of ten pieces mainly concerning fiction and folklore. In the interviews, "That Same Pain, That Same Pleasure" and "The Art of Fiction," as well as in the speech, "Brave Words for a Startling Occasion," Ellison discusses his influences and evolution as a writer, culminating in his novel *Invisible Man*. "Twentieth-Century Fiction and the Black Mask of Humanity" and "Beating That Boy" concern ways that modern fiction writers struggle with how to represent African Americans in fiction. Ellison discusses the ways black Americans, by definition, challenge American cultural assumptions, and the responsibility of black and white writers alike in representing them. "Hidden Name and Complex Fate" is a discussion of the power of names, and of the act of naming, which is by definition the work of the novelist. "Stephen Crane and the Mainstream of American Fiction" is Ellison's introduction to the 1960 release of *The Red Badge of Courage,* in which he lauds the author's skills, focused mainly on his use of moral imperative in his fiction. "Change the Joke and Slip the Yoke" is a response to Stanley Edgar Hyman's assertions about the function of the "darky entertainer" in American culture. In his response, Ellison outlines his thesis that the comical image of the minstrel serves to invert white America's guilt over slavery into laughter, and thus absolve the culture through identification. "Richard Wright's Blues" is Ellison's contention that the autobiographical *Black Boy* fits the definition of the blues, in the sense that the blues amount to the lyrical expression of individual pain and tragedy. "The Word and the Jug," by contrast, is a response to critic Irving Howe's assertion that Wright is a better and more culturally responsible writer than Ellison and James Baldwin. In the essay, Ellison discusses the ways that Wright's writing falls short of major modern fiction because of its adherence to ideology, and he contends that social critics fall prey to the tendency to view minorities as isolated entities, rather than as part of the larger American culture.

Ralph Ellison

Section Two: "Sound and the Mainstream"

Part 2 of *Shadow and Act* is concerned with music, particularly jazz and blues, as expressions of African-American culture. "Living With Music" is Ellison's account of the music in his neighborhood and how, although it can be cause for writer's block, it is integral to his life. "The Golden Age, Time Past" is a nostalgic look at Minton's Playhouse, the site of the evolution of jazz culture in New York. In "As the Spirit Moves Mahalia," Ellison praises and chronicles the rise of Mahalia Jackson, a gospel singer who, despite her mastery of jazz and blues, maintains the church as her forum. "On Bird, Bird-Watching, and Jazz," he speculates on the way that Charlie Parker, although preoccupied with avoiding the role of performer, effectively made his entire life a performance through his infamous wild behavior. Ellison essentially eulogizes jazz guitarist Charlie Christian and blues singer Jimmy Rushing in "The Charlie Christian Story" and "Remembering Jimmy." In "Blues People," Ellison takes writer LeRoi Jones to task for his limited vision in establishing blues in the context of American culture.

Section Three: "The Shadow and the Act"

In the final section of *Shadow and Act*, Ellison considers the way African-American culture is both integrally a part of, but deeply misunderstood by, the mainstream. "Some Questions and Some Answers" is an interview in which Ellison espouses his notion that African-American culture is an outgrowth of and a response to the larger American culture and the ways it is impossible for the two to be mutually exclusive. "The Shadow and the Act" is Ellison's response to several films that depict African Americans in new, though limited, ways. "The Way It Is" summarizes an interview with a middle-aged black woman in an effort to chronicle the effects of World War II, poverty, and discrimination on the average African American. In "Harlem Is Nowhere," the author describes the work of the Lafargue Psychiatric Clinic, a clinic that meets the needs of the chronically mentally ill in Harlem, and the ways that disenfranchisement of the African-American subculture has created conditions that foster mental illness. Finally, "An American Dilemma: A Review" is Ellison's indictment of the attempt at practicing sociology in a vacuum. Once again he contends that African-American culture cannot be understood as simply a social pathology, but as interactive with and inextricably a part of American culture as a whole.

Key Figures

Louis Armstrong

Although no essay in *Shadow and Act* focuses on Louis Armstrong (1900–1971) alone, Ellison makes reference to him many times throughout the collection, both as a blues master and as a distinctive type of musical performer. In several instances, but most explicitly in "On Bird, Bird-Watching, and Jazz," Ellison makes the point that although Armstrong's theatrical, joking, and self-deprecating style is clown-like, it is "basically a make-believe role of clown." Although other jazzmen, such as Charlie Parker and Miles Davis, sought to disassociate themselves with the role of such performance in the name of respecting their racial identity, Ellison asserts that Armstrong's strength of lyric and trumpet redeem his performance and make him "an outstanding creative musician."

Bird

See Charlie Parker

Charlie Christian

In "The Charlie Christian Story," Ellison calls his friend Christian "probably the greatest of jazz guitarists." Originally from Ellison's native Oklahoma City, he led a "spectacular career" with the Benny Goodman Sextet and shares with Ellison his training in classical music as a child in the school band. Ellison goes so far as to charge Christian with giving the guitar its jazz voice, and, in so doing, changing the face of the art forever.

Samuel Clemens

See Mark Twain

Stephen Crane

In "Stephen Crane and the Mainstream of American Fiction," Ellison offers his introduction to the 1960 publication of *The Red Badge of Courage*. The novel is an acknowledged classic, and Ellison hails Crane as the youngest of the nineteenth-century "masters of fiction." The youngest of fourteen children and the son of a Methodist minister, Crane (1871–1900) diverged from his family's religious fundamentalism by immersing himself in all things worldly. Although he was infamous for his adventures and exploits, his writing is sensitive to the individual's process of self-definition in society.

Ralph Waldo Emerson

Ralph Waldo Emerson (1803–1882) was the esteemed abolitionist author, speaker, and poet, after whom Ralph Ellison was named.

William Faulkner

In "Brave Words for a Startling Occasion," Ellison states that as a young writer, he "felt that except for the work of William Faulkner something vital had gone out of American prose after Mark Twain." Ellison names Faulkner (1897–1962) as another "literary ancestor." In "Twentieth-Century Fiction and the Black Mask of Humanity," he takes Faulkner to task for relying too heavily on stereotype in creating black characters for symbolic use, but he suggests "we must turn to him for continuity of moral purpose which made for the greatest of our classics." Later in the collection, he reviews the film version of Faulkner's *Intruder in the Dust* and deems it revolutionary in that "the role of Negroes in American life has been given what, for the movies, is a startling new definition."

Ernest Hemingway

Ernest Hemingway (1899–1961) is another acclaimed twentieth-century writer whom Ellison claims as a "literary ancestor." Although in one of his earlier pieces in "Twentieth-Century Fiction and the Black Mask of Humanity," Ellison charges Hemingway with abandoning moral ideals in fiction in favor of technique, he still considers him a greater artist than his mentor, Richard Wright. He states in "The World and the Jug" that Hemingway is more important to him than Wright because his writing

> . . . was imbued with a spirit beyond the tragic with which I could feel at home, for it was very close to the feeling of the blues, which are, perhaps, as close as Americans can come to expressing the feeling of tragedy.

Irving Howe

Irving Howe is a Jewish-American author of an essay entitled "Black Boys and Native Sons" for the magazine *New Leader*. "The World and the Jug" entails Ellison's two responses to Howe's assertion that because of his ideological commitment, Richard Wright is a superior artist to Ellison and James Baldwin.

Stanley Edgar Hyman

Stanley Edgar Hyman is a friend of Ellison's and, in his words, "an old intellectual sparring partner." In "Change the Joke and Slip the Yoke," Ellison responds to a lecture Hyman prepared for a series at Brandeis University concerning the African-American relationship to folk tradition. Generally, Ellison contends that Hyman oversimplifies the American tradition, particularly when it comes to the practice of blackface, or the "darky" entertainer.

Mahalia Jackson

Mahalia Jackson (1911–1972) was a singer from New Orleans whose performance Ellison reviews in "When the Spirit Moves Mahalia." Ellison asserts that Jackson synthesizes the best of classic jazz and blues artists such as Bessie Smith, but in the venue in which she was raised, the church. According to Ellison, she merges technique and influence so effectively that he considers her "not primarily a concert singer but a high priestess in the religious ceremony of her church."

Charlie Parker

Charlie Parker (1920–1955) is a famous jazz saxophonist and the subject of "On Bird, Bird-Watching, and Jazz." In the essay, Ellison reviews a book on Parker that chronicles the artist's life and exploits. Ellison speculates on the origin of the artist's nickname, Bird, and how it might relate to his famously erratic, often aberrant behavior, and the function of identity in the public eye. He asserts that Parker resisted the role of entertainer, in contrast to artists such as Louis Armstrong, but ironically eliminated his private life by leading such an infamous public one.

Jimmy Rushing

Jimmy Rushing (1901–1972, though some biography sources list 1903 as a birthdate) is an Oklahoma blues singer whom Ellison eulogizes in "Remembering Jimmy." He is remembered for his clear, bell-like voice that he paired with dance, and a lyricism that Ellison identifies as "of the Southwest; a romanticism native to the frontier."

Mark Twain

Mark Twain is the pen name of Samuel Clemens (1835–1910), the celebrated American author of *Tom Sawyer* and *The Adventures of Huckleberry Finn*. The latter, the story of a southern boy on the run with an escaped slave, is considered his masterpiece. Ellison considers Twain his foremost "literary ancestor," a writer whose work captures the colloquial language and climate of frontier America, while holding to a moral ideal of democracy. In "Twentieth-Century Fiction and the Black Mask of Humanity," he applauds Twain's willingness to represent the black character Jim as a whole, flawed human being rather than an idealized version of a man, and throughout the collection cites him as the father of twentieth-century American fiction.

Richard Wright

Richard Wright (1908–1960) is the African-American author of several controversial, groundbreaking works, namely his memoir *Black Boy* and the novel *Native Son*. Wright is recognized as Ellison's mentor, but their relationship was a charged one. On one hand, Ellison lauds Wright's work as an exemplary representation of keeping the blues tradition alive by detailing the pain in one's life. In "Richard Wright's Blues," he also praises Wright's work as an effective means of confronting white America with the brutal reality of the African-American experience. However, later, Ellison asserts several times in *Shadow and Act* that Wright sacrifices good writing in the interest of ideology.

Themes

Frontier

In his introduction to *Shadow and Act*, Ellison asserts that as a Negro American born in Oklahoma in post-Civil War America, he is a "frontiersman." By Ellison's definition, the American frontier is the territory of the individual, the realm in which, like Twain's Huckleberry Finn, he is allowed to seek out his destiny, make rash, "quixotic gestures" and approach the world as full of possibility, unhampered by categorical limitations such as race. Ellison attributes this self-image to his childhood in a community rich in diverse cultural influences in a state unburdened by pre-Civil War affiliations of North or South. Throughout *Shadow and Act*, Ellison uses the image of the frontier as synonymous with or tied to ideas of invention, action, newness, cul-

Topics for Further Study

- Research and read some of the work of Richard Wright. In what ways did Wright and Ellison differ in style and philosophy?

- Investigate the ideology of the black power movement. In what ways might Ellison's politics be scrutinized by organizations affiliated with this movement?

- Consider Ellison's assertions about the ways jazz and blues are musical expressions of African-American culture. In what ways do more recent forms of music, such as rap and hip hop, express the African-American culture of today?

- Choose a work by Twain or Faulkner that features an African-American character. Is the life of this character realistically portrayed?

tural development, and the American ideal of democracy. At several points, for example, he identifies the frontier with passion for the outdoors as depicted in Hemingway's work. At other points, he identifies the frontier with the world of Huckleberry Finn and his quality of self-invention and adventure. In other contexts, he asserts that jazz is a form of the frontier, in the sense that it is an expression and outgrowth of African-American culture, an ever-changing response of the individual to environment, especially in the arena of the jam session, an act of challenge and self-invention. As he explains in the closing of "The Art of Fiction: An Interview," Ellison's understanding of the act of self-representation through writing is an act of shaping culture as he represents his own corner of it. In his words, "The American novel is in this sense a conquest of the frontier; as it describes our experience, it creates it."

Identity

Ellison makes the point that the task of his fiction is to discover exactly who he is, how he defines himself, taking into consideration the filter of American society and his own experience as integrally a part of it. The essays in *Shadow and Act* embody the author's efforts to confront and clarify these issues for himself, and in this capacity, they are preoccupied with the issue of identity on many levels. Throughout his career, Ellison has been criticized for what some take to be his lack of militancy, and for his relationship to the classics of American and European literature, many of which are written by white people. In response, the author has always contended that he is an individual in relationship to his environment, and that his work is committed to resisting stereotype, both black and white. The first section of the collection, "The Seer and the Seen," is particularly devoted to Ellison's ideas about identity as he examines different ways African Americans are perceived by the mainstream. In some of the essays, he discusses the ways that mainstream American society projects a distorted image of African Americans, while in others, such as his portraits of jazz artists, he fleshes out musicians who have previously been viewed as caricatures through their celebrity. While in "Twentieth Century Fiction and the Black Mask of Humanity" he indicts white authors, such as Faulkner, for presenting only limited African-American characters in their fiction, in "The World and the Jug" he takes Wright to task for creating similarly simple characters out of ideological drive. Ellison plays upon the themes of masking, naming, and role-play; he examines the ways in which Americans keep themselves and others bound by such devices but also suggests the endless possibility implicit there. As he asserts in "The Art of Fiction: An Interview," the search for identity is "*the* American theme."

Music

Since Ellison was trained as a composer and raised in a community focused on musical expression, music is central to his identity and his writing. In "Richard Wright's Blues," for example, he defines blues as a means of holding and examining the details of one's pain, and as an expression of African-American life, a means of confronting the mainstream with that pain. He characterizes Wright's memoir *Black Boy* as just such a blues expression. Similarly, elsewhere, such as in "The Golden Age, Time Past," he examines the way jazz expression is an assertion of self, in the sense that it is a relatively new outgrowth of other musical traditions, and, as such, fundamentally American. Several of his essays commemorate the lives of musicians; in "As the Spirit Moves Mahalia,'' for example, he examines the way gospel and blues intersect in one artist's form, while in his review of a biography of Charlie Parker, he fleshes out the American popular image of the musician. In other essays, such as ''The Sound and the Mainstream,'' Ellison's language mirrors the flow of the music he describes; in its own form and in relation to the art of writing, he sees music as critical to the act of African-American expression.

Black and White

As a person of mixed ancestry, black and white, Ellison considers himself a personification of the blend of influences that make up America. His work by definition is about challenging the mythical associations of the polarities of black and white, light and darkness, that are projected upon African Americans in particular. In ''Twentieth-Century Fiction and the Black Mask of Humanity,'' Ellison asserts that historically ''the Negro and the color black were associated with evil and ugliness.'' In several places in *Shadow and Act* he discusses ways in which blackness serves as a metaphor for the buried psychology of all things dark; he asserts that white Americans attribute to African Americans qualities they wish to be disassociated from, such as anger, passion, and sexuality. He examines the ways American culture expresses these stereotypes through literature and film, and how, in his own fiction, he challenges such imagery through depicting a whole, self-contradictory individual. In his commitment to representing himself as a mix of the chaotic influences found in American culture, Ellison draws upon the most obvious metaphors of color to resist simplistic categorization.

Style

Point of View

Many of the pieces that appear in *Shadow and Act* are drawn from progressive, left-leaning publications such as *New Challenge,* associated with the labor/communist parties. Some others are interviews and articles for literary magazines or publications with an educated, cultured bent. Hence, many of the pieces come from a first or third person, didactic point of view. They are straightforward and literal in tone, assuming an informed, educated audience. They also assume interest in and familiarity with the basics of civil rights issues, popular music, literature, and culture. Ellison makes the point that although his novel *Invisible Man* won the National Book Award, most African Americans (at the time of the interview) don't know who he is. This point indicates that although he is African American himself, his ongoing dialogue about the status of race relations in the United States is not necessarily a part of the popular black subculture or the mainstream.

Allusion

One of Ellison's techniques for locating race issues in American culture is by alluding to the work of other writers. In some essays, in particular ''Twentieth-Century Fiction and the Black Mask of Humanity,'' he criticizes Twain, Hemingway, and Faulkner for portraying African Americans as only partial characters, not even human. At other points, generally later in his career, he embraces aspects of these authors' works, and in fact, in ''The World and the Jug'' claims them as his ''literary ancestors,'' writers to whose level he aspires. Ellison demonstrates similar ambivalence about the work of his contemporary, Richard Wright. While in ''Richard Wright's Blues'' he lauds Wright's work as effective confrontation of white America with the brutal conditions for African Americans, in other pieces, he faults Wright for sacrificing quality writing in favor of ideology. These allusions serve as evidence of Ellison's cultural assertions, a springboard for his ideas, and a measure for his own writing.

Historical Context

Ellison's life and the two decades during which *Shadow and Act* was written span a pivotal period in United States history, one full of change and activity. Born only half a century after the end of the Civil War, Ellison's world was still resonating with the effects of the conflict. In the South, Jim Crow laws were in full effect, enforcing strict segregation between blacks and whites. Abolition of slavery crippled the South economically, and rampant poverty was the result. A rise in northern industry after the turn of the century followed and, consequently, so did a migration of southern blacks to northern urban centers.

Compare & Contrast

- **1939:** With the onset of World War II, African Americans call for the desegregation of the U.S. military. While blacks are allowed to serve, they are only allowed to serve in non-combat and support roles. Some gains are made during the war; for example, although it is very controversial, black pilots train at Tuskegee University to fight in the conflict.

  Today: The U.S. military has been entirely desegregated since 1948.

- **1949:** Films such as *Intruder in the Dust* and *Home of the Brave* depict African Americans in supporting roles and as caricatures.

  Today: African Americans, such as Denzel Washington, star in mainstream box office hits and deliver Academy Award–winning performances.

- **1950s:** In the historic *Brown v. Board of Education* case, the Supreme Court rules that racial segregation in education is unconstitutional. Opposition to the ruling is huge, and organizations such as the White Citizens Council effectively keep schools segregated.

  Today: All schools in the United States are desegregated and reflect the racial makeup of their communities. Poorer areas with a higher percentage of minorities, however, tend to have overcrowded schools with poorer quality education.

- **1950s:** A fourteen-year-old boy is murdered in Mississippi for allegedly flirting with a white woman.

  Today: Although such hate crimes are far more rare, they still occur. For example, in 1998, James Byrd Jr., an African-American man from Texas, is dragged to his death behind a truck driven by three white men.

The outcome of such a migration was manifold. On one hand, the 1920s marked a period of artistic experimentation during which African-American culture came into vogue. This national temperament, combined with a trend toward altruism and philanthropy on the part of many wealthy, white northerners, resulted in what is known as the Harlem Renaissance, a period during which African-American art and literature flourished. On the other hand, the movement disrupted family traditions from the South and set many African Americans adrift without family support, and the flood of labor to the North resulted in eventual unemployment and poverty. Two major events eventually helped to improve civil rights for African Americans: the Great Depression, which began with the stock market crash of 1929 and continued throughout the 1930s, bringing poverty to whites and blacks alike; and World War II, which began in 1939 and ended in 1945. During the 1930s, Franklin D. Roosevelt's administration created federally funded job programs like the Works Progress Administration (WPA), and made jobs within these programs available to blacks. In 1937, after strenuous work on the part of the National Association for the Advancement of Colored People (NAACP), Hugo Black became the first African-American appointee to the United States Supreme Court. World War II marked an increased call to desegregate the armed forces, an act that was finalized in 1948 by Harry Truman.

The culmination of events known as the civil rights movement, or black freedom movement, began in 1954 with the outcome of the United States Supreme Court case, *Brown v. the Board of Education,* which declared the racial segregation of education unconstitutional. The year 1955 saw the bus boycott in Montgomery, Alabama, take place; this event eventually resulted in the desegregation of buses in 1956. In 1957, the Reverend Martin Luther King, Jr. was elected president of the Southern Christian Leadership Conference, a group committed to the non-violent direct action and boycotts that characterized the late 1950s and early 1960s. August

1963 marked the March on Washington, at which Dr. King delivered his "I Have A Dream" speech. The march was partially responsible for a new civil rights law proposed by President John F. Kennedy, which was later pushed through after Kennedy's assassination by his successor, President Lyndon B. Johnson. The Civil Rights Act of 1964 prohibited all forms of racial discrimination.

Critical Overview

Shadow and Act was published in 1964, in the wake of the civil rights movement and at the time of the rise of the black power movement. Released only a year after the historic March on Washington, it was met by critics with developed opinions about social reform. Both friends and foes anticipated Ellison's new work because of the response to his novel, *Invisible Man.*

In "Portrait of a Man on His Own," a 1964 *New York Times* review, George P. Elliot writes that *Shadow and Act* "says more about being an American Negro, and says it better, than any other book I know of." He asserts that the last section is "less distinguished" than the first section, "The Seer and the Seen." He goes on to say, however, that it is when Ellison "addresses his attention to his particular experience that what the writer says is of the greatest importance." He continues, saying that the essays "build upon a wisdom—not an intellectual apprehension, but a profound, because experienced, knowledge—of political power and the importance of ideas in shaping society and individuals."

Elliot's enthusiasm, however, does not reflect the whole reception to *Shadow and Act*. In *Improvising America: Ralph Ellison and the Paradox of Form,* C. W. E. Bigsby writes that:

> Those who, in the 1960s and 1970s, proposed their own prescription for cultural and political responsibility . . . found his determined pluralism unacceptable. For although he undeniably concentrated on the black experience in America, he tended to see this experience in relation to the problem of identity, the anxieties associated with the struggle for cultural autonomy, and the need to define the contours of experience.

This idea is echoed in Brent Staples's 1996 review in which he reports, "Black radicals scorned [Ellison] as a white folks' nigger."

The mixed response to *Shadow and Act* is in keeping with response to Ellison's entire body of work. John Wright summarizes this in "Slipping the Yoke," an essay in *Speaking for You: The Vision of Ralph Ellison,* when he writes:

> Ralph Ellison's fiction, essays, interviews, and speeches have been characteristically canny and complex. And both white and black readers of *Invisible Man* and *Shadow and Act* have routinely, even ritually, approached the politics, the art, and the 'racial' values these books codify in terms narrower than those Ellison himself proposes. In consequence, the body of 'conscious thought' he has erected since the 1930s has been left in shadow, artificially isolated from its intellectual roots in Afro-American tradition, and almost invariably denied a critical context as pluralistic in its techniques and cultural references as Ellison's extraordinary eclecticism demands.

Criticism

Jennifer Lynch

Lynch is a teacher and freelance writer in northern New Mexico. In the following essay, she explores themes of self-invention and identity found in Ellison's essays.

In his introduction to *Shadow and Act,* Ellison makes the point that writing is "the agency of my efforts to answer the question: Who am I, what am I, how did I come to be?" When deciding upon a career, he describes wondering "what was the most desirable agency for defining myself." He goes on to describe the essays in the collection as "witness of that which I have known and that which I have tried and am still trying to confront." Ellison is preoccupied with identity—American identity, in particular. As he indicates in the introduction, his essays are "concerned with the nature of the culture and society out of which American fiction is fabricated."

Fabrication is key to Ellison's understanding of American identity and, it follows, American music and fiction; Americans spring from a cultural tradition obsessed with manifest destiny, frontier traditions, and self-invention. Ellison asserts that the real America is constantly unfolding, and as such, the American cultural identity is a thing yet unfinished, always in the process of being invented. Contro-

Jazz bandleader Earl Hines at the Savoy Ballroom in Harlem. Jazz and blues are a recurring theme throughout the essay

versy has surrounded Ellison's work because of his consistent defiance of stereotype and categorization, especially concerning race. As an ethnic blend of black, white, and Native American, he is by definition a mix, and as such inherently American. Bearing this in mind, he asserts that African Americans epitomize the tradition of self-invention, particularly with regard to musical expression. Sprung from the "chaos" of the community in which he was raised, his work reflects his preoccupation with American identity as an act of self-invention.

Ellison contextualizes his essays in his introduction by discussing his childhood and the origins of his writing impulse. He calls his childhood home of Oklahoma City a

> . . . chaotic community, still characterized by frontier attitudes . . . that mixture which often affords the minds of the young who grow up in the far provinces such wide and unstructured latitude, and which encourages the individual's imagination . . . to range widely and, sometimes, even to soar.

Imagination is key to his self-concept; it affords him the freedom to see his world as one of endless possibility, in which he determines his form. The "chaos of Oklahoma" gives rise to Ellison's self-concept as a Renaissance Man, a

master of many art forms. This chaos, he goes on to describe in "That Same Pleasure, That Same Pain", takes the shape of multiple cultural influences, from the classical music of the school band, to southwestern jazz, to European folk dance.

> Culturally everything was mixed, you see, and beyond all question of conscious choices there was a level where you were claimed by emotion and movement and moods which you couldn't often put into words. Often we wanted to share both: the classics and jazz, the Charleston and the Irish reel, spirituals and the blues, the sacred and the profane.

The result is Ellison's sense of endless possibility for his own identity; he reports, "we fabricated our own heroes and ideals catch-as-catch can, and with an outrageous and irreverent sense of freedom."

That freedom is often expressed in jazz and blues terms throughout the text, but especially in the section entitled "Sound and the Mainstream." In "Remembering Jimmy," Ellison states that in his youth, "Jazz and the public jazz dance was a third institution in our lives, and a vital one." He discusses ways that music was critical to his upbringing and sense of self; Ellison himself trained as a composer before he chose a career in writing. By definition, jazz is an outgrowth of other forms of

What Do I Read Next?

- *The Collected Essays of Ralph Ellison* (1995) brings together many of the essays that appear in *Shadow and Act* and *Going to the Territory* with previously unpublished essays and interviews.

- *Invisible Man* (1953) is Ellison's National Book Award–winning novel about a young African-American man's search for identity through his encounters with both southern and northern culture.

- In *The Omni-Americans: Some Alternatives to the Folklore of White Supremacy* (1970), Albert Murray dispels racist mythology with alternative African-American folklore.

- *Uncle Tom's Children* is Richard Wright's 1938 collection of stories depicting the struggles of African Americans before the civil rights movement.

music, including classical music and spirituals, and as such serves as an example of the way African-American culture draws on a blend of influences to create new artistic expressions. As Ellison puts it in "The Charlie Christian Story," "jazz finds its very life in an endless improvisation upon traditional materials." Jazz also serves as a means of self-invention or defining identity for the individual musician. In the same essay, he asserts that "true jazz is an art of individual assertion within and against the group." In "The Golden Age, Time Past," he explains that the jazzman must first learn the fundamentals of his art, and "he must then 'find himself,' must be reborn, must find, as it were, his soul.... He must achieve, in short, his self-determined identity."

Although Ellison makes mention of his college ambition to become a composer, his ultimate means of expressing his identity is as a novelist. The influences he cites in the collection range from the black militant to the traditional in the literary canon and transcend easy categorization. Richard Wright is a stated influence for Ellison, both as a mentor and through offering Ellison opportunities to write for *New Masses,* his first attempt. Wright is known for his absolutist depiction of Bigger Thomas in *Native Son,* a novel aimed at shocking whites into acknowledging the disparity between white and black qualities of life. In "Richard Wright's Blues," Ellison lauds Wright's work as eloquent literary manifestation of the blues "impulse to keep the

painful details and episodes of a brutal experience alive in one's aching consciousness, to finger its jagged grain, and to transcend it." Yet, in "The World and the Jug," Ellison asserts that:

> Wright as a *writer* was less interesting than the enigma he personified . . . he could be so wonderful an example of human possibility but could not for ideological reasons depict a Negro as intelligent, as creative or as dedicated as himself.

Ellison's willingness to express his ambivalence about Wright reflects his resistance to categorization. His simultaneous applause and rejection of a renowned African-American author serves as an assertion of self that is contradictory and complicated. Indeed, he acknowledges in "That Same Pain, That Same Pleasure," it is Wright who instructs Ellison to read the classics, including Conrad, Joyce, and Dostoyevsky, for stylistic instruction.

In "The World and the Jug," Ellison explains that, concerning influence and inspiration, Wright is his "relative" and other writers such as T. S. Eliot, Malreaux, Hemingway, and Faulkner are literary "ancestors." His citation of various authors from diverse traditions and nations reflects Ellison's awareness that, as an American writer, he is a blend of cultural influences, and the blend is a matter of choice and intention. Because they are twentieth-century American novelists, Twain and Hemingway are the most discussed "ancestors" in the text, and both are responsible for what is considered

> **Ellison asserts that the real America is constantly unfolding, and as such, the American cultural identity is a thing yet unfinished, always in the process of being invented.''**

invention in their prose styles. Hemingway is the inventor of his precedent-setting style of short, lean, minimalist sentences, which objectively describe such topics as adventure and war. His prose and thematic material are responsible for the author's public persona as a sportsman and adventurer; in effect, he invents himself, at least in the public eye, by depicting his particular, masculine view of the world. Interestingly, Ellison is as ambivalent about Hemingway as he is about Wright. Although in ''The World and the Jug'' he offers a lyrical explanation for the ways Hemingway inspires him and ''was in so many ways the father-as-artist of so many of us who came to writing during the thirties,'' he is just as willing to indict Hemingway in ''Twentieth-Century Fiction and the Black Mask of Humanity'' for his lack of moral responsibility in his fiction.

Twain, on the other hand, in the same essay, is noted for his introduction of the use of colloquial language and for his revolutionary depiction of an African-American character who is a whole, rounded person. His depiction of Jim in *Huckleberry Finn* is the first American fictional presentation of a black character who is, in Jim's case, at times kind, intelligent, and logical, and at other times, superstitious and foolish. Twain's protagonist, Huckleberry Finn, is an act of invention, too, in that he virtually invents himself by running away and choosing people other than his father to influence or parent him. Twain, like Hemingway, fits Ellison's understanding of the frontier writer both in the content of the work and in the fact that their inventiveness suggests the endless possibility of their art. Thus, they embody Ellison's assertion in ''The Art of Fiction: An Interview'' that ''the American novel is . . . a conquest of the frontier; as it describes our experience, it creates it.''

Whether concerning literature or music, Ellison is explicit throughout *Shadow and Act* about his concern with the construction of American identity through art. He addresses the theme personally by explaining his origins and influences, but the phenomenon of his self-invention is also apparent from the evolution of his work from his earliest pieces in the collection to his latest. This is best evidenced by the preface to ''Twentieth-Century Fiction and the Black Mask of Humanity,'' which was written in 1946. He writes, ''I've left in much of the bias and short-sightedness, for it says perhaps as much about me as a member of a minority as it does about literature.'' In presenting his earlier, less sophisticated work alongside his recent writings throughout the text, Ellison offers a view of his progression as a writer and as an African American in all his complexity. His stated intention in writing is to learn who he is, since, as he asserts in ''The Art of Fiction: An Interview,'' ''the search for identity . . . is *the* American theme.''

Source: Jennifer Lynch, Critical Essay on *Shadow and Act,* in *Nonfiction Classics for Students,* The Gale Group, 2002.

Mark Busby

In the following essay excerpt, Busby focuses on the themes of autobiography and ''the fullness and value of African American culture'' in Shadow and Act.

When Ellison decided to collect his essays, interviews, and speeches written from 1942 to 1964, he turned to one of his favorite ancestors for the title, *Shadow and Act.* T. S. Eliot's ''The Hollow Men,'' perhaps because of the emphasis on a complex dialectical process, provides the allusion:

Between the idea
And the reality
Between the motion
And the act
Falls the Shadow.

Ellison's title suggests several meanings. In the introduction Ellison refers to the title and emphasizes the significance of a writer's need to understand both his own personal past and history when he says that the ''act of writing requires a constant plunging back into the shadow of the past where time hovers ghostlike.'' Writing as act requires a constant interaction with the shadow of the past. A second meaning is suggested by the 1949 essay ''Shadow and Act,'' included in the collection, in which Ellison examines three recent films about African Americans, one based on Faulkner's *Intruder in the Dust*. The film, Ellison suggests, is a shadow of the novel, and films in general involve flickering shadowlike images on a two-dimensional plane.

Shadow and Act contains an introduction and three major divisions: "The Seer and the Seen"—interviews, speeches, and essays on literature; "Sound and the Mainstream"—essays about music and musicians; and "Shadow and Act"—"occasional pieces" concerned "with the complex relationship between the Negro American subculture and North American culture as a whole." Through all three parts Ellison emphasizes the importance of his personal experiences, particularly his Oklahoma past, much quoted in earlier chapters. In fact, some early reviewers labeled the work as autobiography. Both George P. Elliot in the *New York Times Book Review* (25 October 1964) and *R. W. B. Lewis* in the *New York Review of Books* (28 January 1965) called *Shadow and Act* Ellison's "real autobiography."

In the introduction Ellison stresses what Reilly calls his "fictional" generalized autobiography with its "broad frontiersman scheme." There Ellison describes himself and his friends as "frontiersmen" in a territory that emphasized freedom and possibility, explains how they adopted their Renaissance man ideal, points to the significance of southwestern jazz, and, most important, establishes himself as an initiate who ultimately embraced the significant discipline of writing only after undergoing a variety of experiences. "One might say," Ellison writes, "that with these thin essays for wings I was launched full flight into the dark." And as he searched for his craft, he drew from his frontier experience, especially the emphasis on the possibilities of amalgamation, for "part of our boyish activity expressed a yearning to make any—and everything of quality *Negro American;* to appropriate it, possess it, recreate it in our own group and individual images."

Related to Ellison's emphasis on autobiography is a second important theme: the fullness and value of African American culture. Ellison scorns "the notion currently projected by certain specialists in the 'Negro Problem,' which characterizes the Negro American as self-hating and defensive." Like the narrator in *Invisible Man* who learns to reject others' definitions of reality, Ellison learned to repudiate limited definitions of African American life: "I learned that nothing could go unchal-

> " In *Shadow and Act* Ellison draws from his vivid and specific memory to recreate a rich and vibrant culture to juxtapose with the dismal one too often attributed to African American life."

lenged; especially that feverish industry dedicated to telling Negroes who and what they are, and which can usually be counted upon to deprive both humanity and culture of their complexity."

The issues reappear in the first major section, "The Seer and the Seen," concerned primarily with literature. The section contains interviews with Richard G. Stern titled "That Same Pain, That Same Pleasure" originally published in *December* magazine in 1961, and with Alfred Chester and Vilma Howard titled "The Art of Fiction" published in the *Paris Review* in 1955. In the Stern interview Ellison points to many of the same autobiographical details as he does in the introduction: the importance of the frontier past, the power of the imagination, cultural mixture, ("I learned very early that in the realm of the imagination all people and their ambitions and interests could meet"), and the value of African American culture, the "Negro environment which I found warm and meaningful." In the *Paris Review* interview, Ellison talks specifically about the background, style, structure, and imagery of *Invisible Man*.

The first section also includes two speeches, "Brave Words for a Startling Occasion," Ellison's acceptance speech for the National Book Award in 1953, and "Hidden Name and Complex Fate: A Writer's Experience in the United States," an address to the Library of Congress on 6 January 1964 sponsored by the Gertrude Clarke Whittall Foundation. In his acceptance speech, Ellison stressed the relationship between *Invisible Man* and nineteenth-century American fiction, explained his stylistic purpose, and defined democratic principles: "The way home we seek is that condition of man's being in the world, which is called love, and which we term democracy." The speech at the Library of Congress was explicitly autobiographical, as the title indicates, as Ellison reflected upon having been named for Ralph Waldo Emerson and having become a writer. He mused about the questions of identity that one's name suggests, recalled the humor that revolved around his name, and remembered the powerful literary and oral influences that permeated his boyhood before comparing the best nineteenth-century fiction and its direct confrontation with democratic themes to twentieth-century fiction of understatement.

Ellison includes in section 1 three literary essays written prior to the publication of *Invisible Man*. "Beating that Boy," whose title refers to belabored discussions of "the Negro problem," is a 1945 review of Bucklin Moon's *Primer for White Folks*. "Twentieth Century Fiction and the Black Mask of Humanity" (1946) demonstrates Ellison's concerns about the American literary tradition while he worked on *Invisible Man*, especially his thesis that twentieth-century American novelists had turned away from the social and moral function of literature central to nineteenth-century American writers. "Richard Wright's Blues," a review of Wright's *Black Boy* for the *Antioch Review* in 1945, is important because it demonstrates the complexity of Ellison's relationship with Wright. Written before the split with Wright, Ellison found the blues in Wright's autobiography and praised his relative for breaking from the restrictions of both southern society and the cultural possessiveness of black southern culture.

Two essays in the first section are intellectual bouts with white critics. "Change the Joke and Slip the Yoke," published in *Partisan Review* in 1958, is a response to a Stanley Edgar Hyman lecture at Brandeis University. Hyman had identified the trickster and the darky entertainer as folk figures important to African American writers. Ellison disagrees with Hyman, saying that the trickster is a much more universal archetype, and the "'darky' entertainer," Ellison concludes, appealed not to black Americans but to whites for whom blackness had become a metaphor for "the white American's fascination with the symbolism of whiteness and blackness." Ellison points out that the mask of the "'darky' entertainer" was not limited to black folklore, for the American experience was begun in the masquerade as Indians at the Boston Tea Party. In response to Hyman's comments about the narrator's grandfather in *Invisible Man* as the "smart-man-playing-dumb," Ellison notes that the grandfather's ambiguity rather than his mask indicates his importance.

The second and better-known skirmish was with Irving Howe. "The World and the Jug" combines two separate articles written for Myron Kolatch of the *New Leader*, who asked for Ellison's response to Howe's "Black Boys and Native Sons," published in the August 1963 issue of *Dissent*, in which Howe compared Ellison to Wright and Baldwin and found both younger writers lacking. Ellison's second essay responds to Howe's comments about the first piece and therefore takes on an angrier, more combative tone than many of Ellison's other pieces. Ironically Howe had initially charged Ellison with insufficient anger and called for more protest about racism in his work.

Ellison's argument revolves around the distinction between art and propaganda. Protest writing, Ellison asserts, weakens artistic merit if a writer emphasizes protest rather than craft. Judgments about writing should be based on merit, not on whether it includes "racial suffering, social injustice or ideologies of whatever mammy-made variety." But Ellison contends his novel contains protest: "My goal was not to escape, or hold back, but to work through; to transcend, as the blues transcend the painful conditions with which they deal. The protest is there, not because I was helpless before my racial condition, but because I *put* it there."

The second important part of the argument concerns Ellison's belief in the value of African American experience. Social critics such as Howe, Ellison asserts, refuse to see African Americans as full human beings; rather "when he looks at a Negro he sees not a human being but an abstract embodiment of living hell." This limited view ignores the value of African American culture: "To deny in the interest of revolutionary posture that such possibilities of human richness exist for others, even in Mississippi, is not only to deny us our humanity but to betray the critic's commitment to social reality." Consequently, given his attitude about the merit of African American culture, Ellison believes that the most valuable literature that grows from this experience is celebratory: "I believe that true novels, even when most pessimistic and bitter, arise out of an impulse to celebrate human life and therefore are ritualistic and ceremonial at their core. Thus they would preserve as they destroy, affirm as they reject."

Ellison also stresses the importance of African American culture in part 2, "Sound and the Mainstream," with essays about music over such topics as Minton's Playhouse, Mahalia Jackson, Jimmy Rushing, Charlie Bird, Charlie Christian, and LeRoi Jones's book on the blues, *Blues People.* Throughout these essays, Ellison points to the central importance of jazz and the blues on his own work as he highlights music as one of the richest contributions of African American culture to the American amalgamation.

In "Living with Music," for example, he recalls how as a boy he learned about artistic discipline from early Oklahoma jazzmen. From them he came to understand the dynamics of the dialectic between tradition and the individual talent: "I had learned too that the end of all this discipline and technical mastery was the desire to express an affirmative way of life through its musical tradition and that this tradition insisted that each artist achieve his creativity within its frame. He must learn the best of the past, and add to it his personal vision." Similarly Ellison found an interplay between freedom and restriction in Jimmy Rushing's singing. Rushing, like Ellison, was a product of the southwestern frontier, and Ellison believes that Rushing's geographical background was the basis for his individual talent. Ellison's comments on Rushing may just as easily be applied to Ellison himself: "For one of the significant aspects of his art is the imposition of a romantic lyricism upon the blues tradition . . .; a lyricism which is not of the Deep South, but of the Southwest: a romanticism native to the frontier, imposed upon the violent rawness of a part of the nation which only thirteen years before Rushing's birth was still Indian territory. Thus there is an optimism in it which echoes the spirit of those Negroes who, like Rushing's father, had come to Oklahoma in search of a more human way of life." Rushing therefore communicated the blues as "an art of ambivalence" for they "constantly remind us of our limitations while encouraging us to see how far we can actually go."

Besides dramatizing constant tension between freedom and restriction, jazz presents rituals of initiation and rebirth. In his remembrance of Minton's, "The Golden Age, Time Past," Ellison notes that jam sessions there, like the ones he viewed growing up, demonstrated "apprenticeship, ordeals, initiation ceremonies, . . . rebirth." He continues, "For after the jazzman has learned the fundamentals of jazz . . ., he must then 'find himself,' must be reborn, must find, as it were, his soul." Charlie Parker became just such an example of transformation. His nickname, the "Bird," indicated metamorphosis: "Nicknames are indicative of a change from a given to an achieved identity, whether by rise or fall, and they tell us something of the nicknamed individual's interaction with his fellows." As he remade himself and adopted a mask, Parker moved over the line into chaos and became "a sacrificial figure whose struggles against personal chaos, on stage and off, served as entertainment for a ravenous, sensation-starved, culturally disoriented public." The comments about Parker provide insight into Ellison's conceptions of two of his characters, Rinehart and Senator Sunraider/Bliss, figures who tempt chaos as they don masks.

Another leitmotif in this section, important to Ellison's Hickman stories, is the value of history. In his review of LeRoi Jones's *Blues People,* in which he criticizes Jones for reducing blues to ideology, Ellison strikes out against the American tendency to ignore the past: "Perhaps more than any other people, Americans have been locked in a deadly struggle with time, with history. We've fled the past and trained ourselves to suppress, if not forget, troublesome details of the national memory, and a great part of our optimism, like our progress, has been bought at the cost of ignoring the processes through which we've arrived at any given moment in our national existence."

Ellison's title, of course, also points to the importance of history, and the third section is also titled "Shadow and Act." Something of a grab bag, this section includes a 1958 interview with *Preuves,* the title review of films about African Americans, a Hemingway-influenced piece on a Harlem family during World War II, a description of the Lafargue Psychiatric Clinic written in 1948 but unpublished, and an unpublished 1944 review of Gunnar Myrdal's *An American Dilemma.* As a group, these pieces continue some of the earlier themes, but they are less autobiographical than most of the other selections in *Shadow and Act.*

"The Way It Is," the only early *New Masses* article that Ellison decided to include, demonstrates, as the title indicates, Hemingway's influence and Marxist issues as Ellison describes one Harlem family's response to racial injustice and patriotic demands during World War II. "Harlem Is Nowhere" defines the alienation and discontinuity that Harlem residents, dislocated from cultural roots, felt in the 1940s and serves as an important statement of the concerns from which *Invisible Man* developed. Finally, in his review of Myrdal's book,

Ellison again stresses the value of African American life by sharply criticizing the European sociologist for accepting the flawed conclusion that African Americans are the product of social pathology rather than a culture of "great value, of richness."

When *Shadow and Act* appeared in 1964, American racial disharmony was high. Riots in Watts, Detroit, Newark, and other American cities loomed on the horizon. Incendiary comments by Malcolm X, LeRoi Jones, and James Baldwin made many white Americans uncomfortable. So it is not surprising that many reviewers found comfort in Ellison's measured prose. For example, the reviewer for *Choice* (March 1965) called it an" antidote to the more hysterical proclamations coming from the pens of James Baldwin and LeRoi Jones." Ellison was often called "sane" by reviewers, mostly white. In fact, few African American reviewers or journals discussed *Shadow and Act*.

In his review, R. W. B. Lewis, focusing on autobiographical elements, identified Ellison's purpose as a definition of identity: "Inquiring into his experience, his literary and musical education, Ellison has come up with a number of clues to the fantastic fate of trying to be at the same time a writer, a Negro, an American, and a human being." Stanley Edgar Hyman, in a review for the *New Leader* (26 October 1964), emphasized Ellison's concern with values: "In his insight into the complexity of American experience, Ralph Ellison is the profoundest cultural critic that we have, and his hard doctrine of freedom, responsibility, and fraternity is a wisdom rare in our time." Robert Penn Warren, reviewing for *Commentary* (May 1965), found Ellison's concentration on unity from diversity the most important element of *Shadow and Act: "The basic unity of human experience*—that is what Ellison asserts; and he sets the richness of his own experience and that of many Negroes he has known, and his own early capacity to absorb the general values of Western culture, over against what Wright called 'the essential bleakness of black life in America.'"

In *Shadow and Act* Ellison draws from his vivid and specific memory to recreate a rich and vibrant culture to juxtapose with the dismal one too often attributed to African American life. Instead Ellison offers "the glorious days of Oklahoma jazz dances, the jam sessions at Halley Richardson's place on Deep Second, . . . the days when watermelon men with voices like mellow bugles shouted their wares in time with the rhythm of their horses' hoofs." The

figure of the young Ralph Ellison coming out of Oklahoma territory and becoming a famous author is, as Reilly notes, a "fiction," a shaping of experience by art, and it is an American story most powerful. His second collection of essays, published 22 years later, offers a new extension of the old persona.

Source: Mark Busby, "The Mellow Bugler: Ellison's Nonfiction," in *Ralph Ellison,* edited by Warren French, Twayne, 1991, pp. 126–33.

Robert G. O'Meally

In the following essay, O'Meally examines Ellison's intentions in Shadow and Act, *citing Ellison's "single-minded intention to define Afro-American life."*

The initial appeal of *Shadow and Act* seemed to be that here, at last, the "invisible man" would emerge from underground; that here, as one reviewer proclaimed, was Ralph Ellison's "real autobiography." It is true that *Shadow and Act* has autobiographical overtones. Two pieces, the Introduction and "Hidden Name and Complex Fate," are explicitly autobiographical in design. And in the book's reviews and interviews the author draws extensively upon his own experience. Furthermore, by including essays (none retouched) written over a span of twenty-two years, Ellison reveals certain aspects of his development from the twenty-eight-year-old, Marxist-oriented WPA worker of "The Way It Is" (1942) to the seasoned writer of 1964: now he was "not primarily concerned with injustice, but with art."

In his Introduction Ellison offers a sort of apologia, explaining that the essays "represent, in all their modesty, some of the necessary effort which a writer of my background must make in order to possess the meaning of his experience." When the first of the essays appeared, he regarded himself "in my most secret heart at least—a musician," not a writer. "With these thin essays for wings," he notes, "I was launched full flight into the dark." Looking at the publication date printed at the end of each text, we may trace the growth of a young intellectual's consciousness. Thus "their basic significance, whatever their value as information or speculation, is autobiographical." Nonetheless, the book has thematic unities that are even more compelling. A good deal of the cumulative power of *Shadow and Act* derives from its basic contrast of

Harlem's Lenox Avenue; Harlem was Ellison's longtime home and the focus of his experience, and several essays in the collection address Harlem specifically

black American life as seen through the lenses of politics, sociology, and popular culture with black American life as observed and lived by one sensitive, questioning black man.

Shadow and Act, a compilation, has enduring validity as a unified work of art because of its author's single-minded intention to define Afro-American life. Sometimes Ellison gently punctures, sometimes wields an ax, against inadequate definitions of black experience. In place of what he detects as false prophesies, usually uttered by social scientists, Ellison chooses as broad a frame of reference as possible to interpret black experience in richly optimistic terms. "Who wills to be a Negro?" he asks, rhetorically. "*I* do!"

In a number of essays Ellison points out that all too often the white critic treats black art as if it had appeared miraculously, without tradition, as if the black artist just grew like Topsy. To correct for this kind of condescension, Ellison is very careful in his criticism to discuss black music, literature, and the visual arts in the context of tradition: black, American, Western, Eastern, universal. Ellison's warnings notwithstanding, *Shadow and Act* is a singular

> " The writer's job is not to deny but to transmute the loadstone of anger and injustice into art."

achievement. It is not possible to point out another work that deals as fully with Afro-American and American literature and music and politics; and that is varied enough to include tightly drawn literary essays and a formal address alongside breezy interviews and autobiographical reflections. That it all comes together as a well-unified whole is a tribute to its author's power as editor/philosopher/artist.

This is not to suggest that *Shadow and Act* is without precursors. With its emphasis on ritual and folk forms in art, it recalls the writings of Kenneth Burke, André Malraux, and Stanley Edgar Hyman. The political persuasion, which Arthur P. Davis terms "integrationist," as well as the rhetoric remind us of Ellison's support for the freedom movement. As a study of Americana from the expansive perspective of a writer, *Shadow and Act* falls within the tradition of Henry James's *The American Scene* (1907). James Baldwin's *Notes of a Native Son* (1955), which includes book and movie reviews and political commentary as well as documents for an autobiography, provides another context for *Shadow and Act.*

Ellison's book of essays has also inspired others, including Imamu Amiri Baraka's *Home* (1966). Although the perspectives of Ellison and Baraka, who in *Home* professes his strident black nationalism, clash dramatically, their books are very similar in form. Both consist of essays on Afro-American art and politics; both have autobiographical underpinnings. Then too, in that he painstakingly stresses the particular contributions of blacks to American society, Ellison is in his way undoubtedly a black cultural nationalist.

The central theme of "The Seer and the Seen" (the first of the three sections of *Shadow and Act*) is "segregation of the word." White Americans, says Ellison, because of their "Manichean fascination with the symbolism of blackness and whiteness," tend to see the world in black (bad) and white (good). When whites contemplate a "profoundly personal problem involving guilt," the conjured images and characters appear, as it were, darkly. Thus:

It is practically impossible for the white American to think of sex, of economics, his children or women-folk, or of sweeping sociopolitical changes, without summoning into consciousness fear-flecked images of black men. Indeed, it seems that the Negro has become identified with those unpleasant aspects of conscience and consciousness which it is part of the American's character to avoid. Thus when the literary artist attempts to tap the charged springs issuing from his inner world, up float his misshapen and bloated images of the Negro, like the fetid bodies of the drowned, and he turns away, discarding an ambiguous substance which the artists of other cultures would confront boldly and humanize into the stuff of a tragic art.

According to Ellison, certain nineteenth-century writers, notably Herman Melville, Mark Twain, and Stephen Crane, produced classic American fiction because they were able eloquently to confront the "blackness of darkness" on the guilt-shadowed edges of their minds. For them, the black man, even when portrayed in the garb of minstrelsy, represented America's moral concern and quest for freedom. Much of the vitality of *Moby Dick, Huckleberry Finn,* and Crane's short stories derives from the blackness of these works. When other writers left out black characters (or reduced them to the dimensions of badmen, angels, and clowns), these writers presented black characters whose humanity was great and whose principles provided the fiction with a moral context. When other writers ignored or excused Americans' "blackest" political and moral transgressions, these writers faced them directly. "Mark Twain knew that in his America humanity masked its face with blackness."

Ellison writes that, with the Hayes-Tilden Compromise, this moral concern slipped underground. Blacks disappeared almost completely from American fiction; and with them the "deep-probing doubt and a sense of evil" that had immortalized certain nineteenth-century writers. Muckrakers, proletarian writers, and "lost generation" writers raised some doubt about morality. "But it is a shallow doubt, which seldom turns inward upon the writer's own values; almost always it focuses outward, upon some scapegoat with which he is seldom able to identify himself . . . This particular naturalism explored everything except the nature of man."

Even Hemingway's stories, which the young Ellison loved for their descriptions of nature and human emotions, and which he once imitated for their technical excellence, also failed to explore deeply the nature of man. Hemingway authored "the trend toward technique for the sake of technique and production for the sake of the market to the neglect of the human need out of which [these techniques] spring." The understated, hard-boiled novel, "with its dedication to physical violence, social cynicism and understatement," performs on the social level "a function similar to that of the stereotype: it conditions the reader to accept the less worthy values of society, and it serves to absolve our sins of social irresponsibility."

Ellison goes on to consider William Faulkner and Richard Wright, who present a variety of black characters in their fiction. Both recall nineteenth-century writers in their outward and unrelenting concern with America's moral climate. Faulkner's characters, like Mark Twain's, have stereotypical outlines, but Faulkner is willing to "start with the stereotype, accept it as true, and then seek out the human truth which it hides." Wright's characters also verge on the stereotypic: often they are either the usual "bad niggers" of white folklore or the evil, broken blacks of what one critic has called "filthlore" of social-science fiction. Nonetheless, Wright pulls from underground the black character and, with him, the disturbing moral questions that cluster around the black as "seen" by whites. Armed, says Ellison, with the insights of Freud and Marx, Wright sought "to discover and depict the meaning of Negro experience; and to reveal to both Negroes and whites those problems of a psychological and emotional nature which arise between them when they strive for mutual understanding."

Aside from his comments on Wright, Ellison says very little in *Shadow and Act* about Afro-American writing per se. As a boy he was introduced to New Negro poets, and their works inspired pride and excitement over the glamor of Harlem. "And it was good to know that there were Negro writers." But after reading T. S. Eliot, black poetry faded in Ellison's eyes: "The Waste Land" gripped his mind. "Somehow its rhythms were often closer to those of jazz than were those of the Negro poets, and even though I could not understand them, its range of allusion was as mixed and varied as Louis Armstrong." Ellison says that white writers like Eliot, and later Malraux, Dostoevsky, and others, helped to free him from segregation of the mind. Black writers' portraits of blacks were often unsatisfactory, but certain white writers, dealing "darkly" with the complex human condition, led Ellison to realize some of the possibilities for black characters *he* would create. The Invisible Man, of course, is as

much Candide and Stephen Daedalus as he is Richard (of *Black Boy*) or Big Boy (of Sterling Brown's poem, "The Odyssey of Big Boy").

In *Shadow and Act* Ellison spars openly with two literary historians, Irving Howe and Stanley Edgar Hyman. Both "The World and the Jug" and "Change the Joke and Slip the Yoke" began as informal, if heated, rebuttals to articles on *Invisible Man*. "The World and the Jug" germinated through a telephone conversation with Myron Kolatch of the *New Leader*; "Change the Joke and Slip the Yoke" through a letter to Hyman. Irritated by the condescending reductionism he felt to be implicit in their approaches, Ellison took aim with both barrels. In fact, in his attempts to correct what he saw as these critics' distortions of the Afro-American image, he scatters the form and substance of certain of their literary theories, twisting them, sometimes unfairly, to serve his own purposes.

In "The World and the Jug" Ellison takes issue with Howe's essay "Black Boys and Native Sons," which deals what it means to be a black American writer. Ellison objects to the notion that, while Richard Wright kept the faith by maintaining his militant stance, Ellison and Baldwin became overrefined, "literary to a fault." Making Howe a strawman, Ellison labels this critic a sociology-oriented writer who values ideology over art and who is blind to works that are not explicitly political. Howe is also stung for his statement that Wright's release of anger allowed Baldwin and Ellison to express their own anger. "What does Howe know of my acquaintance with violence," writes Ellison, "or the shape of my courage or the intensity of my anger? I suggest that my credentials are at least as valid as Wright's . . . and it is possible that I have lived through and committed even more violence than he." Furthermore, Wright, though a hero and friend, was not as great a literary influence as were Malraux and Hemingway. To say that blacks are influenced only by other blacks assumes that blacks live in a "colored-only" jug with a tight cork. We must remember, however, that the jug is not opaque, but transparent: blacks influence and are influenced by whites and others outside the jug.

Too often, Ellison warns, a writer like Howe, who believes that good art must be overtly *engagé*, shrinks the image of the black man he is purporting to defend. "One unfamiliar with what Howe stands for would get the impression that when he looks at a Negro he sees not a human being but an abstract embodiment of living hell." Thus the raging Bigger

Thomas is preferred to the bemused Invisible Man. Overlooked here is the belief that blacks are unquestionably human and that

> Their resistance to provocation, their coolness under pressure, their sense of timing and their tenacious hold on the ideal of their ultimate freedom are indispensable values in the struggle, and are at least as characteristic of American Negroes as the hatred, fear and vindictiveness which Wright chose to emphasize.

Ellison states succinctly where he differs with Wright (and Howe) regarding the purpose of art:

> Wright believed in the much abused notion that novels are ''weapons''—the counterpart of the dreary notion, common among most minority groups, that novels are instruments of good social relations. But I believe that true novels, even when most pessimistic and bitter, arise out of an impulse to celebrate human life and therefore are ritualistic and ceremonial at their core. Thus they would preserve as they destroy, affirm as they reject.

Ellison says that just as he, and most blacks, have disciplined themselves to live sanely in a hostile America, his novel is a product not of political struggle alone but of disciplined literary struggle. The writer's job is not to deny but to transmute the loadstone of anger and injustice into art.

With its comment on folklore and art, Stanley Edgar Hyman's chapter on *Invisible Man*, published in *The Promised End,* could be seen as derivative of Ellison's own critical work. Yet Ellison takes sharp issue with Hyman in *''Change the Joke.''* In a typical preface he puts his essay in context, explaining that it originated as a letter to ''an old friend and intellectual sparring partner.'' Their two articles, he adds, ''are apt to yield their maximum return when read together.'' Despite this gentle beginning, Ellison is quick to point out that Hyman's conception of how literature draws on folk sources is so much at variance from his own that he ''must disagree with him all along the way.''

Ellison finds fault with the ''racially pure'' aspects of Hyman's discussion. Hyman identifies the ''darky entertainer'' as a figure from black American folklore and as one related to the ''archetypal trickster figure, originating from Africa.'' This minstrel man, a professional entertainer who plays dumb, metamorphoses in Afro-American literature into such characters as the wiley grandfather of *Invisible Man*. This argument offends Ellison by veering toward the claim that black Americans possess idiosyncratic forms directly traceable to an African homeland.

Ellison responds that the black American writer draws on literature of any and all kinds to create character and circumstance. If he uses folklore, it is not because of his ethnic heritage but because he is a student of *Ulysses* and ''The Waste Land'' where folk and myth sources provide structure and resonance. The black writer should not be backed into a corner where the oddments and exotica of folklore are said to preside over the true source of good writing, which is *good writing.*

Ellison adds that when black writers do tap folk sources, they do not use the ''darky'' figures of minstrelsy. Such characters are by no means black folk types but white ones, born of the white American's need to exorcise the true black man and to drape in black certain troubling behavioral patterns and attitudes. When these entertainers show up in American literature they are repulsive to Afro-Americans. Furthermore, masking and ''playing dumb'' are American games, not just black ones. Black characters in novels by American blacks are, Ellison says, as homegrown as their authors. Trace them to Africa, and the critic takes a political position not a literary one.

This hyperbolic statement seems to contradict Ellison's belief that folklore provides a secure base for great literature. But, troubled by the ''segregated'' idea that black writers strictly depend on black sources, and angered by even the dimmest suggestion that as a black writer he himself performed the obscene function of a blackface minstrel man, Ellison threw Hyman a hyperbole. Afro-American folklore provides riches, Ellison says, ''but for the novelist, of any cultural or racial identity, his form is his greatest freedom and his insights are where he finds them.''

So where does the writer find true portraits of Afro-Americans? In black folklore, yes. In churches, barbershops, workgangs, and playgrounds where the lore abounds. But that kind of study can never replace the needed study of images and modes of characterization in literature. And this does appear in the works of Toni Morrison, Ernest J. Gaines, Ishmael Reed, Al Young, Alice Walker, and James A. McPherson—all of whom also use folklore in their fiction—whose characters spring from the Bible, James Fenimore Cooper, Jonathan Swift, Henry James, Zora Neale Hurston, from Ralph Ellison.

When jazz saxophonist Marion Brown taught at the University of Massachusetts, he required his students to read the second section of *Shadow and*

Act, "Sound and the Mainstream." There, he said, you get an idea of the milieu in which the black musician operates. There, too, are several portraits of Afro-Americans at their eloquent best: as musicians, as artists.

"Blues People," a review of Imamu Amiri Baraka's study of black music, is the theoretical cornerstone of *Shadow and Act's* middle section. Baraka, another strawman, is said to strain for militancy and to falsify the meaning of the blues and the background of the bluesman. Afro-Americans of any kind are likely to produce genuine art, notes Ellison, not just dark-skinned, country, lower-class, or militant blacks. Furthermore, Afro-American music may not correctly be considered in isolation from mainstream American music. "The most authoritative rendering of America in music is that of American Negroes." One of Ellison's major points here is that black American musicians, throughout their history in the New World, have functioned not as politicians but as artists, leaders of transcending ritual. "Any effective study of the blues would treat them first as poetry and ritual." To white society, Bessie Smith may have been purely an entertainer, a "blues queen"; but "within the tighter Negro community where the blues were part of a total way of life, and a major expression of an attitude toward life, she was a priestess, a celebrant who affirmed the values of the group and man's ability to deal with chaos." The same is true of other black musicians too, as Ellison carries out the theme in his portraits of Mahalia Jackson, Charlie Parker, Charlie Christian, and Jimmy Rushing.

The piece on Mahalia Jackson, "As the Spirit Moves Mahalia," contains a fine thumbnail sketch of the renowned gospel singer, whose ebullience brought her international fame. Also, though untrained in a formal sense, she is portrayed as a highly conscious artist who extended the gospel form. Disciplined by her experiences in a black southern rural and then black northern urban setting, she was influenced not only by blues and jazz, but by the European classics, flamenco, and certain Eastern forms.

Ellison gives an excellent discussion of black sacred music as the music of ritual. He advises those who would truly understand this singer to hear her in the Afro-American church, where she reigns as "a high priestess in the religious ceremony."

> It is in the setting of the church that the full timbre of her sincerity sounds most distinctly . . . Here it could be seen that the true function of her singing is not

simply to entertain, but to prepare the congregation for the minister's message, to make it receptive to the spirit and, with effects of voice and rhythm, to evoke a shared community of experience.

The recordings are wonderful, but only in church may she sing truly" until the Lord comes." Only in the music's ritual context may the full mystery and meaning of her songs be comprehended.

"Remembering Jimmy" is Ellison's eloquent appreciation of Jimmy Rushing who, like Mahalia Jackson, is portrayed as the leader of a ritual, in this case a secular one: the public dance. The combination of blues, dancers, musicians, and singers "formed the vital whole of jazz as an institutional form, and even today neither part is quite complete without the rest." Rushing's blues and ballads must be experienced in ritual context. So, too, his music is a product of the black neighborhood, his voice seeming to echo something wondrous about the east side of Oklahoma City where he like Ellison got his start. And Rushing's music has political, social, and national implications, reminding Americans of "rockbottom reality" along with "our sense of the possibility of rising about it." Herein lies the force of the blues, "our most vital popular art form," and the universal appeal of an artist/interpreter, Rushing.

Ellison's tribute to another childhood acquaintance in "The Charlie Christian Story" focuses on the jazz musician in American society. In a country where high art is viewed as entertainment, and where the complexities of history are reduced to the clichés of legend, the meanings of jazz are dimly understood. Charlie Christian was exposed to many kinds of music as he grew up. Oklahoma City was a bustling, energetic blues and jazz center where Second Street was comparable to Kansas City's famous Twelfth. Moreover, at school, on the radio, at the movies, and, in Christian's case, at home, classical music as well as popular and folk songs were heard. Many jazz performers, including Christian before he reached New York City, remain local heroes inside the narrow radius of their traveling circuit. But the tradition from which their art springs is a rich and diverse one, tapping blues and classics, folk and high art.

As with Rushing and Jackson, Christian and other jazz artists can be most fully understood in the context of ritual. For jazzmen the public dance is a vital institution. But the "academy"—the principal ritual and testing ground—is the jam session. Here the artists exchange ideas (which then, imitated, drift into the vocabulary of mainstream jazz, leaving their creators anonymous); they also participate in a rite wherein the musician's identity is discovered and asserted. In Ellison's words, "Each true jazz moment . . . springs from a contest in which each artist challenges all the rest; each solo flight, or improvisation, represents (like the successive canvases of a painter) a definition of his identity: as individual, as member of the collectivity and as a link in the chain of tradition." For Ellison, black musicians are tough, astute artists and ritual leaders who teach, purge, destroy, mourn, initiate, delight— and, above all, celebrate.

And black music that is unconnected to these life-sustaining rituals—the church, the dance, the jam session—is liable to be sterile. Such seems the case even with the eloquent saxophone virtuoso, Charlie "Bird" Parker, portrayed in "On Bird, Bird-Watching, and Jazz" as an artist without roots. Though Parker studied and jammed with Kansas City musicians, he (and a generation of imitators) threw off the mask of the dance-hall entertainer only, Ellison says, to become a "white hero" and, ironically, "entertainment for a ravenous, sensation-starved, culturally disoriented public," mostly white. To Ellison, Parker's music reflected the triumph of technique over real feeling (as expressed in sacred and secular ritual) and, finally, adolescent impotence. Of Parker's style, Ellison writes: "For all its velocity, brilliance and imagination there is in it a great deal of loneliness, self-deprecation and self-pity. With this there is a quality which seems to issue from its vibratoless tone: a sound of amateurish ineffectuality, as though he could never quite make it." "Bird lives," in Ellison's view, because he transforms postwar discord and yearning into "a haunting art." Ellison, who obviously is deaf to virtually all jazz beyond Basie and Ellington, says that if Bird could be said to reign as a ritual leader, his was a cult of sad-eyed, self-destructive whites, trying desperately, decadently, to be "hip."

The third and final "movement" of *Shadow and Act*, the one that gives the book its title, is its least focused section. This "eldest" division (containing essays dated 1942, 1944, 1948, 1949, and 1958) comprises two topical essays, a piece on black Hollywood images, a book review, and a self-interview on politics, race, and culture. This mixed section is not, however, a mere grab bag stuffed with old essays unfitted to the rest of the book. Dealing primarily with culture and politics—rather than literature and music—it provides the reader a background against which to evaluate Ellison's discussions of specific art forms and artists.

Also, the essays in this final section are the book's most radical in analysis. In "The Way It Is," published in *New Masses* (1942) Ellison coolly defines the misery and near despair of Harlemites on the home front of the world war fought by a Jim Crow army. In "Harlem Is Nowhere" (unpublished, 1948) he discusses the wretched conditions in Harlem and their effects on the minds of desperate "folk" residents. And in "An American Dilemma: A Review" (unpublished, 1944) he delineates the invidious relation of "philanthropic" big business, social science, and black politics. Here we seem to be in the presence of a Young Turk who hurls elaborate curses from the sidelines of American culture. That two of these essays were not previously published (because of their radical bent?) suggests that Ellison may have yet more gems filed away.

As in the first two thirds of *Shadow and Act*, in this section Ellison deals with the image and role of the Afro-American in the United States. Here again he observes that in terms of culture Afro-Americans are more American than purely African. What binds people of African ancestry throughout the world is "not culture . . . but an identity of passions." "We share a hatred for the alienation forced upon us by Europeans during the process of colonialization and empire are bound by our common suffering more than by our pigmentation." Thus blacks around the world share what one anthropologist has termed a common "culture of oppression" rather than language and other cultural forms and rites. Now we meet Ellison at his stubborn and limiting worse, blindly ignoring the multiplicity of cultural forms shared by peoples of African descent. According to the Ellison of "Some Questions and Some Ancestors," all that blacks in America have in common with blacks in Ghana or South Africa is white oppression.

This is not to say that Afro-Americans do not constitute a distinctive group; nor, as Ellison makes clear elsewhere, does it mean that Afro-Americans are defined simply by their relation to white Americans. In an often-quoted passage from his review of Gunnar Myrdal's *An American Dilemma,* Ellison bristles:

> Can a people (its faith in an idealized American Creed not withstanding) live and develop for over three hundred years simply by *reacting*? Are American Negroes simply the creation of white men, or have they at least helped to create themselves out of what they found around them? Men have made a way of life in caves and upon cliffs, why cannot Negroes have

made a way of life upon the horns of the white man's dilemma?

In fact, black Americans *have* made a way of life which they do not wish to sacrifice entirely, even in their drive for full freedom in America. Ellison accuses Myrdal of presuming that blacks do not participate in "white" culture because they are kept away from it. Ellison offers an important corrective here:

It does not occur to Myrdal that many of the Negro cultural manifestations which he considers merely reflective might also embody a *rejection* of what he considers "higher values." There is a dualism at work here. It is only partially true that Negroes turn away from white patterns because they are refused participation. There is nothing like distance to create objectivity, and exclusion gives rise to counter values. Men, as Dostoevsky observed, cannot live in revolt.

Men tend to prefer the styles and values of their particular cultural group. Sounding somewhat more like Imamu Amiri Baraka than the moderate integrationist, Ellison comments on the effect of integration on black culture:

I see a period when Negroes are going to be wandering around because, you see, we have had this thing thrown at us for so long that we haven't had a chance to discover what in our own background is really worth preserving. For the first time we are given a choice, we are making a choice ... Most Negroes could not be nourished by the life white Southerners live. It is too hag-ridden, it is too obsessed, it is too concerned with attitudes which could change everything that Negroes have been conditioned to expect from life.

Shadow and Act presents explicit and compelling definitions of Afro-American life. The most comprehensive of these appears in "The World and the Jug" (which I talked about earlier in terms of its literary argument):

It is not skin color which makes a Negro American but cultural heritage as shaped by the American experience, the social and political predicament; a sharing of that "concord of sensibilities" which the group expresses through historical circumstance ... Being a Negro American has to do with the memory of slavery and the hope of emancipation and the betrayal by allies and the revenge and contempt inflicted by our former masters after the Reconstruction, and the myths, both Northern and Southern, which are propagated in justification of that betrayal ... It has to do with a special perspective on the national ideals and the national conduct, and with a tragicomic attitude toward the universe. It has to do with special emotions evoked by the details of cities and countrysides, with forms of labor and with forms of pleasure; with sex and with love, with food and with drink, with ma-chines and with animals; with climates and with dwellings, with places of worship and places of entertainment; with garments and dreams and idioms of speech; with manners and customs, with religion and art, with life styles and hoping, and with that special sense of predicament and fate which gives direction and resonance to the Freedom Movement.

Ellison closes this lyrical definition with: "Most important, perhaps, being a Negro American involves a *willed* affirmation of self against all outside pressure—an identification with the group as extended through the individual self which rejects all possibilities of escape that do not involve a basic resuscitation of original American ideals of social and political justice."

As seen by Ellison, the Afro-American's life has been torturous and tragic, but it has also been heroic and rich in form and spirit. Sociologists and sociological critics, indeed critics of all kinds, and writers, black and white, have failed for the most part to focus on black American men and women of flesh and blood. A few writers have seen through the greasepaint stereotypes. In *Shadow and Act* Ellison recommends that those who would truly "know the Negro" study certain nineteenth- and twentieth-century writers (including the Russians) and to learn about black folklore. Moreover, in this abstracted autobiography Ellison surveys his own experience and recommends that blacks be seen (and, especially, that they see themselves) as a group with a special perspective, with beautiful and useful cultural forms, and with a flaming desire for freedom.

Source: Robert G. O'Meally, "Shadow Actor: Ellison's Aesthetics," in *The Craft of Ralph Ellison,* Harvard University Press, 1980, pp. 160–72.

Sources

Bigsby, C. W. E., "Improvising America: Ralph Ellison and the Paradox of Form," in *Speaking for You: The Vision of Ralph Ellison,* edited by Kimberly W. Benston, Howard University Press, 1987, p. 137.

Elliot, George P., "Portrait of a Man on His Own," in *New York Times Book Review,* October 25, 1964.

Staples, Brent, "Indivisible Man," in *New York Times Book Review,* May 12, 1996.

Wright, John, "Slipping the Yoke," in *Speaking for You: The Vision of Ralph Ellison,* edited by Kimberly W. Benston, Howard University Press, 1987, p. 65.

Further Reading

Bloom, Harold, *Ralph Ellison,* Modern Critical Views series, Chelsea House Publishers, 1986.

Bloom's text is a collection of critical essays on Ellison's fiction and non-fiction.

Butler, Robert J., *The Critical Response to Ralph Ellison,* Greenwood Press, 2000.

This work is a collection of critical essays on Ellison's work that were published since the release of his posthumously published work.

Nadel, Alan, *Invisible Criticism: Ralph Ellison and the American Canon,* University of Iowa Press, 1988.

Nadel offers a collection of essays addressing Ellison's ambivalent relationship to other prominent American authors, including Mark Twain, Ernest Hemingway, and William Faulkner.

Woodward, C. Vann, *The Strange Career of Jim Crow,* Oxford University Press, 1966.

Woodward's book is the definitive work detailing the relationship between the civil rights movement and the decades of segregation that preceded it.

A Theory of Justice

John Rawls

1971

A *Theory of Justice* (1971), by John Rawls, is "one of the most influential works in moral and political philosophy written in the twentieth century," according to Samuel Freeman in the *Collected Papers of John Rawls* (1999).

A *Theory of Justice* is Rawls's attempt to formulate a philosophy of justice and a theoretical program for establishing political structures designed to preserve social justice and individual liberty. Rawls writes in reaction to the then predominant theory of utilitarianism, which posits that justice is defined by that which provides the greatest good for the greatest number of people. Rawls proposes a theoretical person who, shrouded in a veil of ignorance, must design a just society without foreknowledge of his or her own status in that society. Rawls asserts that from this objective vantage point, which he calls the original position, the individual will choose a system of justice that adequately provides for those positioned on the lowest rungs of society. The individual will do so because he or she may end up in such a disadvantaged position and will want to be adequately provided for. Rawls draws from earlier theories of political philosophy that posit a social contract by which individuals implicitly agree to the terms on which they are governed in any society. Rawls concludes that such a social contract, formulated from the perspective of the original position, will guarantee a just society without sacrificing the happiness or liberty of any one individual.

Rawls addresses issues of liberty, social equality, democracy, and the conflict of interests between the individual and society.

Author Biography

John Bordley Rawls is one of the most influential philosophers of the twentieth century. He was born on February 21, 1921, in Baltimore, Maryland, the son of William Lee Rawls and Anna Abel (Stump) Rawls. Rawls received a bachelor of arts degree from Princeton University in 1943. During World War II, he served in the military, stationed in the Pacific. He attended Cornell University for a year from 1947–1948 and earned a doctorate from Princeton in 1950. In 1949, he married Margaret Warfield Fox, with whom he had four children.

Throughout his academic career, Rawls held posts in philosophy departments at several prestigious universities in England and the United States, including Princeton University, Oxford University, Cornell University, and the Massachusetts Institute of Technology. He became a professor of philosophy at Harvard University in 1962, where he remained through his semi-retirement as professor emeritus. As an academic, Rawls was active in several national organizations, serving as president of the American Association of Political and Legal Philosophers from 1970–1972, and president of the American Philosophical Association in 1974. He also co-edited the journal *Philosophical Review* from 1956–1959.

Rawls's masterpiece of political philosophy, *A Theory of Justice*, was first published in 1971. Although he wrote numerous articles in academic journals, Rawls did not publish another book until the 1990s. *Justice as Fairness* and *Two Concepts of Rules* both appeared in 1991, followed by *Political Liberalism* in 1993. *John Rawls: Collected Papers*, edited by Samuel Freeman, was published in 1999, and Rawls's *Lectures on the History of Moral Philosophy*, edited by Barbara Herman, was published in 2000. Rawls was awarded the National Humanities Medal by the National Endowment for the Arts in 1999.

In a preface to *Collected Papers*, Freeman observes that Rawls's career as a philosopher has been "guided by a reasonable faith that a just society is realistically possible."

Plot Summary

Justice as Fairness

In *A Theory of Justice*, Rawls begins with the statement that, "Justice is the first virtue of social institution," meaning that a good society is one structured according to principals of justice. Rawls asserts that existing theories of justice, developed in the field of philosophy, are not adequate: "My guiding aim is to work out a theory of justice that is a viable alternative to these doctrines which have long dominated our philosophical tradition." He calls his theory—aimed at formulating a conception of the basic structure of society in accordance with social justice—justice as fairness.

Rawls sets forth to determine the essential principles of justice on which a good society may be based. He explains the importance of principles of justice for two key purposes: first, to "provide a way of assigning rights and duties in the basic institutions of society"; and secondly, to "define the appropriate distribution of the benefits and burdens" of society. He observes that, by his definition, well-ordered societies are rare due to the fact that "what is just and unjust is usually in dispute." He further notes that a well-ordered and perfectly just society must be formulated in a way that addresses the problems of "efficiency, coordination, and stability."

Critique of Utilitarianism

Throughout the twentieth century, the dominant philosophical theory of justice in Western philosophy was utilitarianism. Utilitarianism was first developed in the nineteenth century by "the great utilitarians," whom Rawls lists as David Hume, Adam Smith, Jeremy Bentham, and John Stuart Mill. Utilitarianism essentially posits that a just society is one based on achieving the greatest good, or happiness, for the greatest number of people. However, many theorists have found this principle ultimately unsatisfactory because it implies that the happiness of a minority of people may be justly sacrificed to secure the happiness of the majority. Rawls defines the strict classical doctrine of utilitarianism in terms that capture the fundamental basis of the theory as one that seeks to evaluate societal good in quantitative, mathematical terms:

> The main idea is that society is rightly ordered, and therefore just, when its major institutions are arranged so as to achieve the greatest net balance of satisfaction summed over all the individuals belonging to it.

Rawls's central critique of utilitarian theory is that it makes no distinction between the happiness of any one individual and the total sum happiness of society as a whole. He concludes: "Utilitarianism does not take seriously the distinction between persons."

Critique of Intuitionism

The other predominant school of ethical theory in the twentieth century, intuitionism, is, according to Rawls, equally unsatisfactory. Intuitionism, first developed in the eighteenth century, posits that humans possess an innate, intuitive, sense of justice and morality. Rawls admits, however, that one can never completely get away from a certain degree of intuitionism in developing his own theory of justice as fairness. However, he suggests several tentative means of at least reducing the degree of intuition involved in the process. Primarily, he addresses what he calls the priority problem, whereby intuitionism fails to establish a means of evaluating the relative importance of any one ethical principle over any other. Rawls suggests as a remedy to the priority problem that specific principles of justice be ranked in order of importance, so that the first would take precedence over the second, and so on.

The Social Contract

In formulating his theory of justice as fairness, Rawls draws from an earlier, long-neglected, theory of the social contract, as developed in the seventeenth and eighteenth centuries by Thomas Hobbes, John Locke, Jean-Jacques Rousseau, and Immanuel Kant. Social contract theory assumes that governmental leadership functions on the implicit assumption of an agreement, or social contract, between the ruler and the ruled, according to which the individual willingly sacrifices some personal liberties to secure the greater good of society. Rawls asserts that social contract theory "seems to offer an alternative systematic account of justice that is superior, or so I argue, to the dominant utilitarianism of the tradition."

The Original Position

To devise a system upon which a just society could be based, Rawls proposes a hypothetical man whose choices are made from the standpoint of a veil of ignorance. Rawls imagines a man who must design a society in which he does not know ahead of time what social or economic status he himself will hold. From the perspective of this veil of ignorance as to his own fate, Rawls argues, one can only seek to create a society whereby the least fortunate are provided with adequate means of happiness since one may find oneself in precisely that position. Rawls refers to this hypothetical perspective as the original position. He notes that the hypothetical person in the original position must be assumed to be a rational thinker.

The Two Principles of Justice

According to Rawls, the original position results in the successful achievement of two central principles of justice. The first principle assures that the liberty of the individual may be maximized, given that it does not impinge upon the corresponding freedoms of any other individual. The second principle assures that even the most economically and materially disadvantaged members of society are provided for as best as possible. An important point of this second principle is that Rawls admits room for social and economic inequality, given that those at the lowest end of the spectrum are at least adequately supported.

Key Figures

Saint Thomas Acquinas

Thomas Aquinas (1225–1274) was an Italian theologian of the medieval era who was canonized in 1323. Aquinas based his theological arguments on the ideas of Aristotle. Rawls refers to Aquinas in a discussion of different theories about toleration of religious differences, asserting that Aquinas and the Protestant reformers believed that intolerance of other religions was "a matter of faith."

Aristotle

Aristotle (384–322 B.C.) was the third of the three great Greek philosophers (the others being Plato and Socrates) whose ideas have immeasurably influenced Western thought. Rawls refers to Aristotle in terms of his definition of justice and his concept of perfection. Rawls coins the term "Aristotelian principle" to describe Aristotle's philosophy regarding the relationship between happiness, activity, and enjoyment.

Jeremy Bentham

Jeremy Bentham (1748–1832) was an English philosopher and economist, known as the first and foremost proponent of utilitarianism. His major works include *An Introduction to the Principles of*

Morals and Legislation (1789). Rawls contrasts Bentham's utilitarian theory with his own theory of justice as fairness.

F. Y. Edgeworth

Francis Ysidro Edgeworth (1845–1926) was an Irish economist and statistician, known for his work in applying mathematical principles to the fields of economics and statistics. He also tried to apply mathematics to the theory of ethics. His major works are *New and Old Methods of Ethics* (1877) and *Mathematical Psychics* (1881). Referring to Edgeworth as a utilitarian economist, Rawls discusses his ideas in contrast to those of justice as fairness. Rawls also criticizes Edgeworth's argument for the utility principle on the basis that his basic assumptions are ''unrealistic'' and ''implausible.''

Sigmund Freud

Sigmund Freud (1856–1939) is indisputably recognized as the father of psychoanalytic theory. He was an Austrian Jewish physician, whose theories of psychoanalysis form the basis of psychoanalytic theory. His major works include: *Interpretation of Dreams* (1900), *Five Lectures on Psycho-Analysis* (1910), and *The Ego and the Id* (1923). Rawls mentions Freud in a discussion of the psychology of morals. He argues against Freud's theory of the origin of the sense of justice as rooted in feelings of envy and jealousy.

Thomas Hobbes

Thomas Hobbes (1588–1679) was an English philosopher who was an early figure in developing a utilitarian philosophy of morals. Hobbes's major work is *Leviathon* (1651). His theories regarding the social contract are taken up by Rawls in his own theory of justice as fairness.

David Hume

David Hume (1711–1776) was a Scottish philosopher and economist. He attempted to apply scientific method to an inquiry into human nature, particularly in terms of the concept of knowledge. Rawls mentions that Hume referred to justice as ''the cautious, jealous virtue.'' He makes reference to Hume's works, *A Treatise of Human Nature* (1739) and *An Inquiry Concerning the Principles of Morals* (1751). Rawls discusses his own ideas regarding the circumstances of justice as based in those of Hume. He further mentions Hume in a discussion of the concept of a rational and impartial sympathetic spectator capable of determining the conditions of a just society.

Immanuel Kant

Immanuel Kant (1724–1804) was a German philosopher of the Enlightenment era whose ideas forever transformed philosophical thinking, particularly in the areas of ethics, knowledge, and aesthetics. His work was influential in the later theories of the idealists. Rawls refers frequently to such works by Kant as *The Foundations of the Metaphysics of Morals* and *The Critique of Practical Reason*. He discusses Kant among the theorists who developed the social contract theory. He further mentions Kant in discussion of theories of the ''good'' and the concepts of envy and duty. In a discussion of moral learning, Rawls refers to Kant among several philosophers who believed that morality is a natural, innate quality of humanity. In a section entitled ''The Kantian Interpretation of Justice as Fairness,'' Rawls provides an analysis of the philosophy of Kant in relation to his own theory of justice as fairness.

John Locke

John Locke (1632–1704) was an English philosopher of the Enlightenment era. His major work was *An Essay Concerning Human Understanding*. Rawls also refers to his *Second Treatise on Government*. Rawls states his intention to further develop and refine the theory of the social contract, as earlier discussed by Locke, among others. In a discussion of the basis of morality, Rawls points out that Locke's fundamental principal of morals assumes that God is the legitimate moral authority. He later mentions Locke's advocacy of a limited toleration of religious differences to maintain public order.

Karl Marx

Karl Marx (1818–1883) was a German Jewish economist, historian, and sociologist, whose extraordinarily influential analysis of political and economic history is known as Marxist theory. His major works include *The Communist Manifesto*, written with Friedrich Engels (1848), and *Capital* (three volumes, 1867, 1885, 1894). Rawls briefly mentions various interpretations of Marxist theory, particularly in terms of the relationship between the individual and society.

John Stuart Mill

John Stuart Mill (1806–1873) was an English economic theorist and philosopher known as an influential exponent of utilitarianism. Mill was an early advocate of women's suffrage and was one of the founders of the first women's suffrage society, later known as the National Union of Women's Suffrage Societies, in 1867. Rawls refers to Mill's book *On Liberty* in discussing his ideas about justice, liberty, values, voting rights, and morality. He focuses on Mill's arguments in favor of free institutions, meaning societies designed to allow for personal liberty among individuals. Rawls, however, points out that Mill believed men with greater education and more wisdom should be granted greater power within a democratic society, thus arguing for unequal freedoms among men.

Friedrich Nietzsche

Friedrich Nietzsche (1844–1900) was a highly influential German classical philosopher. His major works include *Thus Spoke Zarathustra* (1883–1885), *Beyond Good and Evil* (1886), and *On the Genealogy of Morals* (1887). In a discussion of the nature of goodness, Rawls mentions that Nietzsche, along with Aristotle, was a theorist of perfectionism, in the sense that he felt the goal of society is the realization of human excellence in art, science, and culture. Rawls observes that Nietzche indicates "that mankind must continually strive to produce great individuals."

Jean-Jacques Rousseau

Jean-Jacques Rousseau (1712–1778) was a highly influential French philosopher and writer whose ideas were a major source of inspiration for the French Revolution of 1789. His major works include *The Social Contract* (1762). Rawls asserts that his aim is to develop and refine the theory of the social contract, as originally conceptualized by Rousseau and other theorists. In a discussion of the issue of religious toleration, Rawls observes that Rousseau, like Locke, advocated limited toleration of diverse religious beliefs. In a discussion of moral learning, Rawls notes that Rousseau believed moral feelings are a natural, innate quality of the mature adult.

Arthur Schopenhauer

Arthur Schopenhauer (1788–1860) was a German philosopher known as an advocate of pessimism. Rawls refers to his *On the Basis of Ethics* (1840) in a brief mention of Schopenhauer's critique of Kantian philosophy.

Henry Sidgwick

Henry Sidgwick (1838–1900) was an English philosopher and writer. His highly influential *Methods of Ethics* (1874) put forth a theory of ethics based on utilitarianism. Sidgwick attempted to define a rational method on which to base ethical decisions. He concluded that there are three possible methods for ethical decision-making: egoism, utilitarianism, and intuitionism. He formulated a theory of universal hedonism, by which the pleasures of the individual and the good of society could be reconciled. Rawls refers to Sidgwick's *Methods of Ethics* throughout *A Theory of Justice*, citing Sidgwick as one of the great classical utilitarian philosophers. Rawls discusses Sidgwick's ideas in contrast to his own theory of justice as fairness. He describes Sidgwick's ideas about institutions of formal justice, noting that Sidgwick maintained that "law and institutions may be equally executed and yet be unjust." Rawls further discusses Sidgwick's critical stance toward the theories of Kant, and his advocacy of the theory of universal hedonism.

Adam Smith

Adam Smith (1723–1790) was a Scottish political economist and social philosopher of the Enlightenment. His major work, *An Inquiry into the Nature and Causes of the Wealth of Nations* (1776), put forth the first systematized theory of political economy. During his lifetime, Smith was internationally recognized for his influence on both social science and economic theory. Rawls refers to Smith in terms of his theory of the invisible hand of market influences, as put forth in *Wealth of Nations.*

Themes

Individual Liberties

In formulating his theory of justice as fairness, Rawls makes clear that the guaranteed freedom of each and every individual is essential to the establishment of a just society. He thus determines that liberty is the first priority in a hierarchy of principles defining justice; he places limitations on individual liberty only insofar as it impinges on the liberty of others. The first principle is stated as: "each person is to have an equal right to the most extensive scheme of equal basic liberties compatible with a similar scheme of liberties for others." In defining what he means by liberty, Rawls points out that there are different types of liberty and that some are

Topics for Further Study

- To what extent do you agree or disagree with Rawls's theory of justice as fairness? Can you suggest an alternative theory?

- Read one of Rawls's articles from the *Collected Papers* (1999). What is his argument? How does it fit in with his theory of justice as fairness? To what extent do you agree or disagree with Rawls's argument in this article?

- Rawls makes reference to a number of influential philosophers (as listed in the Key Figures section of this entry). Pick one of these philosophers and learn more about his life. What were this person's contributions to philosophical thought?

- *A Theory of Justice* was first published in 1971 during an era of great turmoil in American history. Learn more about one of the major events or series of events that took place in the United States between the mid-1960s and mid-1970s. In what ways did this event raise issues relevant to Rawls's conception of a just society?

- Evaluate your own society in accordance with the principles of justice as fairness put forth by Rawls. To what extent is it a just society in its basic political and legal structure? In what ways do you consider it an unjust society? What measures could be taken to make it more just?

more crucial to a just society than others. The most important liberties he describes as first, ''freedom of thought and liberty of conscience,'' and second, ''freedom of person and the civil liberties.'' Rawls further establishes three items that must be accounted for in any definition of liberty: a specification of which individuals are free, a specification of what restrictions they are free from, and a specification of ''what it is they are free to do or not do.'' Rawls provides a list of the essential liberties, which includes: political liberty, freedom of thought, freedom from assault upon the mental or physical well being of the individual, the right to ownership of property, and freedom from arbitrary arrest and seizure. He states that, in accordance with the first principle of justice, all of the above listed liberties are to be guaranteed equally to all individuals.

The Individual versus Society

A central concern in defining a just society is always in regard to the potential for conflict between the interests of the individual and the interests of society as a whole. Rawls points out that the individual must be granted the maximum liberty, but only insofar as it does not have a negative effect on the liberties of others. He asserts that a central flaw in the theory of utilitarianism is that it assumes

the benefit to a majority can justify restrictions on the liberties of any individual or group of individuals. Rawls, on the other hand, avers that there is no justification for limiting the basic liberties of any one individual (granted it does not interfere with those of anyone else). He takes, as an example, the issue of religious tolerance, concluding that a religion that cannot tolerate the co-existence of other religions must be limited, only to protect the fullest expression of all religions.

Social Equality and Inequality

Implicit in Rawls's idea of a just society is that it is one structured so as to maximize social equality. Rawls makes clear that a certain degree of inequality is tolerable, even in a just society. He focuses particularly on inequalities in the distribution of wealth and in the level of political power held by different individuals. He argues that these inequalities are acceptable, given that those on the very lowest rungs of society are guaranteed at least a minimum of financial means, political influence (such as voting), and basic rights. His argument against utilitarianism is in part that it allows for the utter devastation of some members of society, as long as the prosperity and happiness of others is maximized. Rawls, as well as other philosophers before him, have pointed out that there is a degree of inhumanity in this aspect of utilitarian theory, which disregards any concern with social equality. Rawls, on the other hand, proposes a system that allows for limited social inequality.

Democracy

Rawls suggests that the principles upon which a just society is structured are particularly compatible with the form of government known as a constitutional democracy. He prioritizes what he calls the principle of (equal) participation, which ''requires that all citizens are to have an equal right to take part in, and to determine the outcome of'' the political and legal process. He elaborates that this includes the stipulation of one citizen, one vote, and the assurance that elections are fair and free, and regularly held. He adds that the principle of equal participation includes the right of all citizens to run for public office. In addition, ''all citizens should have the means to be informed about political issues.'' Rawls assumes that a democratic society must be structured in accordance with the basic rights of freedom of speech and assembly, and liberty of thought and conscience. In a preface to the 1999 revised edition of *A Theory of Justice*, Rawls expresses his intentions in formulating the theory of justice as fairness, in regard to constitutional democracy:

> The central ideas and aims of this conception I see as those of a philosophical conception for a constitutional democracy. My hope is that justice as fairness will seem reasonable and useful, even if not fully convincing, to a wide range of thoughtful political opinions and thereby express an essential part of the common core of the democratic tradition.

Style

Revision

The results of an ongoing revision process are an important element of Rawls's writing style. Critics frequently comment on *A Theory of Justice* as the representation of an ongoing process of philosophical theorizing on the part of Rawls, which has taken place over the course of some forty years. *A Theory of Justice*, first published in 1971, is actually made up primarily of revised articles Rawls had previously published in academic journals, some going back as early as 1958. Thus, it has been observed that the development and refinement of his ideas between 1958–1971 can be traced within

the text of a single book. Furthermore, Rawls significantly revised *A Theory of Justice* in 1975, to prepare it for translation into other languages; however, these revisions were not incorporated into the English-language version of the text until 1999. Rawls points out that, until the 1999 edition, ''the translated editions . . . have been superior to the original.'' Rawls continued, over the course of some twenty-eight years after the publication of *A Theory of Justice*, to respond to the questions and complaints of many of his critics; thus, the 1999 revised edition incorporates the culmination of these developments into the original 1971 book, in addition to the revisions made for the 1975 translation.

Voice: First Person

Rawls puts forth his argument in the narrative voice of both the *first person singular*—meaning that he uses the pronoun ''I'' to indicate the source of his ideas—and the *first person plural*—meaning that he also uses the pronoun ''we'' to express his ideas. This choice may be contrasted with an approach that assumes an objective, or *third-person* voice by which to put forth a philosophical argument. Rawls appropriately chooses the first person singular narrative voice, which allows him to articulate his ideas in the style of an individual working out a complex, admittedly imperfect, sometimes provisional, philosophy—rather than the definitive, objective conclusions of a *third person* omniscient (all-knowing) narrator. Although Rawls argues in philosophical abstractions, his use of the first person ''I'' is a means of presenting his ideas as the result of an ongoing thought process.

Rawls also uses the first person plural, the pronoun ''we'' in such phrases as: ''We should do what we can to formulate explicit principles.'' In using the first person plural, Rawls draws the reader into his thought processes, inviting the reader to actively participate in thinking through the problems with which Rawls himself is grappling. His use of both singular and plural first person narrative voice represents Rawls's works as an ongoing process of developing and refining his theories in dialogue with both himself and his readers.

Tone

Rawls admits to the reader a certain degree of self-doubt as to whether or not he has succeeded in developing his theory; this is not a weakness in Rawls's writing style but an honest and realistic admission that he, like the reader, is merely one man attempting to make sense of the world—he does not pretend to be putting forth *the* answer to the timeless questions that he is addressing. Thus, he allows himself the opportunity to express doubts about his own ideas, or to admit that some of his ideas have not yet been fully developed. He indicates this in a tone of tentativeness, or self-doubt, throughout the book, using such phrases as: "I shall try to show"; "I wish to develop"; and "It seems desirable at this point . . . to discuss."

Abstract

Rawls opens each of the three main parts of *A Theory of Justice* with an abstract—a condensed description, or summary, of the ideas put forth in that section of the book. Abstracts are frequently included in the opening of academic articles and allow the reader to quickly assess the central argument that follows.

Historical Context

A Theory of Justice was first published in 1971, in the midst of a period of social and political controversy and upheaval in American society. From the mid-1960s through the mid-1970s, major issues of ongoing national concern included: the civil rights movement, the Vietnam War, the nationally declared War on Poverty, the women's liberation movement, and the gay rights movement. Throughout this period, many Americans were concerned with issues of social justice, asking themselves questions similar to the ones that Rawls addresses in *A Theory of Justice*: What is a just society? The variety of controversies that reigned throughout the 1960s and 1970s revolved around this fundamental question, raising such basic issues to a democratic society as social equality and individual liberties.

The Civil Rights Movement

The civil rights movement, which began in the 1950s, was a widespread effort throughout the United States to fight for greater equality for African-American citizens. The civil rights movement can be dated from 1955, when Martin Luther King, Jr., organized a bus boycott in Montgomery, Alabama, to protest segregation—African Americans had been required to sit in the back of buses and to give up their seats to white people. A series of federal actions and legislation designed to expand and protect the rights of African Americans followed throughout the 1950s and 1960s. In 1957, federal troops were sent to Little Rock, Arkansas, to protect

the rights of African Americans to attend integrated public schools. In 1960, Congress passed the Civil Rights Act, which was designed to protect the voting rights of African Americans. The Civil Rights Act of 1964 further ensured far-reaching protection of civil rights to African Americans. The subsequent Voting Rights Act of 1965 even more strongly enforced the ability of African Americans to exercise their right to vote. Nonetheless, ongoing racial inequality provoked violent race riots in major cities throughout the country in the years 1965–1968. The civil rights movement received a tragic blow when Martin Luther King, Jr., was assassinated in the spring of 1968. However, the efforts of the civil rights movement continued, in addition to more radical movements for racial equality, such as the Black Panthers, founded by Huey Newton and Bobby Seale, and the black nationalism of Malcolm X. Inspired by the efforts of African Americans, other ethnic minority groups, such as Latinos and Native Americans, launched organizations to fight for greater equality as American citizens.

The Vietnam War

The Vietnam War took place between a communist North Vietnam and South Vietnam, which was backed by the United States. United States involvement in Vietnam was sanctioned by the passing of the Gulf of Tonkin resolution in 1964. A turning point in American public opinion of the Vietnam War came in 1968 when, as a result of the Tet Offensive, many Americans first perceived that the extent of the communist forces would not make for an easy victory. Massive anti-war demonstrations and large-scale draft evasion grew throughout the late 1960s and early 1970s. In 1970, during a non-violent student protest on the campus of Kent State University, in Ohio, four students were shot dead by the Ohio National Guard. In 1973, a cease-fire agreement was signed, whereby the United States withdrew forces from Vietnam, suffering military defeat after a decade of fighting and the loss of some 58,000 American lives.

The War on Poverty

During the 1960s, President Lyndon B. Johnson initiated extensive legislation designed to enact his declared War on Poverty, as part of his program for a great society. Many benefits were extended to the socio-economically disadvantaged, to ease the burden of economic inequality in the United States. The Housing and Urban Development Act of 1965 was passed to support programs for federal housing.

Compare
&
Contrast

- **1789:** *Introduction to the Principles of Morals and Legislation,* by Jeremy Bentham, delineates the principle of utility, which posits that morality is determined by whatever results in the greatest good for society as a whole, regardless of the fortunes of any individual or group of individuals. This theory goes against intuitionism, a school of thought that implies that humans have an intuitive sense of right and wrong.

  1971: *A Theory of Justice,* by John Rawls, transforms the fields of ethical and political philosphy, posing the first convincing challenge to the dominance of utilitarian thought.

  Today: Ongoing critical response to Rawls, both supportive and dismissive, is a continuing measure of his influence on the field of ethics.

- **Mid-1800s:** Legal, educational, and general social reform occurs in England as a result of corruption and dissatisfaction. A new legal system, largely based on utilitarianism, supplants a system more or less based on natural law.

1960s and 1970s: In the midst of much social and political upheaval, including the civil rights movement, women's liberation movement, gay rights movement, and a nationally declared "War on Poverty," many Americans concern themselves with social justice and its existence within a democratic society.

Today: Discrimination persists in many forms, despite being largely illegal. Welfare reforms attempt to reduce poverty.

- **Mid-1800s:** The Civil War leads to the complete abolishment of legal slavery in the United States.

1960s and 1970s: Legislation is passed to end segregation in the United States. Affirmative action is conceived and is slowly instituted.

Today: Segregation is illegal. Affirmative action is widely instituted and is the subject of many political and legal disputes. The American attempt at civil equality is emulated by other countries, such as South Africa.

The Medicare Bill guaranteed health care coverage for senior citizens. In 1966, the minimum wage was raised, and in 1967, social security pensions were raised. Many other reforms were enacted during this period, focusing on such concerns as educational aid, urban renewal, and mass transportation.

Women's Liberation

The women's liberation movement, inspired by the civil rights movement, was an extensive effort to gain greater equality for women in all areas of society and culture, including work, the family, and politics. The women's liberation movement has been referred to using a variety of terms, including women's lib, the feminist movement, or simply feminism. The women's liberation movement of the 1960s and 1970s is also referred to as second wave feminism, distinguishing it from the first wave feminism of the nineteenth and early-twentieth century women's suffrage movement. The feminist movement has been referred to as a "bloodless revolution" because of the extensive and far-reaching societal changes it accomplished without the use of violence. Early second wave feminists organized consciousness-raising groups, small, loosely organized groups of women, often meeting in private homes to discuss an entire range of concerns affecting women's lives. They were influenced by such early publications as *The Second Sex* (1949), by French writer Simone de Beauvoir, and *The Feminine Mystique* (1963), by Betty Friedan. The National Organization for Women (NOW) was founded in 1966, focusing on reform for women's rights at the public level. The widely circulated motto of the women's lib movement was "the personal is political"—a statement that captured the extent to which feminists perceived that even the most personal experiences, such as family, sex, and relationships, had political implications in regard to women's status in society.

Gay Pride

The gay pride movement is generally dated from the night of June 28, 1969, when gay activists rioted in protest of the arrest of patrons of a gay bar called the Stonewall Inn, in Greenwich Village in New York City. This was the first time in which a public, semi-organized protest by homosexuals had come to national attention, and the organization of a widespread and far-reaching gay pride movement soon followed. Gay Pride Week is now celebrated annually in June, in commemoration of the watershed incident now referred to simply as "Stonewall."

Critical Overview

A Theory of Justice has had tremendous, far-reaching impact on twentieth-century philosophical thought. Rawls is widely credited with breathing new life into the field of political philosophy, which, by the 1950s, had nearly ceased to develop in any significant direction. Victoria Davion and Clark Wolf, in *The Idea of a Political Liberalism* (2000) assert, "By any account, the appearance of [*A Theory of Justice*] was a turning point for political philosophy," adding that it "could not have been more cataclysmic in its effect on the field." As Rex Martin avers, in *Rawls and Rights* (1985), *A Theory of Justice* "is widely regarded as an important and seminal treatise on some of the main topics of moral and political philosophy." Rawls's work also had an important effect on liberal thought. As A. P. Rao asserts, in *Three Lectures on John Rawls* (1981), "Rawls not only brought some freshness into the Anglo-American moral philosophy, but also rescued liberal thinking from sterility, and liberal ideology from impotence."

The book, however, inspired extensive criticism, as well as praise. Brian Barry, in *The Liberal Theory of Justice* (1973), claims, "Rawls's theory of justice does not work and . . . many of his individual arguments are unsound." Yet Barry is quick to add:

> It is, quite simply, a work that anyone in the future who proposes to deal with any of the topics it touches must first come to terms with if he expects the scholarly community to take him seriously.

David Lewis Schaefer, in *Justice or Tyranny?* (1979), offers harsh criticism on the grounds that Rawls's work is not that of true political philosophy, but rather of political ideology. Schaefer asserts, "Rawls's writings . . . embody what I believe to be both a popular yet seriously deficient political ideology and a widely shared yet grossly inadequate understanding of the nature of political philosophy." He goes on to state, "the widespread acclaim that *A Theory of Justice* has received from the academic community despite the book's manifold defects is . . . a disheartening sign of contemporary decay, not only in political philosophy, but in scholarship."

Even Rawls's most ardent admirers find many weaknesses in this seminal work. Robert Paul Wolff, in *Understanding Rawls* (1977), opines that Rawls's central idea in *A Theory of Justice* is "one of the loveliest ideas in the history of social and political theory"; yet, he confirms, "The logical status of the claims in the book never becomes entirely clear."

Whether criticizing or celebrating his theories, none doubt the impact of his ideas on the field of philosophy. Rao notes that the sheer volume of critical response to *A Theory of Justice* has been enormous, remarking that, since the book's first appearance, "Rawls's studies have become a heavy industry." As Davion and Wolf point out:

> Rawls has, for the most part, inspired philosophers not as disciples or followers but as critics and opponents. But even Rawls's most articulate critics have adopted argumentative methods that betray his deep influence. Critical attention of this sort is, we believe, the highest form of scholarly compliment.

They add that, despite the many legitimate criticisms of his ideas, "clearly it is to Rawls's credit that his books and papers continue to inspire controversy and productive disagreement and to generate articulate reasoned response instead of passive doctrinal adherence." Further:

> Among political theorists, there is clearly no overlapping consensus on the success of any particular Rawlsian argument, or even on the idea of an overlapping consensus itself. There is much more agreement on the overwhelming significance of Rawls's contribution to the field and on his enduring influence: Rawls's work has redefined the central issues of political philosophy and raised the standard of rigor and argument for the entire field.

As Rao observes of his widespread and lasting influence, "Rawls has become an integral part of the general intellectual culture, and the ideology, of the Anglo-American world."

Criticism

Liz Brent

Brent has a Ph.D. in American culture, specializing in film studies, from the University of Michigan. She is a freelance writer and teaches courses in the history of American cinema. In the following essay, Brent discusses the principle of equality of opportunity in Rawls's theory of justice as fairness.

A central concern for Rawls is the problem of how to regulate equality of opportunity, given that the potential for any person to succeed in life is in part determined by their inborn, innate talents and abilities, and in part by the social, material, and psychological conditions under which they are raised as children.

Rawls's second principle of justice of fairness states that:

> Social and economic inequalities are to be arranged so that they are both (a) reasonably expected to be to everyone's advantage, and (b) attached to positions and offices open to all.

In other words, a certain degree of social inequality is acceptable, provided that it is ultimately to the benefit of all citizens; for instance, the president in a democratic society has more power than the average citizen, but the vesting of this power in one individual is considered to be beneficial to all citizens in facilitating the functioning of democracy. Rawls explains that there are several ways of interpreting this second principle; he chooses to interpret it in the sense he refers to as democratic equality: that equality means equality of opportunity—that everyone ought to be given an equal opportunity.

However, Rawls observes that fair opportunity cannot regulate the factor of what he calls the natural lottery—meaning the natural talents and abilities accorded to any given individual, merely by accident of birth. He points out that this unequal distribution of natural talents and abilities among individuals is "arbitrary from a moral point of view"; in other words, there is no moral basis for why any one individual should be born with greater intelligence, or greater musical talent (for example), than any other. Rawls makes clear that those with the good fortune to be born with greater natural talents and abilities must recognize that their status is simply the luck of the draw, and not an indication of superiority as a human being: "We do not deserve our place in the distribution of native endowments, any more than we deserve our initial

Rawls draws on Thomas Hobbes's "social contract" theories

starting place in society." He points out that the inequality of innate talents and abilities, which is the condition of the natural lottery, is not an indication that any one person deserves more in life than any other; these inborn inequalities "are simply natural facts." However, society has the ability to accommodate such innate inequalities to maximize the degree of social and material equality enjoyed by each and every citizen: "What is just and unjust is the way that institutions deal with these facts."

Rawls suggests that given that there will always be such innate inequalities in the potential of each individual, society can at least guarantee to each citizen "a formal equality of opportunity in that all have at least the same legal rights of access to all advantageous social positions." He adds that, "all should have a fair chance to attain" any given desirable social position; for example, not only should every citizen be allowed the legal opportunity to become a doctor, but every citizen should be guaranteed a fair chance to achieve the education level necessary to become a doctor.

Rawls elaborates that the social status into which one is born should not hinder the opportunity to realize the individual's natural potential for success in whatever field his or her talents lie: he states

What Do I Read Next?

- In *Rawls: A Theory of Justice and Its Critics* (1990), Chandran Kukathas and Philip Pettit provide analytical discussion of the central critical responses to Rawls's work.

- In *Culture War and Ethical Theory* (1997), Richard F. Von Dohlen discusses Rawls's theories in relation to cultural conflicts facing the United States in the twentieth century.

- In *Pluralism and Consensus: Conceptions of the Good in the American Polity* (1998), Christopher Beem discusses philosophies of liberalism and pluralism, including the theories of Rawls, in relation to American politics and government.

- *John Rawls: Collected Papers* (1999), edited by Samuel Freeman, includes almost all of Rawls's publications (other than his books), arranged in chronological order.

- *Lectures on the History of Moral Philosophy* (2000), edited by Barbara Herman, includes Rawls's lectures on the history of modern ethics from the seventeenth through the twentieth centuries.

"those who are at the same level of talent and ability, and have the same willingness to use them, should have the same prospects of success regardless of their initial place in the social system." He explains, "those with similar abilities and skills should have similar life chances." In other words, society cannot compensate for inequalities in natural talents and abilities—but society should ensure that those with equal talents and abilities be granted equal opportunity to realize their innate potential: "The expectations of those with the same abilities and aspirations should not be affected by their social class."

One of the most important factors in providing this equality of opportunity is "maintaining equal opportunities of education for all." Rawls asserts that the education system is central to establishing equality of opportunity for all citizens: "Chances to acquire cultural knowledge and skills should not depend upon one's class position, and so the school system, whether public or private, should be designed to even out class barriers."

When Rawls speaks of the value of education, he makes clear that it is not merely a matter of training the citizen for economic productivity; more importantly, education is a means of enhancing the quality of life of even the most disadvantaged members of society. He states, "The value of education should not be assessed solely in terms of economic efficiency and social welfare." Rather, "Equally, if not more important, is the role of education in enabling a person to enjoy the culture of his society and to take part in its affairs, and in this way to provide for each individual a secure sense of his own worth."

Rawls, however, admits that even these measures to guarantee equal opportunity cannot compensate for the natural lottery, whereby some are born with greater talents and abilities than others. In addition, he points out that, "the principle of fair opportunity can be only imperfectly carried out, at least as long as some form of family exists." He explains:

> The extent to which natural capacities develop and reach fruition is affected by all kinds of social conditions and class attitudes. Even the willingness to make an effort, to try, and so to be deserving in the ordinary sense is itself dependent upon happy family and social circumstances.

Thus, the ideal of fair equality of opportunity does not address the concern that "the internal life and culture of the family influence, perhaps as much as anything else, affect a child's motivation and his capacity to gain from education, and so in turn his life prospects." Thus, "Even in a well-ordered society that satisfies the two principles of justice, the family may be a barrier to equal chances between individuals." Equal opportunity in education for those with equal innate natural talents and abilities does not compensate for the home life of the child, which may limit his or her potential.

Rawls defines the concept of the natural aristocracy as referring to the greater endowment of natural talents and abilities to some than to others; in other words, this idea asserts that some individuals naturally occupy a greater social status, based on their inborn potential. Rawls asserts that the idea of a natural aristocracy is not necessarily unjust, as long as the elevated privileges awarded to those with greater talent are ultimately used to the benefit of all citizens, including those with lesser natural talent and ability. It is the responsibility of those with greater innate talents and abilities to use these advantages for the benefit of the less privileged members of society. Rawls argues that the natural aristocracy thus can be to the advantage of society as a whole, for "the opportunities of the least favored sectors of the community would be still more limited if these inequalities were removed." Thus, "those who have been favored by nature, whoever they are, may gain from their good fortune only in terms that improve the situation of those who have lost out." Further, any rewards that accrue from this initial vantage point should not be regarded as the natural due of those with the good fortune to possess superior advantages.

To compensate for the unequal distribution of natural talents and abilities, as well as the unequal circumstances into which different individuals are born, Rawls offers the principle of redress. He defines this as the principle that undeserved inequalities call for redress, and adds, "since inequalities of birth and natural endowment are undeserved, these inequalities are to be somehow compensated for." Thus, a greater portion of the resources of a society ought to be directed toward the least advantaged, so that "society must give more attention to those with fewer native assets and to those born into the less favorable social positions." Rawls again points to the education system as a central location for enacting the principle of redress: "In pursuit of this principle greater resources might be spent on the education of the less rather than the more intelligent, at least over a certain time of life, say the earlier years of school."

Rawls thus puts forth a theoretical perspective from which a society may be structured to maximize equality of opportunity while taking into account the inequalities afforded by the natural lottery—

> **It is the responsibility of those with greater innate talents and abilities to use these advantages for the benefit of the less privileged members of society."**

whereby individuals are endowed with an unequal distribution of natural talents and abilities—as well as unequal family, social, and economic circumstances in which to develop these innate talents and abilities.

Source: Liz Brent, Critical Essay on *A Theory of Justice,* in *Nonfiction Classics for Students,* The Gale Group, 2002.

Rex Martin

In the following essay, Martin surveys Rawls's theories of rights.

In this chapter I will first identify the various levels or stages at which Rawls has found talk of rights to be significant (i.e., rights *in* the original position, rights emerging *from* the original position in the principles of justice formulated there, etc.). I then go on to show how Rawls would regard rights at these various levels to be justified. The focus of our discussion will be on rights as embedded in the basic structure of a society. I will try to provide an interpretation of Rawls's claim that such rights are natural rights. Then, last of all, I will consider the implications of this conception of natural rights for global justice.

1. Rawls on Rights and Their Justification

We could conveniently divide Rawls's theory here into a four-part structure. The first and topmost part concerns the so-called primary goods. The second part concerns the formulation of the principles of justice and the choice of a particular set of such principles over alternative ones. (Rawls's preferred set, which he calls the "two principles of justice," would, he thinks, be chosen in the original position.) The next part concerns the institutionalizing of the (two) principles of justice in what Rawls calls the "basic structure" of a society. The last part, then, concerns the actual workings of a society

> Rawls's failure to deal with the analytic issues poses an obstacle to his program as a justification of rights."

so organized and, in particular, some of the institutions and subordinate arrangements that would crop up in such a society—or, at least, in any such society under modern conditions. Interestingly, Rawls refers to rights at each of these four levels.

The primary goods, as we might recall from chapter 1, are goods which, presumptively, any rational person would want, whatever his plan of life or value orientation might be. These goods, abstractly stated, are divided by Rawls into (a) the *social* primary goods—liberty, opportunity and powers, income and wealth, the bases of self-respect—and (b) the *natural* ones—health and vigor, intelligence and imagination. As I suggested in chapter 1, we can view the deliberations of persons in the original position respecting justice as an attempt to define and select preferred principles for allocating or arranging the *social* primary goods among individuals. It is interesting to note that sometimes Rawls includes rights among these primary goods, but sometimes he does not.

In my judgment the listing of rights at this level is confusing and should be dispensed with. Rawls is obviously rather casual on this point. The matter may call for more attention than he has given it, however; for there are two quite distinct reasons why rights as primary goods would be a problematic notion in Rawls's theory of justice.

First, we had established in chapter 1 that the original position, as an arena for the formulation of the principles of justice, could have no features which in and of themselves would be strong enough to generate a principle of justice. For we wanted the eligible principles to follow, not deductively from any descriptive feature of the original position (or any elements initially included in it), but from the arguments that were deployed there. But rights, unlike the other primary goods, are overtly normative entities; moreover, a conventional principle of justice would assert that rights should be respected

or that rights should not be violated. Thus, insofar as rights are among the social primary goods, we could generate a strong—albeit conventional—principle of justice almost immediately out of the primary goods. And there would be no need, then, for the elaborate mechanisms of the theory of justice to allow for the construction of some such principle in the original position. This would violate the constraint that there should be no normative elements of justice introduced into the theory prior to the construction of the preferred principles of justice.

Moreover, rights appear to be a moral category with which utilitarian thinkers have difficulty, as should be evident from chapter 1. So, if rights were to be included among the social primary goods, then this would strongly prejudice the deliberation in favor of a specific sort of moral theory. We would also simultaneously prejudice the event against a utilitarian solution, if it is true that utilitarians have a problem in accounting for basic rights. So, on grounds of the desired normative weakness—or nondeductivity—of the original position model and of the moral neutrality of that model with respect to the competing principles of justice, we should attempt to expunge rights from the list of social primary goods.

This brings me to the second point. To treat rights as primary goods is to regard them as both pretheoretical (i.e., as prior to the theory of justice) and as noninstitutional (since they would antedate the basic structure of a society and, for that matter, all other social institutions). But this seems to beg important questions about the nature of rights, which need to be expressly decided (a point that we shall return to in the next section).

Fortunately, Rawls's inclusion of rights among the social primary goods does not appear to represent anything deep-seated. It is relatively offhand and, apparently, relatively easily set aside. Let us treat rights as effectively purged from the list of such goods, although there is still the interesting question (to which we will return later in this section) of why Rawls would tend to include them.

This takes us to the second stage of our analysis in this section. Rawls argues that in the original position, under conditions of extreme uncertainty in which there are no objective bases for judging probabilities, the two principles would be formulated and selected as the preferred principles.

The important thing, for our purposes, is that the first principle is usually stated by Rawls as itself identifying a right. For example, in his standard statement of the two principles, the first is said to require that "each person is to have an equal right to the most extensive total system of equal basic liberties compatible with a similar system of liberty for all." I would suggest, then, that on this reading the Rawlsian first principle states a basic moral right. And whatever justification attaches to the two principles, as justification through a choice procedure that is both fair and rational, attaches ipso facto to this basic moral right.

The second principle, however, is not formulated by Rawls as a right. Rather, it is characteristically rendered in somewhat different terms: "Social and economic inequalities are to be arranged so that they are both: (a) to the greatest benefit of the least advantaged . . . and (b) attached to offices and positions open to all under conditions of fair equality of opportunity."

The two principles, as they emerge from the original position, are exceedingly abstract. Just as the primary goods belong to what Rawls calls a "thin" theory of the good, so the two principles constitute a "thin" theory of justice. They require to be embodied. Justice is, or should be, a virtue of society, specifically of its basic structure. The object of the two principles is the design or the normative analysis of the basic structure of a society. Included in that structure is a society's political system and its economic system. Each of these, in turn, would be made up of a set of structural elements or institutions (as we saw in chapter 1), with some being described as main institutions (e.g., the political constitution or the supply/demand market) and others as background institutions (e.g., antitrust regulation as a control on the market).

The idea is that a just society would conform to the two principles by building them into its basic structure: institutions are set up which, when operating together, give results that tend to satisfy the two principles over time. These institutions, then, represent a set of middle principles standing between the two principles and the actual operation of a society. The background institutions check tendencies in the main institution which might over time take it away from its original seated disposition; they not only keep the main institution on track—and it, them—but also they remedy its deficiencies, as regards justice. The result is that the "ongoing institutional processes are . . . constrained and the accumulated results of individual transactions continually adjusted."

Rawls references John Stuart Mill's famous work, On Liberty

Rawls repeatedly talks of the two principles, in particular the first one (Equal Basic Liberties), as *assigning* rights and duties. But this is inexact. The two principles assign rights and duties by means of the basic structure. Rawls thinks, for example, that the inclusion of a bill of rights within the constitution is one important way in which the first principle of justice could be institutionalized in a given society. So, the constitution (or some other feature of the basic structure) assigns determinate rights to individual persons; what the first principle does is to "govern"—or better, to *justify*—the business of assigning equal basic rights to individuals. Basic structure rights, in particular those attaching to the main institution(s), are conceived by Rawls as analogous in a variety of ways to natural rights.

The last level in Rawls's theory of rights concerns the legitimate expectations of individual persons. We can assume that these expectations would include those established at the higher levels, as secured by justice. Thus, constitutionally protected political and personal rights as laid down in the basic structure of a society would be legitimate expectations of individuals in that society. And as well, other legitimate expectations would grow up in and around the operation of the various institutions in the basic structure (e.g., the highly detailed list of rights that have grown up around the institutions of trial by jury or of private ownership of property or of equality of opportunity).

But the basic structure is also a framework for the transactions of individuals and associations. Now, individuals do not merely interact (and associations—such as labor unions or corporations or universities—do not merely interact) with the embodied principles and subsequent workings of the basic structure. Individuals also interact with one another and with associations. (The same is true for associations: they interact with one another and with individuals.) Accordingly, rules and practices that are characteristic of these sorts of transactions could be formulated as well. Thus, we could follow a line of devolvement away from the institutions of the basic structure. And here we would encounter a vast variety of subsidiary institutions and practices, of private associations and cooperative ventures. Nonetheless, expectations would attach to the operation of these subsidiary elements and, insofar as the institutions and practices in question were compatible with justice or loosely derivative from it, the expectations would be legitimate ones, as secured or enframed by justice. Thus we can speak of subsidiary rights, as distinct from basic structure rights, of many sorts: rights under this contract or that, of particular organizational structures, of individual family life (e.g., the Martin family), and so on. In general, Rawls encompasses these rights under the heading of fairness or fair play. They are all institutional rights that are justified primarily by their relationship to elements in the basic structure, rather than directly by the two principles of justice themselves. In the absence of reasonably just institutions, we would, of course, have to turn to the two principles; but these could cover only the clear cases (i.e., practices that were grossly unjust, such as slavery, or obviously fair, such as a nonexploitative and voluntary cooperative arrangement or agreement). Since my concern in this study is with basic moral and constitutional rights and their justification, I will have little to say about these subsidiary institutional (or practice) rights.

I have schematically represented Rawls's method of justification as proceeding from the top down. Thus, the top level (deliberation in the original position about the rational and fair distribution of social primary goods) is used to justify the basic moral right that is stated in the first principle of justice; and the first principle of justice is used in turn to justify the constitutional rights that are built into the basic structure of a just society; and these, in turn, play a role of sorts in the justification of all subsidiary rights. But Rawls adds an important control on this procedure by requiring that the justifying principle or theme be matched with certain considered judgments (either in the form of maxims or of paradigm cases) which exhibit or help to exhibit the moral character of that which is to be justified (the "subject" of justification). For example, determination of the constitutional right of persons to be free from the injuries of "cruel and unusual punishment" would involve not merely the first principle of justice and its grounds (the primary goods of liberty and opportunity and of self-respect—i.e., the bases of self-respect) but also considered judgments about punishment and practices that have been associated with it historically (including such matters as mutilation as a form of corporal punishment, public execution and other forms of capital punishment, harsh treatment of those who have not been judged guilty or of those who have been judged insane, the aims of punishment, relevant maxims as to what is legally just, etc.). Rawls calls this matching procedure the method of reflective equilibrium.

In the application of this method a certain amount of to-ing and fro-ing normally results, with adjustments being made in the initial formulation of the justifying principle (or in its range of extension) as well as in our considered judgments. The goal of the method is to bring the two levels—that of justifying principle and that of the practice to be justified (and the material relevant to it)—into alignment.

We can put this point more precisely now by distinguishing between a narrow reflective equilibrium and a wide one. Briefly, a *narrow* reflective equilibrium means that the justifying principle of justice (e.g., the first principle) is matched, more or less on its own, with the considered judgments. A *wide* reflective equilibrium, by contrast, involves matching these judgments not merely with the principle itself but also with the various elements that went into its construction. From chapter 1 we are familiar with these elements as the ones that are organized around the original position "model" in the Rawlsian account of the deliberations about the principles of justice for the basic structure of a society. It is this peculiar sort of coherence between principles and their theoretical backdrop, on the one hand, and considered judgments, on the other, that satisfies the standard of justification in matters of justice and, hence, of rights.

Rawls's account of the justification of rights is subject to most of the criticisms that can be made, more generally, of his theory of justice. Some criticisms, however, can be made specifically of this theory of rights.

Rawls's conception of rights is opaque. He does not attempt an analysis of the concept, and though he uses the term 'rights' freely, he does so without explication. The context is usually unhelpful. Rawls's failure to deal with the analytic issues poses an obstacle to his program as a justification of rights.

Oddly enough, the best place to look for guidance is in Rawls's discussion of what I earlier called subsidiary rights and practices. Thus, although this material may be relatively unimportant to our main project (that of developing a Rawlsian theory of basic moral and constitutional rights), it may, nonetheless, have important implications for what Rawls conceived rights to be. Then, if we can assume that he consistently has meant by 'rights' the same thing throughout, we can extrapolate this discussion to more interesting contexts and thereby have the beginnings of the Rawlsian theory we seek.

I would suggest, then, that a right for Rawls is an individual's legitimate expectation as to what he would receive in a just institutional distribution of social primary goods. The justification of a right, then, would involve establishing the legitimacy of the expectation within the framework of higher-to-lower-level justification under conditions of reflective equilibrium that have already been described, albeit briefly, in this section.

On this reading, liberties as social primary goods could be called rights—not in the original position but, rather, under institutional arrangements imposed by justice. One of Rawls's standard pairings of primary goods—the pairing of rights and liberties—would conform to this usage, though the pairing is confusing since it mixes those things that are primary goods *in* the original position (liberties) with things that could be included there only prospectively (rights). The pairing, then, is anticipatory (and should not be taken literally). It is also revealing—suggesting, as it does, a close tie (almost a conceptual one) between rights and liberties in Rawls's thinking, as if only liberties *could* be rights.

At the same time the reading gives us a reason why Rawls was not inclined to treat the *second* principle of justice as itself a basic moral right or to regard the pattern of just distributions of wealth and social position as a pattern of rights. The reason is

this: though specific liberties can be secured to a determinate degree to *any* given individual (since all share in the basic liberties equally), specific economic or social standings cannot. In economic matters, individuals float between an upper and a lower limit (both of which are determined by the difference principle, the principle that inequalities of wealth and social position must be arranged so that the prospects of the least-advantaged group are maximized). Thus, no given individual has a legitimate expectation of receiving any particular distributive share and, hence, cannot be said to have a right to a particular share. Even the minimum *level* established by the difference principle does not define the legitimate expectation of any given individual (not even those who form the group of the least advantaged); rather the expectation is that of a "representative," or ideal-type, individual. Accordingly, Rawls characteristically withholds the term 'rights' in his discussion of the second principle and its applications. And Rawls's approach here is markedly different from his handling of the first principle and its applications.

But what, exactly, does this Rawlsian conception of rights amount to? I would suggest that two main ideas are determinative here: first, the idea of something distributive or individuatable and, second, the idea of something the distribution of which can be guaranteed.

When it is said that something can be distributed, one means that it can be assigned or parceled out to the individuals in some target group or class. Thus, the towels in a locker room would be, in this sense, distributable to the members of the club, though probably the acoustical properties of the room would not be. Rawls is interested in universal rights, that is, basic moral and constitutional rights; so, the things that someone can have a right to in such cases would have to be things that could be distributed to everyone: that is, the same things to each and everybody in the relevant class (e.g., persons, citizens).

Now, the sand on the beach on some out-of-the-way Pacific island would thus be distributable (assuming that no one owned it), but there is no readily available mechanism to achieve such a distribution; more important, there is no way to guarantee it. This is one reason—probably only one among several—why no one would be inclined to say that people had a right to grains of sand from this beach. Something is, or becomes, a right only when its distribution (we assume it to be a benefit) can be guaranteed, or at least reasonably assured within practical limits, to the individuals who are relevantly said to be the recipients.

Thus, when Rawls speaks of legitimate expectations, he can be interpreted to mean not only that an individual's claims are valid but also that they are reasonable *expectations:* the individual's receiving his share or his due can be counted on because it is built into the structure of things and, we might add, because it is normatively independent of the usual considerations (the public good or the general welfare) that might be urged against it. Rights, for Rawls, are not free-floating claims, of the sort often called moral. They are, rather, details of an institutional arrangement in which the claim and the means for delivering on it are linked closely together.

But at this point we begin to sense a certain amount of tension in Rawls's theory. I will try, in concluding this section, to make this unease explicit.

Some have claimed that Rawls has no place in his theory for moral rights. But the judgment here is hasty, since the first principle, the principle of equal basic liberties, seems itself to be a right in Rawls's account. And since the first principle is developed in the original position, as a principle for the design of the basic structure of a just society, it is prior to any society; the first principle itself cannot, then, be regarded as an institutional right but rather as a prescription for institutional or political rights. And as a prescription, it is moral in character; or so it might be argued. Thus, if the first principle is a right at all, it must be a moral right.

Let us say provisionally, then, that the first principle states a basic moral right: namely, that each person ought to have available the most extensive system of equal basic liberties compatible with a similar system of liberty for all other persons. Having such liberties in a well-ordered society is the legitimate expectation of each person. But what are these liberties?

Now, one could reply that the first principle does not actually specify the liberties in question; it speaks merely of "equal basic liberties." The initial specification of liberties occurs at the point when the basic structure of a society is designed (perhaps with the help of the method of reflective equilibrium). But this is to suggest that the first principle has no essential content of liberties, leaving the determination of "equal basic liberties" to time and circumstance. The first principle becomes, then, merely formal; it says, in effect, once the basic

liberties have been determined in the constitution, they are to be equal for all citizens. But if the meaning of "equal basic liberties" cannot be fixed initially, then the first principle offers inadequate guidance as to precisely what liberties are to be institutionalized. The first principle—and with it, the original position—ceases to be the "Archimedean point" (the phrase is Rawls's) for the critique and design of the basic structure of a society.

The issue that I have been examining is, I think, a serious one for Rawls's theory of equal basic liberties as rights. For if some or even a few basic liberties are by and large specified at a further stage—say, at the design of the basic structure— then the first principle to that degree lacks essential content and stability.

Let us put this point somewhat differently. If the liberties on the list lack specificity or, even worse, fundamental identity, then it is difficult to say that one could have a *right* to them. Rights are, for better or worse, fairly determinate things. There comes a point, as we relax and let go of detail and then of substance, when one can no longer be said to have a legitimate expectation. The thing loses the name of right and becomes something else—an aspiration, perhaps. This line of reply, then, has obvious defects.

Accordingly, one could reply instead that Rawls's first principle of justice establishes a particular "list" of basic liberties; it identifies a specific set of liberties which are to be acknowledged as being held equally by all. (This particular reading has been suggested by Hart.) It is, I think, the correct interpretation; this interpretation of the first principle as specifying a list of basic liberties is made clearer, Rawls says, in revisions that were made for the German edition of his book and in some of his later writings.

The relevant liberties are, Rawls tells us, rights of citizenship and of the person: such things as the right to vote; freedom of speech and assembly; liberty of conscience; the right to own personal property; freedom from slavery, arbitrary arrest, and seizure; and so on. They are standard civil liberties (or rights).

So the tension in Rawls's theory, to which I referred earlier, can now be stated. If, on the one hand, the liberties are specified too loosely, then there is no clear sense in which a person can be said to have a legitimate expectation respecting them. Hence, there would be no *right* to them as defined in the original position but, rather, presumably only in the more determinate institutional setting provided by what Rawls calls the basic structure of a society. On the other hand, were one to say that the basic liberties are rights (as one would be licensed to do, presumably, in the basic structure), then it would appear to be otiose to say of *these* rights that one has a right to them.

So Rawls's way of putting his first principle seems to fail under either option. If the basic liberties lack specificity (in the original position), then one cannot be said to have a legitimate expectation regarding them there; the legitimate expectation arises, so to speak, in some subsequent institutional setting (where they have, presumably, the requisite specificity). Hence, there is no *right* to the basic liberties that is stated by the first principle. But where the liberties have the requisite specificity— as they would have in the basic structure of a society—then they have become rights themselves (i.e., each basic liberty is itself a right), and it is redundant to speak of an additional or supervenient right to such liberties.

The dilemma appears to be that if we feed enough substance into the basic liberties to have a legitimate expectation concerning them, then there's no point in identifying a general right (= the first principle, as stated) alongside them; and if we don't, then we won't have a legitimate expectation, hence no right (regardless of what the first principle states). The first principle, then, seems doomed either to be pointless and trivial or to be inaccurate if taken literally.

The problem here is, perhaps, deeper even than this. In his theory of justice, Rawls operates with two distinct but related categories of analysis: the original position and the basic structure of a society. The original position is quintessentially *moral*. It can be entered by anyone at any time. When people are in the original position they are there, all of them, as free, equal, rational, and moral persons. They are societyless. The original position is a forum for discussion and the formulation of principles. It is a noninstitutional context. The basic structure of a society is quite different in these respects. It supposes a limited and finite population of people whose entire lives will be lived together and who will bequeath, among other things, a set of institutional arrangements to their children. The people here are all inhabitants of some *particular* society and, hence, are co-citizens with one another; as fellow citizens, they are under the *particular*

political (and economic and social) institutions which go to make up the basic structure of that one society, their society. The basic structure of that society is an arena for application, for the building of principles of justice into the ongoing life of that one society in particular. The citizens' principal concern is with institutional design and criticism. The basic structure is necessarily an institutional context.

It is not clear, however, that the notion of rights can flourish in both contexts. Rawls, and many others, have all too easily assumed that it can. Rawls has made it sound as if talk of rights is fluid and can shift effortlessly from the one context to the other. What I have been delineating is at bottom not so much a difficulty that is internal to Rawls's theory (though certain tensions within that theory have helped bring it to light) as it is a fundamental philosophical difficulty in how one talks intelligibly about rights. I will begin the next section with that issue primarily in view, as our main topic for discussion there.

Before we move to that point, however, let me very briefly summarize the main results of our brief introductory survey of rights in Rawls's theory. We have determined that two of the ways in which Rawls talked about rights are dispensable: any listing of rights among the social primary goods was seen to be deeply confused and misleading, hence dispensable for that reason; any reference to rights that individuals might have (toward other individuals or associations) in virtue of legitimate expectations that arose through the workings of institutions that are subordinate to the basic structure (e.g., rights of parishioners or clergy in a church) was seen to be peripheral to our primary concern with basic moral or constitutional rights. That left two main areas for further discussion: (1) the supposed *moral* right stated in the first principle of justice (''each person is to have an equal right to the most extensive total system of equal basic liberties compatible with a similar system of liberty for all'') and (2) the basic liberties themselves as rights. And I have suggested some reasons for saying that these two do not fit well together. If my suggestions were to be accepted—a point that depends on the argument of the next section—then we would drop the idea that the first principle states a right at all. We could reword it, for example, in language reminiscent of the *second* principle, to say that ''political institutions are to be [or should be] so arranged that the most extensive justifiable system of liberties is to be available for each and all.'' We would concentrate then entirely on the idea that the basic liberties named, in effect, in the first principle are rights when embedded in the basic structure of a society. Our whole discussion of rights in Rawls's theory would lead out from that one point. We turn to the first stages of that project, then, in the next section.

2. Natural Rights and the Basic Structure

Rawls is one of the few contemporary philosophers who uses *natural rights* as his standard term (Hart is another). We will assume, though, that he means by natural rights roughly what others have meant by human rights. And I will treat these ways of talking as more or less interchangeable.

We can also assume that Rawls does not mean by natural rights what Thomas Hobbes and John Locke did; for them a natural right was any right that an individual had *in the state of nature*. Such a doctrine would have no appeal to Rawls. He rarely speaks of such a state, and when he does, it is, by and large, to distinguish his account of the original position from that of the state of nature in classical contract theory. In Rawls's view, one would reach such a state only if the participants in the original position failed utterly to achieve a decision on preferred principles of justice and then decided, in effect, that no principle on the short list could be preferred to having no principle at all. A state of nature, rather like the one Hobbes envisioned, would result from that failure; it marks for Rawls the point of ''no agreement.'' There is a deep gulf, then, between natural rights in Rawls's theory, where they are identified by reference to the basic liberties that are listed in the preferred first principle of justice, and the idea in traditional contract theory that such rights are the rights an individual has willy-nilly in a state of nature.

Our main project in this section, then, is to provide an interpretation of what Rawls means by natural rights so understood. I will do this by sketching out an argument to show that the concept of rights (hence that of human or natural rights) implies certain practices or institutional arrangements; thus, the notion of a natural (or human) right as wholly noninstitutional, as logically prior to all practices of formulation and maintenance, is a mistake. It might appear from this that I am actually repudiating the Rawlsian idea of natural rights. But this is not so, for I do not believe Rawls's idea reproduces the traditional conception of natural rights at the crucial points where it breaks down.

Now, supposing my argument to be sound, we are able to settle one important issue raised in the previous section: whether, in Rawls's theory, the notion of rights takes hold at the point of the abstract statement of the first principle in the original position or at the point of *applying* that principle to the basic structure of a society. For I think my argument forces the latter conclusion.

It follows that it is idle to describe the first principle of justice itself as a right (even though Rawls's text can bear such an interpretation). I do not, of course, mean to say that the first principle is thereby pointless but only that the term *right* is dispensable in its formulation. The first principle can be put differently, without using the term *right* at all, and suffer no loss of essential content whatsoever—something that has already been suggested in the previous section.

My argument is designed to show, in short, that it is only when basic liberties are built into the basic structure of a society that they are properly called rights in any significant sense. And this interpretation of natural rights in Rawls's theory—as basic liberties insofar as embedded in the basic structure— is one, I think, that can be gotten from Rawls's texts and that can be supported by sound arguments independently of those texts.

My main contention here is that basic moral rights—natural rights—are basic structure rights (and in that sense constitutional rights). And now to the argument.

Let us begin by turning to one of the main dimensions of what can be called legitimate expectations, that of claims *against* other persons. It is arguable such claims require there to be specific duties which fall on determinate or assignable individuals. Lacking these, claims-against could not take hold and would thereby be defective.

Rawls apparently concurs in this. For we note that Rawls frequently pairs rights and duties. It seems, moreover, that he regards rights as always being correlated with duties—at least in the sense that all rights as legitimate expectations imply duties of second parties (i.e., of persons other than the rightholder). And if this pairing—this correlation— were not in evidence, then the claim-to element (e.g., the claim to a particular liberty) would not in and of itself count as a legitimate *expectation* and, hence, would not be a right for Rawls.

The filling in of the requisite background here need not, however, involve creating new duties (or what have you); it may involve simply hooking on to existing ones. In both cases, though, a fully legitimate expectation, hence a natural or a human right, will combine a valid claim *to* something (e.g., a liberty) with a valid claim on or *against* someone.

Thus, a legitimate expectation includes these two elements (a morally justified claim-to and a morally justified claim-against); but can it be limited to them? The question is whether a legitimate expectation could be limited to being simply a valid claim (as defined by these two elements)—as that and nothing more—and still count as a legitimate expectation, still count as a right. Could one exist, in short, without any sort of social recognition or promotion whatsoever?

In order to answer this question we need to put a certain amount of logical pressure on the notion of a legitimate expectation. The existence of a legitimate expectation in Rawls's sense would probably require, in the simplest case, that there be duties actually incumbent on persons in a particular society and that these could be derived or endorsed in virtue of standards of critical morality. For duties that cannot be acknowledged in a given society—or that cannot be shown to follow, discursively, from accredited principles of conduct which are at least reflectively available to persons in that society—cannot be regarded as proper duties which could normatively bind conduct in that society.

Now, clearly, Rawls's theory is committed to the formulation and social recognition of principles of justice in the original position and to sound arguments, themselves certified publicly there, connecting the principles to goods such as specific liberties and thence to the duties of individual persons.

But we would not want to *restrict* these possible acknowledgments to the original position, for then we would lose all hold on actual persons and on their duties and obligations. There must be some requirement that the duties specified in critical morality (in the original position, for example) carry over into the real world of human action. One cannot have an obligation (or a duty) of which one literally cannot be aware. An actual person's conduct cannot be determined by duty (or obligation) if it is not possible for that person, even upon reflection, to be aware of that duty as a duty.

Now, where the beliefs that people have (including their moral beliefs) effectively block acknowledgment of something as a duty, or as a claim

on the doing of their duty, then we have precisely the unawareness of which I am speaking. Thus, if a duty is removed or a supposed moral reason for performing one's duty is removed, in a given time or place, through such unawareness, then the legitimate expectation dissolves and loses the name of right. For rights imply a significant normative direction of the conduct of others, and that would be missing in the case at hand.

A parallel argument could be developed to show that if a certain claim-to (e.g., to a specific liberty) was similarly unavailable in a given society or could not be understood in that society as following from principles of critical morality, then it could give rise to no legitimate expectation there. Hence it could not be a right, nor could it constitute an element in a right.

So there is an unexpungeable element of "social" recognition built into the Rawlsian idea of rights as legitimate expectations. And I have argued that this factor of social recognition cannot end with the original position but must be extended into actual societies, insofar as they have any prospect of becoming well ordered. Accordingly, questions about basic rights must be addressed from this standpoint, as including both the original position and the basic structure of societies which are well ordered (or at least reasonably that way). This, of course, is Rawls's position' for he requires the elaboration of these would-be basic rights (or legitimate expectations) in the form of social institutions.

Now let us take this one step further, from recognition to maintenance. Here we will canvass the issue of what counts as an exemplification of a natural or human right.

Consider the case of innocent travel. I would argue that the right to travel would be vitiated *as a right* if it were not protected or promoted at all. In such a case the right would be a merely nominal one, a right that existed in name only but not in fact. An ideal-type nominal right is in principle never an enforceable one; enforcement simply does not belong to its nature. Its permanent "recognition" could be assured (the liberty put in writing, enshrined in a declaration or in a bill of rights, honored by lip service), but its perpetual nonenforcement would be equally assured. Such rights do not, as some have suggested, constitute a special class of full-fledged rights. Rather, they constitute a limiting case; they are rights only on paper and nowhere else.

Now, to be sure, nominal rights are rights. The point is, though, that we regard the total absence of promotion and maintenance as infirming a right, as rendering it defective. Nominal rights are rights *in one sense only* (that of recognition), but they fail to function as rights. A merely nominal right gives no normative direction to the conduct of other persons in fact; such persons act as if the right did not exist even on paper. No one of them takes the nominal existence of the right as a reason for doing, or not doing, as the right directs. The right here has in actual practice no justificatory or directive force. Where social recognition effectively counts for so little, the rightholder is without any effective guarantee respecting that which has been recognized and formulated as a moral right. Such a right—when merely nominal—has failed in a crucial respect. It represents at best a marginal and precarious example of a right. On the assumption that any right under serious discussion here is not merely nominal, then, for any particular moral right, there would have to be certain appropriate practices of promotion, protection, enforcement, and so forth, on the part of society, including at least forbearance by (other) private persons. The determination of what is appropriate for a basic moral right then becomes the exact point at issue.

The great natural- and human-rights manifestoes were intended to impose restraints upon governments. Individuals were involved as beneficiaries of these restraints but, for the most part, were not the parties to whom the manifestoes were addressed. The right to a fair trial, which is often given as an example of a natural right (by Rawls and others), is a right that one has against governments in particular, especially one's own. The example is by no means atypical. Whether we look at details of specific rights, as we find them in the great declarations of rights, or at the theory of natural rights (including its actual history), we find that government is in fact the principal addressee.

Thus, I would want to argue that, insofar as the claims-against implicated in natural or human rights are addressed to governments in particular, we have to regard practices of governmental recognition and promotion as being the appropriate form that such social recognition and maintenance must take. To that degree, governmental practices are included within the notion of natural rights. They are (or have become) a part of the concept in question. A natural- or human-rights claim that lacks such recognition and promotion is still a valid claim, but it cannot qualify as a proper natural or human right.

And the issue of whether something is a natural right, or whether such rights ''exist'' or whether people ''have'' them, cannot be decided without consideration of the whole range of relevant practices, which include recognition in law and governmental maintenance of the claimed way of acting or of being treated. Such practices are ingredient in the very notion of what it is for something to be a natural or a human right, or so my argument is meant to show.

Now it may be, I would add, that for some universal moral rights the role of government is incidental or even nonexistent. These rights hold strictly between persons. The moral right to be told the truth (or at least not to be lied to) or the moral right to gratitude for benefits provided or, perhaps, the moral right to have promises kept are examples. Such rights differ from, say, the right not to be killed—even when we're talking about the latter right as held against individuals—in being rights that are maintained exclusively, or almost exclusively, by conscience. They are moral rights merely and in no way claims against the government. Interestingly, though, it is often in these very cases that while we are willing to call such rights moral rights, we would tend to withhold the name of human (or natural) right.

There is a sound basis for saying, then, that natural-rights norms (i.e., valid claims) are addressed to governments primarily. And natural or human rights can be distinguished from other universal moral rights in this very circumstance.

There is an important reason, which needs bringing out, for precisely this restriction. In talk of specifically human or natural rights, it is assumed that human beings live in societies. The goods that are identified in claims-to are here conceived as goods obtained and enjoyed in a social setting. That is, such goods are conceived as provided peculiarly or especially through life in a society. They are not, in short, thought to be attained principally, if at all, on a mere individual-person-to-all-others basis. Here then, where the social context is emphasized, claims against others are for the most part addressed not to individuals as such but, rather, to individuals insofar as they exercise the powers of some assigned agency in that particular social setting. Such claims-against hold, not against everyone individually, but against an organized society; and it is of the institutions—or agencies—of that society that satisfaction is expected.

Admittedly, it is not so much governments as it is organized societies that are selected out by human-

or natural-rights claims. The point, though, is that the basic structures of such societies are correctly regarded as being *politically* organized; and it is governments that typically play, and have played, a major role in such organization. Thus, government enters the natural-rights picture as the organizer, and as one of the major agencies, of the kind of society against which a natural-rights claim is characteristically lodged. Thus, the requirement that natural rights be lodged in the basic structure of a society, that their status as rights of this sort requires such incorporation, seems to follow naturally. And this I take to be the view that Rawls is advancing.

If my analysis is correct or even plausible, we have a reason for the central place that government occupies in our concept of natural or human rights; given this reason, we find it natural that recognition and maintenance by governmental action (the satisfaction principally sought in natural-rights claims) should be relativized to particular societies. For these claims, insofar as we have regard to their primary addressee, are satisfied by political devices (e.g., basic laws) having an appropriately universal scope within a particular society. Such a law would exist when, for example, a freedom to travel on the part of every citizen (or preferably, every person) was recognized in the law of that society and scrupulously enforced. We can call any such operative and universal right (i.e., universal within a given society) a general political or civil right—or, if you will, a constitutional right. The latter, which is the more conventional term, seems serviceable enough.

This particular notion of constitutional rights is easily inserted into Rawls's theory. The rights he has in mind are, on their claim-to side, universal and unconditional (in that a valid moral claim holds good for everyone, or at least for everyone who is alive at a given time—for the ground of the claim is simply a title to something or other that is given to all persons, merely in virtue of their being persons, in accordance with moral principles). This is how I would interpret Rawls's contention that the basic liberties, as determined in the original position, are natural rights. That is, on their claim-to side they are like natural rights in the traditional sense. Such claims are explicitly accommodated in the basic structure of any well-ordered society; and they are, under the requirement of a public sense of institutional justice, not only formulated and acknowledged but also scrupulously maintained there by the particular government involved.

There is, I would note, though, an important asymmetry between the claims-to part and the claims-against part of a complete (or full) valid moral claim. The former may well be universal and virtually without restriction; yet it does not follow automatically here that the claim-against element will be similarly universal. For example, all human beings are, or were at one time, children and all have (or had) the appropriate claims to care and concern: to nourishment, upbringing, and so on. But these claims on the part of each child are principally addressed, not to anyone and everyone, but to that child's parents or guardians in particular. Rights that are thus restricted are called special (rather than general) rights. I want to suggest that something like this functions in the case of human or natural rights; they too are special rights. The claim-to element is unrestricted: it holds for every person (or for every person who is alive at a given time). But the claim-against element is typically restricted: not all persons, but only some (namely, agencies of government), are addressed as principally having the moral duty in question. It is their job to arrange the basic structure so as to incorporate the substance of these claims-to for the benefit of their respective inhabitants.

Indeed, the term *basic structure right,* which I introduced in the previous section, seems to be singularly well suited to capture the peculiar sense of constitutional rights that we want to have in view. The turn to constitutional—or basic structure—rights reflects the fact that human rights typically are special rights and are claimed on moral grounds which hold good for all persons, simply in virtue of their being persons, against particular politically organized societies—specifically, against governments. (Or, as Rawls would probably prefer to say, against one's fellow citizens.) The question of whether a particular valid and universal moral claim has been appropriately responded to by government or by the members of one's society is answered by considering the class of active constitutional rights. Such rights, when molded under the influence of these claims, are the kind of right involved. Their existence is a necessary element in a morally valid claim's being (or becoming) a natural or a human right.

If a particular constitutional right is missing in a given country, then lacking this necessary ingredient, the incipient natural right will fail to jell or it will dissolve, for that country or for that time and place. And we are at best left with a moral claim (presumably valid) that something *should be* a constitutional right.

The basic contention, then, which forms the backdrop of this entire study is that natural or human rights necessarily have an institutional side and that, on this side, they would have in a given society the form of constitutional rights. We recognize, of course, that even in a well-ordered society there may be some constitutional rights which do not have the sort of direct backing, in a valid and universal moral claim as determined from the perspective of the original position, that we have been discussing. These would not, then, be called natural rights. Natural rights are confined to those constitutional or basic structure rights that have the appropriate moral support. I will restrict my discussion in what follows to things that are natural rights in this precise sense.

It is often asked what something that is otherwise a human or natural right would be in a society in which the relevant constitutional right was lacking. The answer is that it would be merely a morally valid claim there. Or to be exact, it would be a valid claim that holds, insofar as practicable, for each and every person in that society, against the government there (and in many cases against private persons also). The claim would hold simply in virtue of its following from accredited moral principles. And the claim would be that the thing identified as the claim-to element (e.g., a given basic liberty as specified in Rawls's first principle) should be established as an operating basic structure or constitutional right in that society.

Any such claim would have an important use insofar as it was or could be acknowledged by people in that society. (And it would most likely be if the conventional morality of that society is such that the first principle would be affirmed when that conventional morality was carefully reflected upon.) For it would provide a realistic and reasonable basis for criticizing the conduct of government or of people generally in that society. Thus, the government could be criticized for failing to promote and maintain a course of action, or a way of being treated, that was incorporated in law as something to be promoted and maintained. Or it could be criticized—that is, the society in question could be criticized—for having failed to take even the first step, that of incorporation into the basic structure and, hence, of authoritative recognition in law. These criticisms would be perfectly sound insofar as they followed from accredited principles (as developed in critical morality, e.g., in the original position) and insofar as they really could be made to connect up with the normative direction that was provided to people in that society by their existing morality or by their system of law.

Thus, for instance, on the assumption that there are morally sound arguments (in the original position, as incorporated in the first principle) against the practice of slavery, we could say that slaves (in the United States in the late eighteenth or early nineteenth century) had a morally valid claim to personal liberty despite what the United States Constitution said or implied (or despite what intellectual defenders of slavery, such as Aristotle, might have said). More important, there was a morally valid claim that this particular liberty should be embodied as a constitutional or civil right (specifically as a right not to be enslaved) for every human person in that society. The intended result of authoritatively acknowledging this claim in that society is that slavery would cease to exist there (but until it did so, the right established by that acknowledgment would be, to some degree, a nominal one). We could expect, then, that the personal liberty would become in time a proper or full-fledged right—that is, an active constitutional or basic structure right there.

The moral soundness of this criticism of slavery does not require that there be some right superordinate to conventional morality or to existing systems of law. Indeed, legally sanctioned slavery may violate no one's rights in those cases where the relevant liberties have not been incorporated as basic structure rights. Nonetheless, the crucial point remains that legally sanctioned slavery is always unjust (a point that I will argue more fully in the next chapter). But whether or not something is a right raises a somewhat different set of questions. Natural rights are not simply demands of justice, not even of distributive justice. Rather, as I have argued in this section, the crucial issue here is whether appropriate practices of recognition and promotion are in place for that kind of right. For without such social recognition and maintenance, whatever was said to be justified, on moral grounds, would not be a proper right.

There is, we see on reflection, an irreducible duality to human or natural rights. On the one side, they are morally validated claims to some benefit or other. On the other side, such rights require recognition in law and promotion by government of the claimed way of acting or of being treated. Neither side is dispensable in a human or natural right.

On its legal side a human or natural right would have the form of a constitutional right. If there are any natural rights at all, it follows that there are active constitutional rights in at least some countries. There will be such rights in all Rawlsian well-ordered societies.

This concludes my line of argument and my use of that argument to interpret Rawls's notion of natural rights. One caveat is, perhaps, in order. Rawls says that "the liberties of equal citizenship must be incorporated into and protected by the constitution"; this is often interpreted as requiring their incorporation into a bill of rights. Thus, it might appear that Rawls's account requires, as a matter of justice, that a well-ordered society have a *written* constitution. But this is a considerable oversimplification. (Though we can say that, where there is a written constitution, it should incorporate the liberties that are listed in the first principle of justice.)

What Rawls's position requires, fundamentally, is the rule of law; with his emphasis on publicity it would follow that such rules will be explicitly formulated—or at least the more important ones are required to be. Among these important laws will be some that are regarded as basic (e.g., laws in a representative—parliamentary—democracy that set the term of a parliament, that identify the frequency of elections, that stipulate how or when a parliament may be dissolved, etc.). Thus, whatever counts as the basic laws in a society, those are to include laws that formulate and afford protection to the basic rights. Accordingly, a country like Great Britain, which has no written constitution, could incorporate universal political—that is, constitutional—rights into its basic laws and thereby conform to Rawls's requirement.

It is even possible to imagine nonlegal sources of constitutional rights. Their principal formulation could occur in a religious book or code or in a work of philosophy (such as Mill's *On Liberty*). Or it could occur in some political document (such as the Declaration of Independence or the *Federalist Papers* or Lincoln's Gettysburg Address) which lies largely outside the law. And it could occur outside the usual legal context of explicit constitutional provisions or valid statutes (as, for one example, the United States Supreme Court's assertion of a fundamental "right of privacy" does or, for another example, as does the considerable codification, by the Executive

Branch, of rights to "affirmative action"). What is important is that basic rights be formulated, that some formulation be authoritatively recognized within the standard political and legal channels of a society, and that, within these channels, government bring its powers to bear so as to promote and maintain the rights that are authoritatively recognized. It is this kind of commitment to basic rights, which can control the political process and is never taken lightly by the political agencies, that Rawls had in mind. (And, we should hasten to add, many of these rights will also normatively direct the conduct of individual citizens as well.)

Rights that are so understood become, literally, a *part* of the basic structure. The way of thinking I have tried to portray here is very like the ancient Greek conception of a constitution (*politeia*) as that which concerns the principal parts of the *polis*—or of the state, as we would call it. If we keep in mind the Rawlsian idea that constitutional rights are basic structure rights, we will not depart too far from this fundamental conception.

This brings us back to the main contention that I have tried to advance in this section: namely, that for Rawls, basic moral rights—natural rights—are basic structure rights (and in that sense constitutional rights). And I have sketched out a rather complex argument, both to interpret Rawls's idea of natural rights and to support his insistence on the explicit formulation by government of rights in the basic structure and of the development there of attendant political institutions for the promotion and maintenance of these rights. I have argued that a theory of natural rights would fail insofar as it leaves out these latter features, of appropriate social recognition and protection, which are essential to any proper right. For without such measures, there could be no basic structure *guarantee* to an individual of what was justifiably claimed as his due, and he could not count on getting what was claimed. There would be no legitimate expectation, hence no true right as part of the basic structure, in the absence of such formulation and maintenance.

Admittedly, the basic liberties are understood as explicitly stated in the first principle of justice (though their formulation there is a rather loose one). This initial formulation does occur, and can only occur, in the original position. But there are no mechanisms for protection in the original position. It is merely anticipated that there will be some such devices. The original position exists simply so that the principles of justice can be *stated* (and can be seen, as stated, to be reasonable and well founded). Hence the liberties that are listed from the perspective of the original position can be, when in the original position, at best merely morally valid claims. Even if we were to waive the requirement of social recognition, letting the formulation of these liberties in the original position stand as surrogate, the rights there would still be analogous to constitutional rights that were merely nominal. This gives the reason, then, why it is empty to regard the first principle of justice, when merely formulated in the original position, as itself a basic right, or as listing basic rights, in any full and significant sense.

But the liberties, as listed in the first principle, can be built into the basic structure of a society, and when they are incorporated in the way I have specified, they become proper rights. They become constitutional rights, parts of the basic structure.

3. Global Justice

For Rawls all natural or fundamental rights, insofar as they are rights, strictly conceived, are necessarily embedded in the basic structure of society—that is, of some *particular* society. The basic liberties are goods of all people, everywhere and at all times. But they are realized as goods only in society—and for any individual, that means in some specific society. Thus, when we look at basic liberties, not as liberties but as constitutional rights, there is an important sense in which they are not ''globalized,'' not spread, as it were, to the four corners of the earth as a single blanket of rights covering all peoples. As proper natural rights such rights enjoy, and can only enjoy, a local existence, in the basic structure of a given society.

Why should this be? Because, as I argued in the previous section, Rawls apparently believes that the basic liberties are inadequately determined—not properly identified or distributed or guaranteed to individuals—in a setting that lacks mechanisms for defining rights: for setting their scope, for adjusting them one to another, for assuring that they will be distributed to actual individuals, for enforcing and protecting that distribution, and so on. Individual political societies—states—have such mechanisms. They are, given their relative independence and self-contained character, the largest such entities, and the most important ones, that do have the appropriate mechanisms. Thus, the same reason which underwrote Rawls's claim that the basic structure of a society is the first subject of justice also underwrites his housing of natural rights—

basic liberties as constitutional rights—within discrete political societies.

The motivation is practical, not logical. The world itself could be the locus of natural rights if there were a world government. But there isn't. There is no basic structure—no political infrastructure—for the globe. The largest viable unit today is the nation state.

This does not mean that a larger, more inclusive political society would be inappropriate, nor does it mean that one should not work to achieve a larger framework. Indeed, if we take seriously the idea that the basic liberties should be rights of all people, then such a global framework might well be indicated. (Though, equally, it might be indicated that the liberties should be incorporated into the basic structure of every existing political society.) But the point is that the possibility of a global framework is very remote at present.

Suppose, though, that one wanted to work now to help globalize the basic liberties as rights at some future date. How should one best go about this? Rawls's answer seems to be—I am theorizing here—that a plausible procedure would be for individual states to strive (where their traditions and institutional development permitted) to conform themselves to justice in their basic structure. This might well constitute a necessary first step. After that, some further move might be possible—perhaps an international association of such states and the development of a new political infrastructure, acting directly on individual persons, within that association. Something like this further move is afoot in western Europe today, though what has resulted so far is much more like a confederation of states than like an individual state.

A good argument could be made, then, that direct moves to a global state—or to a large confederation of inevitably and radically unlike-minded states—from where we are today is not wise. Also, it would not be practical. Nor would it be likely to help achieve anything like the end in view: the globalization of basic liberties as rights for all people everywhere.

All this is useless speculation, however, if we lose sight of the main point. Basic liberties cannot be rights except in a suitable institutional context. They cannot be effective constitutional rights except in the basic structure of a political society. We must confine ourselves, then, to consideration of such basic structures. Insofar as we are interested in institutional design that has any prospect of practical application, we must not outrun the range of existing or feasible basic structures. Thus, we are necessarily concerned with the largest viable political societies—independent states—and their basic structures. This precludes, for the foreseeable future at least, any serious program for designing a global or even an ambitious confederative scheme of basic liberty rights.

The same inhibitions that I have just described, as existing for the basic liberties of the first principle, will also exist for the other primary goods as determined in the second principle (under its two main headings, fair equality of opportunity and the difference principle). The operation of these two features are equally meant to be confined to the basic structures of particular societies. And for the same reason: namely, that today the necessary political infrastructure exists only in these societies and not globally.

It could, of course, be urged that *economically* there is at present a great mutual interdependence among peoples of the earth. But even if global economic interdependence is a fact, two points remain germane.

First, we can speak from the perspective of the original position. The parties there would be concerned about the well-being of persons in *any* society—hence in *all* societies, whether or not these societies and these persons were economically interdependent. The whole point of formulating principles of justice, it seems to me, is to identify areas of appropriate concern for the well-being of persons everywhere insofar as that well-being is a matter of basic fairness. The fact of economic interdependence on a global scale is quite irrelevant to this concern. It can become relevant, but only depending on what the unit of application is. If the unit of application is the existing market (or the multinational firm or capitalist society), then the fact of global economic interdependence is clearly relevant. But if the unit of application of the difference principle is the basic structure of a *political* society, then equally clearly it is not.

The perspective of the basic structure of society is the second one that we can take and must take in order to determine which unit of application is the appropriate one. Suppose the basic structure is as we've already described it (in the earlier discussion in this section of basic liberties); one would have to say in such a case that there is no world-wide political structure that answers to the global eco-

nomic community. Accordingly, there can be no world-wide application of the difference principle today. There cannot be; for that principle, in order to be applied, requires political mechanisms, not merely economic ones. The relevant political mechanisms exist, for now at least, only in independent national states (or perhaps in certain federations of these) but not globally, not in any single, all-encompassing political regime. And what is true for the operation of the difference principle holds also for fair equality of opportunity: the political mechanisms required for its application do not now exist, to any practical degree, except in particular societies, in independent states.

So, the Rawlsian concentration on the basic structure of a particular society, which I have tried to bring out through my analysis of natural rights, limits the application of the preferred principles of justice in a very fundamental way. For direct global application is ruled out—once, that is, we take account of the actual character of the contemporary political world. And I will observe this limitation—in effect a limitation to the basic structure of some particular political society (or state)—throughout my discussion of the application of the two principles of justice.

In the analysis of this and the previous section, we have a setting for Rawls's discussion of basic liberties as rights. I will turn to a more exacting account of these liberties in the next chapter.

Source: Rex Martin, ''A Theory of Justice and Rights,'' in *Rawls and Rights,* University Press of Kansas, 1985, pp. 21–44.

Sources

Barry, Brian, *The Liberal Theory of Justice: A Critical Examination of the Principal Doctrines in ''A Theory of Justice'' by John Rawls,* Clarendon Press, 1973, p. ix.

Davion, Victoria, and Clark Wolf, eds., *The Idea of a Political Liberalism: Essays on Rawls,* Rowman and Littlefield Publishers, Inc., 2000, pp. 1, 3, 14.

Freeman, Samuel, ed., *John Rawls: Collected Papers,* Harvard University Press, 1999, pp. ix, xii.

Martin, Rex, *Rawls and Rights,* University Press of Kansas, 1985, p. vii.

Rao, A. P., *Three Lectures on John Rawls,* Indian Philosophical Quarterly Publications, 1981, p. 1.

Schaefer, David Lewis, *Justice or Tyranny?: A Critique of John Rawls's ''A Theory of Justice,''* Kennikat Press, 1979, pp. ix, 105.

Wolff, Robert Paul, *Understanding Rawls: A Reconstruction and Critique of "A Theory of Justice,"* Princeton University Press, 1977, pp. 3, 16.

Further Reading

Alejandro, Roberto, *The Limits of Rawlsian Justice,* Johns Hopkins University Press, 1998.

Alejandro provides critical discussion of Rawls's theory of justice in relation to the American legal system.

Corlett, J. Angelo, ed., *Equality and Liberty: Analyzing Rawls and Nozick,* St. Martin's Press, 1991.

Corlett provides a collection of essays addressing the themes of justice, equality, and liberty in the works of Rawls and his primary critic, Robert Nozick.

George, Robert P., and Christopher Wolfe, eds., *Natural Law and Public Reason,* Georgetown University Press, 2000.

George and Wolfe provide a collection of essays that focus on the themes of natural law, liberalism, and reason in the work of Rawls.

Walden

Henry David Thoreau

1854

Walden was published in 1854, seven years after Henry David Thoreau ended his stay in a small cabin near Walden Pond. During those years, Thoreau painstakingly revised and polished his manuscript, based on journals he kept while living at the pond. He hoped his book would establish him as the foremost spokesman for the American transcendentalist movement.

In *Walden*, Thoreau condensed events of his twenty-six-month sojourn into one year, for literary purposes. He began and ended his narrative in spring. The eighteen chapters celebrate the unity of nature, humanity, and divinity—a central idea of transcendentalism—and portray Thoreau's life at Walden Pond as an ideal model for enjoying that unity. In solitude, simplicity, and living close to nature, Thoreau had found what he believed to be a better life. In *Walden*, he enthusiastically shares his discoveries so that others, too, may abandon conventional ways and live more sanely and happily.

Walden, however, was a gift more eagerly given than received. Despite some good reviews, the book did not sell well and did nothing to elevate Thoreau's reputation. *Walden* was the second and final book by Thoreau to be published in his lifetime. (His first book, *A Week on the Concord and Merrimack Rivers*, had been published at his own expense and also did not sell well.) It was not until the 1900s that Thoreau and *Walden* found a large, appreciative audience. The book was especially

popular during the enforced simplicity of the Great Depression of the 1930s, and again during the 1960s when individualism, concern for the natural environment, and transcendentalism were important elements in a tidal wave of change that swept through American culture.

Author Biography

Henry David Thoreau was born July 12, 1817, in Concord, Massachusetts. His father, John, worked at various occupations, including farmer, grocer, and pencil manufacturer. His mother, Cynthia, was the daughter of a minister and ran a boarding house to supplement the family's income. Henry was the third of their four children.

Thoreau attended school in Concord and, with financial help from relatives, went on to Harvard University, where he graduated in 1837. By that time, Ralph Waldo Emerson, who would be Thoreau's lifelong mentor and friend, had moved to Concord. Emerson and Thoreau were members of a thriving group of transcendentalists that included Bronson Alcott (father of author Louisa May Alcott), Margaret Fuller, and others. (The core of transcendentalist philosophy is the idea that divinity and truth reside throughout creation and are grasped intuitively, not rationally.)

Rather than settling into one of the professions for which Harvard had prepared him, Thoreau moved from job to job, trying everything from teaching to being a handyman. He wanted time to walk outdoors, to think, and to write, and he was happy to live simply so that he could work little. He had a gift for surveying, an occupation that he enjoyed because it allowed him to be outdoors and to interact more with nature than with people. Throughout his life, when he needed to take temporary work to make money, Thoreau often turned to surveying.

By the early 1840s, Thoreau was regularly contributing poems and essays to *The Dial,* the transcendentalist journal edited by Emerson. Thoreau was living with Emerson and his wife at this time, doing chores and helping to run the household. In March 1845, Thoreau began building a cabin on land belonging to Emerson beside Walden Pond near Concord. He lived there from July 1845 until September 1847 and kept a journal—already a long-established habit. After leaving the cabin at Walden Pond, he lived briefly in Emerson's home again (while Emerson was traveling overseas) and after that lived for the rest of his life in his parents' home. He never married.

In 1849, Thoreau published, at his own expense, his first book, *A Week on the Concord and Merrimack Rivers*, an account of a trip taken in 1839. The book was not a success; it took Thoreau several years to pay for its publication.

From 1847 to 1854, Thoreau revised and polished his manuscript for *Walden*, based on his journals. He hoped that this book would elevate his status as a writer and as a transcendentalist philosopher to the level that Emerson was respected. When it was finally published in 1854, however, *Walden* received a lukewarm response and did not sell well. In his later years, Thoreau turned his attention to writing against slavery.

Thoreau died at home in Concord on May 6, 1862, at the age of forty-four, of tuberculosis. He was little known and little mourned. Many of his neighbors in Concord and his literary peers saw him as an extremist, and he was often the object of insult and ridicule. In his eulogy, Emerson rightly said, ''The country knows not yet . . . how great a son it has lost.''

Plot Summary

Chapter One: ''Economy''

Thoreau begins by telling readers that he is writing to answer why he chose to live alone for more than two years in a small, simple cabin near Walden Pond. Much of the chapter is devoted to explaining that the way most people live, spending all their time and energy working to acquire luxuries, does not lead to human happiness and well-being. Thoreau writes that he prefers having time to walk in nature and to think much more than working long hours to pay for big houses, large tracts of land, herds of animals, or other property. He goes so far as to say that the ownership of such things is actually a disadvantage, as one who owns them must take care of them, while one who owns little has more freedom to do as he or she pleases. This is why Thoreau chose to live simply and cheaply in a house he built for himself: in simplicity and economy he found freedom. Finally, Thoreau describes how he built his house. He includes exact figures showing how much he spent on materials (twenty-eight dollars and twelve and one-half cents).

Chapter Two: "Where I Lived, and What I Lived For"

Continuing the idea set forth in the first chapter, Thoreau writes that he once considered buying a farm. He realized, though, that a person did not have to own a farm to enjoy those things about it that are most valuable, such as the beauty of its landscape. Thoreau concludes: "But I would say to my fellows, once for all, as long as possible live free and uncommitted. It makes little difference whether you are committed to a farm or the county jail." He urges his readers to simplify their lives as well so that they may live fully and freely.

Thoreau describes the area around his cabin and how much he enjoyed the peaceful natural surroundings. He answers the question why he lived there:

> I went to the woods because I wished to live deliberately, to front only the essential facts of life, and see if I could not learn what it had to teach, and not, when I came to die, discover that I had not lived.

Chapter Three: "Reading"

Here Thoreau makes a case for reading good books. He points out that the best books are "the noblest recorded thoughts of man" and that such books can take readers nearer to heaven. He complains that hardly anyone reads these books. Instead, he writes, people who are perfectly capable of reading the classics waste their time on unchallenging and worthless popular stories. He calls society to task for failing to be a "patron of the fine arts."

Chapter Four: "Sounds"

Thoreau writes that reading must be complemented by direct experience. This is in keeping with his transcendentalist philosophy, which emphasizes direct, intuitive experience of nature, truth and the divine.

In this chapter, Thoreau focuses on the sounds he experiences at Walden, from the singing of birds to the whistle of a train, and on how these sounds affect his mood. The sounds of animals especially cause him to feel the unity and joy of all things.

Chapter Five: "Solitude"

Thoreau makes his case that the companionship of nature is more fulfilling than that of humans, and that he could not possibly be lonely in nature because he is a part of it. The plants and animals are his friends and, amid the peace of nature, God himself is the author's visitor:

Henry David Thoreau

> I have occasional visits . . . from an old settler and original proprietor, who is reported to have dug Walden Pond, and stoned it, and fringed it with pine woods; who tells me stories of old time and of new eternity; and between us we manage to pass a cheerful evening with social mirth and pleasant views of things.

Chapter Six: "Visitors"

Calling himself "no hermit," Thoreau writes that he did have visitors during his years at Walden. He describes at length a Canadian woodchopper who often did his work in the woods around Thoreau's cabin. Thoreau got to know the man and liked him because he lived simply and in harmony with nature. However, Thoreau eventually realized that "the intellectual and what is called spiritual man in him were slumbering as in an infant."

Other visitors included children, whom Thoreau liked for their innocence and enthusiasm, and "half-witted men from the almshouse." The latter, Thoreau writes, were in many cases wiser than the men who were running the town, and he "thought it was time that the tables were turned."

Chapter Seven: "The Bean Field"

The author describes his bean field and how he worked it. As usual, Thoreau gives both practical details and a mystical report of his agricultural project. He explains just how he worked his field and how much profit he made from it. He also asserts that the sun and the rain are the true cultivators and that woodchucks and birds have as much right to their share of the harvest as Thoreau has to his.

Chapter Eight: ''The Village''

Thoreau often walked into the village, he reports, to hear just a little of its incessant gossip. A little news and gossip, he found, was entertaining, while more than a little numbed the soul. He did not like to stay long or to partake in too much of village life.

He reports that on one visit to the village he was arrested and put in jail (but soon released) for failing to pay taxes. He refused to pay, he explains, as a protest against the legality of slavery.

Chapter Nine: ''The Ponds''

Most of this chapter is devoted to a detailed description of Walden Pond and the idyllic times Thoreau enjoyed in and around it. The author again describes the unity of nature, self, and divinity that he experiences there. He makes clear that the pond has a special kind of spiritual purity, calling it ''God's Drop.'' He also describes other nearby ponds.

Chapter Ten: ''Baker Farm''

This chapter contrasts Thoreau's joyful, contented, and easy life with the life of one of his neighbors in the woods, John Field. Field is an Irish laborer who works long days turning the soil for area farmers. Thoreau sees that Field works himself to exhaustion to pay the rent on his rustic hut and to feed his family. He explains to Field that there is another way to live—the way that Thoreau has chosen. Thoreau can see, though, that Field is not willing to give up the chase for ''luxuries'' such as coffee and beef, so he leaves Field alone, grateful that he himself has found a better way to live.

Chapter Eleven: ''Higher Laws''

Like the last chapter, this one presents a basic contrast. First, Thoreau acknowledges his own animal instincts, apparent, for example, when he sees a woodchuck and is ''strongly tempted to seize and devour him raw.'' Then he describes his spiritual instinct toward ''higher'' things. Both are to be accepted as part of human nature, he says, but as a person matures, the spiritual should wax while the

animal wanes. In fact, Thoreau believes that the entire human race is evolving from animal to spiritual consciousness. Because killing and eating animals is an expression of the lower, animal instinct, Thoreau stopped hunting and ate very little meat or fish. ''I have no doubt that it is a part of the destiny of the human race, in its gradual improvement, to leave off eating animals,'' he writes.

Chapter Twelve: ''Brute Neighbors''

Following what has become a pattern, Thoreau again takes up the same idea explored in the previous chapter, but explores it in a new way. This chapter begins with a dialogue between a Hermit and a Poet. Thoreau makes clear that these two characters represent himself and a visitor who used to come to his cabin. The gist of the dialogue is that the Poet—the visitor—tempts the Hermit to leave his meditations and go fishing. The Hermit wonders, ''Shall I go to heaven or a-fishing?'' and ends by going fishing. In this battle between the animal and the spiritual natures of man, the animal has won.

The rest of the chapter describes many animals that lived around Thoreau. In observing them, Thoreau concludes that both the animal and the spiritual natures coexist in animals and that animals experience no conflict between the two.

Chapter Thirteen: ''House-Warming''

Thoreau prepared for winter by collecting wild apples, grapes, and nuts and by winterizing his house. He built a chimney (he had been cooking on a fire outdoors) and plastered his cabin to keep out the cold wind. By the time this work was finished, the pond was frozen, and Thoreau delighted in observing the ice itself and the bottom of the pond, which he could clearly see through the ice.

Chapter Fourteen: ''Former Inhabitants; and Winter Visitors''

In deep winter, nature slept and visitors rarely came to Thoreau's cabin. He acknowledges that this extreme solitude was a challenge. ''For human society I was obliged to conjure up the former occupants of these woods,'' he writes.

The author tells about three former slaves and their homes in the woods; about the Stratton and Breed families, the latter ruined by rum; and about Wyman the potter and Hugh Quoil, an alcoholic who was said to have fought at the Battle of Waterloo. Walks in the dark, quiet winter woods, and the infrequent human visitors of winter are also recalled.

Chapter Fifteen: "Winter Animals"

Thoreau describes walking on the frozen ponds, from which he could see the woods at new angles, and his observations of wildlife in winter. Squirrels, rabbits, and other creatures lived around, under, and above his cabin, and he threw them corn and potato peels to help them through the winter.

Chapter Sixteen: "The Pond in Winter"

Thoreau recalls using his surveying skills to map Walden Pond and to measure its depth—one hundred seven feet. He tells of a large crew of laborers coming to harvest the pond's ice, which would be shipped to faraway places and sold. This idea of Walden being spread over the Earth is mirrored in Thoreau's writing. He read the Bhagavad Gita (a Hindu scripture) in the mornings, which made him think of "pure Walden water mingled with the sacred water of the Ganges."

Chapter Seventeen: "Spring"

The thawing of the pond and the stirring of animals signaled spring, and Thoreau reports that he felt in himself the same revitalization that he saw taking place all around him. Once again, he exults in nature. At the end of this chapter, Thoreau gives the date on which he left his life in the woods but does not say why he left.

Chapter Eighteen: "Conclusion"

Near the beginning of this chapter, Thoreau summarizes what he learned during his time in the woods:

> If one advances confidently in the direction of his dreams and endeavors to live the life which he has imagined, he will meet with a success unexpected in common hours. He will put some things behind, will pass an invisible boundary; new, universal, and more liberal laws will begin to establish themselves around and within him. . . . In proportion as he simplifies his life, the laws of the universe will appear less complex, and solitude will not be solitude, nor poverty, nor weakness weakness.

Thoreau ends his narrative by urging readers to apply to their own lives what he has shared with them. He counsels them to explore inner, rather than outer, worlds: "Be a Columbus to whole new

continents and worlds within you, opening new channels, not of trade, but of thought." He is confident that new ways of thinking will lead to new, fulfilling ways of living.

Key Figures

The Canadian Woodchopper

The woodchopper does his work in Walden Woods, and he and Thoreau often visit. He is a big, strong, good-natured man who works hard and is content with his life although he makes little money. He knows how to read and enjoys reading the works of Homer even though he doesn't understand them. After getting to know the woodchopper, Thoreau concludes, "The intellectual and what is called spiritual man in him were slumbering as in an infant."

James Collins

James Collins is an Irishman who works for the railroad and lives in a shanty near where Thoreau builds his cabin. Thoreau buys Collins's shanty for $4.25 and disassembles it to use the boards and nails in his cabin. On the morning of the transfer of ownership, Thoreau sees Collins and his family on the road, with all their possessions wrapped up in one large bundle.

John Field

John Field is an Irishman who lives with his wife and children in a hut near the Baker Farm. During a rainstorm Thoreau goes to take shelter in the hut, which he thinks is vacant, but finds Field and his family there. Thoreau can see that John works very hard as a "bogger" (someone who turns the soil for farmers) to support his family and yet lives very poorly. Thoreau explains his own way of life, hoping that John will adopt it and thus live better while working less. He tells John if he would give up luxuries such as coffee and butter, he could give up his toil. He wouldn't need to buy boots if he quit his job, Thoreau says, and he could easily catch fish in the pond and sell them for the little money he would need. John and his wife seem to consider this briefly but, according to Thoreau, they are unable to understand how they could live as Thoreau suggests. "It was sailing by dead reckoning to them, and they saw not clearly how to make their port,'' he writes.

Brister Freeman

Brister Freeman was a former slave who lived on Brister's Hill before Thoreau's stay in the woods. He was an apple-grower. He is a character in the book because during the winter, when there are few visitors, Thoreau thinks about the woods' former residents to occupy his mind. In effect, his past neighbors become present company. Thoreau reports that he has read Brister's epitaph in the cemetery.

Fenda Freeman

The wife of Brister Freeman, Fenda was a fortune teller.

The Hermit

The Hermit is one of two fictional characters in the book and clearly represents Thoreau. The Hermit has a dramatic dialogue with The Poet, in which The Poet comes to visit The Hermit and tempts him to leave his solitary meditations and go fishing. The Hermit succumbs to this temptation and goes fishing with The Poet, temporarily allowing his desire for worldly and sensual pleasures to overcome his desire for spiritual experience.

Cato Ingraham

Cato was another former slave who lived in Walden Woods before Thoreau. His former master had provided him with land to live on and a house. Cato planted walnut trees on his land so that he would have an asset in his old age, but Thoreau reports that a white man somehow took Cato's walnuts from him.

The Poet

The Poet is one of two fictional characters in the book and represents a visitor from the village. The Poet has a dramatic dialogue with The Hermit, in which The Poet tempts The Hermit to leave his solitary meditations and go fishing.

Hugh Quoil

Hugh Quoil was another past resident of the woods who had lived in the place once occupied by Wyman the potter. It was rumored that Quoil had fought at Waterloo. He had a certain sophistication but was an alcoholic. Thoreau says that ''All I know of him was tragic'' and describes what he saw when he visited Quoil's cabin after his death: ''His pipe lay broken on the hearth. . . . The skin of a woodchuck was freshly stretched upon the back of the house, a trophy of his last Waterloo; but no warm cap or mittens would he want more.''

Henry David Thoreau

Thoreau is the book's narrator. An eccentric philosopher and lover of nature, Thoreau builds a cabin near Walden Pond, intending to live in solitude as an experiment in simplicity and spiritual exploration. ''My greatest skill has been to want but little,'' Thoreau writes. He grows food, both for his own needs and to sell for the little money he requires. He reads and entertains occasional visitors. He spends many hours walking in the woods around his cabin, closely observing the landscape and animals. In this communion with nature, he also finds communion with the divine.

Thoreau is both irritable and humorous, often simultaneously, and he is a man of contradictions. He compares human beings to muskrats and vermin, and the only thing he likes less than people is people organized in the form of institutions. ''Wherever a man goes, men will pursue and paw him with their dirty institutions, and, if they can, constrain him to belong to their desperate odd-fellow society,'' he complains. Yet he admits that he walks into the village often to hear news and gossip, and when deep winter keeps all visitors away, he conjures up memories and stories of past residents of the woods to keep him company.

Wyman

Another former resident of the woods whom Thoreau recalls, Wyman was a potter who sold his wares in the village. Thoreau reports that Wyman and his descendants were so poor that the tax collector would come around and find nothing of value to take except a pot or two. Wyman, like Thoreau, lived on the land as a squatter.

Zilpha

Zilpha was a former slave who lived in Walden Woods before Thoreau stayed there. Zilpha earned her meager living by spinning cloth, singing as she spun. During the War of 1812, English soldiers burned her small home and all her animals. ''She led a hard life, and somewhat inhumane,'' Thoreau writes.

Topics for Further Study

- Would you want to spend a year or two living as Thoreau lived at Walden Pond? Why or why not?

- Thoreau refers to Greek and Roman gods and goddesses and to Hindu gods and scriptures throughout *Walden*. Do research to learn about these two religious systems and then explain why you think Thoreau made frequent references to them. What aspects and elements of these religions make them compatible with Thoreau's ideas?

- Thoreau kept detailed financial records to show how much money he earned and how much he spent on various things. What does this tell you about him? Does this trait seem consistent with other aspects of Thoreau's philosophy and behavior, or not? Explain your answer.

- Spend a period of time—an hour or a day—in natural surroundings and away from other people as much as possible. Your "Walden" may be a backyard or a park. Take notes on what you observe. Later, write an essay about your experience in which you include both information from your notes and reflections about how the experience affected you.

- Imagine that you are Thoreau and have just been set down in the middle of an airport in a big American city in the twenty-first century. Write a page in your journal describing what you see, hear, and feel.

Themes

Unity

According to Thoreau's transcendentalist philosophy, nature, humanity, and God are unified. His transcendent God is also immanent—present in every raindrop, blade of grass, and animal as well as in every human being. Further, one of the best ways for human beings to experience their own unity with God is to observe nature. In the woods one day, he writes:

> I was suddenly sensible of such sweet and beneficent society in Nature, in the very pattering of the drops, and in every sound and sight around my house, an infinite and unaccountable friendliness all at once like an atmosphere sustaining me.

Explaining why he loves the company of nature, Thoreau writes, "Am I not partly leaves and vegetable mould myself?" This theme of unity occurs throughout the book, often through metaphors, similes, and personifications that equate nature, humans and the divine. "I may be either the driftwood in the stream or Indra [a Hindu deity] in the sky looking down on it," he declares. Watching hawks circle above him, he sees them as "the embodiment of my own thoughts." Hearing bullfrogs, he thinks of them as "the sturdy spirits of ancient wine-bibbers and wassailers, still unrepentant, trying to sing a catch in their Stygian lake." (In Greek myth, the River Styx is in Hades; the souls of the dead are rowed across it.) When whippoorwills sing, he writes that they "chanted their vespers," attributing to them a knowledge of and reverence for God.

The goal of the transcendentalist is to experience God within. Thoreau exulted that living immersed in nature at Walden Pond allowed him to attain this goal often.

Solitude

For Thoreau, living outside of human community is the complement to living immersed in nature. One must withdraw from human company to truly experience oneness with nature and, therefore, with God. "I love to be alone," he declares.

Thoreau sometimes had visitors at his cabin and sometimes walked into the village to hear news and observe people (much as he observed animals;

in one passage he compares watching people in the village to watching muskrats in the woods). But, he writes, "I find it wholesome to be alone the greater part of the time. To be in company, even with the best, is soon wearisome and dissipating."

Human society moves too fast for Thoreau and centers around things that are of no interest to him: acquiring large homes and luxuries, giving fancy dinner parties, gossiping, and working long hours to pay for things. He sees most people as being spiritually asleep, and feels he has nothing in common with them.

In answer to those who asked if he was lonely, Thoreau writes that he had much company in his solitude. "Every little pine needle expanded and swelled with sympathy and befriended me," he assures readers. He even asserts that he was visited by God "in the long winter evenings" and by Mother Nature—"a ruddy and lustful old dame" who told him fables and invited him to walk in her garden.

Individualism

The idea of individualism is closely related to Thoreau's transcendentalism. According to this philosophy, human beings need no priests, scriptures, or traditions to know God, because God resides in each individual and can be found by being true to oneself.

Thoreau's own strong sense of individualism shows throughout the book, as he rejects virtually all the conventions of his time and place to find his own way of living. His ascetic, nearly vegetarian diet of cheap, local foods was as uncommon as his choice to go off and live rustically in the woods.

Encouraging individualism, Thoreau writes what has become one of the most enduring ideas in all his work: "If a man does not keep pace with his companions, perhaps it is because he hears a different drummer. Let him step to the music which he hears, however measured or far away."

Style

First-Person Narration

Thoreau wrote *Walden* in the first person. He explains on the first page that, although "I" is omitted from most books, "it is, after all, always the first person that is speaking." In addition, he explains that the book is all about Thoreau himself. "I should not talk so much about myself if there were anybody else whom I knew as well," he assures readers.

Because of its first-person narration, and because it is based on journals, readers often assume that *Walden* was written "off the cuff" or that its organization is informal or accidental. Nothing could be further from the truth. Thoreau spent seven years after his stay at Walden rewriting and revising his manuscript. He structured the book to suit his dual purposes of explaining how he lived and of urging readers to apply his experiences to their own lives. He compressed twenty-six months into one year for his narrative, beginning and ending in spring, the season of rebirth. Within the general structure of a one-year span, Thoreau organized his material by topic, rather than strictly chronologically. For example, the chapter "The Village" comes during the "summer" season of the book, but not every incident related in it actually took place during summer.

Description

Walden is rich in densely detailed descriptive passages that make use of so much figurative language and imagery that they are poetic. Thoreau's descriptions of the landscape and the wildlife around him are a testament to his close observations of nature. He uses lively, precise words and unusual phrases to convey the sights and sounds of nature. To cite one example of many, he writes that on a summer afternoon the

> . . . hawks are circling about my clearing; the tantivy of wild pigeons, flying by twos and threes athwart my view, or perching restless on the white pine boughs behind my house, gives a voice to the air; a fish hawk dimples the glassy surface of the pond and brings up a fish; a mink steals out of the marsh before my door and seizes a frog by the shore; the sedge is bending under the weight of the reed-birds flitting hither and thither; and for the last half-hour I have heard the rattle of railroad cars, now dying away and then reviving like the beat of a partridge.

References to Persons and Literature

Evidence that Thoreau has read the world's great books, as he urges his readers to do, is liberally sprinkled throughout *Walden*. He demonstrates familiarity with the Bible and with the Vedas and the Bhagavad Gita of Hinduism; with the Greek and Roman gods and goddesses; with Homer and

Aeschylus in the Western canon and with poets of the Middle East; and with the rulers, explorers, and scientists of his own time and of the past.

These wide-ranging references reinforce the theme of unity. Thoreau shows that the scriptures and the great men of different cultures and different times have much in common and can be cited in support of the same ideas.

Humor

The author's seriousness of purpose and his sense of urgency in conveying his ideas do not smother Thoreau's sense of humor, which makes frequent appearances in *Walden.* Criticizing the impracticality of formal education, Thoreau writes, ''To my astonishment I was informed on leaving college that I had studied navigation!'' and declares that he would have learned more by sailing once around the harbor. On his opinion that people keep their homes overheated in winter and wear too many clothes, he writes:

> By proper Shelter and Clothing we legitimately retain our own internal heat; but with an excess of these, or of Fuel, that is, with an external heat greater than our own internal, may not cookery be said to begin?

Historical Context

New England Transcendentalism

Transcendentalism took root in New England in the mid-1830s in reaction against the rationalism (emphasis on intellectual understanding) of the Unitarian Church. The philosophy centered on the premise that divine truth is present in all things and that truth, or God, is known through intuition, not through the rational mind. From this core proceeded the belief that all of nature, including all humans, is one with God.

The term ''transcendental'' was borrowed from German philosopher Immanuel Kant (1724–1804), who wrote in his well-known work *Critique of Practical Reason,* ''I call all knowledge transcendental which is concerned, not with objects, but with our mode of knowing objects so far as this is possible a priori'' (meaning, independent of sensory experience). American transcendentalism was thus clearly linked to similar philosophies that existed in Europe, and it also shared important ideas with Eastern philosophies and religions, including Hinduism. The New England transcendentalists read the Bhagavad Gita (which Thoreau reports that he read in the mornings) and the Vedas (which Thoreau references several times), among other Eastern scriptures.

The New England transcendentalists did not confine themselves to literary pursuits but also tried to put their philosophy into practice. Some, such as Bronson Alcott and Elizabeth Peabody, focused on educational reform. Peabody and Margaret Fuller applied the principles of transcendentalism to the crusade for women's rights. The group created two experimental communities, Fruitlands and Brook Farm.

It is the writing of Thoreau and of Emerson that has been the most enduring product of American transcendentalism. Thoreau's ideas about nonviolent resistance to oppression were very important both to Mahatma Gandhi's campaign against the British in India in the early 1900s, and to the American civil rights movement of the 1960s.

The Building of the Railroads

Thoreau writes at length of the train that passes the western shore of Walden Pond. He hears its whistle and the rattle of its cars along the tracks. He thinks about the people and the freight on the train, about where the train began the day and where it will deliver its goods, and about how trains are changing the pace and the way of life in America.

In the 1840s and 1850s, the entire nation was caught up in the drama of building the railroads. While only forty miles of track were laid between 1820 and 1830, by 1850 there were 9,022 miles of operating track in the country. The railroads were changing everything. Trains made the thriving steamboat industry obsolete, because they could transport freight and people much more directly and quickly. (This industrial struggle contributed to the tensions that led to the Civil War because the northern companies owned the railroads and southern companies owned the steamboats.) Better transportation meant cheaper goods and greater variety, so the railroads encouraged the desire for luxuries that Thoreau was preaching against. Railroads also increased the pace of life and led to Americans keeping more exact schedules as business and travel began to depend on the inflexible schedules of the trains. In sum, the railroads carried mainstream

Compare
&
Contrast

- **1850s:** Walden Pond (about half a mile long and with a total area of about sixty-one acres) and much of the land immediately around it are owned by Ralph Waldo Emerson. While the land was once heavily forested, many of the trees are being cut down as fuel. The particularly cold winter of 1851–1852 takes a heavy toll on Walden Woods. The few local residents are described by Thoreau in *Walden,* including a fortune teller, a potter, and railroad workers. People who live in Concord, a mile and a half away, come out to the pond to fish and swim, and they use the surrounding land for hunting, berry picking, and picnicking, as well as for a source of fuel.

  Today: Walden Pond and the land around it are a National Historical and Literary Landmark owned by the state of Massachusetts. (The Emerson family donated the land to the state in 1922 so that it would be preserved.) The land is the site of the Thoreau Institute, which has a twelve-thousand-square-foot Education Center and a five-thousand-square-foot Research Center on the grounds, housing a reading room, archives, staff offices, and other facilities. About 750,000 people visit the site each year. Walden Pond is still used for swimming.

- **1850s:** In *Walden,* Thoreau recalls hearing trains' whistles as they passed the western end of Walden Pond during his stay, and he describes the many ways in which railroads are changing American life. By 1850, there are 9,022 miles of operable track, virtually all built in the last twenty years. On February 22, 1854—the year in which *Walden* is published—a train travels from the East Coast to the Mississippi River for the first time.

  Today: The United States has 230,000 miles of operable track, 1.2 million freight cars, and twenty thousand locomotives.

- **1850s:** Transcendentalism, which borrows elements of Eastern philosophies and religions, has a devoted following in Massachusetts and influences many American intellectuals and writers.

  Today: Yoga is increasingly popular throughout the United States. Yoga is the Sanskrit word for ''union.'' The various schools of yoga taught today have some commonalities with transcendentalism, such as the beliefs that each individual soul is directly linked to God and that truth is everywhere present in creation and can be experienced intuitively, rather than rationally. While millions of Americans practice only one element of yoga—its regimen of physical postures and exercises—a growing number are adopting the broader philosophy and more of its practices, such as meditation and vegetarianism.

American society ever farther from the kind of life Thoreau celebrates in *Walden.*

Critical Overview

Walden was widely reviewed when it first appeared. This attention was due not to Thoreau's reputation (he had only one other published book, and it had not sold well) but to his publisher's energetic promotion of the book and to the support of Thoreau's well-known friend Emerson. Many publications printed excerpts of *Walden* to herald its arrival.

Most reviews were positive. ''It is a strikingly original, singular, and most interesting work,'' wrote a reviewer in the *Salem Register.* The *Lowell Journal and Courier* noted, ''The press all over the country have given the most flattering notices of it'' and predicted, ''without doubt it will command a very extensive sale. It surely deserves it.''

Deserving or not, the book did not sell well. About seven hundred fifty copies were sold in the first year after publication. And not all notices were

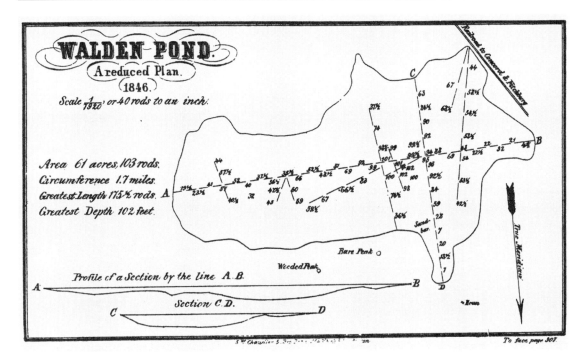

Hand-drawn map of Walden Pond

positive. A reviewer for the *Boston Daily Journal* wrote,

> Mr. Thoreau has made an attractive book. . . . But while many will be fascinated by its contents, few will be improved. As the pantheistic doctrines of the author marred the beauty of his former work, so does his selfish philosophy darkly tinge the pages of Walden.

Walden went out of print in 1859 and was not available again until after Thoreau's death. It was not until the early 1900s that scholars and readers began to reconsider the book. Thoreau surely would have been disappointed by the perspective of *The Cambridge History of English and American Literature,* which portrayed him as an American Robinson Crusoe and dismissed the book's philosophical component. "The reader who takes up the book with the idea that he is going to enjoy another *Robinson Crusoe* will not be pleased to find that every now and then he will have to listen to a lay sermon or a lyceum lecture," the authors wrote. "It is the adventurous, *Robinson Crusoe* part that is imperishable."

While it is true that to this day that *Walden* is often categorized as nature writing, some modern critics and readers have appreciated its philosophy. On the hundredth anniversary of its original publication, the esteemed author E. B. White wrote in the *Yale Review* that, while many of his contemporaries were dismissive of *Walden*, White himself felt that "a hundred years having gone by, *Walden*, its serenity and grandeur unimpaired, still lifts us up. . . ." He called the book "an original omelette from which people can draw nourishment in a hungry day."

In 1996, Nicholas Bagnall reviewed a new edition of *Walden* in *New Statesman.* Nichols echoed the early twentieth-century opinion of *The Cambridge History of English and American Literature.* "I was . . . hooked on Thoreau's fine indignation and the swagger of his prose," Nichols wrote. "His observations on nature . . . which make the bulk of his book, are both lyrical and exact." But Nichols went on to characterize Thoreau's philosophizing in the book as a "relentless search for epigrams" that offered nothing new or notable.

Criticism

Candyce Norvell

Norvell is an independent educational writer who specializes in English and literature. She holds degrees in linguistics and journalism and has done

What Do I Read Next?

- *"Walden" and Other Writings,* edited by Brooks Atkinson and with an excellent introduction by Ralph Waldo Emerson, is a collection of Thoreau's major works, including additional nature writing and political essays such as "Civil Disobedience" and "A Plea for Captain John Brown." First published in 1937, the collection was republished in a new edition in 2000.

- *Essays: First and Second Series* (1990), edited by Douglas Crase, collects the major essays of Thoreau's mentor and friend, Ralph Waldo Emerson. These essays were originally published in two separate volumes in 1841 and 1844, and they express philosophies and attitudes very similar to those found in *Walden.*

- *My First Summer in the Sierra* (1911), by John Muir, is the most popular work of the famous conservationist and, along with *Walden,* is a classic American nature journal. Muir was just a young man in 1869, when he spent the summer helping to drive a large flock of sheep through the Sierra Nevada Mountains. Years later, when his diary of that summer was published, it inspired thousands of Americans to visit the area that later became Yosemite National Park.

- *Pilgrim at Tinker Creek* (1974), by Annie Dillard, is sometimes cast as a modern *Walden.* In it, Dillard records observations made over the course of a year at Tinker Creek in the Blue Ridge Mountains of Virginia. The book won a Pulitzer Prize for nonfiction.

- *Leaves of Grass* (1855), by Walt Whitman, was published the year after *Walden.* It celebrates nature and the American landscape in poetry much as Thoreau's work does in prose.

- *Little Women* (1868) is a classic novel based on the childhood of its author, Louisa May Alcott, the daughter of New England transcendentalist Bronson Alcott, who was Thoreau's friend. The book tells the story of the March family, following daughters Meg, Jo, Beth, and Amy from childhood to adulthood. The Marches are transcendentalists who value self-reliance, individualism, compassion, and education above material and social achievement.

---

graduate work in theology. In this essay, she discusses Thoreau's frequent references to Christianity and Hinduism throughout Walden.

Walden is a book of contrasts. Thoreau contrasts summer and winter, village and woods, the animal and spiritual natures that struggle within every human being, and many other pairs of opposites. One recurring and important contrast is that between Christianity—especially as taught and practiced in America at the time Thoreau was writing—and Hinduism. Like other New England transcendentalists, Thoreau was an avid reader of Hindu scriptures, and he quotes them and refers to them often in *Walden.* Like virtually all Americans of his time, he was also familiar with the Bible and with how the Christian denominations of his day interpreted it. What is particularly interesting is how he uses this dual knowledge. Most references to Christian scriptures, doctrines, and practices are either irreverent or disapproving, while Hindu scriptures and beliefs are presented with reverent appreciation.

Neither Thoreau's disdain for contemporary Christianity nor his appreciation of Hinduism is surprising. The popularity of transcendentalist ideas in New England arose out of discontent with what some saw as the strict and uninspiring doctrines of the Unitarian Church, so there was a natural conflict between transcendentalists and organized Christianity. Further, a fundamental difference between transcendentalism and Christianity can be traced to Hinduism: While orthodox Christian doctrine holds that God is transcendent (existing beyond creation) but not immanent (existing within creation; i.e., present within all created things and beings, including humans), transcendentalism borrows the Hindu concept that God is both transcendent and immanent.

The difference is important. The Christian belief that God does not dwell in humans leads to the belief in the need for some kind of divinely appointed intermediary—such as a savior or a priest—to establish a relationship between people and God. In contrast, the Hindu and transcendentalist belief in the immanence of God leads to the doctrine that every person can, without the need for an intermediary, experience the divine within himself or herself.

The transcendentalist belief in every person's ability to know God outside of institutional religion is a perfect complement to Thoreau's individualism and his general dislike of institutions. He found in the scriptures and doctrines of Hinduism a religious teaching that was well suited to his personality and his philosophy of life. Everything about the Christianity of his time, with its emphasis on institutions, conformity, and obedience to church authorities, was in conflict with them.

Thus, Thoreau makes more than one mocking reference to the Westminster Shorter Catechism, the "manual" of Christian doctrine that was used to teach young people in many churches. According to the catechism, the primary purpose of human life is "to glorify God and enjoy him forever." In one reference to it, Thoreau writes, "Our hymn books resound with a melodious cursing of God and enduring him forever."

Thoreau denigrates a Methodist newspaper of his day, called *Olive-Branches*. He writes that people who want to read a newspaper should read the best one available rather than *Olive-Branches* or other "pap."

The comment that "Men are generally still a little afraid of the dark, though the witches are all hung, and Christianity and candles have been introduced" manages all at once to be jocular and disapproving (it was, of course, in the name of Christianity that the witches had been hung) and dismissive (neither Christianity itself nor its assaults on others had succeeded in freeing humanity from its age-old fears).

In a later passage, Thoreau takes aim at the exclusivism of the Christianity practiced in his society. He says that the local farm hand "who has had his second birth and peculiar religious experience" may think that such experiences are limited

> Just as his contemporaries used the Bible as a guide for their daily lives, Thoreau turned to the Hindu scriptures."

to people who believe just as he does, but "Zoroaster, thousands of years ago, traveled the same road and had the same experience; but he, being wise, knew it to be universal and treated his neighbors accordingly." Thoreau goes on to point out that Zoroaster, as the founder of Zoroastrianism, the oldest of the world's great religions, may be said to have "invented and established worship among men." His point is that human beings sincerely worshipped God thousands of years before the founding of the Christian church. Thoreau concludes the passage by suggesting that Christians should "humbly commune with Zoroaster . . . and . . . with Jesus Christ himself, and let 'our church' go by the board."

(While he doesn't mention it, Thoreau must have been aware, from his study of the Hindu scriptures, that even the term "second birth" or "born again" is not exclusive or original to Christianity. Hinduism uses the very same term, with some similarity in meaning.)

In the above passage and in others, Thoreau makes a distinction between the founder of Christianity and institutionalized Christianity. In the passage above, he makes clear that he values the teachings of Jesus Christ but not those of "our church." In "Reading," a chapter in which he urges readers to read the great books, he gives the Bible a place alongside his beloved Vedas (Hindu scriptures), writing:

> That age will be rich indeed when those relics which we call Classics, and the still older and more than classic but even less known Scriptures of the nations, shall have still further accumulated; when the Vaticans shall be filled with Vedas and Zendavestas [the scriptures of Zoroastrianism] and Bibles. . . . By such a pile we may hope to scale heaven at last.

Though Thoreau acknowledges the value of Christian teachings when stripped of their churchly attachments, it is the Hindu books that inspire him. "In the morning, I bathe my intellect in the stupendous and cosmogonal philosophy of the Bhagavad

Gita,'' he rhapsodizes, ''in comparison with which our modern world and its literature seem puny and trivial.'' It is the Gita, he writes, that contains the perennial truths sought by all humankind across time and space, and it is the Gita that informs and elevates his own life. While Thoreau's contemporaries, upon going to draw water at a well, might think of biblical characters who performed similar duties, Thoreau goes to his well and meets ''the servant of the Brahmin . . . come to draw water for his master, and our buckets as it were grate together in the same well. The pure Walden water is mingled with the sacred water of the Ganges.''

Just as his contemporaries used the Bible as a guide for their daily lives, Thoreau turned to the Hindu scriptures. In preaching the sacredness and importance of the morning hours, Thoreau writes, ''The Vedas say, 'All intelligences awake with the morning.''' On the subject of diet, he writes, ''I am far from regarding myself as one of those privileged ones to whom the Ved refers when it says that 'he who has true faith in the Omnipresent Supreme Being may eat all that exists.'''

Thoreau was born a Westerner, but his own ''second birth''—the shift of his ambitions from those of the animal nature to those of the spiritual nature—made him, philosophically and spiritually, an Easterner.

Source: Candyce Norvell, Critical Essay on *Walden*, in *Nonfiction Classics for Students,* The Gale Group, 2002.

Robert Fanuzzi

In the following essay excerpt, Fanuzzi explores how Thoreau "describes not just an imagined city but how cities became imaginary" in Walden.

A second look at *Walden* suggests that Thoreau went to the country to find the city. He admits that his seclusion is motivated by necessity, since the opportunities for ''beautiful living'' once characteristic of civilized society are now found only ''out of doors, where there is no house and no housekeeper.'' Thus secluded, he finds ''a good port'' from which to conduct his ''private business,'' a railroad line to link a ''citizen of the world'' to national and international marketplaces, a cosmopolitan alternative to Concord's unlettered, ''provincial'' culture, and even—through Ellery Channing's companionship—the bonhomie of Broadway. Perhaps most important, he determines that by cultivating Catonian civic virtue, he has reacquired

the integrity to ''sustain . . . the manliest relations to men'' forfeited by his neighboring yeomen. In sum, every historic association of the city was present at Walden Pond—except, of course, the city itself.

The city is indeed both present and absent in *Walden*. It exists through references and allusions to city life, which is to say it exists as metonymy. This city has no geographical equivalent and in fact disclaims its status as locality, for Thoreau's intent is to use historically identified conventions of urbanism to conceive a space that corresponds to his imagination. Still retaining his sense of place, he wants this space to be habitable. When he asks in the midst of the woods, ''What sort of space is that which separates a man from his fellows and makes him solitary?,'' his metaphor adumbrates a sphere of autonomy bounded only by the means of its articulation. Throughout *Walden*, he deliberately designates those activities proper to this sphere—thinking, walking, writing, reading, thinking—and circumscribes them as art, which he defines as the ''struggle to free himself from this low state.'' Like other contemporary utopian reforms, his artistic realization contains the promise of a living space in which one may find the virtue, prosperity, and liberty not found in other environs. With a ''mission'' that Benjamin terms ''the emancipation from experiences,'' Thoreau strolls through the woods as the flaneur: an aesthetic consciousness whose individualized perception and mode of expression constitute his experience of place.

If Thoreau had lived in Boston, it would be easier to endow him with an urban imagination, though as my opening paragraph suggests, it is surely possible to contrast his project with pastoralism. The greater challenge that *Walden* poses is to see the imagination that Thoreau exercised so freely not only as spatial logic but as a construction of social space and, even more particularly, as a historical incidence of urbanism. In *Walden*, Thoreau creates what urbanists call a development history for the imagination, accounting for the creation of avowedly figural forms by the same changes in social morphology that were transforming the built and unbuilt landscape of eastern Massachusetts into centers or subsidiaries of an equally new social form, the urban-industrial complex. He attributes the liberation of the imagination directly to urbanization, but the same process provided the negative conditions for artistic production. Indeed, describing the emergence of the imagination as a spatialized form for Thoreau meant projecting an invisible space existing only as traces or inferences of representation. In *Walden*, this prospect is realized as an imagined city symbolizing a civic tradition with its attendant social spaces that was disappearing from Concord's increasingly urbanized environs. Though Thoreau stood by this tradition and detested its compromise, he did not resist the processes of historical and morphological change. On the contrary, he exploited them, transforming mutable civic space into its timeless utopian representation. Thoreau's civic project was, in fact, to intensify the awareness of artistic representation—a prospect which Paul Ricoeur defines as the operation of the utopian—in order to mark a disjunction in the progress of liberalism between the material development of cities and its invisible moral and political abstractions. Because Thoreau situated himself in the midst of this conflict, *Walden* describes not just an imagined city but *how* cities became imaginary. We can consider this event to be as crucial to the emergence of Thoreau's artistic consciousness as to the future of urban space, keeping in mind Benjamin's judgment of Baudelaire: "He envisioned blank spaces which he filled in with his poems. His work cannot merely be categorized as historical like anyone else's, but it intended to be so and understood itself as so. . . ."

Thoreau's aspiration towards idiosyncrasy notwithstanding, the unique history that *Walden* tells is the emergence of aesthetic forms from the conventions and traditions of civic life. Indeed, his determination to recreate this life in the midst of the woods lays bare the enabling assumption of an artistic sensibility: that a city is a construct of consciousness, imagined through the awareness of individuality, if not alienation, that city life engenders. While urbanism thus defined is central to our conception of modernism, the tendency to interpret urban space as the medium of the imagination is already extant in the place names for many of the locales of nineteenth-century literature: in addition to Baudelaire's Paris, Whitman's New York, Crane's Bowery, Dickens's London, and so on. The distinctiveness of Thoreau's Walden Pond among these "unreal cities" is that it brings to the fore the contradiction between the experience of place and the actual place, so that both the imaginative processes and the means of representation are defamiliarized. That is, they are foregrounded and thematized as locales in themselves. For Thoreau, this defamiliarization promises an unprecedented and unbounded sphere of experience, but he will also insist that this "sort of space" shares the

> The greater challenge that *Walden* poses is to see the imagination that Thoreau exercised so freely not only as spatial logic but as a construction of social space and, even more particularly, as a historical incidence of urbanism."

structure, conditions, and even the history of a spatialized social form.

We are introduced to this contradiction early in *Walden*, when Thoreau quite deliberately juxtaposes associations of city and country. After berating his townsmen for their industriousness, he announces that his "purpose in going to Walden Pond was . . . to transact some private business." Then he invites a comparison between his solitary life of rustic simplicity and the far-flung, multitudinous affairs of the international mercantile trader. In assuming this identity, Thoreau is also borrowing its native habitat. According to political historian Gary Nash, the international merchant would have been a politically active Whig or Federalist, committed to liberalizing developments in government and trade and usually situated in an Atlantic port city like Boston, Baltimore, New York, or Philadelphia. Thoreau contends that Walden Pond is likewise "a good place for business" because of its "good port and good foundation," as well as its ice-trade-convenient railroad connection. In "Sounds," he will say that the railroad, transporting exotic goods from free and distant markets, makes him akin to the international merchant, a "citizen of the world." He evidently wants to build not just a city on a hill but a commercial society by a pond, "the germ," he says, "of something more."

In borrowing an urban locale, Thoreau is also reclaiming a political history. Through their alliance with restive manufacturers and disenfranchised artisans, the liberal Whig traders of the eighteenth century made the Atlantic commercial city into the center of political resistance against monopolies, mercantilism, and colonialism. By comparing himself to the urban merchant, Thoreau perpetuates a complementary vision of freedom: the autonomy promised the urban commercial classes in a postcolonial, laissez-faire economy. We may read his intention ''to transact some private business with the fewest obstacles'' as a similar link between political and economic freedom. This linking would have been compatible with his reigning ambition in *Walden* and in many of his essays, which was to establish the relevance of the nation's democratic revolution to antebellum America; but here he seeks to recreate the appropriate social space for continued struggle through detailed historical references to the eighteenth-century commercial city. In the spirit of the urban Whigs Trenchard and Gordon, Thoreau envisions this space as a free society of trade and commerce, politically and geographically beyond the reach of an intrusive state. The taxation that he seemed to oppose so capriciously represented what these liberals feared most: the intervention of statist policies—whether they financed trade monopolies, the slave trade, or a system of railroads—in the properly private affairs of civil society.

For Thoreau, this kind of uncivil, neomercantilist economy signifies a structural change in the polity, a reorganization of social space that gives the state its own space, the all-inclusive yet personalized space of the nation. He detects the expansion of this space in the sentiments of citizens who ''think it essential that the *Nation* have commerce, and export ice, and talk through a telegraph, and ride thirty miles an hour,'' but he will protect an ideal of civil autonomy rooted in eighteenth-century urban liberalism. When he says that such citizens are ''content to live like baboons,'' he applies a venerable term of moral opprobrium—corruption—to Jefferson's laboring yeomen.

Thoreau's praise of the cosmopolitan merchant, on the other hand, is unstinting; he affects envy, almost wonder, for what amounts to ''a demand for universal knowledge.'' But he is determined to let neither the location of Walden Pond nor the passage of time deprive him of the intelligence, freedom, and prosperity available to the eighteenth-century urban bourgeoisie. He builds his identification with this class by undermining both the pastoral tradition of American letters and the nationalist history it projected. Whereas Bryant and even Emerson celebrated nature as the extension and progress of positive sovereignty, Thoreau represents nature according to the self-negating provisions of civil society. That is, he considers Walden Pond to be natural insofar as it is a completely privative realm, free of superfluous obstacles and unconditioned by an in-trusive alien power. Thoreau calls life in this realm ''primitive and frontier life'' not because it is wild but precisely because it is governed by ''the essential laws of man's existence,'' which he finds recorded in ''the old day books of the merchants.'' Not surprisingly, these laws instruct Thoreau in the ways of bourgeois society: what is natural and necessary is ''all that man obtains by his own exertions.'' Under this condition, he disqualifies the labor of his neighboring farmers, who work not for themselves but for the holders of their mortgages on their homes and farms. So he is forced to commend the unencumbered wigwam, the virtues of uncultivated fields, and the political economy of squirrels. His deprecation of baboons notwithstanding, animals furnish Thoreau with perhaps his most explicitly self-justifying image of the bourgeoisie: their orderly yet consummately free lives follow only the dictates of natural, invisible laws. He makes special allowances when he adds Fuel and Clothing to the animals' necessities of Food and Shelter, but he considers any life that obeys intrinsic imperatives to be both a moral and material improvement over that of Concord townsmen.

Walden ultimately recommends that the conscientious citizen devote himself to ''more sacred laws,'' but Thoreau's attachment to a legally constituted dominion in heaven or on earth perpetuates a historically urban form of society in the absence of a corresponding urban space. Thoreau was well aware of the historical discrepancy, but he means the invocation of an antecedent social form to annul the influence of the state by providing a permanent haven from positive law. In this sense, he is using the pastoral to revive, replay, and infinitely extend eighteenth-century urbanization, which created not only the infrastructure of public dissent but an invisible realm called civil society, which, as Habermas says, was governed by ''anonymous laws functioning in accord with an economic rationality immanent, so it appears, in the market.'' Though Habermas does not historicize the urban development that created this realm, he does make the rise of a ''town'' consciousness, in opposition to that of a ''court,'' coincident with the codification of civil laws that have exclusive administrative jurisdiction over economic and social exchanges. Thoreau places himself under these ''more liberal laws'' and hopes that they can again convene an autonomous society in the midst of the woods. In commending Walden Pond for its ''good port,'' he is making a glancing reference to the shared history of liberal capitalism and urban development, though he maintains that the commercial city rising from Walden Pond would be built ''on piles of your own driving.''

Thoreau repeatedly argues a classically liberal ideal of individual autonomy, but he does not abstract even the discussion of inward nature from the infrastructure and institutions of an urbanized social form. His conception of a morally guided subject, obedient to ''the laws of his own being,'' is derived from the self-governing commercial society, while his concern for the state of ''true integrity'' links him more particularly to the Whig-Federalist city's civic sphere, which fused the republican politics of disinterested virtue with an economically constituted social space. From the Revolution to the antebellum era, the commercial city was indeed the sphere in which the new nation's republican pretensions were given institutional form, often most effectively translated by the Whig-Federalist commercial classes. The lyceums, atheneums, libraries, and salons that composed the antebellum era's ''republican institutions'' were first developed in Atlantic port cities; with no attempt to disguise the city's principal indigenous activity, their wealthy patrons celebrated them as ''cultural ornaments to mercantile society.'' In conjunction with Federalist architecture's French neo-classicism, these ''cultural ornaments'' fueled the post-Revolutionary city's comparison of itself to the classical polis, although this was more true for Philadelphia and Boston than for single-mindedly mercantile New York; the former two competed with one another for the title ''Athens of America.'' Within the institutions of this civic sphere, self-seeking burghers could transcend their interests and exercise their rational faculties. Perhaps even more importantly, an unruly populace would learn how to govern itself by the laws of reason.

The Jacksonian era may have envisioned a form of society in the image of the rural majority, but in *Walden* the Whig-Federalist city plan is recovered and extended. In ''Reading,'' Thoreau proposes that Concord proper be developed along the lines of a classically Federalist city, replete with indigenous salons, galleries, libraries, lyceums, and other educational facilities. He exhorts the citizens of Concord not to adopt a ''provincial'' life but to ''act collectively in the spirit of our [prospective] institutions'' and ''take the place of the noblemen in Europe.'' This ambition to create ''noble villages of men'' is in keeping with a principal objective of the early republic, which was to authorize its sovereignty through the education of a rational public capable of governing itself. But in practical terms,

this imperative is also an impetus for city-building, for the republican project of political education entailed the development of a cosmopolitan center capable of receiving information, influences, and goods, as Thoreau insists, from distant ports. ''Reading'' resituates republicanism in an urban tradition and suggests that the Transcendentalists' project of self-culture derives from its plans for civic development.

Jefferson's abhorrence of cities has led us to equate republicanism with the country, but politics and geography are often difficult to equate, especially during the early national period in New England. If agrarianism was celebrated as a republican ideal, it was promoted by the same Federalist urban merchants who were building and promoting the port city. In Boston, a group known as the Essex Junto was particularly effective in investing rural life with the same power to inculcate virtue that the urban institutions aimed at. The country seats and adjoining farms that dotted the eastern Massachusetts landscape were considered not as alternative economies in their own right but as necessary adjuncts to market exchanges that guaranteed the exchanges' virtue and their contribution to the public good. Agrarianism served urban commercial interests even more explicitly when it was accompanied by a program of political education. In lectures such as ''The Duty of the Farmer to His Calling'' and ''Why a Massachusetts Farmer Should Be Content,'' farmers were told by an urban elite that they were the pillars of the republic and that their thrift, frugality, and increasingly unprofitable industry furnished the moral basis of a predominantly commercial society.

Thoreau may have sought respite from modern society in natural environs, but his plans for Walden Woods and vicinity reflect the traditional land-use patterns of the urban Federalist. In ''Where I Lived, and What I Lived for,'' he reports that he roamed the countryside as a self-appointed real-estate broker, financier, and landscape architect of imaginary country seats; he then reinterprets this conventional pattern of subdivision as the simple experience of sitting. To further link his ''*sedes*'' to the development plans of the commercial class, he speculates that ''the future inhabitants of this region, wherever they may place their houses, may be sure that they had been anticipated.''

Like the urban Federalist, Thoreau does not mean to associate himself with present or future farmers. His dedication to husbandry, on display in

"The Bean Field," is in fact inspired by a civic tradition cultivated in the eighteenth century by the Anglo-American urban bourgeoisie. As J. G. A. Pocock reports, Whig liberals adopted the Catonian ideal of an agrarian republic to argue that virtue, the selfless participation of a citizen in the life of his polity, could be exercised by the members of an urbanized commercial society whose profits advanced the interests of the public. Their inspiration for an actively moral citizenry came from the classical polis, though as first developed in the seventeenth century, "country" ideology did attempt to secure England's status as a republic by invoking a natural basis for virtue in nondependent landholding. But as Britain evolved into an international trading empire, "country" signified an opposition political party whose model republic was less associated with nature than with free commerce. Against speculative, debt-inducing, and state-sponsored monopolist ventures, proponents of a liberalized marketplace envisioned a virtuous society governed by laws of just commerce, of wide distribution of capital, and of equitable exchange. To ameliorate the influence of financial interests in the government, to mitigate the power of the state, and to establish the authority of the public, *Cato's Letters* proposed "agrarian law or something like it." The polity entailed by these laws corresponded not to a farm but to an idealized commercial society whose market exchanges exemplified classical ideals of citizenship.

We readily accept Thoreau's investment in classical politics as determining his relation to pastoralism and agrarianism; as Horkheimer says, his "escape into the woods was conceived by a student of the Greek polis rather than by a peasant." What we should add to this truism is that his understanding of the civic tradition is mediated by the civil discourse of the urban bourgeoisie. Thoreau likewise refuses to distinguish between virtue and commerce, arguing instead that the value of rural life comes from its contribution to civil commerce. In this sense, he too pursues agrarianism, "or something like it." In "The Bean Field," he archly notes the derision his bastardized husbandry elicited from locals and reserves his pride not for his agricultural expertise and certainly not for his noble toil but for $8.72, "the result of my experience in raising beans." This narrowly economic assessment might seem at variance with the disinterested ideals of agrarian republicanism, but Thoreau's interest in farming is to prove Cato's dictum: "the profits of agriculture are particularly pious or just."

Such profits are conducive to virtue because they can be obtained without debt, without state capitalization, and particularly without submission to the "slave-driver" within. To the extent that husbandry allows him to maintain his independence from a neomercantilist, slave-driving economy, Thoreau has fulfilled the promise of urban liberalism and made commerce into a medium of virtuous citizenship. In this context, "country" does not denote a natural setting or even a natural economic order. On the contrary, Whigs used agrarian republicanism to place the imprimatur of the civic ideal on their commercial city. By Thoreau's time, this city does not exist in nature, so he is in the strange position of having to imagine a civic space *as* nature—or, to use an important eighteenth-century distinction, as *second* nature. Through his ersatz agriculture—indeed, through an imitation of nature—Thoreau wants his readers to look beyond his immediate environs and imagine the unrealized, nonlocalizable realm of the commercial city, wherein profit was in proportion to virtue. There they would find not only the advantages of civilization but the evidence of their own imagination.

Source: Robert Fanuzzi, "Thoreau's Urban Imagination," in *American Literature*, Vol. 68, No. 2, June 1996, pp. 321–29.

John Carlos Rowe

In the following essay excerpt, Rowe examines how Thoreau likens human language to other natural phenomena in Walden.

> *To learn means: to become knowing. In Latin, knowing is* qui vidit, *one who has seen, has caught sight of something, and who never again loses sight of what he has caught sight of. To learn means: to attain to such seeing. To this belongs our reaching it; namely, on the way, on a journey. To put oneself on a journey, to experience, means to learn.*

—Heidegger, "Words," *On the Way to Language*

> *I have sought to re-name the things seen, now lost in chaos of borrowed titles, many of them inappropriate, under which the true character lies hid. In letters, in journals, in reports of happenings I have recognized new contours suggested by old words so that new names were constituted.*

—William Carlos Williams, *In the American Grain*

Walden is Thoreau's perfect form; it has the mathematical precision of a musical composition. Thoreau certainly appears to demonstrate in this work the radically formalized truth he had foreseen in an earlier work: "The most distinct and beautiful statement of any truth must take at last the mathe-

Thoreau's room at Walden

matical form." *Walden* is "addressed to poor students," who love to play its verbal games and diagram its architectonic order in the place of healthier sport. Such economy and control are rare in the literature of the American Renaissance, which seems better represented by the outwanderings of Whitman or the divine rage of Melville. There is little voyaging here; this is a book of construction and possession: "In most books, the *I,* or first person, is omitted; in this it will be retained; that, in respect to egotism, is the main difference. We commonly do not remember that it is, after all, always the first person that is speaking." All radiates concentrically from this artificial "I," whose insistent presence organizes and determines what we might see. Thoreau has much to say against ownership, but in this book he appropriates nature and brings it within his compass. The writing defines and encloses a Transcendental fiefdom; *Walden* legalizes the everlasting wholeness of natural creation. All seasons speak the same truth in but varied manifestations, so that the poet need only lift the corners of his veils to disclose the divinity in things.

This is a book of discovery, but not of creation. Perhaps it is no accident that the most extended literary discussion concentrates on "Reading" rather than on writing. Of course, Thoreau emphasizes the intimate bond between the two activities: "Books must be read as deliberately and reservedly as they were written." Yet, *Walden* is primarily intended as a Baedeker to the order of nature, the primacy of which remains unquestioned. Writing is sacred and mystical in its universal appeal and endurance, but nonetheless secondary to the literal text of nature: "It is the work of art nearest to life itself." "Reading" quickly gives way to "Sounds" more basic to "the language which all things and events speak without metaphor, which alone is copious and standard." William Drake writes, "The step from 'Reading' to 'Sounds' is that from the language of men to the 'language' of things, from what can be said *about* nature, to nature itself." The classics play an important role throughout *Walden*, but they must be put aside in the early stages of Thoreau's ritualized self-purification: "I did not read books the first summer; I hoed beans."

Walden betrays the desire for an established metaphysical center to determine human behavior and organize knowledge. The metaphors of building and clothing appear to offer human beings the freedom of a creative imagination, but such activities are themselves merely techniques for discovering and obeying the dictates of an authoritative Being. Fishing, diving, and mining are basic to this

> *Walden* **betrays the desire for an established metaphysical center to determine human behavior and organize knowledge.''**

work of reconnaissance: ''My instinct tells me that my head is an organ for burrowing, as some creatures use their snout and fore-paws, and with it I would mine and burrow my way through these hills. I think that the richest vein is somewhere hereabouts; so by the divining rod and thin vapors I judge; and here I will begin to mine.'' Such deep diving intends to bring to light what is hidden, freeing what has been imprisoned in humans by their faulty methods of perception and cognition. *Awakening* is the avowed aim of *Walden*, and it means the *arising* of truth into consciousness by means of a systematic removal of barriers in order to open a path. For Thoreau, to awaken is to ''come into being'' rather than to ''bring into being.'' Language facilitates such discovery only to the extent that it serves a prior perception and thus may be made ''pertinent'' to reality. Metaphor is employed ironically to reveal the ''commonsensical'' in everyday speech and thus to free us to receive the tangible, literal spirituality that only nature presents. As Drake remarks, ''To say that nature has a language, is itself a metaphor. Metaphor as Thoreau speaks of it always defines human experience, *within human bounds.*'' Thus, in a work that is nothing but metaphor, Thoreau struggles to destroy the metaphorical in order to allow the presence of the indwelling god to emerge.

The achievement of *Walden* is the result of this confidence that the natural origin of language escapes the symbolism of words and remains eternally and creatively present. In such a bookish work there is remarkably little reflection upon language itself, as if the natural facts were sufficient for the grammar of our lives. There is something disturbingly evasive in such passages as the following from ''Higher Laws'': ''Every man is the builder of a temple, called his body, to the god he worships, after a style purely his own, nor can he get off by hammering marble instead. We are all sculptors and painters, and our material is our own flesh and blood and bones. Any nobleness begins at once to refine a

man's features, any meanness or sensuality to imbrute them.'' Substituting the body for the materials of the sculptor, Thoreau disparages the symbolic mode of the traditional artist. True art speaks directly in and through natural existence, spontaneously manifesting itself in the life of the artist.

And yet, such sophistry is purchased only by means of an elaborate metaphoric structure yoking temple and body, style and behavior. Thoreau is able to elide the conventional distinctions between body and soul, substance and spirit, only by means of a language that operates by syntagmatic associations and paradigmatic substitutions essential to figurative language. Thoreau may employ language in *Walden* more cleverly than in any of his other works, but he scrupulously avoids the problematic of language itself. Emerson insists that ''Nature is the symbol of spirit,'' thus suggesting a correspondence between the production of words as ''signs of natural facts'' and the recognition of ''natural facts'' as the ''symbols of particular spiritual facts.'' Emerson's view involves a rich and varied language coordinated with natural symbolism; Thoreau's insistence on the ultimate literality of natural facts reduces language to a secondary representation.

There are, of course, many ways in which *Walden* can be read as an extended meditation on the use and abuse of language. In *The Senses of Walden,* Stanley Cavell employs Wittgenstein to interpret *Walden* as the discovery of ''what writing is and, in particular, what writing *Walden* is.'' *Walden* certainly abounds with evidence that self-knowledge is as much a linguistic process as a purely natural one; in fact, the entire work turns on the doubling of the place of Walden in its textual realization. The awakening promised in the epigraph and the spring that concludes the work's seasonal cycles are metaphors for the composition of the text; the dwelling that Thoreau builds is ultimately a house of words. Yet, the aim of this ''wording of the world'' is a simplicity and clarity that result in the resolution of true self-knowledge.

The discipline of Thoreau's deliberation is equivalent to Wittgenstein's goal of learning how what we say is what we mean. Thoreau relies, however, on his confidence in a fundamental language of Nature from which human speech derives; Wittgenstein's problems are compounded by the fact that his investigations must remain totally within the domain of ordinary language. Wittgenstein must repeat the basic Kantian move of bracketing the thing-in-itself as unknowable, thus shifting the concern of understanding to the development of such internal linguistic distinctions as literal and figurative, grammatical and performative, conventional and original. In *Walden*, Thoreau decidedly does not bracket the thing-in-itself, even though he acknowledges the difficulty of expressing it. Cavell brilliantly suggests that Thoreau provides in *Walden* that "deduction of the thing-in-itself" that Kant "ought to have provided" as "an essential feature (category) of objectivity itself, viz., that of *a world apart from me in which* objects are met." Transcendental deduction, however, can be performed only on a system of representation; Thoreau's ability to offer such a deduction of objectivity depends upon his confidence in the "language" of Nature, on the possibility of an "objective" language. Thus, Thoreau can assert in *Walden* what Kant in the three critiques only subjunctively "wished" for: that the order of the mind has a structural identity with the order of Nature.

The objectivity of Nature in *Walden* thus secretly governs the subjectivity of human language, which eternally symbolizes that literal origin. Cavell argues that "the externality of the world is articulated by Thoreau as its nextness to me." This idea of the proximity of man and Nature determines Cavell's understanding of philosophical unity in Thoreau: "Unity between these aspects is viewed not as a mutual absorption, but as perpetual nextness, an act of neighboring or befriending." I shall develop a similar notion of metaphysical difference in my Heideggerian reading of *A Week on the Concord and Merrimack Rivers*, which draws, as Cavell's reading of *Walden* does, on Thoreau's paradoxical "friendship" (itself a metaphor for self-consciousness) as a complex of proximity and distance. However, I employ Heidegger's metaphor of the "between" (of earth and sky, of man and nature, of beings and Being), which differs crucially from "nextness."

The "neighborhood" of man and Nature is made possible by the authority of the language of Nature, whose objective and literal presence always exceeds human speech. When we say what we mean, when we speak deliberately, we approach the simplicity of such natural language, and words become facts. But the "between" of man and Nature describes a different space of human dwelling, because this between constitutes a relation that does not exist as a possibility prior to human language. In *Walden*, the language of Nature makes possible human speech, but the human language of *A Week* invents the idea of Nature as part of the

measurement of our being. The grounding of human language in an inexpressible natural presence is symbolized in *Walden* in terms of building: a house, a self, a neighborhood with what *is*. The displacement of natural presence into the "difference" of human language in *A Week* is expressed in metaphors of voyaging, of traveling the between of beings and Being that is measured only by such movement. This "bridging" and "crossing" is the essential activity of metaphor. The text of *Walden* celebrates its departure from Walden as the realization of the natural experiment; the text of *A Week* celebrates the return to Concord as a "fall" into that language that has forever displaced the Nature it set out to discover.

In this description of the spring thaw flowing down the railroad cut, Thoreau offers one of the most extended and self-conscious verbal plays in *Walden*. The intricate blending of natural energies is a metaphor for the act of composition as an interpretation of specific phenomena in Nature: "As it flows it takes the forms of sappy leaves or vines, making heaps of pulpy sprays a foot or more in depth, and resembling, as you look down on them, the laciniated lobed and imbricated thalluses of some lichens; or you are reminded of coral, of leopards' paws or birds' feet, of brains or lungs or bowels, and excrements of all kinds." At such a moment language appears to call forth not only the intricate relations of the natural scene but also the pure metaphorics of such relations. Such poetry seems to constitute the truth of Nature by means of an integrated verbal display that challenges the self-sufficiency of natural phenomena. Everything observed seems to contribute to the production of signs that announce their metaphorical powers. Such technical descriptions as "laciniated lobed and imbricated thalluses of some lichens" signify through poetic complexes of alliteration, assonance, consonance, condensation, and syllabic rhythm. Yet, at such a critical moment Thoreau hesitates and then retreats, insisting that the true "artistry" remains external and divine: "I am affected as if in a peculiar sense I stood in the laboratory of the Artist who made the world and me,—had come to where he was still at work, sporting on this bank, and with an excess of energy strewing his fresh designs about."

Metaphor has made such vision possible, but it is quickly rejected in favor of "such a foliaceous mass as the vitals of the animal body." And as if checking the dangerous excess implied in the verbal dance, Thoreau insists on dissecting words themselves to reveal their natural grounding, effectively emptying them of their autonomous powers:

> No wonder that the earth expresses itself outwardly in leaves, it so labors with the idea inwardly. The atoms have already learned this law, and are pregnant by it. The overhanging leaf sees here its prototype. *Internally,* whether in the globe or animal body, it is a moist thick *lobe,* a word especially applicable to the liver and lungs and the *leaves* of fat (λειβω, labor, lapsus, to flow or flow or slip downward, a lapsing; λοβοσ, globus, lobe, globe; also lap, flap, and many other words,) *externally* a dry thin *leaf,* even as the *f* and *v* are a pressed and dried *b.* The radicals of lobe are *lb,* the soft mass of the *b* (single lobed, or B, the double lobed,) with a liquid *l* behind it pressing it forward. In globe, *glb,* the gutteral *g* adds to the meaning the capacity of the throat.

Thoreau's phonemic, phonetic, and etymological analyses serve to restrain the flight of metaphor and situate the imagination within the "facts" of nature. Language is reduced to the physical associations of words and things that reveal a hidden natural form. *Walden* clearly argues for a natural principle of growth and unfolding that denies any sense of completion or closure, but language imitates that organic development only by means of a formal precision with respect to external facts that restricts imaginative play by narrowing the range of authentic (or pertinent) meanings. Emerson avoids some of these dangers by insisting that art is "a nature passed through the alembic of man. Thus in art does Nature work through the will of a man filled with the beauty of her first works." For Emerson, both natural and linguistic symbolisms require a reciprocal interpretation, whereas Thoreau insists on the *presence* of unmediated truth in the earth's "living poetry."

Thus, in *Walden* every impulse to discuss poetics is quickly diverted back to the controlling meditation on the permanence and variety of natural forms. The mastery of this work relies largely on Thoreau's insistence that language and thought would be indistinguishable from natural phenomena if we fully understood our being. In his study of Thoreau, James McIntosh argues that the principal drama in *Walden* is the struggle of the "I" to sustain his integrity in the face of an encompassing natural order. Revisions made between 1847 and 1852 seem to indicate that in the process of composition Thoreau grew "less anxious to write of himself as a part of nature, more intent on asserting his intelligent separateness." But the very diversity and activity that individualize the narrator and his style merely confirm the determining power of the underlying natural forms. The anxiety of alienation is neatly resolved as the *illusion* of separation that properly honed senses may see beyond. Every verbal strategy seems designed to measure and refine the a priori ground of being in nature.

Source: John Carlos Rowe, "The Being of Language: The Language of Being," in *Henry David Thoreau,* edited by Harold Bloom, Modern Critical Views series, Chelsea House Publishers, 1987, pp. 145–51.

Paul Schwaber

In the following essay excerpt, Schwaber describes how readers can "perceive experientially Thoreau's psychic and moral growth" in Walden.

When a man is able to live his philosophy, it becomes more than a theoretical construction of his mind. It becomes his attitude, his way of having experience. Few men achieve this unification of mind, aspiration, and event. Too few, perhaps, even try. Yet some do; and as any reader of our literature knows, one of the very few masterpieces of American writing, Thoreau's *Walden*, has as its subject precisely this attempt.

Though apparently an account of Thoreau's two-year sojourn at Walden Pond, *Walden* reveals his coming of age during the years in which he wrote it. It can be read, therefore, as Henry David Thoreau's spiritual autobiography for the years 1845 to 1854. *Walden* is, of course, more than an account or an autobiography. It is a work of art. Because of its artistry, we are able to perceive experientially Thoreau's psychic and moral growth, and we can begin to understand the relevance of his growth to us.

In 1845 Thoreau built a hut near Walden Pond and moved into it as a practical expediency: he wanted to live inexpensively in order to write and think. He also wanted to feel that he was living excellently. As he explained in the most famous passage in the book, "I went to the woods because I wished to live deliberately, to front only the essential facts of life, and see if I could not learn what it had to teach, and not, when I came to die, discover that I had not lived. I did not wish to live what was not life, living is so dear; nor did I wish to practice resignation, unless it was quite necessary." To live essentially meant first of all to distinguish between labor which a man must do in order to survive and respect himself, and labor which he does without realizing that it is aimed at acquiring or preserving things which impede his life because they are not worth the effort they entail. Thoreau thought his neighbors in Concord sacrificed too much of their life energy to this latter type of busy-ness, and he characterized it astutely as "doing penance in a thousand remarkable ways." His interest was in living, not merely in making more than a living. He objected to a man wasting his mind and soul in incessant labor which was intended, ironically enough, to provide for a fuller life. Thoreau thought life too short to postpone it. Perhaps therefore he devoted his first chapter, "Economy," to his radical distinction between essentials and inessentials, or, as he would have believed, between practicalities and impracticalities.

For it was just such a practical problem he faced. He tells us cryptically that his purpose in going to Walden was "to transact some private business with the fewest obstacles." He never tells us directly what this "private business" was, but we may fairly deduce that it had largely to do with protecting, strengthening, and reconstituting his soul. He was then twenty-eight years old and had not yet been able to find a way of getting his living without injuring his spirit. After graduating from Harvard, he taught school, lived with the Ralph Waldo Emersons, lectured before the Concord Lyceum, published in the *Dial,* and went to Staten Island as a tutor in the house of Emerson's brother William; while in New York he tried to break into the literary market there, but he met with little success; finally he returned home to Concord to work in his father's pencil factory. By none of his varied attempts at earning a living had he managed to live his chosen life as a writer and as a man. The move to Walden afforded a good solution to his economic problem. It seems also to have been an admirable gesture toward the solitude that this young man needed to grow from an apprentice philosopher and a spiritual youth to an independent adult.

Thoreau tells us early in *Walden* that he aspired to live a noble life though most men live mean ones, and, to judge from the resolute tone of the opening chapter, he has a pretty fair idea of how stubbornly he—Henry David Thoreau—has had to proceed toward his goal. Furthermore, he knows the specific qualities of the life to which he aspired. What becomes clear through the course of the book, and what commands our respect for the man and the lessons he would teach us, is that he slowly, patiently, even arduously, attains that life he values and by which he judged the lives of his neighbors to be insufficient models for him to follow.

What did Thoreau judge to be the salient qualities of essential life—once, that is, a man has attended honorably to life's physical necessities?

> **Thoreau thus rejected the practices and assumptions of his neighbors in Concord with good cause. He had the courage to be as radical, or as eccentric, as he had to be."**

Though he spends a good deal of the first chapter sniping at inessentials, he points to two compendious values. The first is self-reliance, the quality of soul to which a man wins through by consciously struggling for it: "I am resolved," he writes with exaggerative humor and undoubted seriousness, "that I will not through humility become the devil's attorney. I will endeavor to speak a good word for the truth." A self-reliant man can bear to be free, and only such a man is ready to love and respect other men: "I am wont to think that men are not so much the keepers of herds as herds are the keepers of men, the former are so much freer." "Most men, even in this comparatively free country, through mere ignorance and mistake, are so occupied with the factitious cares and superfluous coarse labors of life that its finer fruits cannot be plucked by them. . . Actually, the laboring man has not leisure for a true integrity day by day; he cannot afford to sustain the manliest relations to men."

The second of Thoreau's compendious values is more elusive, doubtless because it cannot be taken by frontal assault, however arduous: "In any weather, at any hour of the day or night, I have been anxious to improve the nick of time, and notch it on my stick too; to stand on the meeting of two eternities, the past and the future, which is precisely the present moment; to toe that line." Near the end of the book he reiterates: "We should be blessed if we lived in the present always, and took advantage of every accident that befell us, like the grass which confesses the influence of the slightest dew which falls on it; and did not spend our time in atoning for the neglect of past opportunities, which we call doing our duty." The present moment fully lived does not admit of penance for past deeds or omissions; nor does it admit of postponement now in favor of future gratifications, whether secular or religious. The present is not for self-chastisement or even for earnest and studious attempts to make the future better. In short, a man lives well only when he is at peace with himself, which is to say when he is without anxiety; and Thoreau knew that for some people anxiety is a "well nigh incurable disease." As he wrote in his journal, "It would be glorious to see mankind at leisure for once."

To the lives of quiet desperation that he refused to imitate he contrasted a life of joyous and manly independence in the present. Instead of committing himself to responsibilities of past and future, such as "inherited farms, houses, barns, cattle, and farming tools," commitments which enslave a man's spirit, Thoreau asserted proudly that he was a "sojourner" in the woods and in civilized society. A skeptical, canny, and withal hopeful man, he insisted on finding for himself what life was about by living it: "Here is life, an experiment to a great extent untried by me; . . . [M]an's capacities have never been measured, . . . [we cannot] judge of what he can do by any precedents, so little has been tried." The sojourner and experimenter alone can feel pleasure, the feeling that more than all others eluded his contemporaries; Thoreau remarked that their very games concealed "stereotyped but unconscious despair. . . There is no play in them." He insisted that a man's life should include the joy that can come only with living—which includes working—as a man should. And joy for Thoreau meant lyrical participation and even playfulness: "Children, who play life, discern its true law and relations more clearly than men, who fail to live it worthily, but who think that they are wiser by experience, that is by failure." "I had this advantage, at least, in my mode of life, over those who were obliged to look abroad for amusement, to society and the theater, that my life itself was become my amusement and never ceased to be novel."

II

Thoreau thus rejected the practices and assumptions of his neighbors in Concord with good cause. He had the courage to be as radical, or as eccentric, as he had to be. His protest, to use Whitehead's phrase in a new context, was "a protest on behalf of value." The goal he set for himself was compounded of utilitarian skills and spiritual ease. He envisioned a life of manly independence, which he understood to be the prerequisite for freedom and love, and of full experience of the ripeness of the moment lived.

I have said that in *Walden* we see Thoreau move toward and, I think, reach the goal he set for himself in the early part of the book. That movement is the great moral development of the book. And that moral development is central to the book's aesthetic excellence.

So much perceptive comment has been written in recent years in appreciation of *Walden*'s artistry—its stylistic aptness and its structural and imagistic unity—that one must wonder if he has anything more to add. I need only mention here how the themes of wildness and civilized control, privacy and sociability, freedom and servitude, and joy and despair alternate and interrelate; how images of night and sleep are contrasted with those of morning and wakefulness, and how these images become metaphors for spiritual conditions; how Thoreau's two-year experience at Walden and some of his subsequent experiences are presented as transpiring in one year; and how the passage of the year from summer to spring is made to coincide symbolically with the details of Thoreau's activity and with the rebirth of his spirit. I would suggest, however, that Thoreau's rebirth of spirit accords with the life he values and that the moral development of the book thus provides its dramatic unity. As we read on in *Walden* we became witnesses to Thoreau's dramatic, though quiet, psychic development. It is reflected in the changes that are evident in his tone of voice and in the quality and type of his responses to the things about him.

At the beginning of the book Thoreau speaks as a man apart, though, as the act of writing itself and even his acerbic humor would suggest, he is never cut off entirely from some good feeling for his fellow men. He writes, as he is the first to admit, about himself and what he did. His tone as he tells of moving out of Concord to Walden Pond alternates between defiance, scolding, and preaching; it is always resolute. One assumes that he is so insistent because he knows the truth and wants to be heard. But why so harsh a tone? Why so argumentative a rebellion? He seems to attack his neighbors' way of life and to defend his own at least as much as he celebrates it. Perhaps he is not so sure of himself as he would like to be. His distinction between a professor of philosophy (one who has subtle thoughts and professes what is admirable) and a philosopher (one who lives admirably) is helpful. To be a philosopher is "so to love wisdom as to live according to its dictates, a life of simplicity, independence, magnanimity, and trust. It is to solve some of the problems of life not only theoretically, but practically." In the long first chapter of *Walden*, Thoreau breaks idols, teaches, and asserts, but to use his own distinction, he sounds more like a professor than a philosopher:

> I see young men, my townsmen, whose misfortune it is to have inherited farms, houses, barns, cattle, and farming tools; for these are more easily acquired than gotten rid of . . . Who made them serfs to the soil? . . . They have got to live a man's life, pushing all these things before them, and get on as well as they can. How many a poor immortal soul have I met well-nigh crushed and smothered under its load, creeping down the road of life, pushing before it a barn seventy-five feet by forty, its Augean stables never cleansed, and one hundred acres of land, tillage, mowing, pasture, and wood lot.

This is the tone of a reformer of others rather than of himself. Thoreau can be astute in his social criticism, as he is in the passage just quoted or when he attacks the factory system of production for having as its object not necessary and useful goods for men but profits for corporations. But it was not as a reformer of systems or of other men that Thoreau wished to live; and, as can be seen from his statements about philanthropy and abolition in the first chapter, he thought that the only reform that was both honorable and possible was self-reform. Whatever influence he might have on other men would be the result of the example and not the form of his self-reform. "I never dreamed of any enormity greater than I have committed. I never knew, and never shall know, a worse man than myself." The man's honesty is breathtaking. Henry David Thoreau was problem enough for him to solve. Yet his tone in the first chapter suggests that when he went to Walden he was only within shouting distance of the mode of life he valued most highly.

Mid-way through the book, in "The Village," Thoreau provides further suggestion of a deep inner uneasiness which has yet to be assuaged. He writes that walking in the village seemed to him like running a gauntlet and that at such times the woods afforded him snug haven. By the time he reaches the concluding chapter, however, he has grown significantly. Not that he is unrecognizable. He still confronts us as a moral teacher who exhorts us to live well. What has changed is his attitude. He encourages rather than scolds; he is assertive but not biting. He is, above all, magisterially confident for himself and presumably for all who have attended to him. He is not sentimentally optimistic, for he has directed his eye inward and he remembers what he has seen. Instead he is stubbornly and stoically hopeful: "However mean your life is, meet it and live it; . . . Love your life, poor as it is." Though he remains at odds with the habitual and wrong attitudes and

institutions of men, he is not nearly as prickly as he has been. He seems more aware of the humanity of his listeners than formerly and no longer to be alone in the universe of men; he writes as if he can assume agreement or sympathy in at least some of his readers. And it is these men of kindred spirit—his sympathetic readers—whom he invites to the most perilous task of all, the exploration of their own souls: "Herein are demanded the eye and the nerve. Only the defeated and deserters go to wars, cowards that run away and enlist."

Having begun by lecturing somewhat shrilly and telling of his move away from his townsmen to care for his embattled soul, Thoreau ends his book by returning to town and by reaching out, in his own way, to his neighbors. A wiser, stronger, and shrewder man than he had been, he is now more at peace with himself because more in tune with his aspirations and, therefore, more amiably disposed toward the men and women with whom he will be living again. Now at last he can brag for mankind "as lustily as chanticleer in the morning." The final words of *Walden* glisten with hope and possibility, with courage, and with implied will: "[S]uch is the character of that morrow which mere lapse of time can never make to dawn. The light which puts out our eyes is darkness to us. Only that day dawns to which we are awake. There is more day to dawn. The sun is but a morning star."

Source: Paul Schwaber, "Thoreau's Development in *Walden,*" in *Criticism,* Vol. V, No. 1, Winter 1963, pp. 64–70.

Sources

Bagnall, Nicholas, Review of *Walden,* in *New Statesman,* December 5, 1997, p. 57.

"New Publications," in *Boston Daily Journal,* August 10, 1854, p. 1.

"New Publications," in *Salem Register,* August 10, 1854, p. 2.

Trent, W. P., J. Erskine, S. P. Sherman, and C. Van Doren, eds., "Thoreau, Walden," in *The Cambridge History of English and American Literature in 18 Volumes,* Vol. 16, Oxford University Press, 1907–21.

"Walden; or, Life in the Woods," in *Lowell Journal and Courier,* August 10, 1854, p. 2.

White, E. B., "A Slight Sound at Evening," in *The Points of My Compass,* HarperCollins Publishers, Inc., 1962.

Further Reading

Myerson, Joel, *The Cambridge Companion to Henry David Thoreau,* Cambridge University Press, 1995.

In addition to essays covering all of Thoreau's major works, this volume also includes essays discussing the author's friendship with Ralph Waldo Emerson, his changing reputation over the years, and other topics.

Richardson, Robert D., Jr., *Henry Thoreau: A Life of the Mind,* University of California Press, 1986.

This well-reviewed and highly regarded biography includes discussions of *Walden* and Thoreau's other major works.

Smith, David Clyde, *The Transcendental Saunterer: Thoreau and the Search for Self,* Frederic C. Beil, Inc., 1997.

Smith, a Thoreau scholar, focuses on Thoreau's walking—it is said that he spent more time walking than doing anything else—and how it influenced his life, his writing, and his philosophy.

Versluis, Arthur, *American Transcendentalism and Asian Religions,* Oxford University Press on Demand, 1997.

Part of the Oxford Press Religion in America series, this book covers the beginning of Transcendentalist Orientalism in Europe and the complete history of American Transcendentalism to the twentieth century, with a focus on how Asian religions and cultures have influenced transcendentalism in the West.

Glossary of Literary Terms

A

Abstract: Used as a noun, the term refers to a short summary or outline of a longer work. As an adjective applied to writing or literary works, abstract refers to words or phrases that name things not knowable through the five senses. Examples of abstracts include the *Cliffs Notes* summaries of major literary works. Examples of abstract terms or concepts include "idea," "guilt" "honesty," and "loyalty."

Absurd, Theater of the: See *Theater of the Absurd*

Absurdism: See *Theater of the Absurd*

Act: A major section of a play. Acts are divided into varying numbers of shorter scenes. From ancient times to the nineteenth century plays were generally constructed of five acts, but modern works typically consist of one, two, or three acts. Examples of five-act plays include the works of Sophocles and Shakespeare, while the plays of Arthur Miller commonly have a three-act structure.

Acto: A one-act Chicano theater piece developed out of collective improvisation. *Actos* were performed by members of Luis Valdez's Teatro Campesino in California during the mid-1960s.

Aestheticism: A literary and artistic movement of the nineteenth century. Followers of the movement believed that art should not be mixed with social, political, or moral teaching. The statement "art for art's sake" is a good summary of aestheticism. The movement had its roots in France, but it gained widespread importance in England in the last half of the nineteenth century, where it helped change the Victorian practice of including moral lessons in literature. Oscar Wilde is one of the best-known "aesthetes" of the late nineteenth century.

Age of Johnson: The period in English literature between 1750 and 1798, named after the most prominent literary figure of the age, Samuel Johnson. Works written during this time are noted for their emphasis on "sensibility," or emotional quality. These works formed a transition between the rational works of the Age of Reason, or Neoclassical period, and the emphasis on individual feelings and responses of the Romantic period. Significant writers during the Age of Johnson included the novelists Ann Radcliffe and Henry Mackenzie, dramatists Richard Sheridan and Oliver Goldsmith, and poets William Collins and Thomas Gray. Also known as Age of Sensibility

Age of Reason: See *Neoclassicism*

Age of Sensibility: See *Age of Johnson*

Alexandrine Meter: See *Meter*

Allegory: A narrative technique in which characters representing things or abstract ideas are used to convey a message or teach a lesson. Allegory is typically used to teach moral, ethical, or religious lessons but is sometimes used for satiric or political purposes. Examples of allegorical works include Edmund Spenser's *The Faerie Queene* and John Bunyan's *The Pilgrim's Progress.*

Allusion: A reference to a familiar literary or historical person or event, used to make an idea more easily understood. For example, describing someone as a ''Romeo'' makes an allusion to William Shakespeare's famous young lover in *Romeo and Juliet.*

Amerind Literature: The writing and oral traditions of Native Americans. Native American literature was originally passed on by word of mouth, so it consisted largely of stories and events that were easily memorized. Amerind prose is often rhythmic like poetry because it was recited to the beat of a ceremonial drum. Examples of Amerind literature include the autobiographical *Black Elk Speaks,* the works of N. Scott Momaday, James Welch, and Craig Lee Strete, and the poetry of Luci Tapahonso.

Analogy: A comparison of two things made to explain something unfamiliar through its similarities to something familiar, or to prove one point based on the acceptedness of another. Similes and metaphors are types of analogies. Analogies often take the form of an extended simile, as in William Blake's aphorism: ''As the caterpillar chooses the fairest leaves to lay her eggs on, so the priest lays his curse on the fairest joys.''

Angry Young Men: A group of British writers of the 1950s whose work expressed bitterness and disillusionment with society. Common to their work is an anti-hero who rebels against a corrupt social order and strives for personal integrity. The term has been used to describe Kingsley Amis, John Osborne, Colin Wilson, John Wain, and others.

Antagonist: The major character in a narrative or drama who works against the hero or protagonist. An example of an evil antagonist is Richard Lovelace in Samuel Richardson's *Clarissa,* while a virtuous antagonist is Macduff in William Shakespeare's *Macbeth.*

Anthropomorphism: The presentation of animals or objects in human shape or with human characteristics. The term is derived from the Greek word for ''human form.'' The fables of Aesop, the animated films of Walt Disney, and Richard Adams's *Watership Down* feature anthropomorphic characters.

Anti-hero: A central character in a work of literature who lacks traditional heroic qualities such as courage, physical prowess, and fortitude. Anti-heros typically distrust conventional values and are unable to commit themselves to any ideals. They generally feel helpless in a world over which they have no control. Anti-heroes usually accept, and often celebrate, their positions as social outcasts. A well-known anti-hero is Yossarian in Joseph Heller's novel *Catch-22.*

Antimasque: See *Masque*

Antithesis: The antithesis of something is its direct opposite. In literature, the use of antithesis as a figure of speech results in two statements that show a contrast through the balancing of two opposite ideas. Technically, it is the second portion of the statement that is defined as the ''antithesis''; the first portion is the ''thesis.'' An example of antithesis is found in the following portion of Abraham Lincoln's ''Gettysburg Address''; notice the opposition between the verbs ''remember'' and ''forget'' and the phrases ''what we say'' and ''what they did'': ''The world will little note nor long remember what we say here, but it can never forget what they did here.''

Apocrypha: Writings tentatively attributed to an author but not proven or universally accepted to be their works. The term was originally applied to certain books of the Bible that were not considered inspired and so were not included in the ''sacred canon.'' Geoffrey Chaucer, William Shakespeare, Thomas Kyd, Thomas Middleton, and John Marston all have apocrypha. Apocryphal books of the Bible include the Old Testament's Book of Enoch and New Testament's Gospel of Peter.

Apollonian and Dionysian: The two impulses believed to guide authors of dramatic tragedy. The Apollonian impulse is named after Apollo, the Greek god of light and beauty and the symbol of intellectual order. The Dionysian impulse is named after Dionysus, the Greek god of wine and the symbol of the unrestrained forces of nature. The Apollonian impulse is to create a rational, harmonious world, while the Dionysian is to express the irrational forces of personality. Friedrich Nietzche uses these terms in *The Birth of Tragedy* to designate contrasting elements in Greek tragedy.

Apostrophe: A statement, question, or request addressed to an inanimate object or concept or to a nonexistent or absent person. Requests for inspiration from the muses in poetry are examples of apostrophe, as is Marc Antony's address to Caesar's corpse in William Shakespeare's *Julius Caesar:* ''O, pardon me, thou bleeding piece of earth, That I am meek and gentle with these butchers!. . .Woe to the hand that shed this costly blood!. . .''

Archetype: The word archetype is commonly used to describe an original pattern or model from which all other things of the same kind are made. This term was introduced to literary criticism from the psychology of Carl Jung. It expresses Jung's theory that behind every person's ''unconscious,'' or repressed memories of the past, lies the ''collective unconscious'' of the human race: memories of the countless typical experiences of our ancestors. These memories are said to prompt illogical associations that trigger powerful emotions in the reader. Often, the emotional process is primitive, even primordial. Archetypes are the literary images that grow out of the ''collective unconscious.'' They appear in literature as incidents and plots that repeat basic patterns of life. They may also appear as stereotyped characters. Examples of literary archetypes include themes such as birth and death and characters such as the Earth Mother.

Argument: The argument of a work is the author's subject matter or principal idea. Examples of defined ''argument'' portions of works include John Milton's *Arguments* to each of the books of *Paradise Lost* and the ''Argument'' to Robert Herrick's *Hesperides.*

Aristotelian Criticism: Specifically, the method of evaluating and analyzing tragedy formulated by the Greek philosopher Aristotle in his *Poetics.* More generally, the term indicates any form of criticism that follows Aristotle's views. Aristotelian criticism focuses on the form and logical structure of a work, apart from its historical or social context, in contrast to ''Platonic Criticism,'' which stresses the usefulness of art. Adherents of New Criticism including John Crowe Ransom and Cleanth Brooks utilize and value the basic ideas of Aristotelian criticism for textual analysis.

Art for Art's Sake: See *Aestheticism*

Aside: A comment made by a stage performer that is intended to be heard by the audience but supposedly not by other characters. Eugene O'Neill's *Strange Interlude* is an extended use of the aside in modern theater.

Audience: The people for whom a piece of literature is written. Authors usually write with a certain audience in mind, for example, children, members of a religious or ethnic group, or colleagues in a professional field. The term ''audience'' also applies to the people who gather to see or hear any performance, including plays, poetry readings, speeches, and concerts. Jane Austen's parody of the gothic novel, *Northanger Abbey,* was originally intended for (and also pokes fun at) an audience of young and avid female gothic novel readers.

Avant-garde: A French term meaning ''vanguard.'' It is used in literary criticism to describe new writing that rejects traditional approaches to literature in favor of innovations in style or content. Twentieth-century examples of the literary *avant-garde* include the Black Mountain School of poets, the Bloomsbury Group, and the Beat Movement.

B

Ballad: A short poem that tells a simple story and has a repeated refrain. Ballads were originally intended to be sung. Early ballads, known as folk ballads, were passed down through generations, so their authors are often unknown. Later ballads composed by known authors are called literary ballads. An example of an anonymous folk ballad is ''Edward,'' which dates from the Middle Ages. Samuel Taylor Coleridge's ''The Rime of the Ancient Mariner'' and John Keats's ''La Belle Dame sans Merci'' are examples of literary ballads.

Baroque: A term used in literary criticism to describe literature that is complex or ornate in style or diction. Baroque works typically express tension, anxiety, and violent emotion. The term ''Baroque Age'' designates a period in Western European literature beginning in the late sixteenth century and ending about one hundred years later. Works of this period often mirror the qualities of works more generally associated with the label ''baroque'' and sometimes feature elaborate conceits. Examples of Baroque works include John Lyly's *Euphues: The Anatomy of Wit,* Luis de Gongora's *Soledads,* and William Shakespeare's *As You Like It.*

Baroque Age: See *Baroque*

Baroque Period: See *Baroque*

Beat Generation: See *Beat Movement*

Beat Movement: A period featuring a group of American poets and novelists of the 1950s and 1960s—including Jack Kerouac, Allen Ginsberg, Gregory Corso, William S. Burroughs, and Lawrence Ferlinghetti—who rejected established social and literary values. Using such techniques as stream of consciousness writing and jazz-influenced free verse and focusing on unusual or abnormal states of mind—generated by religious ecstasy or the use of drugs—the Beat writers aimed to create works that were unconventional in both form and subject matter. Kerouac's *On the Road* is perhaps the best-known example of a Beat Generation novel, and Ginsberg's *Howl* is a famous collection of Beat poetry.

Black Aesthetic Movement: A period of artistic and literary development among African Americans in the 1960s and early 1970s. This was the first major African-American artistic movement since the Harlem Renaissance and was closely paralleled by the civil rights and black power movements. The black aesthetic writers attempted to produce works of art that would be meaningful to the black masses. Key figures in black aesthetics included one of its founders, poet and playwright Amiri Baraka, formerly known as LeRoi Jones; poet and essayist Haki R. Madhubuti, formerly Don L. Lee; poet and playwright Sonia Sanchez; and dramatist Ed Bullins. Works representative of the Black Aesthetic Movement include Amiri Baraka's play *Dutchman*, a 1964 Obie award-winner; *Black Fire: An Anthology of Afro-American Writing*, edited by Baraka and playwright Larry Neal and published in 1968; and Sonia Sanchez's poetry collection *We a BaddDDD People*, published in 1970. Also known as Black Arts Movement.

Black Arts Movement: See *Black Aesthetic Movement*

Black Comedy: See *Black Humor*

Black Humor: Writing that places grotesque elements side by side with humorous ones in an attempt to shock the reader, forcing him or her to laugh at the horrifying reality of a disordered world. Joseph Heller's novel *Catch-22* is considered a superb example of the use of black humor. Other well-known authors who use black humor include Kurt Vonnegut, Edward Albee, Eugene Ionesco, and Harold Pinter. Also known as Black Comedy.

Blank Verse: Loosely, any unrhymed poetry, but more generally, unrhymed iambic pentameter verse (composed of lines of five two-syllable feet with the first syllable accented, the second unaccented). Blank verse has been used by poets since the Renaissance for its flexibility and its graceful, dignified tone. John Milton's *Paradise Lost* is in blank verse, as are most of William Shakespeare's plays.

Bloomsbury Group: A group of English writers, artists, and intellectuals who held informal artistic and philosophical discussions in Bloomsbury, a district of London, from around 1907 to the early 1930s. The Bloomsbury Group held no uniform philosophical beliefs but did commonly express an aversion to moral prudery and a desire for greater social tolerance. At various times the circle included Virginia Woolf, E. M. Forster, Clive Bell, Lytton Strachey, and John Maynard Keynes.

Bon Mot: A French term meaning "good word." A *bon mot* is a witty remark or clever observation. Charles Lamb and Oscar Wilde are celebrated for their witty *bon mots*. Two examples by Oscar Wilde stand out: (1) "All women become their mothers. That is their tragedy. No man does. That's his." (2) "A man cannot be too careful in the choice of his enemies."

Breath Verse: See *Projective Verse*

Burlesque: Any literary work that uses exaggeration to make its subject appear ridiculous, either by treating a trivial subject with profound seriousness or by treating a dignified subject frivolously. The word "burlesque" may also be used as an adjective, as in "burlesque show," to mean "striptease act." Examples of literary burlesque include the comedies of Aristophanes, Miguel de Cervantes's *Don Quixote,*, Samuel Butler's poem "Hudibras," and John Gay's play *The Beggar's Opera*.

C

Cadence: The natural rhythm of language caused by the alternation of accented and unaccented syllables. Much modern poetry—notably free verse—deliberately manipulates cadence to create complex rhythmic effects. James Macpherson's "Ossian poems" are richly cadenced, as is the poetry of the Symbolists, Walt Whitman, and Amy Lowell.

Caesura: A pause in a line of poetry, usually occurring near the middle. It typically corresponds to a break in the natural rhythm or sense of the line but is sometimes shifted to create special meanings or rhythmic effects. The opening line of Edgar Allan Poe's "The Raven" contains a caesura following "dreary": "Once upon a midnight dreary, while I pondered weak and weary. . . . "

Canzone: A short Italian or Provencal lyric poem, commonly about love and often set to music. The *canzone* has no set form but typically contains five or six stanzas made up of seven to twenty lines of eleven syllables each. A shorter, five- to ten-line "envoy," or concluding stanza, completes the poem.

Masters of the *canzone* form include Petrarch, Dante Alighieri, Torquato Tasso, and Guido Cavalcanti.

Carpe Diem: A Latin term meaning "seize the day." This is a traditional theme of poetry, especially lyrics. A *carpe diem* poem advises the reader or the person it addresses to live for today and enjoy the pleasures of the moment. Two celebrated *carpe diem* poems are Andrew Marvell's "To His Coy Mistress" and Robert Herrick's poem beginning "Gather ye rosebuds while ye may. . . ."

Catharsis: The release or purging of unwanted emotions— specifically fear and pity—brought about by exposure to art. The term was first used by the Greek philosopher Aristotle in his *Poetics* to refer to the desired effect of tragedy on spectators. A famous example of catharsis is realized in Sophocles' *Oedipus Rex,* when Oedipus discovers that his wife, Jacosta, is his own mother and that the stranger he killed on the road was his own father.

Celtic Renaissance: A period of Irish literary and cultural history at the end of the nineteenth century. Followers of the movement aimed to create a romantic vision of Celtic myth and legend. The most significant works of the Celtic Renaissance typically present a dreamy, unreal world, usually in reaction against the reality of contemporary problems. William Butler Yeats's *The Wanderings of Oisin* is among the most significant works of the Celtic Renaissance. Also known as Celtic Twilight.

Celtic Twilight: See *Celtic Renaissance*

Character: Broadly speaking, a person in a literary work. The actions of characters are what constitute the plot of a story, novel, or poem. There are numerous types of characters, ranging from simple, stereotypical figures to intricate, multifaceted ones. In the techniques of anthropomorphism and personification, animals—and even places or things—can assume aspects of character. "Characterization" is the process by which an author creates vivid, believable characters in a work of art. This may be done in a variety of ways, including (1) direct description of the character by the narrator; (2) the direct presentation of the speech, thoughts, or actions of the character; and (3) the responses of other characters to the character. The term "character" also refers to a form originated by the ancient Greek writer Theophrastus that later became popular in the seventeenth and eighteenth centuries. It is a short essay or sketch of a person who prominently displays a specific attribute or quality, such as miserliness or ambition. Notable characters in lit-

erature include Oedipus Rex, Don Quixote de la Mancha, Macbeth, Candide, Hester Prynne, Ebenezer Scrooge, Huckleberry Finn, Jay Gatsby, Scarlett O'Hara, James Bond, and Kunta Kinte.

Characterization: See *Character*

Chorus: In ancient Greek drama, a group of actors who commented on and interpreted the unfolding action on the stage. Initially the chorus was a major component of the presentation, but over time it became less significant, with its numbers reduced and its role eventually limited to commentary between acts. By the sixteenth century the chorus—if employed at all—was typically a single person who provided a prologue and an epilogue and occasionally appeared between acts to introduce or underscore an important event. The chorus in William Shakespeare's *Henry V* functions in this way. Modern dramas rarely feature a chorus, but T. S. Eliot's *Murder in the Cathedral* and Arthur Miller's *A View from the Bridge* are notable exceptions. The Stage Manager in Thornton Wilder's *Our Town* performs a role similar to that of the chorus.

Chronicle: A record of events presented in chronological order. Although the scope and level of detail provided varies greatly among the chronicles surviving from ancient times, some, such as the *Anglo-Saxon Chronicle,* feature vivid descriptions and a lively recounting of events. During the Elizabethan Age, many dramas— appropriately called "chronicle plays"—were based on material from chronicles. Many of William Shakespeare's dramas of English history as well as Christopher Marlowe's *Edward II* are based in part on Raphael Holinshead's *Chronicles of England, Scotland, and Ireland.*

Classical: In its strictest definition in literary criticism, classicism refers to works of ancient Greek or Roman literature. The term may also be used to describe a literary work of recognized importance (a "classic") from any time period or literature that exhibits the traits of classicism. Classical authors from ancient Greek and Roman times include Juvenal and Homer. Examples of later works and authors now described as classical include French literature of the seventeenth century, Western novels of the nineteenth century, and American fiction of the mid-nineteenth century such as that written by James Fenimore Cooper and Mark Twain.

Classicism: A term used in literary criticism to describe critical doctrines that have their roots in ancient Greek and Roman literature, philosophy, and art. Works associated with classicism typically exhibit restraint on the part of the author, unity of design and purpose, clarity, simplicity, logical organization, and respect for tradition. Examples of literary classicism include Cicero's prose, the dramas of Pierre Corneille and Jean Racine, the poetry of John Dryden and Alexander Pope, and the writings of J. W. von Goethe, G. E. Lessing, and T. S. Eliot.

Climax: The turning point in a narrative, the moment when the conflict is at its most intense. Typically, the structure of stories, novels, and plays is one of rising action, in which tension builds to the climax, followed by falling action, in which tension lessens as the story moves to its conclusion. The climax in James Fenimore Cooper's *The Last of the Mohicans* occurs when Magua and his captive Cora are pursued to the edge of a cliff by Uncas. Magua kills Uncas but is subsequently killed by Hawkeye.

Colloquialism: A word, phrase, or form of pronunciation that is acceptable in casual conversation but not in formal, written communication. It is considered more acceptable than slang. An example of colloquialism can be found in Rudyard Kipling's *Barrack-room Ballads:* When 'Omer smote 'is bloomin' lyre He'd 'eard men sing by land and sea; An' what he thought 'e might require 'E went an' took—the same as me!

Comedy: One of two major types of drama, the other being tragedy. Its aim is to amuse, and it typically ends happily. Comedy assumes many forms, such as farce and burlesque, and uses a variety of techniques, from parody to satire. In a restricted sense the term comedy refers only to dramatic presentations, but in general usage it is commonly applied to nondramatic works as well. Examples of comedies range from the plays of Aristophanes, Terrence, and Plautus, Dante Alighieri's *The Divine Comedy,* Francois Rabelais's *Pantagruel* and *Gargantua,* and some of Geoffrey Chaucer's tales and William Shakespeare's plays to Noel Coward's play *Private Lives* and James Thurber's short story ''The Secret Life of Walter Mitty.''

Comedy of Manners: A play about the manners and conventions of an aristocratic, highly sophisticated society. The characters are usually types rather than individualized personalities, and plot is less important than atmosphere. Such plays were an important aspect of late seventeenth-century English comedy. The comedy of manners was revived in the eighteenth century by Oliver Goldsmith and Richard Brinsley Sheridan, enjoyed a second revival in the late nineteenth century, and has endured into the twentieth century. Examples of comedies of manners include William Congreve's *The Way of the World* in the late seventeenth century, Oliver Goldsmith's *She Stoops to Conquer* and Richard Brinsley Sheridan's *The School for Scandal* in the eighteenth century, Oscar Wilde's *The Importance of Being Earnest* in the nineteenth century, and W. Somerset Maugham's *The Circle* in the twentieth century.

Comic Relief: The use of humor to lighten the mood of a serious or tragic story, especially in plays. The technique is very common in Elizabethan works, and can be an integral part of the plot or simply a brief event designed to break the tension of the scene. The Gravediggers' scene in William Shakespeare's *Hamlet* is a frequently cited example of comic relief.

Commedia dell'arte: An Italian term meaning ''the comedy of guilds'' or ''the comedy of professional actors.'' This form of dramatic comedy was popular in Italy during the sixteenth century. Actors were assigned stock roles (such as Pulcinella, the stupid servant, or Pantalone, the old merchant) and given a basic plot to follow, but all dialogue was improvised. The roles were rigidly typed and the plots were formulaic, usually revolving around young lovers who thwarted their elders and attained wealth and happiness. A rigid convention of the *commedia dell'arte* is the periodic intrusion of Harlequin, who interrupts the play with low buffoonery. Peppino de Filippo's *Metamorphoses of a Wandering Minstrel* gave modern audiences an idea of what *commedia dell'arte* may have been like. Various scenarios for *commedia dell'arte* were compiled in Petraccone's *La commedia dell'arte, storia, technica, scenari,* published in 1927.

Complaint: A lyric poem, popular in the Renaissance, in which the speaker expresses sorrow about his or her condition. Typically, the speaker's sadness is caused by an unresponsive lover, but some complaints cite other sources of unhappiness, such as poverty or fate. A commonly cited example is ''A Complaint by Night of the Lover Not Beloved'' by Henry Howard, Earl of Surrey. Thomas Sackville's ''Complaint of Henry, Duke of Buckingham'' traces the duke's unhappiness to his ruthless ambition.

Conceit: A clever and fanciful metaphor, usually expressed through elaborate and extended comparison, that presents a striking parallel between two seemingly dissimilar things—for example, elaborately comparing a beautiful woman to an object like a garden or the sun. The conceit was a popular device throughout the Elizabethan Age and Baroque Age and was the principal technique of the seventeenth-century English metaphysical poets. This usage of the word conceit is unrelated to the best-known definition of conceit as an arrogant attitude or behavior. The conceit figures prominently in the works of John Donne, Emily Dickinson, and T. S. Eliot.

Concrete: Concrete is the opposite of abstract, and refers to a thing that actually exists or a description that allows the reader to experience an object or concept with the senses. Henry David Thoreau's *Walden* contains much concrete description of nature and wildlife.

Concrete Poetry: Poetry in which visual elements play a large part in the poetic effect. Punctuation marks, letters, or words are arranged on a page to form a visual design: a cross, for example, or a bumblebee. Max Bill and Eugene Gomringer were among the early practitioners of concrete poetry; Haroldo de Campos and Augusto de Campos are among contemporary authors of concrete poetry.

Confessional Poetry: A form of poetry in which the poet reveals very personal, intimate, sometimes shocking information about himself or herself. Anne Sexton, Sylvia Plath, Robert Lowell, and John Berryman wrote poetry in the confessional vein.

Conflict: The conflict in a work of fiction is the issue to be resolved in the story. It usually occurs between two characters, the protagonist and the antagonist, or between the protagonist and society or the protagonist and himself or herself. Conflict in Theodore Dreiser's novel *Sister Carrie* comes as a result of urban society, while Jack London's short story "To Build a Fire" concerns the protagonist's battle against the cold and himself.

Connotation: The impression that a word gives beyond its defined meaning. Connotations may be universally understood or may be significant only to a certain group. Both "horse" and "steed" denote the same animal, but "steed" has a different connotation, deriving from the chivalrous or romantic narratives in which the word was once often used.

Consonance: Consonance occurs in poetry when words appearing at the ends of two or more verses have similar final consonant sounds but have final vowel sounds that differ, as with "stuff" and "off." Consonance is found in "The curfew tolls the knells of parting day" from Thomas Grey's "An Elegy Written in a Country Church Yard." Also known as Half Rhyme or Slant Rhyme.

Convention: Any widely accepted literary device, style, or form. A soliloquy, in which a character reveals to the audience his or her private thoughts, is an example of a dramatic convention.

Corrido: A Mexican ballad. Examples of *corridos* include "Muerte del afamado Bilito," "La voz de mi conciencia," "Lucio Perez," "La juida," and "Los presos."

Couplet: Two lines of poetry with the same rhyme and meter, often expressing a complete and self-contained thought. The following couplet is from Alexander Pope's "Elegy to the Memory of an Unfortunate Lady": 'Tis Use alone that sanctifies Expense, And Splendour borrows all her rays from Sense.

Criticism: The systematic study and evaluation of literary works, usually based on a specific method or set of principles. An important part of literary studies since ancient times, the practice of criticism has given rise to numerous theories, methods, and "schools," sometimes producing conflicting, even contradictory, interpretations of literature in general as well as of individual works. Even such basic issues as what constitutes a poem or a novel have been the subject of much criticism over the centuries. Seminal texts of literary criticism include Plato's *Republic,* Aristotle's *Poetics,* Sir Philip Sidney's *The Defence of Poesie,* John Dryden's *Of Dramatic Poesie,* and William Wordsworth's "Preface" to the second edition of his *Lyrical Ballads.* Contemporary schools of criticism include deconstruction, feminist, psychoanalytic, poststructuralist, new historicist, postcolonialist, and reader- response.

D

Dactyl: See *Foot*

Dadaism: A protest movement in art and literature founded by Tristan Tzara in 1916. Followers of the movement expressed their outrage at the destruction brought about by World War I by revolting against numerous forms of social convention. The Dadaists presented works marked by calculated madness and flamboyant nonsense. They stressed total freedom of expression, commonly through primitive displays of emotion and illogical, often senseless, poetry. The movement ended shortly after the war, when it was replaced by surrealism. Proponents of Dadaism include Andre Breton, Louis Aragon, Philippe Soupault, and Paul Eluard.

Decadent: See *Decadents*

Decadents: The followers of a nineteenth-century literary movement that had its beginnings in French aestheticism. Decadent literature displays a fascination with perverse and morbid states; a search for novelty and sensation—the "new thrill"; a preoccupation with mysticism; and a belief in the senselessness of human existence. The movement is closely associated with the doctrine Art for Art's Sake. The term "decadence" is sometimes used to denote a decline in the quality of art or literature following a period of greatness. Major French decadents are Charles Baudelaire and Arthur Rimbaud. English decadents include Oscar Wilde, Ernest Dowson, and Frank Harris.

Deconstruction: A method of literary criticism developed by Jacques Derrida and characterized by multiple conflicting interpretations of a given work. Deconstructionists consider the impact of the language of a work and suggest that the true meaning of the work is not necessarily the meaning that the author intended. Jacques Derrida's *De la grammatologie* is the seminal text on deconstructive strategies; among American practitioners of this method of criticism are Paul de Man and J. Hillis Miller.

Deduction: The process of reaching a conclusion through reasoning from general premises to a specific premise. An example of deduction is present in the following syllogism: Premise: All mammals are animals. Premise: All whales are mammals. Conclusion: Therefore, all whales are animals.

Denotation: The definition of a word, apart from the impressions or feelings it creates in the reader. The word "apartheid" denotes a political and economic policy of segregation by race, but its connotations— oppression, slavery, inequality—are numerous.

Denouement: A French word meaning "the unknotting." In literary criticism, it denotes the resolution of conflict in fiction or drama. The *denouement* follows the climax and provides an outcome to the primary plot situation as well as an explanation of secondary plot complications. The *denouement* often involves a character's recognition of his or her state of mind or moral condition. A well-known example of *denouement* is the last scene of the play *As You Like It* by William Shakespeare, in which couples are married, an evildoer repents, the identities of two disguised characters are revealed, and a ruler is restored to power. Also known as Falling Action.

Description: Descriptive writing is intended to allow a reader to picture the scene or setting in which the action of a story takes place. The form this description takes often evokes an intended emotional response—a dark, spooky graveyard will evoke fear, and a peaceful, sunny meadow will evoke calmness. An example of a descriptive story is Edgar Allan Poe's *Landor's Cottage,* which offers a detailed depiction of a New York country estate.

Detective Story: A narrative about the solution of a mystery or the identification of a criminal. The conventions of the detective story include the detective's scrupulous use of logic in solving the mystery; incompetent or ineffectual police; a suspect who appears guilty at first but is later proved innocent; and the detective's friend or confidant— often the narrator—whose slowness in interpreting clues emphasizes by contrast the detective's brilliance. Edgar Allan Poe's "Murders in the Rue Morgue" is commonly regarded as the earliest example of this type of story. With this work, Poe established many of the conventions of the detective story genre, which are still in practice. Other practitioners of this vast and extremely popular genre include Arthur Conan Doyle, Dashiell Hammett, and Agatha Christie.

Deus ex machina: A Latin term meaning "god out of a machine." In Greek drama, a god was often lowered onto the stage by a mechanism of some kind to rescue the hero or untangle the plot. By extension, the term refers to any artificial device or coincidence used to bring about a convenient and simple solution to a plot. This is a common device in melodramas and includes such fortunate circumstances as the sudden receipt of a legacy to save the family farm or a last-minute stay of execution. The *deus ex machina* invariably rewards the virtuous and punishes evildoers. Examples of *deus ex machina* include King Louis XIV in Jean-Baptiste Moliere's *Tartuffe* and Queen Victoria in *The Pirates of Penzance* by William Gilbert and Arthur Sullivan. Bertolt Brecht parodies the abuse of such devices in the conclusion of his *Threepenny Opera.*

Dialogue: In its widest sense, dialogue is simply conversation between people in a literary work; in its most restricted sense, it refers specifically to the speech of characters in a drama. As a specific literary genre, a "dialogue" is a composition in which characters debate an issue or idea. The Greek philosopher Plato frequently expounded his theories in the form of dialogues.

Diction: The selection and arrangement of words in a literary work. Either or both may vary depending on the desired effect. There are four general types of diction: ''formal,'' used in scholarly or lofty writing; ''informal,'' used in relaxed but educated conversation; ''colloquial,'' used in everyday speech; and ''slang,'' containing newly coined words and other terms not accepted in formal usage.

Didactic: A term used to describe works of literature that aim to teach some moral, religious, political, or practical lesson. Although didactic elements are often found in artistically pleasing works, the term ''didactic'' usually refers to literature in which the message is more important than the form. The term may also be used to criticize a work that the critic finds ''overly didactic,'' that is, heavy-handed in its delivery of a lesson. Examples of didactic literature include John Bunyan's *Pilgrim's Progress,* Alexander Pope's *Essay on Criticism,* Jean-Jacques Rousseau's *Emile,* and Elizabeth Inchbald's *Simple Story.*

Dimeter: See *Meter*

Dionysian: See *Apollonian and Dionysian*

Discordia concours: A Latin phrase meaning ''discord in harmony.'' The term was coined by the eighteenth-century English writer Samuel Johnson to describe ''a combination of dissimilar images or discovery of occult resemblances in things apparently unlike.'' Johnson created the expression by reversing a phrase by the Latin poet Horace. The metaphysical poetry of John Donne, Richard Crashaw, Abraham Cowley, George Herbert, and Edward Taylor among others, contains many examples of *discordia concours.* In Donne's ''A Valediction: Forbidding Mourning,'' the poet compares the union of himself with his lover to a draftsman's compass: If they be two, they are two so, As stiff twin compasses are two: Thy soul, the fixed foot, makes no show To move, but doth, if the other do; And though it in the center sit, Yet when the other far doth roam, It leans, and hearkens after it, And grows erect, as that comes home.

Dissonance: A combination of harsh or jarring sounds, especially in poetry. Although such combinations may be accidental, poets sometimes intentionally make them to achieve particular effects. Dissonance is also sometimes used to refer to close but not identical rhymes. When this is the case, the word functions as a synonym for consonance. Robert Browning, Gerard Manley Hopkins, and many other poets have made deliberate use of dissonance.

Doppelganger: A literary technique by which a character is duplicated (usually in the form of an alter ego, though sometimes as a ghostly counterpart) or divided into two distinct, usually opposite personalities. The use of this character device is widespread in nineteenth- and twentieth- century literature, and indicates a growing awareness among authors that the ''self'' is really a composite of many ''selves.'' A well-known story containing a *doppelganger* character is Robert Louis Stevenson's *Dr. Jekyll and Mr. Hyde,* which dramatizes an internal struggle between good and evil. Also known as The Double.

Double Entendre: A corruption of a French phrase meaning ''double meaning.'' The term is used to indicate a word or phrase that is deliberately ambiguous, especially when one of the meanings is risque or improper. An example of a *double entendre* is the Elizabethan usage of the verb ''die,'' which refers both to death and to orgasm.

Double, The: See *Doppelganger*

Draft: Any preliminary version of a written work. An author may write dozens of drafts which are revised to form the final work, or he or she may write only one, with few or no revisions. Dorothy Parker's observation that ''I can't write five words but that I change seven'' humorously indicates the purpose of the draft.

Drama: In its widest sense, a drama is any work designed to be presented by actors on a stage. Similarly, ''drama'' denotes a broad literary genre that includes a variety of forms, from pageant and spectacle to tragedy and comedy, as well as countless types and subtypes. More commonly in modern usage, however, a drama is a work that treats serious subjects and themes but does not aim at the grandeur of tragedy. This use of the term originated with the eighteenth-century French writer Denis Diderot, who used the word *drame* to designate his plays about middle- class life; thus ''drama'' typically features characters of a less exalted stature than those of tragedy. Examples of classical dramas include Menander's comedy *Dyscolus* and Sophocles' tragedy *Oedipus Rex.* Contemporary dramas include Eugene O'Neill's *The Iceman Cometh,* Lillian Hellman's *Little Foxes,* and August Wilson's *Ma Rainey's Black Bottom.*

Dramatic Irony: Occurs when the audience of a play or the reader of a work of literature knows something that a character in the work itself does not know. The irony is in the contrast between the intended meaning of the statements or actions of a character and the additional information understood by the audience. A celebrated example of dramatic irony is in Act V of William Shakespeare's *Romeo and Juliet,* where two young lovers meet their end as a result of a tragic misunderstanding. Here, the audience has full knowledge that Juliet's apparent ''death'' is merely temporary; she will regain her senses when the mysterious ''sleeping potion'' she has taken wears off. But Romeo, mistaking Juliet's drug-induced trance for true death, kills himself in grief. Upon awakening, Juliet discovers Romeo's corpse and, in despair, slays herself.

Dramatic Monologue: See *Monologue*

Dramatic Poetry: Any lyric work that employs elements of drama such as dialogue, conflict, or characterization, but excluding works that are intended for stage presentation. A monologue is a form of dramatic poetry.

Dramatis Personae: The characters in a work of literature, particularly a drama. The list of characters printed before the main text of a play or in the program is the *dramatis personae.*

Dream Allegory: See *Dream Vision*

Dream Vision: A literary convention, chiefly of the Middle Ages. In a dream vision a story is presented as a literal dream of the narrator. This device was commonly used to teach moral and religious lessons. Important works of this type are *The Divine Comedy* by Dante Alighieri, *Piers Plowman* by William Langland, and *The Pilgrim's Progress* by John Bunyan. Also known as Dream Allegory.

Dystopia: An imaginary place in a work of fiction where the characters lead dehumanized, fearful lives. Jack London's *The Iron Heel,* Yevgeny Zamyatin's *My,* Aldous Huxley's *Brave New World,* George Orwell's *Nineteen Eighty-four,* and Margaret Atwood's *Handmaid's Tale* portray versions of dystopia.

E

Eclogue: In classical literature, a poem featuring rural themes and structured as a dialogue among shepherds. Eclogues often took specific poetic forms, such as elegies or love poems. Some were written as the soliloquy of a shepherd. In later centuries, ''eclogue'' came to refer to any poem that was in the pastoral tradition or that had a dialogue or monologue structure. A classical example of an eclogue is Virgil's *Eclogues,* also known as *Bucolics.* Giovanni

Boccaccio, Edmund Spenser, Andrew Marvell, Jonathan Swift, and Louis MacNeice also wrote eclogues.

Edwardian: Describes cultural conventions identified with the period of the reign of Edward VII of England (1901–1910). Writers of the Edwardian Age typically displayed a strong reaction against the propriety and conservatism of the Victorian Age. Their work often exhibits distrust of authority in religion, politics, and art and expresses strong doubts about the soundness of conventional values. Writers of this era include George Bernard Shaw, H. G. Wells, and Joseph Conrad.

Edwardian Age: See *Edwardian*

Electra Complex: A daughter's amorous obsession with her father. The term Electra complex comes from the plays of Euripides and Sophocles entitled *Electra,* in which the character Electra drives her brother Orestes to kill their mother and her lover in revenge for the murder of their father.

Elegy: A lyric poem that laments the death of a person or the eventual death of all people. In a conventional elegy, set in a classical world, the poet and subject are spoken of as shepherds. In modern criticism, the word elegy is often used to refer to a poem that is melancholy or mournfully contemplative. John Milton's ''Lycidas'' and Percy Bysshe Shelley's ''Adonais'' are two examples of this form.

Elizabethan Age: A period of great economic growth, religious controversy, and nationalism closely associated with the reign of Elizabeth I of England (1558–1603). The Elizabethan Age is considered a part of the general renaissance—that is, the flowering of arts and literature—that took place in Europe during the fourteenth through sixteenth centuries. The era is considered the golden age of English literature. The most important dramas in English and a great deal of lyric poetry were produced during this period, and modern English criticism began around this time. The notable authors of the period—Philip Sidney, Edmund Spenser, Christopher Marlowe, William Shakespeare, Ben Jonson, Francis Bacon, and John Donne—are among the best in all of English literature.

Elizabethan Drama: English comic and tragic plays produced during the Renaissance, or more narrowly, those plays written during the last years of and few years after Queen Elizabeth's reign. William Shakespeare is considered an Elizabethan dramatist in the broader sense, although most of his work was produced during the reign of James I. Examples of Elizabethan comedies include John

Lyly's *The Woman in the Moone,* Thomas Dekker's *The Roaring Girl, or, Moll Cut Purse,* and William Shakespeare's *Twelfth Night.* Examples of Elizabethan tragedies include William Shakespeare's *Antony and Cleopatra,* Thomas Kyd's *The Spanish Tragedy,* and John Webster's *The Tragedy of the Duchess of Malfi.*

Empathy: A sense of shared experience, including emotional and physical feelings, with someone or something other than oneself. Empathy is often used to describe the response of a reader to a literary character. An example of an empathic passage is William Shakespeare's description in his narrative poem *Venus and Adonis* of: the snail, whose tender horns being hit, Shrinks backward in his shelly cave with pain. Readers of Gerard Manley Hopkins's *The Windhover* may experience some of the physical sensations evoked in the description of the movement of the falcon.

English Sonnet: See *Sonnet*

Enjambment: The running over of the sense and structure of a line of verse or a couplet into the following verse or couplet. Andrew Marvell's ''To His Coy Mistress'' is structured as a series of enjambments, as in lines 11–12: ''My vegetable love should grow/Vaster than empires and more slow.''

Enlightenment, The: An eighteenth-century philosophical movement. It began in France but had a wide impact throughout Europe and America. Thinkers of the Enlightenment valued reason and believed that both the individual and society could achieve a state of perfection. Corresponding to this essentially humanist vision was a resistance to religious authority. Important figures of the Enlightenment were Denis Diderot and Voltaire in France, Edward Gibbon and David Hume in England, and Thomas Paine and Thomas Jefferson in the United States.

Epic: A long narrative poem about the adventures of a hero of great historic or legendary importance. The setting is vast and the action is often given cosmic significance through the intervention of supernatural forces such as gods, angels, or demons. Epics are typically written in a classical style of grand simplicity with elaborate metaphors and allusions that enhance the symbolic importance of a hero's adventures. Some well-known epics are Homer's *Iliad* and *Odyssey,* Virgil's *Aeneid,* and John Milton's *Paradise Lost.*

Epic Simile: See *Homeric Simile*

Epic Theater: A theory of theatrical presentation developed by twentieth-century German playwright Bertolt Brecht. Brecht created a type of drama that the audience could view with complete detachment. He used what he termed ''alienation effects'' to create an emotional distance between the audience and the action on stage. Among these effects are: short, self-contained scenes that keep the play from building to a cathartic climax; songs that comment on the action; and techniques of acting that prevent the actor from developing an emotional identity with his role. Besides the plays of Bertolt Brecht, other plays that utilize epic theater conventions include those of Georg Buchner, Frank Wedekind, Erwin Piscator, and Leopold Jessner.

Epigram: A saying that makes the speaker's point quickly and concisely. Samuel Taylor Coleridge wrote an epigram that neatly sums up the form: What is an Epigram? A Dwarfish whole, Its body brevity, and wit its soul.

Epilogue: A concluding statement or section of a literary work. In dramas, particularly those of the seventeenth and eighteenth centuries, the epilogue is a closing speech, often in verse, delivered by an actor at the end of a play and spoken directly to the audience. A famous epilogue is Puck's speech at the end of William Shakespeare's *A Midsummer Night's Dream.*

Epiphany: A sudden revelation of truth inspired by a seemingly trivial incident. The term was widely used by James Joyce in his critical writings, and the stories in Joyce's *Dubliners* are commonly called ''epiphanies.''

Episode: An incident that forms part of a story and is significantly related to it. Episodes may be either self-contained narratives or events that depend on a larger context for their sense and importance. Examples of episodes include the founding of Wilmington, Delaware in Charles Reade's *The Disinherited Heir* and the individual events comprising the picaresque novels and medieval romances.

Episodic Plot: See *Plot*

Epitaph: An inscription on a tomb or tombstone, or a verse written on the occasion of a person's death. Epitaphs may be serious or humorous. Dorothy Parker's epitaph reads, ''I told you I was sick.''

Epithalamion: A song or poem written to honor and commemorate a marriage ceremony. Famous examples include Edmund Spenser's

"Epithalamion" and e. e. cummings's "Epithalamion." Also spelled Epithalamium.

Epithalamium: See *Epithalamion*

Epithet: A word or phrase, often disparaging or abusive, that expresses a character trait of someone or something. "The Napoleon of crime" is an epithet applied to Professor Moriarty, arch-rival of Sherlock Holmes in Arthur Conan Doyle's series of detective stories.

Exempla: See *Exemplum*

Exemplum: A tale with a moral message. This form of literary sermonizing flourished during the Middle Ages, when *exempla* appeared in collections known as "example-books." The works of Geoffrey Chaucer are full of *exempla*.

Existentialism: A predominantly twentieth-century philosophy concerned with the nature and perception of human existence. There are two major strains of existentialist thought: atheistic and Christian. Followers of atheistic existentialism believe that the individual is alone in a godless universe and that the basic human condition is one of suffering and loneliness. Nevertheless, because there are no fixed values, individuals can create their own characters—indeed, they can shape themselves—through the exercise of free will. The atheistic strain culminates in and is popularly associated with the works of Jean-Paul Sartre. The Christian existentialists, on the other hand, believe that only in God may people find freedom from life's anguish. The two strains hold certain beliefs in common: that existence cannot be fully understood or described through empirical effort; that anguish is a universal element of life; that individuals must bear responsibility for their actions; and that there is no common standard of behavior or perception for religious and ethical matters. Existentialist thought figures prominently in the works of such authors as Eugene Ionesco, Franz Kafka, Fyodor Dostoyevsky, Simone de Beauvoir, Samuel Beckett, and Albert Camus.

Expatriates: See *Expatriatism*

Expatriatism: The practice of leaving one's country to live for an extended period in another country. Literary expatriates include English poets Percy Bysshe Shelley and John Keats in Italy, Polish novelist Joseph Conrad in England, American writers Richard Wright, James Baldwin, Gertrude Stein, and Ernest Hemingway in France, and Trinidadian author Neil Bissondath in Canada.

Exposition: Writing intended to explain the nature of an idea, thing, or theme. Expository writing is often combined with description, narration, or argument. In dramatic writing, the exposition is the introductory material which presents the characters, setting, and tone of the play. An example of dramatic exposition occurs in many nineteenth-century drawing-room comedies in which the butler and the maid open the play with relevant talk about their master and mistress; in composition, exposition relays factual information, as in encyclopedia entries.

Expressionism: An indistinct literary term, originally used to describe an early twentieth-century school of German painting. The term applies to almost any mode of unconventional, highly subjective writing that distorts reality in some way. Advocates of Expressionism include dramatists George Kaiser, Ernst Toller, Luigi Pirandello, Federico Garcia Lorca, Eugene O'Neill, and Elmer Rice; poets George Heym, Ernst Stadler, August Stramm, Gottfried Benn, and Georg Trakl; and novelists Franz Kafka and James Joyce.

Extended Monologue: See *Monologue*

F

Fable: A prose or verse narrative intended to convey a moral. Animals or inanimate objects with human characteristics often serve as characters in fables. A famous fable is Aesop's "The Tortoise and the Hare."

Fairy Tales: Short narratives featuring mythical beings such as fairies, elves, and sprites. These tales originally belonged to the folklore of a particular nation or region, such as those collected in Germany by Jacob and Wilhelm Grimm. Two other celebrated writers of fairy tales are Hans Christian Andersen and Rudyard Kipling.

Falling Action: See *Denouement*

Fantasy: A literary form related to mythology and folklore. Fantasy literature is typically set in nonexistent realms and features supernatural beings. Notable examples of fantasy literature are *The Lord of the Rings* by J. R. R. Tolkien and the Gormenghast trilogy by Mervyn Peake.

Farce: A type of comedy characterized by broad humor, outlandish incidents, and often vulgar subject matter. Much of the "comedy" in film and television could more accurately be described as farce.

Feet: See *Foot*

Feminine Rhyme: See *Rhyme*

Femme fatale: A French phrase with the literal translation ''fatal woman.'' A *femme fatale* is a sensuous, alluring woman who often leads men into danger or trouble. A classic example of the *femme fatale* is the nameless character in Billy Wilder's *The Seven Year Itch,* portrayed by Marilyn Monroe in the film adaptation.

Fiction: Any story that is the product of imagination rather than a documentation of fact. characters and events in such narratives may be based in real life but their ultimate form and configuration is a creation of the author. Geoffrey Chaucer's *The Canterbury Tales,* Laurence Sterne's *Tristram Shandy,* and Margaret Mitchell's *Gone with the Wind* are examples of fiction.

Figurative Language: A technique in writing in which the author temporarily interrupts the order, construction, or meaning of the writing for a particular effect. This interruption takes the form of one or more figures of speech such as hyperbole, irony, or simile. Figurative language is the opposite of literal language, in which every word is truthful, accurate, and free of exaggeration or embellishment. Examples of figurative language are tropes such as metaphor and rhetorical figures such as apostrophe.

Figures of Speech: Writing that differs from customary conventions for construction, meaning, order, or significance for the purpose of a special meaning or effect. There are two major types of figures of speech: rhetorical figures, which do not make changes in the meaning of the words, and tropes, which do. Types of figures of speech include simile, hyperbole, alliteration, and pun, among many others.

Fin de siecle: A French term meaning ''end of the century.'' The term is used to denote the last decade of the nineteenth century, a transition period when writers and other artists abandoned old conventions and looked for new techniques and objectives. Two writers commonly associated with the *fin de siecle* mindset are Oscar Wilde and George Bernard Shaw.

First Person: See *Point of View*

Flashback: A device used in literature to present action that occurred before the beginning of the story. Flashbacks are often introduced as the dreams or recollections of one or more characters. Flashback techniques are often used in films, where they are typically set off by a gradual changing of one picture to another.

Foil: A character in a work of literature whose physical or psychological qualities contrast strongly with, and therefore highlight, the corresponding qualities of another character. In his Sherlock Holmes stories, Arthur Conan Doyle portrayed Dr. Watson as a man of normal habits and intelligence, making him a foil for the eccentric and wonderfully perceptive Sherlock Holmes.

Folk Ballad: See *Ballad*

Folklore: Traditions and myths preserved in a culture or group of people. Typically, these are passed on by word of mouth in various forms—such as legends, songs, and proverbs— or preserved in customs and ceremonies. This term was first used by W. J. Thoms in 1846. Sir James Frazer's *The Golden Bough* is the record of English folklore; myths about the frontier and the Old South exemplify American folklore.

Folktale: A story originating in oral tradition. Folktales fall into a variety of categories, including legends, ghost stories, fairy tales, fables, and anecdotes based on historical figures and events. Examples of folktales include Giambattista Basile's *The Pentamerone,* which contains the tales of Puss in Boots, Rapunzel, Cinderella, and Beauty and the Beast, and Joel Chandler Harris's Uncle Remus stories, which represent transplanted African folktales and American tales about the characters Mike Fink, Johnny Appleseed, Paul Bunyan, and Pecos Bill.

Foot: The smallest unit of rhythm in a line of poetry. In English-language poetry, a foot is typically one accented syllable combined with one or two unaccented syllables. There are many different types of feet. When the accent is on the second syllable of a two syllable word (con- *tort*), the foot is an ''iamb''; the reverse accentual pattern (*tor* -ture) is a ''trochee.'' Other feet that commonly occur in poetry in English are ''anapest'', two unaccented syllables followed by an accented syllable as in inter-*cept*, and ''dactyl'', an accented syllable followed by two unaccented syllables as in *su*-i- cide.

Foreshadowing: A device used in literature to create expectation or to set up an explanation of later developments. In Charles Dickens's *Great Expectations,* the graveyard encounter at the beginning of the novel between Pip and the escaped convict Magwitch foreshadows the baleful atmosphere and events that comprise much of the narrative.

Form: The pattern or construction of a work which identifies its genre and distinguishes it from other genres. Examples of forms include the different genres, such as the lyric form or the short story form, and various patterns for poetry, such as the verse form or the stanza form.

Formalism: In literary criticism, the belief that literature should follow prescribed rules of construction, such as those that govern the sonnet form. Examples of formalism are found in the work of the New Critics and structuralists.

Fourteener Meter: See *Meter*

Free Verse: Poetry that lacks regular metrical and rhyme patterns but that tries to capture the cadences of everyday speech. The form allows a poet to exploit a variety of rhythmical effects within a single poem. Free-verse techniques have been widely used in the twentieth century by such writers as Ezra Pound, T. S. Eliot, Carl Sandburg, and William Carlos Williams. Also known as *Vers libre*.

Futurism: A flamboyant literary and artistic movement that developed in France, Italy, and Russia from 1908 through the 1920s. Futurist theater and poetry abandoned traditional literary forms. In their place, followers of the movement attempted to achieve total freedom of expression through bizarre imagery and deformed or newly invented words. The Futurists were self-consciously modern artists who attempted to incorporate the appearances and sounds of modern life into their work. Futurist writers include Filippo Tommaso Marinetti, Wyndham Lewis, Guillaume Apollinaire, Velimir Khlebnikov, and Vladimir Mayakovsky.

G

Genre: A category of literary work. In critical theory, genre may refer to both the content of a given work—tragedy, comedy, pastoral—and to its form, such as poetry, novel, or drama. This term also refers to types of popular literature, as in the genres of science fiction or the detective story.

Genteel Tradition: A term coined by critic George Santayana to describe the literary practice of certain late nineteenth- century American writers, especially New Englanders. Followers of the Genteel Tradition emphasized conventionality in social, religious, moral, and literary standards. Some of the best-known writers of the Genteel Tradition are R. H. Stoddard and Bayard Taylor.

Gilded Age: A period in American history during the 1870s characterized by political corruption and materialism. A number of important novels of social and political criticism were written during this time. Examples of Gilded Age literature include Henry Adams's *Democracy* and F. Marion Crawford's *An American Politician.*

Gothic: See *Gothicism*

Gothicism: In literary criticism, works characterized by a taste for the medieval or morbidly attractive. A gothic novel prominently features elements of horror, the supernatural, gloom, and violence: clanking chains, terror, charnel houses, ghosts, medieval castles, and mysteriously slamming doors. The term ''gothic novel'' is also applied to novels that lack elements of the traditional Gothic setting but that create a similar atmosphere of terror or dread. Mary Shelley's *Frankenstein* is perhaps the best-known English work of this kind.

Gothic Novel: See *Gothicism*

Great Chain of Being: The belief that all things and creatures in nature are organized in a hierarchy from inanimate objects at the bottom to God at the top. This system of belief was popular in the seventeenth and eighteenth centuries. A summary of the concept of the great chain of being can be found in the first epistle of Alexander Pope's *An Essay on Man,* and more recently in Arthur O. Lovejoy's *The Great Chain of Being: A Study of the History of an Idea.*

Grotesque: In literary criticism, the subject matter of a work or a style of expression characterized by exaggeration, deformity, freakishness, and disorder. The grotesque often includes an element of comic absurdity. Early examples of literary grotesque include Francois Rabelais's *Pantagruel* and *Gargantua* and Thomas Nashe's *The Unfortunate Traveller,* while more recent examples can be found in the works of Edgar Allan Poe, Evelyn Waugh, Eudora Welty, Flannery O'Connor, Eugene Ionesco, Gunter Grass, Thomas Mann, Mervyn Peake, and Joseph Heller, among many others.

H

Haiku: The shortest form of Japanese poetry, constructed in three lines of five, seven, and five syllables respectively. The message of a *haiku* poem usually centers on some aspect of spirituality and provokes an emotional response in the reader. Early masters of *haiku* include Basho, Buson, Kobayashi

Issa, and Masaoka Shiki. English writers of *haiku* include the Imagists, notably Ezra Pound, H. D., Amy Lowell, Carl Sandburg, and William Carlos Williams. Also known as *Hokku.*

Half Rhyme: See *Consonance*

Hamartia: In tragedy, the event or act that leads to the hero's or heroine's downfall. This term is often incorrectly used as a synonym for tragic flaw. In Richard Wright's *Native Son,* the act that seals Bigger Thomas's fate is his first impulsive murder.

Harlem Renaissance: The Harlem Renaissance of the 1920s is generally considered the first significant movement of black writers and artists in the United States. During this period, new and established black writers published more fiction and poetry than ever before, the first influential black literary journals were established, and black authors and artists received their first widespread recognition and serious critical appraisal. Among the major writers associated with this period are Claude McKay, Jean Toomer, Countee Cullen, Langston Hughes, Arna Bontemps, Nella Larsen, and Zora Neale Hurston. Works representative of the Harlem Renaissance include Arna Bontemps's poems ''The Return'' and ''Golgotha Is a Mountain,'' Claude McKay's novel *Home to Harlem,* Nella Larsen's novel *Passing,* Langston Hughes's poem ''The Negro Speaks of Rivers,'' and the journals *Crisis* and *Opportunity,* both founded during this period. Also known as Negro Renaissance and New Negro Movement.

Harlequin: A stock character of the *commedia dell'arte* who occasionally interrupted the action with silly antics. Harlequin first appeared on the English stage in John Day's *The Travailes of the Three English Brothers.* The San Francisco Mime Troupe is one of the few modern groups to adapt Harlequin to the needs of contemporary satire.

Hellenism: Imitation of ancient Greek thought or styles. Also, an approach to life that focuses on the growth and development of the intellect. ''Hellenism'' is sometimes used to refer to the belief that reason can be applied to examine all human experience. A cogent discussion of Hellenism can be found in Matthew Arnold's *Culture and Anarchy.*

Heptameter: See *Meter*

Hero/Heroine: The principal sympathetic character (male or female) in a literary work. Heroes and heroines typically exhibit admirable traits: idealism, courage, and integrity, for example. Famous heroes and heroines include Pip in Charles Dickens's *Great Expectations,* the anonymous narrator in Ralph Ellison's *Invisible Man,* and Sethe in Toni Morrison's *Beloved.*

Heroic Couplet: A rhyming couplet written in iambic pentameter (a verse with five iambic feet). The following lines by Alexander Pope are an example: ''Truth guards the Poet, sanctifies the line,/ And makes Immortal, Verse as mean as mine.''

Heroic Line: The meter and length of a line of verse in epic or heroic poetry. This varies by language and time period. For example, in English poetry, the heroic line is iambic pentameter (a verse with five iambic feet); in French, the alexandrine (a verse with six iambic feet); in classical literature, dactylic hexameter (a verse with six dactylic feet).

Heroine: See *Hero/Heroine*

Hexameter: See *Meter*

Historical Criticism: The study of a work based on its impact on the world of the time period in which it was written. Examples of postmodern historical criticism can be found in the work of Michel Foucault, Hayden White, Stephen Greenblatt, and Jonathan Goldberg.

Hokku: See *Haiku*

Holocaust: See *Holocaust Literature*

Holocaust Literature: Literature influenced by or written about the Holocaust of World War II. Such literature includes true stories of survival in concentration camps, escape, and life after the war, as well as fictional works and poetry. Representative works of Holocaust literature include Saul Bellow's *Mr. Sammler's Planet,* Anne Frank's *The Diary of a Young Girl,* Jerzy Kosinski's *The Painted Bird,* Arthur Miller's *Incident at Vichy,* Czeslaw Milosz's *Collected Poems,* William Styron's *Sophie's Choice,* and Art Spiegelman's *Maus.*

Homeric Simile: An elaborate, detailed comparison written as a simile many lines in length. An example of an epic simile from John Milton's *Paradise Lost* follows: Angel Forms, who lay entranced Thick as autumnal leaves that strow the brooks In Vallombrosa, where the Etrurian shades High over-arched embower; or scattered sedge Afloat, when with fierce winds Orion armed Hath vexed the Red-Sea coast, whose waves o'erthrew Busiris and his Memphian chivalry, While with perfidious hatred they pursued The sojourners of

Goshen, who beheld From the safe shore their floating carcasses And broken chariot-wheels. Also known as Epic Simile.

Horatian Satire: See *Satire*

Humanism: A philosophy that places faith in the dignity of humankind and rejects the medieval perception of the individual as a weak, fallen creature. "Humanists" typically believe in the perfectibility of human nature and view reason and education as the means to that end. Humanist thought is represented in the works of Marsilio Ficino, Ludovico Castelvetro, Edmund Spenser, John Milton, Dean John Colet, Desiderius Erasmus, John Dryden, Alexander Pope, Matthew Arnold, and Irving Babbitt.

Humors: Mentions of the humors refer to the ancient Greek theory that a person's health and personality were determined by the balance of four basic fluids in the body: blood, phlegm, yellow bile, and black bile. A dominance of any fluid would cause extremes in behavior. An excess of blood created a sanguine person who was joyful, aggressive, and passionate; a phlegmatic person was shy, fearful, and sluggish; too much yellow bile led to a choleric temperament characterized by impatience, anger, bitterness, and stubbornness; and excessive black bile created melancholy, a state of laziness, gluttony, and lack of motivation. Literary treatment of the humors is exemplified by several characters in Ben Jonson's plays *Every Man in His Humour* and *Every Man out of His Humour.* Also spelled Humours.

Humours: See *Humors*

Hyperbole: In literary criticism, deliberate exaggeration used to achieve an effect. In William Shakespeare's *Macbeth,* Lady Macbeth hyperbolizes when she says, "All the perfumes of Arabia could not sweeten this little hand."

I

Iamb: See *Foot*

Idiom: A word construction or verbal expression closely associated with a given language. For example, in colloquial English the construction "how come" can be used instead of "why" to introduce a question. Similarly, "a piece of cake" is sometimes used to describe a task that is easily done.

Image: A concrete representation of an object or sensory experience. Typically, such a representation helps evoke the feelings associated with the object or experience itself. Images are either "literal" or "figurative." Literal images are especially concrete and involve little or no extension of the obvious meaning of the words used to express them. Figurative images do not follow the literal meaning of the words exactly. Images in literature are usually visual, but the term "image" can also refer to the representation of any sensory experience. In his poem "The Shepherd's Hour," Paul Verlaine presents the following image: "The Moon is red through horizon's fog;/ In a dancing mist the hazy meadow sleeps." The first line is broadly literal, while the second line involves turns of meaning associated with dancing and sleeping.

Imagery: The array of images in a literary work. Also, figurative language. William Butler Yeats's "The Second Coming" offers a powerful image of encroaching anarchy: Turning and turning in the widening gyre The falcon cannot hear the falconer; Things fall apart. . . .

Imagism: An English and American poetry movement that flourished between 1908 and 1917. The Imagists used precise, clearly presented images in their works. They also used common, everyday speech and aimed for conciseness, concrete imagery, and the creation of new rhythms. Participants in the Imagist movement included Ezra Pound, H. D. (Hilda Doolittle), and Amy Lowell, among others.

In medias res: A Latin term meaning "in the middle of things." It refers to the technique of beginning a story at its midpoint and then using various flashback devices to reveal previous action. This technique originated in such epics as Virgil's *Aeneid.*

Induction: The process of reaching a conclusion by reasoning from specific premises to form a general premise. Also, an introductory portion of a work of literature, especially a play. Geoffrey Chaucer's "Prologue" to the *Canterbury Tales,* Thomas Sackville's "Induction" to *The Mirror of Magistrates,* and the opening scene in William Shakespeare's *The Taming of the Shrew* are examples of inductions to literary works.

Intentional Fallacy: The belief that judgments of a literary work based solely on an author's stated or implied intentions are false and misleading. Critics who believe in the concept of the intentional fallacy typically argue that the work itself is sufficient matter for interpretation, even though they may concede that an author's statement of purpose can be useful. Analysis of William Wordsworth's *Lyrical Ballads* based on the observations about poetry he makes in his "Preface" to the second edition of that work is an example of the intentional fallacy.

Interior Monologue: A narrative technique in which characters' thoughts are revealed in a way that appears to be uncontrolled by the author. The interior monologue typically aims to reveal the inner self of a character. It portrays emotional experiences as they occur at both a conscious and unconscious level. images are often used to represent sensations or emotions. One of the best-known interior monologues in English is the Molly Bloom section at the close of James Joyce's *Ulysses*. The interior monologue is also common in the works of Virginia Woolf.

Internal Rhyme: Rhyme that occurs within a single line of verse. An example is in the opening line of Edgar Allan Poe's "The Raven": "Once upon a midnight dreary, while I pondered weak and weary." Here, "dreary" and "weary" make an internal rhyme.

Irish Literary Renaissance: A late nineteenth- and early twentieth-century movement in Irish literature. Members of the movement aimed to reduce the influence of British culture in Ireland and create an Irish national literature. William Butler Yeats, George Moore, and Sean O'Casey are three of the best-known figures of the movement.

Irony: In literary criticism, the effect of language in which the intended meaning is the opposite of what is stated. The title of Jonathan Swift's "A Modest Proposal" is ironic because what Swift proposes in this essay is cannibalism—hardly "modest."

Italian Sonnet: See *Sonnet*

J

Jacobean Age: The period of the reign of James I of England (1603–1625). The early literature of this period reflected the worldview of the Elizabethan Age, but a darker, more cynical attitude steadily grew in the art and literature of the Jacobean Age. This was an important time for English drama and poetry. Milestones include William Shakespeare's tragedies, tragi-comedies, and sonnets; Ben Jonson's various dramas; and John Donne's metaphysical poetry.

Jargon: Language that is used or understood only by a select group of people. Jargon may refer to terminology used in a certain profession, such as

computer jargon, or it may refer to any nonsensical language that is not understood by most people. Literary examples of jargon are Francois Villon's *Ballades en jargon,* which is composed in the secret language of the *coquillards,* and Anthony Burgess's *A Clockwork Orange,* narrated in the fictional characters' language of "Nadsat."

Juvenalian Satire: See *Satire*

K

Knickerbocker Group: A somewhat indistinct group of New York writers of the first half of the nineteenth century. Members of the group were linked only by location and a common theme: New York life. Two famous members of the Knickerbocker Group were Washington Irving and William Cullen Bryant. The group's name derives from Irving's *Knickerbocker's History of New York.*

L

Lais: See *Lay*

Lay: A song or simple narrative poem. The form originated in medieval France. Early French *lais* were often based on the Celtic legends and other tales sung by Breton minstrels—thus the name of the "Breton lay." In fourteenth-century England, the term "lay" was used to describe short narratives written in imitation of the Breton lays. The most notable of these is Geoffrey Chaucer's "The Minstrel's Tale."

Leitmotiv: See *Motif*

Literal Language: An author uses literal language when he or she writes without exaggerating or embellishing the subject matter and without any tools of figurative language. To say "He ran very quickly down the street" is to use literal language, whereas to say "He ran like a hare down the street" would be using figurative language.

Literary Ballad: See *Ballad*

Literature: Literature is broadly defined as any written or spoken material, but the term most often refers to creative works. Literature includes poetry, drama, fiction, and many kinds of nonfiction writing, as well as oral, dramatic, and broadcast compositions not necessarily preserved in a written format, such as films and television programs.

Lost Generation: A term first used by Gertrude Stein to describe the post-World War I generation of

American writers: men and women haunted by a sense of betrayal and emptiness brought about by the destructiveness of the war. The term is commonly applied to Hart Crane, Ernest Hemingway, F. Scott Fitzgerald, and others.

Lyric Poetry: A poem expressing the subjective feelings and personal emotions of the poet. Such poetry is melodic, since it was originally accompanied by a lyre in recitals. Most Western poetry in the twentieth century may be classified as lyrical. Examples of lyric poetry include A. E. Housman's elegy ''To an Athlete Dying Young,'' the odes of Pindar and Horace, Thomas Gray and William Collins, the sonnets of Sir Thomas Wyatt and Sir Philip Sidney, Elizabeth Barrett Browning and Rainer Maria Rilke, and a host of other forms in the poetry of William Blake and Christina Rossetti, among many others.

M

Mannerism: Exaggerated, artificial adherence to a literary manner or style. Also, a popular style of the visual arts of late sixteenth-century Europe that was marked by elongation of the human form and by intentional spatial distortion. Literary works that are self-consciously high-toned and artistic are often said to be ''mannered.'' Authors of such works include Henry James and Gertrude Stein.

Masculine Rhyme: See *Rhyme*

Masque: A lavish and elaborate form of entertainment, often performed in royal courts, that emphasizes song, dance, and costumery. The Renaissance form of the masque grew out of the spectacles of masked figures common in medieval England and Europe. The masque reached its peak of popularity and development in seventeenth-century England, during the reigns of James I and, especially, of Charles I. Ben Jonson, the most significant masque writer, also created the ''antimasque,'' which incorporates elements of humor and the grotesque into the traditional masque and achieved greater dramatic quality. Masque-like interludes appear in Edmund Spenser's *The Faerie Queene* and in William Shakespeare's *The Tempest*. One of the best-known English masques is John Milton's *Comus*.

Measure: The foot, verse, or time sequence used in a literary work, especially a poem. Measure is often used somewhat incorrectly as a synonym for meter.

Melodrama: A play in which the typical plot is a conflict between characters who personify extreme good and evil. Melodramas usually end happily and emphasize sensationalism. Other literary forms that use the same techniques are often labeled ''melodramatic.'' The term was formerly used to describe a combination of drama and music; as such, it was synonymous with ''opera.'' Augustin Daly's *Under the Gaslight* and Dion Boucicault's *The Octoroon, The Colleen Bawn,* and *The Poor of New York* are examples of melodramas. The most popular media for twentieth-century melodramas are motion pictures and television.

Metaphor: A figure of speech that expresses an idea through the image of another object. Metaphors suggest the essence of the first object by identifying it with certain qualities of the second object. An example is ''But soft, what light through yonder window breaks?/ It is the east, and Juliet is the sun'' in William Shakespeare's *Romeo and Juliet*. Here, Juliet, the first object, is identified with qualities of the second object, the sun.

Metaphysical Conceit: See *Conceit*

Metaphysical Poetry: The body of poetry produced by a group of seventeenth-century English writers called the ''Metaphysical Poets.'' The group includes John Donne and Andrew Marvell. The Metaphysical Poets made use of everyday speech, intellectual analysis, and unique imagery. They aimed to portray the ordinary conflicts and contradictions of life. Their poems often took the form of an argument, and many of them emphasize physical and religious love as well as the fleeting nature of life. Elaborate conceits are typical in metaphysical poetry. Marvell's ''To His Coy Mistress'' is a well-known example of a metaphysical poem.

Metaphysical Poets: See *Metaphysical Poetry*

Meter: In literary criticism, the repetition of sound patterns that creates a rhythm in poetry. The patterns are based on the number of syllables and the presence and absence of accents. The unit of rhythm in a line is called a foot. Types of meter are classified according to the number of feet in a line. These are the standard English lines: Monometer, one foot; Dimeter, two feet; Trimeter, three feet; Tetrameter, four feet; Pentameter, five feet; Hexameter, six feet (also called the Alexandrine); Heptameter, seven feet (also called the ''Fourteener'' when the feet are iambic). The most common English meter is the iambic pentameter, in which each line contains ten syllables, or five iambic feet, which individually are composed of an unstressed syllable followed by an accented syllable. Both of the following lines from Alfred, Lord Tennyson's

''Ulysses'' are written in iambic pentameter: Made weak by time and fate, but strong in will To strive, to seek, to find, and not to yield.

Mise en scene: The costumes, scenery, and other properties of a drama. Herbert Beerbohm Tree was renowned for the elaborate *mises en scene* of his lavish Shakespearean productions at His Majesty's Theatre between 1897 and 1915.

Modernism: Modern literary practices. Also, the principles of a literary school that lasted from roughly the beginning of the twentieth century until the end of World War II. Modernism is defined by its rejection of the literary conventions of the nineteenth century and by its opposition to conventional morality, taste, traditions, and economic values. Many writers are associated with the concepts of Modernism, including Albert Camus, Marcel Proust, D. H. Lawrence, W. H. Auden, Ernest Hemingway, William Faulkner, William Butler Yeats, Thomas Mann, Tennessee Williams, Eugene O'Neill, and James Joyce.

Monologue: A composition, written or oral, by a single individual. More specifically, a speech given by a single individual in a drama or other public entertainment. It has no set length, although it is usually several or more lines long. An example of an ''extended monologue''—that is, a monologue of great length and seriousness—occurs in the one-act, one-character play *The Stronger* by August Strindberg.

Monometer: See *Meter*

Mood: The prevailing emotions of a work or of the author in his or her creation of the work. The mood of a work is not always what might be expected based on its subject matter. The poem ''Dover Beach'' by Matthew Arnold offers examples of two different moods originating from the same experience: watching the ocean at night. The mood of the first three lines— The sea is calm tonight The tide is full, the moon lies fair Upon the straights. . . . is in sharp contrast to the mood of the last three lines— And we are here as on a darkling plain Swept with confused alarms of struggle and flight, Where ignorant armies clash by night.

Motif: A theme, character type, image, metaphor, or other verbal element that recurs throughout a single work of literature or occurs in a number of different works over a period of time. For example, the various manifestations of the color white in Herman Melville's *Moby Dick* is a ''specific'' *motif*, while the trials of star-crossed lovers is a ''conventional'' *motif* from the literature of all periods. Also known as *Motiv* or *Leitmotiv*.

Motiv: See *Motif*

Muckrakers: An early twentieth-century group of American writers. Typically, their works exposed the wrongdoings of big business and government in the United States. Upton Sinclair's *The Jungle* exemplifies the muckraking novel.

Muses: Nine Greek mythological goddesses, the daughters of Zeus and Mnemosyne (Memory). Each muse patronized a specific area of the liberal arts and sciences. Calliope presided over epic poetry, Clio over history, Erato over love poetry, Euterpe over music or lyric poetry, Melpomene over tragedy, Polyhymnia over hymns to the gods, Terpsichore over dance, Thalia over comedy, and Urania over astronomy. Poets and writers traditionally made appeals to the Muses for inspiration in their work. John Milton invokes the aid of a muse at the beginning of the first book of his *Paradise Lost:* Of Man's First disobedience, and the Fruit of the Forbidden Tree, whose mortal taste Brought Death into the World, and all our woe, With loss of Eden, till one greater Man Restore us, and regain the blissful Scat, Sing Heav'nly Muse, that on the secret top of Oreb, or of Sinai, didst inspire That Shepherd, who first taught the chosen Seed, In the Beginning how the Heav'ns and Earth Rose out of Chaos. . . .

Mystery: See *Suspense*

Myth: An anonymous tale emerging from the traditional beliefs of a culture or social unit. Myths use supernatural explanations for natural phenomena. They may also explain cosmic issues like creation and death. Collections of myths, known as mythologies, are common to all cultures and nations, but the best-known myths belong to the Norse, Roman, and Greek mythologies. A famous myth is the story of Arachne, an arrogant young girl who challenged a goddess, Athena, to a weaving contest; when the girl won, Athena was enraged and turned Arachne into a spider, thus explaining the existence of spiders.

N

Narration: The telling of a series of events, real or invented. A narration may be either a simple narrative, in which the events are recounted chronologically, or a narrative with a plot, in which the account is given in a style reflecting the author's artistic concept of the story. Narration is sometimes used as a synonym for "storyline." The recounting of scary stories around a campfire is a form of narration.

Narrative: A verse or prose accounting of an event or sequence of events, real or invented. The term is also used as an adjective in the sense "method of narration." For example, in literary criticism, the expression "narrative technique" usually refers to the way the author structures and presents his or her story. Narratives range from the shortest accounts of events, as in Julius Caesar's remark, "I came, I saw, I conquered," to the longest historical or biographical works, as in Edward Gibbon's *The Decline and Fall of the Roman Empire,* as well as diaries, travelogues, novels, ballads, epics, short stories, and other fictional forms.

Narrative Poetry: A nondramatic poem in which the author tells a story. Such poems may be of any length or level of complexity. Epics such as *Beowulf* and ballads are forms of narrative poetry.

Narrator: The teller of a story. The narrator may be the author or a character in the story through whom the author speaks. Huckleberry Finn is the narrator of Mark Twain's *The Adventures of Huckleberry Finn.*

Naturalism: A literary movement of the late nineteenth and early twentieth centuries. The movement's major theorist, French novelist Emile Zola, envisioned a type of fiction that would examine human life with the objectivity of scientific inquiry. The Naturalists typically viewed human beings as either the products of "biological determinism," ruled by hereditary instincts and engaged in an endless struggle for survival, or as the products of "socioeconomic determinism," ruled by social and economic forces beyond their control. In their works, the Naturalists generally ignored the highest levels of society and focused on degradation: poverty, alcoholism, prostitution, insanity, and disease. Naturalism influenced authors throughout the world, including Henrik Ibsen and Thomas Hardy. In the United States, in particular, Naturalism had a profound impact. Among the authors who embraced its principles are Theodore Dreiser, Eugene O'Neill, Stephen Crane, Jack London, and Frank Norris.

Negritude: A literary movement based on the concept of a shared cultural bond on the part of black Africans, wherever they may be in the world. It traces its origins to the former French colonies of Africa and the Caribbean. Negritude poets, novelists, and essayists generally stress four points in their writings: One, black alienation from tradi-

tional African culture can lead to feelings of inferiority. Two, European colonialism and Western education should be resisted. Three, black Africans should seek to affirm and define their own identity. Four, African culture can and should be reclaimed. Many Negritude writers also claim that blacks can make unique contributions to the world, based on a heightened appreciation of nature, rhythm, and human emotions—aspects of life they say are not so highly valued in the materialistic and rationalistic West. Examples of Negritude literature include the poetry of both Senegalese Leopold Senghor in *Hosties noires* and Martiniquais Aime-Fernand Cesaire in *Return to My Native Land.*

Negro Renaissance: See *Harlem Renaissance*

Neoclassical Period: See *Neoclassicism*

Neoclassicism: In literary criticism, this term refers to the revival of the attitudes and styles of expression of classical literature. It is generally used to describe a period in European history beginning in the late seventeenth century and lasting until about 1800. In its purest form, Neoclassicism marked a return to order, proportion, restraint, logic, accuracy, and decorum. In England, where Neoclassicism perhaps was most popular, it reflected the influence of seventeenth- century French writers, especially dramatists. Neoclassical writers typically reacted against the intensity and enthusiasm of the Renaissance period. They wrote works that appealed to the intellect, using elevated language and classical literary forms such as satire and the ode. Neoclassical works were often governed by the classical goal of instruction. English neoclassicists included Alexander Pope, Jonathan Swift, Joseph Addison, Sir Richard Steele, John Gay, and Matthew Prior; French neoclassicists included Pierre Corneille and Jean-Baptiste Moliere. Also known as Age of Reason.

Neoclassicists: See *Neoclassicism*

New Criticism: A movement in literary criticism, dating from the late 1920s, that stressed close textual analysis in the interpretation of works of literature. The New Critics saw little merit in historical and biographical analysis. Rather, they aimed to examine the text alone, free from the question of how external events—biographical or otherwise—may have helped shape it. This predominantly American school was named "New Criticism" by one of its practitioners, John Crowe Ransom. Other important New Critics included Allen Tate, R. P. Blackmur, Robert Penn Warren, and Cleanth Brooks.

New Negro Movement: See *Harlem Renaissance*

Noble Savage: The idea that primitive man is noble and good but becomes evil and corrupted as he becomes civilized. The concept of the noble savage originated in the Renaissance period but is more closely identified with such later writers as Jean-Jacques Rousseau and Aphra Behn. First described in John Dryden's play *The Conquest of Granada,* the noble savage is portrayed by the various Native Americans in James Fenimore Cooper's ''Leatherstocking Tales,'' by Queequeg, Daggoo, and Tashtego in Herman Melville's *Moby Dick,* and by John the Savage in Aldous Huxley's *Brave New World.*

O

Objective Correlative: An outward set of objects, a situation, or a chain of events corresponding to an inward experience and evoking this experience in the reader. The term frequently appears in modern criticism in discussions of authors' intended effects on the emotional responses of readers. This term was originally used by T. S. Eliot in his 1919 essay ''Hamlet.''

Objectivity: A quality in writing characterized by the absence of the author's opinion or feeling about the subject matter. Objectivity is an important factor in criticism. The novels of Henry James and, to a certain extent, the poems of John Larkin demonstrate objectivity, and it is central to John Keats's concept of ''negative capability.'' Critical and journalistic writing usually are or attempt to be objective.

Occasional Verse: poetry written on the occasion of a significant historical or personal event. *Vers de societe* is sometimes called occasional verse although it is of a less serious nature. Famous examples of occasional verse include Andrew Marvell's ''Horatian Ode upon Cromwell's Return from England,'' Walt Whitman's ''When Lilacs Last in the Dooryard Bloom'd''— written upon the death of Abraham Lincoln—and Edmund Spenser's commemoration of his wedding, ''Epithalamion.''

Octave: A poem or stanza composed of eight lines. The term octave most often represents the first eight lines of a Petrarchan sonnet. An example of an octave is taken from a translation of a Petrarchan sonnet by Sir Thomas Wyatt: The pillar perisht is whereto I leant, The strongest stay of mine unquiet mind; The like of it no man again can find, From East to West Still seeking though he went. To mind unhap! for hap away hath rent Of all my joy the very

bark and rind; And I, alas, by chance am thus assigned Daily to mourn till death do it relent.

Ode: Name given to an extended lyric poem characterized by exalted emotion and dignified style. An ode usually concerns a single, serious theme. Most odes, but not all, are addressed to an object or individual. Odes are distinguished from other lyric poetic forms by their complex rhythmic and stanzaic patterns. An example of this form is John Keats's ''Ode to a Nightingale.''

Oedipus Complex: A son's amorous obsession with his mother. The phrase is derived from the story of the ancient Theban hero Oedipus, who unknowingly killed his father and married his mother. Literary occurrences of the Oedipus complex include Andre Gide's *Oedipe* and Jean Cocteau's *La Machine infernale,* as well as the most famous, Sophocles' *Oedipus Rex.*

Omniscience: See *Point of View*

Onomatopoeia: The use of words whose sounds express or suggest their meaning. In its simplest sense, onomatopoeia may be represented by words that mimic the sounds they denote such as ''hiss'' or ''meow.'' At a more subtle level, the pattern and rhythm of sounds and rhymes of a line or poem may be onomatopoeic. A celebrated example of onomatopoeia is the repetition of the word ''bells'' in Edgar Allan Poe's poem ''The Bells.''

Opera: A type of stage performance, usually a drama, in which the dialogue is sung. Classic examples of opera include Giuseppi Verdi's *La traviata,* Giacomo Puccini's *La Boheme,* and Richard Wagner's *Tristan und Isolde.* Major twentieth- century contributors to the form include Richard Strauss and Alban Berg.

Operetta: A usually romantic comic opera. John Gay's *The Beggar's Opera,* Richard Sheridan's *The Duenna,* and numerous works by William Gilbert and Arthur Sullivan are examples of operettas.

Oral Tradition: See *Oral Transmission*

Oral Transmission: A process by which songs, ballads, folklore, and other material are transmitted by word of mouth. The tradition of oral transmission predates the written record systems of literate society. Oral transmission preserves material sometimes over generations, although often with variations. Memory plays a large part in the recitation and preservation of orally transmitted material. Breton lays, French *fabliaux,* national epics (including the Anglo- Saxon *Beowulf,* the Spanish *El Cid,* and the Finnish *Kalevala*), Native American myths and legends, and African folktales told by plantation slaves are examples of orally transmitted literature.

Oration: Formal speaking intended to motivate the listeners to some action or feeling. Such public speaking was much more common before the development of timely printed communication such as newspapers. Famous examples of oration include Abraham Lincoln's ''Gettysburg Address'' and Dr. Martin Luther King Jr.'s ''I Have a Dream'' speech.

Ottava Rima: An eight-line stanza of poetry composed in iambic pentameter (a five-foot line in which each foot consists of an unaccented syllable followed by an accented syllable), following the abababcc rhyme scheme. This form has been prominently used by such important English writers as Lord Byron, Henry Wadsworth Longfellow, and W. B. Yeats.

Oxymoron: A phrase combining two contradictory terms. Oxymorons may be intentional or unintentional. The following speech from William Shakespeare's *Romeo and Juliet* uses several oxymorons: Why, then, O brawling love! O loving hate! O anything, of nothing first create! O heavy lightness! serious vanity! Mis-shapen chaos of well-seeming forms! Feather of lead, bright smoke, cold fire, sick health! This love feel I, that feel no love in this.

P

Pantheism: The idea that all things are both a manifestation or revelation of God and a part of God at the same time. Pantheism was a common attitude in the early societies of Egypt, India, and Greece—the term derives from the Greek *pan* meaning ''all'' and *theos* meaning ''deity.'' It later became a significant part of the Christian faith. William Wordsworth and Ralph Waldo Emerson are among the many writers who have expressed the pantheistic attitude in their works.

Parable: A story intended to teach a moral lesson or answer an ethical question. In the West, the best examples of parables are those of Jesus Christ in the New Testament, notably ''The Prodigal Son,'' but parables also are used in Sufism, rabbinic literature, Hasidism, and Zen Buddhism.

Paradox: A statement that appears illogical or contradictory at first, but may actually point to an underlying truth. ''Less is more'' is an example of a paradox. Literary examples include Francis Bacon's statement, ''The most corrected copies are commonly the least correct,'' and ''All animals are equal, but some animals are more equal than others'' from George Orwell's *Animal Farm*.

Parallelism: A method of comparison of two ideas in which each is developed in the same grammatical structure. Ralph Waldo Emerson's ''Civilization'' contains this example of parallelism: Raphael paints wisdom; Handel sings it, Phidias carves it, Shakespeare writes it, Wren builds it, Columbus sails it, Luther preaches it, Washington arms it, Watt mechanizes it.

Parnassianism: A mid nineteenth-century movement in French literature. Followers of the movement stressed adherence to well-defined artistic forms as a reaction against the often chaotic expression of the artist's ego that dominated the work of the Romantics. The Parnassians also rejected the moral, ethical, and social themes exhibited in the works of French Romantics such as Victor Hugo. The aesthetic doctrines of the Parnassians strongly influenced the later symbolist and decadent movements. Members of the Parnassian school include Leconte de Lisle, Sully Prudhomme, Albert Glatigny, Francois Coppee, and Theodore de Banville.

Parody: In literary criticism, this term refers to an imitation of a serious literary work or the signature style of a particular author in a ridiculous manner. A typical parody adopts the style of the original and applies it to an inappropriate subject for humorous effect. Parody is a form of satire and could be considered the literary equivalent of a caricature or cartoon. Henry Fielding's *Shamela* is a parody of Samuel Richardson's *Pamela*.

Pastoral: A term derived from the Latin word ''pastor,'' meaning shepherd. A pastoral is a literary composition on a rural theme. The conventions of the pastoral were originated by the third-century Greek poet Theocritus, who wrote about the experiences, love affairs, and pastimes of Sicilian shepherds. In a pastoral, characters and language of a courtly nature are often placed in a simple setting. The term pastoral is also used to classify dramas, elegies, and lyrics that exhibit the use of country settings and shepherd characters. Percy Bysshe Shelley's ''Adonais'' and John Milton's ''Lycidas'' are two famous examples of pastorals.

Pastorela: The Spanish name for the shepherds play, a folk drama reenacted during the Christmas season. Examples of *pastorelas* include Gomez

Manrique's *Representacion del nacimiento* and the dramas of Lucas Fernandez and Juan del Encina.

Pathetic Fallacy: A term coined by English critic John Ruskin to identify writing that falsely endows nonhuman things with human intentions and feelings, such as "angry clouds" and "sad trees." The pathetic fallacy is a required convention in the classical poetic form of the pastoral elegy, and it is used in the modern poetry of T. S. Eliot, Ezra Pound, and the Imagists. Also known as Poetic Fallacy.

Pelado: Literally the "skinned one" or shirtless one, he was the stock underdog, sharp-witted picaresque character of Mexican vaudeville and tent shows. The *pelado* is found in such works as Don Catarino's *Los effectos de la crisis* and *Regreso a mi tierra.*

Pen Name: See *Pseudonym*

Pentameter: See *Meter*

Persona: A Latin term meaning "mask." *Personae* are the characters in a fictional work of literature. The *persona* generally functions as a mask through which the author tells a story in a voice other than his or her own. A *persona* is usually either a character in a story who acts as a narrator or an "implied author," a voice created by the author to act as the narrator for himself or herself. *Personae* include the narrator of Geoffrey Chaucer's *Canterbury Tales* and Marlow in Joseph Conrad's *Heart of Darkness.*

Personae: See *Persona*

Personal Point of View: See *Point of View*

Personification: A figure of speech that gives human qualities to abstract ideas, animals, and inanimate objects. William Shakespeare used personification in *Romeo and Juliet* in the lines "Arise, fair sun, and kill the envious moon,/ Who is already sick and pale with grief." Here, the moon is portrayed as being envious, sick, and pale with grief— all markedly human qualities. Also known as *Prosopopoeia.*

Petrarchan Sonnet: See *Sonnet*

Phenomenology: A method of literary criticism based on the belief that things have no existence outside of human consciousness or awareness. Proponents of this theory believe that art is a process that takes place in the mind of the observer as he or she contemplates an object rather than a quality of the object itself. Among phenomenological critics

are Edmund Husserl, George Poulet, Marcel Raymond, and Roman Ingarden.

Picaresque Novel: Episodic fiction depicting the adventures of a roguish central character ("picaro" is Spanish for "rogue"). The picaresque hero is commonly a low-born but clever individual who wanders into and out of various affairs of love, danger, and farcical intrigue. These involvements may take place at all social levels and typically present a humorous and wide-ranging satire of a given society. Prominent examples of the picaresque novel are *Don Quixote* by Miguel de Cervantes, *Tom Jones* by Henry Fielding, and *Moll Flanders* by Daniel Defoe.

Plagiarism: Claiming another person's written material as one's own. Plagiarism can take the form of direct, word-for- word copying or the theft of the substance or idea of the work. A student who copies an encyclopedia entry and turns it in as a report for school is guilty of plagiarism.

Platonic Criticism: A form of criticism that stresses an artistic work's usefulness as an agent of social engineering rather than any quality or value of the work itself. Platonic criticism takes as its starting point the ancient Greek philosopher Plato's comments on art in his *Republic.*

Platonism: The embracing of the doctrines of the philosopher Plato, popular among the poets of the Renaissance and the Romantic period. Platonism is more flexible than Aristotelian Criticism and places more emphasis on the supernatural and unknown aspects of life. Platonism is expressed in the love poetry of the Renaissance, the fourth book of Baldassare Castiglione's *The Book of the Courtier,* and the poetry of William Blake, William Wordsworth, Percy Bysshe Shelley, Friedrich Holderlin, William Butler Yeats, and Wallace Stevens.

Play: See *Drama*

Plot: In literary criticism, this term refers to the pattern of events in a narrative or drama. In its simplest sense, the plot guides the author in composing the work and helps the reader follow the work. Typically, plots exhibit causality and unity and have a beginning, a middle, and an end. Sometimes, however, a plot may consist of a series of disconnected events, in which case it is known as an "episodic plot." In his *Aspects of the Novel,* E. M. Forster distinguishes between a story, defined as a "narrative of events arranged in their time- sequence," and plot, which organizes the events to a ''sense of causality.'' This definition closely mirrors Aristotle's discussion of plot in his *Poetics.*

Poem: In its broadest sense, a composition utilizing rhyme, meter, concrete detail, and expressive language to create a literary experience with emotional and aesthetic appeal. Typical poems include sonnets, odes, elegies, *haiku,* ballads, and free verse.

Poet: An author who writes poetry or verse. The term is also used to refer to an artist or writer who has an exceptional gift for expression, imagination, and energy in the making of art in any form. Well-known poets include Horace, Basho, Sir Philip Sidney, Sir Edmund Spenser, John Donne, Andrew Marvell, Alexander Pope, Jonathan Swift, George Gordon, Lord Byron, John Keats, Christina Rossetti, W. H. Auden, Stevie Smith, and Sylvia Plath.

Poetic Fallacy: See *Pathetic Fallacy*

Poetic Justice: An outcome in a literary work, not necessarily a poem, in which the good are rewarded and the evil are punished, especially in ways that particularly fit their virtues or crimes. For example, a murderer may himself be murdered, or a thief will find himself penniless.

Poetic License: Distortions of fact and literary convention made by a writer—not always a poet—for the sake of the effect gained. Poetic license is closely related to the concept of ''artistic freedom.'' An author exercises poetic license by saying that a pile of money ''reaches as high as a mountain'' when the pile is actually only a foot or two high.

Poetics: This term has two closely related meanings. It denotes (1) an aesthetic theory in literary criticism about the essence of poetry or (2) rules prescribing the proper methods, content, style, or diction of poetry. The term poetics may also refer to theories about literature in general, not just poetry.

Poetry: In its broadest sense, writing that aims to present ideas and evoke an emotional experience in the reader through the use of meter, imagery, connotative and concrete words, and a carefully constructed structure based on rhythmic patterns. Poetry typically relies on words and expressions that have several layers of meaning. It also makes use of the effects of regular rhythm on the ear and may make a strong appeal to the senses through the use of imagery. Edgar Allan Poe's ''Annabel Lee'' and Walt Whitman's *Leaves of Grass* are famous examples of poetry.

Point of View: The narrative perspective from which a literary work is presented to the reader.

There are four traditional points of view. The ''third person omniscient'' gives the reader a ''godlike'' perspective, unrestricted by time or place, from which to see actions and look into the minds of characters. This allows the author to comment openly on characters and events in the work. The ''third person'' point of view presents the events of the story from outside of any single character's perception, much like the omniscient point of view, but the reader must understand the action as it takes place and without any special insight into characters' minds or motivations. The ''first person'' or ''personal'' point of view relates events as they are perceived by a single character. The main character ''tells'' the story and may offer opinions about the action and characters which differ from those of the author. Much less common than omniscient, third person, and first person is the ''second person'' point of view, wherein the author tells the story as if it is happening to the reader. James Thurber employs the omniscient point of view in his short story ''The Secret Life of Walter Mitty.'' Ernest Hemingway's ''A Clean, Well-Lighted Place'' is a short story told from the third person point of view. Mark Twain's novel *Huck Finn* is presented from the first person viewpoint. Jay McInerney's *Bright Lights, Big City* is an example of a novel which uses the second person point of view.

Polemic: A work in which the author takes a stand on a controversial subject, such as abortion or religion. Such works are often extremely argumentative or provocative. Classic examples of polemics include John Milton's *Aeropagitica* and Thomas Paine's *The American Crisis.*

Pornography: Writing intended to provoke feelings of lust in the reader. Such works are often condemned by critics and teachers, but those which can be shown to have literary value are viewed less harshly. Literary works that have been described as pornographic include Ovid's *The Art of Love,* Margaret of Angouleme's *Heptameron,* John Cleland's *Memoirs of a Woman of Pleasure; or, the Life of Fanny Hill,* the anonymous *My Secret Life,* D. H. Lawrence's *Lady Chatterley's Lover,* and Vladimir Nabokov's *Lolita.*

Post-Aesthetic Movement: An artistic response made by African Americans to the black aesthetic movement of the 1960s and early '70s. Writers since that time have adopted a somewhat different tone in their work, with less emphasis placed on the disparity between black and white in the United States. In the words of post-aesthetic authors such as Toni Morrison, John Edgar Wideman, and Kristin Hunter, African Americans are portrayed as looking inward for answers to their own questions, rather than always looking to the outside world. Two well-known examples of works produced as part of the post-aesthetic movement are the Pulitzer Prize-winning novels *The Color Purple* by Alice Walker and *Beloved* by Toni Morrison.

Postmodernism: Writing from the 1960s forward characterized by experimentation and continuing to apply some of the fundamentals of modernism, which included existentialism and alienation. Postmodernists have gone a step further in the rejection of tradition begun with the modernists by also rejecting traditional forms, preferring the anti-novel over the novel and the anti-hero over the hero. Postmodern writers include Alain Robbe-Grillet, Thomas Pynchon, Margaret Drabble, John Fowles, Adolfo Bioy-Casares, and Gabriel Garcia Marquez.

Pre-Raphaelites: A circle of writers and artists in mid nineteenth-century England. Valuing the pre-Renaissance artistic qualities of religious symbolism, lavish pictorialism, and natural sensuousness, the Pre-Raphaelites cultivated a sense of mystery and melancholy that influenced later writers associated with the Symbolist and Decadent movements. The major members of the group include Dante Gabriel Rossetti, Christina Rossetti, Algernon Swinburne, and Walter Pater.

Primitivism: The belief that primitive peoples were nobler and less flawed than civilized peoples because they had not been subjected to the tainting influence of society. Examples of literature espousing primitivism include Aphra Behn's *Oroonoko: Or, The History of the Royal Slave,* Jean-Jacques Rousseau's *Julie ou la Nouvelle Heloise,* Oliver Goldsmith's *The Deserted Village,* the poems of Robert Burns, Herman Melville's stories *Typee, Omoo,* and *Mardi,* many poems of William Butler Yeats and Robert Frost, and William Golding's novel *Lord of the Flies.*

Projective Verse: A form of free verse in which the poet's breathing pattern determines the lines of the poem. Poets who advocate projective verse are against all formal structures in writing, including meter and form. Besides its creators, Robert Creeley, Robert Duncan, and Charles Olson, two other well-known projective verse poets are Denise Levertov and LeRoi Jones (Amiri Baraka). Also known as Breath Verse.

Prologue: An introductory section of a literary work. It often contains information establishing the situation of the characters or presents information about the setting, time period, or action. In drama, the prologue is spoken by a chorus or by one of the principal characters. In the ''General Prologue'' of *The Canterbury Tales,* Geoffrey Chaucer describes the main characters and establishes the setting and purpose of the work.

Prose: A literary medium that attempts to mirror the language of everyday speech. It is distinguished from poetry by its use of unmetered, unrhymed language consisting of logically related sentences. Prose is usually grouped into paragraphs that form a cohesive whole such as an essay or a novel. Recognized masters of English prose writing include Sir Thomas Malory, William Caxton, Raphael Holinshed, Joseph Addison, Mark Twain, and Ernest Hemingway.

Prosopopoeia: See *Personification*

Protagonist: The central character of a story who serves as a focus for its themes and incidents and as the principal rationale for its development. The protagonist is sometimes referred to in discussions of modern literature as the hero or anti-hero. Well-known protagonists are Hamlet in William Shakespeare's *Hamlet* and Jay Gatsby in F. Scott Fitzgerald's *The Great Gatsby.*

Protest Fiction: Protest fiction has as its primary purpose the protesting of some social injustice, such as racism or discrimination. One example of protest fiction is a series of five novels by Chester Himes, beginning in 1945 with *If He Hollers Let Him Go* and ending in 1955 with *The Primitive.* These works depict the destructive effects of race and gender stereotyping in the context of interracial relationships. Another African American author whose works often revolve around themes of social protest is John Oliver Killens. James Baldwin's essay ''Everybody's Protest Novel'' generated controversy by attacking the authors of protest fiction.

Proverb: A brief, sage saying that expresses a truth about life in a striking manner. ''They are not all cooks who carry long knives'' is an example of a proverb.

Pseudonym: A name assumed by a writer, most often intended to prevent his or her identification as the author of a work. Two or more authors may work together under one pseudonym, or an author may use a different name for each genre he or she publishes in. Some publishing companies maintain ''house pseudonyms,'' under which any number of authors may write installations in a series. Some authors also choose a pseudonym over their real names the way an actor may use a stage name. Examples of pseudonyms (with the author's real name in parentheses) include Voltaire (Francois-Marie Arouet), Novalis (Friedrich von Hardenberg), Currer Bell (Charlotte Bronte), Ellis Bell (Emily Bronte), George Eliot (Maryann Evans), Honorio Bustos Donmecq (Adolfo Bioy-Casares and Jorge Luis Borges), and Richard Bachman (Stephen King).

Pun: A play on words that have similar sounds but different meanings. A serious example of the pun is from John Donne's ''A Hymne to God the Father'': Sweare by thyself, that at my death thy sonne Shall shine as he shines now, and hereto fore; And, having done that, Thou haste done; I fear no more.

Pure Poetry: poetry written without instructional intent or moral purpose that aims only to please a reader by its imagery or musical flow. The term pure poetry is used as the antonym of the term ''didacticism.'' The poetry of Edgar Allan Poe, Stephane Mallarme, Paul Verlaine, Paul Valery, Juan Ramoz Jimenez, and Jorge Guillen offer examples of pure poetry.

Q

Quatrain: A four-line stanza of a poem or an entire poem consisting of four lines. The following quatrain is from Robert Herrick's ''To Live Merrily, and to Trust to Good Verses'': Round, round, the root do's run; And being ravisht thus, Come, I will drink a Tun To my *Propertius*.

R

Raisonneur: A character in a drama who functions as a spokesperson for the dramatist's views. The *raisonneur* typically observes the play without becoming central to its action. *Raisonneurs* were very common in plays of the nineteenth century.

Realism: A nineteenth-century European literary movement that sought to portray familiar characters, situations, and settings in a realistic manner. This was done primarily by using an objective narrative point of view and through the buildup of accurate detail. The standard for success of any realistic work depends on how faithfully it transfers common experience into fictional forms. The realistic method may be altered or extended, as in stream of consciousness writing, to record highly subjec-

tive experience. Seminal authors in the tradition of Realism include Honore de Balzac, Gustave Flaubert, and Henry James.

Refrain: A phrase repeated at intervals throughout a poem. A refrain may appear at the end of each stanza or at less regular intervals. It may be altered slightly at each appearance. Some refrains are nonsense expressions—as with ''Nevermore'' in Edgar Allan Poe's ''The Raven''—that seem to take on a different significance with each use.

Renaissance: The period in European history that marked the end of the Middle Ages. It began in Italy in the late fourteenth century. In broad terms, it is usually seen as spanning the fourteenth, fifteenth, and sixteenth centuries, although it did not reach Great Britain, for example, until the 1480s or so. The Renaissance saw an awakening in almost every sphere of human activity, especially science, philosophy, and the arts. The period is best defined by the emergence of a general philosophy that emphasized the importance of the intellect, the individual, and world affairs. It contrasts strongly with the medieval worldview, characterized by the dominant concerns of faith, the social collective, and spiritual salvation. Prominent writers during the Renaissance include Niccolo Machiavelli and Baldassare Castiglione in Italy, Miguel de Cervantes and Lope de Vega in Spain, Jean Froissart and Francois Rabelais in France, Sir Thomas More and Sir Philip Sidney in England, and Desiderius Erasmus in Holland.

Repartee: Conversation featuring snappy retorts and witticisms. Masters of *repartee* include Sydney Smith, Charles Lamb, and Oscar Wilde. An example is recorded in the meeting of ''Beau'' Nash and John Wesley: Nash said, ''I never make way for a fool,'' to which Wesley responded, ''Don't you? I always do,'' and stepped aside.

Resolution: The portion of a story following the climax, in which the conflict is resolved. The resolution of Jane Austen's *Northanger Abbey* is neatly summed up in the following sentence: ''Henry and Catherine were married, the bells rang and every body smiled.''

Restoration: See *Restoration Age*

Restoration Age: A period in English literature beginning with the crowning of Charles II in 1660 and running to about 1700. The era, which was characterized by a reaction against Puritanism, was the first great age of the comedy of manners. The finest literature of the era is typically witty and urbane, and often lewd. Prominent Restoration Age writers include William Congreve, Samuel Pepys, John Dryden, and John Milton.

Revenge Tragedy: A dramatic form popular during the Elizabethan Age, in which the protagonist, directed by the ghost of his murdered father or son, inflicts retaliation upon a powerful villain. Notable features of the revenge tragedy include violence, bizarre criminal acts, intrigue, insanity, a hesitant protagonist, and the use of soliloquy. Thomas Kyd's *Spanish Tragedy* is the first example of revenge tragedy in English, and William Shakespeare's *Hamlet* is perhaps the best. Extreme examples of revenge tragedy, such as John Webster's *The Duchess of Malfi,* are labeled "tragedies of blood." Also known as Tragedy of Blood.

Revista: The Spanish term for a vaudeville musical revue. Examples of *revistas* include Antonio Guzman Aguilera's *Mexico para los mexicanos,* Daniel Vanegas's *Maldito jazz,* and Don Catarino's *Whiskey, morfina y marihuana* and *El desterrado.*

Rhetoric: In literary criticism, this term denotes the art of ethical persuasion. In its strictest sense, rhetoric adheres to various principles developed since classical times for arranging facts and ideas in a clear, persuasive, appealing manner. The term is also used to refer to effective prose in general and theories of or methods for composing effective prose. Classical examples of rhetorics include *The Rhetoric of Aristotle,* Quintillian's *Institutio Oratoria,* and Cicero's *Ad Herennium.*

Rhetorical Question: A question intended to provoke thought, but not an expressed answer, in the reader. It is most commonly used in oratory and other persuasive genres. The following lines from Thomas Gray's "Elegy Written in a Country Churchyard" ask rhetorical questions: Can storied urn or animated bust Back to its mansion call the fleeting breath? Can Honour's voice provoke the silent dust, Or Flattery soothe the dull cold ear of Death?

Rhyme: When used as a noun in literary criticism, this term generally refers to a poem in which words sound identical or very similar and appear in parallel positions in two or more lines. Rhymes are classified into different types according to where they fall in a line or stanza or according to the degree of similarity they exhibit in their spellings and sounds. Some major types of rhyme are "masculine" rhyme, "feminine" rhyme, and "triple" rhyme. In a masculine rhyme, the rhyming sound falls in a single accented syllable, as with "heat" and "eat." Feminine rhyme is a rhyme of two syllables, one stressed and one unstressed, as with "merry" and "tarry." Triple rhyme matches the sound of the accented syllable and the two unaccented syllables that follow: "narrative" and "declarative." Robert Browning alternates feminine and masculine rhymes in his "Soliloquy of the Spanish Cloister": Gr-r-r—there go, my heart's abhorrence! Water your damned flower-pots, do! If hate killed men, Brother Lawrence, God's blood, would not mine kill you! What? Your myrtle-bush wants trimming? Oh, that rose has prior claims— Needs its leaden vase filled brimming? Hell dry you up with flames! Triple rhymes can be found in Thomas Hood's "Bridge of Sighs," George Gordon Byron's satirical verse, and Ogden Nash's comic poems.

Rhyme Royal: A stanza of seven lines composed in iambic pentameter and rhymed *ababbcc.* The name is said to be a tribute to King James I of Scotland, who made much use of the form in his poetry. Examples of rhyme royal include Geoffrey Chaucer's *The Parlement of Foules,* William Shakespeare's *The Rape of Lucrece,* William Morris's *The Early Paradise,* and John Masefield's *The Widow in the Bye Street.*

Rhyme Scheme: See *Rhyme*

Rhythm: A regular pattern of sound, time intervals, or events occurring in writing, most often and most discernably in poetry. Regular, reliable rhythm is known to be soothing to humans, while interrupted, unpredictable, or rapidly changing rhythm is disturbing. These effects are known to authors, who use them to produce a desired reaction in the reader. An example of a form of irregular rhythm is sprung rhythm poetry; quantitative verse, on the other hand, is very regular in its rhythm.

Rising Action: The part of a drama where the plot becomes increasingly complicated. Rising action leads up to the climax, or turning point, of a drama. The final "chase scene" of an action film is generally the rising action which culminates in the film's climax.

Rococo: A style of European architecture that flourished in the eighteenth century, especially in France. The most notable features of *rococo* are its extensive use of ornamentation and its themes of lightness, gaiety, and intimacy. In literary criticism, the term is often used disparagingly to refer to a decadent or over-ornamental style. Alexander Pope's "The Rape of the Lock" is an example of literary *rococo.*

Roman a clef: A French phrase meaning "novel with a key." It refers to a narrative in which real persons are portrayed under fictitious names. Jack Kerouac, for example, portrayed various real-life beat generation figures under fictitious names in his *On the Road.*

Romance: A broad term, usually denoting a narrative with exotic, exaggerated, often idealized characters, scenes, and themes. Nathaniel Hawthorne called his *The House of the Seven Gables* and *The Marble Faun* romances in order to distinguish them from clearly realistic works.

Romantic Age: See *Romanticism*

Romanticism: This term has two widely accepted meanings. In historical criticism, it refers to a European intellectual and artistic movement of the late eighteenth and early nineteenth centuries that sought greater freedom of personal expression than that allowed by the strict rules of literary form and logic of the eighteenth-century neoclassicists. The Romantics preferred emotional and imaginative expression to rational analysis. They considered the individual to be at the center of all experience and so placed him or her at the center of their art. The Romantics believed that the creative imagination reveals nobler truths—unique feelings and attitudes—than those that could be discovered by logic or by scientific examination. Both the natural world and the state of childhood were important sources for revelations of "eternal truths." "Romanticism" is also used as a general term to refer to a type of sensibility found in all periods of literary history and usually considered to be in opposition to the principles of classicism. In this sense, Romanticism signifies any work or philosophy in which the exotic or dreamlike figure strongly, or that is devoted to individualistic expression, self-analysis, or a pursuit of a higher realm of knowledge than can be discovered by human reason. Prominent Romantics include Jean-Jacques Rousseau, William Wordsworth, John Keats, Lord Byron, and Johann Wolfgang von Goethe.

Romantics: See *Romanticism*

Russian Symbolism: A Russian poetic movement, derived from French symbolism, that flourished between 1894 and 1910. While some Russian Symbolists continued in the French tradition, stressing aestheticism and the importance of suggestion above didactic intent, others saw their craft as a form of mystical worship, and themselves as mediators between the supernatural and the mun-

dane. Russian symbolists include Aleksandr Blok, Vyacheslav Ivanovich Ivanov, Fyodor Sologub, Andrey Bely, Nikolay Gumilyov, and Vladimir Sergeyevich Solovyov.

S

Satire: A work that uses ridicule, humor, and wit to criticize and provoke change in human nature and institutions. There are two major types of satire: "formal" or "direct" satire speaks directly to the reader or to a character in the work; "indirect" satire relies upon the ridiculous behavior of its characters to make its point. Formal satire is further divided into two manners: the "Horatian," which ridicules gently, and the "Juvenalian," which derides its subjects harshly and bitterly. Voltaire's novella *Candide* is an indirect satire. Jonathan Swift's essay "A Modest Proposal" is a Juvenalian satire.

Scansion: The analysis or "scanning" of a poem to determine its meter and often its rhyme scheme. The most common system of scansion uses accents (slanted lines drawn above syllables) to show stressed syllables, breves (curved lines drawn above syllables) to show unstressed syllables, and vertical lines to separate each foot. In the first line of John Keats's *Endymion,* "A thing of beauty is a joy forever:" the word "thing," the first syllable of "beauty," the word "joy," and the second syllable of "forever" are stressed, while the words "A" and "of," the second syllable of "beauty," the word "a," and the first and third syllables of "forever" are unstressed. In the second line: "Its loveliness increases; it will never" a pair of vertical lines separate the foot ending with "increases" and the one beginning with "it."

Scene: A subdivision of an act of a drama, consisting of continuous action taking place at a single time and in a single location. The beginnings and endings of scenes may be indicated by clearing the stage of actors and props or by the entrances and exits of important characters. The first act of William Shakespeare's *Winter's Tale* is comprised of two scenes.

Science Fiction: A type of narrative about or based upon real or imagined scientific theories and technology. Science fiction is often peopled with alien creatures and set on other planets or in different dimensions. Karel Capek's *R.U.R.* is a major work of science fiction.

Second Person: See *Point of View*

Semiotics: The study of how literary forms and conventions affect the meaning of language. Semioticians include Ferdinand de Saussure, Charles Sanders Pierce, Claude Levi-Strauss, Jacques Lacan, Michel Foucault, Jacques Derrida, Roland Barthes, and Julia Kristeva.

Sestet: Any six-line poem or stanza. Examples of the sestet include the last six lines of the Petrarchan sonnet form, the stanza form of Robert Burns's "A Poet's Welcome to his love-begotten Daughter," and the sestina form in W. H. Auden's "Paysage Moralise."

Setting: The time, place, and culture in which the action of a narrative takes place. The elements of setting may include geographic location, characters' physical and mental environments, prevailing cultural attitudes, or the historical time in which the action takes place. Examples of settings include the romanticized Scotland in Sir Walter Scott's "Waverley" novels, the French provincial setting in Gustave Flaubert's *Madame Bovary,* the fictional Wessex country of Thomas Hardy's novels, and the small towns of southern Ontario in Alice Munro's short stories.

Shakespearean Sonnet: See *Sonnet*

Signifying Monkey: A popular trickster figure in black folklore, with hundreds of tales about this character documented since the 19th century. Henry Louis Gates Jr. examines the history of the signifying monkey in *The Signifying Monkey: Towards a Theory of Afro-American Literary Criticism,* published in 1988.

Simile: A comparison, usually using "like" or "as", of two essentially dissimilar things, as in "coffee as cold as ice" or "He sounded like a broken record." The title of Ernest Hemingway's "Hills Like White Elephants" contains a simile.

Slang: A type of informal verbal communication that is generally unacceptable for formal writing. Slang words and phrases are often colorful exaggerations used to emphasize the speaker's point; they may also be shortened versions of an often-used word or phrase. Examples of American slang from the 1990s include "yuppie" (an acronym for Young Urban Professional), "awesome" (for "excellent"), wired (for "nervous" or "excited"), and "chill out" (for relax).

Slant Rhyme: See *Consonance*

Slave Narrative: Autobiographical accounts of American slave life as told by escaped slaves. These works first appeared during the abolition movement of the 1830s through the 1850s. Olaudah Equiano's *The Interesting Narrative of Olaudah Equiano, or Gustavus Vassa, The African* and Harriet Ann Jacobs's *Incidents in the Life of a Slave Girl* are examples of the slave narrative.

Social Realism: See *Socialist Realism*

Socialist Realism: The Socialist Realism school of literary theory was proposed by Maxim Gorky and established as a dogma by the first Soviet Congress of Writers. It demanded adherence to a communist worldview in works of literature. Its doctrines required an objective viewpoint comprehensible to the working classes and themes of social struggle featuring strong proletarian heroes. A successful work of socialist realism is Nikolay Ostrovsky's *Kak zakalyalas stal* (*How the Steel Was Tempered*). Also known as Social Realism.

Soliloquy: A monologue in a drama used to give the audience information and to develop the speaker's character. It is typically a projection of the speaker's innermost thoughts. Usually delivered while the speaker is alone on stage, a soliloquy is intended to present an illusion of unspoken reflection. A celebrated soliloquy is Hamlet's "To be or not to be" speech in William Shakespeare's *Hamlet.*

Sonnet: A fourteen-line poem, usually composed in iambic pentameter, employing one of several rhyme schemes. There are three major types of sonnets, upon which all other variations of the form are based: the "Petrarchan" or "Italian" sonnet, the "Shakespearean" or "English" sonnet, and the "Spenserian" sonnet. A Petrarchan sonnet consists of an octave rhymed *abbaabba* and a "sestet" rhymed either *cdecde, cdccdc,* or *cdedce.* The octave poses a question or problem, relates a narrative, or puts forth a proposition; the sestet presents a solution to the problem, comments upon the narrative, or applies the proposition put forth in the octave. The Shakespearean sonnet is divided into three quatrains and a couplet rhymed *abab cdcd efef gg.* The couplet provides an epigrammatic comment on the narrative or problem put forth in the quatrains. The Spenserian sonnet uses three quatrains and a couplet like the Shakespearean, but links their three rhyme schemes in this way: *abab bcbc cdcd ee.* The Spenserian sonnet develops its theme in two parts like the Petrarchan, its final six lines resolving a problem, analyzing a narrative, or applying a proposition put forth in its first eight lines. Examples of sonnets can be found in Petrarch's *Canzoniere,* Edmund Spenser's *Amoretti,* Elizabeth Barrett

Browning's *Sonnets from the Portuguese,* Rainer Maria Rilke's *Sonnets to Orpheus,* and Adrienne Rich's poem ''The Insusceptibles.''

Spenserian Sonnet: See *Sonnet*

Spenserian Stanza: A nine-line stanza having eight verses in iambic pentameter, its ninth verse in iambic hexameter, and the rhyme scheme ababbcbcc. This stanza form was first used by Edmund Spenser in his allegorical poem *The Faerie Queene.*

Spondee: In poetry meter, a foot consisting of two long or stressed syllables occurring together. This form is quite rare in English verse, and is usually composed of two monosyllabic words. The first foot in the following line from Robert Burns's ''Green Grow the Rashes'' is an example of a spondee: Green grow the rashes, O

Sprung Rhythm: Versification using a specific number of accented syllables per line but disregarding the number of unaccented syllables that fall in each line, producing an irregular rhythm in the poem. Gerard Manley Hopkins, who coined the term ''sprung rhythm,'' is the most notable practitioner of this technique.

Stanza: A subdivision of a poem consisting of lines grouped together, often in recurring patterns of rhyme, line length, and meter. Stanzas may also serve as units of thought in a poem much like paragraphs in prose. Examples of stanza forms include the quatrain, *terza rima, ottava rima,* Spenserian, and the so-called *In Memoriam* stanza from Alfred, Lord Tennyson's poem by that title. The following is an example of the latter form: Love is and was my lord and king, And in his presence I attend To hear the tidings of my friend, Which every hour his couriers bring.

Stereotype: A stereotype was originally the name for a duplication made during the printing process; this led to its modern definition as a person or thing that is (or is assumed to be) the same as all others of its type. Common stereotypical characters include the absent- minded professor, the nagging wife, the troublemaking teenager, and the kindhearted grandmother.

Stream of Consciousness: A narrative technique for rendering the inward experience of a character. This technique is designed to give the impression of an ever-changing series of thoughts, emotions, images, and memories in the spontaneous and seemingly illogical order that they occur in life. The

textbook example of stream of consciousness is the last section of James Joyce's *Ulysses.*

Structuralism: A twentieth-century movement in literary criticism that examines how literary texts arrive at their meanings, rather than the meanings themselves. There are two major types of structuralist analysis: one examines the way patterns of linguistic structures unify a specific text and emphasize certain elements of that text, and the other interprets the way literary forms and conventions affect the meaning of language itself. Prominent structuralists include Michel Foucault, Roman Jakobson, and Roland Barthes.

Structure: The form taken by a piece of literature. The structure may be made obvious for ease of understanding, as in nonfiction works, or may obscured for artistic purposes, as in some poetry or seemingly ''unstructured'' prose. Examples of common literary structures include the plot of a narrative, the acts and scenes of a drama, and such poetic forms as the Shakespearean sonnet and the Pindaric ode.

Sturm und Drang: A German term meaning ''storm and stress.'' It refers to a German literary movement of the 1770s and 1780s that reacted against the order and rationalism of the enlightenment, focusing instead on the intense experience of extraordinary individuals. Highly romantic, works of this movement, such as Johann Wolfgang von Goethe's *Gotz von Berlichingen,* are typified by realism, rebelliousness, and intense emotionalism.

Style: A writer's distinctive manner of arranging words to suit his or her ideas and purpose in writing. The unique imprint of the author's personality upon his or her writing, style is the product of an author's way of arranging ideas and his or her use of diction, different sentence structures, rhythm, figures of speech, rhetorical principles, and other elements of composition. Styles may be classified according to period (Metaphysical, Augustan, Georgian), individual authors (Chaucerian, Miltonic, Jamesian), level (grand, middle, low, plain), or language (scientific, expository, poetic, journalistic).

Subject: The person, event, or theme at the center of a work of literature. A work may have one or more subjects of each type, with shorter works tending to have fewer and longer works tending to have more. The subjects of James Baldwin's novel *Go Tell It on the Mountain* include the themes of father-son relationships, religious conversion, black life, and sexuality. The subjects of Anne Frank's

Diary of a Young Girl include Anne and her family members as well as World War II, the Holocaust, and the themes of war, isolation, injustice, and racism.

Subjectivity: Writing that expresses the author's personal feelings about his subject, and which may or may not include factual information about the subject. Subjectivity is demonstrated in James Joyce's *Portrait of the Artist as a Young Man,* Samuel Butler's *The Way of All Flesh,* and Thomas Wolfe's *Look Homeward, Angel.*

Subplot: A secondary story in a narrative. A subplot may serve as a motivating or complicating force for the main plot of the work, or it may provide emphasis for, or relief from, the main plot. The conflict between the Capulets and the Montagues in William Shakespeare's *Romeo and Juliet* is an example of a subplot.

Surrealism: A term introduced to criticism by Guillaume Apollinaire and later adopted by Andre Breton. It refers to a French literary and artistic movement founded in the 1920s. The Surrealists sought to express unconscious thoughts and feelings in their works. The best-known technique used for achieving this aim was automatic writing—transcriptions of spontaneous outpourings from the unconscious. The Surrealists proposed to unify the contrary levels of conscious and unconscious, dream and reality, objectivity and subjectivity into a new level of "super-realism." Surrealism can be found in the poetry of Paul Eluard, Pierre Reverdy, and Louis Aragon, among others.

Suspense: A literary device in which the author maintains the audience's attention through the buildup of events, the outcome of which will soon be revealed. Suspense in William Shakespeare's *Hamlet* is sustained throughout by the question of whether or not the Prince will achieve what he has been instructed to do and of what he intends to do.

Syllogism: A method of presenting a logical argument. In its most basic form, the syllogism consists of a major premise, a minor premise, and a conclusion. An example of a syllogism is: Major premise: When it snows, the streets get wet. Minor premise: It is snowing. Conclusion: The streets are wet.

Symbol: Something that suggests or stands for something else without losing its original identity. In literature, symbols combine their literal meaning with the suggestion of an abstract concept. Literary symbols are of two types: those that carry complex associations of meaning no matter what their con-

texts, and those that derive their suggestive meaning from their functions in specific literary works. Examples of symbols are sunshine suggesting happiness, rain suggesting sorrow, and storm clouds suggesting despair.

Symbolism: This term has two widely accepted meanings. In historical criticism, it denotes an early modernist literary movement initiated in France during the nineteenth century that reacted against the prevailing standards of realism. Writers in this movement aimed to evoke, indirectly and symbolically, an order of being beyond the material world of the five senses. Poetic expression of personal emotion figured strongly in the movement, typically by means of a private set of symbols uniquely identifiable with the individual poet. The principal aim of the Symbolists was to express in words the highly complex feelings that grew out of everyday contact with the world. In a broader sense, the term "symbolism" refers to the use of one object to represent another. Early members of the Symbolist movement included the French authors Charles Baudelaire and Arthur Rimbaud; William Butler Yeats, James Joyce, and T. S. Eliot were influenced as the movement moved to Ireland, England, and the United States. Examples of the concept of symbolism include a flag that stands for a nation or movement, or an empty cupboard used to suggest hopelessness, poverty, and despair.

Symbolist: See *Symbolism*

Symbolist Movement: See *Symbolism*

Sympathetic Fallacy: See *Affective Fallacy*

T

Tale: A story told by a narrator with a simple plot and little character development. Tales are usually relatively short and often carry a simple message. Examples of tales can be found in the work of Rudyard Kipling, Somerset Maugham, Saki, Anton Chekhov, Guy de Maupassant, and Armistead Maupin.

Tall Tale: A humorous tale told in a straightforward, credible tone but relating absolutely impossible events or feats of the characters. Such tales were commonly told of frontier adventures during the settlement of the west in the United States. Tall tales have been spun around such legendary heroes as Mike Fink, Paul Bunyan, Davy Crockett, Johnny Appleseed, and Captain Stormalong as well as the real-life William F. Cody and Annie Oakley. Literary use of tall tales can be found in Washington Irving's *History of New York,* Mark Twain's *Life on the Mississippi,* and in the German R. F. Raspe's *Baron Munchausen's Narratives of His Marvellous Travels and Campaigns in Russia.*

Tanka: A form of Japanese poetry similar to *haiku.* A *tanka* is five lines long, with the lines containing five, seven, five, seven, and seven syllables respectively. Skilled *tanka* authors include Ishikawa Takuboku, Masaoka Shiki, Amy Lowell, and Adelaide Crapsey.

Teatro Grottesco: See *Theater of the Grotesque*

Terza Rima: A three-line stanza form in poetry in which the rhymes are made on the last word of each line in the following manner: the first and third lines of the first stanza, then the second line of the first stanza and the first and third lines of the second stanza, and so on with the middle line of any stanza rhyming with the first and third lines of the following stanza. An example of *terza rima* is Percy Bysshe Shelley's ''The Triumph of Love'': As in that trance of wondrous thought I lay This was the tenour of my waking dream. Methought I sate beside a public way Thick strewn with summer dust, and a great stream Of people there was hurrying to and fro Numerous as gnats upon the evening gleam,. . .

Tetrameter: See *Meter*

Textual Criticism: A branch of literary criticism that seeks to establish the authoritative text of a literary work. Textual critics typically compare all known manuscripts or printings of a single work in order to assess the meanings of differences and revisions. This procedure allows them to arrive at a definitive version that (supposedly) corresponds to the author's original intention. Textual criticism was applied during the Renaissance to salvage the classical texts of Greece and Rome, and modern works have been studied, for instance, to undo deliberate correction or censorship, as in the case of novels by Stephen Crane and Theodore Dreiser.

Theater of Cruelty: Term used to denote a group of theatrical techniques designed to eliminate the psychological and emotional distance between actors and audience. This concept, introduced in the 1930s in France, was intended to inspire a more intense theatrical experience than conventional theater allowed. The ''cruelty'' of this dramatic theory signified not sadism but heightened actor/audience involvement in the dramatic event. The theater of cruelty was theorized by Antonin Artaud in his *Le Theatre et son double (The Theatre and Its Double),* and also appears in the work of Jerzy Grotowski, Jean Genet, Jean Vilar, and Arthur Adamov, among others.

Theater of the Absurd: A post-World War II dramatic trend characterized by radical theatrical innovations. In works influenced by the Theater of the absurd, nontraditional, sometimes grotesque characterizations, plots, and stage sets reveal a meaningless universe in which human values are irrelevant. Existentialist themes of estrangement, absurdity, and futility link many of the works of this movement. The principal writers of the Theater of the Absurd are Samuel Beckett, Eugene Ionesco, Jean Genet, and Harold Pinter.

Theater of the Grotesque: An Italian theatrical movement characterized by plays written around the ironic and macabre aspects of daily life in the World War I era. Theater of the Grotesque was named after the play *The Mask and the Face* by Luigi Chiarelli, which was described as ''a grotesque in three acts.'' The movement influenced the work of Italian dramatist Luigi Pirandello, author of *Right You Are, If You Think You Are.* Also known as *Teatro Grottesco.*

Theme: The main point of a work of literature. The term is used interchangeably with thesis. The theme of William Shakespeare's *Othello*—jealousy—is a common one.

Thesis: A thesis is both an essay and the point argued in the essay. Thesis novels and thesis plays share the quality of containing a thesis which is supported through the action of the story. A master's thesis and a doctoral dissertation are two theses required of graduate students.

Thesis Play: See *Thesis*

Three Unities: See *Unities*

Tone: The author's attitude toward his or her audience may be deduced from the tone of the work. A formal tone may create distance or convey politeness, while an informal tone may encourage a friendly, intimate, or intrusive feeling in the reader. The author's attitude toward his or her subject matter may also be deduced from the tone of the words he or she uses in discussing it. The tone of John F. Kennedy's speech which included the appeal to ''ask not what your country can do for you'' was intended to instill feelings of camaraderie and national pride in listeners.

Tragedy: A drama in prose or poetry about a noble, courageous hero of excellent character who, because of some tragic character flaw or *hamartia*, brings ruin upon him- or herself. Tragedy treats its subjects in a dignified and serious manner, using poetic language to help evoke pity and fear and bring about catharsis, a purging of these emotions. The tragic form was practiced extensively by the ancient Greeks. In the Middle Ages, when classical works were virtually unknown, tragedy came to denote any works about the fall of persons from exalted to low conditions due to any reason: fate, vice, weakness, etc. According to the classical definition of tragedy, such works present the "pathetic"—that which evokes pity—rather than the tragic. The classical form of tragedy was revived in the sixteenth century; it flourished especially on the Elizabethan stage. In modern times, dramatists have attempted to adapt the form to the needs of modern society by drawing their heroes from the ranks of ordinary men and women and defining the nobility of these heroes in terms of spirit rather than exalted social standing. The greatest classical example of tragedy is Sophocles' *Oedipus Rex*. The "pathetic" derivation is exemplified in "The Monk's Tale" in Geoffrey Chaucer's *Canterbury Tales*. Notable works produced during the sixteenth century revival include William Shakespeare's *Hamlet, Othello,* and *King Lear*. Modern dramatists working in the tragic tradition include Henrik Ibsen, Arthur Miller, and Eugene O'Neill.

Tragedy of Blood: See *Revenge Tragedy*

Tragic Flaw: In a tragedy, the quality within the hero or heroine which leads to his or her downfall. Examples of the tragic flaw include Othello's jealousy and Hamlet's indecisiveness, although most great tragedies defy such simple interpretation.

Transcendentalism: An American philosophical and religious movement, based in New England from around 1835 until the Civil War. Transcendentalism was a form of American romanticism that had its roots abroad in the works of Thomas Carlyle, Samuel Coleridge, and Johann Wolfgang von Goethe. The Transcendentalists stressed the importance of intuition and subjective experience in communication with God. They rejected religious dogma and texts in favor of mysticism and scientific naturalism. They pursued truths that lie beyond the "colorless" realms perceived by reason and the senses and were active social reformers in public education, women's rights, and the abolition of slavery. Promi-

nent members of the group include Ralph Waldo Emerson and Henry David Thoreau.

Trickster: A character or figure common in Native American and African literature who uses his ingenuity to defeat enemies and escape difficult situations. Tricksters are most often animals, such as the spider, hare, or coyote, although they may take the form of humans as well. Examples of trickster tales include Thomas King's *A Coyote Columbus Story,* Ashley F. Bryan's *The Dancing Granny* and Ishmael Reed's *The Last Days of Louisiana Red.*

Trimeter: See *Meter*

Triple Rhyme: See *Rhyme*

Trochee: See *Foot*

U

Understatement: See *Irony*

Unities: Strict rules of dramatic structure, formulated by Italian and French critics of the Renaissance and based loosely on the principles of drama discussed by Aristotle in his *Poetics*. Foremost among these rules were the three unities of action, time, and place that compelled a dramatist to: (1) construct a single plot with a beginning, middle, and end that details the causal relationships of action and character; (2) restrict the action to the events of a single day; and (3) limit the scene to a single place or city. The unities were observed faithfully by continental European writers until the Romantic Age, but they were never regularly observed in English drama. Modern dramatists are typically more concerned with a unity of impression or emotional effect than with any of the classical unities. The unities are observed in Pierre Corneille's tragedy *Polyeuctes* and Jean-Baptiste Racine's *Phedre*. Also known as Three Unities.

Urban Realism: A branch of realist writing that attempts to accurately reflect the often harsh facts of modern urban existence. Some works by Stephen Crane, Theodore Dreiser, Charles Dickens, Fyodor Dostoyevsky, Emile Zola, Abraham Cahan, and Henry Fuller feature urban realism. Modern examples include Claude Brown's *Manchild in the Promised Land* and Ron Milner's *What the Wine Sellers Buy.*

Utopia: A fictional perfect place, such as "paradise" or "heaven." Early literary utopias were included in Plato's *Republic* and Sir Thomas More's *Utopia,* while more modern utopias can be found in

Samuel Butler's *Erewhon,* Theodor Herzka's *A Visit to Freeland,* and H. G. Wells' *A Modern Utopia.*

Utopian: See *Utopia*

Utopianism: See *Utopia*

V

Verisimilitude: Literally, the appearance of truth. In literary criticism, the term refers to aspects of a work of literature that seem true to the reader. Verisimilitude is achieved in the work of Honore de Balzac, Gustave Flaubert, and Henry James, among other late nineteenth-century realist writers.

Vers de societe: See *Occasional Verse*

Vers libre: See *Free Verse*

Verse: A line of metered language, a line of a poem, or any work written in verse. The following line of verse is from the epic poem *Don Juan* by Lord Byron: "My way is to begin with the beginning."

Versification: The writing of verse. Versification may also refer to the meter, rhyme, and other mechanical components of a poem. Composition of a "Roses are red, violets are blue" poem to suit an occasion is a common form of versification practiced by students.

Victorian: Refers broadly to the reign of Queen Victoria of England (1837–1901) and to anything with qualities typical of that era. For example, the qualities of smug narrowmindedness, bourgeois materialism, faith in social progress, and priggish morality are often considered Victorian. This stereotype is contradicted by such dramatic intellectual developments as the theories of Charles Darwin, Karl Marx, and Sigmund Freud (which stirred strong debates in England) and the critical attitudes of serious Victorian writers like Charles Dickens and George Eliot. In literature, the Victorian Period was the great age of the English novel, and the latter part of the era saw the rise of movements such as decadence and symbolism. Works of Victorian literature include the poetry of Robert Browning and Alfred, Lord Tennyson, the criticism of Matthew Arnold and John Ruskin, and the novels of Emily Bronte, William Makepeace Thackeray, and Thomas Hardy. Also known as Victorian Age and Victorian Period.

Victorian Age: See *Victorian*

Victorian Period: See *Victorian*

W

Weltanschauung: A German term referring to a person's worldview or philosophy. Examples of *weltanschauung* include Thomas Hardy's view of the human being as the victim of fate, destiny, or impersonal forces and circumstances, and the disillusioned and laconic cynicism expressed by such poets of the 1930s as W. H. Auden, Sir Stephen Spender, and Sir William Empson.

Weltschmerz: A German term meaning "world pain." It describes a sense of anguish about the nature of existence, usually associated with a melancholy, pessimistic attitude. *Weltschmerz* was expressed in England by George Gordon, Lord Byron in his *Manfred* and *Childe Harold's Pilgrimage,* in France by Viscount de Chateaubriand, Alfred de Vigny, and Alfred de Musset, in Russia by Aleksandr Pushkin and Mikhail Lermontov, in Poland by Juliusz Slowacki, and in America by Nathaniel Hawthorne.

Z

Zarzuela: A type of Spanish operetta. Writers of *zarzuelas* include Lope de Vega and Pedro Calderon.

Zeitgeist: A German term meaning "spirit of the time." It refers to the moral and intellectual trends of a given era. Examples of *zeitgeist* include the preoccupation with the more morbid aspects of dying and death in some Jacobean literature, especially in the works of dramatists Cyril Tourneur and John Webster, and the decadence of the French Symbolists.

Cumulative
Author/Title Index

Nationality/Ethnicity Index

Subject/Theme Index